Rear Admiral Richmond Kelly Turner enroute to Kwajalein on board USS Rocky Mount, *January 1944.*

The Amphibians Came to Conquer

THE STORY OF
ADMIRAL
RICHMOND KELLY TURNER

I

by
VICE ADMIRAL
GEORGE CARROLL DYER
USN (Retired)

With an introduction by
Rear Admiral
ERNEST McNEILL ELLER
USN (Retired)

Prologue

In a letter to the Director of Naval History, 9 November 1956, Admiral Kelly Turner wrote as follows:

> But the matter of my writing a book—and particularly a history of all past amphibious warfare—is quite a different thing, and one which I would not care to undertake. Before retiring in 1947, I did give serious thought to writing an account of the amphibious operations in which I participated, but decided against doing so for several reasons.
>
> In the first place, writing history is quite a field in itself, and one with which I am unfamiliar. I definitely would not attempt it by the use of a 'ghost'. Look at all the lousy books that ghosts have produced since the war! Again, it would have meant living in Washington for several years, of digging into many thousands of documents written by other officers as well as by my staff and myself, and of which I do not have copies. Finally, I scarcely could have avoided controversy, and giving myself 'breaks' that perhaps would be undeserved.
>
> So, Judge, the whole thing simply did not appeal to me then, and appeals to me even less now. Future professional historians will write what they feel like writing anyhow, whether truthful or not. So I'm willing to let them disagree among themselves!

When I had my first interview about this book with Kelly Turner, he told me with a grin:

> When Judge told me that you were willing to undertake the task, I thought,
>   'Well, he's just enough of a son-of-a-bitch to do a good job.'
> So, I told Judge 'all right'.

Acknowledgements

During the nine years that the author of this factual study of the life of Admiral Richmond Kelly Turner worked on these volumes, hundreds of all ranks and ratings in the Armed Forces have been interviewed. My very real thanks go to each one of them for their contribution to this work, but particularly to those who had the intestinal fortitude to permit themselves to be quoted when they had something critical to say about the subject.

To the Director of Naval History, Rear Admiral E. M. Eller, who initiated this factual study, who encouraged me to undertake it and then patiently, very patiently, waited for the end product, more than thanks is due. My warmest gratitude extends to him.

The long seige of my efforts was mostly carried through in the Navy's Classified Operational Archives, whose physical location shifted frequently, but the courtesy of Dean Allard who heads the Archives Division and of Mrs. Mildred Mayeux, research assistant, who was a thousand times helpful, never shifted. They are real gems in the naval historical research field.

To Mr. Paul A. Sweeney of the Office of Naval Operations, who took my maps and diagrams and made them come alive with his cartographic art, my deepest thanks.

To my friends of many years, Vice Admiral T. G. W. Settle and Captain John E. Dingwell, who read the manuscript and pointed out my errors, thanks again for their patience and real help.

To a former Ships Writer of mine, Chris A. Miller, who persisted through his retirement years in the decipherment of my handwriting and the typing (and then retyping) thanks ten times over. And to Mrs. Jean Ellinger who typed the final smooth copy so well, an accolade.

Last, but not least, my wife of 48 years bore with me and my writing chore with remarkable understanding, year after year after year, and my public thanks to her.

George C. Dyer

GEORGE C. DYER

Foreword

THE AMPHIBIANS CAME TO CONQUER

This book is a story of a fighting man—Kelly Turner—of the maturing United States Navy, and of the people who helped develop the man into a fighting admiral. It is also a story of the seagoing part of the amphibious operations of World War II in which Kelly Turner fought.

Since Kelly Turner was a United States Naval Officer and fought only in the Pacific Ocean in World War II, this book deals primarily with the amphibious matters of the World War II Pacific campaigns. But it does not pretend to tell the whole story of our naval war or the amphibious campaigns in the Pacific from 1942 to 1945. After all, it took that distinguished historian, Samuel E. Morison, nine of his 14 volume *History of United States Naval Operations in World War II* and 18 years to do that chore.

Kelly Turner's claim to permanent naval distinction arises out of his contributions to the amphibious phases of World War II in the South and Central Pacific Oceans. So this volume moves from Pacific island to Pacific atoll to Pacific island again, as our bone crushing amphibious operations cleared the stepping stones to Tokyo.

It also tells a bit of the state of the purely naval aspects of the amphibious art when World War II started. And, more importantly, what happened as the war moved along to improve the art, as Kelly Turner and a million other Americans brought their minds to bear on "the most difficult problem" in warfare, an amphibious operation.

During the 24 years since World War II ended, most of the titans of the World War II Navy—namely Leahy, King, Nimitz, Halsey, Edwards—have told their last anecdote and voyaged over the line into their last snug harbor. In an effort to get a well-rounded picture of Kelly Turner and of the various amphibious operations, those of the titans (Nimitz, Kinkaid, Spruance) still alive when this was being researched and many of his other seniors and principal subordinates have been consulted about a vast variety of matters in connection with which they were in a position to witness events or to have informed opinions.

Keeping in mind that the historian's rule is that the pale ink of a contemporary record is better than the best memory, still there are some facts and many important opinions never committed to that contemporary record. At least that was this biographer's own experience during service through three wars in the United States Navy. So it is only fair to say that the contents of this book are colored by the facts revealed and opinions expressed by those consulted, as well as by the basic contemporary record.

Every major amphibious operation in the South and Central Pacific campaigns was born and bred among strong men of strong professional opinions. The student of amphibious warfare and of the Navy will benefit from mention of those differing opinions, for he must prepare himself to operate successfully in an atmosphere of strong professional judgments in any future arena of war.

George C. Dyer

GEORGE C. DYER
PENDENNIS MOUNT
ANNAPOLIS, MARYLAND

April 23, 1969

Contents

VOLUME I

Chapter		Page
	Prologue	v
	Acknowledgements	vii
	Foreword	ix
	Introduction	xix
I	The First Thirty Years of "Kelly"; 1885–1915	1
II	Ten Years of Big Ship Gunnery; 1916–1926	51
III	Early Years of a Decade of Service in the Naval Aeronautical Organization; 1927–1932	87
IV	In and Out of Big Time Naval Aviation; 1932–1940	115
V	Planning for War with Germany or Japan, or Both; 1940–1941	153
VI	1941 Naval Organization, Doctrine and Landing Craft Developments for Amphibious War	201
VII	WATCHTOWER; One for Ernie King	229
VIII	CACTUS Bound	277
IX	Success, Then Cliff Hanging	319
X	SAVO—The Galling Defeat	355
XI	Logistics, the Heart of the Six Months Battle; August 1942–February 1943	403
XII	HUDDLE Slowly Scuttled	435
XIII	Polishing Skills in the Russells	457
XIV	Planning for Paring the Japanese Toenails in New Georgia	481
XV	Tough Toenails Paring; 30 June 1943 to 15 July 1943	533

VOLUME II

XVI	To the Central Pacific and Tarawa	597
XVII	The Pushover—Makin	651
XVIII	That Real Toughie—Tarawa	683
XIX	At Long Last "The Perfect One," The Marshalls	733
XX	Roi—Namur, and The Frosting on the Cake—Eniwetok	801
XXI	The Nut Cracker; Saipan—Tinian—Guam	853
XXII	The Nut Cracker After the Fall of Saipan; Tinian—Guam	925
XXIII	Iwo Jima; Death at Its Best	969
XXIV	Okinawa and Four Stars	1053
XXV	End of the War and United Nations Organization Duty	1113
XXVI	The Last Long Mile	1137
	Appendix A—*USS Richmond K. Turner*	1175
	Appendix B—A Note on Primary Sources	1179
	Appendix C—The Last Word	1181
	Bibliography	1185
	Index	1191

Illustrations and Charts

(Illustrations identified by numbers preceded by 80-G are official U.S. Naval photographs in the National Archives; those numbered with NR&L(M) prefixes are in the historical collection in the U.S. Naval Photographic Center, Washington, D. C.; those numbered with NH prefixes, and those identified as from the Turner Collection, are in the Naval History Division, Washington, D.C.)

VOLUME I

	Page
Rear Admiral Turner enroute to Kwajalein	frontispiece
Richmond Kelly Turner at fifteen	7
Invitation to reception, 1900	8
High school graduation	10
USS Milwaukee	31
Ensign Turner and niece	34
Kelly Turner and his bride-to-be	37
Ensign Turner in landing force uniform	44
Lieutenant (jg) Turner at San Pedro de Macoris	47
Commander Turner at about 45	82
Commander Turner, Executive Officer of USS Saratoga	117
USS Astoria woodcut	143
Funeral procession for late Ambassador Saito	144
Sailors carrying ashes	145
Captain Turner, Mr. Arita, and Joseph Grew	147
Turner-drafted despatch	178–79
Beardall memorandum	180
Central and South Pacific Area (chart)	231
Solomon Islands, Santa Cruz Islands (chart)	236
South Pacific island garrisons (chart)	237
Lines of communication (chart)	250
South Pacific distance chart	251
Captain James H. Doyle, USN	271
Kelly Turner at Tongatabu, Tonga Islands	278
Organization of the South Pacific Force	280
Organization of Permanent Forces of PHIBFORSOPAC	281
Rear Admiral Turner and Major General Vandegrift	289
Amphibious Force, TF 62 organization for WATCHTOWER	291
COMSOPAC organization for WATCHTOWER	292
Expeditionary Force, TF 61 organization for WATCHTOWER	292
Top Echelon organization for WATCHTOWER	293
On the bridge of USS McCawley	299

	Page
The Fiji Islands (chart)	306
The Solomons and Southern Approaches (chart)	314
The Solomon Islands (chart)	320
Guadalcanal-Tulagi (chart)	322
Task Force 62 Cruising Disposition (chart)	324
Guadalcanal and the Russell Islands (chart)	325
Landing Objectives—Tulagi-Gavutu (chart)	331
Marine landing at Tonga Island	334
Transport Area, Guadalcanal (chart)	335
Mineswept Areas, Guadalcanal (chart)	339
Japanese attacks, Guadalcanal	347
Japanese high-level attacks, Guadalcanal	349
Battle of Savo Island (chart)	356
Plane sightings of Japanese Cruiser Force (chart)	363
Vice Admiral Gunichi Mikawa, IJN	366
Ship disposition at Savo Island (chart)	376
Disposition of Patrol and Screening Groups at Savo (chart)	379
Multiple Approach Route—Savo (chart)	381
Rear Admiral Turner at sea, 1942	409
Guadalcanal supply lines (chart)	418
Santa Cruz Island (chart)	436
Officers and Men of the Staff Allowance, COMPHIBFORSOPAC	459
Movement to CLEANSLATE (chart)	461
Russell Islands (chart)	469
Airfield Banika Island	471
The Bismarck Barrier (chart)	482
New Georgia and Rendova Island (chart)	486
TOENAILS Operation Area (chart)	489
Japanese Defense Organization for Bismarck Barrier	491
Training Seabees at Noumea, New Caledonia	495
Rear Admiral Turner with Seabee officers	496
Vangunu and New Georgia Islands (chart)	497
Colonel Henry D. Linscott, USMC	508
Officers' Quarters, Guadalcanal	510
SOPAC Naval Organization for TOENAILS	514
The Admiral's Head	517
Lieutenant Colonel Frank D. Weir, USMC	519
Staff of Commander Amphibious Force South Pacific	521
Task Force 31 organization for TOENAILS	524
1st Echelon Western Group (TU 31.1)	526
Eastern Force organizatios for TOENAILS	526
The day's catch	529
Lieutenant Charles Stein (SC), USN	529
New Georgia Group (chart)	534
Assault Force organization for TOENAILS	535

	Page
New Georgia Island, Onaiavisi Entrance (chart)	540
Rendova Harbor (chart)	543
Road at East and West Beaches, Rendova	544
Rendova-New Georgia Area (chart)	546
LCI(L) Group 14 landing craft, Rendova Harbor (chart)	553
Men of the 24th Construction Battalion	557
Japanese air attack, 30 June 1943 (chart)	558
Eastern Force organization for TOENAILS	563
Viru Harbor (chart)	568
Vangunu Island and Wickham Anchorage (chart)	573
Zanana Beach, New Georgia Island (chart)	578
Rice Anchorage, New Georgia Island (chart)	580
Bairoca Road, Munda, New Georgia	584
Cargo unloaded at Munda	588

VOLUME II

	Page
Fifth Amphibious Force Emblem	602
Rear Admiral Turner, Fall 1943	605
USS *Pennsylvania* (BB-38)	610
Marshall and Gilbert Islands (chart)	612
Gilbert Islands (chart)	615
Central Pacific (chart)	615
CINCPAC's Operation Plan—GALVANIC	629
Central Pacific Forces, Fifth Fleet Operation Plan—GALVANIC	630
Assault Force, TF 54 Operation Plan—GALVANIC	631
Northern Attack Force, TF 52 Operation Plan—GALVANIC	633
Makin Atoll (chart)	650
Southwest Butaritari Island (chart)	660
Makin Atoll, Gilbert Islands (chart)	664
Butaritari Island, Yellow Beach Two (chart)	670
Tarawa Atoll (chart)	683
Betio Island (chart)	689
Landing craft allocation, Betio (chart)	695
Red Beaches, Betio Island (chart)	698
Japan to the Gilberts (chart)	735
The Marshall Islands (chart)	738
Kwajalein Atoll (chart)	750
Fifth Fleet Command organization for FLINTLOCK	754
Joint Expeditionary Force, TF 51 organization for FLINTLOCK	754
Southern Attack Force, TF 52 organization for FLINTLOCK	755
Fifth Amphibious Force Staff	759
Blockhouse "BRUCE" on Roi Island	764
Southern Kwajalein Atoll (chart)	768
Gea and South Passes (chart)	768
Roi-Namur (chart)	772
Majuro or Arrowsmith Atoll (chart)	774

	Page
USS Rocky Mount, Marshall Islands	780
Gea Pass (chart)	784
Landing beaches, Kwajalein Island (chart)	794
Northern Kwajalein (chart)	801
USS Appalachian (AGC-1)	804
Landing Plan-IVAN and JACOB (chart)	805
Roi-Namur Fire Support Areas (chart)	814
Blockhouse at Red Beach Three, Roi Island	818
Marines waiting to advance at Green Beach Two	819
Eniwetok Atoll (chart)	824
Rear Admiral Harry W. Hill and Brigadier General Thomas E. Watson	828
Engebi Island (chart)	835
Eniwetok Island (chart)	835
Parry Island (chart)	840
Pacific distance chart	858
Lower Marianas distance chart	858
Vice Admiral Turner, 6 June 1944	863
Vice Admiral Turner at the Saipan attack	866
Northeast coast of Saipan	867
Saipan (chart)	871
Fifth Fleet, TF 50 organization for FORAGER	874
Joint Expeditionary Force, TF 51 organization for FORAGER	875
Northern Attack Force, TF 52 organization for FORAGER	877
Fortification, Saipan (chart)	890
Landing positions, Saipan (chart)	904
Landing craft and transports	908
Saipan attack	917
Guam (chart)	926
Southern Guam (chart)	936
Coral-filled log cribs off Agana	938
Wire fence roll obstructions, Agana	941
Barbed wire entanglement at Agana	942
Japanese anti-boat battery, Bangi Point	947
Tinian Island (chart)	951
Tinian flag raising ceremonies, 1944	963
Vice Admiral Turner, Commodore Theiss, Captain Patten	967
Admiral King's handwritten memo	977
USS Eldorado at Iwo Jima	985
Vice Admiral Turner dictating to his writer	986
Nanpo Shoto Group (chart)	988
Iwo Jima (chart)	990
Vice Admiral Turner enroute to Iwo Jima	992
Command organization for DETACHMENT	995
Fifth Fleet organization for DETACHMENT	996
Joint Expeditionary Force for DETACHMENT	997

	Page
"Every Man a Lookout"	1007
Assault commanders in *USS Rocky Mount*	1012
Landing beach at Mount Suribachi	1017
Bombardment of Mount Suribachi	1019
Landing craft, East Beach	1022
Congestion of supplies	1026
LST-764 unloading at Iwo Jima	1026
Road construction at Iwo	1029
Bulldozers	1031
Preassembled Marston matting	1034
Unloading at Red Beach	1034
View from Mount Suribachi	1036
Turner's request for pre-landing bombardment	1043
Spruance's reply to Turner re pre-landing bombardment	1044
Turner with Captain Whitehead and Commodore Theiss	1057
Distance chart, Ryukyu Islands	1060
Okinawa (chart)	1067
Kerama Retto—Okinawa Area (chart)	1068
Command organization, Okinawa	1070
Pacific Ocean Area, Okinawa	1070
Fifth Fleet organization for Okinawa	1071
Joint Expeditionary Force Command for Okinawa	1073
Military leaders, *USS Eldorado* off Okinawa	1085
Hagushi assault landing	1090
USS Teton Okinawa operation	1092
LST-884 at Kerama Retto after kamikaze attack	1101
USS Leutze after kamikaze attack	1103
Oil painting of Admiral Turner	1107
Mrs. Turner at Navy Day Luncheon, 1945	1116
Portrait of Admiral Turner	1118
Military Staff Committee of United Nations	1120
Vice Admiral and Mrs. John Ballantine	1123
Major General Leslie Groves and Admiral Turner	1126
Mrs. Turner and her dogs	1129
Admiral Turner visits the *Eldorado*	1151
Admiral Turner and Captain Peden, 1954	1155
Richmond Kelly Turner on *Time* magazine cover	1164

Introduction

Admiral Dyer has created a unique book about a unique man in these pages filled with the clear understanding, the seeking for truth and the salty language of a true sailor. He has done this by years of indefatigable persistence not unlike that of his subject—a man never known to quail before a barrier or to shrink from work, danger or hardship. In fact, those on the receiving end of his amphibious typhoon soon learned that Admiral Kelly Turner didn't even know the word barrier.

Of the millions of Americans who greatly served our times afloat and ashore in the Pacific in World War II, few did not know of Kelly Turner, one of history's ablest military leaders. He was a man greatly admired by many, greatly loved by some and greatly hated by others. He was a genius, a relentless driver of himself as well as of everyone under him, an unusual leader who could integrate into his computer brain more details of an operation than the experts on his staff knew. At the same time he could make the big decision instantly and then carry it through with unrelenting drive. He had the rare ability to see all the trees and at the same time comprehend the forest. "Terrible Turner," as many called him, was terrible indeed to the enemy, as well as to some of those under him who did not measure up to his almost impossible standards of effectiveness.

Admiral Dyer's fascinating biography of this remarkable naval leader has many appeals. Not the least is his unremitting effort to get at the truth and frankness in relating it. He pulls no punches showing Turner just as this tough and fearless leader wanted to be shown—without camouflage. Thus the dark cruises in company with the bright. Note a few of the statements about Kelly Turner picked at random from the book:

 a. A "fresh caught" ensign who served in Kelly Turner's spit and polish cruiser before World War II recalls vividly: "Captain Turner was the meanest man I ever saw, and the most competent naval officer I ever served with."

 b. A splendid Marine officer who served first on the Staff of Major General Holland M. Smith, USMC and then on Turner's staff recollects: "Admiral Turner had an almost unbelievable capacity for work. He drove himself without mercy, and he expected and demanded the same of those around him. I never saw him relax or take his ease."

c. General Holland M. (Howling Mad) Smith, Turner's able counterpart in the Marines writes: "Kelly Turner is aggressive, a mass of energy and a relentless task master. The punctilious exterior hides a terrific determination. He can be plain ornery. He wasn't called 'Terrible Turner' without reason.

"He commanded the FIFTH AMPHIBIOUS FORCE, while I commanded the Expeditionary Troops which went along with the Navy and our partnership, though stormy, spelled hell in big red letters to the Japanese."

As a young officer, many years his junior, I had not heard of Kelly Turner before World War II. His name hove in sight for me with his well-executed landing on Guadalcanal and subsequent bitter defeat in the Japanese surprise night attack of what we then called the first battle of Savo—and of which as part of my duties on Admiral Nimitz's staff, I prepared the CINCPAC action report. The same questions about this battle that Admiral Dyer so well explains without bias, but with care to present all of the evidence, likewise deeply concerned us at the time. Yet I think most agreed with the decision that the defeat did not mean that Admiral Turner would be relieved.

In November 1942 on a trip to Guadalcanal and elsewhere in the Pacific related to training, battle lessons, and improvements in ordnance and gunnery, I first met Admiral Turner in his flagship at Noumea. Subsequently I rode with him in his flagship, as in the Gilberts operation, or visited him from another ship in later mighty amphibious assaults including Okinawa that swept awesomely across the Pacific like successive typhoons. I saw him often at Pearl Harbor in the planning stages of these far-reaching campaigns as we and his staff worked closely on bombardment plans, shore fire control parties, tactics, training, and other facets of amphibious operations like underwater demolition teams. The initial team developed late in the planning for the Gilberts operations evolving from intelligence on boat mines close inshore and the problem of reefs interfering with movement to the beaches. The first makeshift team, hurriedly assembled, served such good purpose in the Gilberts operation that a full program sprang from it.

No man could have been more courteous, gentlemanly and kind than Admiral Turner was to me, a visitor and observer in his domain. At the

Introduction

same time I could see the relentless tenacity with which he cracked his whip over those who formed his team. He drove them ruthlessly but none more so than himself, as Admiral Dyer clearly brings out.

If I were to measure the traits that make a leader succeed, I would place at the top courage and drive (the will to win), faith in Divine guiding power, preparation and knowledge, integrity. If a leader has these, few things short of death can stop him. If to them he adds generosity of spirit, compassion and patience with people, overlaid on his own impatience to succeed, he will be greatly loved.

Though often lacking this last noble trait, Admiral Turner had the qualities necessary to succeed to an eminent degree. Nothing fazed him. Difficulty and danger stirred him to his most brilliant endeavor. He seemed to fear neither death nor the devil and hurled himself into the forefront of the greatest peril. On one of the operations I remember being shown by the flag censor an outgoing letter from a sailor on the flagship. It read something like this, "We are getting ready to sail on a big operation. I don't know where we are going but this is probably your last letter from me. Terrible Turner is on board and where he goes you are lucky if you come back."

Admiral Turner obviously had compassion and understanding of men. His own swift grasp of the whole picture, however, his customary near perfection in action, his relentless urge to hit ever faster and harder, resulted in lashing impatience against those who couldn't steam at his flank speed 18 hours a day.

The United States needed a leader of his capacity in the rough, tough and complex amphibious game in the Pacific. After victory, we also needed to get a clear account of this man and his methods against the unknown crises the future would bring. Years ago upon relieving Rear Admiral John B. Heffernan in this job, I found an excellent program of command studies underway on two of our senior naval leaders who had played key roles in shaping events from World War I on. To these we happily were able to add many others in full or partial studies by joining in the Columbia University Oral History Program through the generous aid of Allan Nevins.

In addition to these oral history studies, some leaders covered personal recollections of the momentous events of World War II at least in part by published works as in the case of Admirals Leahy, King, Halsey and Mitscher. Admirals Nimitz, Spruance and Turner, three titans in any history of war, steadfastly refused to record anything. Each had personal reasons that repeated efforts could not shake. We kept trying. At last when we found the right officer to prepare his command study, but near the end of his voyage on earth's troubled seas, Admiral Turner gave in.

Sadly, early in the study Admiral Turner embarked upon his last great expedition—to storm the gates of the Beyond. Very soon thereafter Admiral Spruance, his close friend and neighbor as well as companion through many valiant days, agreed to enter the program. This resulted in the excellent book *Admiral Raymond A. Spruance, USN, A Study in Command* by Vice Admiral E. P. Forrestel, USN (Retired). Admiral Nimitz went part way, but, for reasons one must respect, even to the end, would not enter into a full command study.

Admiral Turner knew that he had in Admiral Dyer an officer of great sagacity, excellent balance and judgment, wide experience in both planning and operations—a man like himself, tenacious for the truth. He desired and knew that Admiral Dyer would spare no effort to find the facts and to present them as he found them, let the chips fall where they may. In the interesting pages that follow, the reader will swiftly note these characteristics of the sailor-author along with seagoing language filled with the tang of salt spray.

It has been a deep pleasure working with Admiral Dyer through the years and watching this exhaustive study evolve—a study that could be of immense benefit to the Navy as it serves the nation in the trials of the future. We have made all our resources available to him, including the matchless records of World War II. We have helped in every way possible but he has done the work. His own tireless spirit drove him on in sickness and in health through thousands of hours of work. He did much of his research in our Classified Operational Archives aided by our admirable staff there under Dr. Dean Allard. Along with myself, Dr. Allard was among those who read and made recommendation on the manuscript which Admiral Dyer accepted or rejected. Miss Sandra Brown contributed immeasurably in preparing the final manuscript for publishing. Mr. John Gallagher of the Printing and Publications Division of the Office of the Chief of Naval Operations deserves special credit for his assistance. But to repeat, this is Admiral Dyer's own work, developed with his own hand without any variation other than his acceptance of some of our suggestions.

The United States Navy's overwhelming and invariably successful amphibious assaults of World War II, which this fine book covers for those directed by that master of the art, Richmond Kelly Turner, did not come solely from the courage, skill and bold leadership that illumined all of them. These qualities of the spirit marvelously shown by hundreds of thousands of Ameri-

Introduction

cans made the assaults succeed. However, the unbroken chain of successes in the Central Pacific where Turner's driving will reigned, in the Southwest Pacific under Admiral D. E. Barbey (Uncle Dan the amphibious man) and in the Atlantic under another master, Admiral H. Kent Hewitt, rested on the marked advantages sea based power had gained over that ashore with every step in invention and technology. Together they had strikingly increased the ancient advantages of navies of mobility, flexibility, surprise and awesome concentration of striking power.

From the first decades of the 19th century to these last ones of the 20th, the gradually accelerating and now exploding industrial-scientific revolution has profoundly changed the world. It has had far-reaching impact upon every aspect of man's life but nowhere more than in the weapons by which aggressors try to spread the rule of tyranny and by which wise men of democracies keep strong if they expect to survive.

One of the most significant results of the repeated scientific-technological revolutions has been the steady growth in ability of power based at sea to overcome that ashore. Over a century ago the introduction of steam (and much later the internal-combustion engine) freed the attack by ships from the vagaries of wind and tide and speeded up every part of an amphibious operation. Indeed the increased capability and precision that steam brought to attack from the sea came at just the right time to play an overwhelming role in Union victory in the Civil War—insuring a united nation for the great needs and stresses of our times.

Several significant developments besides steam increased relative strength afloat in the Civil War. These included armor that gave ships something of the resistance of forts, much larger guns providing enormous concentrations of heavy mobile artillery that seldom could be matched ashore, and the beginning of rifling that increased the range of attack making it harder for fixed guns to hit distant maneuvering ships.

After the Civil War many other developments followed. It is sufficient to mention a few of the most influential. At the turn of the century the submarines came into the Fleet to enlarge seapower's advantages of secrecy and surprise; in amphibious operations they provided means for undetected scouting and reconnaissance. The airplane, evolving with the internal combustion engine, when based afloat on the moving airfields of carriers gave large concentrations of power and opened vast new horizons for navies. In World War II, radar and the influence fuse joined a long line of advances in fire control, including ancestors of today's computers, that brought large progress in accuracy and effect of gunfire. This particularly benefited the ship in combat with shore fortifications because of its ability to maneuver and dodge at high speed whereas its target ashore was immobile.

Other developments favoring assault from the sea included increased size and efficiency of attack transports that provided swift movement of armies over long sea distances. Likewise, specialized landing ships and craft of many types developed to speed the assault troops to the beach. Closing the shore, they enjoyed a volume of protective fire never before attained. In most of Admiral Turner's operations the concentration of fire from ships large and small, from planes off support carriers cruising nearby, and from the troops' amphibians, including tanks, was so devastating that, if it did not knock out, it stunned the defenders. Hence the first waves of troops met practically no resistance coming in, or at the beach. After the capture of Guam, for example, Major General Geiger, USMC, commanding the Landing Force sent this message:

> . . . I wish to express . . . my appreciation for continuous and effective support rendered. The enemy was never able to rally from the initial bombardment and the continual gunfire support kept him in a state of confusion to the end of the campaign. Naval gunfire contributed largely in keeping losses of the Landing Forces to a minimum and in bringing the Guam Campaign to an early and successful close. . . .
>
> The positions where we landed were heavily fortified. . . . Our naval gunfire and air bombardments were so effective that scarcely a shot was fired at our first four LVT waves until after they were on the beach. At least half of the total amount of fixed defenses were destroyed, and more than that in the vicinity of the landing. Probably 80% of the troops defending the beach either were killed or retreated to other positions.

The foregoing and much more unfold in Admiral Dyer's thorough study as he tells the story of the growth of the Amphibious Navy's ships and craft, the development of the amphibious art, and the awesome effect of Terrible Turner's amphibious typhoon "slightly controlled and irresistible." Not least among the study's merits is the fact that in it for the first time we find individually named the smaller ships and craft of the amphibious task forces, and their commanders, who fought under Turner through the rugged campaigns of the South and Central Pacific.

Admiral Turner fearlessly rode the crest of danger. Where the greatest risks and toil awaited, there he was found leading the attack. Americans owe him a large debt for his achievements that so remarkably shaped history. And we owe gratitude to Admiral Dyer who has so carefully and well

Introduction

portrayed Admiral Turner's methods, his growth in experience, and the accomplishments of the amphibians of the Pacific Fleet which Turner so well developed and led.

How much these meant to the United States and freedom then. How much the complex overall Navy in which the amphibious force merges as a key element means today. Yet, we find most Americans complacently accepting the phenomenal rise in Soviet sea power in the last decade, while we cut back our own Navy, as a matter of no importance. Hopefully, Admiral Dyer's able work will help to bring better understanding.

E. M. ELLER
Director of Naval History

CHAPTER I

The First Thirty Years of "Kelly" 1885–1915

Kelly Turner spent 43 active years on the Navy List. He left his mark on the Navy and on his brother officers, both seniors and juniors, for he flayed about a bit in our Navy. But most of all, he flayed the Japanese, from early August in 1942 until mid-August in 1945.

When Kelly finished with the Japanese, they were licked. When Kelly finished his active service and moved on to the retired list of the Navy, the Navy was not licked, but it was quieter and never quite the same.

His multitudinous friends, and even his foreign enemies were unanimous in their appraisal of one aspect of his character. For the Japanese in a radio broadcast on 21 February 1945 said:

> The true nature of an alligator is that once he bites into something, he will not let go. Turner's nature is also like this.[1]

This is the story of a man who once he bit into something, would not let go.

THE TURNER CLAN[2]

Let us look into Kelly Turner's family origins to find a clue explaining this characteristic.

His forebears, the Kellys and the Turners were an energetic and a restless lot. They moved out of the British Isles and west across the Atlantic Ocean.

---
[1] *Foreign Broadcast Intelligence Service Bulletin;* 28 February 1945.
[2] Information on the Turner Clan from:
(a) James Turner's Bible (oldest son of John Turner); (b) John Turner's Bible from his children. Presented on his 73rd birthday 27 October 1873 (second son of John Turner); (c) B. I. Griswold, *History of Fort Wayne, Indiana* (1917); (d) Turner Family Magazine, January 1916; (e) Records of Caroline County, Maryland; (f) Newspaper clippings, 24 November 1879 to 19 October 1932, from various California and Ohio newspapers; (g) History of the Turner Clan as compiled by Richmond Kelly Turner; (h) Interviews with and letters of Miss L. Lucile Turner, Carmel, California, 1961–1963. Hereafter Miss L. Turner.

They kept moving west across the New Country until the Pacific Ocean barred further western movement. Then they churned up and down the Pacific Coast.

The particular Turner progenitors with whom we are concerned migrated from Westmoreland in Northwest England prior to the middle of the 1720's and settled on the Chesapeake Bay side of the Eastern Shore of Maryland. They received a 12-mile square land grant in Caroline County between the Choptank River and Tuchanoe Creek. This is about 50 miles, as the crow flies, due east of the Capitol in Washington, D.C.

The Turners had been farmers and millers in England and they were farmers, millers and traders in Colonial Maryland. They also were Protestant and members of the Church of England. John Turner, great grandfather of Richmond Kelly Turner bit into Methodism in 1765. This outraged the elders of the clan, who gave John the hard choice of reconverting or losing his land heritage. He was a good alligator, gave up his land heritage, and stayed a Methodist. This decision entailed a short move westward in Maryland to Talbot County on Chesapeake Bay.

In 1827, a little over a hundred years after the Turners had first settled in the New World, young farmer John Turner,[3] grandfather of the Admiral, up anchored from Maryland and moved west. He first settled south of Columbus, Ohio, near Circleville, and then in 1833 in Whitley County in northeast Indiana. Here, on 10 April 1843, Enoch Turner, father of Richmond Kelly Turner, was born.

In 1844, the John Turners moved on westward to Iowa. Five years later the big decision was made to undertake the long overland trek to California after a preparatory winter period at Council Bluffs, Iowa.

Departing on 3 April 1850, in company with a family named Blosser, and proceeding via Salt Lake City, the John Turners with six children arrived in Stockton, California, in late August 1850. They brought supplies for the gold mines in what were the latter days of the "Gold Rush." For some months after arrival, John Turner continued in that freighter trade, although the older sons engaged in gold mining on the north bank of the Calaveras River, near San Andreas, California. The family then reverted to farming, first on a section of land in San Joaquin County (where the town, Turner, named for the family lies on Route 50), and then, 20 years later, near Woodville in Tulare County in South Central California.

Enoch Turner, the sixth son and eleventh of John Turner's twelve children,

---

[3] Born Talbot County, Maryland, 27 October 1800, married Mary Bodfield, 27 August 1821.

The First Thirty Years

moved to Oregon after the Civil War, during which his mother had died.[4] His brother Thomas was a printer on the Portland *Oregonian*. On 2 July 1867, Enoch married Laura Francis Kelly [5] in East Portland. He was 24 and a school teacher at the time. The tradition of large families was carried on by Enoch Turner and Laura Kelly. Grandfather Samuel Kelly had had 12 children and the Clinton Kellys 13. Great grandfather John Turner also had had 12, and in turn, his son, John Turner, had had nine children.

Eighteen years after the marriage, on 27 May 1885, Richmond Kelly Turner was born in East Portland, Oregon, the seventh of eight children, three boys and five girls. Grandfather John Turner was 85 when this grandson was born. He was to see the young alligator when, in the next year, he persuaded his son, Enoch, to return to California to help him run his ranch near Woodville, which was becoming a burden because of his years.

Surviving portraits and other data of the Turner clan show their physical characteristics to have been an upright and spare physique, with straight black or brown hair, dark eyes and an occasional hooked nose. In general, they were tough physically and long-lived, the first one transplanted from England reputedly having hung on until reaching the age of 104 (1760). John Turner died in 1891 at age 91;[6] his oldest son James at 102;[7] but his son Enoch, Admiral Turner's father, died in 1923 at a young 80.[8]

The 19th century Turners were a severe clan. They raised their children in the tradition of "Spare the rod, and spoil the child." They were always moving westward toward more primitive living conditions. As farmers and ranchers, they battled nature for long, long hours each day, and with very few mechanical assists. These stern conditions left a mark on the Twentieth Century Turners.

Enoch Turner believed in the value of education and stressed it to his children. Five of the seven, who reached adulthood, prepared for and taught school. One taught for 50 years, another for 37. Since every naval officer is constantly schooling young Americans, it can be added that the youngest son, Richmond Kelly, also was in education for 40 years. For the urge to master knowledge was ingrained in this youngest son from as early as he could remember.[9]

---

[4] 3 March 1863, French Camp, California, 3 miles west of Turner, California.
[5] Born 15 March 1847. Died Anaheim, California, 13 October 1918.
[6] 22 December 1891, Woodville, Tulare County, California.
[7] 18 October 1932, Turner's Station, California.
[8] 16 November 1923, San Diego, California. Buried Parkview Cemetery, Stockton, California.
[9] Interviews with Admiral Richard K. Turner, USN (Ret.), Monterey, California, Mar. 1960. Hereafter Turner.

KELLY CLAN[10]

It will be no surprise that an enterprising Protestant Kelly came from Ireland, settled in Pennsylvania near Philadelphia, and by the early 1740's started a numerous Kelly clan on the development of the New World. This was a period which the *Encyclopaedia Britannica* says was marked by immigration from Ireland of "poorer Protestants ruined by heavy rents and the commercial acts."[11]

In the early 1750's the Colony of Virginia recruited many Scots, Irish and Germans, recently arrived in the New World, to settle on the western border of Virginia to form barrier communities against Indian attacks. One of the Irish so recruited was Thomas Kelly who moved to Botetourt County (north of Roanoke) where he farmed his homestead.

Thomas Kelly fulfilled the purpose of his recruitment when he participated in the French-Indian Wars of 1754–1760, during which France and England fought for the control of the Ohio Valley. Certificate #5808 of the Botetourt County Court, Virginia, now in the possession of the Turner family (and sighted by the author), certifies that he served as a corporal in the militia of Virginia and in Captain Dickenson's Company of Rangers for the protection of the Colony of Virginia during 1757, 1758, and 1759.

The fighting capabilities of the Irish found further employment during the Revolutionary War, when Thomas Kelly served in Moylan's Cavalry, Continental Line, Fourth Pennsylvania Regiment of Light Dragoons. As partial compensation for these services, Thomas Kelly received a grant of land in Greenbrier County in the western part of Virginia (now eastern West Virginia).

However, land did not hold the Thomas Kellys in Virginia, for about 1800 they moved on from Greenbrier County to a place near Somerset in Pulaski County, Kentucky. There it is duly recorded that Samuel Kelly, third son of Thomas who had been born in Botetourt County, Virginia, on 7

---

[10] Information on the Kelly clan is from:

(a) Pennsylvania Archives, 5th series. Vols III and IV; (b) Lewis Preston Summers, *Annals of South-West Virginia, 1790–1800* (Abingdon, Virginia: By the author, 1929), pp. 91, 373, 379, 384; (c) James P. Haltigan, *The Irish in the American Revolution and Their Early Influence in the Colonies* (Washington, D.C.: By the author, 1908); (d) Laura Francis Kelly Turner, Pamphlet (Portland, Oregon: By the author, 1901). Mrs. Turner, the Admiral's mother, was interested in genealogy. Early dates in her pamphlet were based on inquiries made and data collected during a visit east in 1882.

[11] *Encyclopaedia Britannica*, 14th ed., Vol. XII, p. 610.

The First Thirty Years

February 1776, was married to a Nancy Canada at Clifty Creek, Pulaski County, Kentucky, on 3 September 1807. Nancy Canada was ten years younger than her husband, having been born 7 April 1786.

In 1847, Grandfather Clinton Kelly, the eldest son of the Samuel Kellys was 39.[12] He lost two wives through early death, and had married a third, Moriah Maldon Crain, on 11 March 1840. She bore the future mother of the Admiral.

Clinton Kelly was a successful farmer, a lay preacher in the Methodist Church, and dead set against the practice of slavery. He made the quite natural alligator decision to hold on to his belief and to leave the slave state of Kentucky and move on westward to territory where slavery did not exist.

Clinton Kelly and two brothers, Albert and Thomas, built wagons, collected horses, oxen and necessary traveling effects, and in the fall of 1847, the three families went to Independence, Missouri, to make final preparations for an overland trip to The Dalles, Oregon, the next spring. On 1 May 1848, accompanied by four other families, they set out in 12 wagons. The first night a bad hailstorm scattered the stock. All the stock were later found except those belonging to Albert Kelly, so Albert turned back. The remaining six families, with Clinton Kelly as the leader of the caravan, made the trip successfully, shipping their freight by raft from The Dalles to Oregon City, Oregon.

In the spring of 1849, Grandfather Kelly bought 640 acres of land in what is now East Portland, Oregon, for 50 dollars, and planted a crop of potatoes.[13] Grandfather Clinton Kelly became a leader in his community, and remembering that he had given the land for the first school, a grateful East Portland named a high school after him, "The Clinton Kelly High School of Commerce."[14] The 227th ship launched by the Oregon Shipbuilding Company during World War II was named the *Clinton Kelly*.[15] The Clinton Kelly Memorial Church is a lasting monument of his zeal and of his assurance of the vitality of his Christian faith.

Laura Francis Kelly, Mother of the Admiral and the fourth child of Clinton, was born in Pulaski County, Kentucky, prior to the movement of the family to Oregon.

---

[12] Born Clifty Creek, Pulaski County, Kentucky, 15 June 1808.
[13] Now bounded by East 26th, East 42nd, Hogate and Division, East Portland.
[14] Powell Blvd and 40th Avenue, East Portland.
[15] Launched 31 July 1943.

RICHMOND

Admiral Turner's first name "Richmond" came from his mother's youngest brother, Richmond Kelly. Why Laura Kelly's brother was named Richmond is not known, but it is family legend that it came from the Duke of Richmond. The Duke was a great sympathizer and worker for the cause of the American Colonies (and for the cause of Ireland), and an early Kelly had received the name Richmond in his honor. This name had been carried along.[16]

The 14th Edition of the *Encyclopaedia Britannica,* under the heading "Earls and Dukes of Richmond" states:

> Charles, 3rd Duke of Richmond, 1734–1806 . . . In the debates on the policy that led to the War of American Independence Richmond was a firm supporter of the colonists. Richmond also advocated a policy of concession in Ireland, with reference to which he originated the famous phrase 'a union of hearts.' [17]

Admiral Turner informed the author that his mother was a warm supporter of the Irish and of their efforts for independence during the early 20th century.[18]

Admiral Turner's brothers and sisters usually referred to him as "Rich" and family letters to him carried this salutation. His boyhood letters are signed "The Kid," up to age 14 and then until about 1925 are either signed "Richmond" or "Rich." After that they are signed "Rich" or "Kelly." [19]

The John Turner Clan and the Clinton Kelly Clan each were closely knit clans. When Richmond Kelly Turner died, the Kelly Clan, in annual meeting assembled, passed a proper memorial resolution, stating that it was "Fitting and proper that the members of the Kelly Clan take note of his passing and briefly review his life and career."

RICHMOND KELLY TURNER

Young Turner received his grammer grade and high schooling in California, mainly in Stockton, although there was a period when his father was

---

[16] Turner; Miss L. Turner.
[17] *Encyclopaedia Britannica,* 14th ed., Vol. XIX, p. 293.
[18] Turner.
[19] Family letters 1898–1940 (Miss L. Turner). Earliest letter dated 20 Nov. 1898 to "Dear Old Mama" (RKT then aged 13).

Richmond Kelly Turner at fifteen, 1900.

> To
> Mr. and Mrs. Turner,
> Stockton,
> Calif.-
> The teachers and pupils of the Lafayette Eighth Grade desire your presence and that of your family at a reception tendered by them to your son, Richmond, in honor of his success in the Examiner contest.
> The reception will be held in Miller's Memorial Hall, tomorrow evening, June 6,

Invitation to reception.

typesetting and later editing a small weekly in Fresno, during which time, he attended school there.

He was 13 when the Spanish-American War commenced. In Fresno, where he was in 1898, he recalled that he went frequently to the Armory to hear the drummers and speakers bidding young men to enlist. However, he formed no predilection for the Navy at that time.[20]

In 1900, the *San Francisco Examiner,* as a circulation promotion project, sponsored the holding of a competitive examination amongst boys from the eighth grade through junior in high school, in the *Examiner's* circulation area. Subjects covered in the examination were United States History, Civics, and English Composition.

The top 15 contestants were selected to attend both the Republican and Democratic National Political Conventions of 1900. The group, all boys, witnessed the re-nomination of William McKinley in Philadelphia and that of William Jennings Bryan in Kansas City, Missouri. Richmond Kelly Turner

---
[20] Turner.

was one of this very fortunate group of 15 representing Fremont School of Stockton, where he was then in the eighth grade.[21]

In 1901, a cousin suggested that young Turner try for the Naval Academy, as a local appointment existed. Despite the success in the previous competitive examination, the tests for the Naval Academy included geometry, which he had not yet taken in high school, so he decided he was unprepared to tackle the examination without more schooling.[22]

In 1902, the Turner family moved south briefly to Santa Ana, California. The transfer letter for "Richmond Turner" reads as follows:

> STOCKTON HIGH SCHOOL
> May 26, 1902
>
> TO THE PRINCIPAL, SANTA ANA HIGH SCHOOL
>
> This will introduce to you Mr. Richmond Turner who is desirous of entering your High School. He is within a month of promotion from our Junior Class. As a student, he is strong, thorough, and painstaking. Had he remained with us until the end of June, he would have been promoted to the middle class with honorary mention. We regret to part with such a student and feel sure that you will find him a young man of marked ability.
>
> Very respt,
> D. A. MOBLEY
> Prin. S.H.S.

TO THE NAVAL ACADEMY

Early in 1904, Enoch Turner was back north and operating a print shop in Stockton. He called his son's attention to an article in the local newspaper announcing that competitive examinations would be held for appointment by the local (Sixth District) Congressman, James Carion Needham, to both the Naval Academy at Annapolis and the Military Academy at West Point.[23]

By an Act of Congress approved 3 March 1903, the number of appointments to the Naval Academy by each Senator, Representative, and Delegate in Congress had been increased temporarily from one to two, in order to provide officers for the enlarged United States Fleet, which President Theodore Roosevelt was urging the Congress both to authorize and to provide the tax money for. In passing the Act for the enlargement of the Naval Academy, Congress had prescribed that the appointments were to be made as deter-

---
[21] *San Francisco Examiner*, 1943; Miss L. Turner.
[22] Turner.
[23] *Ibid.*

Richmond Kelly Turner at his high school graduation, 1904.

The First Thirty Years

mined by the Secretary of the Navy; but so that ultimately each Senator, Congressman, and Delegate might recommend one person for appointment as midshipman during each Congress.[24] So Congressman Needham's vacancy was similar to one which many Congressmen had in the year 1904.

It might be noted here, however, that the Congress took a dim view of this increase as a long-continued measure, and provided that on 30 June 1913, the appointments would revert to one midshipman in the Naval Academy at any one time for each Congressman. Fortunately for the United States Navy in World War I, this diminution in appointments never took place.[25]

After a couple of days of wrestling with the problem of his future, and primarily because of the modest state of the family exchequer, which did not match his burning desire for a first-rate college education, young Turner decided to make a try for an appointment. This decision was made despite his mother's general, and strongly stated, objections to all war and its trappings and her youngest son's involvement therein. He started doing extra studying. Without tutorage, but with an assist from the Naval Academy in the form of a pamphlet with copies of previous examinations, he won the appointment from a group of eighteen candidates.[26]

Looking over the examinations which young Turner took for the *Examiner* contest and the ones which candidates for admittance to the Naval Academy took during the years 1903–1907, and then giving these examinations a quick comparison with those taken by prospective midshipmen of recent years, the vast changes in the examination processes for the same basic subjects are immediately apparent. The present educational examination system frequently supplies correct answers and requires only their identification amongst error, while the horrendous ones of yester-year required substantive knowledge, such as:

> Briefly describe the work of the following men in connection with the colonial history of the United States
> Captain John Smith
> John Winthrop
> Roger Willliams
> Lord Baltimore
> William Pitt
> James Wolfe
> Give an account of:
> Admiral Coligny

---
[24] *U.S. Naval Academy Register,* 1901–1902, 1903–1904, 1905–1906, 1906–1907.
[25] *Ibid.*
[26] Turner.

Warren Hastings
Nathaniel Hawthorne

Despite this hazard and that of having to name in proper order all the waters passed through in making a voyage from Yokohama, Japan, to Saint Louis, Missouri, via Hongkong and the Suez Canal, 297 physically qualified young Americans took their places in the rear ranks of the Regiment of Midshipmen during the summer of 1904. Among them was Richmond Kelly Turner, who had done very well in all subjects except geography, in which he had perhaps failed to mention the Straits of Bab-el-Mandeb as he entered the steaming waters of the Red Sea, en route to far away Saint Louis.

MIDSHIPMAN TURNER

Richmond Kelly Turner became a midshipman on 13 June 1904. He was erect, long limbed and slender (6 feet, 1¾ inches tall and 150 pounds), black haired, well featured, and sober faced.

When the Class of 1908 entered the Naval Academy in 1904, Captain Willard H. Brownson, U. S. Navy, Class of 1865, was Superintendent. Captain Brownson, U. S. Navy, was a well-known naval figure, destined to have the distinction of continuing on as Chief of the Bureau of Navigation for some five months and 16 days after his retirement for age.

Two years previously (by Act of Congress approved 1 July 1902) the title of the young gentlemen under instruction at the Naval Academy had been changed from naval cadets to midshipmen. The latter name had a long seagoing background, while the word "cadet," in use only from 1883 to 1902, was strictly Army in its connotations. The change was both welcome and sensible.

And the previous year, the Congress had further provided that all candidates at time of examination for the Naval Academy, must be between the ages of 16 and 20, instead of between 15 and 20 as had been prescribed since the Act of 4 March 1889. This latter change tended to equalize just a bit the educational level of the entering midshipmen.

As candidate Turner walked through the massive gate of the Naval Academy "in whose shadow an armed sentinel ever paces to and fro" to become Midshipman Turner and to be paid 500 dollars per year, he was to discover that the physical Naval Academy was in the process of being completely rebuilt to its present monumental aspect. The "Old Quarters" dating from 1845 and the "New Quarters" dating from 1870, were being replaced by Bancroft Hall, a large dormitory named after the 1845 Secretary of the Navy, George Bancroft. Large classroom buildings with commodious and modern teaching facilities and named after naval officers who had made their mark in the educational (Mahan), inventive (Dahlgren), engineering (Isherwood), or command aspects (Sampson, Schley) of the Navy, were growing apace.

> The work on the new buildings has progressed in as satisfactory a manner as could be expected during the past year, considering the almost unprecedented severity of the winter. . . . [and the living quarters for the midshipmen] should be ready for occupancy on 20 September 1904.[27]

The Old Academy was a hodgepodge, in arrangement of buildings, in types of architecture, and in the varying inadequacies of the facilities. But the primary reason for the complete rebuilding was to be found in the blossoming of the United States into a world power under the leadership of Presidents William McKinley and Theodore Roosevelt. To provide the military power to support its new world position, the Navy was being expanded.

The Secretary of the Navy would soon report to the President that "Never before were so many warships launched by this or any other nation in one year."[28] And never before had there been so many midshipmen under instruction at the Naval Academy.

The number of graduates of the Naval Academy had slowly increased from 34 in 1890 to 62 in 1904. The total number of midshipmen at the Naval Academy in 1890 had been 241 but now at the start of the 1904–1905 Academic Year there were 823 midshipmen in the Naval Academy; 114 were in the capable First Class, 133 in the blossoming Second Class, 279 were "Sprightly Youngsters," and 297 neophytes were in the Plebe Class, of which Midshipman Turner was a hard working part.[29]

From these figures it is apparent that the Class of 1908 was the second of the very large classes needed to man the "Great White Fleet" to enter the Naval Academy.[30]

---

[27] (a) U.S. Navy Department, *Annual Report of the Secretary of the Navy for the Year 1904* (hereafter SECNAV, *Annual Report*) (Washington: Government Printing Office, 1904), p. 43, Captain Willard H. Brownson, USN, June 6, 1904 to Chief of the Bureau of Navigation in *Report of Chief of the Bureau of Navigation*, 1904 (hereafter CHBUNAV, *Annual Report*). (b) *Lucky Bag* (Naval Academy Graduating Class Book), 1908, p. 171.
[28] SECNAV, *Annual Report*, 1904, p. 3.
[29] *U.S. Naval Academy Register*, 1890–1891, 1904–1905.
[30] Ships of the United States Navy were painted white.

14   *Amphibians Came To Conquer*

PLEBE YEAR (1904–1905)

Plebe Year opened Midshipman Turner's eyes to the world of the Navy, which was agreeably busy with trying to keep the Caribbean peace, and zealously busy with acute professional problems incident to healthy and vigorous growth.[31]

In 1904, naval interest in the political-military arena centered in the fiscally unsound and politically unstable Dominican Republic. In professional development naval interest centered in the recent decision to shift from coal to oil for generating steam for propulsion purposes, and in installing wireless telegraph stations on shore and on ships.[32]

The Navy at this time, maintained a cruiser-gunboat squadron in the waters of the Caribbean, available to proceed on short notice to Santo Domingo, as the Dominican Republic was then known, or to Panama, recently involved with gaining its independence from Colombia. As the year 1904 ended, the Commander of the Caribbean Squadron optimistically reported that a conference held on board the *USS Detroit* in Dominican waters when the revolution was at its height resulted in "the peace since that time." He added that conditions now were "not without promise of stability." [33]

It was also in 1904 that the Chief of the Bureau of Steam Engineering recommended that the Navy undertake the expensive, but beneficial, change from coal to oil giving the same reasons as are now given for the shift from oil to nuclear energy, i.e., extention of the steaming radius, attainment of maximum speed at short notice and ability to steam for long periods at high speed. At the same time both the Secretary of the Navy and Chief of the Bureau of Navigation noted that the average age of captains in command of battleships was 57, and recommended a system of promotion be introduced for lowering this age. They both also recommended that the rank of vice admiral be authorized and given to the Commanders in Chief of the North Atlantic and Asiatic Fleets.[34]

While the headline events in Santo Domingo were taking place well outside the Academy walls, a lean and erect 19-year-old westerner was being

---

[31] Turner.
[32] SECNAV, *Annual Report*, 1904, p. 18.
[33] CHBUNAV, *Annual Report*, Encl. H-2, p. 72 in SECNAV *Annual Report*, 1904. Commander Caribbean Squadron, Rear Admiral C. D. Sigsbee, USN.
[34] (a) *Ibid.*, pp. 5–7; (b) SECNAV, *Annual Report*, pp. 8, 9, 15, 18.

paternally molded into Midshipman Turner, United States Navy, within the Academy walls.

In sports, although he had played guard on grade school football teams, at the Academy he went out for baseball and track. "Previous to 1904, only inter-class track meets had been held at the Naval Academy. . . . In the Spring of 1905 a large number of candidates from all classes appeared." Midshipman Turner was one of that large number, and made the track team that year, running the hurdles.[35]

The Superintendent's prediction in regard to the living quarters proved reasonably accurate. At the start of the 1904–1905 Academic Year, "the northeast wing of Bancroft Hall went into commission" allowing half the midshipmen to take apartments in Bancroft Hall. Turner's Battalion (six companies) continued to live in "Old Quarters," "an unsightly structure perhaps, but fragrant with the very romance and spirit of the days of yore."[36]

The Regiment of Midshipmen was organized into two battalions of six companies each, with about 75 midshipmen in a company. Everyone in the company got to know everyone else, and classmates, in four years, formed strong opinions in regard to the others in their class.[37]

Physical hazing of plebes was a problem at the Naval Academy in 1904–1905 despite the fact that the Congress recently had passed a law forbidding it, and the official naval policy, as well as unofficial officer belief were strongly against it.

Awareness of interest at higher levels in physical hazing is shown by the Superintendent's remarks in his 1904 and 1905 Annual Reports to the Chief of Bureau of Navigation: "I can state to the Department, the practice of hazing is now one of the past;" "No case of hazing has occurred in the past year."[38]

Admiral Turner's remembrance was that he personally was not physically hazed during plebe academic year until January 1905 when 1906 became the first class. This class started physical hazing on a broad scale again and it continued until November 1905. In that month, a Midshipman Branch of the second class (1907) died following a fist fight with a Midshipman

---

[35] *Lucky Bag*, 1906, pp. 224, 225.
[36] *Ibid.*, 1905, pp. 102, 125; *Ibid.*, 1907, p. 107.
[37] (a) *Naval Academy Registers;* (b) Turner.
[38] (a) Superintendent of the Naval Academy, *Annual Report*, p. 43 in CHBUNAV, *Annual Report*, 1904; (b) *Ibid.*, p. 445 in SECNAV, *Annual Report*, 1905; (c) RKT to Mother, letter, 7 Jan 1906. "One time last year I did the sixteenth 342 times."

Meriwether of the third class (1908) arising out of hazing administered to Meriwether by Branch during 1908's plebe year.

From then on throughout Midshipman Turner's second and first class years, there was no general physical hazing of plebes.

> Most of the stuff in the papers is a pack of lies. . . .
> The fuss is being raised by a lot of newspapers and old women like the Secretary of the Navy and others.[39]

But, mental hazing or "running" of plebes continued throughout his four years as a midshipman.

The urgency of the need for additional junior officers to man the ballooning number of ships in the Fleet was brought home to the Naval Academy when the first class (1905) was suddenly graduated on 30 January 1905, four months ahead of time. While the second class (1906) took over the duties and privileges of the first class, this only resulted in a change to stronger and more high-handed masters for Midshipman Turner and his fellow plebes, despite the Superintendent's belief that "No case of hazing has occurred during the past year." The Class of 1908 remained in its lowly state both in name and in privileges until June 1905.[40] Of the 297 plebes in 1908, 256 finished Plebe Year successfully and became "youngsters." Eleven obtained 85 percent of the maximum mark of 4.0 and "starred." Midshipman R. K. Turner stood 14th. He stood number 1 in English and Law, 17 in Military Efficiency, 23 in Modern Languages, but only number 111 in Conduct.[41]

At the end of Plebe Year, one of Turner's classmates who played a major role in World War II was "found deficient, allowed an examination, passed and continued with the class."[42] This was Mark A. Mitscher who encountered later academic difficulties and, after "taking the six year course," graduated with the Class of 1910.

As the Academic Year ended, and the midshipmen prepared for the Summer Practice Cruise, the 1905 *Lucky Bag* noted:

> Though the new Academy is by no means near completion, some of the buildings not having yet been started, even in its present condition the magnificence of the finished project can be clearly discerned.

---

[39] *Ibid.*
[40] (a) CHBUNAV, *Annual Report*, p. 445 in SECNAV, *Annual Report*, 1905; (b) *Lucky Bag* 1905.
[41] *U.S. Naval Academy Register*, 1905–1906.
[42] *Ibid.*

The First Thirty Years 17

The yearbook added, possibly with the Congressional abolition of hazing in mind:

> With the passing of the Old Academy, not only the old buildings have disappeared, but also the old customs and the old life.

More specifically the 1905 *Lucky Bag* noted of the Class of 1908:

> Bedad, yer a bad un'
> Now turn out yer toes'
> Yer belt is unhookit,
> Yer cap is on crookit,
> Ye may not be drunk,
> But bejabers, ye look it.[43]

YOUNGSTER CRUISE

The 1905 Summer Practice Cruise for the midshipmen of the Naval Academy was made by the 6,000-ton second class battleship *USS Texas* (Flagship), four monitors, the *USS Terror, USS Arkansas, USS Florida*, and *USS Nevada*, two small cruisers, the *USS Newark* and *USS Atlanta*, the old but famous *USS Hartford*, and the Naval Academy Station Ship, the *USS Severn*. The last two had sails only.[44] Even without the *Severn* and *Hartford*, this was a patch-work of ships of rather varied formation keeping qualities.

These ships, except the Naval Academy Station Ship, normally comprised the Coast Squadron of the North Atlantic Fleet. Rear Admiral Francis W. Dickens, U. S. Navy, was the Coast Squadron Commander. Rear Admiral Robley D. Evans (Fighting Bob) was Commander in Chief of the North Atlantic Fleet.

The schedule of the cruise was about as uninteresting from the viewpoint of midshipmen anxious to see the world, as it was practical for naval authorities to make. Ports visited were: Solomon's Island, Maryland; Gardiner's Bay, Long Island; Rockland, Eastport, and Bangor, Maine; and New London, Connecticut. According to the *Lucky Bag* "We saw the same old New England towns." The summer was marked by "the seasick cruise up to Gardiner's Bay, a little work, more play, good times ashore," and "at the end of the cruise, the *Severn* caught in a Nor'easter and driven out to sea, where untold mental and physical agonies were experienced." [45]

---

[43] *Lucky Bag*, 1905, pp. 127, 146.
[44] (a) *U.S. Naval Academy Register*, 1905–1906; (b) RKT to Mother, letter, 4 Jun. 1905.
[45] *Lucky Bag*, 1907, p. 164; Ibid., 1908, p. 276.

However, the cruise was notable for one reason. From 7 June 1905, to 17 June 1905, the Practice Squadron held Joint Exercises, or "war maneuvers," with the United States Army in the Chesapeake Bay area.

> Leaving Solomon's we started in to show up the Army. We captured Baltimore, Washington and Fortress Monroe, the Army getting the decision, most of the sleep and about all the grub.[46]

This exercise fitted into Naval Academy drills which "Sometimes included practice amphibious landings across the Severn River." [47] Before they finished their careers, these fledgling officers were to hold many more Joint Exercises with the Army—a few in World War I and many in World War II.

The *USS Atlanta*, in which Midshipman Turner cruised until 15 July 1905, was commanded by Commander William F. Halsey, U. S. Navy (Class of 1873), father of Fleet Admiral W. F. Halsey, U. S. Navy (Class of 1904) of World War II fame. Commander Halsey was the original "Bull" Halsey—so named because of his bull throated voice and the frequent use of that voice in directing his requirements to anyone topside on the 175 to 308 feet between the stem and stern of the *USS Chesapeake, USS Atlanta*, or *USS Des Moines*, all of which ships he commanded on Midshipmen Practice Cruises.[48]

The *Atlanta* was a 20-year-old protected cruiser of about 3,200 tons displacement and 13 knots top speed which, although part of the Coastal Squadron, had been laid up in reserve status at Annapolis during the six months prior to the 1905 cruise. Notwithstanding the fact that she had been the first of the *Boston*-class cruisers of the "New Navy" to be commissioned (19 July 1886) and a ship of which the Navy was always very proud, she did not compare in modernity with the cruisers built since the Spanish American War, then actively operating in other subdivisions of the Atlantic Fleet.[49]

However, Admiral Turner remembered Youngster Cruise as "what first convinced him that he was for a life in the Navy, and that the Navy had a place in it for him"; even though his reaction to sleeping in a hammock was

---

[46] *Ibid.*, 1906, p. 78.

[47] Ernest J. King and Walter M. Walker, *Fleet Admiral King, A Naval Record* (New York: W.W. Norton & Co., 1952), p. 73. Hereafter *King's Record*. Reprinted by permission of W.W. Norton & Co., Inc.

[48] Interview with Admiral J. O. Richardson, USN, Class of 1902, U.S. Naval Academy, December 1961. Hereafter Richardson. The *USS Chesapeake*, a steel hulled, square rigger, was a training ship for midshipmen. Renamed *USS Severn*.

[49] U.S. Naval History Division, *Dictionary of American Fighting Ships*, Vol. I (Washington: Government Printing Office, 1959), p. 203.

"Darn a hammock, they are about the awkwardest things to sleep in that I ever struck." [50]

The 1908 *Lucky Bag* recorded a different event for making one decide for the Navy:

> The event of plebe year, however, that remains most vivid in our minds today was the Army game; it was then we first felt the call of the Navy and realized that we were in it and for it. How we cheered and yelled and, yes, cried as the Army defeated us 11–0 in a hard fought game.

YOUNGSTER YEAR (1905–1906)

According to the 1908 Midshipmans yearbook, "Our Youngster Year saw the death of the old Naval Academy life and the birth of the new." Richmond Turner in a letter to his mother reported: "The Sup is trying to bilge all that he can, as he can't handle so many [midshipmen] easily." [51]

In 1905, the Navy continued active in Santo Domingo, and the Navy received a new Secretary of the Navy, Charles J. Bonaparte.

The increase in the naval power of the United States was not without its critics, who believed that an increased Navy would merely drag us into wars. The previous Secretary of the Navy thought it desirable to meet this criticism in his Annual Report to the President by remarking:

> ... while doubtless, we shall always be in the lead in every international movement to promote peace, it is much better for us to be at all times so well prepared for war that war will never come.[52]

The new Secretary, since his last name had strong military connotations, thought to quiet the critics by taking yet another tack, foreseeing quite erroneously:

> It is reasonable to anticipate that their numbers [of ships in our Navy] will be reduced, and even reduced materially, within the next five years.

Perhaps to temper this unhappy thought as far as his subordinates in the Navy were concerned, he added:

> Without giving our Navy undue praise, it may be fairly described as of great promise.[53]

---

[50] (a) Turner; (b) RKT to Mother, letter, 4 Jun. 1905.
[51] (a) *Lucky Bag*, 1908, p. 274; (b) RKT to Mother, letter, 7 Jan. 1906.
[52] SECNAV, *Annual Report*, 1904, p. 4.
[53] *Ibid.*, 1905, pp. 23, 25.

Commenting on the unsolved and vexing problem of desertion, the new Secretary offered the sage suggestion that:

> Desertion is, in my opinion, due substantially to two causes—either bad men or bad officers.[54]

Sidestepped in this analysis were the miserable pay scale for the enlisted personnel, harsh living and working conditions, and skeletonized manning of ships.[55]

Forty more of Turner's classmates were dropped out during the academically tough Youngster Year and only 216 were passed through to the Second Class. Turner finished number 7, and only three men in his class starred—which is an indication of the difficulty of the Youngster Year. Turner stood number 1 in Mechanical Processes and number 5 in Military Efficiency. His low mark again was in Conduct, where he stood number 149.[56]

SECOND CLASS YEAR (1906–1907)

The summer of 1906 saw the midshipmen gaily off to Funchal, in the Madeira Islands, and to Horta on Fayal Island in the Azores. They were embarked in the cruisers of the 5th Division of the U. S. Atlantic Fleet. This division consisted of the third class protected cruisers *USS Minneapolis* (C-13), *USS Denver* (C-14), *USS Des Moines* (C-15), and the *USS Cleveland* (C-19). Turner, a second classman, was lucky enough to be in the *Denver*, a brand new cruiser (commissioned May 1904) of about the same tonnage as the *Atlanta* but faster (16.5 knots), and with a modern armament of ten 5-inch, 50-caliber guns. The *Des Moines* and the *Cleveland* were sister ships of the *Denver*, while the *Minneapolis* was a larger and faster (21 knots) cruiser of 7,400 tons that had earned her spurs in the Spanish American War.[57]

The *USS Denver* was commanded by Commander J. C. Colwell, U. S. Navy (Class of 1874). Colwell was one of the unfortunate ones retired by the Plucking Board the following year, on June 1907, in the interests of increasing the flow of promotion to commander. Colwell and his contem-

---

[54] *Ibid.*, 1905, p. 10.

[55] Basic pay with allowances for a first class seaman with four years total service was $21 per month versus $246 per month today; watch and watch was normal seven days a week routine; Captain's weekly personnel inspection was held Sunday morning.

[56] *U.S. Naval Academy Register,* 1906–1907. Those attaining an average of 85 percent wore stars on the collar of their uniform.

[57] *Dictionary of American Fighting Ships,* Vol. I, pp. 203–222.

poraries had spent 27 years of commissioned service before reaching, in 1903, the comfortable grade of commander where he was to enjoy only four brief years in this grade.

Six commissioned line officers and two past midshipmen formed the 3,200-ton *Denver's* complement of line officers. Today's destroyers of only slightly greater tonnage have a complement of not less than 17 commissioned line officers.

Besides the two foreign ports ("Madeira, the place seemed like God's own garden," and "of all the ends of the world, Horta is the worst") the midshipmen visited Frenchman's Bay and Bar Harbor, Maine; Newport, Rhode Island; and New London, Connecticut.

Not all midshipmen enjoyed the privilege of visiting foreign ports for:

> Just at the end of the year, when we learned we were going abroad, the hazing restrictions were handed out in large and small packages—many of us were confined for months to the academic limits and to the practice ships because we upheld a system we honestly believed was for the best interests of the Academy and the Service.[58]

Midshipman Turner was not one of those restricted. He enjoyed his first "trip abroad" and stayed out of trouble, although he remembered well the heady Madeira wine. "Yes, Madeira Isle is very fine; nothing so good as Madeira wine." [59]

The Second Class Cruise was marked also by "unpleasant memories of rolling ships, wave-swept decks, and of future admirals manning the rails wishing only to die, with the winds howling through the rigging in derision." The Midshipmen Squadron Practice Cruise on the way to the Madeira Islands had to heave to while the storm abated.

On the return voyage from the Azores, there was heavy weather again, and "only salt horse and hard tack to eat," according to one version and "dog biscuit, salt horse of the vintage of '69 and syrup," according to another.[60]

Along with most of his classmates, Midshipman Turner suffered the experience of being seasick the first time he was in a real North Atlantic storm. His recollection of it was vivid.

> You know there are twelve grades of wind, from No. 1 a light breeze to No. 12 a hurricane. The storm we had was a No. 10 and lasted six days.

---

[58] *Lucky Bag,* 1907.
[59] (a) *Lucky Bag,* 1907; and 1908, pp. 277–78; (b) RKT to Mother, letter, 18 Oct. 1906; (c) Turner.
[60] *Lucky Bag,* 1907, p. 197; *Ibid.,* 1908, pp. 275, 277.

> Oh it is great to be out on the bounding, pounding, howling, raging deep at such a time—just fine! I know of no pleasure greater than to be gazing down into the green, foamy, crawling shining water and wonder if the fish that got your last meal enjoyed it any more than you did, and you know there's no help for it either; you know that the blooming old ship won't go down and so give you a little relief. Those old freaks who decided that hell is of fire, had it all wrong. I'm sure it's much more like a storm at sea on a warship. When you realize that on one day we constantly rolled over to an angle of 37 degrees on each side of the perpendicular, perhaps you can imagine that a sailor's life is not what it's cracked up to be.
>
> After we got into smooth water the most popular song on board went like this:
>
>> 'A farmer's life, a farmer's life,
>> A farmer's life for me, for me,
>> If I could lead a farmer's life
>> How happy I would be.' [61]

Early in Second Class Year, Midshipman Turner wrote to his mother:

> Well you never saw half as busy a man as I am now, and as I expect to be all the rest of the year. I have written over fifty letters in the last week and a half to other colleges and universities concerning games for our baseball team next spring . . . . and on top of this, I have been trying to get the work on the "Lucky Bag" well underway. This is rather hard to do. It is a thing that must be created rather than just put together. . . .
>
> Second class year is, deservedly I have discovered, given the name of being the very hardest year in the Academy. I have been boning very steadily since coming back and find that it takes all my concentrating to get anything out of the stuff—Watson's Physics—Theoretical Mechanics (with problems by J Gow) . . . Biegs Naval Boilers, Naval Engines and Machines . . . Exterior Ballistics and the Elastic Strength of Guns, both intensely theoretical and both with formulas anywhere from one foot to ten in length.[62]

Richmond was a good correspondent with his mother with seven letters during the two and a half months of the summer cruise. He confided in one letter:

> We of the Navy are worse gossips than a bunch of women. That and hard work is about all we do.[63]

Only 14 midshipmen were dropped out of the 1908 class during Second Class Year. Midshipman Turner still stood number 7, and was the last man to achieve the enviable stars on his collar that denoted academic ex-

---

[61] RKT to Mother, letter, 8 Nov. 1906.
[62] RKT to Mother, letter, 14 Oct. 1906.
[63] RKT to Mother, letter, 18 Oct. 1906.

cellence. Other than in conduct, in which he stood number 65, he was not lower than 27th in any subject.

To Midshipman Turner, Second Class Year was "one of turmoil," with 1907 graduating in three sections, the largest number 86, in September 1906, a moderate size group of 50 in January 1907, and the last 72 from the academic bottom of the class, in June 1907.[64]

FIRST CLASS CRUISE

> Of that cruise, it need only be said that it was the most pleasant experience of our Naval Academy career. Jamestown, Norfolk, New York, Poughkeepsie, New London, Baltimore and Washington were all on the itinerary and everyone thoroughly enjoyed the yachting trip.[65]

The visit to Jamestown was occasioned by the 1907 Jamestown Exhibition and participation by the Midshipmen Practice Cruise in "the most noble pageant of recent years," a Fleet Review by President Theodore Roosevelt.

The Class of 1908 made its pleasant but unglamorous First Class Midshipmen's Practice Cruise during the summer of 1907 in three monitors, the *Arkansas*, *Florida*, and *Nevada*, all less than five years in commission, and in Dewey's flagship at the Battle of Manila Bay, the fine armored cruiser *Olympia* of 8,500 tons. The famous *Olympia*, initially commissioned on 5 February 1895, mounted what, in 1907, was still considered a modern battery, consisting of four 8-inch 35-caliber guns and ten 5-inch 40-caliber guns.

On the other hand, the low powered and awkward appearing monitors were never popular with the seagoing Navy for they dived under more waves than they rode over and according to the 1908 *Lucky Bag* "rolled through 365° at every swell." They mounted six guns on their 3,200 tons displacement. These monitors were built during the 30-year era when Congress legislated the detailed characteristics of our naval ships, and during the early years of that era when Congress was unwilling to authorize seagoing ships capable of offensive action in the sea lanes of the world and authorized only "sea going coastal line ships" or "harbor defense ships."[66]

---

[64] (a) Turner; (b) *Naval Register*, 1908.
[65] *Lucky Bag*, 1908, p. 279.
[66] *Dictionary of American Naval Fighting Ships*, Vol. I, pp. 189–91, 203, 207. *Naval Act of 5 Aug. 1882, Naval Act of 3 Mar. 1885, Naval Act of 3 Aug. 1886, Naval Act of 19 Jul. 1892, Naval Act of 2 Mar. 1895, and Naval Act of 4 May 1898.*

The harbor defense monitors assigned to his cruise were later to have their names changed to *Ozark, Tallahassee,* and *Tonapah,* respectively. Midshipman First Class R. K. Turner, luckily, was assigned to the *Olympia,* for not only was she a respectable appearing man-of-war that gave a sense of pride to her ship's company, but attached thereto was one Lieutenant Ernest J. King, U. S. Navy, the future Commander in Chief, U. S. Fleet and Chief of Naval Operations during World War II. Lieutenant King was an instructor in ordnance and gunnery at the Naval Academy, temporarily on duty in the *Olympia* for the Summer Practice Cruise. Turner admired the brainy, professionally alert and strict disciplinarian Lieutenant King. Presumably, King personally thought enough of Turner to join with others to recommend him for battalion command during the coming year.[67]

A member of the Class of 1910 did not look upon Midshipman Turner with the same kind eyes as Lieutenant King. He writes:

> We were shipmates in the *Olympia* on my youngster cruise in 1907. He was overbearing and split. Unpleasant to be on watch with. Inspired, I am sure by a sense of duty—which he understood required him to be 'Commanding.' [68]

FIRST CLASS YEAR (1907–1908)

Much to Midshipman Turner's surprise, in view of his conduct standing during the previous three years (number 111, 149, and 65), but to his considerable delight, he was given four stripes and named to command the 2nd Battalion at the commencement of First Class Academic Year. This was high honor indeed.[69]

Harry Booth Hird who stood number 14 in efficiency and graduated number 30 in the class was the "Five Striper" and Midshipman Commander of the Regiment of Midshipmen, and Edmund Randall Norton who stood number 39 in efficiency and graduated number 2 in the class was the other "Four Striper" and in command of the 1st Battalion.

Both Hird and Norton turned their attention to specialties of the naval profession; the first became an engineer, the latter a naval constructor. Both retired as captains; the first voluntarily in 1939, after 31 years of post-Academy service, and the latter in 1943, with physical disability after 35 years' service.[70]

---
[67] Turner.
[68] Member Class of 1910 to GCD (the author), letters, 24 Feb. 1962.
[69] Turner.
[70] *U.S. Naval Register,* 1939, 1943; *U.S. Naval Academy Register,* 1908.

And for the future midshipman contemplating the relationship between his efficiency and conduct while at the Naval Academy, with his future success in the Navy, it should be noted that the midshipman in the Class of 1908 who stood number one in efficiency for his four years at the Academy, Edward James Foy, was one of the 22 officers in the Class of 1908, who became a rear admiral on the active list of the Navy. As for the midshipman who ended up his four years in 1908, standing number one in conduct, William Hurton Piersel, it was his misfortune to be found physically disqualified upon graduation and to be required to submit his resignation.[71]

Midshipman Turner was a very busy young gentleman his First Class Year. Besides the detailed tasks which any battalion commander has in controlling and leading four hundred young Americans, he was editor of the *Lucky Bag*, the annual of each Naval Academy graduating class. Because of this assignment, he enjoyed "late lights," and the privilege of working after the 10 p.m. taps for "All Hands."

To these duties were added the fun of managing the baseball team which won nine straight games, but lost the important one to Army, 5 to 6. He soon learned that there was always more to be done than the day permitted, and the necessity of tying together the loose ends of every task before checking it off in his mind, as a satisfactory completion. He also had a strong urge to improve his academic standing, and this meant further intensive mental work.[72]

The effort was rewarded by a class standing of number 4 for First Class Year, and number 5 for the four-year course.

The Academic Year was also one of constant physical change in the Naval Academy as old classroom buildings on the prospective sites of new ones had to be torn down, so that classes were shifted from here to there to meet the day-to-day situation.

The Class of 1908 was the only class during the period from 1901 to 1908 to graduate as a unit in the month and year anticipated at the time of entrance of the class into the Naval Academy. During most of these years, the muster role of the Regiment of Midshipmen and the midshipmen officers therefore were as flexible and fast moving as an accordion.

Mid-term graduations took place in 1905 and there were two graduations in 1906 and 1907, with the size of the Brigade and its midshipmen leaders changing accordingly.

---

[71] Piersel, now Commander, USNR (Ret.).
[72] Turner.

The 1908 *Lucky Bag* indicated that Midshipman Turner had organizational and editorial skill, as well as a way with words. It made its bow to culture by having 21 cartoons each amusingly based on an extract from Shakespeare, and by including in the write-up on each graduate a bit of poetry or a descriptive phrase from a standard classical author. The one on the page devoted to "Spuds" Turner reads:

> Something there is more needful than expense.
> And something previous even to taste—tis sense,
> Good sense which only is the gift of heaven,
> And though no science, fairly worth the seven.
>
> Pope

As editor of the *Lucky Bag,* it would seem a safe surmise that there would be nothing in the individual write-up on Midshipman Turner which Editor Turner did not sanction. It was, in fact, almost a publisher's blurb:

> from California, with the Westerner's frankness and good nature love of adventure and fondness for the good old American game of 'draw' [poker] . . . Has served the class well in different capacities and is deservedly popular . . . A busy man, with hardly time to catch a smoke . . . A good athlete, but doesn't like to train . . . An all-around man and a good fellow.

The "good nature" and "good fellow" were probably the furthest deviation from the truth as some of his classmates saw "Spuds" Turner. Their present remembrance of an association of nearly 60 years ago may be summed up in the words:

> I respected his strong character and his brain power, and his very marked abilities, but never liked him.[73]

A classmate, and the first officer in 1908 to attain the rank of Four Stars and as such to command a fleet in World War II, remarked regarding their Academy days.

> Kelly Turner always wanted to be a leader, and probably aspired to be President of the Class of 1908. So whenever 1908 had a business meeting, he was always on his feet with suggestions to be made. Jack Shafroth was much the same.[74]

That Midshipman Turner could relax and be good natured and a good fellow when the occasion suggested it—is indicated by his service on the

---

[73] Interviews with three of eight members of Class of 1908, 1961, 1962, 1963.

[74] (a) Interview with Admiral Thomas C. Kinkaid, USN (Ret.) 20 May 1963. Hereafter Kinkaid; (b) Vice Admiral J. F. Shafroth, graduated number 80 in the Class of 1908.

The First Thirty Years

Class Supper Committee and his giving the toast to "Athletics" on that wildly festive occasion.[75]

The good sense of the editor was shown when the Class of 1908 dedicated its *Lucky Bag* to Commander William Shepherd Benson, Head of the Department of Discipline, who was destined to be the first of an impressive line of Chiefs of Naval Operations. Commander Benson contributed these mellow words to the 1908 *Lucky Bag:*

> We shall feel that our work has not been vain, if perchance it helps you of 1908 to realize the true worth of Friendship and the part it plays in the life of the Class, the Academy, and the Service.

First Class Year was a year which gave Midshipman Turner the feeling that even the minor cogs in the Navy have "to work their hearts out" to satisfy their superiors, and "to be happy with themselves." [76]

Midshipman Turner left Bancroft Hall and his four years as a midshipman with a good taste in his mouth.

> And when our course is over
> And we leave old Bancroft Hall
> We'll go on leave a singing
> It's a good world after all.[77]

A treasured keepsake of these four years included the following letter in long-hand:

> My dear Mr. Turner
> I acknowledge with hearty thanks your handsome gift of:
>
> The *Lucky Bag* of 1908
>
> It is most interesting and entertaining too.
> If the handsome young faces carry out their indications, there are fine men in the Class, and our country will be the safer for them.
> With heartfelt good wishes for you and for the "Class of 1908,"
> I am faithfully yours,
> GEORGE DEWEY

May 27, 1908.

INSTRUCTORS AT THE NAVAL ACADEMY

From 1904 to 1908, instruction at the Naval Academy was primarily in the hands of naval officers, except in Mathematics and English which were

---

[75] *Lucky Bag*, 1908.
[76] Turner.
[77] *Lucky Bag*, 1908, p. 279.

usually by civilian instructors. The over-all Academy ratio was roughly two officers to one civilian instructor.[78] According to the Naval Academy Superintendent, due to the continual shortage of officers in the Navy, and the continual shortage of money to hire civilian instructors, "it has been necessary to avail ourselves of the services of the senior class as instructors in Mathematics, in Applied Mathematics, and in English." [79]

During the period when Midshipman Turner was at the Naval Academy, duty at that institution was considered highly desirable by the top flight officers of the "Line of the Navy." Such duty offered an excellent opportunity for the daily exercise of leadership qualities as well as providing an opportunity for professional study and personal broadening of technical competence. For example, during his three year duty at the Naval Academy, Ernie King read military history and naval history voraciously.[80]

More than a fair share of the heavy cream of the Line officers of the Navy of the ranks from lieutenant to commander were to be found at the Naval Academy. This is evidenced by the fact that during the period 1904–1908 a total of six future Chiefs of Naval Operations and/or future Commanders in Chief of the United States Fleet were on duty at the Naval Academy among the 58 to 65 Line officers instructing midshipmen in professional and cultural subjects and in the Command and Discipline Department.

Future Chiefs of Naval Operations were:

W. S. BENSON
W. V. PRATT
W. D. LEAHY
E. J. KING

Future Commanders in Chief, United States Fleet were:

H. A. WILEY
W. V. PRATT [81]
A. J. HEPBURN
E. J. KING [82]

It also might be remarked that during this period there were from 58 to

---
[78] *Naval Academy Registers*, 1904–1908.
[79] CHBUNAV, *Annual Report*, p. 45 in SECNAV, *Annual Report*, 1904.
[80] *King's Record*, p. 74.
[81] Held CNO Office subsequently to that of CINCUS.
[82] Held combined office and title, Commander in Chief United States Fleet and Chief of Naval Operations.

The First Thirty Years

65 Line officers instructing midshipmen in professional and cultural subjects and in the Command and Discipline Departments. The number of future Flag officers among the 58 to 65 Line officer instructors varied from 18 to 23, depending upon which of the years from 1904 to 1908 is chosen.[83] Any naval command with a nucleus of from 30 percent to 40 percent potential Flag officers is fortunate indeed. This fact indicates the great importance attached 50 to 60 years ago to the training of midshipmen.

Victory at sea in World War I, World War II, and the Korean War can be attributed, in a considerable measure, in this writer's opinion, to the excellence of this fundamental schooling and training, and the high caliber of those managing and conducting these tasks.

GRADUATION

On 30 March 1908, Midshipman Turner wrote his mother—then visiting his oldest brother, Izer Turner, teaching school at Lingayen, in the Philippines:

> I have requested to be assigned to duty on the *Colorado,* an armored cruiser, now on the Pacific Coast. She is one of a squadron of eight ships and this squadron is expected to be sent to China in the Fall, so I'll probably be able to see you then, as they will visit Manila, of course.
>
> * * * *
>
> I expect to have a final mark for the year of about 3.60, which will give me a mark for the course of about 3.47 with a standing either sixth or seventh. With that standing, I could probably get into the Construction Corps, but I prefer the Line.[84]

On 5 June 1908, Midshipman Turner was graduated, his diploma stating "with distinction," and was ordered, not to the *Colorado* and the Armored Cruiser Squadron of the Pacific Fleet, but to a smaller cruiser, the *USS Milwaukee.* The *Milwaukee* in the 3rd Division and the 2nd Squadron was a new 9,700-ton, 22-knot, protected cruiser officially designated as a "Cruiser, First Class" and one of the 25 cruisers and gunboats which together with 23 torpedo boats and torpedo boat destroyers, made up the United States Pacific Fleet, then under the command of Rear Admiral John H. Dayton, U. S. Navy. While the *Milwaukee's* protection of 5-inch armor was light, she fairly bristled with guns. Her main battery consisted of fourteen 6-inch

---
[83] *U.S. Naval Academy Registers,* 1904–1908; *U.S. Naval Registers,* 1908–1936.
[84] RKT to Mother, letter, 30 Mar. 1908.

50-caliber guns; her secondary battery of eighteen 3-inch 50-caliber guns and twelve 3-pounders. This vast array of 44 topside guns caught the eye immediately. There was a promise of plenty for a young man with a first-rate mind and a strong body to learn and do. And it can be assumed that Captains Charles A. Gove and Charles C. ("Squinchy") Rogers, both of the Class of 1876, and both later Flag officers, were quite determined that the four or five past midshipmen in the *Milwaukee's* officer allowance would carry their share of the load.

Looking back on his four years at Annapolis, Admiral Turner said: "I liked the Naval Academy. Most of those in my class who didn't were young." [85]

PAST MIDSHIPMAN

In 1908, midshipmen successfully completing the course at the Naval Academy were ordered to sea duty in a semi-probationary status for two years before being eligible for a Presidential commission as ensigns in the United States Navy. They were officers in a qualified sense, were titled "Past Midshipman" and were subject to much rotation in their divisional assignments on board ship. They received continued close supervision in endless hard work, minor personal consideration, and tantalizingly small pay ($1,400.00 per year). Their rewards included a possible rearrangement of relative standing on the naval list with their classmates, based on performance of duty when promoted to ensign, denial of the normal ten percent increase of pay for officers serving at sea, and denial of permission to marry.

This last feature of a past midshipman's life was the most distasteful to Past Midshipman Turner. In his senior year at high school, he had fallen in love with a schoolmate, Harriet (Hattie) Sterling.[86] "I love Hattie and I can't get used to the idea of staying away from her." [87] This one real love of Richmond Kelly Turner's life was nurtured by separation for the first six years of his naval career, before marriage on 3 August 1910, in Stockton,

---

[85] Turner.

[86] Daughter of Mr. & Mrs. John Calhoun Sterling, born Carmanche, Calaveras County, California, 9 May 1888; RKT to GCD, letter, 4 Nov. 1960.

[87] RKT to Mother, letter, 16 Nov. 1908. On 4 June 1905 he had reported to his mother having taken to the June Ball a "Miss Ethel Naylor of Baltimore, a perfect beauty with the most wonderful eyes."

Midshipman Turner's first ship, USS Milwaukee.

Turner Collection

California. He had hoped·very strongly that marriage would come sooner. As early as the fall of 1906, Midshipman Turner had written:

> When I graduate, that is still nineteen months off, I think we will be commissioned ensigns instead of waiting a couple of years longer, and that means five or six hundred dollars a year difference.[88]

But Congress was slow to move on the recommendation of the Navy Department and the Class of 1908 served their two years as past midshipmen —officers, but not commissioned officers.

Harriet Sterling, as her husband, was of pioneer California stock, her paternal grandmother having come to California in 1864 by way of the Isthmus of Panama, after her grandfather, John Calhoun Sterling, was killed in the Civil War. Harriet Sterling's maternal grandparents reached California in 1849 and 1852, William Henry Lyons via Cape Horn, Georgia Allen by wagon train.[89]

Harriet Turner brought one immediate change to her husband's life. She called him "Kelly"—and the Navy soon followed suit. Her womanly reason —she didn't like the name "Richmond" or its shortened form "Rich" and detested his *Lucky Bag* nickname "Spuds." [90] The latter nickname had been given Midshipman Turner reportedly because he had several mole growths on his face which looked like incipient potatoes.[91]

THE FIRST YEARS

Past Midshipman Turner served in four ships during his first year out of the Naval Academy, and it was not until he arrived in the roomy 13,680-ton armored cruiser *West Virginia* in July 1909, that the Bureau of Navigation let him stay long enough to really make his mark.

In 1908, the old Bureau of Navigation was in desperate straits for officers. The Great White Fleet of 16 battleships, the backbone of the Navy, and six torpedo boat destroyers had sailed from Hampton Roads, Virginia, in December 1907 for its record-breaking, flag-showing and muscle-flexing "Voyage Around the World." The ships of the Great While Fleet were manned by a full allowance of officers and men. Since the whole Navy was

---
[88] RKT to Mother, letter, 18 Oct. 1906.
[89] (a) Interview with Mrs. Harriet S. Turner, March 1960. Hereafter Mrs. Turner; (b) Miss L. Turner.
[90] Mrs. Turner.
[91] Interview with James M. Doyle (Class of 1909), classmate for two years, Jan. 1964.

under strength in officers, this left those ships not lucky enough to make the voyage less than just scrimpily officered. The Bureau kept robbing Peter to pay Paul. The *Milwaukee* with an approved complement of 36 officers on commissioning 11 May 1906, and officered by nine commissioned line officers, seven past midshipmen, and nine staff and warrant officers when the Great White Fleet shoved off, was brought down to six commissioned line officers, four past midshipmen, and nine staff and warrant officers during 1908.[92]

During this first year, and after spending four months in the *Milwaukee*, Past Midshipman Turner happily served for seven weeks in the 270-ton harbor tug *Active* (YT-14) at the Mare Island Navy Yard. Here, he was reasonably close to Stockton and the love of his life. Then he was bounced back to the *Milwaukee* for a short month and in January 1909 was assigned for six months to the *Preble* (DD-12), one of the 16 original torpedo boat destroyers of about 480 tons authorized by the Congress during the Spanish American War, and whose keel had been laid down way back in April 1899.

Duty in the *Milwaukee* was mainly as a Junior Division Officer and as Junior Watch Officer, within an ever decreasing number of Line officers and past midshipmen. Under the principle of rotation of duties, Past Midshipman Turner served in the Gunnery Department under Gunnery Officer, Lieutenant Edward B. (Dad) Fenner, later a Flag officer, and then for three months as First Assistant Engineer in the Engineering Department under Lieutenant Earl P. Jessop. With the exception of his three "additional duty" engineering assignments in the Navy's early torpedo boats and torpedo boat destroyers, and one month in the *West Virginia* as Second Assistant, this was his only real engineering detail in almost 40 years of active duty. He enjoyed engineering duty but even more, he enjoyed working with Navy guns, whether they were small, medium or large, but he particularly enjoyed his life in the Navy with the big guns.[93]

Duty in the harbor tug *Active* was in the combined billets of Executive Officer, Senior Engineer, and Navigator; and in the *Preble* and *Davis* in the combined billets of Executive Officer and Engineer Officer.

In July 1909, Past Midshipman Turner commenced a three-year cruise in the Armored Cruiser Squadron, about which the old song went:

> Here's to the cruisers of the Fleet
>   So goldurn fast, they're hard to beat,

---

[92] *Naval Registers,* 1907, 1908, 1909.
[93] (a) Turner; (b) RKT to Mother, letter, 8 Nov. 1909.

Ensign Turner and his niece aboard USS West Virginia

    The battleships, they may be fine,
      But me for a cruiser every time.

             *   *   *   *   *

    The officers are a bunch of drunks.
      They keep their white clothes in their trunks.
    They stand their watches in their bunks.
      In the Armored Cruiser Squadron.

  In the period of our Navy when there was a touch of truth as well as a touch of poetry in this doggerel, Past Midshipman Turner and then Ensign Turner stood out as one of the low powered beacon lights, in the Armored Cruiser Squadron and in the good ship *West Virginia*.

The First Thirty Years

In a Navy that was officially wet, and unofficially dripping in spots, he drank hard liquor very sparingly, he worked unceasingly, he had brains and applied them, and he kept his eye on the true gunnery target—progress of the Navy.

In a period of our Navy's long history, when there was no selection for promotion to any rank, when seniors were apt to spread the cold truth and nothing but the truth on officers' semi-annual fitness reports, when ship's companies were small, and every officer was well known to his captain, the fitness reports of this young officer; while lacking the whipped cream topping of the fitness reports of the ensigns of the 1960's, were indicative of the Navy's best young officers of any year or age.

> [1] A thoroughly good man and excellent officer, steady and reliable. [2] Even tempered, energetic, active and painstaking. [3] Exceptionally able and efficient.[94]

As a makee learn officer, he was a captain's dream of what a young officer should have—interest, brains, and a willingness to work.

> I haven't told you about my new guns. . . . There was a new deal . . . my six 3-inch [guns] were taken away and I got four 6-inch in their place. . . . I consider myself extremely lucky, as there isn't another midshipman in the Fleet, if indeed there is in the entire Navy, with so important a battery.[95]
>
> I'll have to get a little sleep as I have averaged not more than five or six hours a day for a couple of weeks.[96]
>
> Everyday since we left the Golden Gate has been one brim full of interest and hard work.[97]

The Armored Cruiser Squadron, like the "Cruising, boozing boys of SUBDIVNINE" (Submarine Division Nine) was always on the move. In September 1909, they headed for New Guinea, but more particularly for the Admiralty Islands, part of the Bismarck Archipelago about 400 miles northwest of the Solomons. According to Kelly:

> The trip down to Admiralty Islands was more in the nature of a reconnaissance than anything else. Strictly on the q.t., the United States Government is on the lookout for more coaling stations in this part of the world, and those islands seem to promise well, if we can only buy them from Germany, which I doubt very much.
>
> The Intelligence Board of the Fleet, of which I am, or was, one of the assistants, gathered a lot of information without letting the trader there know

---

[94] Extracts from fitness reports, *USS West Virginia*.
[95] RKT to Mother, letter, 3 Oct. 1909.
[96] RKT to Mother, letter, 28 Nov. 1909.
[97] RKT to Mother, letter, 3 Oct. 1909.

anything about it, and some of us made a very complete chart of the harbor [Nares in Western Manus Island], a thing that had never been done before. We were four days making it, all of which were spent out in a small steam launch, unprotected from the heat. And let me tell you it gets hot down there, right underneath the sun. [Latitude 2° South] [98]

Later he wrote:

> Since leaving Honolulu, except for one day in Manila, I have spent every bit of time on board ship, doing nothing but stand my watches and work on my guns. It has been mighty interesting, too, I can tell you, though, hard and tedious work as the guns on this ship are old and have to have a lot of doctoring to get results from them. But as it was my first target practice [as a Gun Division Officer] and as I have a lot to learn about guns, I haven't minded a bit . . . even over losing about fifteen pounds in weight since leaving the States. . . . Tomorrow we put to sea and fire at a moving target exactly the same conditions that we would have in battle. . . . We stood first in night practice out of all the ships in the Navy, and we are hoping to do as well tomorrow.[99]

VISITING JAPAN

The visit of the Great White Fleet to Japan in October 1908 had been a great personal triumph for President Theodore Roosevelt's "Walk softly and carry a big stick" diplomacy, since as one historian points out:

> The visit was undoubtedly successful in creating great good will and in quieting talk of war between the two countries.[100]

In January 1910, Rear Admiral Uriel Sebree, U. S. Navy (Class of 1867), brought the Armored Cruiser Squadron of the Pacific Fleet to Japan for a further good will visit. From the depths of the *West Virginia* steerage, Past Midshipman Turner observed:

> I didn't go ashore very much as I am studying for my exams. . . . Nagasaki was very pleasant, climate good, and the people very pleasant to us. . . . The Japanese are a really civilized people.[101]

There were times in the years ahead, when he might have wished to question this last judgment.

---

[98] RKT to Mother, letter, 28 Nov. 1909.
[99] RKT to Mother, letter from Olongapo, P. I., undated.
[100] Dudley W. Knox, *A History of the United States Navy* (New York: G. P. Putnam's Sons, 1947), p. 378.
[101] RKT to Mother, letter from Yokohama, Japan, 17 Jan. 1910.

The First Thirty Years 37

PROMOTION TO ENSIGN

When promoted to ensign in June 1910, Past Midshipman Turner retained his relative standing of number 5 in the Class of 1908. The Naval Examining Board, wrestling with the records of 178 past midshipmen, shuffled the precedence of the bottom half of the Class of 1908 considerably. In the top half, fewer and less drastic changes were made, the earliest rearrangement shifting graduate number 12 ahead of graduate number 11.[102]

However, in another four years Lieutenant (junior grade) Turner would become the number one Line officer in the Class of 1908 in the *Naval Register*—when one officer senior to him resigned his commission and the other three Line officers his senior transferred to the Naval Construction Corps.

Two hundred of the Class of 1908 received diplomas of graduation. Six resigned at graduation time and 13 had resigned as past midshipmen. Three had been dismissed from the Naval Service and 178 were promoted to en-

---

[102] *Naval Register*, 1911.

NH 69097

Kelly Turner and his bride-to-be, 1910.

sign, although three, due to general courts martial, were in markedly inferior positions on the Lineal List of the Line of the Navy.[103]

His marriage in early August 1910 increased Ensign Turner's financial problems with only a small measure of surcease from the larger pay check his commissioned rank carried. His pay now totaled $170 per month as an ensign on sea duty with over five years' total naval service.

NAVY PAY

Just before Midshipman Turner graduated, the Congress on 13 May 1908, had been pleased to grant a very small increase of pay to a limited portion of the Naval Service, the first pay increase since 1 July 1899. The new pay law increased the pay of Midshipman Turner from $500 to $600 per year, of Past Midshipman Turner from $950 to $1,400 per year, and of Ensign Turner from $1,400 to $1,700 per year. The past midshipmen were judged to have been extremely fortunate, since commanders and captains at sea continued to draw for another 12 years the same meager base pay as they had under the old 1899 pay bill.

Richmond Kelly Turner was raised in frugal circumstances. He had a sound appreciation of the value of money, including the dollars of the United States Government. For example, in December 1898, he wrote to his Father:

> I have a position carrying papers at $3 a month. Saturday, I bought a hat $1.85, two shirts @ $.50, and [spent] $.45 on the trip to and around San Francisco.
>
> I send a little Christmas present which I hope you will enjoy.[104]

He early learned the availability and uses of credit by the officers and gentlemen of the Naval Service.

> I had to put off paying for Hattie's present, but that's all right, as I got her a better one than if I'd paid cash.[105]

But, on his first visit to Japan after buying a bolt of white silk for his prospective bride's dress, he wrote:

> It makes me mad clear through to see so many nice things to buy, without the wherewithal to purchase.[106]

---

[103] *Ibid.*, 1908, 1909, 1910, 1911.
[104] RKT to Papa, letter, 26 Dec. 1898.
[105] RKT to Mother, letter, 7 Jan. 1906.
[106] RKT to Mother, letter, 17 Jan. 1910.

The First Thirty Years

On his second visit to the island of Hawaii and a year after marriage, the pangs of the pocketbook were still with him, as he remarked:

> I shan't go up to Kilauea, the volcano which is rather more active now than usually, as the trip costs about six dollars and I can't spare the money." [107]

Each of his 1909 to 1911 letters available have some mention of financial problems. Nevertheless, his concern in regard to these never matched his pleasure over career successes in the Navy, and did not approach his concern over the care and happiness of his wife, who closely balanced the Navy as his main source for continued happy living.

HAWAII—PEARL HARBOR, 1911

The Navy continued to satisfy the Turner clan's basic need to be on the move.

The *West Virginia* continued to cruise about the Pacific Ocean; the Navy continued to use the Naval Academy marking system where 4.0 was the mark for perfection; and Ensign Turner continued to receive 3.8's, 3.9's, and 4.0's and complimentary remarks from his Commanding Officers in his fitness reports.

In late 1911, the *West Virginia,* as part of the Armored Cruiser Squadron, took part in the ceremonies in connection with the first opening of what was to become Ten-Ten Drydock, the 1,010-foot drydock at Pearl Harbor.

> The *California* officially opened Pearl Harbor the other day, and Prince Kalianaole [sic] gave a brief luau, or barbecue in honor of the guests. There were all kinds of native chow and stuff to eat, and the old Queen Lilianokealaui [sic] was there. She still maintains her old court and sat on a sort of throne in a pergola, with an attendant waving one of those big tassel fans, that you see in Egyptian pictures, over her, and surrounded by her court, a Chamberlain and Ladies and Gentlemen in Waiting, armed with guitars and ukuleles. She is over seventy and a toothless, fat old thing.[108]

TORPEDO BOAT DESTROYERS

On 12 June 1912, Ensign Turner having arrived in the *West Virginia* from a torpedo boat destroyer was detached to duty in a torpedo boat

---
[107] RKT to Mother, letter, 15 Dec. 1911.
[108] RKT to Mother, letter, 15 Dec. 1911.

destroyer. Ensign Turner had requested duty in "one of the ships of the Pacific Torpedo Flotilla" on 19 September 1911.[109]

During this period, 1908–1913, in the life of a developing and growing Navy, torpedo boats and torpedo boat destroyers had considerable allure for young officers. These small, cramped, and speedy crafts (22–29 knots) offered the opportunity to officers in their first five years of seagoing duty to be heads of departments and commanding officers—instead of far down on the totem pole of major shipboard responsibility. Past Midshipman Turner served six months in the *Preble* (TBD-12) in 1909. Ensign Turner in March and April 1912 served in the diminutive 155-ton *Davis* (TB-12) in a temporary duty status. Commencing in June 1912 he served a year as Executive Officer and, at the end of his sea cruise, and, for a brief nine weeks, in command of the much larger *Stewart* (TBD-13).[110]

The *Davis* was only 50 paces (148 feet) long and had but 1,750 horsepower in her Lilliputian engines to provide her with 23 knots. The *Preble* and *Stewart* were a hundred feet longer, displaced 420 tons and needed all their 7,000 horsepower to make 28–29 knots. The torpedo boats normally had an ensign and a past midshipman aboard while the larger torpedo boat destroyers required two commissioned officers and one past midshipman to keep them operating now and then.

It was during this 1912–1913 period that Ensign Turner's fitness reports showed that his eyes and interests had begun to turn to the broader aspects of a naval officer's self-training. He wrote: "I have read books by Mahan, Darriens, Knapp and Logan." [111]

Gradually over the next few years Ensign Turner read all of Mahan's main works and listed this fact in the appropriate place in his fitness report. His commanding officers in the torpedo boat destroyers, only a class or two senior to him, were duly impressed and continued to sprinkle a generous quota of 4.0's on his fitness reports and always reported him "forceful, active, and painstaking," three useful characteristics for the naval officer.

MAKING A SERVICE REPUTATION 1913–1925

The 12 years from 1913 to 1925 saw Lieutenant (junior grade) Turner

---

[109] CHBUNAV, letter 6312–15, 3 Oct. 1911.
[110] (a) BUNAV Orders, 6312–19, 21 Mar. 1912 and 6322–19, 11 Jun. 1912; (b) SECNAV, N–31–H, 29 Jul. 1913.
[111] Fitness Reports, 1912, 1913.

The First Thirty Years

acquire an excellent "Service reputation" and the three stripes of a commander. There was some very thin ice which he barely and luckily got over, while serving on a staff and while in command of a destroyer. Breaking through thin ice in the Navy during this period was not only dangerous, it was darn likely to be fatal. For during this period, the Navy, many years in advance of the Army, fostered and adapted the selective system of promotion for all grades above the rank of lieutenant commander.

As Fleet Admiral King wrote, the 1916 Selection Law had

> an immediate effect on the Service, for until that time longevity had been the yardstick by which naval officers reached high command. The matter of selecting only the best, and eliminating the others, had been discussed throughout the Navy for some years.[112]

Since all seagoing Line officers had the same basic education, and the same fundamentals of military character acquired at the Naval Academy, it was obvious that to "be amongst the best" for future selection, it was necessary, at the minimum, to acquire further education and to use it to the maximum. This Lieutenant (junior grade) Turner set about doing.[113]

The Navy had for many years required its officers to take broad gauge professional examinations upon each promotion to a higher grade. These tough examinations were highly effective in self education and in keeping all seagoing Line officers up to date in all professional aspects of their complex careers. The professional examinations covered such fringe matters as international law and military law, as well as the basic professional requirements of theoretical navigation, practical navigation, electrical engineering, steam engineering, seamanship, ordnance, and gunnery.

But in addition to this self education, postgraduate instruction was open to an outstanding few in the Bureaus and at Navy Yards. The establishment of the Naval Postgraduate School in 1912 at the Naval Academy greatly expanded the opportunity for further formal education of young officers. After one year of intensive study at Annapolis, the students were sent on to Harvard, Columbia, Massachusetts Institute of Technology, University of Chicago, or the University of Michigan for their master's degree in mechanical, electrical, diesel, radio, chemical, or various aspects of ordnance engineering.

---

[112] *King's Record*, p. 103. Reprinted by permission of W.W. Norton & Co., Inc.

[113] The *Naval Register*, 1914, lists 34 officers who had completed postgraduate courses in ordnance and 23 who had completed postgraduate courses in engineering, beginning with graduates of the Class of 1898.

PROMOTION TO JUNIOR LIEUTENANT

In June 1913, Ensign Turner passed his examinations and became one of the 150 junior lieutenants from the Class of 1908 commissioned in the Navy. Fourteen of his classmates had resigned their naval commissions while ensigns; three had been retired because of physical disability; one had been dismissed; and one had unhappily run away from the Navy and been declared a deserter. However, the Line of the Class of 1908 in the Navy had suffered further losses. Two classmates transferred to the Marine Corps, two to the Civil Engineer Corps, one to the Mathematics Corps, one to the Supply Corps and the three who stood number 1, 2, and 3 upon graduation transferred to the Construction Corps. Out of two hundred graduates, in five short years, only 75 percent remained in the Line.

On 1 January 1908, there were but 1,270 Line officers in the Navy including 307 past midshipmen. Only 84 of these were captains, and besides Admiral George Dewey there were no more than twenty other Flag officers. By 1 January 1913 the total number of Line officers had increased to 1,708.[114] During the interim, Past Midshipman Turner had been examined and promoted to ensign on 6 June 1910. He was promoted to junior lieutenant on 6 June 1913.

Acquiring a first flight service reputation with these 105 important people in the Navy, the captains and Flag officers depended upon doing something worthwhile where they could see or hear about it. This could be accomplished in the Navy-wide Gunnery Competition or in the Engineering Competition which had been started in the Navy in 1902 and in 1907 respectively. It could be accomplished in command of a ship. It could be accomplished on the staff of a Flag officer. It had to be accomplished where the greatest number of officers were stationed—that is in the Fleet. Shore duty was a place where you prepared yourself for more effective duty afloat and got away from as soon as possible. You could lose your reputation ashore, but you could not make it there. Unless under instruction, shore duty was something you enjoyed and swept under the rug and forgot about.

To illustrate how small the number of officers was on shore duty, in the Office of the Chief of Naval Operations on 1 January 1916, there were only 39 Line officers; in the Bureau of Navigation, 11 Line officers; and in the Bureau of Ordnance, 14 officers. Yet the Navy had 1,984 Line officers.[115]

---
[114] *Naval Registers*, 1908, 1913.
[115] *Naval Register*, 1 Jan. 1916.

SHORE DUTY AND LOVE

Ensign Turner twice was an applicant for postgraduate work at the School of Marine Engineering while in the *West Virginia*. As hoped for by him:

> I have a bare chance to get something pretty good this Fall and we want to be ready. I have a chance to get detailed to the School of Marine Engineering, a graduate school held at Annapolis. And as it is for two years, and all of it ashore, naturally we are anxious to go if possible. Then after that, if I do well enough, after one more cruise at sea, I may be able to get the detail permanently and never go to sea again. It is something that I am very much interested in, and I am getting to the point where I am tired of being a sort of parasite, but want to do something real; I want to have a part in the real progress of the world, to have my work more constructive than destructive, as it is now.[116]

Ensign Turner buttered his second request for postgraduate engineering instruction with a statement that he had had 13 months and 15 days of engineering duty in his four years since graduation, and with commendatory letters from his Commanding Officer and other officers served with in the *West Virginia, Preble, Milwaukee,* and *Active*.

This yen for perpetual shore duty under the guise of being an engineer, unfortunately for the Japanese, did not live much beyond the honeymoon period.

The first of his 1908 classmates, Harry B. Hird, the "five striper" at the Naval Academy, to be ordered to the Postgraduate School was ordered in 1912 for instruction in marine engineering, and became an "engineering duty only" officer. Ensign Turner was not so ordered. Perhaps the Bureau was influenced by what one of the officers, Lieutenant Commander E. P. Jessop, U. S. Navy, wrote in regard to Ensign Turner:

> From watching the Engineering Class at the Academy for two years, I find that about twenty percent of them applied for it because they desired to make themselves better officers for the Service, the remainder because they could put themselves in a position to escape watchstanding, get shore duty out of turn, or expecting to get additional education at the expense of the Government and then resign.

He had read Ensign Turner's mind—but in balance he added:

> You could not make a better choice than Turner. He is bright, and has good executive ability naturally and is industrious, all of which qualities, I consider essential.[117]

---

[116] (a) RKT to Mother, letter, 3 Jun. 1911; (b) RKT to SECNAV, official letters requesting assignment to School of Marine Engineering, 27 Jan. 1911 and 28 May 1912.
[117] RKT, *Official Record*.

Ensign Turner in landing force uniform.

POSTGRADUATE INSTRUCTION

Past Midshipman Turner had dreamed about having his first shore duty in Hawaii:

> When the time comes for my first shore duty I am surely going to ask to be sent to this place [Honolulu] because then, when Hattie and I are married, I can conceive of no more beautiful place to spend two honeymoon years.[118]

---
[118] RKT to Mother, letter from Honolulu, T. H., 3 Oct. 1909.

Ensign Turner had dreamed again about having shore duty before his initial five years' sea service was completed, and particularly he had dreamed about it in January 1911, and in May 1912, when he officially requested shore duty via the postgraduate route. However, it was not until 30 September 1913, that Lieutenant (junior grade) Turner with five years of sea service and watchstanding under his belt, reported into the Naval Academy for postgraduate instruction in Ordnance. Three years later, and after several disturbing sea duty interruptions, he had his postgraduate degree, and was headed for a job in the Gunnery Department of the Flagship of the U. S. Atlantic Fleet, the good ship *Pennsylvania*. However, the interruptions at sea gave him his first amphibious training, since he had been a midshipman.

In the fall of 1913, there were 13 of the Class of 1908 and one officer who had come up from the ranks in the "Under Instruction, Naval Academy" category. Ten of Lieutenant (junior grade) Turner's classmates came from the first 15 percent of the 1908 graduating class. Four were taking the postgraduate courses in Ordnance, the rest in Engineering or Electrical Engineering. The competition was bound to be intelligent, determined, and tough.[119]

Lieutenant (jg) Turner almost didn't stay at postgraduate instruction. The Bureau of Navigation, having in August 1913 ordered him to postgraduate duty, five months later, discovered that he had not signed an "Agreement of Post Graduate students to serve eight years in the Navy." So the Bureau sent him the form to sign.

Lieutenant (junior grade) Turner bounced it back with the following letter:

> 1. Returned herewith unsigned is Enclosure (A) transmitted to me with Bureau's letter above referred to.
> 2. This agreement is unsigned for the following reasons: that I was ordered to the Post Graduate Course without having requested the assignment, and did not at the time know of the existence of the agreement nor that its projection was contemplated; that I believe the agreement should be presented at the time of issuing orders to this duty and an opportunity be given for a free decision at that time without detriment to the officer concerned, instead of at this time when several months have been spent in the course with no knowledge of the existence of the agreement; that while I have every intention never to leave the Navy, I desire not to engage unqualifiedly to remain in the Navy. . . .[120]

The Bureau could easily have judged this letter harshly and bounced its author to the Asiatic Station, since the other three Ordnance students signed

---
[119] *Naval Register*, 1 Jan. 1914.
[120] BUNAV letter 25545/145D of 6 Mar. 1914 and RKT reply.

it. But instead, the Bureau of Navigation showed compassion and with a soft answer signed by "Victor Blue, from South Carolina too," the 48-year-old Chief of Bureau, accepted Turner's substitute statement that he had "every desire to remain in the Navy my whole life" and intended "to continue my service in the Navy of the United States for a period of at least eight (8) years."

TO THE CARIBBEAN

The first six months of postgraduate education flowed smoothly otherwise, until all of a sudden on 24 April 1914, Lieutenant (junior grade) Turner was detached by commercial telegram to sea duty in the 1,000-ton, 1,100-horsepower *Marietta*.

The years 1913 to 1916 were years of revolution and counter revolution in the Dominican Republic, and of United States involvement in the safety of United States lives and property investment resulting therefrom. Provisional President Jose Bordas of the Dominican Republic, in office since 13 April 1913, for a term "no longer than one year," refused to step down at the end of his provisional term, and a new and strongly supported revolution against him broke out, augmenting the small revolution proclaimed on 1 September 1913, over his sale of control of the National Railways.[121]

The good gunboat *Marietta* was part of the Cruiser Squadron, U.S. Atlantic Fleet, under Rear Admiral William B. Caperton, U.S. Navy, which the Navy Department made available to support the State Department's "Gunboat Diplomacy" in Santo Domingo in April 1914.

The only major trouble with the *Marietta* was that she was in that nebulous condition labeled "in reserve" and assigned to training the New Jersey Naval Militia with only one officer, a chief boatswain, on board. Her state of war readiness, in mid-April 1914 thus was questionable. The Bureau of Navigation, in 1914, as in other years of sudden demands for officers, stripped the Postgraduate School to officer the *Marietta* and additional ships needed for Santo Domingo, noting that "there are only 329 officers on shore duty other than Postgraduate School and War College."[122]

Lieutenants (junior grade) Turner and H. Thomas Markland, the latter also an ordnance student, were sent to the *Marietta* post haste. They brought

---
[121] Sumner Welles, *Naboth's Vineyard*, Vol. II (New York: Payson and Clark, LTD, 1928), chs. XI–XIII.
[122] CHBUNAV, *Annual Report*, 1914, p. 146.

the total of commissioned officers to six, and Lieutenant (junior grade) Turner was the Gunnery Officer of the six 4-inch guns with which the ship was armed. Besides being given additional duty as Paymaster for the ship, when the Paymaster had to be hospitalized ashore, Lieutenant (junior grade) Turner was the Landing Force Officer.

The *Marietta* in August 1914, was at San Pedro de Macoris—a seaport on the southeast coast of the island and about 40 miles east of the capital city, called Santo Domingo in 1914. On the beach the government forces and the rebels were maneuvering for advantage. Lieutenant Turner took quick action. He reported that:

> On [August 2, 1914] at about 3:20 p.m., an engagement having commenced between the government forces and the revolutionists, I left this ship . . . in charge of a Landing Force [totaling 50] consisting of one infantry section of twenty six men, and one officer, Ensign H. V. McCabe, seventeen men with two Colt's Automatic Machine Rifles, three signalmen, three pioneers, two men forming an ammunition party and a medical party of one hospital steward and two stretchermen in the charge of Assistant

NH 69102

Lieutenant (jg) Turner at San Pedro de Macoris, Dominican Republic, August 1914

Surgeon T. A. Fortescue. This force at once occupied the northwest corner of the cement walled enclosure belonging to the Santa Fe Sugar Company in which were gathered about one thousand refugees. . . . I established outposts . . . . no armed forces were within the neutral zone when the landing occurred, and none attempted to enter until about 3:30 the next morning. . . .

The firing between the two forces continued briskly for about an hour and a half, many rifle bullets passing over or falling within the neutral zone. . . . There was one casualty. . . . Firing continued intermittently until moonset, at 3:00 a.m., when it increased for about an hour, and then gradually died away. . . .

* * * *

Occasional shots only were fired in town during the day. . . . The refugees were very much pleased that we were there; government troops with whom we came in contact were uniformly courteous.

The Landing Force returned to the ship at 7:10 p.m. August 3rd.[123]

The rest of the story is told in the fitness report entry of Commander W. Pitt Scott, U. S. Navy:

Marietta Landing Force under command of Lieutenant Turner was landed to enforce respect for a neutral zone by the Government Forces and the rebels during an attack by the rebels on San Pedro de Macoris, the rebels having previously refused to agree to respect such a zone. This duty continuing on the 2nd and 3rd of August was performed by Lieutenant Turner in a highly credible manner and was entirely successful in its purpose.[124]

At least as much to the point were the eleven 4.0's in the Fitness Report.

During this period, his mother wrote a letter to President Woodrow Wilson, on 23 July 1914, protesting her son's detachment from postgraduate instruction and sending him to the miniature war. Mrs. Turner addressed the letter to the President because she believed the President was one

who considers no matter too small for his careful attention." [125]

The Secretary of the Navy, Josephus Daniels, signed the pleasant refusal of the request:

I regret it would not be practicable to relieve him now.[126]

But, at the end of 1914, with the trouble in the Dominican Republic settled, temporarily at least, the *Marietta* came back to the United States and

---

[123] Report of Lieutenant (junior grade) R. K. Turner to Commanding Officer, *USS Marietta*, Aug. 4, 1914.

[124] (a) RKT Fitness Report, 9/30/14; (b) San Pedro de Macoris is on the south coast of Dominican Republic 50 miles east of Santo Dominico.

[125] Letter in RKT official personal file.

[126] Copy of SECNAV letter in RKT official personal file.

The First Thirty Years

soon thereafter, Lieutenants (junior grade) Turner and Markland returned to the calm of their text books and instruction courses.[127]

During this postgraduate period, Turner wrote an article published in the 20 May 1916, *Scientific American* titled, "The Size of Naval Guns: Are Twelve 14-inch or Eight 17-inch Guns to be Preferred?" Turner set forth the problem, explored it, and analyzed it, and without definitely saying so, seemed to favor the larger guns. Another article titled "Classes of Naval Guns" is marked "submitted to several magazines but refused."

Within this same period of study and learning, Turner read papers or gave lectures before the student officers on Terrestrial Magnetism, Principles of Gun Construction, The Chemistry of Smoky Powders, and Optical Instruments and Appliances.

He was busy as a bee and liking it.[128]

---
[127] 26 January 1915.
[128] Turner.

CHAPTER II

Ten Years of Big Ship Gunnery 1916–1926

THE NAVY 1914 STYLE

As Lieutenant (junior grade) Turner finished up his first ten years in the Navy, Josephus Daniels was firmly in the saddle as Secretary of the Navy, proving it by signing junior officers' orders, and attending to other minutiae of administration.[1]

The Navy had grown and prospered in those ten years. The total enlisted force on 30 June 1904 was 29,321 and ten years later it was 52,293. Line officers had increased from 1,050 to 1,880.[2]

Congress, "that forward looking body," had recently authorized three new dreadnaughts and six new torpedo boat destroyers, and a "seagoing submarine . . . first of its kind."[3]

The Secretary, despite the blood letting going on in Europe, envisioned along with Tennyson that the good hour soon cometh when:

> the war-drum throbb'd no longer, and the battle-flags were furled,
> In the Parliament of man, The Federation of the world.[4]

The Secretary, in his wisdom, also gave approval to the sentiments of Admiral Sir Percy Scott of the Royal Navy who believed that "the submarine was the most effective ship of the navy of the future" and he advised

> a cessation in the rapid construction of dreadnaughts and the utilization of the money thus spent in building large numbers of submarines.[5]

The General Board of the Navy, that small but select body of elder statesmen, in opposition, reiterated its opinion that:

---

[1] Josephus Daniels' original signature on (a) RKT's 1913 orders to postgraduate duty, (b) orders granting RKT leave in 1913, (c) detachment from *Marietta* in 1914, and (d) a leave request in September 1915.
[2] (a) SECNAV, *Annual Reports*, 1904–1914; (b) *Naval Registers*, 1904 and 1914.
[3] SECNAV, *Annual Report*, 1 Dec. 1914, p. 5.
[4] *Ibid.*, p. 52.
[5] *Ibid.*, pp. 8–9.

command of the sea can only be gained and held by vessels that can take and keep the sea in all times and in all weathers and overcome the strongest enemies that can be brought against them.[6]

Fortunately for the Navy in World War I, World War II, and the Korean War, Congress bought this truism and has continued to buy it, irrespective of the military characteristics or name of the particular "vessel" needed at any particular year date to take and keep the seas.

Even if the professional Navy would not support the spending of all its allotted share of the taxpayers' money on submarines, it did go ahead with their progressive development, and at the same time, it did urge and did make progress in the even newer field of aviation.

Aviation had received its first really effective approval in the Navy when Admiral George Dewey, President of the General Board, recommended to the Secretary of the Navy in October 1910, that "the problem of providing space for airplanes or dirigibles be considered in all new designs for scouting vessels."

By January 1914, airplanes had flown off and onto temporary platforms erected on naval ships and there existed an "Office of Aeronautics" in the Division of Operations, Navy Department. The Navy had 12 airplanes and qualified naval aviators in equally small numbers.[7]

The establishment of an aeronautics station at Pensacola, Florida, and the organization of a naval flying school there was undertaken in January 1914. Since then,

> a steady increase of aircraft on a large scale is a fixed policy of the department.[8]

and during the next few months

> the *Mississippi* . . . carried aircraft to Vera Cruz and for 43 days made daily flights without regard to weather or other conditions.[9]

Besides needling the Navy about submarines, the Secretary of the Navy was prodding the Navy in the personnel management and educational fields. He stated:

> a. The Secretary has given less thought to guns than to the man behind the gun.

---

[6] *Ibid.*, p. 9.
[7] DCNO (Air) and CHBUWEP, *United States Naval Aviation 1910–1960*, NAVWEPS–00–801P–1, pp. 2–8. Take-off from *Birmingham* (CS–2) 4 November 1910; Landing on *Pennsylvania* (ACR–4) 18 January 1911.
[8] SECNAV, *Annual Report*, 1914, pp. 12–13.
[9] *Ibid.*, p. 12.

b. Every ship should be a school.

c. It must be true in the American Navy that every sailor carries an admiral's flag in his ditty box.[10]

The educational urge caught on like wildfire, but the Secretary's personal desire and order to put all sailormen into pajamas each night was a great flop as anyone serving in the Navy 50 years later will attest.

The professional Navy had long urged the Secretary to enunciate a policy that "Henceforth all the fighting ships which are added to the Fleet will use oil. . . ."[11] When this was done, it was obvious that technical engineering education in the mass must be undertaken in the Navy, and that the 11 existing technical schools would have to be expanded many times, and many more officers would have to be employed ashore in areas of technical training.

Since the Line of the Navy was 75 percent on sea duty, change in this seagoing condition was in the offing. An unsteady flow of promotion, then as always, was another problem. The Chief of the Bureau of Navigation noted:

> An abnormal condition exists in the Line of the Navy and to some extent in the Staff Corps.[12]

The abnormal condition was that there were only about 40 yearly promotions out of the grade of junior lieutenant, while 140 ensigns were being promoted into the grade of junior lieutenant each year, at the completion of three years of service as ensigns. The junior lieutenants and ensigns constituted almost 60 percent of the Line of the Navy.

Resignations of past midshipmen and now ensigns, who saw no future promotion beyond lieutenant commander until in their middle fifties had been running at a high rate, as has been noted for the class of 1908 with 13 resigning as past midshipmen and 14 resigning as ensigns. The result was seen on board the ships in Mexican waters during the 1914 Vera Cruz seizure and occupation, about which the Chief of the Bureau of Navigation said:

> Half of the Heads of Departments [on the battle ships] were lieutenants. Practically all officers on ships in Mexican waters, except Heads of Departments [and above] were in the grade of ensign.[13]

A description of the 1914 Navy would not be complete without mention-

---

[10] *Ibid.*, pp. 6–35.

[11] *Ibid.*, p. 17.

[12] CHBUNAV, *Annual Report*, in SECNAV *Annual Report*, 1914, pp. 144–45.

[13] *Ibid.*, p. 145.

ing a marked change taking place in the relationship between quarter deck and forecastle. As seen through the rose tinted glasses of the Secretary, in this area:

> There is being established between the Commanding Officers and men a confidential intimacy, which far from undermining discipline, ennobles it further by an enlightened consciousness of solidarity and sacrifice.[14]

TO SEA DUTY

In March 1916, the Bureau of Navigation thoughtfully advised Lieutenant (junior grade) Turner that he would be assigned to the *Pennsylvania* (BB-38) upon completion of his postgraduate instruction on 30 June 1916.

The *Pennsylvania* was brand new, due to be first commissioned on 12 June 1916, and to be the flagship of the United States Atlantic Fleet, with Admiral Henry T. Mayo on board and flying his four star flag.

The detail was a feather in Lieutenant (junior grade) Turner's cap, and brought him into favorable contact again with Lieutenant Commander E. J. King, Deputy Chief of Staff to Admiral Mayo. There are many disadvantages to flagship duty, but one of the real advantages, in those days, at least, was that the senior officers in the ship and on the Flag officer's staff were apt to have been carefully chosen, and more than apt to prosper in their future climb up the Navy ladder.

Although only a junior grade lieutenant in 1916, Turner was to become, within 15 months, first a Turret Officer, then the Assistant Gunnery Officer of the *Pennsylvania,* and then in late 1917, when only a senior lieutenant of one year seniority, the Gunnery Officer of the *Michigan* (BB-27).

He had the good fortune to have Captain Henry B. Wilson, a future Commander in Chief of the United States Fleet, as his captain in the *Pennsylvania,* and Captain Carlo B. Brittain, an up-coming Flag officer, as his captain in the *Michigan.*

One of his first flight shipmates in the *Pennsylvania* was Lieutenant Raymond A. Spruance, Class of 1907, later to be his immediate boss during the Central Pacific campaigns in 1943–1945.

The *Pennsylvania,* on a displacement of 31,400 tons, mounted twelve 14-inch 45-caliber guns in her main battery and twenty-two 5-inch 51-caliber guns in her secondary battery, and made 21 knots. The *Michigan* was six

---

[14] SECNAV, *Annual Report,* 1914, p. 6.

years older, 15,000 tons less displacement, 150 feet shorter, three knots slower, and mounted only eight 12-inch 45-caliber guns in her main battery. But she was a real gunnery prize for an officer who had been a senior lieutenant only a year.

Neither the *Pennsylvania* nor the *Michigan* lucked into battleship operation in the European Theater of war during World War I. The British thought it prudent to add only coal burning American battleships to their Home Fleet, because of their shortage of oil, and the *Pennsylvania* burned oil. The *Michigan,* a coal burner, was just too old and too slow to be needed or wanted. Instead, these two battleships trained and trained and trained secondary battery gun crews to act as the Armed Guards of hundreds of merchant ships and to man the guns on the recently converted, and far fewer, regular transports of the Armed Services. The training of gun crews was largely carried out in the Southern Drill Grounds off the entrance to Hampton Roads and near Base 2 at Yorktown, Virginia, and off Base 10 at Port Jefferson, New York, in Long Island Sound. This repetitive training entailed taking green recruits by the thousands and teaching them to man, operate, shoot and take care of a 3-, 4- or 5-inch gun.

In January 1917—eight and a half years out of the Naval Academy—Richmond Kelly Turner put on the two stripes of a senior lieutenant. His seniority dated from 29 August 1916, the date when the law introducing promotions by selection into the upper ranks of the Line of the Navy became effective. This law also markedly increased (by 20 percent) the number of senior lieutenants authorized in our Navy.

World War I brought temporary promotion of Turner to lieutenant commander in late December 1917 (dating from 15 October 1917) and just three months after reporting in as Gunnery Officer of the *Michigan*. This welcome step required the second of two upgrading in uniform stripes in one calendar year.

GUNNERY AND MORE GUNNERY

Although Lieutenant Commander Turner was one of the very junior Gunnery Officers in the Atlantic Fleet, this did not deter him from presenting, via official channels to the Chief of Bureau of Ordnance, his ideas on the improvement of the fire control apparatus for the big guns of the ships of the Fleet.

The Chief of Bureau, in replying to the letter indicated an aroused curiosity regarding the ideas, and requested travel orders be issued to bring Turner to Washington, saying:

> The Bureau has now received what it considers excellent suggestions from a Gunnery Officer of the Atlantic Fleet in regard to its director scope.[15]

This was the lever which, before the year 1918 was out, moved Lieutenant Commander Turner from the old, old *Michigan,* whose keel was laid in 1906 onto the *Mississippi* (BB-41), of the newest class of battleships in the Fleet.

> Kelly relieved Jonathan S. Dowell as Gunnery Officer. We were good friends and proud of being the junior heads of department in the latest battleship. Our departments got along fine together, no friction.[16]

Captain William A. Moffett was one of the *Mississippi's* two skippers while Turner was aboard and this officer was to exercise great influence on the later career of his Gunnery Officer.

During his three years as Gunnery Officer of three different ships, Kelly Turner continued to grind out 4.0's on his fitness reports, except in "Neatness of person and dress." His failure to buy new uniforms at yearly intervals as the water of time flowed steadily under the bridge, a failure presumed by this scribe to be due to the fact that he was always traveling financially close to the wind, caused, on at least a dozen occasions, various truthful reporting seniors to spoil the panorama of 4.0's on his fitness reports by dropping in a 3.4 or 3.7 or even a 3.0 opposite "neatness of person and dress."

It was noted on his fitness reports during this three-year period in gunnery work that he had given lectures before the Atlantic Fleet Gunnery Officers on such diverse subjects as "Principles of Gun Design" and "Notes on Director Scopes." He was described in the remarks section of his fitness reports as "exceedingly able and thoroughly conscientious in the performance of duty . . . Self reliant, with excellent judgment . . . valuable, whenever scientific reasoning is required . . . Hard working, conscientious and loyal. . . . There is nothing in the way of praise for this officer's work that could be left unsaid."

Some of his ensign shipmates in the *Michigan* and *Mississippi,* when asked to comment 45 years later, also expressed similar opinions in regard to Lieutenant Commander Turner's knowledge, ability and accomplishments.

---

[15] BUORD to CO MICHIGAN and BUNAV letter, 14 Feb. 1918.

[16] Captain Philip Seymour, USN (Ret.), to GCD, letter, 12 Mar. 1964. Seymour was Chief Engineer of the *Mississippi* in 1918.

They also remembered more readily the undivided attention to Uncle Sam's chores which he had demanded of all within the range of his piercing eyes, and the stern mannerisms and tongue lashings with which he had boat-swained his juniors.[17]

One shipmate wrote:

> I got to know Turner at the end of World War I on the *Mississippi*, when he was Gunnery Officer and I was Exec; he was a strong character and a very able naval officer by this stage of his distinguished career.[18]

Another shipmate in the *Mississippi*, an ensign in 1918, gave this appraisal:

> Kelly was a dynamic officer, when I first saw him, and remained such as long as I knew him, but there probably have never been any 'Funny Ha Ha' stories about him.
>
> Dorothy and I entertained him in our home for dinner one evening in Norfolk, while he was skipper of a cruiser. Our colored cook of the moment was helping us get rid of cocktails, etc., (unbeknownest to us), and consequently the dinner was a shambles, when it was *finally* served, but I doubt that it was 'funny' to Kelly. Few things were. But he always got the job done.[19]
>
> For the period in question—June to October 1918—Kelly was the gun boss on the *Michigan*, I serving as J.O. in Turret 2.
>
> Kelly was the boss—you never had a thought otherwise. He completely dominated the running of the ship. With a war on, gunnery was bound to be the No. 1 activity as opposed to a peacetime one of titivating ship, and the Captain and Executive Officer gave him a free hand—that hand that had such a sure touch. Kelly had the admiration and respect of all on board which generated complete confidence in his leadership. His great industry (he came closer to working 18 hours a day than any person I have ever known) and brilliant intellect justified beyond a doubt the high regard in which we held him.
>
> His leadership did not engender fear but rather a healthy respect for the qualities I have outlined. It was not borne of much, if any, personal magnetism. I don't recall his ever showing any mean or petty streak when some shortcoming came to his notice.
>
> He was unselfish, the good of the Navy was his only thought.
>
> I do not recall any tall tales that occurred at this time, although certainly there must have been some. It was all serious business at Yorktown. I do not recall RKT having any hobbies or indulging in much recreation—as I have said, he was all serious business.[20]

---

[17] Interview with Captain E. H. Kincaid, USN (Ret.) 5 Dec. 1961.

[18] Captain Paul P. Blackburn (Class of 1904) to GCD, letter, 13 Jan. 1964. Captain Blackburn, last survivor of Turner's 1908 officer shipmates in *Milwaukee*.

[19] Rear Admiral Joseph R. Lannom, USN (Ret.), to GCD, letter, Feb. 1964.

[20] Rear Admiral Grayson B. Carter, USN (Ret.), to GCD, letter, 25 Feb. 1964. Hereafter G. B. Carter.

That this domination of the *Michigan* did not impress all in the steerage can be judged by the following "45 year after" recollection.

> As far as Turner goes, I draw a complete blank. I can't remember him at all [not even] what his job was.[21]

The following letters, one personal the other official, tell more of the World War I story. The official one also bears the pencil notation "No dice" and the initials "RKT."

U.S.S. Arizona,
Navy Yard, New York, N.Y.,
September 30, 1919.

DEAR ADMIRAL:

Replying to your letter of September 29, 1919, it gives me pleasure to state that I served under your command in command of the U.S.S. *Michigan* from June 20, 1918 until September 7, 1918, when I was detached and ordered to command the U.S.S. *Arizona.* During this time the *Michigan* was operating in Chesapeake Bay preparing for and going through with the various forms of target practice. It will be noted that the ship was very successful at Short Range Battle Practice and won the ship control "E". About August 1, 1918 the *Michigan* was ordered to the Navy Yard, League Island for overhaul and made the passage at night, in company with the U.S.S. *Louisiana,* escorted by one destroyer, as the enemy's submarines were then operating off the coast. The *Michigan* remained at the Navy Yard for overhaul until I was detached.

While the *Michigan* was in a very efficient condition while I was in command, I cannot help but feel that the credit is due to my predecessor, Captain C. B. Brittain, U. S. Navy, to the Executive Officer, Commander George J. Meyers, U. S. Navy, and to the Gunnery Officer, Lieutenant Commander Richmond K. Turner, U. S. Navy. I found the ship in a fine condition and merely carried on.

I am,

Very sincerely yours,
(signed)   J. H. DAYTON,
Captain, U. S. Navy.

Rear Admiral J. H. Glennon, U.S.N.,
Commandant Third Naval District

CBB/HO

UNITED STATES ATLANTIC FLEET
U.S.S. Pennsylvania, Flagship
Navy Yard, New York, N.Y. 3 October 1919.

From: Rear Admiral C. B. Brittain, U. S. Navy
To: Bureau of Navigation (BOARD OF AWARDS)

---

[21] Mr. Peyton S. Cochran, to GCD, letter, 2 Mar. 1964. Cochran was an ensign in the *Michigan* June 1918 to September 1918.

Via: Captain J. H. Dayton, U.S.N. (*U.S.S. Arizona*)
Subject: Lieutenant Commander Richmond K. Turner, U.S.N., recommended for war service recognition by the Board of Awards.

1. I recommend Lieutenant Commander Richmond K. Turner, U. S. Navy, for the Distinguished Service Medal as having distinguished himself by specially meritorious service to the Government in a duty of great responsibility while serving under my command on board the *U.S.S. Michigan* as Gunnery Officer of that vessel from September, 1917, to 10 June 1918.

2. Lieutenant Commander Turner displayed ability, zeal and energy in a specially meritorious degree in maintaining the battle efficiency of the Gunnery Department of the *U.S.S. Michigan* in a high degree of preparedness. At the same time he rendered specially meritorious service in organizing and training for transfer to other vessels large numbers of recruits and other men for war service. Only such service as was rendered by this officer as above indicated could have, under the circumstances, maintained the *U.S.S Michigan*, a battleship of the first line, in the high degree of battle efficiency that she was in during the period covered and I accordingly recommend him for the Distinguished Service Medal.

3. In June, 1918, I was succeeded in command of the *Michigan* by Captain J. H. Dayton, U.S.N., and this letter is forwarded through that officer for such endorsement as he may see fit to make.

C. B. Brittain

WAR'S END AND SHORE DUTY

In June 1919, World War I was well over. Josephus Daniels, still the Secretary of the Navy, was singing the Navy's praises to the President and to the Congress, and distributing Navy Crosses, a personal heroism medal, on a helter-skelter basis but particularly to Commanding Officers who had lost their ships to enemy action. This sad practice was continued on by his successors during World War II.

The Distinguished Service Medal and Navy Cross Medal distribution met courageous moral and official resistance from Vice Admiral William S. Sims. The various operational and administrative judgments of the Navy Department during the war years also evoked a large amount of critical comment by those who had largely spent the short war at sea in positions of responsibility.

Before the spitball throwing subsided within the Navy, Congress decided to look into the squabble, and conducted, over many months, an investigation of the Service, and more particularly the Navy Department, its organization and its war functioning. This newsworthy chore was undertaken by a subcommittee of the Senate Committee on Naval Affairs, and soon took on political overtones.

A fair share of the spitballs had been aimed at Secretary Daniels. He rose to the occasion with magnificent eclat, proclaiming all those who questioned any aspect of the total victory achieved at sea, or the sagacity or timing of the naval decisions prior to this victory, or the organization of the headquarters which supported it logistically, as only wanting to deprive the Secretary of the Navy of his proper range of authority and of detailed decision-making.

This inglorious publicization of the unhappiness of many of the Navy's senior officers with their publicity wise civilian Secretary, made many lieutenant commanders consider leaving the Navy, but not Lieutenant Commander Turner.[22]

The Chief of the Bureau of Ordnance, Rear Admiral Ralph Earle, on 5 June 1919, nominated Lieutenant Commander Turner to the Bureau of Navigation for duty as relief of Commander Harvey Delano (Class of 1906) at the Naval Gun Factory, Navy Yard, Washington, D.C. Josephus Daniels personally signed Turner's orders to this effect on 20 June 1919.

This second tour of shore duty after a short three years at sea was an interesting tour. It included a chance to inspect officially the renowned British battle cruiser HMS *Renown* carrying six 15-inch guns in her main battery, a size of gun not in use in the United States Navy, to visit the surrendered German battleship *Ostfriesland,* and learn of German fire control, to make numerous trips to the Fleet to observe various target practices, and to visit a large number of industrial plants dealing with various parts of ordnance equipment.

In July 1920, along with the rest of his class, Turner took and passed his examinations for permanent lieutenant commander, to date from 7 December 1919.

KNICKERBOCKER DISASTER

During mid evening of 28 January 1922, the roof of the Knickerbocker Theater in the city of Washington, collapsed on its movie-viewing occu-

---

[22] Turner.

pants due to an overweight of snow, caused by a two-foot snowfall. Ninety-eight of the approximately 1,000 movie fans died.

A Fire and Rescue Party was ordered out of the Washington Navy Yard about 2300 and this was supplemented twice during the night by supporting parties and equipment. Lieutenant Commander Turner, alerted about 2300 by Commander Husband E. Kimmel, later of Pearl Harbor fame, but then the Officer of the Day at the Navy Yard, sent off the first party of about 25 men with their rescue equipment at 2345 and followed with additional acetylene torches, tanks of acetylene gas, hack saws, sledges and other essentials about 0100, 29 January. Lieutenant Commander Turner remained in charge of the naval efforts at the theater until relieved about 0800.[23]

For this work, he participated in the general commendation signed by Edwin Denby, Secretary of the Navy.

5306–137
THE SECRETARY OF THE NAVY
Washington, 9 February, 1922.

From: Secretary of the Navy
To: Commandant, Navy Yard, Washington, D. C.
Subject: Commendation for services in connection with rescue work among the victims of Knickerbocker Theater disaster in this city.

1. The Department has noted with much gratification the prompt response and splendid services of the officers and men under your command on the occasion of the Knickerbocker Theater disaster on the night of Saturday, January 28th, last. All reports received speak in the most flattering terms of the fine work performed by the naval personnel, and while some individuals particularly distinguished themselves, it was impossible, owing to the confusion and necessity for incessant efforts on the part of every one present, to obtain the names of all such persons.

2. For this reason, and in order not to single out a few for distinction where others whose names were unknown rendered equally splendid service, the Department takes this occasion to extend, through you, to all members of your command and of the *U.S.S. Mayflower,* who participated in the work in question, its warm praise and sincere commendation of their fine performance of duty.

EDWIN DENBY
Secretary of the Navy.

During this shore duty period Lieutenant Commander Turner also com-

---

[23] RKT to Officer of Day, Washington Navy Yard, official report, 30 Jan. 1922.

pleted the correspondence course in "Strategy and Tactics" of the Naval War College. The famous William S. Sims not only signed the routine letter sending off the certificate of completion but also sent off a special "great credit" letter.

No. 238
Pl–Cl–JW

NAVAL WAR COLLEGE
Newport, Rhode Island, 8 April, 1922.

To: Lieutenant Commander Richmond K. Turner, U.S. Navy, U.S. Naval Gun Factory, Navy Yard, Washington, D.C.

Subject: Completion of War College Correspondence Course

1. The records show that you have completed the Correspondence Course with great credit.

I wish to congratulate you on the results of your work, and on the perseverence you have shown, and trust that you will make known to other officers the benefit you may have derived, in order that they may realize the vast importance of training in their profession, which can be obtained by study of this sort, and in no other way.

WM. S. SIMS,
Rear Admiral, U. S. Navy, President

In addition to the Naval War College correspondence course, Lieutenant Commander Turner wrote two articles for the Naval Institute during this period, "A Fighting Leader For the Fleet" and "Gun Defense Against Torpedo Planes." The first appeared in the April 1922 issue of the *Proceedings,* and the latter article, jointly authored with Lieutenant Theodore D. Ruddock, was printed in October 1922, after Turner had gone to sea duty.

TO THE CALIFORNIA

Three years soon passed, and on 17 July 1922, Rear Admiral John H. Dayton, Commandant, signed Lieutenant Commander Turner's detachment orders, sending him to the new battleship *California* (BB-44). The pride of the Mare Island Navy Yard had her keel laid in October 1916, but was not commissioned until 10 August 1921. She carried twelve 14-inch 50-caliber guns in her main battery, the same armament as Turner had supervised in the *Mississippi.* The *California* shortly was to take over from the *New Mexico* (BB-40) the honor of being the flagship of the Pacific Fleet. Admiral

E. W. Eberle was the respected Commander in Chief. The skipper of the *California* was Captain Lucius A. Bostwick, Class of 1890, in the near future to be among those selected to Flag officer.

Commander William R. Furlong, later to become Chief of the Bureau of Ordnance, was the Fleet Gunnery Officer, and Commander Willis W. Bradley, Jr., Class of 1907, was the Gunnery Officer from whom Lieutenant Commander Turner took over. One of Turner's classmates, Henry Frederick D. Davis, who had graduated but three numbers behind Turner, was the Chief Engineer of the *California,* and another, Ernest W. McKee, was Fleet Athletic Officer.

Another of the *California* officers was Paul S. Theiss of the Class of 1912, who later was to be his Executive Officer in his cruiser command, and then Chief of Staff to Turner during a major part of the Central Pacific Campaign in World War II.

The *California* was moving along in her first full year in commission, a very successful year during which she was awarded the Battle Efficiency trophy for 1921–1922.

The 1922–23 Supply Officer of the *California* recalls:

> It was unwise to cross Kelly unless one was fully cognizant of his own position and believed in the correctness of his own stand.
>
> He was a dynamic and forceful officer who was fully cognizant of what he wished to accomplish, with due consideration of other Heads of Department who equally desired to promote the best interests of the ship.
>
> I found him far easier to get along with than his predecessor, Bradley. I do not recall that Kelly overstepped his position, but was forceful in requiring cooperation of other departments.[24]

Highly praiseworthy fitness reports from Captain—later Rear Admiral—John H. Dayton, were to be anticipated at the Washington Navy Yard after the very favorable relationship with Turner in the *Michigan*. However, when Turner reported to the *California,* and Captain Bostwick picked up the chore, there was a new fitness report form from the Bureau of Navigation, and a nudge from that Bureau to make the reports more realistic.

In the 19 qualities on which all officers were marked, Captain Bostwick appraised Lieutenant Commander Turner superior in seven, above average in eight and average in four—cooperative qualities, patience, education and

---

[24] Interview with Captain Walter D. Sharp (Supply Corps), 13 Mar. 1964. Sharp was a commander when Turner, a lieutenant commander, reported to the *California*.

loyalty of subordinates. Only the appraisal of average in education can be questioned, and this only in view of the postgraduate training Lieutenant Commander Turner had received. There were only 24 of the 111 of his classmates still on the Navy List who had completed formal postgraduate training.

A shipmate of this period relates:

> I was an ensign and assigned to the Plotting Room in the *California.* When the new Gunnery Officer had been aboard a few days, I paid my 'get acquainted' call on him. In due time he asked me whether we were having any kind of problem in the Plotting Room. I said everything was going pretty well except we were having certain 'circuit trouble' and proceeded to give him the details. He listened attentively—Then he said 'I suggest you look at the back of a particular switch board, which he designated, the fourth switch up from the bottom and the third one in. The trouble should be there.' I bowed out, and with the firecontrol electrician checked out this particular switch—found it had troubles, which were corrected. From then on, we had no more of this type of 'circuit trouble.' I was mightily impressed since there were several hundred switches in the Plotting Room.
>
> The next time I had a chance to talk to the Gunnery Officer, I asked him how he knew just where our trouble was located. He answered: 'I designed the board.'
>
> He was really something.[25]

By the time Lieutenant Commander Turner was detached from the *California* on 15 June 1923, Captain Bostwick rated Turner superior in 12 and average in only one—"patience." There could be no factual complaint about that appraisal of his patience.

And the Skipper had these comments to add along the way.

> Great energy and force of character, an energetic worker, and of excellent executive ability.
>
> In his own conduct and bearing, he sets an excellent example to his subordinates in devotion to duty and industry.

STAFF DUTY

In May 1923, the following letter was received by Lieutenant Commander Turner and as will be told shortly—led to placing his naval career in jeopardy.

---

[25] Interview with Admiral Walter F. Boone, USN (Ret.), 29 May 1964.

> NAVY DEPARTMENT
> OFFICE OF NAVAL OPERATIONS
> Washington, 19 May 1923.
>
> MY DEAR TURNER:
>
> How would you consider the job of Gunnery Officer in the Scouting Fleet, on the staff of Admiral McCully, who is to command that fleet about 1 July? I am only writing this to get your wishes in the matter and more or less feel that if it is agreeable to you, Admiral McCully would be very glad to have you.
>
> On the receipt of this and after making up your mind, send me a telegram at my expense to this effect: "Gladly accept detail," or "Prefer not take advantage of your offer."
>
> I am going to ask you to keep this *matter strictly confidential.*
>
> Yours sincerely,
> Chauncey Shackford,
> *Captain, U. S. Navy, Director of Gunnery Exercises and Engineering Performances.*

The answer was "gladly accept detail" and orders were issued on 13 June 1923, to accomplish this change. Turner reported on 29 June 1923.

Vice Admiral Newton A. McCully, Class of 1887, Commander Scouting Fleet, was a warrior of the old school. Toughened by duty as Commander Naval Forces Operating in Russia and later as Head Naval Mission to Russia, this strong minded and capable Flag officer brought to his duty an extremely active body, honest mind, and the moral courage to speak his convictions.

His flagship in the Atlantic was normally the coal burning 26,000-ton *Wyoming* (BB-32), first commissioned in 1912, and occasionally the slightly older *Florida* (BB-30), or *Utah* (BB-31). The routine of the Scouting Force in 1923–1924 called for much time to be given to training exercises in gunnery, engineering and communications, cruising Naval Reserves and midshipmen, an annual amphibious exercise, and then the big Fleet Problem with the whole United States Fleet.

Vice Admiral McCully wrote on Lieutenant Commander Turner's first fitness report.

> Lieutenant Commander Turner is probably one of the most capable and best equipped Gunnery Officers in the Navy. He is forceful and extremely energetic.

When six more months had passed into the propeller wash, Vice Admiral McCully opined:

> His remarkable ability is founded on thorough study and full consideration of

any question. His judgment is extraordinarily sound. Very tenacious of his opinions. Which at times takes the appearance of intolerance of the opinions of others.

By the time three more months slid under the forefoot, Vice Admiral McCully's opinion had further hardened and he wrote:

> Individual ability too strong to make a good subordinate. With increased rank and experience this defect undoubtedly will disappear, as his intelligence is of too high an order for him not to see its advantages.
>
> As Fleet Gunnery Officer, and with the exception mentioned in [paragraph] 12, and which was aggravated perhaps by a similar defect in Commander Scouting Fleet, his work could hardly be excelled. . . . In actual war, he would be invaluable . . . being thoroughly capable, resolute and bold.

Since the Navy Regulations required that any fitness reports containing unfavorable statements or marks be referred to the officer reported on, this fitness report was referred officially to Turner for statement. On 25 August 1924, he brought his side of the controversy to a quick official demise by endorsing the report: "I do not desire to make a statement."

But to make sure that Lieutenant Commander Turner got the point, as well as the fitness report, Vice Admiral McCully sat down and penned the following personal letter:

> 26 July, 1924.
>
> At Sea
>
> My dear Turner:
>
> I am forwarding you a Fitness Report to which you may take exception. However, I wish you to know that I never failed to appreciate your really extraordinary qualities and consider it quite as much my fault as yours that we could not hit it off better.
>
> I am under many obligations to you for the fine work you did while with us, and always felt that anything turned over to you would be most thoroughly worked out, and that the essence of the result could not be improved on by anyone. I shall remember particularly your assistance during the Battle of Panama, and your remarks to me "You will never get a better chance at them" in the morning of the 18th.
>
> In case of war this would make me desire to have you with me again. You may attach this letter to the Fitness Report if you see fit, and I think it might be advisable.
>
> With kind regards, and a sincere affection.
>
> Very faithfully yours,
> N. A. McCully.

Fortunately for Kelly Turner's peace of mind, this last fitness report was not submitted until after the 1924 Selection Board for commander had completed its chores, stored its ditty box, and dispersed.

SELECTION TO COMMANDER

Commander Scouting Fleet, in the *Wyoming* (flagship) together with *Arkansas, New York,* and *Texas* made the 1924 summer practice cruise with the midshipmen of the Naval Academy embarked, visiting ports in England, France, Netherlands, as well as Gibraltar and the Azores. Without much notice, Lieutenant Commander Turner learned he was not to make this very pleasant cruise, and on 28 May 1924 was ordered out of the flagship to the *Florida* to await detachment to other duty.[25]

Being dropped from the Scouting Fleet Staff just before he was to come up for selection to commander was a distinct blow to Lieutenant Commander Turner, but it was softened by his being ordered in command of a ship, the destroyer *Mervine*.

Normally, in 1924, all lieutenant commanders of the Line, including naval aviators, would have had a full command cruise under their belts by the time they reached the zone where they would actually be considered for selection to the grade of commander.

An examination of the annual *Naval Registers* from 1920 to 1925 shows that during these years, the Bureau of Navigation was working steadily through the appropriate Naval Academy classes, seeing to it that one and all had a chance to qualify themselves for selection to command rank by demonstrating their capabilities in command of aircraft squadrons, destroyers, submarines, minecraft, gunboats, seaplane tenders, or other small auxiliaries.

Lieutenant Commander Turner had had just the briefest sort of command cruise—two months in the *USS Stewart* from 7 July 1913 until 14 September 1913, when he was a junior lieutenant. It was obvious that his record needed bolstering in the "exercise of command area."

The 1 January 1925 *Naval Register* shows 12 officers in the Class of 1908 getting in a late lieutenant commander destroyer command cruise, including the class's two future four star admirals, Kinkaid and Turner.

In those benighted days, selection lists came out in late May or early June. During early June 1924, in fact just before Lieutenant Commander Turner

---

[25] COMSCOFLT to RKT, orders, 28 May 1924.

was finally detached from the Staff, Scouting Fleet, on 17 June 1924, the selection list for commander was approved by the President and promulgated by the Navy Department. The very, very good news was that the top 11 officers in 1908 had been considered and all had been selected. It could be said in the case of Lieutenant Commander Richmond Kelly Turner that the 1924 commander Selection Board had been willing to take the intention, in lieu of the actual deed of demonstrated success in a small ship command, before promotion to commander.

CLASS OF 1908 ON THE ROAD TO COMMANDER

The period from June 1913 to late 1916 by which time the Class of 1908 had been promoted to senior lieutenant was one of further rapid diminution of the Class of 1908 in the Line of the Navy. Ten were physically retired, although some of the physical disabilities apparently were not dangerous to longevity, as five of those ten are still alive nearly 50 years later. Three were dismissed from the Naval Service, two resigned and death took two, one (Richard C. Saufley) being the first naval aviation casualty from the class, and the 14th aviator in all the Navy to win naval wings.

One hundred thirty-three made senior lieutenant and the name Richmond Kelly Turner appeared at the top of the list of Line officers of the Class of 1908 in the 1917 annual *Naval Register*. That name was to remain in that position for the next 25 *Naval Registers*.

During the short year when the Class of 1908 wore the two stripes of a senior lieutenant, two more names had to be crossed out. One was a physical retirement and the other was the first naval officer lost in World War I, Lieutenant Clarence C. Thomas. He died on 28 April 1917, following the loss of the 2,551-ton tanker the *SS Vacuum*, sunk by a submarine off the coast of England.

With the end of World War I, there was an unusual flood tide of ten resignations. These were surprising, because each of these officers had devoted over 10 years to the naval profession, the comfortable rank of lieutenant commander had been reached, a temporary wartime pay increase had been received and this increase was in the process of being made permanent by the Congress.

The flood tide of resignations was largely based on the flood tide of naval disarmament talk, which culminated in the Limitation of Naval Armament

Conference. This conference met in Washington on 12 November 1921, and drafted a treaty that was signed on 6 February 1922 and ratified by all the signatory powers by July 1923. During 1921–1922, 376 ships of the United States Navy were placed out of commission, and the total of enlisted personnel was reduced to 86,000. On 31 December 1921 all permanent officers with a wartime temporary advancement in rank, some 1,059, were reverted by departmental fiat to their permanent rank. In addition, some 700 Naval Reserve officers were ordered to inactive duty, and over a thousand enlisted men were reverted from temporary officer rank to their permanent enlisted ranks. These events, leaving less than 20 officers of the Naval Reserve on active duty, and no temporarily commissioned enlisted men, raised doubts as to the future of the naval profession, and led to the thoughtful resignations.

It was a period of great discouragement for the officer corps of the Navy. There was a shortage of over a thousand officers of the Line in the Navy. The budget did not allow adequate money for purchase of fuel oil, with the result that "the movement of ships was restricted far below that which is necessary to maintain efficiency in the Fleet and to train new personnel in seagoing habits." [26]

Ships were undermanned, and they were not going to sea. Strange as this may seem to the naval officer of the mid-1960's, it made many naval officers of the early 1920's most unhappy.

By the time the Selection Board of 1924 and 1925 started looking over Lieutenant Commander Turner and his classmates, there were 109 on the Line of the Navy list remaining out of the 131 who had made the rank of lieutenant commander initially. One hundred were selected to the grade of commander. This was selection at its easiest. In fact it couldn't be called selection. It was a modified form of plucking those whose records indicated they were the less able 10 percent. But the promise of tougher hurdles lay ahead, and only 50 percent of the 1908 graduating class was still around working at seagoing chores.

THE 1924 SEAGOING NAVY

The 1924 United States Fleet had four major components in U. S. waters. These were the Battle Fleet, operating in the Pacific, the Scouting Fleet

---

[26] SECNAV, *Annual Report*, 1923, pp. 10, 12.

operating in the Atlantic, and the Control Force and the Fleet Base Force operating in both oceans.

The Battle Fleet contained battleships, destroyers and aircraft squadrons, while the Scouting Fleet had fewer and older battleships, a lesser number of destroyers, but all the new light cruisers. The Control Force had the old cruisers, some destroyers, part of the mine squadrons, and the submarines. The Fleet Base Force had mine squadrons, a few destroyers and the logistic support ships of the Train.

According to the Fleet's Annual Report:

> The amount of time allotted to the year's work (of the Fleet) is approximately as follows:
>
> | | |
> |---|---|
> | Tactical Exercises | 10 weeks |
> | Cruising | 10 weeks |
> | Gunnery Exercises | 12 weeks |
> | Upkeep and Overhaul | 18 weeks |
> | Holidays | 2 weeks |
>
> Possibly unforeseen calls will encroach upon the overhaul time. This is the common tendency.[27]
>
> Much has been said in conference and in correspondence concerning the instability of officer personnel. . . . Such a condition is inevitable.[28]

The 1924–1925 year was the second year of Visual Signalling Competition and of Radio Competition between ships of the Fleet. These competitions added to the previously long existing gunnery and engineering competitions, and expanded cruising schedules meant that ship employment schedules, in fact, were "very crowded." This crowding led the Commander in Chief (Admiral Robert E. Coontz) to recommend that interruptions to the training of the Fleet "must be limited to national celebrations, and specifically to the Fourth of July and Navy Day."

Among the events logged by the Commander in Chief were:

   a. The Japanese Training Squadron of three cruisers, visited San Francisco during the year.
   b. Ten ships of the Fleet rendered assistance to the Army-Around-The-World fliers.
   c. A shift from Magdalena Bay on the Southwest Coast of Lower California, Mexico to Lahaina Bay, in Maui, Hawaii, as a training base for the Battle Fleet was made, on a trial basis.[29]

---

[27] CINCUS, *Annual Report*, 1924, para. 92.
[28] *Ibid.*, para. 51.
[29] *Ibid.*, paras. 64, 65, 77, 79.

Recognition of the need for cohesiveness of the seagoing personnel marked this era.

> The importance of the association of the personnel of the Fleet during Fleet concentration periods, not only for the training of the various subordinate units in cooperative action for the effective use of the Fleet as a whole, but also for the exchange of ideas, for the coordination of opinion, and, for the rectification and reduction to writing of Fleet Instructions and indoctrination has been clearly demonstrated.[30]

These were also the years when the groundwork for the successes of the Navy during World War II were being laid. Admiral Coontz noted:

> The early completion and addition to the Fleet of aircraft carriers, cruisers, and submarines is recommended.[31]
>
> An increase of ten thousand (10,000) men is required now if the advance in Fleet training is to continue. Without this training material preparedness is futile and belief in our readiness to perform our missions a delusion.[32]

The logistical problems of a war with Japan were recognized at this early date:

> Fleet logistics as bearing upon mobility have been developed, and underway fueling exercises for cruisers and destroyers were included in the 1925 Fleet problems for the second time.[33]

* * * * *

> After a study of Fleet operations extending over many years, and after executing numerous operations in simulation of war conditions, the Commander in Chief is impressed with the complete dependence of the combatant vessels of the United States Fleet upon the service rendered by auxiliaries. . . .
>
> The slow speed of the auxiliaries . . . is the greatest single element of weakness in the United States Fleet today. . . . Whatever may be the number and characteristics of the combatant vessels, they cannot be used to the full extent of their speed, radius of action, and offensive power, unless they can be accompanied by auxiliaries.[34]

One of the three main objectives of the Commander in Chief, Admiral Robert E. Coontz, was stated to be:

> Development of the Train to the end that it may refuel, re-victual, re-stock and repair combatant units on the high seas.[35]

---

[30] *Ibid.*, 1925, para. 59.
[31] *Ibid.*, 1924, para. 164(f).
[32] *Ibid.*, 1925, para. 192(a).
[33] *Ibid.*, 1924, para. 24; *Ibid.*, 1925, para. 44.
[34] *Ibid.*, 1925, para. 171(i).
[35] *Ibid.*, 1924, para. 16.

Plain speaking in official reports was the practice, and the most important element leading to improvement of the Navy. For example,

> of all the classes of ships in the Fleet, the submarines are the worst inherently for the purposes required. Their design appears to be obsolete and faulty, and they are not reliable.[36]

In the years ahead, submarines could and would be improved, although it took a good bit of doing.

Lieutenant Commander Turner fitted into this pattern of the 1924 Navy perfectly. He loved to work and he loved competition. He had an innate desire to excel.

THE MERVINE (DD-322)

Turner's new command, the *Mervine,* was named for a naval officer who served on active duty until he was 71, his last command being the Gulf Squadron in the early days of the Civil War. Rear Admiral Mervine's most famous exploit was his landing, when a captain, as the head of a detachment at Monterery, Upper California, on 7 July 1847 and, under the orders of Commodore John D. Sloat, taking possession of that place and "California," in the name of the United States.

The *Mervine* was one of the later numbers of the World War I destroyer building program, actually having been built in 1919 and 1920 and commissioned on 28 February 1921. She mounted four 4-inch 50-caliber guns, one 3-inch 23-caliber gun, and had twelve 21-inch torpedo tubes in four nests of three each. Her normal displacement was 1,215 tons, and she had Curtis geared turbines, which theoretically would provide a speed of 35 knots.

The *Mervine* was assigned to Destroyer Division 35 of Destroyer Squadron 12 of the Destroyer Squadrons, Pacific Fleet. Rear Admiral Frank H. Schofield, Class of 1890, was in command of the Destroyer Squadrons. Captain John G. Church, Class of 1900, was the boss man of the 20 destroyers in Squadron 12.

Destroyer Division 35, in that 1924 mid-summer did not have a regularly detailed division commander when Lieutenant Commander Turner reported, although the *Robert Smith* (DD-324), was designated division flagship. The senior Commanding Officer in the division, Commander John N. Ferguson, Class of 1905, was not in her, but was in the *Selfridge* (DD-320).

---
[36] *Ibid.,* para. 114.

There were 103 destroyers in commission in the Navy in July 1924 and 38 of them were in the Battle Fleet. The new 7,500-ton light cruisers of the *Omaha* class were starting to join the Fleet, and the "experiment of substituting bunks for hammocks" was being tried in the larger ships of the Navy.[37]

The memory of the Honda disaster of September 1923 in which seven destroyers were stranded and two temporarily grounded by running ashore in a fog on the California coast was fresh in every destroyer man's mind.

The *Mervine*, along with the rest of the division was in the Puget Sound area, when on 28 July 1924, Lieutenant Commander Turner assumed command, the previous Commanding Officer, Lieutenant Commander Robert M. Hinckley, having already gone to shore duty. The Executive Officer was Lieutenant Frederick D. Powers, Class of 1914, and the ship had one more than her full allowance of seven officers.

As the officer personnel situation eased, the Department ordered Commander Theodore A. Kittinger, Class of 1901, as Commander, Destroyer Division 35. Commander Kittinger had missed stays in his first chance at selection to temporary commander in August 1917, and when later selected, served out World War I junior to a number of the Class of 1902 on the Navy List. On the reversion of all officers to their permanent rank on 1 January 1922, he regained his original seniority within the Class of 1901. Considered for selection to Captain in the same year that Turner was selected to Commander, Kittinger was not amongst those picked for promotion that year nor by any later Selection Board.

While Turner was in command, the *Mervine* participated with the other destroyers of Destroyer Division 35, Destroyer Squadron 12 and Destroyer Battle Force in the scheduled ship training, division training, squadron training, and force training incident to the Fleet schedule of tactical and strategical training and competitive exercises.

The *Mervine* also participated in Fleet Problem V, 2–11 March 1925. This was the first Fleet Problem to incorporate actual aircraft operations from a carrier, the *USS Langley*. Aircraft patrol squadrons had participated since 1923 in scouting and search during Fleet Problems, as had observation planes from battleships and cruisers. These aircraft had also simulated carrier aircraft bombing operations for several years, but the 1925 Fleet Problem opened the tide gate of seagoing aviation advancement.

Early detachment from the *Mervine* denied Lieutenant Commander

---

[37] SECNAV, *Annual Report,* 1924.

Turner a chance to participate in the 1925 Joint Amphibious training exercise which the Commandant of the Marine Corps described as:

> The outstanding activity of the year was the Joint Army and Navy Problem No. 3 held off Hawaii. . . . The exercises which took place at Hawaii were completely successful from the standpoint of the Marines. The plan worked to perfection and the landing was accomplished.[38]

Planning by the Marines had been on the basis of 40,000 troops. Fifteen hundred Marines represented the 40,000.

The extent that these operations raised the planning interest of Lieutenant Commander Turner in air and amphibious operations is unknown, since all the official records of the *Mervine,* except the Ship's Log, have been destroyed by the pitiless burners of the Record Depositories.

On 8 April 1925, six days before Lieutenant Commander Turner was to be relieved, the *Mervine,* while anchored in San Francisco Bay, dragged anchor in the late afternoon and fetched up across the bow of the battleship *Colorado,* "the latter's bow striking at the forward end of the deck house."

Collisions in 1925 generally meant Boards of Investigation or Courts of Inquiry and all too frequently these were followed by general courts martial for the unwitting or negligent. Fast paper work and a "slight" collision might forestall such a personal career disaster.

The Commander in Chief Battle Fleet's despatch report read:

> 7008 Art 1556 *Mervine* dragged anchor and collided with bow of *Colorado.* No serious damage sustained. Request technical availability at Navy Yard, Mare Island for new mast complete, and two radio antennae spreaders and other incidental material. . . . Diver will examine port propeller Thursday 1805.

So it appeared that higher authority rated the damage "not serious," but to forestall a Board of Investigation, it was essential to convince them that there had been no negligence, and soon.

The comprehensive *Mervine* report to the Commander in Chief, United States Fleet regarding the collision was dated 8 April, the day of the incident, and despatched before midnight. The closely reasoned statement by the Commanding Officer supported by statements of the Officer with the Day's Duty, and the only officer aboard, and of eight enlisted men gave the following account of the incident.

The Commanding Officer on 3 April 1925 had issued "Special Instructions for San Francisco Bay" which started out with the statement: "The current in

---

[38] Commandant Marine Corps, *Annual Report,* 1925.

San Francisco Bay is dangerous." It also included instructions as to how to detect dragging of the anchor, who was to carry out this duty, and what to do if dragging occurred.

The Acting Executive Officer, Lieutenant (jg) Samuel W. Canan in his accompanying statement stated he had published this order to "All Hands," and personally instructed the chief petty officers, signalmen and men standing gangway watches regarding it, and given copies to each of the officers standing Day's Duty. Each of the deck petty officers in his statement confirmed receiving this instruction.

The Commanding Officer was not on board "having left at 1120 to attend the Chamber of Commerce luncheon and not having returned." Following the luncheon, he played golf at the Presidio. Ensign Everett H. Browne, Class of 1923, the Chief Engineer of the *Mervine,* had the Day's Duty and was in command at the time of the casualty.

At 1556 the dragging was noted and immediately reported. Ensign Browne acted promptly. He sent a messenger ashore for the Commanding Officer. He heaved around on the port chain, went ahead on the engines at 1616 (as soon as the engines were ready) but "just barely missed clearing the *Colorado.*" "The *Colorado* personnel did everything possible to prevent damage, veering chain promptly. . . . Especial credit is due the Engineer Force in starting up the main engines so quickly after being notified."

> Ensign Browne is a very promising young officer, of a high type, zealous, active and capable, and has already rendered excellent service as Engineer Officer of this vessel. The Commanding Officer has confidence in his ability and judgment. . . . [He] appears to have erred in not dropping the second anchor as soon as he saw the vessel was dragging.[39]

How the seniors in the chain of command viewed this letter is not known but what is known is that a Board of Investigation was held but as far as Lieutenant Commander Turner and Ensign Everett Hale Browne were concerned, nothing of a disciplinary nature ever came of it. And that was luck of the first water.

The Board of Investigation of three commanders was headed by the Division Commander, Commander Theodore A. Kittinger, and convened on 13 April 1925. Ensign Browne testified that he "did not think you could heave in on one anchor and veer on the other at the same time," with only the one capstan with which destroyers were fitted. This combined with the fact that he had noted that "the starboard anchor chain was faked out on

---

[39] CO *Mervine* to CINCUS, letter, 8 Apr. 1925.

deck being painted," when he had made an early afternoon inspection and that he did not know that it had been reshackled to the anchor until a minute or so before the collision, had caused him to delay ordering the starboard anchor let go.

Lieutenant Commander Turner testified that the dragging of the anchor was due to "a round turn around the fluke of the anchor," and that Ensign Browne

> was Officer of the Deck of the *Mervine* on a previous occasion in San Diego when the vessel dragged her anchor. He noted the dragging as soon as it occurred and reported it to Lieutenant (jg) Canan—Lieutenant (jg) Canan got underway and shifted anchorage without damage of any kind.
> I have great confidence in Ensign Browne.

The Board of Investigation found "no responsibility for the dragging" and that the "spare anchor was not let go in due season, nor were the engines used to maximum capacity."[40]

The Board of Investigation asked by the Convening Authority to give "the Board's opinion as to the responsibility for the collision" stated it was due to "the lack of judgment on the part of the acting Commanding Officer." The Convening Authority, while not disagreeing with this as the technical reason for the collision, took a broader view and indicated the basic reason lay in the error of the Commanding Officer in having entrusted Ensign Browne to the charge of the ship:

> His ability and performance as an Engineer Officer appears to have led his Captain to suppose a corresponding ability in other line duties, in which he actually lacked experience.[41]

However, no copy of the Board of Investigation was attached to Turner's official record, which was personal and official consideration of a generous order.

Commander Destroyers Battle Fleet approved the Board's report, and informed seniors in the chain of command, by including a copy of newly issued Circular Letter, that he had reaffirmed the timeless requirement that

> no officer is entrusted with charge of a ship at anchor or at moorings, until that officer has been instructed, trained, and examined as to knowledge and competence as a seaman.[42]

From the Navy Directories of 1924 and 1925 it appears that only two

---
[40] Board of Investigation, Report of Collision *USS Mervine-USS Colorado*, 13 Apr. 1925.
[41] COMDESRON, Battle Fleet to CINC, Battle Fleet, letter, 30 Apr. 1925.
[42] COMDESRON, Battle Fleet to DESRON, Battle Fleet, letter, 24 Apr. 1925.

ship's officers served with Turner throughout his eight and a half months' cruise in the *Mervine*. These durable officers were Lieutenant (junior grade) Samuel W. Canan, Class of 1920, and Ensign Everett H. Browne, Class of 1923. The Executive Officer, Gunnery Officer, and Communication Officer, however, all served more than seven of the eight and a half months, and the Communication Officer, Ensign William B. Ammon, who came aboard shortly after Turner, went on to become a Flag officer on the active list of the Navy, and Director of Naval Communications. Rear Admiral Ammon died before this book got well underway.

When asked to say what stood out in their memories from the period of their service in the *Mervine* with Turner, one shipmate wrote:

> His invincible determination to make a happy efficient destroyer over into a taut battleship.[43]

Another remembered

> his sincere regret in being detached from duty in the *Mervine*. He had strived so hard to make his first command a success.[44]

Describing Turner another wrote:

> Intellectually brilliant, but impatient with average guys slow to grasp his theories, intolerant of opinions at variance with his, there was only one way to do a thing—the Turner way. Mostly, he was right, sometimes wrong and always very hard to convince.[45]

All the living officers who served more than a dog watch (a very short period) in the *Mervine* under Turner were queried in regard to Turner. It can be recorded as a fact that the *Mervine* is not remembered as a "happy ship" by several of her officers who served under Lieutenant Commander Turner, and that all her officers remember that some were not at all happy with their captain. He was "rank poison" to one.

Others mentioned Turner's "positiveness," his "excellent leadership" and his "determination." [46]

When asked to rate Lieutenant Commander Turner on a scale made up of:

1. Tops,

---

[43] Commander Frederick D. Powers, USN (Ret.), to GCD, letter, 9 Mar. 1964. Hereafter Powers.
[44] Commander Everett H. Browne, USN (Ret.), to GCD, letter, 10 Apr. 1964. Hereafter Browne.
[45] Captain Joseph U. Lademan, USN (Ret.), to GCD, letter, 9 Mar. 1964. Hereafter Lademan.
[46] (a) Commander Samuel W. Canan, USN (Ret.), to GCD, letter, 22 Mar. 1964; (b) Commander Roy R. Darron, USN (Ret.), to GCD, letter, 18 Mar. 1964; (c) Commander Everett H. Browne, USN (Ret.), to GCD, letter, 10 Apr. 1964.

2. Quite all right,
3. So, so,
4. The NUTS,

ratings were from one to four, with two placing him in category one, and two placing him in category four. It is perhaps significant that the two who served with him the longest rated him "Tops."

His Executive Officer believed Turner's strongest point was

> work, work, work of all kinds and everybody's work as well as his own.

His Gunnery Officer thought Turner's strongest point was a

> brilliant, forceful, theoretical mind.

Another named his "fairness," and still another "a personal hard worker."

Turner's weakest points were believed to be his "refusal to delegate authority" and his "impatience and intolerance with other points of view," that he was "a detail artist," or "a driver not a leader." One said: "In my opinion he had no weakness, unless you would call his driving urgency one."

One officer recalled that members of the ship's company were heard to ask each other "When do we get a bugler?" or "When will the *Mervine* get her cage mast?" both of which were the dog marks of a battleship. However, discipline in the *Mervine* was remembered as "average" or "good" and by two as "excellent," although the Executive Officer thought that his captain at mast was "harsh at times and over lenient at others."

> RKT lived by the 'Book.' His punishments at mast were exactly what the Book called for—no more—no less. He believed in swift and impartial punishment. No delay, no waiting for the convening of a court-martial. No back log of mast reports.
>
> In approaching the Nest in San Diego Harbor one afternoon, RKT at the Conn, the forward throttleman answered the annunciator with ⅔ speed ahead instead of ⅔ speed astern, which caused a slight bump between the *Mervine* and the ship at the Nest, and made for a poor landing. The other ship just happened to be the flagship of the Division Commander, with the Division Commander on deck.
>
> RKT sent for me and directed the forward throttleman be brought to mast as soon as the plant was secured. When RKT came down from the bridge, all was in readiness. He asked the throttleman, an Engineman second class, for an explanation, and the man stated that he had made a mistake.
>
> RKT said 'Fireman, first class; go aft.'
>
> This is an example of his swift but fair punishment.[47]

---

[47] Browne.

As a ship handler, Turner was remembered as "excellent" by most and as "not too hot" or "inclined to place too much emphasis on a range and bearing plot, and little or no regard for the seaman's eye" by another. This officer wrote he "wanted every landing to be a mooring problem." [48]

The Chief Engineer related this story:

> When preparing for a Full Power Run, the usual procedure is to work up to speed gradually, warming up each piece of machinery uniformly, and then settling the plant down to just below the required speed. This took about two hours and when I was ready, I went to the Bridge to report to RKT.
>
> This particular morning the visibility was low, about 5 miles, and when I requested permission to start the run, this was denied, due to visibility. The plant was in excellent operating condition, and after several denials to start the run, I was impatient and asked 'Captain, what's the difference between 32 and 33 knots in this visibility?' He replied, 'One knot, young man, one knot.' [49]

The Gunnery Officer recalled the following incident:

> Turner was an Ordnance P.G. He had designed a gyro stabilized sight for the type of gun director installed on the *Mervine* and his word was law in all matters connected with her fire control system. While the ship was in drydock shortly after he took command, he devised a method for obtaining the inclination of the gun roller paths that differed radically from procedures prescribed in the instructional pamphlets of those days. Using data obtained from a complicated arrangement of vertical battens and theodolites, Turner computed the settings to compensate for the inclination of the roller paths at each gun and told me to check them after we were underway to see if they were correct. After the first check I reported that the settings were way off, showing him the results plotted on a large sheet of cross section paper. He said I was making some mistake and told me to do it again. This went on for almost a month and my room was filling up with sheets of paper half the size of my bunk all proving that his computed settings were no good. Finally, I persuaded him to come up to the director with me. He watched a few checks being made, then, saying we'd probably made some mistake in the original data, promptly discarded what, for me, had been a troublesome theory. He was a hard man to convince. [50]

The Executive Officer recalled that he became distraught over what he considered Turner's harsh opinions of his and the other officers' performance of duty and over the remark of one of the Officers' of the Deck that he

---

[48] Powers, Lademan, Canan, Darron, Browne.
[49] Browne.
[50] Lademan.

wanted to push Turner overboard, and would have done so if he thought he could get away with it. As a result, the Division Medical Officer and then the Squadron Medical Officer talked with the Executive Officer who was ordered to the Naval Hospital and to Waiting Orders with no duty assignment for several months.[51]

However, no matter how "unforgiving and severe" Turner was, surprisingly enough no officer was suspended from duty for any of the hundred and one causes or incidents which in those days resulted in such suspensions. All the officers convinced their next promotional examining board of their professional qualifications and were promoted. This included the Executive Officer. But, the Chief Engineer remembered:

> It was common 'No. 4 Smokestack Gossip' that RKT and the Division Commander were not compatible. There was such a contrast in character and temperament between the two. The Division Commander took great pride in being the 'King of the Passovers' and was marking time until he was retired and was not very tolerant toward an officer of the ability of RKT and his conscientious efforts. If there was any 'extra duty' to be performed by any ship in the Division, the assignment usually fell to the *Mervine*.[52]

The Division Commander undoubtedly was aware of the lack of calm leadership exercised by Lieutenant Commander Turner and of the turmoil within the officer ranks of the *Mervine*. Bad news, and that includes inadequate leadership, works up as well as down in the Navy. Commander Kittinger viewed Lieutenant Commander Turner's performance of duty dimly, but not so dimly as did some of the ship's officers. He marked him in command ability 3.2 or 3.5. "This officer seems to have average ability" was his only remark on one fitness report, and on another he wrote only: "This officer possesses about average ability except in Ordnance in which he is superior."

On three different fitness reports, Commander Kittinger marked his brainy subordinate "average" in 19 different categories, including "intelligence," "above average" in none, and "superior" in none.

Never having gotten around to questioning Admiral Turner before his sudden death, in regard to this phase of his naval service, this scribe cannot add anything to this unusual series of fitness reports except to say they in no way painted a complete picture of the officer and man. He was many things, but never "average."

---

[51] Powers.
[52] Browne.

Whatever trials and tribulations Lieutenant Commander Turner had with his Division Commander, he never gave vent of them to me.

The official part of the eight and a half months' cruise in the *Mervine* is covered by the despatch quoted below:

> From Commander Destroyer Squadrons, Battle Fleet to Bureau of Ordnance 0129 For Commander R. K. Turner. The *Mervine* stands fourth in battle efficiency. My appreciation and my hearty congratulations on this excellent performance 2125.

Fourth out of 103 was not bad, and Rear Admiral Schofield, a future Commander in Chief, was a good man to impress. The personal side was covered in a letter written to this same Force Commander:

> NAVY DEPARTMENT
> NAVAL EXAMINING BOARD
> *Washington, 27 May 1925.*
>
> REAR ADMIRAL F. H. SCHOFIELD, U.S.N.,
> *Commanding Destroyer Squadrons,*
> Battle Fleet, *U.S.S. Omaha, Flagship,* c/o Postmaster, San Francisco, Calif.
>
> MY DEAR SCHOFIELD:
>
> I was pleased to find that Lieutenant Commander Richmond K. Turner of the Mervine in his examination for promotion to Commander made marks of over 3.56 in all subjects.
>
> You are surely having a most interesting and instructive cruise. All of us here attached to desks envy you and all the others who have been with the Fleet.
>
> Very sincerely yours,
> SUMNER E. W. KITTELLE

One of Turner's officers in the *Mervine* wrote:

> I don't know if Turner was given to introspection before *Mervine*, but he must have done some thorough going self-analysis after. Only so, could he have changed and produced his later record of accomplishment.[53]

This scribe does not know either. But considering the fact that he had been "asked off" of Vice Admiral McCully's staff and sent to the *Mervine*, it would have been quite normal if Lieutenant Commander Turner had asked himself many questions during the 1924–1925 period of his naval service, and come up with some good answers.

---

[53] Powers.

TO THE BUREAU OF ORDNANCE

In late March 1925, after only eight months in command, Lieutenant Commander Turner was ordered to the Bureau of Ordnance for duty. He was relieved by Lieutenant Commander Penn L. Carroll, Class of 1909, just back from duty with the Naval Mission to Brazil. Turner drew a dead horse of one month's pay—$325—on 14 April 1925 to finance the trip to Washington and requested one month's leave.

On 17 June 1925, Rear Admiral C. C. Bloch, Chief of the Bureau of

Commander Turner at about 45.

Ordnance, delivered with congratulations, Turner's commission as a commander. In 1925, a commission as a commander in the Navy was a license to sit at the feet of the Navy great and learn, and a franchise to start molding those about him in his own image.

Commander Turner's duty in the Bureau of Ordnance was as Head of the Design and Turret Mount and Machinery Sections. During the 18 months that he held this assignment, he was frequently away on temporary duty witnessing tests of new ordnance material of both the Army and the Navy, as well as "witnessing Joint Coast Artillery—Air Service Anti-aircraft tests." This detail was highly satisfying to Commander Turner. There were "about 20 officers in the Bureau, about half of whom later became Flag officers; a highly intelligent group, hard working, and accomplishing a lot of progress with pretty limited funds." [54]

Rear Admiral Bloch described his subordinate in his fitness reports as "Hard worker, forceful, active, sound judgment and strong opinions." In the periodic fitness reports, Rear Admiral Bloch marked Turner superior in 14 characteristics and above average in the five others.

A contemporary, who worked in the same field of effort, reports as follows:

> In 1925 when I was on duty in the Naval Gun Factory in the old Navy Yard, Washington, Kelly Turner was Head of the Design and Turret Mount and Machinery Sections in the former Bureau of Ordnance. The Naval Gun Factory was doing the experimental work in connection with new turret mounts and machinery designs and it was necessary for me, and the other officers directly connected, to work closely with those in the Bureau.
>
> However, I had to draw the line sharply, when Kelly Turner started giving orders directly to my subordinates as to what was to be done or how it was to be done. He was always ready to take charge anywhere anytime.[55]

TO PENSACOLA

A shipmate in the *Mervine,* Darron, reports that when he put in for flight training, Lieutenant Commander Turner told him, "If I were a younger man, I'd request aviation too." Kelly got no younger, but in 1927 he qualified as a naval aviator.

Admiral Turner's personally approved biography states that he went

---
[54] Turner. Future Flag officers were J. O. Richardson, T. S. Wilkinson, O. M. Hustvedt, O. C. Badger, C. H. Wright, C. H. Jones, and W. H. P. Blandy.
[55] Kinkaid.

into aviation because he was "interested in the rise of aviation as a vital factor in warfare." [56] Amplifying this in 1960, he said:

> I was interested in going into aviation for some years, prior to applying for aviation training. When in 1918–1919, I was Gunnery Officer of the *Mississippi* (BB-41) Captain Moffett was Commanding Officer, and he was much interested in Naval Aviation. [Note: From the *Mississippi*, Captain Moffett went to duty in Naval Operations as Director of Naval Aviation.] While I was in the *Mississippi* a fly off platform was built on the top of #2 turret. So it was quite natural that I should take a real interest in planes flying off any of my turrets.[57]
>
> When in 1923, I was on Admiral McCully's staff as Gunnery Officer and Aviation Officer, I was strong for aviation. Later when I was in the Bureau of Ordnance in 1925–1926, Admiral Moffett and I used to walk down together to the Old Navy Department from 3000 Connecticut Avenue. One day while we were walking down, he suggested to me that I apply. I took the physical examination, passed and applied.[58]

Three months later, the Bureau of Navigation got around to replying: "Note has been made of your request and it will be given consideration." [59] But, Admiral Moffett's continual efforts to have first flight senior officers go into naval aviation, put Commander Turner into the same aviation training class as Captain Ernest J. King.

Commander Turner reported for instruction in flying at the Naval Air Station, Pensacola, on 3 January 1927 and successfully completed the course on 30 August 1927. Three members of the Class of 1908, including Turner, were in the school, but he was the only one whose mental and physical reflexes were still limber enough to absorb the essential skills, and become a naval aviator.

One of his instructors, 35 years later, opined:

> Kelly was a good flyer, and very sharp in the classroom. He worked at things hard and caught on rapidly.[60]

Another of Turner's instructors wrote:

> I remember the Great Man's entrance on the Pensacola scene very well. At that time, I was running the torpedo plane school and teaching ground aviation ordnance. As each new class arrived, we, in ground school, had to help out during the solo period. Ralph Davison, Superintendent of Flight Training assigned Kelly to me as one of my four students.

---

[56] Official Biography, Turner.
[57] Turner.
[58] Turner. Application dated 4 June 1926.
[59] BUNAV to RKT, letter, cer 6312–144, Nav 312–D of 2 Sep. 1926.
[60] Interview with VAdm M. K. Greer, USN (Ret.), 12 Dec. 1961.

Kelly's reputation had preceded him, a hard man, EJK's favorite, etc. We instructors were all Lieutenants who, before flight, had to sign the Bevo list. (I hereby certify that I have not partaken of intoxicating spirits during the past 24 hours.) Flight instruction had not reached the precision in technique that came a year or so later when Barrett Studley [61] wrote the Instructor's Manual. The average of instruction was poor and some of us knew it.

Kelly was formally friendly as we met on the beach of old Squadron One. A gray haired grim man who took himself seriously—I told him about course rules and my proposed procedure and he seemed impatient as if he knew all about it.

He wore a student helmet, hard, with ear pieces for a speaking tube from a canvas mouth piece hung around my neck. Instructors rode the front seat of the NY-1 single float, whirlwind engine seaplane. Biplane, of course, top speed about 75, I guess and landing speed well below 50.

At first, he was inclined to argue with me about the errors he made. I remember this well, for during the second or third hour of instruction I landed the plane and told him in no uncertain terms that he had better do what I said or he wouldn't get by. From then on, he was amenable to all suggestions and he soloed without difficulty.

I remember one time when we had a strong west wind right down the beach, and I stalled the plane at about 1000 feet so that we came down almost vertically as I would give short bursts of throttle to avoid spinning. After he soloed and was being given a check by Ray Greer,[62] he caught hell for trying to do something similar. . . .

Admiral Upham asked him to submit a report criticizing constructively flight training and the Pensacola command. I remember that he is reported to have said that he had never seen a station run so well,—and by lieutenants. But it shows the prestige he had with those seniors.[63]

---

[61] Lieutenant, USN, died 3 March 1941.
[62] Now Vice Admiral M. R. Greer, USN (Ret.).
[63] Admiral Austin K. Doyle, USN (Ret.), to GCD, letter, 5 Jan. 1961. Hereafter Arty Doyle.

CHAPTER III

Early Years of a Decade of Service in the Naval Aeronautical Organization 1927–1932

AN OLD MAN IN A YOUTH ORGANIZATION

When Commander Turner left Pensacola in November 1927, he headed for one of the more difficult assignments in the mushrooming Naval Aeronautical Organization. He was 42, a newly found naval aviator and his first flying billet was to be in command of the Aircraft Squadrons of one of the three major subdivisions of the United States Fleet, the United States Asiatic Fleet.

Not that Air Squadrons, Asiatic Fleet was a large organization. It distinctly was not. But the Department was planning on its marked expansion, and it was highly desirable that this expansion take place from a sound base.[1]

A more cautious handling of Commander Turner's limited aviation abilities would have been to billet him in some part of the Naval Aeronautical Organization where, for the first few months, he might exercise his wings under senior aviators who could be expected to offer a word of counsel from time to time. There were five Flag officers, and a dozen captains and commanders senior to him, qualified as naval aviators or naval observers at this time.[2]

In these days when the Naval Aeronautical Organization encompasses eight or nine thousand aircraft, depending upon the Administration's assess-

---

[1] (a) CINC Asiatic, *Annual Reports,* 1928 and 1929 with departmental endorsements thereon. Hereafter referred to as Asiatic *A.R.;* (b) COMAIRONS, Asiatic, *Annual Reports,* 1928 and 1929. Hereafter referred to as COMAIRONS *A.R.;* (c) BUAER, Endorsement to Asiatic, *A.R.,* 1929.

[2] *Register of Commissioned and Warrant Officers of the United States Navy and Marine Corps,* January 1928. Hereafter referred to as *Naval Register.*

ment of the degree of heat of the Cold War,[3] it is well to recall that, on 1 December 1927, there were only 876 heavier-than-air (HTA) aircraft in the Navy.[4] Of these, just 26 were on the Asiatic Station. Fourteen of the 26 were in VF-1017 and VO-107 with the 3rd Brigade of Marines in China, and six VO seaplanes were shipborne in Light Cruiser Division Three. Both the Marine Brigade and the Cruiser Division were on duty in the Asiatic Fleet and on the China Coast, in a temporary status.[5]

Only the six Martin Torpedo seaplanes (T3M-2) assigned to VT Squadron five were directly under the command of Commander Aircraft Squadrons, Asiatic Fleet, along with the flagship, *USS Jason,* and the tenders, *USS Avocet* and *USS Heron.*[6]

But irrespective of the size of the command, the Asiatic Station, in 1928, was a beacon toward which those naval officers seeking to practice the more turbulent aspects of their profession could well turn.

THE SITUATION IN CHINA 1927–1929

The mere fact that the 3rd Brigade of Marines with Major General Smedley Butler, USMC, commanding, and Light Cruiser Division Three with Rear Admiral J. R. Y. Blakely, USN, commanding, were temporarily in the Asiatic Command and that 3,000 Marines were in Peking and Tientsin, and 1,000 in Shanghai was indicative that China was boiling with "Antiforeign agitation and civil war."[7] "Chinese Nationalism and Russian Communism walked and worked hand in hand." Americans in China, reportedly "were in a state of high tension and were much concerned about the welfare of their persons and their property."[8] Three cruisers, 17 destroyers, 11 submarines, four tenders, four minesweepers, one transport, and one oil tanker were stationed in northern China during this period in addition to the regular Yangtze River gunboats.

The Commander in Chief of the United States Asiatic Fleet was also

---

[3] DCNO(AIR) and CHBUWEPS, *United States Naval Aviation 1910–1960,* NAVWEPS–00–80P–1, Appendix IV. Hereafter referred to as NAVWEPS–00–80P–1.

[4] *United States Navy Directory,* January 1, 1928, p. 140.

[5] Asiatic, A.R., 1928, pp. 20, 22. Third Brigade Marines status changed from Temporary to Permanent status 1 March 1928. Light Cruiser Division Two relieved Light Cruiser Division Three on 30 May 1928.

[6] *Navy Directory,* Jan. 1928, p. 130.

[7] *Encyclopaedia Britannica,* 14th ed., vol. V, p. 545; (b) SECNAV, *Annual Report,* 1928, pp. 4, 5.

[8] (a) Asiatic, A.R., 1928, p. 3; *ibid.,* 1929, p. 10; (b) SECNAV, A.R., 1928, p. 5.

concerned. That wise old man and Old China Hand, Admiral Mark L. Bristol, opined:

> A new spirit has been born in the hearts of the Chinese people of all classes. By some it is called Nationalism, and others call it Radicalism, Communism, or Bolshevism. . . . The term self-assertiveness is probably a better name for it, than any of the above. . . . In general, the foreigner has shown little consideration in his dealings with the Chinese in the past. It is likely the Chinese will show less in his dealings with the white race in the future.[9]

The year 1927 had ended in China on a social note and a blood purge. Both included the name of Chiang Kai-shek, the leader of the Kuomintang Armies in the march north into Central China.

Returning to Shanghai from Tokyo on 10 November 1927, Chiang Kai-shek married a sister of Mrs. Sun Yat-sen, by name Mei-ling Soong, on 1 December 1927.[10] This brought Chiang into close alliance with the financially powerful Soong family, and enabled him to claim both the mantle of the dead Sun Yat-sen and the leadership of the Nationalists.

The attempted communist coup d'etat at Canton on 11 December 1927 provided a more than valid reason for the Nationalist authorities to close all U.S.S.R. consulates on account of their part in this attempted communist take over. The Russian Vice Consul and other Russians were shot.[11]

The "Rape of Nanking" on 24 March 1927 had turned the bulk of moderate elements of the Kuomintang away from their Soviet Union advisors. The Russians were blamed for working up the soldiers in the Nationalist armies to a high pitch of hatred against foreigners in general, as well as against foreign schools, churches, and hospitals. Chiang Kai-shek, in December 1927, was anxious to widen the break of his former personal ties with the communists, both foreign and domestic, to become the acknowledged leader of the midde-of-the-road Chinese, and to halt the disintegration of the Chinese governmental structure.[12]

When Commander Turner arrived at Manila on 19 January 1928, it appeared for a time that China might simmer down as Chiang Kai-shek was soon appointed Commander in Chief of all the Chinese Armies, and announced a moderate policy. However, this hope was short lived. Conflict

---
[9] Asiatic, A.R., 1928, p. 7. Admiral Bristol, when a commander, was on the Asiatic Station in 1911–1913.
[10] Asiatic, A.R., 1928, p. 8.
[11] (a) Asiatic, A.R., 1928, p. 16; (b) Encyclopaedia Britannica, vol. V, p. 546.
[12] Ibid., p. 545.

continued between conservative leaders and radical leaders, the "followers and students of the Soviet Russian advisors who came to China to assist the revolution." [13] Added to this turbulence was the Japanese-generated conflict at Tsinan in Shantung Province, in May 1928. A partial Japanese re-occupation of Shantung Province along the Tsingtao-Tsinan railroad followed.

The situation was turbulent enough so that the Commander in Chief of the Asiatic Fleet thought it fit to report to the Department:

> Concentration, protection, and evacuation plans have been worked out for all Chinese cities where any numbers of Americans reside, at the various ports along the Chinese Coasts, and up the Yangtze River.[14]
> Acts and threatened acts against foreigners had thrown all foreigners into a state of panic from which most of them have not yet recovered.[15]

To state the matter conservatively, 1928 and 1929 were interesting years for a naval officer with a deep interest in world politics to be on the China Station.

AIRCRAFT SQUADRONS ASIATIC 1928–1929

Aircraft Squadrons, U. S. Asiatic Fleet had formed in February of 1924, when the Secretary of the Navy's General Order 533 of 12 July 1920, providing for an Air Force, as one of the type of commands within each of the three major Fleets, was finally effectuated for the Asiatic Fleet.[16]

The Naval Aeronautical Arm of the Navy had been extended organizationally into the two continental based Fleets beginning in January 1919, when the *USS Shawmut* (CM-4) was designated as flagship of the Air Detachment, U. S. Atlantic Fleet.[17] This organization had been activated on 3 February 1919 when 39-year-old Captain George W. Steele, U. S. Navy, Class of 1900, assumed command. Captain Steele, although not a graduate of Pensacola, had been an assistant to the Director of Naval Aviation in Naval Operations before taking over this sea detail. He was an intelligent supporter of naval aviation and showed his continuing interest in its development by qualifying as a lighter-than-air pilot in 1923.[18]

---

[13] Asiatic, *A.R.*, 1929, p. 6.
[14] *Ibid.*, 1928, p. 33.
[15] *Ibid.*, 1929, p. 11.
[16] (a) *Navy Directory*, May 1924; (b) General Orders of Navy Department; (c) Interview with Vice Admiral M. R. Greer, USN (Ret.), 12 Dec. 1961. Hereafter Greer.
[17] NAVWEPS–00–80P–1, p. 30.
[18] (a) Archibald D. Trumbull and Clifford L. Lord, *History of United States Naval Aviation* (New Haven: Yale University Press, 1949), p. 150. Hereafter Trumbull and Lord; (b) *Official Naval Biography*, of officer concerned. Hereafter *Official Biography*.

Steele's command consisted of six H-16 flying boats under Lieutenant Bruce G. Leighton, U. S. Navy, Class of 1913, as "Airboat Squadron Commander," a Kite Balloon Division of six balloons on as many ships, and an airplane division of three land planes on the famous *Shawmut*, later to be sunk as *Oglala* on 7 December 1941.[19] All 3,805 tons of her had been converted into an aircraft tender after 11 years passenger-freight service in the Fall River Line, and 18 months as a converted minelayer.[20]

It was 10 months later, before the *Aroostook* (CM-3), a sister ship of the *Shawmut* was taken from the Mine Force of the Pacific Fleet and made the flagship and tender for the Air Detachment, Pacific Fleet.[21] She got off to a running start with Captain Henry C. Mustin, Class of 1896, (number 11 naval aviator certificate) as Detachment Commander and skipper of the flagship. Commander John H. Towers (number three naval aviator certificate) was the Executive Officer.[22]

The hunt for just any kind of a ship, which could undertake the duties of an aircraft tender and flagship on the Asiatic Station had taken much longer. Finally, the old collier *Ajax* (AC-14) of 9,250 tons, built in Scotland for the coal trade in 1890, and 34 years and two wars later serving the United States Navy alongside the dock in Cavite, Philippine Islands, was chosen. She was hauled into the stream in February 1924. Her designation was changed to AGC-15, and her assignment was changed from the Receiving Ship for the 16th Naval District to flagship of Aircraft Squadrons, U. S. Asiatic Fleet. Lieutenant Commander Charles S. Keller, U. S. Navy, who commanded the *Ajax* as Receiving Ship, temporarily continued in command, awaiting the arrival of an officer versed in aviation.

Six Douglas Torpedo (DT-2) aircraft of Torpedo Squadron 20 were ferried out to Cavite aboard the USS *Vega* (AK-17) and arrived in Cavite in mid-February 1924 after a 40-day passage from San Diego, California.[23] They were the backbone and sinew of Aircraft Squadrons, Asiatic.

Everything in supporting resources for the Squadron over the next few years was in the nature of an improvisation. "Aircraft Squadrons Asiatic exists solely to provide a groundwork to be built upon" was the way Admiral

---

[19] (a) *Navy Directory*, 1919; (b) NAVWEPS–00–80P–1, p. 30.

[20] Bureau of Construction and Repair, *Ships Data, U.S. Naval Vessels* (Washington: Government Printing Office, 1938). Hereafter *Ships Data*.

[21] (a) *Dictionary of American Naval Fighting Ships*, Vol. I, p. 64. Hereafter DANFS, I; (b) *Navy Directory*, 1919.

[22] (a) *Ibid.*; (b) NAVWEPS–00–80P–1, Appendix I, p. 195.

[23] (a) *Navy Directory*, 1924; (b) Greer; (c) DANFS, I, p. 17.

W. A. Moffett, Chief of the Bureau of Aeronautics, described the situation to his Aide.[24]

It was 24 June 1924, before Commander Albert C. Read, U. S. Navy, reported aboard the *Ajax* to take command of that ship, Aircraft Squadron, Asiatic and VT Squadron 20. Read was Class of 1907, holder of naval pilot certificate number 24, and had been skipper of the NC-4 on the first eastward trans-Atlantic flight, 16–27 May 1919.[25] He had just come from two years at the Naval War College. By previous training and experience, Read could be judged outstandingly well qualified to get naval aviation development off to a good start in the Asiatic Fleet and make a contribution to its task of showing the flag in and about the important Far East area.

In assigning naval aviators, the Navy Department gave Commander Read some real help. For in the eight officer complement were George D. Murray, Marshall R. Greer, and Frederick W. McMahon, all of whom served the Navy in later years as Flag officers.[26]

By early 1925 the *Heron*, a 950-ton *Bird* class minesweeper, had been taken from "out of commission" status and converted to a small seaplane tender (AVP-2), and added to the Aircraft Squadrons command.[27]

The important change in Aircraft Squadrons, Asiatic, was to take place in mid-1925. Because the Navy was rapidly shifting from coal to oil for its propulsion, the services of the big 19,000-ton collier *Jason* (AC-12), were no longer needed in the Fleet Base Force operating in the Atlantic. Without being fitted as a "heavier-than-air aircraft" tender, she was sent out to Manila to relieve the antiquated and disintegrating *Ajax*.[28]

A change had been desirable from the day the *Ajax* was designated an aircraft tender. Her topside space was so limited that only two assembled aircraft could be carried on board. The remaining four were boxed and stowed in the holds. Additionally, she was worn out with sea service. Before the year was out, this became painfully evident during a typhoon-afflicted voyage between Guam and the China coast. Reluctantly, but immediately, she was surveyed as unsafe, condemned as unfit, and sold.[29]

---

[24] Interview with Captain George Dorsey Price, USN (Ret.), San Diego, California, 12 Oct. 1961. Hereafter Price.

[25] (a) Official Biography, Read; (b) Trumbull and Lord, p. 168; (c) NAVWEPS–00–80P–1, Appendix II.

[26] (a) *Navy Directory*, 1924; (b) *Naval Register*, 1947.

[27] (a) *Navy Directory*, 1925; (b) *Ships Data*, 1938.

[28] (a) *Ibid.*; (b) *Navy Directory*, 1925; (c) Greer.

[29] (a) *Ibid.*; (b) *Ships Data*, 1938; (c) DANFS, I.

The *Jason* was 21 years younger than the *Ajax*, with twice the displacement. But she was not ideal as an aircraft tender.

As Commander of Aircraft Squadrons, Asiatic, reported to the Navy Department:

> The *Jason* is a collier assigned as an aircraft tender and flagship. No materiel nor personnel changes, other than the addition of a small Flag complement have been made. . . . [She is] wholly inadequate as a tender for the Air Squadrons.[30]

As a further supplement, another *Bird*-class minesweeper, the *Avocet* (AVP-4) had been added to the squadron early in September 1925, having been freshened up to act as a seaplane tender, after being taken from "out of commission" status.[31]

By 1928, the command of Aircraft Squadrons, Asiatic, had passed through the hands of two non-aviators, Commander Ernest Frederick (Class of 1903) and Commander Raymond F. Frellsen (Class of 1907). This occurred because, with only a dozen commanders in the Navy designated as naval aviators, none had been made available to the Commander in Chief, Asiatic, for the command.[32]

Commander Frellsen, having been detached at the end of September 1927, had already arrived back in the States before Commander Turner sailed on the *SS President Monroe* from San Francisco on 16 December 1927, for the four and a half week voyage to Manila, Philippine Islands.

PROBLEMS AHEAD

In January 1928, not only was the flagship without a regularly detailed Commanding Officer, but the Executive Officer, Lieutenant Commander Karl E. Hintze, U. S. Navy (Class of 1913), was awaiting departure for the States as soon as his relief, Lieutenant Commander Walter M. A. Wynne, U. S. Navy (Class of 1915) came aboard. In addition to the doctor, a paymaster, and his clerk, there were two junior grade lieutenants and an ensign to keep the 162-man ship's organization producing.[33]

---

[30] COMAIRONS, *A.R.*, 1928, p. 1.

[31] (a) *Navy Directory*, 1926–1927; (b) DANFS, I, p. 78.

[32] Four of the commander naval aviators commanded or were executives of ships (*Lexington, Saratoga, Wright, Langley*); three commanded Naval Air Stations (Hampton Roads, Pearl Harbor, Pensacola); two were on Staffs AIRBATFOR, AIRSCOFOR; three were in Navy Department.

[33] (a) *Navy Directory*, Jan. 1928; (b) Turner; (c) Price; (d) COMAIRONS, *A.R.*, 1928, p. 23.

In the other major unit of the command, Lieutenant Commander George D. Price, U. S. Navy, was in command of VT-5A, the current designation for what previously had been called VT Squadron 20, and there were only three other naval aviators in the squadron.

So, upon arrival, Commander Turner found much to be done. This was not only because the Squadron and its flagship had been required to operate under-manned in officers and men, but because a change was taking place in the type of aircraft the Squadron operated. VT Squadron Five A was just being provided with six new Martin torpedo airplanes (T3M-52), a type which started coming off the assembly lines in July 1926. The orders from the Department were that four were to be in commission and two in reserve.[34]

The hand-to-mouth existence of the Navy in the lean-national defense days of the Coolidge Administration is illustrated by a quote from Commander Turner's official report. The new torpedo planes, he noted, "were received without any spare parts whatsoever." These T3M-2s were one engine tractor biplanes with twin floats, built by Martin in 1926–27. "Spares did not begin to arrive until March" 1928.[35] Not only was the supply end of logistics spotty, but adequate personnel were lacking. Only five aviators, including Commander Aircraft Squadrons, and 33 enlisted men were assigned to the squadron.

There was also a lean ration of bread and butter flight orders for the flight crews. Only eight flight orders for the squadron were allowed and "several enlisted men in the Squadron fly regularly, but have no flight orders." In due time Commander Turner's efforts persuaded the Department to raise this quota of flight orders to 14 against his recommended 22.[36]

The four aviators in the Squadron were glad to have an aviator in command because they believed his voice would carry more weight than the previous non-aviators at the Fleet staff level, he would understand their many problems more quickly, and would be more apt to be sympathetic to them. But their real desire was for a naval aviator who had been in naval aviation as long or longer than they had been. Someone who would anticipate the aviator's problems and do something to avoid their even arising. Commander Turner was accepted with an "It's bound to be better now"—but the big question mark was "How much better?" [37]

---

[34] (a) Asiatic, A.R., 1928, para. 241, 281, 287, 295; (b) COMAIRONS, A.R., 1928, pp. 22, 23, 24; (c) NAVWEPS–00–80P–1, p. 210.
[35] COMAIRONS, A.R., 1928, pp. 20, 28, 29.
[36] (a) COMAIRONS, A.R., 1928, p. 25; Ibid., 1929, p. 39; (b) Asiatic, A.R., 1929, p. 68.
[37] Price.

Service in the Naval Aeronautical Organization

The most obvious handicap of the Aircraft Squadrons, Asiatic, was the lack of a proper tender. The second handicap, which had to be accepted, was the 1922 Washington Treaty for the Limitation of Naval Armaments. This treaty included provisions that the status quo, at the time of signing of the treaty, would be maintained by the United States in regard to its naval bases west of Hawaii. Therefore, no measures could be taken "to increase the existing naval shore facilities for the repair and maintenance of Naval Forces" in the Philippine Islands.[38]

It was distressingly obvious that facilities to permit the operation from the beach of the seaplanes of the Squadron would violate the provisions of the treaty. One of the aviators in the Squadron at this time in 1928, Lieutenant George Dorsey Price (Class of 1916), recalls an incident arising during the typhoon season when the planes had made a routine operating flight to Olongapo and were moored overnight in Olongapo Bay. The squadron was warned the next day of the near approach of a typhoon which had veered suddenly to head for Manila from its original path to the east of Luzon.

In order to save their aircraft, the plane crews, with some shoreside assistance and hastily-laid ramps, hauled the seaplanes up on the beach at the Naval Station Olongapo. Here the pontoons were filled with water and the planes lashed down. When the typhoon had passed, the planes were floated, and returned to their tenders at Manila.

About three weeks later, the squadron commander was informed that the Japanese Government had complained to the United States Government that the Navy had violated the 1922 Washington Treaty by increasing the facilities for plane handling at the Naval Station, Olongapo. The squadron commander was required to provide factual data to the Governor General's Office, so that an appropriate response could be made to the Japanese.[39]

The general hazard of weather and the specific hazard of typhoons to aircraft were a constant worry to the new squadron commander. He expressed his anxieties in these words:

> Too great emphasis cannot be placed on the dangers of plane operations on this station due to typhoons. Unless planes can be hoisted out of the water or anchored down on shore or on board ship during typhoons, they will almost certainly be wrecked.
>
> Under present conditions, it is impracticable to operate planes from the

---

[38] Washington Treaty for the Limitations of Naval Armaments, 1922, Article XIX.
[39] Price.

vicinity of Manila during the rainy season. Cavite is unsuitable as a seaplane base at any time of the year.[40]

During his 16 months on station, two planes were lost and one was badly damaged due to crack-ups in rough water landings, which proved to be beyond the skill of the pilots, or the structure of the planes.[41]

With shoreside seaplane facilities out of question, Commander Turner immediately turned his attention to drafting plans to convert the 17-year-old *Jason* (AC-12) to a heavier-than-air aircraft tender. He soon formulated two major projects to alter the *Jason*. Project One would fit her to base 12 planes on board and Project Two would permit 30 planes to be based on board.[42]

Project One was urgent because, beginning on July 1, 1928, the *Jason* was to base six T3M-2 aircraft and a flag unit of two UO Chance Vought observation aircraft in full commission, and carry three more T3M-2 aircraft in reserve.[43]

Admiral Bristol, the Commander in Chief, was quick and positive in helping the project along. He advised the Chief of Naval Operations:

> The *Jason* is unsuitable in her present condition as an aircraft tender, but could be made so with the alterations to be recommended. These include additional quarters for officers and men, the conversion of the coal bunkers into fuel oil stowage, storerooms and magazines; the installation of gasoline stowage, of new generators, and the possible removal of the coaling booms, substituting two cranes; with these changes, the *Jason* could maintain the following planes:—18VT; 6VO; and 6VF.[44]

Although mentioned last in priority by the Commander in Chief, the change dearest to the naval aviator's heart was one which would remove the coal hoisting gear of the *Jason* and provide modern plane handling booms, with winch controls, permitting fast and delicate handling of the planes. On 30 April 1928, one of the new Martin torpedo planes was dropped 30 feet by the coal handling gear "necessitating a major overhaul of both plane and engine." [45]

Money for all naval purposes was modest in fiscal 1928 and fiscal 1929, but Project One was accomplished at Cavite Navy Yard in the late spring of 1929. Project Two was lost in the financial depression which began in the

---

[40] COMAIRONS, A.R., 1928, pp. 3, 4, 10, 20.
[41] *Ibid.*, p. 11; *Ibid.*, 1929, p. 22.
[42] (a) Asiatic, A.R., 1928, pp. 24, 31, 53; (b) COMAIRONS, A.R., 1928, p. 19.
[43] (a) *Ibid.*, 1928, p. 2; *Ibid.*, 1929, pp. 4, 20; (b) Asiatic, A.R., 1929, p. 58.
[44] *Ibid.*, 1928, pp. 24, 31; *Ibid.*, 1929, p. 58.
[45] (a) COMAIRONS, A.R., 1928, p. 11; (b) Price.

fall of 1929, as was the proposed patrol plane increase on the Asiatic Station to 18.

The *Jason*, burning "old and slack" Chinese coal and making a competitive score in the Fleet Engineering competition of only 75.00 at her best cruising speed of 11.6 knots, was to be nursed along until mid-1932. Then, together with many other ships, she succumbed to drastically reduced naval appropriations, and was placed out of commission, taking most of Aircraft Squadrons, Asiatic, to the same boneyard.[46]

So although Commander Turner was largely responsible for initiating the remodeling of the collier *Jason* into an aircraft tender, the length of his tour in command did not permit him to witness the undertaking of the actual alterations or to publish the official change in designation.[47]

Commander Turner received a distinct boost up the ladder from his tour on the Asiatic Station. This was far from routine, as many an officer dampened his promotion opportunities on that fast stepping station. He was extremely lucky to have Admiral Mark L. Bristol as the Commander in Chief, Asiatic Fleet, and as his immediate senior. Admiral Bristol, a non-naval aviator, but an officer of recognized ability and strong character, had been Director of Naval Aviation in the Navy Department from 1913 to 1916, and was the originator of the phrase "Take the Air Service to Sea." [48]

One of Turner's earnest desires was to take the Aircraft Squadrons to sea and to conduct air reconnaissance of the sea areas around and about the main islands of the Philippines. Primarily this was because "there are no charts for aerial navigation of the Philippines" and there was little information regarding possible seaplane bases from which large seaplanes could be operated in time of war.[49] Both of these deficiencies could be corrected while at the same time Commander Turner would acquire an opportunity to "act independently with no mother hen superior peering over his shoulder." [50]

This policy fitted into Admiral Bristol's plans, and the desire of the Chief of Naval Operations, Admiral Charles F. Hughes, U. S. Navy, for data to prepare aviation charts in the Philippine Islands. Admiral Bristol had caused

---

[46] (a) Asiatic, A.R., 1929, p. 58; (b) COMAIRONS, A.R., 1928, p. 7; Ibid., 1929, p. 14; (c) Trumbull and Lord, p. 276.
[47] *Jason* was built at Maryland Steel Company as Fleet Collier 12 in 1911. Changed designation AC–12 to AV–2 on January 21, 1930. Stricken from Navy List May 19, 1936. *Ships Data*, 1938.
[48] Trumbull and Lord, p. 36.
[49] (a) Turner; (b) Asiatic, A.R., 1928, p. 43.
[50] Turner.

Commander Light Cruiser Division Three, Rear Admiral J. R. Y. Blakely, U. S. Navy, to visit and report upon Malampaya Sound, Palawan; Tawi Tawi Bay, Tawi Tawi; and Dumanquilas Bay and Davao Gulf, Mindanao. These large water areas, all 500 to 600 miles south of Manila were examined "with a view to their utilization as Advanced Bases for the U. S. Fleet." [51]

These visits and the subsequent reports to the Navy Department were to provide the detailed data necessary to permit filling out the War Plans of that date calling for the U. S. Fleet to move from the continental United States to an Advance Base in the Southern Philippines, in the early days of a war with Japan.[52]

AIR RECONNAISSANCE

It was apparent that if the Aircraft Squadrons could conduct aerial reconnaissance over and around some of the larger islands in the Philippines and determine the availability of suitable protected areas outside the typhoon belt from which seaplanes could operate, a substantial amount of information would accrue, upon which to base detailed offensive and defensive war operations of the U. S. Fleet.[53]

During the period July 1, 1927 to April 20, 1929, therefore, four to six planes of Aircraft Squadrons, Asiatic, carried out aerial and photographic reconnaissance covering:

   a. West Coast of Luzon from Cape Bolinao at the entrance to Lingayen Gulf to San Bernadino Strait 400 miles to the southeast
   b. East Coast of Luzon
   c. Mindoro Island
   d. Burias, Marinduque, Masbate and Ticao Island
   e. Mindanao, except East Coast
   f. Visayas, except East Coast
   g. All major ports of the Philippines [54]

In addition while based at Chefoo, China, "reconnaissance flights were made from Chefoo to Chinwangtao for the purpose of obtaining photographs of the coastline and landmarks, for the Hydrographic Office." Later

---
[51] Asiatic, *A.R.*, 1928, p. 41.
[52] *Orange War Plan*, 1924.
[53] Asiatic, *A.R.*, 1928, p. 37.
[54] COMAIRONS, *A.R.*, 1928, p. 9; *Ibid.*, 1929, p. 19.

an aerial survey of the Nanking area was made.[55] During all these flights, Commander Turner carried more than his share of the load. He showed an eagerness to fly which matched that of his subordinates, eight to 16 years younger, and he showed a high degree of skill for one of his years. He also showed a complete unwillingness to accept past performance of the Aircraft Squadrons as a standard for the present or future.[56]

The squadron was kept pounding away at the wearisome, but rewarding, task of air reconnaissance, until at the time of his relief, Commander Turner was able to report "all operations contemplated in connection with the preparation of airway charts have been completed." [57]

During 1928 and 1929, the Commander in Chief also was requesting all merchant ships transiting the general Asiatic Station area to send in a report at the end of each voyage showing the type of weather encountered each day, and to answer:

    a. What speed could a destroyer maintain?
    b. What speed could a submarine maintain?
    c. Could a destroyer or submarine oil from a tanker?
    d. Could airplanes land or take off?

With this data properly synthetized and plotted on the monthly pilot charts of the North Pacific Ocean and, acting on the assumption that the masters of the ships had not answered questions where they lacked competence, it was possible to plan more accurately for a naval campaign in the Western Pacific.[58]

JOINT MANEUVERS

Admiral Bristol was energetic and air-minded. He had come away from his eight years' duty as High Commissioner in Turkey, with a well-founded reputation for diplomacy. This was helpful in continuing and expanding Joint Exercises with the Army, in which both Army and Naval aircraft played a regular role. Major General Douglas MacArthur, USA, was commander of the Army's Philippine Department. He was to be the next Chief of Staff of the Army.

Joint maneuvers between the Army and Navy were a tradition on the

---
[55] *Ibid.*, p. 19.
[56] Price.
[57] COMAIRONS, *A.R.*, 1929, p. 19.
[58] Asiatic, *A.R.*, 1929, p. 42.

Asiatic Station, but they waxed and waned depending on the spirit of cooperation between the top echelons of command. Admiral Bristol in his first yearly summary of operations after taking command reported:

> Measures have been taken with the Army authorities to greatly extend the scope of these Joint maneuvers for next year (July 1, 1928 to June 30, 1929).

His future plans specifically included "scouting for the approach of the Fleet by combined Army-Navy planes, followed by a combined air attack." [59]

These operations brought Commander Turner into close working relations with the senior officers of the Army Air Corps, and with the staff of the Commander in Chief, as well as with Admiral Bristol himself. In due time and after much preliminary communication training, during which "reliable radio ranges between planes up to 200 miles" were achieved, the planned operations were carried out on 12, 13, and 15 November 1928. The November 15 operation resulted in the following despatch to the Chief of Naval Operations.

> Setting a precedent in the Asiatic Station, and it is believed for the first time in history, Army and Navy planes in a single formation, under a unified command performed a simulated attack on an assumed hostile fleet.
> COMAIRONS with six T3M2 planes, 2 UO planes, 8 Army pursuit planes, 6 Army attack planes, and 6 Army bombers at 0800, 15 November 1928 made rendezvous at Corregidor, and, acting on the information supplied by 4 Army scouts, delivered a simultaneous attack, involving torpedoing, bombing and strafing on the light cruisers, which were defended by their own planes and a force of fifteen destroyers, at a point about 30 miles to the southwest of Corregidor.
> The operation appeared successful in every phase and was marked by excellent radio communication and coordination.
> A total of 32 planes simultaneously conducted the operation, in addition to the six defending planes of the attacked crusiers.
> This maneuver marks a distinct advance in the efficiency of the defense of the Philippine Islands and it is believed the spirit of cooperation existing between the Army and Navy Air Services could not be higher.[60]

The Secretary of the Navy was quick to snap back with:

> The Department is much gratified at success of Joint Air Operations and especially because of the high spirit of cooperation existing between Army and Navy in Philippines.[61]

This was followed by a warm congratulatory personal letter to Com-

---

[59] (a) *Ibid.*, 1928, p. 36; (b) COMAIRONS, A.R., 1929, p. 6.
[60] Paraphrased copy of a coded despatch, COMAIRONS, A.R., 1929, p. 28.
[61] SECNAV to CINC, Asiatic, Plain Language message 0019–0847 of November 1928.

mander Turner from the Assistant Secretary of the Navy for Air, Edward P. Warner, which concluded with "I hope there will be opportunity for many more such studies and practices, both in your command and elsewhere." [62] A copy of this letter was placed in Commander Turner's official record.

By April 1929, Commander Turner was able to report: "There have been ten occasions when operations have been held by this squadron with units of the Army, since 1 July 1928." [63] These included Joint Board Problems 1 and 3 as set forth in Joint Board No. 350. And Admiral Bristol, at the end of the 1929 fiscal year, in commenting on Fleet training during the previous 12 months said:

> One of the most interesting features has been the development of combined Army-Navy aircraft operations.[64]

He summed up the matter with these words:

> Cooperation between the Army and Navy air forces has been excellent and great advancement made in combined operation.[65]

WAR PLANS

A tour of the Asiatic Station at this time also provided an excellent opportunity for an analysis of war operations in the Philippines. That Commander Turner was so minded is indicated by what he wrote in April 1929:

> It is customary amongst Naval officers to consider it practically settled that the ORANGE [Japanese] forces in the case of an ORANGE-BLUE War, will be landed on the shores of Lingayan Gulf. The existing ASIATIC FLEET operating plan covers this contingency in considerable detail.[66]

Commander Turner did not controvert this surmise, which proved to be 100 percent correct. But he thought, and was forthright enough to say so in a carefully reasoned three-page letter, that the possibility of a Japanese landing in a southern arm of Lamon Bay, called Lopez Bay, "should be again studied" by the Navy as an alternative Japanese landing objective. Lopez Bay was 125 miles by rail and road southeast of Manila. There the water was smooth and the beaches good. Turner believed that "this matter has not

---

[62] ASSECNAV, letter, January 26, 1929.
[63] COMAIRONS, A.R., 1929, pp. 6, 11.
[64] Asiatic, A.R., 1929, p. 26.
[65] Ibid., p. 44.
[66] COMAIRONS, Asiatic to CINC, Asiatic, letter, FE 14/FC–4/FF6/AV, 20 Apr. 1929.

received the attention from the Navy it merits." He noted that "the Army has held maneuvers in Eastern Luzon at this point." He further opined:

> The use of Naval forces, in case of a hostile landing on the East Coast of Luzon has been insufficiently investigated [and] prepared for.[67]

This proposal, however, did not result in immediate action. Due to the Army being unwilling to hold combined operations during a period when the Asiatic Fleet was normally in the Philippines for the fiscal year 1929, Admiral Bristol sadly reported "No combined operations with the Army were carried out other than those with the combined aircraft." He strongly believed in and recommended that "Combined Army-Navy problems involving the defense of the Philippine Islands be carried out and that such problems be formulated in Washington." [68] In this way the Army Command in the Philippines would be required to carry them out.

The United States Army continued to regard Lopez Bay as a likely Japanese landing area, and the Army was quite right. The Japanese made their secondary landing at Lopez Bay on 24 December 1941, two days after the main Japanese landing had taken place at Lingayen Gulf. Major General George M. Parker, Jr., USA, with the South Luzon Force (two divisions) was in that area to oppose the landing at Lopez Bay. All three of the Japanese assault forces for the 7,000-man secondary landing came ashore in Lopez Bay.[69]

Commander Turner's knowledge, perspicacity, initiative, and forthrightness in this matter must have strengthened his seniors' regard for his judgment in regard to other planning and operational matters once the war operations of the Japanese had started.

OPERATIONAL TRAINING

The normal schedule for the Asiatic Fleet in 1928–1929 was for the Fleet to spend the four winter months in operational and gunnery training, based in the Philippines; the four summer months on similar training, based in North China; and the four remaining months, cruising and "showing the Flag" in all the principal ports from the Dutch East Indies to Japan. Fleet

---

[67] *Ibid.*
[68] Asiatic, *A.R.,* 1929, pp. 27, 44.
[69] Louis Morton, *The Fall of the Philippines,* Vol. IV in subseries *The War in the Pacific* of series UNITED STATES ARMY IN WORLD WAR II (Washington: Office of the Chief of Military History, Department of the Army, 1953), Chs. VI–VII.

and Type exercises were held during passage between ports and Joint exercises when in the Philippine area.[70]

An impressive schedule of exercises was carried out in 1928–1929 despite the fact that the shadow of the Great Depression had already fallen on the Navy and some exercises were cancelled "due to the necessity of conserving fuel oil." [71]

Despite the fact that "water conditions on the Asiatic Stations are frequently too rough for the present type of seaplane," VT Squadron Five A flew nearly 800 hours in fiscal year 1928 and 1,000 hours in fiscal 1929. More than 100 of these latter hours were in night flying.[72] A compulsory requirement for night flying by all naval aviators had been promulgated by the Chief of Naval Operations on 16 January 1929 to become effective 1 July 1930. Each naval aviator was required to pilot an aircraft for 10 hours of night flying involving at least 20 landings.

Always anxious to be the first over any hurdle, Commander Turner on 30 March 1929, reported to the Bureau that he had met both requirements and submitted the supporting data. The Bureau of Navigation was hardhearted. They pointed out that some of his night flying had been prior to 16 January and that he had completed only 9 hours and 45 minutes of night flying time after that date.[73]

It was during this cruise that Commander Turner's appetite for intelligence data was whetted. The lack of current informational data especially oriented to the needs of naval aviators on the Asiatic Station, and the lack of foreign intelligence both bothered him. He had been able to do something about the first problem, and he tried to do something about the intelligence. He noted in his Annual Report, that he had sent into the Department "twenty intelligence reports," and he recommended that the Office of Naval Intelligence issue a new intelligence portfolio for the Far East Area.[74]

On the way back to the continental United States, Commander Turner was given authority by the Bureau of Navigation to enter Japan. He spent two weeks there with the United States Naval Attache at Tokyo, Japan, getting himself better grounded with the military resources of the Japanese Empire, and receiving educated guesses on its probable political and military

---

[70] Asiatic, A.R., 1929, p. 23.
[71] (a) Ibid.; (b) COMAIRONS, A.R., 1928, 1929.
[72] (a) Ibid., 1928, pp. 7–8; 1929, p. 15. (b) Asiatic, A.R., 1928, p. 39.
[73] (a) CNO, letter, A21/P11/1/29 Ser. 0116 of 16 Jan. 1929; (b) BUNAV, Ser. 6312 167–Nav 311–MF of May 22, 1929.
[74] COMAIRONS, A.R., 1929, p. 31.

intentions. These two weeks counted as leave. Mrs. Turner had preceded him to the United States.[75]

However, the tour on the China Station was not all beer and skittles. In the 16 months of command, four planes, out of an operating force never numbering more than eight, were lost. One of the tenders, the USS *Avocet*, grounded on the beach at Chefoo, China, as described in the following report:

> One summer night, while the *Jason* lay at Chefoo, a gale came up and ships began to drag anchor. I and Commander Turner had already retired ashore for the night. A rumor came to me at our hotel that the *Avocet* was aground on Chefoo beach. I went out and verified this and then returned to our hotel and told Turner. Without any grumbling he turned out and together we went to the beach and began salvage operations. My duties next morning were to take the heavy *Jason*, anchor as near the *Avocet* as safety permitted, get out hawsers to the *Avocet* and keep them under tension. With the aid of some sand sucking gear, the *Avocet* came off easily. No aid was requested from outside our own organization.[76]

In the Navy of 1928, planes and ships were carefully guarded pieces of government property, for which officers had a high degree of personal responsibility. Each of these events was followed by a Court of Inquiry or Board of Investigation and, in the *Avocet* case, a General Court Martial.[77]

While Commander Turner was happy to report that "for the first time since the establishment of the Aircraft Squadrons, the planes have fully completed all the gunnery exercises required in the Navy-wide gunnery competition during the gunnery year," he added that "the scores made were very poor," and the results were "unsatisfactory." So, the gunnery of the squadron was dismal. To a former gunnery officer of no mean skill, this was a bitter pill to swallow. Previously "not one of the aviators on board had ever launched a torpedo from a plane. . . . No officer attached to VT Squadron Five A was sufficiently familiar with the general methods of gunnery training to supervise this important and arduous work." There had been handicaps, but there was also progress. The best that could be said was that the future should be more propitious, based on the training accomplished.[78]

Special pleading to the Fleet Staff had produced an increase of three Line

---

[75] (a) CINC, Asiatic to Commander Turner, orders, 16 Mar. 1929. (b) Turner.

[76] Lieutenant Commander Walter M. A. Wynne, USN (Ret.) to GCD, questionnaire answers, 18 Mar. 1962.

[77] COMAIRONS, *A.R.*, 1928, p. 11; 1929, p. 22.

[78] (a) *Ibid.*, 1929, p. 11; (b) Turner.

lieutenants and four warrant officers on board the *Jason*, but only much letter writing persuaded the Department to provide a 50 percent increase in naval aviators on the far China Station.

Officer turnover had been painfully rapid. In 16 months there had been four changes in Executive Officers of the flagship. One served under Commander Turner only one month and another only four months before returning to the United States at the expiration of their cruise on the Asiatic Station. Additionally there had been four Engineer Officers, three First Lieutenants, two Gunnery Officers, and two Communications Officers between 1 July 1928 and 1 April 1929.[79]

HOMEWARD BOUND

Having drawn a two-months dead horse, amounting to $816.66 (today this would amount to $2,800.00), having paid the 20 peso fee to become a permanent absentee member of the Manila Golf Club, and having shipped his Essex Sedan stateside for a mere $125, Commander Turner went aboard the *SS President Madison* on 20 April 1929 with a feeling of some elation as he carried a message given him that day by a spokesman for the ship's company of the command which read:

> To Commander R. K. TURNER, *U.S. Navy*
>
> With sincere and grateful appreciation of the high quality of leadership and spirit of good fellowship you consistently exhibited as our Commander, the Aircraft Squadrons Asiatic wish you God speed and bon voyage. May you enjoy a pleasant and satisfactory tour of duty in your new assignment. May good fortune and happy landings always be your portion.
>
> Au Revoir.[80]

Not that there had been no dissent.

One of the junior lieutenant aviators in the squadron balanced out the picture with the following words:

> He was capable and energetic, a good flyer with good aviation judgment; [the Squadron was] efficient, fairly smart as an outfit. [Commander Turner] was interested in tactics. He could foresee war with Japan. [The

---

[79] (a) Navy Directory 1928, 1929; (b) COMAIRONS, A.R., 1929, pp. 11, 37. (c) Interview with Captain E. B. Rogers, USN (Ret.), 10 Oct. 1961. Following an assignment as Commanding Officer S–40, Rogers, then a Lieutenant Commander, served as Executive Officer USS *Jason* from November 1928 to March 1929. He relieved Lieutenant Commander Walter M. A. Wynne, USN (Class of 1915). Hereafter Rogers.

[80] Personal files of R. K. Turner.

main accomplishment was] surveying sites in the Philippines which could be made into aircraft landing areas in the future. [He remembered his AIRONS Commander as] Ambitious and the Prussian Type. [His main interest was] to advance himself through hard work. He demanded hard work and efficiency from others, but drove himself harder. [He] was unpopular with a considerable number of junior officers and a few seniors.[81]

One of his executive officers in the *Jason* described his 44-year-old skipper as follows:

> Kelly Turner had a strong mind and lots of drive. He was up at dawn and still going strong at ten that night. If he had an objective in mind, he would seek to reach it, exploring any and all ways. He would accept no half-way job of any kind from an officer subordinate. He drove, and would not listen to excuses, and certainly not always to reason. You either met his standards or got to hell out of the way.
>
> His primary weakness was his lack of consideration and cooperation down the ladder to the wardroom.
>
> He was a bold seaman and an excellent ship handler. The *Jason* was a big old tub with inadequate power. Turner took her into holes on the East Coast of Luzon, which required a very high degree of skill. The *Jason* had no sonic depth finder, and the charts were old and inadequate, but he dodged coral heads adeptly and frequently.
>
> The *Jason* had good discipline. The men got a fair shake at mast, but Kelly Turner was no molly-coddler.
>
> He was about as far from a beach hound as one could get. He played golf with me and with Russ Ihrig (Skipper of the *Heron*) on week-ends. He was a long iron hitter. With a number 7 iron, he could drive nearly 200 yards."[82]

Along the lines of the latter comments, another officer added:

> He played a fair game of golf and liked golf. He stuck strictly to the rules.[83]

One of the Commanding Officers of seaplane tenders, the *Heron,* who served a full year with Commander Turner says:

> It was my opinion, and common consensus of Squadron Officers, I believe, that Kelly was tops in all respects as a Squadron Commander. He was obviously a fine planner from the aviation survey projects he laid out. He was an aggressive operations commander. I know from his inspection procedures that he was a thorough and highly competent administrator. My impression from Squadron and *Jason* officers was that he was taut and perhaps

---

[81] Captain Crutchfield Adair, USN (Ret.) to GCD, questionnaire answers, 23 Apr. 1962. Hereafter Adair.
[82] Rogers.
[83] Adair.

tough, but fair, although intolerant of inefficiency to the point where some thought he was a sundowner.[84]

The Executive Officer of the *Jason* who served longest with him (10 months) reports:

> Before I reported for duty on the *Jason*, the advice to me was to watch out for Commander Turner. He was a Son-of-a-bitch.
> Kelly Turner turned out to be a close approximation to what I consider an officer and gentleman should be. One who could lead in any direction. He had no weak points, but instead a variety of strong ones which would only come in focus as occasion required. . . .
> To the enlisted personnel, he had for them the aura of the master about him. . . . For the officers, he was the gentleman's gentleman. . . . Hence, he never once lost the respect of any of the personnel he came in contact with, officers or men.[85]

Admiral Mark Bristol took a kindly view of Commander Turner in the regular fitness reports. He recognized his weaknesses, marking him average in patience and self-control, but superior in most other qualities, and in the various reports penned these descriptive phrases:

> Active mind and desire to be doing something is very gratifying.
> A very good mind which he keeps working with a very desirable imagination.
> He never hesitates to undertake anything.

BUREAU OF AERONAUTICS

Commander Turner's cruise on the Asiatic Station was 12 months shorter than the normal two and a half years. The shortening of this pleasurable and stimulating command duty arose because of the familiar Navy "Daisy Chain."

In early 1928, Captain Ernest J. King was Assistant Chief of the Bureau of Aeronautics. "When fur flew" between King and the Chief of Bureau, Rear Admiral Moffett, King promptly was ordered to command the Naval Air Station, Naval Operating Base, Hampton Roads, Virginia.[86] To replace King, Admiral Moffett decided to fleet up his Planning Officer, Commander J. H. Towers. To keep the daisy chain moving, and to fill the important billet of Plans Officer in the Bureau, the decision was made to take advan-

---

[84] Commodore Russell H. Ihrig, USN (Ret.) to GCD, questionnaire answers, Feb. 1962.
[85] Wynne.
[86] *King's Record*, p. 211.

tage of Commander Turner's planning ability and bring him back early from the Asiatic Station.

Rear Admiral Moffett had headed the Bureau of Aeronautics for nine years. Moffett was an "energetic personality" who "invariably knew what he wanted in the most definite way." [87] For this reason, doing the advance planning for him was not an easy task, since no matter what an extensive estimate of the situation might show to be a desirable course of action, Admiral Moffett was apt to have already made a couple of 10 league mental strides along his own throughway from here to there in the particular area under consideration.[88]

In July 1929, when Turner reported, the Bureau of Aeronautics had 42 officers assigned to it, of which six were in the Plans Division. Commander Marc A. Mitscher, a former classmate, and Lieutenant Commander Charles E. Rosendahl (Class of 1914) and a lighter-than-air enthusiast, were Commander Turner's principal assistants, but there was also a recent shipmate, Lieutenant Commander George D. Price who had commanded Squadron VT Five A in Aircraft Squadrons, Asiatic.[89]

The Air Arm of the Navy was growing although the great economic depression of the early 1930's was to slow the pace for several years. Naval appropriations for the year ahead were 366 million, but before Commander Turner would get to sea again they would be down to 318 million for fiscal year 1933.[90]

There were 5,458 officers in the Line of the Navy of which 520 were naval aviators. Of all officers in the Navy 50 percent were on shore duty, 50 percent on sea duty. The Marines were in Nicaragua where operations against the bandits continued, and in Haiti, where a "state of unrest which for a time threatened the internal peace" continued. Although 84,500 men manned the Navy, this number was soon to be cut back to 79,991 by 30 June 1931.[91] Out of a grand total of 928 planes available to the Navy, 425 planes were attached to the United States Fleet.[92]

The Chief of the Bureau of Aeronautics would soon object to the reduction to two million dollars of money available for "experiments," half "for the development of details of" and half for the purchase of "experimental

---

[87] *Ibid.*, p. 207.
[88] Turner.
[89] *Naval Register*, July 1929.
[90] SECNAV, *Annual Reports*, 1929, 1930, 1933.
[91] SECNAV, *Annual Report*, 1928, pp. 23, 24, *Ibid.*, 1929, pp. 157, 159, *Ibid.*, 1930, pp. 5, 6.
[92] *Ibid.*, 1930, pp. 8, 567.

aircraft and engines." The Chief of the Bureau of Construction and Repair would soon report that "designs of two types of 40-foot motor launches for landing in the surf have been completed." [93]

One incident of Commander Turner's desk tour in the Plans Office which was connected with the reduced expenditure of research funds is interesting. A classmate of Kelly Turner's, resigned from the Navy, Eugene E. Wilson, relates this tale in connection with trying to interest the Navy in letting the British manufacture the controllable pitch propeller, the gear shift of the air.

> When I approached the Bureau of Aeronautics [to get approval of letting a foreign manufacturer have the plan], I ran smack into a cold front. Control of research and development had been usurped by the Plans Division, now under my Academy and Columbia classmate, Commander R. K. Turner. 'Spuds' Turner was a fighting man, an E. J. King type, and a tough customer. He was to become immortal as 'Terrible Turner of Tarawa' in World War II, but he was scarcely my choice for BUAERO's Research and Development. He and I had had a run in in Guantanamo Bay on the Destroyer Tender *Bridgeport,* when he was Gunnery Aide on the Staff of the CinC. In the absence of my skipper, he tried to bawl me out in public for one of his own blunders, and I ordered him off the ship. Now, he not only avowed 'no interest' in the new propeller, but he stormed up and down the corridor bawling me out for wasting money on a useless gadget.[94]

When the Chief of the Bureau of Aeronautics, Rear Admiral Moffett, agreed with Wilson, who in 1930 was President of Hamilton Standard Propellers of Pittsburgh, and signed the papers approving the giving to de Havillands, a British aircraft company, the plans to build the controllable pitch propeller, then Turner "was really hoist on his own petard," according to Wilson. The "gadget" turned out to be invaluable.

As Chief of the Planning Division, Bureau of Aeronautics, Commander Turner was a regular member of the Aeronautical Board, a Joint Board of the Army and Navy, and one of the first vehicles for Joint action by the Services. The Aeronautical Joint Board was:

> Specifically charged with the preparation of plans to prevent competition in the procurement of material, when the Chiefs of the respective Services have been unable to reach an agreement; consideration in respect of projects for experimental stations on shore, coastal air stations, and for stations to be used jointly by the Army and Navy; and the consideration of all estimates for appropriations for the aeronautical programs of the Army and Navy with a view to the elimination of duplication. . . . the Joint Board

---

[93] *Ibid.,* pp. 576; 261.
[94] Eugene E. Wilson, *The Gift of Foresight* (n.p., author, 1964), pp. 284–86.

during the past year has submitted 30 unanimous reports and recommendations for the approval of the two Secretaries.[95]

Having gotten his feet pleasantly wet in Joint maneuvers with the Army Air Corps on the Asiatic Station resulting in a Secretarial commendation, Commander Turner was particularly willing to work with the Army as a member on the Joint Board.[96]

The next few years flew by, and they moved Commander Turner from strictly naval matters into the arena of political-military affairs. This was a major broadening step in his over-all development, since in this latter field a military officer becomes a trustee of the essential interests of the country.

In 1931, the Big Powers were going through one of their perennial disarmament binges. The Washington Treaty for the Limitations of Naval Armaments, concluded in February 1922, and signed by France, Italy, Japan and the United Kingdom as well as by the United States, had started an incomplete and unequal limitation of naval armaments among the major naval powers. This limitation was very popular not only in the countries directly affected, but in those countries whose navies were small. Statesmen and politicians talked continuously of expanding the limitations.

In 1925, the United States joined in the unfruitful discussions of that year by the Preparatory Commission for the Reduction and Limitation of Armaments—sea, land, and air—fathered by the League of Nations. Two years later, a three-power naval conference between Japan, the United Kingdom, and the United States, convened in Geneva, but the conferees failed to expand the naval armament limitations of the 1922 Washington Treaty. France and Italy declined to join in this 1927 naval disarmament effort, but did join in the London Naval Conference of 1930. They refused, however, to accept the limitations placed on auxiliary tonnage by the 1930 London Treaty.

Having accomplished a minor advance in naval limitation in 1930, the United States' effort turned in 1931 to the broader field of all military disarmament. In early 1931, a Draft Convention for Limitations and Reduction of Armaments, drawn up by a Preparatory Commission assembled under the auspices of the League of Nations, was referred by the State Department to the Navy Department for comment. The disarmament convention was to meet at Geneva on 2 February, 1932.

The General Board of the Navy, which consisted of its senior statesmen, considered the subject matter for some eight months and submitted its

---

[95] SECNAV, *Annual Report,* 1929, p. 72.
[96] Turner.

recommendations to the Secretary of the Navy in a weighty 104-page document. The General Board recommended to the Secretary of the Navy for adoption the following statement of policy as Navy Department policy, and its forwarding to the Secretary of State.

> The Department is opposed, as unsafe and inadvisable, to reduction by example, or by any method which does not consider all elements of national armament.
>
> The Navy Department believes that the first and most important problem in the movement toward limitation and reduction of armaments is to effect general agreement in 1932 which will bring nations into a worldwide system of limitation of armaments stabilized at the lowest level obtainable without undue friction or misunderstanding.[97]

Commander Turner was directed in March 1931 to

> report to the Senior Member present, General Board, Navy Department, for temporary duty in connection with preparation for the next disarmament conference at Geneva in 1932.[98]

For nine months, Commander Turner carried water on both shoulders by serving in the Planning Division of the Bureau of Aeronautics and with the General Board. At night he was studying and learning the positions taken or advanced by all the participating nations in the disarmament discussion. During the day he was trying to devise plans for a shrinking purse to cover expanding naval air operations.

On 27 November 1931 he was detached from all duty in the Bureau of Aeronautics and in due time proceeded to Geneva, Switzerland, where he remained until 22 July 1932. Admiral Turner's most significant remembrance of this conference was that the British had recommended and argued long and hard for the abolition of aircraft carriers from the navies of the signatory powers. The records of the conference indicate that this proposal was advanced by the British on 29 February 1932.

Commander Turner's efforts, and those of his seniors, were fruitless. The 1932

> conference was soon lost in a maze of conflicting proposals, each nation seeking to improve its own relative status by suggesting the reduction or abolition of those weapons essential to potential opponents and the retention of those considered necessary to its own national defense.[99]

And perhaps more succinctly, it can be said that the conference foundered

---
[97] General Board, letter 438–2–Serial 1521–C–Oct. 1931, p. 5.
[98] BUNAV, letter, NAV–3–N–6312–187 of 11 Mar. 1931.
[99] *Encyclopaedia Britannica,* Vol. XIII, p. 843B.

on the Japanese invasion of Manchuria in September 1931, the threatened withdrawal of Germany from the conference which actually took place in September 1932, and the absence of the largest land power nation in Europe, the Soviet Union, from membership in the League of Nations.

The world-wide economic depression was having a significant effect in every democratically run country in reducing the willingness of the peoples representatives to spend tax money on armaments. The United States Navy was enduring markedly reduced steaming and training activity. A large number of the ships were sitting day after day alongside of docks in Navy yards in "rotating reserve." The small nucleus of professional officers and men had their low pay further cut, the first year by 8.33 percent and then, the next year by 12.5 percent.

This period was remembered as somber and depressing.

> Forced by this circumstance [the depression] to effect rigid economies, the expansion of naval aviation was slowed, the aircraft inventory was barely sufficient to equip operating units, research and development programs suffered, and operations were drastically curtailed.[100]
>
> The Bureau of Aeronautics was asked to keep the budget inside 32 million for 1932.[101]

However, there were two important advances in making naval aviation an integral part of the U. S. Fleet. Toward the end of Commander Turner's detail in aviation planning, the keel for the USS Ranger (CV-4), first ship of the U. S. Navy to be designed and constructed as an aircraft carrier, was laid down, September 1931, and the underway recovery of seaplanes by battleships and cruisers became a reality through planned development of the towing sled.

Equally important was the new policy, enunciated in November 1930 by the Chief of Naval Operations, Admiral W. V. Pratt, 16 months after Commander Turner took over the Plans Division, by which the majority of large naval air stations were assigned to and operated under Fleet command instead of under Shore and Bureau of Aeronautics command.

Admiral Turner felt that he had been most fortunate to have been picked in 1931 for the technical advisor detail at Geneva. It gave him the opportunity to work closely with Ambassador Hugh Gibson and with the diplomatically trained members of the General Board, such as former Commanders in Chief of the Asiatic Fleet, Admirals Mark L. Bristol and Charles B.

---

[100] NAVWEPS–00–80P–1, p. 65.
[101] Trumbull and Lord, p. 276.

McVay, and the senior naval member of the Advisory Group sent to Geneva, Rear Admiral A. J. Hepburn, later Commander in Chief of the United States Fleet.[102]

Commander Turner felt he had profitted greatly. And fortunately he came out of it with three good pieces of paper, the most important of which were orders to the carrier *Saratoga* (CV-3) as Executive Officer. The *Saratoga* was one of the only two real battle line carriers in the Navy, the other being the *Lexington* (CV-2). The other two pieces of paper were commendatory letters from Secretary of State H. L. Stimson and from the Chairman of the American Delegation, Hugh Gibson. The latter is reproduced herewith.

Geneva, Switzerland
July 27, 1932

The Honorable the SECRETARY OF STATE.
Washington

SIR: I have the honor to refer to the services of Commander Richmond K. Turner, Naval Adviser to the American Delegation to the General Disarmament Conference. Commander Turner's technical knowledge and skill in handling all matters pertaining to air questions rendered his services of great value to the Delegation. He was often called upon to present the views of this Delegation during the meetings of the Air Commission, and he rendered this service most effectively.

I desire to commend his services most highly to both the Department of State and the Navy Department, and should be pleased if a copy of this despatch were made available for the records of the Navy Department.

Respectfully yours,

(Signed) HUGH GIBSON

AS A SPEECHMAKER

During this tour of shore duty, Commander Turner was in considerable demand as a speechmaker. He received five sets of official orders from the Bureau of Navigation for this purpose in 1930, which should have been something of a record considering the parsimony of the Bureau in doling out travel funds during those money-hungry days.

Commander Turner talked to the Naval Postgraduate School on:

    a. Aircraft Policies of the Army and Navy

---

[102] Turner.

 b. Programs and Projects of Naval Aviation
 c. Naval Five-Year Program

He talked also to the Coast Artillery School, the Air Corps Tactical School, and the Marine Corps School. And he was invited back the next year.

Whether it was Commander Turner, Captain Turner, or Rear Admiral Turner, the man was no flamboyant orator. If, however, one was interested in learning about the subject talked on, he was not only first-rate to listen to, but superior. For he always had the facts in his mind and on the tip of his tongue. The facts were arranged logically to support major conclusions. He spoke with marked intensity and with a minimum of note referencing and hemming and hawing. He was a great success during question periods, since he quickly tautened the bowline around the necks of those whose queries indicated lack of attention to what had been said once, but dealt painstakingly with those who sought to explore areas in the speech not covered fully, or to question the reasoned deductions.

As Patrick J. Hurley, Secretary of War, wrote:

> It is reported that the lectures were very interesting, instructive, and capably delivered, and that their quality indicated a thorough knowledge of the subjects covered.[103]

He was an effective speaker because he was unpretentious, direct and informed.

---

[103] CHBUNAV to RKT, letter, 31 Mar. 1931, forwarding commendatory letter from SECWAR.

CHAPTER IV

In and Out of Big Time Naval Aviation 1932–1940

EXECUTIVE OFFICER—SARATOGA (CV-3)

The United States Fleet had been reorganized in April 1931, and the use of the terms Battle Fleet and Scouting Fleet discontinued. Under the reorganization, there was a large Battle Force in the Pacific Ocean with battleships, carriers, destroyers, minecraft, and shore-based patrol squadrons, and a smaller Scouting Force in the Atlantic Ocean with no minecraft and fewer of all the other types, but strong in cruisers. There was a widely dispersed Submarine Force to supersede the Control Force, and a Base Force, the latter performing expanded duties of the former logistic Train, and including a few shore-based aircraft squadrons, largely patrol aircraft.

The *Saratoga* was half of the aircraft carrier strength in the mighty Battle Force, sharing that honor with the *Lexington.* The third carrier in the United States Navy, the ex-collier *Jupiter,* now the *Langley,* was in the Scouting Force. The number of battleships on 1 July 1931 was at a new low, as only 12 battleships were in full commission, and the number of enlisted personnel in the whole Navy was down to the post World War I low of 79,700.

Just to make the modern naval officer's mouth water at the thought, the percentage of reenlistments in 1933 was over 90 percent, and to shed a tear, the 15 percent pay cut was in effect and officers did not receive any increase of pay when promoted or when completing stipulated periods of naval service.[1]

Fleet Problem XIV was to be held in 1933 in the area between the Hawaiian Islands and the Pacific Coast, and Fleet Problem XV was held in 1934 in the Caribbean.

---
[1] SECNAV, *Annual Report,* 1933, pp. 8, 14, 16.

The Captain of the *Saratoga* was Rufus F. Zogbaum. In his nostalgic book *From Sail to Saratoga,* he wrote, in the early 1950s:

> My executive officer was a man who has since become famous in commanding many of the great amphibious operations in the Pacific War, Kelly Turner, sometimes referred to in newspapers as 'Terrible Turner.' He had taken over his new duties at the same time as I had taken command, so we had both to get acquainted with the ship as well as with one another, and to plan how she was best to be run under our new regime.
>
> New brooms generally sweep too clean, and so, after all the publicity the *Saratoga* had lately gotten in the newspapers, on account of her grounding, we decided to proceed with caution in any reforms we intended to make. In my first talk with Turner, I felt we were in complete accord, that with this able and brilliant second-in-command I could leave him all the details that go with the executive's job. Although he was aggressive, dominant and could see quickly the best way of doing things and demanded they should be done thus and with despatch, I never found anything 'terrible' about Kelly Turner.[2]

Captain Zogbaum was of the same Naval Academy class of 1901 as Ernie King. He had gone to Pensacola as a junior captain at age 49, the same age as King ventured into aviation. He had completed the aviation course about 18 months after Turner and King. He was justly proud of qualifying as a naval aviator, and of his fine command, the *Saratoga.*

Commander Turner was Executive Officer of the *Saratoga* for 18 months from the day after Christmas 1932 until 11 June 1934, and served throughout Captain Zogbaum's command tour.

On the final fitness report which Captain Zogbaum gave Commander Turner, he wrote:

> No Commanding Officer could ask for a better Executive. . . . Recently selected for Captain and should go far in the Naval Service.

TO WORK AS EXEC

One of the outstanding senior lieutenants in the *Sara* remembered:

> I was the Assistant Gunnery Officer on the *Saratoga* when R.K.T. came aboard as Exec. When his orders to the ship were posted I seem to recall rumors going around to the effect that he was somewhat a sundowner.
>
> He had the single-minded devotion to duty which I sense in Russ Ihrig [Commodore Russell M. Ihrig]. He wanted things done as they should be

---

[2] Rufus Fairchild Zogbaum, *From Sail to Saratoga, A Naval Autobiography* (Rome: author's wife, 1956).

Commander Richmond Kelly Turner, Executive Officer of the USS Saratoga (CV–3), 1 October 1933.

done—right the first time—and he followed up his orders. The *Sara* was to be the best ship in the Fleet and her boats were one way of showing this. He demanded a spick and span crew and brass work that winked, canvas scrubbed and bleached, with lots and lots of real sailormade awnings, turksheads and rope mats. None of this was in the nature of make-work, however. He felt that a good ship had good boats and vice versa. To be sure that he was always a man who had his wits about him when duty called he did not drink on week days, and his weekend drinking was so moderate as to be almost abstemious. Under his eye, we did a good job when Long Beach was hit by the quake.[3]

---
[3] Rear Admiral Charles B. Hunt, USN (Ret.), to GCD, letter, 1 Apr. 1965.

Another shipmate of early aviation days remembered:

> While Exec of the *Saratoga*, Kelly was a legend. It is said he studied music so that he could give the band hell.[4]

Before the 1932 Christmas holidays were over, the new Executive Officer had gathered together all the naval aviators of the squadrons attached to the *Saratoga* and told them:

> You are all naval aviators, and from what I hear, darn good ones. But from now on, you have got to also be naval officers![5]

The practice under the previous Executive, a classmate of Turner's, Commander A. H. Douglas, had been for the squadron aviators to do their flying and a very minimum of shipkeeping and watch standing. Kelly put them all on the ship's watch lists, the younger ones as Junior Officer of the Watch or as Officer of the Deck, the senior ones on a Squadron Watch List similar to the ship's Head of Department Watch List. The squadron officers took their duty turns with the ship's officers, a day of watch duty every fourth day, but watches so scheduled to give them eight hours off watch before flying.

This broad concept of officer seagoing and ship qualification endeared Commander Turner, neither to the officers, nor to their wives when the *Saratoga* was in port. However, the policy paid big, big dividends in formation handling skills and in self-confidence during World War II when a number of these aviators increased in rank markedly and, by CINCPAC fiat, automatically senior to all non-flying officers in surface ship commands in the same unit or group and thus the task unit or task group commander. This *Saratoga* policy spread its wings softly throughout the aeronautical organization of the Fleet during later pre-World War II years.

The cruise in the *Saratoga* included all the usual chores borne by Executive Officers of that 1933–1934 period including much umpiring of other ships, most frequently the *Lexington,* gunnery and torpedo practices, and much inspecting and writing of reports.

This latter aspect resulted in Commander Turner receiving two official letters of praise from the Commander in Chief of the United States Fleet, Admiral David F. Sellers, one stating that his report had shown "a broad tactical knowledge."[6]

In late March 1934, Commander Turner learned that his services were

---

[4] Arty Doyle.

[5] Interviews with Vice Admiral William M. Callaghan, USN, and Rear Admiral Carl K. Fink, USN, both lieutenants in the *Saratoga* in 1932–1933, 2 Mar. 1966.

[6] CINCUS to Commander Turner, letters, A16–3/3817 of 29 Dec. 1933 and 11–G–O of 16 May 1934.

being sought for duty on their staff by two Flag officers, each a qualified aviation observer, rather than a qualified naval aviator. The two were Rear Admiral Henry V. Butler, a rear admiral of the upper half, and currently away from aviation and commanding Battleship Division Three, Battle Force, and Rear Admiral Alfred W. Johnson, a rear admiral of the lower half and currently commanding Aircraft, Base Force. Aircraft, Base Force, contained all the aircraft patrol squadrons of the major Fleet air bases.

However, Rear Admiral Butler was slated to fleet up to vice admiral and take over Aircraft, Battle Force, containing the two largest carriers of the Fleet, and their healthy contingents of fighting aircraft. The problem was further complicated by the desire of the Department to do its own detailing. As described by Mrs. Turner:

> Kelly is still at sea about his job. Admiral Butler wants him for his Chief of Staff, and, of course he is crazy for the job. The Bureau wants another man, and the thing is still hanging fire.
>
> His relief has been ordered. The Butler job will keep him away until December. If he goes to Admiral Johnson's Staff, he will be back in Coronado for six weeks, and then go to Alaska for three months. I am afraid there will be so much fuss they will just order him to some shore job.[7]

But feminine intuition proved wrong and on 11 May 1934, the Bureau of Navigation ordered Commander Turner detached from the *Saratoga* in June and assigned him as Chief of Staff to Commander Aircraft, Battle Force. The orders were delivered in Gonaives, Haiti, on 17 May and executed in New York City on 11 June 1934.

THE FEMININE FRONT

The problems in 1934 of the childless Navy wife with a seagoing husband are timeless, as indicated by the following abstracts from Mrs. Turner's letter:

> It is so dead here [Long Beach], and everyone is so blue, it is awful.
>
> I can't seem to fill up the days.
>
> I started taking steam baths and massage at the club, and it made a new woman of me. Lost eight pounds. . . . Must go to the dressmaker. I lost so much weight, all my clothes are falling off.
>
> Ming [the dog] expects her puppies any day now. I am hoping they will come so that I can go to the Riverside Dog Show Sunday.[8]

---

[7] Mrs. Turner to Miss L. Turner, letter, 12 Apr. 1934.
[8] *Ibid.*

THE 1934 SEAGOING NAVY

The Naval Directories of 1 July 1924 and 1 July 1934 list "Ships of the Navy in Commission" as follows:

	1924	1934
Battleships, first line	18	15
Heavy cruisers, first line	0	14
Heavy cruisers, second line	5	0
Lightcruisers, first line	8	10
Lightcruisers, second line	3	0
Aircraft carriers, first line	0	3
Aircraft carriers, second line	1	1
Minelayers, second line	2	1
Destroyers, first line	103	102
Light minelayers	6	4
Submarines, fleet	0	3
Submarines, first line	77	50
Submarines, second line	3	0
Gunboats	9	8
Auxiliaries (large)	52	30
Total	291	241

In the 10 years from 1924, the Fleet had shrunk, particularly in numbers of enlisted personnel, and in submarines and auxiliary strength. But, and it was a great big BUT, in 1934, there were 46 new ships building compared with only 17 building in 1924.

Besides new and better ships, another essential for fighting a major war, a professionally trained officers corps, also was being slowly but steadily built up. The number of Line officers had increased from about 4,700 in 1924 to 5,800 in 1934, nearly 25 percent. Thus gradually the professional corps that could instruct the tens of thousands of Naval Reserve officers who would instruct the millions of citizen sailors during World War II, was being gathered together.

The Commander in Chief of 1934, David F. Sellers, as had Admiral Coontz in 1924, thought that "the replacement of our obsolete submarines" was the first and primary deficiency of the Fleet, needing correction. In 1934 "suitable tactical flagships for submarine squadrons operating with the Fleet," and "suitable tenders specially designed to facilitate the operation of patrol planes" edged out faster ships "in the Train" as the second most urgent deficiency needing to be corrected. However, in connection with the 1934 Train, the Commander in Chief stated:

> It is essential that we should have faster oilers. Either the Navy should build them or we should subsidize private interests to build them.[9]

This latter suggestion, in effect, bore real fruit several years later, when the Maritime Commission built the 18-knot *Cimarron* (AO-22), and the Navy acquired her.

1934 was a year of major progress toward the proficiencies needed from 1942 to 1945, and from 1950 to 1953. Fleet Problem XV was conducted in the Pacific Ocean approaches to the Canal Zone area and continued in the Caribbean during April-May 1934. A tentative cruising doctrine for a trans-Pacific campaign was developed and published. "Three day" Fleet tactical exercises were held at intervals of six weeks, and "in all during the year twenty Fleet tactical exercises were conducted." Actual carrier air attacks with hundred pound bombs were carried out on the de-armed ex-battleship *Utah,* which represented enemy carriers and was part of the enemy task force. Reminiscent of the Coral Sea Battle of 1942, the *Utah* was located only after the planes passed through a "wide belt of dense fog." At this time also abbreviated plain language contact reports were used for the first time in tactical exercises.[10]

The Fleet Marine Force, which had been established in December 1933 by Navy Department General Order, picked up the amphibious tasks of the former Expeditionary Force, and more closely integrated these tasks into the daily work of the Fleet. Unfortunately, in February 1934, the 5th Reinforced Battalion of the Fleet Marine Force, embarked in ships of the Train, could not carry out a planned amphibious landing on San Clemente Island due to bad weather and lack of a "safe, landing beach."

All destroyers were fueled at sea, and all ships of the Fleet transited the Panama Canal in 47 hours. Further progress under Admiral Sellers towards success in World War II was evidenced by these three extracts from the Commander in Chief's Annual Report:

> Intelligence units on individual ships for the interception of enemy messages and the taking of direction finder bearings of enemy ships were formed.
> Throughout the year, the Commander-in-Chief has endeavored to interest the younger officers in tactics. He has searched for merit in the junior grades

---

[9] (a) CINCUS, *A.R.*, 1924, pp. 6, 7, 8; (b) *Ibid.*, 1934, pp. 7, 8.
[10] *Ibid.*, pp. 12, 13, 14, 15, 18.

and given warm commendation when it has been earned by some outstanding performance.[11]

Voice radio was being tested in the Fleet.[12]

However, voice radio was slow to catch hold in the Fleet.

AIRCRAFT BATTLE FORCE (1934–1935)

Commander Turner had a highly successful year as Chief of Staff to Commander Aircraft, Battle Force. When he reported for this duty in June 1934, Aircraft, Battle Force, consisted of three carriers, the *Lexington, Saratoga,* and the old *Langley,* carrying all together 15 squadrons of aircraft, totalling 169 planes, as well as the short-lived dirigible *Macon,* due to be lost 12 February 1935.

In the spring of 1935, the 15,000-ton aircraft carrier *Ranger* completed her final trials and joined, bringing five squadrons of aircraft totaling 77 planes with her.

The value of night flying skill for naval aviators had been impressed upon Commander Turner, and he was able to persuade his Admiral of a widespread need for this skill in his command, the largest seagoing naval aircraft command in the world.

So, as one old-time skilled naval aviator wrote:

> As C/S for Admiral Butler, he [Turner] left his mark by starting the practice of having all squadrons alternate working only at night.[13]

This again paid big dividends to the Navy in World War II.

TO THE NAVAL WAR COLLEGE

As Commander Turner's sea cruise drew to a close, the question as to where he would do his upcoming shore duty must have been high in his mind. No clues on his desires were found by this writer, except that his fitness reports showed that his preference of duty was for duty and instruction at the Naval War College. And as a member of the senior class, to the Naval War College he was ordered, being detached in time to drive across country and report in late June 1935.

---

[11] *Ibid.,* pp. 16, 17, 19.
[12] *Ibid.,* p. 29.
[13] Doyle.

PROMOTION TO CAPTAIN

Selections to captain from the Class of 1908 extended over three years. The 1933, 1934, and 1935 Selection Boards all worked on 1908. Since Turner was selected by the 1933 Board and since he was not ordered before the naval examining board until just after he arrived at the War College, he had 18 months of pleasant relaxation knowing that he was over the hump and just waiting to make his number, which he did on 1 July 1935.

The years 1933, 1934, and 1935 were lean for the Line of the Navy. All up and down the Navy List, as far as percentage of officers selected was concerned, only a bit better than one out of every two lieutenants, lieutenant commanders, and commanders were being chosen to continue their careers in the Navy.

The top of 1908 did well with the 1933 Selection Board with 14 out of the top 16 being selected. The next year, 27 out of the middle 50 were lucky, but in 1935 only seven out of 25 from the bottom of the class were tapped. In each of the two latter years, one commander was picked up by the Selection Board, after having missed the boat once.

So of the 100 who made commander eight years before, only 50 reached the charmed grade of captain. Forty-two of the 50 were promoted in 1936, 28 years after graduation from the Naval Academy, which is about the time the Line officer of today starts wondering whether he will make three stars.

THE NAVAL WAR COLLEGE

The students at Naval War College during the 1930's were a cross section of the Navy. It was far from being a place where only officers "going places" in the Navy or "the brains" were detailed by the Bureau of Navigation. The War College was a perfect place to send officers whom the Bureau wished to put in a specific slot the following summer, and needed to be kept on ice for the ensuing year. It also was a perfect place to send an officer for whom, at the moment, the Navy had no appropriate detail. Unfortunately, it also was a place where an officer, whom nobody in command really wanted at the moment, or anytime, could be kept for a year, with the hope that a turn in his health or the ceaseless pruning of the Selection Boards would eliminate him as a detailing problem.

And of course, there were always in each class at the Naval War College a small number of eager beavers, who yearned for a broader appreciation of the political, economic, and psychological problems of the world and a keener knowledge of the strategical military aspects of any future world conflicts, whether between *Blue* (United States) and *Black* (Germany) or even *Orange* (Japan) and *Blue*. Despite the Bureau of Navigation's frequent circular letters that no request for the War College was necessary, or desired, these eager beavers requested such duty.

NAVAL AVIATION AND THE NAVAL WAR COLLEGE

In the five years, June 1930–1935, before Commander Turner became a student at the Naval War College, there had been only one naval aviator on the staff of more than 20 officers of that institution. In the Line student body of 70 to 90 officers there was only one naval aviator in three out of these five years. Throughout this period, there were over 800 naval aviators in the Navy, out of a total averaging 5,500 officers in the Line of the Navy. The number of students at the Naval War College during each of these five years was approximately one out of 60 to one out of 80 of the Line of the Navy, but the number of naval aviator students during three of these five years was only one out of 800 naval aviators, and always less than one out of 160.

Bearing in mind the reluctance of the Bureau of Aeronautics to designate any of its charges for a detail outside the Naval Aeronautics Organization, it was a minor miracle that Commander Turner was so designated.

This divergence between the Naval War College and the Naval Aeronautical Organization had a large part of its basis in the slowness with which the "Damage Rules" of the Naval War College, used in all Fleet Problems and tactical exercises, came to recognize the potency of the air bomb and the accuracy with which carrier aircraft delivered it. Thus, one aviator wrote:

> I had the old *Sara* Air Group as we headed for Pearl on the annual cruise. We were ordered to attack the 'enemy,' three *California*'s and three *Idaho*'s. We came in from 22,000 feet, effected complete surprise with 74 a/c and roughly 54 half ton bombs. Squadrons of the group had won all the gunnery trophies that year. The Chief Umpire, going by War College rules, slowed one BATDIV two knots!!!
> So you can see the thinking at that time at the Naval War College.[14]

Admiral Turner recalled that duty at the Naval War College was "much to his liking."[15] The President of the Naval War College was Rear Admiral

---

[14] Admiral Austin K. Doyle, USN (Ret.), to GCD, letter, 28 Mar. 1964.
[15] Turner.

Edward C. Kalbfus, who was to fly four stars, when he next went to sea. Captains Frank H. Sadler, Milo F. Draemel, Raymond A. Spruance, and Robert A. Theobald were members of the War College Staff, and Commanders Walden L. Ainsworth, Lawrence F. Reifsnider, Alvin D. Chandler, Bernhard H. Bieri, and Edmund D. Burroughs were all members of his Senior Class. All these were to be Flag officers during World War II. Another member of Turner's class was Lieutenant Colonel DeWitt Peck, USMC. The latter served with Turner in War Plans in Naval Operations and on COMINCH Staff in 1941–1942, as well as a General officer in the Solomons in 1942–1943.

Captain Turner, while a student at the Naval War College, submitted his main thesis, on "The Foreign Relations of the United States." He pointed out in the thesis the need for a clearly stated national policy for the United States and softly stated that such a policy did not now exist but was "in a state of flux." He added:

> The reason for the better definition of the policies of certain other powers is that in the gamble of European politics their very existence as nations is at stake, while the United States, besides trying to protect its foreign trade, is chiefly concerned in keeping out of wars which, in no respect, threaten its real security.

This secure condition of the United States did not continue for long after 1936, because of the rampaging Adolph Hitler.

DUTY ON THE NAVAL WAR COLLEGE STAFF

As early as it was decently possible, February 1936, Captain Turner's orders from duty "under instruction" to duty on the War College staff in June 1936 were issued.

One of Captain Turner's productive chores at the Naval War College, and which he looked back upon with pride, was the drafting of a letter in 1937 to the Chairman of the General Board for signature by the President of the Naval War College on the subject of "New Destroyer Construction" for the 1939 Building Program.

At this time, when the United States was still bound by the total tonnage allowances of the Naval Disarmament Treaties, there was considerable pressure to plan to build in 1939 and 1940, within the highly restricted available authorized destroyer tonnage, a larger number of small destroyers in lieu of a smaller number of large destroyers. It was said that the larger number of small destroyers would more adequately meet the overseas convoy tasks, as well as the anti-submarine and anti-aircraft problems of the Fleet.

The specific problem upon which the opinion of the Naval War College was requested by the General Board covered the desirability of building 42 destroyers of 1,200 standard treaty displacement tons in lieu of 32 destroyers of 1,600 standard treaty displacement tons, or some intermediate number of an intermediate tonnage.

The War College reply, after analyzing the problem, set forth the following counsel:

> Superior seakeeping qualities and long radius are the strategic characteristics which ought to be considered fundamental in the determination of design of destroyers for the United States Navy,

and

> Larger ships would be more efficient in unfavorable weather, and could keep the sea for longer periods of time.
>
> [The 1600-ton ship was] favored, but it should be given a maximum speed of from 38 to 40 knots. [in lieu of the 35 knots being considered] [16]

The influence of this letter, which Turner drafted, on the General Board is unknown, but it is a fact that the "1939 Building Program Destroyer Characteristics," as approved, called for destroyers of 1,630-ton standard displacement.[17]

That this tonnage was none too great for the ships expected to keep the seas in the Western Pacific and provide anti-aircraft and anti-submarine protection to Task Forces, was evidenced when one destroyer of this 1,630-ton displacement, the *Spence* (DD-512), along with two of the lesser 1,200-ton type, *Hull* (DD-350) and *Monaghan* (DD-354), were lost in a typhoon which the Third Fleet plowed through on 18 December 1944.

A contemporary at the Naval War College furnishes these opinions in regard to Captain Turner:

> In the first year of our association there, he was like myself a student. He no doubt had in mind staying on on the staff the following year or two. He was very active and came up with fine papers and solutions to the problems, but didn't see eye to eye with the strategical section which at that time was headed up by Theobald. For one thing Turner did not think that Theobald was giving

---

[16] (a) Chairman of the General Board to President, Naval War College, letter, GB 420–9 of 9 Jul. 1937; (b) President, Naval War College to Chairman of the General Board, letter, 1 Sep. 1937.

[17] SECNAV to General Board, letter, ser 4510 of 16 Dec. 1937.

the proper weight to air and its possibilities. He considered Theobald a bit unimaginative and hide bound, and did not hesitate to intimate as much. In the lecture question periods and during the critiques, he was very effective, and when he had a different point of view, could expound it well. There were some interesting clashes between these two men, particularly over the role that air would have in the event of war in the Pacific, and looking back on it, there is little doubt that Turner was more often more prophetic than Theobald.

In the two years as head of the Strategic Section of the Staff, Turner did much to revamp the problems and this part of the course to bring it in line with the most probable developments in naval expansion and the paths that this might take. The problems and staff presentations had not changed much for several years and were getting a bit stale. A look at the problems used during Turner's time will show that he had a good idea of what the war in the Pacific would be like. He moved away from the idea that the war would center around the battleships, and intensified the interest in air operations and amphibious campaigns. He also outlined a new series of staff presentations, of which he delivered a good number, which will no doubt still be in the archives of the College. For one thing he insisted that the staff be able to present their subjects without reading them and this made for more interesting sessions. As was to be expected he was very good in conducting critiques and had more consideration for the opinion of the others than his predecessor had had.[18]

Another contemporary related:

> I was a student at the Naval War College in 1937 and went to the staff there just as Turner was leaving in June 1938. He was highly effective on the staff—an excellent moderator when strategical and tactical situations were being discussed by the students. He had a sharp tongue, was quite humorless, but well read and intensely interested in the work of the College.[19]

Specific lectures delivered by Captain Turner at the Naval War College in order to fulfill his instructional duties were legion, but he had special pride in "Operations for Securing Command of the Seas." In this lecture, besides covering the strictly naval aspects of the problem, he took a long look forward and stressed the need for developing and establishing an organization and a system of *national* strategy and *national* tactics in order to provide realistic guidance for handling "the particular problems which may confront American naval officers."

Therefore, the rough patterns of the National Security Council and the

---

[18] Vice Admiral Bernhard H. Bieri to GCD, letter, 17 Sep. 1960. Rear Admiral Theobald commanded the North Pacific Force and Task Force Eight commencing May 21, 1942. Turner's naval aviator predecessor at NWC was his classmate, Commander Archibald H. Douglas, whom he had also relieved in the *Saratoga*.

[19] Interview with Commodore Ralph S. Wentworth, USN (Ret.), 9 Mar. 1964.

Joint Chiefs of Staff were dimly outlined in this two-day lecture of 9–10 July 1937.

KELLY TURNER AT 51

This seems a good time to introduce a thumb-nail sketch of the Kelly Turner character at this stage of his career with 29 years of commissioned service behind him.

> At that time (1936) he was a newly appointed Captain about 51 years of age. He was about six feet tall and in apparent excellent physical condition, lean and quick acting. He gave the impression of being very alert, was military in bearing and actions, and was well groomed.
>
> He was serious and devoted to his profession. Being very forceful and when convinced, of strong convictions, he was inclined to be abrupt and sometimes tactless, but he was intellectually honest and if one had a point, he could be convinced. He was aggressive and decisive. He had great ability to express himself clearly and well, not only on paper but verbally. He made no point of trying to make people like him, but he commanded a high degree of respect by the manner in which he mastered his profession and performed his duties. There was no doubt in my mind, even at that time, that he was an aggressive, competitive, combatant type, and that when and if the opportunity came, he would know how to do, and do a good job. When we in the Staff were given a job, he let us do it. He was free with good ideas but not insistent that one use them if one had any himself. I profited much professionally from my association with him at this time.
>
> As to his drinking habits, I can say that I never noted that he used it to excess. I attended quite a number of stag affairs over the two and a half years that I was there and Turner was at most of them. To my recollection, he handled his liquor well.[20]

The officer who relieved Captain Turner as Head of the Strategic Section of the Staff of the Naval War College wrote:

> I went to the Naval War College as a student in June, 1937. Turner was Head of the Strategy Section of the College Staff. I felt that I learned a great deal from him during the year ending May 1938.
>
> I remained on the War College Staff until late May 1940, serving the last year as Head of the Strategy Section.
>
> This experience was invaluable to me in the commands I held in World War II and later.
>
> I observed convincing evidence during my tour at the College of the out-

---
[20] Bieri.

standing contributions Admiral Turner had made to the course of instruction.[21]

TO STAY OR NOT TO STAY IN AVIATION

Captain Turner was aware of the fact that he had trod on many toes in getting his fellow aviators "up on the step" and in line abreast with the seagoing capabilities of the rest of the general Line officers during his duty in the *Saratoga* and on Aircraft Battle Force Staff. He had never been a popularity hound and never intended to be one, but he was keenly aware of criticism, even when he refused to let it temper his actions. He was aware that on a Flag Selection Board, the opinions of the naval aviator members carried great weight with the non-aviator as to which naval aviators should or should not be selected.[22]

He also longed to get back to a ship where guns were the first order of importance and not the last. He also thought that if he had a large non-aviation combatant command, he would be a better Flag officer if he should be selected and later have a command in the top echelons of the Navy. He looked at the Navy List and saw that Captain Patrick N. L. Bellinger, Naval Aviator Number 18, was just two numbers senior to him, Newton H. White, a designated naval aviator since 1919 only one number senior to him, and Albert C. Read, Naval Aviator Number 24, not too much further up the Navy List. A Johnny-come-lately naval aviator might not fare too well in that competition. So he made up his mind to seek a non-aviation detail on his next sea cruise, as indicated in the following correspondence:

> NAVY DEPARTMENT
> BUREAU OF AERONAUTICS
> *Washington, 31 August 1936.*
>
> DEAR TURNER:
>
> In connection with preparation of the Captain's slate for several years in the future, I would like to recommend to the Bureau of Navigation that you remain on your present duty until about June 1938. The *Wasp* should be completed in the Fall of 1938 and it is my present intention to recommend you for command. However, it appears practicable to assign you to the *Ranger* in June '38 if that would be preferable from your standpoint. Please advise me which assignment would be most agreeable to you.

---

[21] Interview with Admiral John Leslie Hall, USN (Ret.), 2–3 Nov. 1961.
[22] Richardson.

Trusting that you are enjoying your present duty and with best regards, I remain,

Very sincerely yours,

A. B. Cook,
Rear Admiral, U.S.N.

Captain R. K. Turner, USN,
U.S. Naval War College, Newport, R. I.

P.S. The *Saratoga, Lex, Yorktown* and *Enterprise* in June 1938 will all be commanded by officers senior to you.

Note: The *Wasp* was a comparatively small 14,800-ton 29-knot carrier, whose contract date of completion was November 22, 1938, but which due to delays, was not actually commissioned until April 25, 1940. The *Ranger* was of approximately the same tonnage.

Naval War College
5 September 1936.

My dear Admiral,

Thank you for your letter of 31 August, and for your consideration with regard to my choice between command of the *Wasp* and *Ranger*. I had expected that circumstances would require my remaining here until the summer of 1938.

There is, however, a serious difficulty with regard to my next sea assignment, at least from my own standpoint. This difficulty is due to the fact that I will have only one captain's cruise before I come up for selection for admiral. Naturally, it is very important for me that my cruise be such as will meet two conditions; 1st, that it will best fit me for flag rank; and 2nd, that it will give me a record of well-rounded service such as will appeal to the Selection Board.

In 1938 I will have been continuously in aviation for nearly twelve years. If I then go to sea in command of a carrier, in 1942 when I come up for selection my continuous aviation service will probably have been sixteen years.

This does not seem to me to be a very good record with which to go before the Board. I therefore intend next year to request officially, as I have already done on my report of fitness, to be sent in command of a battleship. Kinkaid tells me that my seniority in 1938 will probably give me a good chance for a battleship.

This decision should by no means be construed as due to a waning interest in aviation. On the contrary, I am more than ever convinced that we still have a long way to go to exploit its full value to the Navy. I certainly hope to get a later chance to have more aviation duty, which to me has been far more interesting than any other.

There will doubtless be an ample number of officers in 1938 for all the aviation commands. This is as it should be, in order that aviators may from time to time have an opportunity to obtain straight line service . . . a rotation absolutely essential, if they are to fit themselves for general command duty in the grades of captain and admiral. In my opinion, the most serious personnel problem facing us is the development of a plan whereby we can give our splendid young aviators enough general line duty to fit them for the highest positions, as the Navy by no means can afford to lose what in many respects is its best element. Possibly my return to general service may influence others to take the same step.

I talked this over with Mitscher in June, but didn't wish to bother you with it at the time.

I hope you will forgive this long letter to a busy man. Again with thanks, and best regards and wishes,
  Very sincerely,
                 R. K. TURNER

Note: Commander Mark A. Mitscher in June 1936 was Head of the Flight Division, Bureau of Aeronautics.

The first quoted letter above, the one from the Chief of Bureau of Aeronautics, only a little over a year after Turner had gone ashore, brought the matter of his staying or not staying in aviation to a head. Admiral Turner's 1960 reaction to stories about his being heaved out of the aeronautical organization was strong.

> Anyone who says I was assed out of aviation, doesn't know the facts, and you can consider the statement was generally father to the wish. Cook may have been worrying about his promising me the *Wasp* and he may have been joyous over my request for a battleship or cruiser, but if he had any thoughts of heaving me out of aviation, I beat him to the punch by many many months.[23]

The rest of the official record reads as follows:

            NAVAL WAR COLLEGE
        Newport, Rhode Island, 12 November 1937.

MY DEAR ADMIRAL,

Today I have submitted an official request for my next sea cruise to be in command of a battleship or heavy cruiser, rather than an aircraft carrier. You may remember that I took this matter up with you last spring and you indicated that you were agreeable to the proposal. The reason I am submitting an official request is to have the record show that this step will be taken on my own volition.
  Very sincerely,
                 R. K. TURNER

Rear Admiral A. B. Cook, USN,
Chief of Bureau of Aeronautics,
Navy Department,
Washington, D. C.

---
[23] Turner.

NAVAL WAR COLLEGE
Newport, Rhode Island, 8 November 1937.

From: Captain R. K. Turner, U. S. Navy,
To: The Chief of the Bureau of Navigation,
Via: The President, Naval War College.

Subject: Request concerning command assignment for next sea cruise.

1. There are several matters in connection with my next assignment to sea duty which I desire to bring to the notice of the Bureau.

2. I will complete my normal tour of shore duty in the spring of 1938. Assuming a two year sea cruise, followed by a normal three year shore tour, I will not go to sea again until 1943. In that year I will have completed thirty-five years of service since graduation from the Naval Academy. It is apparent, therefore, that I am likely to have but one sea cruise in my present grade before my class appears for selection to flag rank.

3. I have performed duty in the Aeronautic Organization of the Navy since 1 January, 1927. If I continue in this Organization during my next sea cruise, I will come up for selection after a period of sixteen years of continuous aviation duty. Even though, during this time, my actual duties have been little different from those performed by other members of my class, I believe that my apparent lack of general line experience might operate to reduce my chances for selection. Furthermore, a variation in duty at this stage of my career would also tend to increase my usefulness as a flag officer, should I be selected as such.

4. For the above reason, I request that during my next sea cruise I be assigned to the command of a vessel not in the Aeronautic Organization. I would prefer the command of a battleship; but if my seniority will not entitle me to this assignment, I request command of a heavy cruiser. In either case, I desire command of a vessel in the active part of the Fleet.

5. As I will have but one captain's cruise, it must necessarily be at least two years in length in order to establish eligibility for promotion. Because my total sea service is somewhat less than the average for my class, and because of my desire for a maximum of command experience, I earnestly request that the Bureau permit me to remain at sea for as long as possible in excess of two years.

6. This letter should in no manner be construed as indicating a lessening of my interest in aviation, as such is not the case. In order to remain eligible for aviation duty at a later period, I request that the Bureau continue in effect my present designation as naval aviator.

R. K. TURNER

Copy to: Naval War College,
            Bureau of Aeronautics.

NAVAL WAR COLLEGE
Newport, Rhode Island, 12 November 1937.

MY DEAR SHARP,

I have just submitted an official request for command of a battleship or heavy cruiser during my next sea cruise, rather than command of an aircraft carrier. You may recall our conversation on this subject last spring. The reason for the official request is merely to show that I will not have been "assed" out of aviation, but am leaving of my own volition.

With best wishes,
            Very sincerely,

R. K. TURNER

Captain Alexander Sharp, U. S. Navy,
Bureau of Navigation,
Washington, D. C.

Note: Captain Sharp was the Captain Detail Officer in the Bureau of Navigation.

In December 1937, at Captain Turner's annual aviation physical examination, the absence of adequate ocular accommodation was noted and in February 1938, the Bureau of Navigation officially informed Captain Turner that he was "qualified for duty involving flying only when accompanied by a co pilot." The defect was not an unusual one for a man nearing age 53, but Captain Turner was a man who didn't like defects in others, much less in himself.

No matter what the record shows, it is almost a standing tradition of naval aviators that Kelly Turner was thrown out of aviation. The "heave ho" story will not down. According to one aviator:

> I am positive that Kelly's imperturbable stubbornness as Chief of Staff for Henry Butler played a large part in his failure to stay in aviation. Butler's Flag Lieutenant committed suicide, thereby unjustly giving Turner's critics the chance to say he had been too tough on everyone.[24]

But after reading the correspondence on this subject the same officer wrote:

> I have always thought, as have others, that Jack Towers was the one to deprive Kelly of his rightful command of a large carrier. I am glad to know differently.[25]

---

[24] A. K. Doyle to GCD, letter, 1961.
[25] A. K. Doyle to GCD, letter, 1964. Note: Captain John H. Towers was Assistant Chief of the Bureau of Aeronautics when Captain Turner was issued orders to sea duty in February 1938.

HIGH PRAISE FROM ABOVE

Before Captain Turner left the Naval War College, Rear Admiral Edward C. Kalbfus and Rear Admiral Charles P. Snyder, the two Presidents of the Naval War College under whom he had served, had written on his fitness reports:

> a superior officer in every respect . . . a keen analytical mind and in an assiduous search for the truth . . . has made a substantial contribution to the College . . . Widely read . . . an accomplished strategist and tactician.

TO THE ASTORIA

The 16 December 1933 copy of *Plane Talk,* the ship's paper of the *Saratoga,* printed Commander Turner's picture and the "hearty congratulations of the ship's company on his selection to Captain." The lead article was headlined "Astoria Launched Today."

Four years and nine months later, the *Astoria* and Captain Turner got together again.

The *Astoria* (CA-34) was a 10,000-ton heavy cruiser, carrying nine 8-inch 55-caliber guns in three turrets, and eight 5-inch 25-caliber guns in her anti-aircraft battery. She was reasonably new, having been commissioned in April 1934 and was currently assigned to Cruiser Division Six of the Cruisers, Scouting Force. The *Minneapolis* was the flagship of the division. Rear Admiral Royal E. Ingersoll was the Division Commander, and Rear Admiral Gilbert J. Rowcliff (1902) was Commander Cruisers, Scouting Force.

> I first met Kelly Turner a couple of hours after he reported on board. It was Sunday. I was the Supply Duty Officer. He sent for me and asked if we carried No Oxide in stock. (I was not the GSK pay clerk.) I told him I would find out. I returned a half-hour later and informed him that we did not, but that I had prepared a requisition for a supply to be delivered either at Panama or Guantanamo, ports we were departing for the following day (certainly soon afterwards). He signed the requisition. The next morning, when the regular clerk returned and I told him about the Captain's desires, he informed me he had about five hundred pounds in stock, but carried under a Navy stock number not its commercial name No Oxide. What to do? It was 8:05, I went to the Captain's cabin and asked his orderly if I might speak to him. He was having breakfast. I was ushered into his cabin. 'Captain,' I said, tremulously I fear, because his reputation had preceded him, 'I've come to tell you that you have the most stupid chief pay clerk in the Navy serving

under you.' His eyes crinkled, then his face became one huge grin. 'Well, do I now?' he asked. I then told him of my discovery and that I had destroyed the requisition. I suppose I still had the undertaker look on my face, because he laughed aloud. Then, suddenly, he became quite serious. 'What made you say what you did?' he asked. 'Because I'm disgusted having muffed the first job you gave me.' He grinned again. 'You outsmarted me. You said about yourself exactly what I would have said about you, had I found out about this before you told me.' Needless to say, the Captain believed what I told him after that.[26]

Turner had three Executive Officers during his two years in the *Astoria*—a bad sign for any Commanding Officer. The first was Commander Paul S. Theiss who reported to the *Astoria* a couple of months prior to Turner's reporting on 10 September 1938. Theiss was a former shipmate and a good friend. An alert and knowledgeable sailorman aboard the *Astoria* at the time writes:

> The other gentleman who might have much good to say about Turner would be Paul S. Theiss, one of Turner's XO's in *Astoria*. Conversely, it would be my guess that Turner had genuine respect for Theiss. My reasons for saying this is that Turner normally addressed Theiss as "Paul" when talking to the latter (this was unusual for Turner). The other reason that Turner might have been happy with Theiss is that Theiss was an insomniac thereby able to devote most of 24 hours a day to his job—this would fit in well for Turner, and I believe it did. I know Theiss slept very little for as a QM I had watches on the bridge every night underway. The normal path going on and off watch was such that I could see into the Exec's room. Regardless of the time of night, the Exec was usually sitting at his desk, fully clothed, either working or catnapping. I have never known Theiss to place a call to be awakened in the night call book. No doubt Theiss did sleep in his bunk but I venture to say that it was not very often. I recall also that sometimes during WWII, Theiss was reconnected with Turner at sea, either on his staff or Captain of Turner's flagship. A good bet would be that Turner asked for Theiss and, if so, because Theiss would work much longer than most people's physical capacity could endure on a continuous basis.[27]

Rear Admiral Theiss's death in 1956 at a young 66 and long before work on this book started, removed one who knew much about Richmond Kelly Turner.

Unfortunately, after 26 years' commissioned service, and without having

---

[26] Commander Roy O. Stratton (SC), USN (a Chief Pay Clerk in 1939), to GCD, letter, 4 Aug. 1962. Hereafter Stratton.

[27] Lieutenant Commander Vicenzo Lopresti to GCD, letter, 12 Sep. 1963. Lopresti was a seaman and quartermaster third class under Turner, having entered the Navy 6 January 1936. Hereafter Lopresti.

been on board long enough to receive a regular fitness report from Turner, Commander Theiss, the first time his class was considered, failed of selection to captain as "best fitted" that December and was ordered to shore duty the following June. He was selected to captain as "fitted" by the next Selection Board in December 1939 and retained on active duty.[28] Theiss's failure of selection in 1938 actually could not be attributed to Captain Turner in any way, since Turner did not arrive in the *Astoria* until ten days after the regular 31 August 1938 fitness reports had gone into the Department, the last semi-annual fitness report before the 1938 Selection Board met in December.

The second and third Executive Officers were Commanders Marion Y. Cohen, and C. Julian Wheeler. Cohen, Class of 1914, relieved Theiss 15 June 1939, and, by his own official request, in order to better handle a family problem, left in December 1939 for command of San Diego based Destroyer Division 70, when relieved by Wheeler, Class of 1916. Commander Cohen was named "best fitted" captain by his first Selection Board, in a list when only four of the bottom 15 commanders of the Class of 1914, where he was positioned on the Navy List, were so picked. So it can be deduced that Commander Cohen earned more than just highly satisfactory fitness reports from Captain Turner as did Wheeler, who also cleared the hurdle to "best fitted" captain at the first try. Wheeler is still around and comments as follows:

> The *Astoria* under Turner's command was what is known in the Navy as a taut ship. It always stood well in the various competitions we had at that time and was well thought of in the Division.
>
> Due to his brilliance and ability, Admiral Turner was at his best under stress. He was thoroughly in command of the situation at all times.
>
> When relaxed he entered into the spirit of the occasion and joined in the fun, whatever it was. I consider him one of the ablest naval officers of our time.[29]

A lower decks observer reports:

> Turner's reputation reached the fo'c's'le before he took command of *Astoria*. A crew member had served with him previously and he soon got the word around. Suffice to say 'Turn-to Turner' was the word. Apparently this phrase was hitched to him some years previously as it may have been hitched to other naval officers. Anyway, it was an inkling as to what to expect. This meant much, because Captain C. C. Gill (Turner's predecessor) was, indeed, a relaxed, 'no-strain,' pleasant little gentleman.
>
> *Astoria*, of course, was Turner's first major command and command he did.

---

[28] For explanation of 'best fitted' and 'fitted' selection, see pages 267–69.
[29] Rear Admiral C. Julian Wheeler, USN (Ret.), to GCD, letter, 17 Mar. 1964.

The first day underway, after having been ashore several years, was a routine evolution. He came up to the bridge, solicited no advice, took the conn and performed as well as anyone could in getting underway and settled down in formation enroute to the training area off San Clemente Island. This pattern persisted for the following two years. He expected that everyone connected with an evolution knew his part perfectly and executed it efficiently. He, in turn, knew all the parts.

Turner never forgot for a moment what he was after and how he was going to get it. He drove himself at full speed with absolute and sincere dedication for the Navy. Turner was going after Admiral stars and of course he got them —no one deserved them more. However, in pursuing his aims—personal and dedicated—he no doubt left a bad taste in many officers' mouths as to his ability and as to his relations with them as gentlemen. He was absolutely intolerant of delay, inefficiency, and laxness among his officers. Impatience was exhibited immediately with an ensuing 'chewing out' on the spot regardless of rank or rating in the immediate vicinity. This of course runs against the traditional 'Commend publicly and censure privately.'

I recall vividly when *Astoria* was coming onto range for a shoot and Turner asked his XO if he had studied the OGE and familiarized himself with the details of the shoot. The XO replied in the negative, after which Turner forthwith ordered the XO from the bridge for immediate study of the exercise. The XO returned in a few minutes with OGE in hand and asked the Captain if he expected him to learn all about the exercise *now*, indicating that it was an awful lot to digest. Turner replied in no uncertain terms that that was his intent and further that he was amazed that he was questioned about the intent when in the first place the XO should be ready to take over command at any time regardless of evolution in progress and therefore he should have known all about the exercise previously. I heard all this . . . I was manning a pelorus.

D. R. Maltby, a QM striker, performed incorrectly on a particular occasion for which he was called by Turner for explanation. Maltby gave his story that he had been ordered to do such and such. Apparently the situation changed between order and execution whereby common sense would indicate a changed situation and Turner pointed it out to Maltby. He asked Maltby if he recognized the new situation whereby execution of the order would be stupidity. Maltby answered in the affirmative after which Turner in a kindly paternalistic manner informed Maltby thus: 'One of the greatest glories of being an American sailor is that your officers give you the credit for having the ability to think for yourself.' Maltby was very impressed.

There was some humor in Turner and he could smile and laugh. An incident I recall happened at Captain's Mast. Approximately six men were before Turner for 'shooting craps'. Turner went down the line asking each if he was 'shooting craps'. Each admitted guilt except one colored boy who said he wasn't 'shooting craps'. Turner turned to a witness to ascertain whether the boy was involved in the game. The witness replied that he definitely was in there with money sticking out of his hands. Turner then asked the colored boy for explanation of his statement. The colored boy answered, 'No such, Captain, ah wasn't shooting no craps, ah was jus fadin.' At this, all semblance of solemnity and dignity went over the side for Turner burst out laughing as did all around him. Suffice to say that each was punished lightly.

I mentioned previously that Turner was after Admiral's stars. He left no stone unturned in pursuance of his aim. He probably was the worst example for training officers in shiphandling. I recall no occasion, but there probably were some, when Turner allowed an officer to get the ship underway and form up; nor do I recall an occasion during tactical maneuvers when Turner did not take the conn. I suppose the reasoning was that good maneuvering would evoke a 'well done' from the OTC (usually an admiral). Turner would have each 'well done' certified as a true copy by the Communications Officer with addition thereon of the particular event for the 'well done' after which the copy would be mailed to the Chief of the Bureau of Navigation for insertion in his record. Turner's record must have been full of those messages.[30]

An officer who served in the *Astoria* for over three years and under four different captains, remarked:

> Kelly Turner's driving ambition was not getting to be an admiral, but was to get the job done in as nearly perfect manner as it could be done. Perfection was his goal.[31]

The Heads of Departments had varying opinions of their Captain, but they all testified to the high efficiency and capabilities of the *Astoria* during Turner's command.[32] They recalled his "thoroughness," "brilliant mind," "long hours" and "hard work." To one he was "very strict, very impatient, intolerant of any mistakes, sharp tongued" but "fair." To another, he was "easily understood, and when his requirements were definitely understood, easily followed." To still another, he was "exceptionally smart, but by the same token he expected everyone else to be in the same category." It was recalled that he went on camping trips, fishing trips, and picnics, golfed, and engaged in gardening. One who fished with Turner found him companionable, but felt that his real hobby was his career.

All except one department head thought their cruise with Turner was a big help in their future careers. This one reported: "The only unsatisfactory

---

[30] Lopresti. Note: There were no "well done" despatches in Turner's official record.

[31] Interview with Rear Admiral Donald W. Gladney, Jr., USN (Ret.), 20 Apr. 1964. Gladney was Senior Watch Officer and Plotting Room Officer in 1938–40. Hereafter Gladney.

[32] Questionnaire answers from Rear Admirals D. M. McGurl, B. W. Decker, N. D. Brantly, J. K. B. Ginder; Captains S. S. Bunting, K. L. Forster, D. E. Willman, and Lieutenant Commander Harry R. Hubbard, USN (Ret.), to GCD. Hereafter *Astoria* Heads.

fitness report in my record.... It was a rough and tough existence, but I learned a lot about life." Another recalled "that most officers disliked Captain Turner," but "that if you did your job and made no excuses when you did not, he respected you." He "was ready to help you, if you asked for his advice." By and large, the Heads of Department thought the Captain's efforts and detailed interests unduly spilled over into their own particular areas of responsibility at one time or another. "Inclined to expect the impossible, he was in retrospect, fair, although it didn't seem so at the time."

Memories of these Heads of Departments recalled only two officers who were suspended from duty during the two years, one a Head of Department. Another observer in the *Astoria* writes:

> The *Astoria* was directed to Guam to assist the merchant ship *Admiral Halsted* which was grounded in Apra Harbor; *Astoria* pulled her off. Upon leaving Guam the *Astoria* steamed close to Saipan and Rota taking many, many photographs with large cameras taken aboard at Annapolis by Navy photographers who embarked as passengers. The photographs of Saipan and Rota were for the purpose of determining whether the islands were fortified contrary to mandate. A four-engine Japanese plane circled the *Astoria* during which time Turner kept telling the photographers to attempt to photograph such that four engines could be seen. When the photo mission was completed the *Astoria* then proceeded to search the track area which Richard Halliburton was to traverse from the Orient to the U.S. in a Chinese junk. The ship's planes searched 250,000 square miles of ocean area—results were negative. The photographers also photographed Yokosuka Naval Base just prior to arriving in Yokohama. Apparently the Japanese detected this because when *Astoria* steamed out a smoke screen was laid by the Japanese between *Astoria* and Yokosuka Base.[33]

* * * *

> When Admiral Turner choked to death on a piece of chicken, 'Time' published his death notice. In the short notice it mentioned that Turner 'profaned his way across the Pacific' during the war. I was a little surprised at this characterization. The inference would be that Turner was a profane man. This I don't believe. I know he swore occasionally but I'm sure that unless he changed radically, he was far from being a profane man.[34]

* * * *

> On the other side of the coin it can be said that Turner's enlisted men were uppermost in his mind and no problem was too trivial for his concern when it applied to his men. He was kind and almost fatherly to his crew but always firm and consistent. He always gave reasons 'why' when one of his men was in trouble or had problems.[35]

---

[33] Stratton.
[34] Lopresti.
[35] Stratton.

None of the 12 *Astoria* officer shipmates questioned checked "profane" as a Turner characteristic. They all checked Turner as "hardworking," "brilliant," "impatient," and "fair." One wrote that "he was a dedicated patriot and put his patriotism ahead of personal glory."

MISSION TO JAPAN

On 26 February 1939, a recent Japanese Ambassador to the United States, Hiroshi Saito, died in Washington, D. C., and the United States Government decided to send his body back to Japan on board an American Man-of-War. Presumably this was to repay a 14-year-old courtesy by the Japanese cruiser *Tama* which brought the body of the late Ambassador Edgar A. Bancroft to San Francisco, arriving 22 August 1925.[36]

But it was this and a little more, because Saito was no longer the Ambassador to the United States when he died.

Just why the Commander in Chief picked the *Astoria* to perform this chore is not known, but Admiral Bloch did know Captain Turner quite well, and, as has been related, thought highly of him.

According to our Ambassador to Japan, Mr. Joseph C. Grew, the late Ambassador Saito "knew our country in a way very few foreigners have ever come to know it" and had done "much constructive work." Grew expressed genuine regret at his passing.[37] In any case, Captain Turner was directed to do whatever was within his control to ensure that the Japanese became aware of the genuine regret of this country at the death of Ambassador Saito.[38]

While the *Astoria* was in Norfolk improving her logistic readiness for the long cruise ahead, Czechoslovakia was dismembered and Bohemia and Moravia became German "protectorates." Hitler's Germany annexed the port of Memel while the *Astoria* was in the Canal Zone on 22 March, and the Italians invaded Albania just after the ship left Honolulu. Two hundred and five members of the United States House of Representatives had just endangered the military readiness of the country by refusing to authorize the fortification of Guam. The world's political scene was changing faster than the *Astoria* was moving and Captain Turner whose interest in the

---

[36] SECNAV, *Annual Report*, 1925.
[37] Speech as reported *The Trans Pacific*, Tokyo, 20 Apr. 1939.
[38] (a) Turner; (b) Official Report from USS *Astoria*, CA34/A15/A4–3/(1002) of 2 Jun. 1939. Hereafter *Saito Report*.

political-military area had been whetted by his tour at Newport must have been hard put to keep abreast, or to guess what might come next.

Along with many other naval officers, Captain Turner did not trust the Japanese public pronouncements, nor did he believe in the bright idea originated at a high level that paying a special honor to a dead Japanese diplomat would cause the Japanese Army officers, in the saddle in Japan, to alter the policies which the majority of Americans disliked, but about which they were not prepared to do anything realistic.

But orders were orders, and he honestly wished and tried to show official good will and to reflect the position of the State Department throughout the special assignment.[39]

> The Captain played the visit straight. I acted as his Aide during the visit and it was my impression that he believed the mission could and would accomplish good if everyone in the *Astoria* did his part well.[40]

Captain Turner officially alerted the ship's company of the *Astoria* in regard to their demeanor during the days ahead while carrying out this somber ceremonial chore, with a memorandum published on 18 March 1939, the day the *Astoria* received the Ambassador's ashes in an urn at Annapolis.

This was just a few weeks after the Japanese had shown their predatory intentions in Southeast Asia by occupying the large Chinese island of Hainan off northern French Indo China, and just days before they were to raise their flag over the big old walled city of Nanchang in Southeast China, and to annex the Spratly Islands in the South China Sea.

The memorandum read as follows:

A MISSION OF HONOR

Today the United States pays honor to the memory of a distinguished diplomat, Hiroshi Saito, the late former ambassador of Japan to the United States. Born in 1886, and educated at the Tokyo Imperial University and the Nobles College, he entered the Japanese Foreign Service in 1911. His first assignment was as attache of the Japanese Embassy in Washington, so that, strange to say, both his first and last duty abroad were in America.

Hiroshi Saito served in the various positions of Secretary, Consul, Minister, and Ambassador, some of his posts being Seattle, London, The Hague, Geneva, and Washington. He achieved success as a writer and public speaker. He was highly popular with his associates, and, working always for the good of his own country, until the day of his death never varied from his purpose of promoting good relations between Japan and the United States.

It is, of course, unnecessary for the Captain to say that he is deeply sensible

---

[39] Turner.
[40] Gladney.

of the honor of having the *Astoria* selected to transport to his final repose the remains of this diplomat so highly renowned and esteemed throughout the world, and especially in America. All hands on board assuredly join in this feeling, and are gratified at becoming the means chosen by the President for expressing respect for Hiroshi Saito.

Let us, then, during the ceremonies today and the long voyage ahead, never fail to show our respect to the memory of the late former Ambassador, and our cordiality toward the foreign guest who accompanies the remains of his former chief.

R. K. TURNER
Captain, U. S. Navy.

Madame Saito, showing great good judgment, refused the offer of the Department of State, that she accompany her husband's remains on the *Astoria*.

The ship's paper, *The Astorian*, carried this account.

THE ASTORIA IN JAPAN
by R. B. Stiles

After participating in Fleet Problem XX in the Caribbean, the *Astoria* suddenly got underway on 3 March 1939 from Culebra, Virgin Islands for Norfolk, Va. After taking on a capacity load of stores and fuel, she proceeded to Annapolis, Md., and left there on 18 March bound for Yokohama, Japan, with the ashes of the late ex-ambassador Hiroshi Saito. The ashes were accompanied by Naokichi Kitazawa, Second Secretary of the Japanese Embassy in Washington, on the trip to Japan.

After two days in Balboa, C.Z., while various high officials and a delegation from the Japanese colony in Panama paid their respects to Saito's ashes, the *Astoria* got underway for Honolulu, T.H., on 24 March. Arriving there on 4 April, simultaneously with the *Tatuta Maru* on which Mrs. Saito and her two daughters were crossing to Japan, the *Astoria* tied up to the dock and various officials of Honolulu boarded to pay their respects. Two days in Honolulu and the *Astoria* left Diamond Head astern on the last lap of her twenty-nine day, 10,000-mile trip, across two oceans from Annapolis, to Yokohama. She crossed the International Dateline on 9–11 April, and escorted by three Japanese destroyers, entered Yokohama harbor on 17 April with the Stars and Stripes at half mast, and the Japanese ensign flying from the fore. The 21-gun salute fired by the *Astoria* was answered by *H.I.J.M.S. Kiso*.

This formal entrance of the *Astoria* into Japan was described aptly by the reporter for a Tokyo English language newspaper with these words:

As grey as the leaden dawn from which she emerged, the *Astoria*, escorted

Naval Aviation, 1932–1940

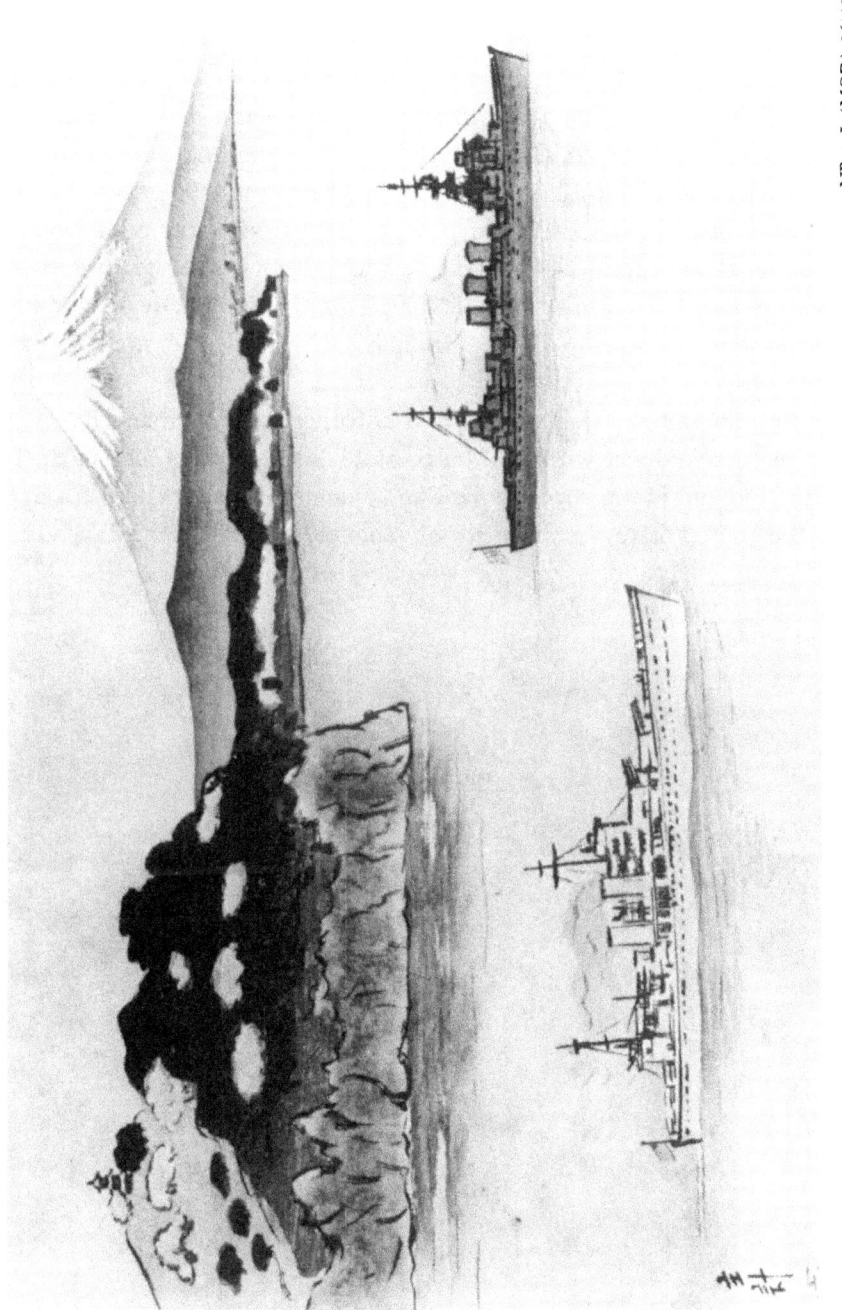

USS Astoria bearing the ashes of late Ambassador Hiroshi Saito entering Yokohama Harbor, Japan. HIJMS Kiso is in the background. Woodcut was presented by the Japanese Navy Department to the crew of USS Astoria, 27 April 1939.

by three Japanese destroyers, steamed slowly into Yokohama Harbor at 8:10 in the morning.[41]

Of the four ships which entered Tokyo harbor together on that morning, only the *Hibiki* survived the war, although she was damaged by a mine in late March 1945. The Japanese destroyer *Sagiri* was the first to go, sunk by a Dutch submarine off Borneo on the day before Christmas 1941. The *Astoria* was the next. She was one of the first to populate Ironbottom Sound north of Guadalcanal in August 1942, and she was joined in that graveyard by the *Akatsuki* sunk by United States naval gunfire from Rear Admiral Callaghan's Support Group, Task Group 67.4, during the night of 13 November 1942.

To make the *Astoria*'s visit stirring and unforgettable, the many Japanese who wished to avoid war with the United States, joined with those Japanese who wished to find in the *Astoria*'s visit an acceptance or an implied forgiveness by the United States Government of Japanese aggression in Manchuria,

---

[41] *The Trans-Pacific*, Tokyo, Thursday, 20 Apr. 1939.

Turner Collection

Street funeral procession in Tokyo for late Ambassador Saito.

U. S. Navy sailor men carrying the ashes of late Ambassador Saito.

and in central China, including the sinking of the gunboat *Panay* and the rape and pillage of Nanking.

The State funeral was as formalized and impressive as Orientals can make such a cheerless occasion. Tens of thousands lined the streets. It was the "double cherry blossom season" in Japan. Once it was over, the Japanese good will demonstration rolled up like a South China Sea cloudburst. Poets wrote verses, musicians composed lyrics, the Tokyo newspapers covered the event with massive minutiae. Everyone was friendly. Thousands visited the *Astoria* at Yokosuka.

In Admiral Turner's effects were three phonograph records with special English and Japanese renderings of an "Ode by Yone Nogushi dedicated to Captain Richmond Turner of the *Astoria*," a "Welcome *Astoria*" march and a lyric "Admiral Saito's Return," with special soprano solo.

The lyric:

> This day the storms forget to rave,
> The angels walk from wave to wave
> This ship glides gently over the foam,
> That brings the noble envoy home.

The ode:

> Pale blossoms greet you
> Seaman from afar
> Who bring him home
> Where all his memories are.

The march:
> Welcome you men with hearts so true
> America's best—America's pride
> You show that tho the winds blow
> That peace and goodwill the storm can ride.

Upon arrival, Ambassador Grew had informed Captain Turner that he was trying hard to facilitate the State Department's purposes of the visit, and to accomplish these, he felt it necessary to channel the Japanese people's enthusiasm and wave of friendliness for the United States into quiet waters. Suggested remarks for each occasion upon which Captain Turner was to speak were handed to him to parrot.[42] A heavy official party schedule was established.

The United States Ambassador entertained Captain Turner, the Executive Officer, Commander Theiss, and seven officers at a dinner which the Japanese War Minister, General Itagaki, and a chief supporter of the Anti-Comintern Pact of 1936 attended. The Japanese Foreign Minister, Mr. Hachiro Arita, a strong proponent of the Greater East Asia Co-Prosperity Sphere, gave a tea for the Captain and 35 officers, and the Navy Minister, Admiral Mitsumasa Yonai, later Prime Minister and unsuccessful proponent of the "go slow" policy in antagonizing the United States, gave a full dress Japanese dinner for the Captain and 20 officers. This party was much enjoyed as were other courtesies extended by the Japanese Navy.[43]

Captain Turner played his delicate part with a skill which pleased the American Ambassador. Speeches with every meaningless, friendly redundant word of condolence or of thanks carefully chosen were endless. Sprigs of cherry blossoms were handed to Captain Turner at all functions. The Imperial Family cabled President Roosevelt a message of appreciation.

Mr. Arita said on one occasion:
> Sympathy opens the hearts of men. The spontaneous expression of sympathy of the American people for Japan has so impressed the Japanese people that their gratitude is beyond description.[44]

On another occasion these non-prophetic words flowed from Mr. Arita:
> We are fully aware that nothing must be left undone to preserve and to strengthen the happy relations already existing between America and Japan, which have been maintained unbroken throughout the years since the memo-

---
[42] Gladney.
[43] Ibid.
[44] Arita, Speech, *Tokyo Advertiser*, 21 Apr. 1939.

rable visit of Commodore Perry. We are firmly resolved to do our utmost to attain the noble ideals to which Mr. Saito devoted his ceaseless efforts.[45]

The speakers of both houses of the Japanese Parliament gave a luncheon; the Emperor gave a tea in the Imperial Gardens, which Turner did not attend; the Navy Vice Minister, Vice Admiral Isoroki Yamamoto, and the Vice Chief of the Navy General Staff, Vice Admiral Mineichi Koga, gave dinners. These, combined with a luncheon by the American Japanese Society, a Garden Party by the Foreign Office, official overnight sightseeing tours, radio broadcasts to the States, and the big return party by the *Astoria* to all whom the Captain was indebted, filled the nine days in Japan to overflowing. The Secretary of the Navy had allowed Captain Turner only $300 to cover all his official entertaining in Japan.

Captain Turner's memorandum on this subject ends with: "26 April: Sail for Shanghai, Thank God!"

---

[45] *Ibid.*, 20 Apr. 1939.

NH 69109

Captain Richmond Kelly Turner; Mr. Hachira Arita, Japanese Foreign Minister; and Joseph Grew, United States Ambassador to Japan.

The *Astoria's* newspaper records the lower deck impression of the visit.

> Official calls, ceremonies, and the transfer of the ashes to Tokyo on the 17th, and on the 18th the crew began to realize the gratitude felt and importance attached by the Japanese to the *Astoria's* mission in Japan. Thirty thousand yen were appropriated for the entertainment of the *Astoria's* men; presents and tokens of gratitude began to pour in to the Foreign Office from people in every walk of life; a sightseeing tour for each watch was arranged by the City of Tokyo; a garden party with entertainment, beer and sake flowing freely and a Japanese girl as partner for each man at the lunch and entertainment; a 200-mile bus and train trip to Shimoda, the sight of Commodore Perry's visit in 1854 to negotiate for the opening of Japan to foreign commerce, bus and train fares free and all doors open to the name *USS Astoria* on the blue hats. Everyone was shown a royal good time and all were reluctant to leave when the *Astoria* left the cheers, 'sayonaras' and 'bonzais' from the crowd on the dock behind, and pointed her bow across the East China Sea for Shanghai on 26 April.[46]

An officer who made the cruise wrote a five-page letter to his mother describing the wonderful spirit of good will poured forth by the Japanese people. Extracted from this letter are several paragraphs of particular interest:

> This was the first indication that we had of the genuine gratitude of the people of Japan for bringing Mr. Saito's ashes back in a 10,000-ton cruiser. . . .
>
> It developed later, in discussions with various people who are supposed to know the political set-up in Japan, that the Japanese Government itself was not all in sympathy with the movement, but that the people were grateful.
>
> It seems that Mr. Saito had been kicked out of his post in Washington for apologizing for the sinking of the gunboat *Panay* before his Government ordered him to do so, and that the Government was unkindly disposed toward him. Some high dignitaries in the Government really looked upon our transportation of Mr. Saito's ashes as an insult by President Roosevelt, since he had sent a cruiser with one whom they had 'dismissed from office.'
>
> * * * * *
>
> We received quite an ovation from the crowd and an elderly Japanese lady who must easily have been seventy or eighty years of age stepped out of the crowd, took my hand and kissed it, saying something in Japanese which I could not understand. I felt very little and meek indeed, and could do nothing but salute and thank her.

The *Astoria* was presented with embroidered pictures and paintings, a silver plaque and a porcelain statue which were distributed appropriately to the Captain's cabin, the wardroom, and the Warrant Officers' Mess room.

---

[46] *The Astorian.*

Captain Turner was presented with a cloisonne vase by the Navy Minister and a Daimyo robe from the Foreign Minister "under circumstances that did not admit of refusal."

The Japanese Government followed up the *Astoria's* visit by considering the presentation of decorations to Captain Richmond K. Turner and Commander Paul S. Theiss. The Navy Department did not perceive any objection and "the honor contemplated is appreciated." [47]

The Japanese took this step despite a written protest by Vice Admiral Oikawa, Commander in Chief of the Japanese Fleet in China, that the *Astoria* had failed to salute his flag when passing his flagship in the lower Yangtze en route out of Shanghai for Hongkong. Captain Turner's attention was called to the presence of the Japanese flagship but—perhaps piqued by the previous last-minute Japanese cancellation of an arranged exchange of calls with the Admiral—said "to hell with it" and proceeded on his way.[48]

After leaving Japan, the *Astoria* had a pleasurable cruise to China, and on back to the West Coast via the Philippines and Guam. After the war, one footnote to history was added by Admiral Turner on the cruise:

> I wonder if you know that Yokoyama, the Jap Junior Aide for the *Astoria*, was the representative of the Jap Navy in the surrender on the *Missouri?* In the photos taken from MacArthur's position, he is in the rear rank, the left hand figure. I saw a good deal of him in Washington in 1940–41.[49]

END OF BIG SHIP COMMAND CRUISE

The Navy Department let Captain Turner remain in the *Astoria* for a full two-year command cruise, and when he went ashore in October 1940, at age 55, he was credited with a reasonably healthy total of 18 years and 8 months of sea duty. Some captains in the Class of 1908 had acquired as much as 21 years of sea duty by this time, and the average for the Class was about 19 years and 6 months.[50]

One Head of Department reminiscences included: "When he was detached and left the ship, a chorus of boos echoed from the hawse pipe to the flagstaff." [51] Several others gathered on the quarterdeck, near the head of the gangway ladder, deny this categorically, but say, in effect, there was "no

---

[47] SECNAV to SECSTATE, letter, Op–13/PS May 24/00/P15390529 of 25 May 1939.
[48] Warburton.
[49] RKT to Rear Admiral Audley L. Warburton, USN (Ret.), letter, 18 Jan. 1950.
[50] *Navy Register,* 1941.
[51] *Astoria* Heads.

question but many breathed a sigh of relief that the Turner command cruise had come to an end."

A further sidelight about this occasion, recalled by one young officer, who as a freshly graduated ensign was serving as Assistant Navigator in the *Astoria* in October 1940, reads as follows:

> When Captain Turner left the ship, we were all paraded at the gangway ready to say our farewells, when Admiral Fletcher's barge approached. He came aboard, shook the Captain's hand and said, 'Well, Kelly, we never got along, but you always gave me a good ship.'
> Captain Turner was the meanest man I ever saw, and the most competent naval officer I ever served with. [52]

THE DIVISION COMMANDERS LOOK BACK

Turner had two Division Commanders while in the *Astoria,* Royal E. Ingersoll and then Frank Jack Fletcher. Both were still alive with vigorous opinions as they neared eighty.

Rear Admiral Ingersoll's 1938–1939 official fitness report opinions of Turner included:

> Captain Turner handled the extensive entertainment program while in Japan with commendable ease, skill and grace. He spoke well and was a credit to the Navy. . . . I can always count on the *Astoria* doing the right thing in any situation. . . . The *Astoria* is a splendid ship, clean, efficient, happy, taut and smart.

Rear Admiral Fletcher in 1940 wrote:

> Captain Turner is one of the most intelligent and forceful men in the Service. His ship is efficient and unusually well handled. I mark him 'outstanding' in the literal meaning of the word.

Twenty-five years and a long war later, neither Flag officer had changed his mind about Kelly Turner's fitness for top command in the Navy or his great capacity for effective work. Admiral Fletcher added:

> Any Captain who relieved Kelly Turner was in luck. All he would have to do is back off on the thumb screws a bit to have the perfect ship.[53]

Admiral Ingersoll remembered:

> I had never served with Kelly Turner until he joined Cruiser Division Six. He ran a taut but smart ship, beautifully handled in formation and at other

---
[52] Commander Tom H. Wells, USN (Ret.) to GCD, letter, 4 Dec. 1969.
[53] Interview with Admiral Frank Jack Fletcher, USN (Ret.), 25 May 1963. Hereafter Fletcher.

times, and always on its toes. You didn't have to tell Turner much. He was usually one jump ahead of you.

I later served with him in Operations when he had War Plans, and I was Vice Chief. He did a magnificent job.

I remember making an inspection of the *Astoria*. She was wonderfully clean. I had put the heavy cruiser *San Francisco* in that class of cruisers into commission the same year as the *Astoria* went into commission, and knew wherever dirt might be found. The main blowers were mounted up on massive circular steel angle irons with small openings around the periphery and keeping them clear underneath was very difficult because it was so hard to get at this space. I looked under them all on the *Astoria* this day. At one particular blower, I noticed a piece of string sticking out, so I grabbed it and hauled on it. Out came, at the end, one of Walt Disney's dogs 'Pluto on Wheels.' It was fun to watch Turner's expression and the way his lower jaw dropped. We all really laughed at that surprise.

During the war, he was the right man at the right place.

One other thing I remember about the *Astoria*. I ordered a General Court Martial for their Chaplain who got drunk and overstayed his shore leave. That was the second court-martial of a Chaplain I had as Commander Cruiser Division Six, and both were dismissed.[54]

As for Admiral Turner's remembrance of the *Astoria*, he wrote to a shipmate:

Poor old *Astoria*. It was a bitter pang on the forenoon of August 9, 1942, to stand on the *McCawley's* bridge while under heavy air attack, and watch that brave, lovely little ship burn and sink. That's one memory that will never leave me—but I'm glad to say that there are many other matters concerning the *Astoria*, that I remember with the greatest pleasure.[55]

---

[54] Interview with Admiral Royal Eason Ingersoll, USN (Ret.), 26 March 1964. Hereafter Ingersoll.
[55] RKT to Rear Admiral Warburton, letter, 28 Jan. 1950.

CHAPTER V

Planning for War With Germany or Japan or Both 1940–1941

BACKGROUND FOR WAR PLANNING

It seemed to some officers that the publicized policy of the civilian heads of the government and the vocal opinion of certain mid-western Congressmen at various times prior to World War I and World War II was that, while the military were supposed to win any war which the United States got into and the Congress then authorized, there was to be no counter-offensive war planning of any kind and no defensive war planning for a war against any specific country, nor for a defensive war allied with any specific country.

President Woodrow Wilson actually had forbidden the Joint Board, the pre-1942 Joint War Planning Agency, to meet when he learned they were working hard in the pre-Vera Cruz days planning on what to do should the United States get involved in a war with Mexico. This suspension lasted from 1914 through World War I and into 1919.

Secretary Daniels forbad the creation of a War Plans Division within the Office of the Chief of Naval Operations, when that office was created by Congress in 1915 over his opposition. There was a Director of Plans, but not until Mr. Daniels had left office and World War I was over, was there a War Plans Division and a Director of War Plans.

It was not until 1936 that the Navy found enough moral courage and officer personnel to establish billets for War Plans Officers on the staffs of the principal Fleet, Force, and subordinate seagoing commands and on the shoreside staffs of the logistically essential District Commandants, and it was not until 1941 that the designation started appearing in the command rosters.

Despite these powerful handicaps, the press of world events by 1938 indicated to all naval officers, who would open their eyes and see, that the future held dangers for the United States unless it would stand and fight. How, when, where, and with whom as allies to fight were not questions which could be answered unilaterally by the United States Navy, but most officers had strong opinions.

So, War Planning was rated highly by the Line of the Navy as 1940 came up over the horizon and many of its best officers welcomed details therein. For this reason, as well as a natural interest in political-military matters, and desire to follow through on the strategical training received at the Naval War College, Captain Turner was pleased when he was tapped for the Director of War Plans billet in the Office of Chief of Naval Operations.[1]

Neither Admiral Harold R. Stark, Chief of Naval Operations in 1940, nor Rear Admiral Royal E. Ingersoll, his senior assistant, could remember in detail how Captain Turner came to be picked for the War Plans desk. Each gave the credit to the other, with an assist to Captain Abel T. Bidwell, the Director of Officer Personnel in the Bureau of Navigation.[2] Both of these officers used the same expression to summarize their present opinions of the detail: "The right man."

On 14 September 1940, Captain Turner was relieved of command of the *Astoria* by Captain Preston B. Haines of the Class of 1909. He drew his usual dead horse, this time amounting to $698.37 and departed from the *Astoria,* in Pearl Harbor, for Washington.

The new billet offered a tacit promise of further promotion, since for 18 years, starting with Clarence S. Williams in 1922, all the regular occupants of the Director of War Plans chair except the captain he was about to relieve, who had not been reached by the 1939 Selection Board, achieved Flag rank. And most of its occupants had moved on to the upper echelons of the Navy. There were William R. Shoemaker, William H. Standley, Frank H. Schofield, Montgomery Meigs Taylor, and more recently William S. Pye and Royal E. Ingersoll to emulate and surpass.

Captain Turner reported on 19 October 1940. He was selected for Flag officer by the December 1940 Selection Board. By special Presidential fiat, on 8 January 1941, he assumed the rank, but not the pay, of a rear admiral.[3]

In October 1940 Secretary of the Navy Frank Knox had been in his job three months, and Admiral Stark had been in his important billet as Chief

---
[1] Turner.
[2] (a) Interview with Admiral Harold R. Stark, USN (Ret.), 16 Feb. 1962. Hereafter Stark; (b) Ingersoll.
[3] FDR to RKT, letter, 8 Jan. 1941.

of Naval Operations for 14 months. Rear Admiral Ingersoll was Stark's "Assistant," later called Vice Chief. Rear Admiral Walter S. Anderson was Director of Naval Intelligence, Rear Admiral Herbert F. Leary was Director of Fleet Training, and Rear Admiral Alexander Sharp was Director of the Naval Districts Division. Rear Admiral Roland M. Brainard was Director of Ship Movements and Rear Admiral Leigh Noyes was Director of Communications. These divisions and War Plans were the principal centers of authority and power in Naval Operations.

Within the War Plans Division, there was much talent including Turner's successor as Director of War Plans, Captain Charles M. Cooke, together with Captains Oscar Smith, Charles J. Moore, Harry W. Hill, Frank L. Lowe, Edmund D. Burroughs, and Commanders John L. McCrea, Forrest P. Sherman, and Walter C. Ansel. In the United States Fleet, Commander Vincent R. Murphy (1918) and later Commander Lynde D. McCormick (1915) were the War Plans Officers, while in the Asiatic Fleet, Captain William R. Purnell acted as such until Commander William G. Lalor (1921) was so designated. At lower Fleet echelons, War Plans was generally an additional duty assignment for the Operations Officer. Commander Heber H. McLean (1921) was ordered to Admiral King's staff as War Plans Officer when the Atlantic Fleet was formed up. All of these officers went on to fight the war which they were engaged in planning against, some in positions of major responsibility.

When Captain Turner arrived in Washington, the major portion of the United States Fleet (Admiral James O. Richardson, Commander in Chief) was in Pearl Harbor. A Two Ocean Navy had been authorized by the Congress on 19 July 1940, but the Atlantic Fleet had not yet been formed up. The old Atlantic Squadron, about to become the Patrol Force and under Rear Admiral Hayne Ellis in the *Texas,* had been carrying out the increasingly complex naval tasks of the Atlantic. Many naval officers thought some of the tasks were highly irregular and others saw a violation of the United States laws of neutrality. By Presidential order, all were keeping quiet about it.

The Germans were still basking in the downfall of France, and had ports on the Atlantic Ocean from which to operate their submarines. Italy was about to invade Greece. The Havana Conference of June 1940, on the surface at least, had gained the support of all the American republics for a non-neutral neutrality policy of the United States, as well as for an agreement that territory in the Americas could not be transferred from one non-

American nation to another despite any changes in management at the home offices in Europe.

The "Destroyers for Naval Bases" arrangement was finalized on 2 September 1940, and Rear Admiral John W. Greenslade was out in the hustings developing recommendations for base facilities which would permit a better United States defense of the Panama Canal, and better United States offensive actions against German submarines. When Rear Admiral Greenslade submitted his Board's recommendations on this subject, he was put to developing a set of recommendations for the location and development of naval bases for a Two Ocean Navy.

One of the first major tasks which Captain Turner faced was to meet the request of Rear Admiral Greenslade who

> orally requested an indication of the views of the Chief of Naval Operations as to general strategic matters which might influence the conclusion to be reached by the Board.[4]

In view of the fact that the Communists—in effect a non-American foreign power—have now taken over Cuba, the 1940 opinion of the War Plans Officer, and of the Chief of Naval Operations is worth quoting:

> 16. The Caribbean, the southern flank of the Atlantic position, is doubtless the most important single strategic area which the United States has within its power to control permanently. Its security is essential for defense against attack from the eastward upon the Panama Canal, Central America, Mexico and the southern United States. It is the most advanced location from which offensive operations can be undertaken for the protection of South America, or for the disruption of enemy communication lines along the African Coast. Its importance to the United States can be realized by imagining a situation in which a strong foreign power would be firmly ensconced therein. . . .
>
> 17. The distances around the eastern rim of the Caribbean are such that it does not seem possible to provide for an adequate defense of the region by the development of a single operating base area. Preferably, base areas would be developed in the vicinity of the Northwestern end, in the center, and at the south eastern end of the rim. The positions that naturally suggest themselves are around Guantanamo and Jamaica, around Porto Rico, and around Trinidad. . . .[5]

ARE WE READY?

The General Board on 1 July 1940, in answer to the pertinent question of the Secretary of the Navy "Are We Ready?" had said "No" in a clear

---
[4] CNO to Rear Admiral John W. Greenslade, letter, Ser 045112 of 29 Nov. 1940.
[5] *Ibid.*

and unmistakable manner, and supplied 35 pages of details to support its conclusion. Many of these details related to the War Plans Division. This was a reaffirmation of a similar conclusion they had arrived at on 31 August 1939. By 14 June 1941, when the General Board again studied the question, some rays of light were barely visible on the horizon but the Board adhered to its opinion: "The Naval Establishment is not ready for a serious emergency."[6]

It is against these seasoned official statements that events between 19 October 1940 and 7 December 1941 must be related.

JOINT BOARD—WAR PLANNING

The Joint Board, a 1903 creation of the Secretary of War and Secretary of the Navy, and initially an advisory board only, had over the years developed into the principal war planning agency of the War and Navy Departments, particularly in the areas of Joint operations and coordination and control of military and naval forces. It produced an excellent publication, *Joint Action Army–Navy*.

As Director of War Plans in Naval Operations, Captain Turner became the Naval Member of the Joint Planning Committee of the Joint Board. Brigadier General L. T. Gerow, Chief of Army War Plans Division, was the Army member, but frequently Colonel Joseph T. McNarney, Air Corps, U.S. Army, signed as the Army Member. According to Turner:

> The greatest single problem that concerned the Joint Board and the Joint Planners in the Fall of 1940 was the lack of any clear lines of national policy to guide the direction of military efforts to prepare for a war situation.
> The State Department had no political War Plan.
> Therefore the Army and Navy themselves undertook a broad study of the global political situation and prepared a draft letter which was designed to be the basis for consultation and agreement between the State, War, and Navy Departments. . . .[7]

The two officers who turned out the "Study of the Immediate Problems concerning Involvement in War" in late December 1940 were Turner and McNarney.[8] They urged a copy of the study be furnished Mr. Sumner Welles, and after his recommendations had been received, and revisions made, they suggested that the Secretaries of State, War, and Navy consider

---
[6] General Board No. 425, Sers 1868 of 31 Aug. 1939, 1959 of 1 Jul. 1940, and 144 of 14 Jun. 1941.
[7] RKT, address delivered at National War College, 28 Jan. 1947.
[8] JB No. 325, Ser 670 of 21 Dec. 1940.

the study with a view to its submission to the President for formal approval. Their estimate "sought to keep in view the political realities in our own country" where "the strong wish of the American people at present seems to be to remain at peace."

The Turner-McNarney study paper was touched off by a "Memorandum on National Policy" from Admiral Stark to the Secretary of the Navy dated 12 November 1940. This memorandum later became known as "Plan Dog" since it offered four possible plans of action by the United States in the event of a two-ocean war, Plan A, B, C, or D, and recommended Plan D, a strong offensive war in the Atlantic and a defensive war in the Pacific.

The Joint estimate of Turner and McNarney is a remarkable document in many respects, particularly in forecasting the timing and the various factors which brought the United States into war.

It stated:

> With respect to Germany and Italy, it appears reasonably certain that neither will initiate open hostilities with the United States, until they have succeeded in inflicting a major reverse on Great Britain in the British Isles or in the Mediterranean.
>
> With respect to Japan, hostilities prior to United States entry into the European War or to the defeat of Britain may depend upon the consequences of steps taken by the United States to oppose Japanese aggression. If these steps seriously threaten her [Japan's] economic welfare or military adventures, there can be no assurance that Japan will not suddenly attack United States armed forces.

In connection with a war with Japan, they forecast:

> Such a war might be precipitated by Japanese armed opposition should we:
>   1. Strongly reinforce our Asiatic Fleet or the Philippine garrison.
>   2. Start fortifying Guam.
>   3. Impose additional important economic sanctions.
>   4. Greatly increase our material . . . aid to China.

Or by:

>   5. A definite indication that an alliance with the British or Dutch had been consummated.
>   6. Our opposition to a Japanese attack on British or Dutch territory.
>
> It might be precipitated by ourselves in case of overt Japanese action against us, or in case of an attempt by Japan to extend its control over Shanghai, or Indo-China.

Believing as these planners did, it can now be understood why the Asiatic Fleet was not reenforced and the Philippine Garrison more rapidly built up

Planning for War, 1940–1941 159

in the 12 months between December 1940 and December 1941, despite the pleas of the military commanders responsible for defense in the Far East area.[9]

The paper also pin-pointed the reality of the danger of imposing "important" economic sanctions, the effect of which the Japanese formally stated was the immediate cause of their deciding upon war, in order to ensure their industrial livelihood. And made clearer now is the background reason for the many false denials made during 1941 that there were definite contingent arrangements with the Dutch and British for the defense of the Dutch-Malaysia area.

The rapidity with which Japan overran Malaysia is often stated to have been a surprise to the military. But, Turner and McNarney offered the opinion:

> Provided the British and Dutch cooperate in a vigorous and efficient defense of Malaysia, Japan will need to make a major effort with all categories of military force to capture the entire area. The campaign might even last several months.

Since Singapore surrendered on 15 February 1942 and Java surrendered 9 March 1942, the forecast was uncannily accurate.

The hazard of orienting United States forces toward the Pacific was indicated.

> Should we prepare for a full offensive against Japan . . . the length of time required to defeat Japan would be considerable. . . .
> If Great Britain should lose in Europe, we would then be forced to re-orient toward the Atlantic, a long and hazardous process.
> For this reason, and in view of the existing situation in Europe, the Secretaries of State, War and Navy are of the opinion that war with Japan should be avoided if possible. Should we find that we cannot avoid war, then we should undertake only a limited war.

Their specific recommendations were:

> 1. The United States . . . should pursue a course that will most rapidly increase the military strength of both the Army and the Navy . . . and refrain from any steps that will provoke a military attack upon us by any other power.
> 2. The United States ought not willingly engage in any war against Japan.
> 3. That, if forced into a war with Japan, the United States should, at the same time, enter the war in the Atlantic, and should restrict operations in the mid-Pacific and the Far East in such a manner as to permit the prompt move-

---

[9] CNO to SECNAV, Op–12–WCB, letter, Ser 08212 of 17 Jan. 1941, subj: Recommendations concerning further reinforcement of the U. S. Asiatic Fleet.

ment to the Atlantic of forces fully adequate to conduct a major offensive in that ocean.[10]

These recommendations foretold the "Victory in Europe First" defense plans and the United States Declaration of War on Germany and Italy on 11 December 1941.

PLANS DIVISION WORK LIST

Admiral Turner in a lecture at the National War College in 1946, stated:

> On October 19, 1940, when I reported to Admiral Stark, the Chief of Naval Operations, he gave me two orders:
>
> 1. The first order was that, in view of his expectation of an early Japanese offensive in the Pacific, the Navy needed an immediate temporary plan for a major war in the Pacific, with a strong defense of Hawaii, and increased support for our Asiatic Fleet.
>
> 2. The second order by Admiral Stark was that, since he believed a collapse of the United Kingdom would be extremely serious for the United States, the United States should at once hold staff conversations with the United Kingdom with a view to making an Allied War Plan that could be made effective quickly, should the political situation indicate intervention.

These will be dealt with in inverse order.

ABC CONFERENCE AND AGREEMENT

The day after Christmas 1940, the Director of Naval Intelligence and the Chief of the Bureau of Aeronautics were directed to furnish data needed in examining the possible operation of naval forces of the United States from Iceland and Scotland under the assumption of the United States "having entered the war on 1 April 1941."

The first sentence of this memorandum read:

> As you may be aware, the War and Navy Department will shortly engage in staff conversations with British Officers for the purpose of reaching agreements as to the possible fields of military responsibility and methods of military collaboration of the two nations, should the United States decide to ally itself with the British Commonwealth in the War against Germany.[11]

---

[10] JB No. 325, Ser 670 of 21 Dec. 1940.
[11] Director of War Plans to Director Naval Intelligence, Chief of BUAER–OP–12–CTB, memorandum, Ser 052212 of 26 Dec. 1940.

By and large this was the first "on the line" statement whereby other divisions of Naval Operations were informed of the definite cast of United States die to be ready, at least with plans, for a war against Germany. Many preliminary steps for such an eventuality had been inferred by the officers in these divisions from various specific directives covering precise action to be taken in definite circumstances. This directive was an umbrella.

The Staff conversations mentioned in the above memorandum actually opened in Washington on 29 January 1941, and it was primarily to provide the Navy War Plans Officer with a more suitable rank for his part in this conference that the President (against the wishes of his naval advisors) directed that Captain Turner wear the uniform of a rear admiral.[12] The British Navy showed up with four Flag and General officers, but the United States Navy had to be content with two Flag officers, one underpaid.

The British had first proposed the conference to Rear Admiral Robert L. Ghormley, our Special Naval Observer in London, way back in June 1940, and it could be considered a certainty that they would arrive splendidly prepared to argue their case.

In order to obtain a firm statement of the British kick-off position for our planning staff, we asked for "an estimate of the military situation of the British Commonwealth" as a preliminary to the staff discussions. The British, anxious to engage the United States in military talks, provided it.

Rear Admiral Turner and Colonel McNarney drafted the "Joint Instructions for Army and Navy Representatives for Holding Staff Conversations with the British including an agenda for the Conversations." The agenda included a statement of the "basic national military position" of the United States. The recommendations included:

> In order to avoid commitment by the President, neither he nor any of his cabinet should officially receive the British representatives.[13]

Neither did the President directly approve the statement of "basic national military position" although he was furnished a copy. At a White House conference of the Secretaries of State, War, and Navy, the Chief of Staff, the Chief of Naval Operations, and others on 16 January 1941, the President in effect, did approve the "basic national military position" set forth in the Turner-McNarney memo of 21 December 1940, by refraining from making any adverse comment thereon when it was mentioned and discussed. This

---

[12] U.S., Congress, *Hearings Before the Joint Committee on the Investigation of the Pearl Harbor Attack* (79th Cong., 1st Sess., part 4), p. 1983. Hereafter *Pearl Harbor Hearings*.

[13] JB No. 325, Ser 674 of 21 Jan. 1941.

gave its authors, as well as their military superiors, confidence in undertaking their important negotiations with the British.[14]

RAINBOW WAR PLANS

When Captain Turner reported to the CNO for duty in the War Plans Division in October 1940, there were five major United States War Plans, known as *Rainbow One, Two, Three, Four,* and *Five,* in various stages of completion.

A brief description of their character follows.

Rainbow One sought to prevent violation of the letter or spirit of the Monroe Doctrine by guarding closely the Western Hemisphere, while at the same time protecting the vital interests of the United States, its possessions and its seaborne trade, wherever these might be.

Rainbow Two had as its basic purpose the accomplishment of *Rainbow One,* and additionally, while *not* providing "maximum participation in continental Europe," defeating enemy forces in the Pacific and sustaining the interests of the Democratic Powers in the Pacific.

Rainbow Three aimed to carry out the mission of *Rainbow One* and to protect the United States' vital interests in the Western Pacific by securing control in the Western Pacific.

Rainbow Four proposed to accomplish *Rainbow One* without allies or helpful neutrals by occupying allied areas in the Western Hemisphere, and by defending the Western Hemisphere only as far south as the Brazilian bulge, and if necessary falling back in the Pacific as far as Hawaii.

Rainbow Five's initial basic purpose was to project the Armed Forces of the United States to the Eastern Atlantic and to either or both of the African or European continents as rapidly as possible, consistent with the mission of *Rainbow One* in order to effect the decisive defeat of Germany or Italy or both. Later drafts oriented the purpose, in effect, to winning World War II with Europe the primary theater of effort.[15]

Events occurring in Europe during the 1939–1941 period of actual drafting of these plans caused certain basic assumptions to vary and to fluctuate, and similarly, but to a lesser extent, the detailed purposes.

The initial Joint Board directive to the Joint Planning Committee to develop these five war plans was dated 30 June 1939, just two months and

---
[14] Turner.
[15] JB No. 325, Ser 642 of 30 Jun. 1939.

a day before World War II started with the German attack on Poland. *Rainbow Two* had been recommended for addition to the earlier drafts of four prospective tasks of the Planning Committee, on 21 June 1939.[16]

Within the next 16 months, two plans, *Rainbow One* and *Rainbow Four*, had been completed by the Joint Planning Committee, pushed up the line, and approved by the President. *Rainbow One* was written in the remarkable time of 45 days, approved by the Joint Board and the Secretaries of War and Navy on 14 August 1939, and then held by the President for two months before receiving his blessing. The Navy published and distributed a Navy Basic War Plan, *Rainbow One*. The Army did not publish a supporting plan for *Rainbow One*, putting their efforts into *Rainbow Four* since that plan envisaged a stronger Army effort than *Rainbow One*.

When France started to crumble and Italy jumped into the war, *Rainbow Four* was rushed to completion by the Joint Planning Committee and approved by the Joint Board on 7 June 1940. Again the President sat on a War Plan for two months before, on 14 August 1940, giving his approval. The Army prepared but did not issue a supporting plan for *Rainbow Four* while the Navy started but did not finalize a supporting Plan. This lack of follow-through came about, presumably because both Services were reluctant to promulgate such a pure "Fortress America" stand, politically popular as it might be.

In regard to these War Plans, Vice Admiral Turner during the Hart Inquiry on 3 April 1944 testified:

> I shared the opinion with many others that the war plans which were in existence during 1940 [*Rainbow One* and *Rainbow Four*] were defective in the extreme. They were not realistic, they were highly theoretical, they set up forces to be ready for use at the outbreak of war, or shortly after, which could not possibly have been made available. . . .[17]

The Joint Planning Committee prepared but did not submit to the Joint Board a Joint Army and Navy Basis War Plan *Rainbow Two*. This plan, which in effect provided for the United States to fight a Western Pacific war, while England and France fought a European war, became less and less a reality as Germany showed her prowess over these two prospective allies.

The Joint planners were never able to agree on a *Rainbow Three,* which provided for active defense in the Western Hemisphere and an offensive

---

[16] JPC to JB OP-12-B-6, letter of 21 Jun. 1939; subj: JB No. 325.
[17] *Pearl Harbor Hearings*, part 26, p. 268.

for securing control in the Western Pacific, primarily because Army planners could not accept the basic thought that:

> our national policy requires the United States maintain a strong position in the Western Pacific....
> The Army members believe that it would be both futile and unwise even to mention in the Joint Estimate as a serious suggestion for a peacetime course of action that the garrison of the Philippines be increased.[18]

However, since a Navy War Plan for a war in the Pacific seemed essential to the Chief of Naval Operations, the Navy drafted and issued Navy Basic War Plan *Rainbow Three* (WPL–43). This Plan was not concurred in by the War Department.[19]

The above four War Plans had a relatively short life. *Rainbow One* deserves praise because it was a major prop in getting the shoreside Navy expanded rapidly toward a tremendous wartime capability, since the Plan called for a military might to protect the vital interests of the United States wherever they might be located. The plan was cancelled by the Joint Board on 5 May 1942. *Rainbow Two,* which gave first priority to our defeat of Japan, and the many requirements for an agreed upon offensively minded *Rainbow Three* were cancelled on 6 August 1941, since well before that date it had been accepted by both Services that Germany was the primary enemy and Europe the primary theater. *Rainbow Four,* the "Hold America" War Plan, lost its basic requirement when it became evident that Great Britain and the Soviet Union were going to hold against Germany. It was cancelled by the Joint Board on 5 May 1942.

RAINBOW FIVE

A month after Captain Turner had arrived in Naval Operations, and 18 months after Colonel Clark's memorandum, referenced above, the Army planners still felt that they were unable to make any major military commitments in the Far East because of a lack of realistic capacity.[20] The Navy planners, and the Chief of Naval Operations, by November 1940 had accepted that view. While many sharp differences of opinion with the Army

---

[18] Col. F. S. Clark, War Plans Division, General Staff, memorandum for Director of War Plans, 17 Apr. 1939.

[19] Pearl Harbor *Hearings,* part 26, p. 268. Advance copies WPL 43 were sent to CINCUS, 17 December 1940 by officer messenger. Issued by the Navy Department on 9 January 1941.

[20] Acting Assistant Chief of Staff WPD. Memorandum for Chief of Staff, 13 Nov. 1940, Subj: Comments on Plan Dog.

planners continued, the basic concept of the future war which the United States would wage was close to being a jointly agreed upon one. This concurrence permitted an agreed upon draft of *Rainbow Five* to be hammered out in five months.

Admiral Ingersoll, the #2 in Naval Operations in 1940–41, and later Commander in Chief, Atlantic Fleet, told this author:

> One thing you should mention is that Kelly Turner wrote *Rainbow Three* and the first supporting draft for *Rainbow Five*.[21]

Rainbow Five, the famous and quite excellent War Plan placed in effect on 7 December 1941, immediately following the Pearl Harbor attack, was approved initially by the Joint Board on 14 May 1941. A revised draft was approved only four weeks before the United States was fully in World War II.

Vice Admiral Turner testified in regard to *Rainbow Five* on 3 April 1944:

> While the Navy Department believed that our major military effort, considered as a whole, should initially be against Germany—that view, I may add, was also held by the War Department—we were all in agreement that the principal naval effort should be in the Pacific . . . . our strongest naval concentration and naval effort ought to be in the Central Pacific.[22]

THE PRE-WORLD WAR II PLANNING EFFORT

During the period of two and a half years from June 1939 to December 1941, the Navy published and promulgated three major War Plans in detail —*Rainbow One, Rainbow Three,* and *Rainbow Five*. The Army published and distributed only one, *Rainbow Five*, but certainly the essential one. It was a tremendous Service-wide planning effort.

The War Department had planning problems in connection with the *Rainbow* Plans. Mark S. Watson in his official Army history of this effort says:

> But in the case of the undermanned and underequipped Army, these plans were far from realistic, and hence were little more than Staff studies. This theoretical approach was inescapable, in view of the weakness of forces which would be available on war's sudden arrival. Most of the plans defined ultimate offensives, but with awareness that they would require forces that would be available only long after war should start. This meant that comprehensive planning, which is the only planning of importance, had made far less head-

---

[21] Ingersoll.
[22] *Pearl Harbor Hearings*, part 26, p. 266.

way in the Army than in the Navy. The latter had an impressive force-in-being—the U. S. Fleet, which was continuously at sea in some phase of operational training.[23]

RKT AND ADMIRAL NOMURA

On 11 March 1941, the Japanese Ambassador, Admiral Kichisaburo Nomura, at a cocktail party given in his honor by the Japanese Naval Attache, talked with Rear Admiral Turner briefly and suggested that he would like to converse with him at greater length. Admiral Nomura telephoned Turner the next day and arranged for the further meeting on the same day.

In his five-page report of this conversation, Turner reported that Nomura had stated "his mission was to prevent war between Japan and the United States" and that "the best interests of the two countries were to maintain peace." He "was exploring the ground, as best he could in order to find a basis on which the two nations could agree." [24]

Nomura placed the blame for the war in China and other strong measures on the "younger radical element" of the Japanese Army. He said: "The senior officers of the Japanese Navy, on the contrary, had been and still are in favor of peace with the United States." Nomura recognized "the value of a peaceful conquest" versus a wartime conquest of areas in Southeast Asia. "Japan has not now, and never has had, any desire to extend control over the Philippines."

When Rear Admiral Turner explained the special relationship existing between the United States and Great Britain, Nomura said:

> All Japanese Naval officers understood this thoroughly, but unfortunately, Japanese Army officers did not. He had tried to explain this to them, but they would not believe him. In his opinion the presence of the United States Fleet in Hawaii, particularly in combination with the British, forms a stabilizing influence for affairs in the Pacific.

Rear Admiral Turner came away from the interview with the opinion:

> I believe he is fully sincere, and that he will use his influence against further aggressive moves by the military forces of Japan.

Rear Admiral Turner was not alone in that belief. He and others in

---

[23] Mark S. Watson, *Chief of Staff: Prewar Plans and Preparation,* Vol. I in subseries *The War Department* of series UNITED STATES ARMY IN WORLD WAR II (Washington: Historical Division, Department of the Army, 1950), p. 87.
[24] RKT to CNO, Report of conversation with Japanese Ambassador, 13 Mar. 1941.

Washington through the breaking of Japanese coded messages were reading the Japanese Ambassador's report of his conversation with Turner and others in the Ambassador's despatches to the Japanese Foreign Office. Unfortunately, diplomatic Japanese despatches prior to 1 July 1941 are not printed in the Pearl Harbor Report, so it is not possible to compare the two participants' reports on the 12 March conversation to their seniors.

The 12 March 1941 Turner conversation with Admiral Nomura was followed by another on 20 July 1941 which Turner duly reported.[25] Admiral Nomura, late on this particular afternoon, and with what to him was a hot piece of Japanese Army news had tried to visit Admiral Stark, but had not found him at home, so he called at Rear Admiral Turner's residence. The main purpose of his visit was to watch the Navy ripples on the Potomac, when a Japanese land mine went off in the Far East, for the news was that "within the next few days Japan expected to occupy French Indo China." From the strength of its ripples, Admiral Nomura could hope to obtain a naval estimate whether the United States would go to war with Japan as a result.

Actually the Indo China occupation took place the following day, 21 July 1941. The Japanese Army just had not let their Foreign Office in on the exact date. Yet, the top echelon in Naval Operations already had been alerted on 19 July 1941 by decoding a Japanese diplomatic message of 14 July that the Japanese Army soon would move into Indo China.[26] So Rear Admiral Turner was not surprised by Admiral Nomura's news.

Turner's report said Nomura made these points:

    a. He had accepted the duty as Ambassador only after great insistence by his friends, particularly high ranking naval officers and the more conservative group of Army officers.

    b. It is essential that Japan have uninterrupted access to necessary raw materials.

    c. Japan's economic position is bad and steadily getting worse.

    d. Japan must make some arrangement through which support of the Chungking regime will be reduced.

    e. Essential for Japan's security is the more or less permanent stationing of Japanese troops in Inner Mongolia in order to break the connection between Russia and China.

    f. Within the next few days Japan expects to occupy French Indo China. . . . This occupation has become essential.

    g. Japan contemplates no further move to the South for the time being.

---

[25] DWP to CNO, OP-12-CTB, letter, Ser 083412 of 21 Jul. 1941.
[26] *Pearl Harbor Hearings*, part 12, pp. 2–3.

h. The one great point upon which agreement might be reached, he again emphasized, as the inherent right of self defense.

Turner's report made the following points:

a. The occupation of Indo-China by Japan is particularly important for the defense of the United States, since it might threaten the British position in Singapore and the Dutch position in the Netherland East Indies.

b. It can thus be seen what a very close interest, from a military viewpoint, the United States has in sustaining the status quo in the southern position of the Far East.

c. Japan really had very little to fear from American, British, or Dutch activities in the Far East.

The last statement proved all too accurate and probably too revealing, for the Japanese Army acted boldly. For example, they bombed the *USS Tutuila* (PR-4), a river gunboat, at Chungking, China, on 30 July 1941.

Admiral Nomura and the Director of War Plans had other meetings, as did Counselor Terasaki of the Japanese Embassy. These were mentioned in Japanese diplomatic messages of 30 September 1941, 14 October 1941, and 16 October 1941 (Parts 1 and 2) with direct quotes of Turner's remarks.[27]

Both Admirals, Stark and Turner, were personally appreciative of the difficult position of Nomura. By frankly stating their personal reactions to the Japanese actions and proposals, they sought to provide him with a clear understanding, uncluttered with diplomatic double-talk, of an informed and interested American's reaction.[28] Both of these Flag officers believed in Nomura's honest intentions during the negotiations and lack of any prior knowledge of the Pearl Harbor attack.[29]

FAMILY PROBLEMS

While these momentous events were underway, Kelly Turner took the time to tell his sister of some Turner family problems:

We are having terrible things in our family. I think I may have told you that our dogs have been very sick with what the doctor says is a 'cold' but which is very like the intestinal influenza for humans, though much more severe. The new little puppy (a grand little dog) died of it last week, and

---

[27] *Ibid.*, part 12, pp. 45, 68, 72, 73.
[28] Stark.
[29] Stark; Turner.

today Mikko died. Ming is extremely sick, and I do not believe that she will live, though I don't tell Harriet that.

My darling Harriet is in the depths, naturally. Ming has been sick for nearly four weeks, and Harriet is simply worn out from worry and nursing. She doesn't sleep well, and is very thin, and worn. She has had *such* a terrible year—five of her lovely dogs dying, her mother's death, the suicide of a very dear friend, and the tragic death of her very best friend, Marian Ross. Here in Washington are no women she has ever been very close to, and my work is so confining and my hours so long that she simply gets no distraction from her difficulties. She is fine and brave about it all as anyone could be, but all these things have depressed her greatly. I try to do what I can, but she is alone a great deal, and worries a lot. The Melhorns are going to stay with us a few days next month, and then the Cutts for a short time, and that should help somewhat.[30]

ESCORT OF CONVOYS

In the Atlantic theatre, where another war was raging, Rear Admiral Turner also played a role of great importance. On 17 January 1941, he advised the CNO that the Navy in the Atlantic would be ready to escort convoys from the East Coast to Scotland by 1 April 1941.[31]

On 20 March 1941, the Secretary of the Navy signed a Turner-drafted memorandum to the President on the tasks of the United States Naval Forces in the Atlantic, in case of a decision to escort convoys. This memorandum ended with the statement:

> Our Navy is ready to undertake it [convoying] as soon as directed, but could do it more effectively were we to have six to eight weeks for special training.[32]

This was about 22 months after the start of the war in Europe.

The SS *Robin Moor*, a United States merchant ship with a general cargo, bound for South Africa was sunk by a German submarine on 21 May 1941. But, it was 19 July 1941 before CINCLANT issued his orders to escort convoys, and convoys between the East Coast and Iceland were organized and escorted. It was 16 September 1941 before trans-Atlantic convoys were escorted by the Atlantic Fleet ships.

It was Admiral Turner's opinion that had the Germans made a few submarine attacks in the Pacific Ocean, prior to 7 December 1941, the Pacific

---

[30] RKT to Miss LLT, letter, 9 Feb. 1941. Captain Kent C. Melhorn (Medical Corps), USN, and Captain Elwin F. Cutts, USN (Class of 1908).
[31] DWP to CNO, letter, 17 Jan. 1941.
[32] SECNAV to President, memorandum, 20 Mar. 1941.

Fleet would have been better prepared for World War II and might have been more adequately alerted on 7 December 1941.[33]

MR. HARRY HOPKINS HELPS THE NAVY

Admiral Turner thought that Mr. Harry Hopkins made a major contribution to getting the United States ready for war, by his ability to persuade the President to take steps which the Service Chiefs had been unable to persuade him to undertake.[34] The following extracts from a 29 April 1941 letter from the Director of War Plans to the Chief of Naval Operations is supporting evidence.

> 1. In the course of a luncheon conversation with Mr. Harry Hopkins, he desired to be informed as to exactly what steps might be taken on the assumption that the United States might be in the war on August 1st. . . .
> 2. In reply, I recommended:
>   a. a detachment of the Pacific Fleet, be sent at an early date to the Atlantic. . . .
>   b. that enough antiaircraft guns and pursuit aircraft be diverted from deliveries to the British and assigned to the United States Army as might be necessary to outfit the ground and air defense units which would protect United States bases in the British Isles. . . .
>   c. immediately taking over approximately thirty transports, freighters, and tankers. . . .
>   d. a sufficient expansion of Navy and Marine Corps personnel to provide for the above ships and for bringing all units up to full strength.
> 3. Mr. Hopkins expressed the opinion that, if these matters were presented to the President, the latter would give directions to carry them out. . . .[35]

On 22 April 1941, the President had approved the increase of enlisted strength of the regular Navy to 232,000. This was an increase from a regular Navy strength of 145,000 established on 8 September 1939, when the President declared a "Limited National Emergency." The President had authority to move the 232,000 figure to 300,000 when he declared an "Unlimited National Emergency" and it was towards this objective that he was being nudged by the Director of War Plans.

It was another three weeks, 22 May 1941, before the Chief of Naval Operations signed the detailed request to the President, covering the "thirty

---
[33] Turner.
[34] *Ibid.*
[35] DWP to CNO, OP–12–VED, letter, Ser 050712 of 29 Apr. 1941.

transports, freighters and tankers" that Turner mentioned to Mr. Hopkins. Fourteen additional combat loading transports were specifically requested.

In the Atlantic Ocean, at this time, the Navy had but three transports fitted for combat loading, and in the Pacific Ocean but three more, with a total of six more transports being converted. The Army had four transports fitted for combat loading in the Atlantic and none in the Pacific with four more transports converting. There were eight more Army or Navy transports not fitted for combat loading, which according to CNO's memorandum "were required to support our existing overseas garrisons with equipment and replacement personnel."[36]

This letter produced an approval, on 24 May 1941, for the construction or acquisition of 550,000 tons of auxiliary shipping. Final approval also was received in the first part of May from the President for the transfer of one aircraft carrier, three battleships, four cruisers and 18 destroyers to the Atlantic from the Pacific, a transfer he had originally approved and then in large part rescinded in early April.[37]

Finally, in mid-April 1941, the Director of War Plans drafted, the CNO signed, and the President had with great skill, strengthened, clarified, and approved a "Project for Western Hemisphere Defense Plans." This project required the strengthening of the Atlantic Fleet, and soon emerged as WPL–50. Presumably, Mr. Harry Hopkins had helped in this and in all these other matters.[38]

TO THE AZORES OR ICELAND

At the same time as these desirable actions were taken by the President, he ordered the Army and the Navy to be prepared to seize the Azore Islands by 22 June 1941. Since the Joint Plan for this operation showed a need for 41 combat loaded transports and cargo ships, the inadequacy of the CNO request of May to the President for only 14 additional combat loading transports was soon apparent. However, when the Azores seizure was cancelled about 4 June 1941, it does not seem, from the official records located, that any new request went out from the Director of War Plans for more

---

[36] (a) OP–12B memorandum of 6 May 1941, subj: Army Navy Transports available in May 1941; (b) CNO to President, memorandum, Ser 059412 of 22 May 1941.

[37] (a) CNO to CINCPAC, OP–38, memorandum, Ser 06538 of 7 Apr. 1941; (b) OPNAV to CINCPAC memorandum, Ser 132019 of 13 May 1941.

[38] CNO to SECNAV, memorandum, 16 Apr. 1941. Retyped to include changes made by the President.

transports. Had Rear Admiral Turner more clearly visualized then the pressing needs for transports and tankers in the early stages of World War II, he would have pressed his case for them even harder.[39]

The Army War Plans Division and the Navy War Plans Division were agreed in their dislike for the Azores occupation, but the Army was the more reluctant to see one of its only two amphibiously trained combat divisions disappear over the horizon for occupation duties before a war had even started. The Azores Occupation Force was scheduled to total about 28,000 troops, with the Army and the Marine Corps each to supply 14,000 troops.

The British had 25,000 troops in Iceland and when the President on 4 June 1941, changed the objective from the Azores to Iceland, he assigned the occupation task to the Army. When the Army begged off temporarily, the Marines received the nod on 5 June 1941, and a 4,000-man Marine brigade sailed in four transports and two cargo ships via Argentia, Newfoundland on 22 June 1941.

It was not until September 1941 that sizable Army forces arrived in Iceland and took over command and, during the next five months, relieved the Marines and assumed the duties of the United States Forces in Iceland.

Rear Admiral Turner was in the White House again during the week of 16 June 1941 in connection with the Iceland occupation, but no report of this visit has been located in the files. Presumably, however, it strengthened his favorable impression of Mr. Harry Hopkins.[40]

In July, he also had business with the nation's top political authorities. As Mrs. Turner described it:

> Kelly had a very exciting day. First the Vice President asked him for lunch. There were just the two of them, and Mr. Wallace wanted to ask a lot of questions. Later Admiral King, Admiral Stark, the Secretary and Kelly all had a conference with the President. . . .
>
> The burning question now is what are the Japs going to do, and what we will do?[41]

STATE OF MIND—MAY 1941

One thing that continually irritated the Director of War Plans in the first months of 1941, was what he labeled the "Army planners defensive atti-

---

[39] Turner.

[40] Robert E. Sherwood, *Roosevelt and Hopkins, An Intimate History* (New York: Harper and Brothers, 1948), p. 302.

[41] Mrs. RKT to Lucile Turner, letter, 18 Jul. 1941.

tude." [42] In May, therefore, he persuaded the Chief of Naval Operations to sign an official letter to the Chief of Staff which contained these critical words:

> 9. No plans whatsoever exist for Joint Overseas expeditions, nor for naval cooperation with Army effort in support of Latin-American Governments.
> 10. If the United States is to succeed in *defeating* the Axis forces, it must act on the offensive, instead of solely on the defensive.[43]

HAIRBRAINED SCHEMES OF THE PRESIDENT

Admiral Turner also recalled that:

> Stark spent a lot of time knocking down the hairbrained schemes of the President in regard to the Navy.[44]

When Admiral Stark was questioned in regard to this, he smiled and said:

> Maybe I wouldn't call them hairbrained schemes, but there were many I didn't believe sound and we did spend a lot of time trying to prove this, or provide better alternatives, or determine just what would be needed to carry the project out. The President had a great habit of 'trying one on the dog.' [45]

During the 1941 period of German consolidation of position in Central Europe and the Balkans and prior to the German invasion of the Soviet Union on 22 June, the question as to where they would hit next was a constant one. The value to the Germans of certain pieces of real estate to facilitate their movement towards the Americas, particularly South America, was evident, and this generally raised the question of its prior seizure or reenforcement by American arms. Sooner or later the President would drop a remark in regard to it, and then the pressure would be on the War Plans Division for an estimate on such a situation or for a plan to meet it.

Immediately after the President had directed the relief of the British forces in Iceland, the War Plans Division drafted a memorandum to the Secretary of the Navy for signature by the CNO on the strategic value to the United States, of Iceland, the Azores, the Canary Islands, the Cape Verde Islands, and French West Africa.[46]

---

[42] Turner.
[43] CNO to COS, OP–12–VED, letter, Ser 058212 of 22 May 1941, subj: Analysis of plans for overseas expeditions.
[44] Turner.
[45] Stark.
[46] CNO to SECNAV, OP–12–VED, letter, Ser 067012 of 10 Jun. 1941.

The memorandum started out with:

> Before the United States embarks on any program of the occupation of overseas positions in the Atlantic, I wish to bring to your attention certain strategic aspects of the various positions named. . . .

The memorandum then discussed the subject under two conditions:

> a. Great Britain in the war and,
> b. Great Britain defeated.
>
> Were the United Kingdom to be forced out of the war, it would be strategic folly for the United States to attempt to hold Iceland [and] . . . . out of the question for the United States to try to hold the Canary Islands.

With the United Kingdom still in the war, Iceland and the Azores were important, but the Cape Verde Islands much less so.

> It would be essential that we be able at all times, to exert a strong naval and air effort along the line Natal—Dakar, which would be impossible were our Fleet to be pinned to the defense of outlying positions further North.

Another Presidential throw-out of April 1941 held up to the strong light of reason by Turner would have initiated a

> northern cruise by units of the Pacific Fleet . . . (a striking group of one aircraft carrier, a division of heavy cruisers and one squadron of destroyers, with tankers as necessary), to proceed from Pearl to Attu, Aleutian Islands then to Petropavlovsk in Siberia for a three-day visit.

The War Plans Officer recommended "that the cruise not be made at present." [47]

Before the year 1941 was out, the President was suggesting using naval aircraft carriers to deliver aircraft to Russia. This was deemed "inadvisable" by the War Plans officer since it incurred "risks which I consider cannot be justified." It was pointed out that the Japanese had eight carriers in the Pacific and United States had but three, and that:

> you will recall my recently telling Kimmel and Hart to execute preliminary deployments, and to go on the alert in view of a possible break with Japan.[48]

The original letter to the President on this matter as drafted by Turner and as modified and then signed by Stark showed some difference in Stark's and Turner's appraisal of Japan's intentions or at least of the willingness of these officers to bring their appraisals to the attention of the President.

---

[47] DWP to CNO, memorandum of 10 Apr. 1941, subj: Project for northern cruise by units of Pacific Fleet.

[48] CNO to President, letter, Ser 0132812 of 14 Nov. 1941, subj: Delivery of Aircraft to Russia. Preliminary Draft of this letter.

Turner wrote that Kimmel and Hart had been alerted "against an attack by Japan." Stark softened that to "against a possible break with Japan," a very great difference when one considers the Pearl Harbor attack.

THE ATLANTIC CONFERENCE

The Atlantic Conference was held in Argentia Harbor, Newfoundland, from 10–15 August 1941. Rear Admiral Turner was one of the very small working naval staff that accompanied Admiral Stark to the conference. There were only two from War Plans, Turner and Commander Forrest Sherman, Chief of Naval Operations in 1950–51.

According to Mrs. Turner:

> Kelly had two weeks leave granted and we were to leave on [August] first. Two nights before he came home and said that he couldn't go. . . .
>
> He says Churchill is splendid, very simple and easy to approach and very much smaller than his pictures show.
>
> Everything is such a mess though, and no leadership. . . . I am so glad Kelly got to go and he had a fine two weeks rest.[49]

BRITISH-AMERICAN PACIFIC PLANNING

The Atlantic Conference had broad effects in both the War and Navy Departments on their planning for future contingencies. It cracked the door to Combined Planning with the British, but U.S. Naval planners proceeded very cautiously, insofar as the Pacific Ocean was concerned.

A letter which Rear Admiral Turner wrote to Rear Admiral V. H. Danckwerts of the British Joint Staff Mission in Washington is informative in regard to the status of Combined Planning with the British in early October, 1941. It also illustrates the security consciousness of the Chief of Naval Operations.

> In reply to the reference [Your secret letter No. 107/41 of Sept. 25, 1941] you are informed that we have given very careful study to the Admiralty's proposals for a new Far East Area agreement as shown in ADB-2. . . .
>
> While neither the Army nor the Navy has reached a final decision, at the present time they are inclined to believe that, until such time as a really practicable combined plan can be evolved for the Far East Area, it will be better

---

[49] Mrs. RKT to Lucile Turner, letter, 18 Aug. 1941.

to continue working under an agreement for coordination of effort by the system of mutual cooperation. . . .

As a matter of fact, the military situation out there has changed considerably since last Spring, and will change more after the United States reenforcements, now planned, arrive in the Philippines. The Army has a rather large plan of reenforcements, and the Navy expects, in January, to send out there six more submarines, one more patrol plane squadron, and two squadrons of observation-scout planes.

* * * * *

I think you have no need for fears that the Pacific Fleet will remain inactive on the outbreak of war in the Pacific. You can reassure the Australians on this point. I regret, however, that in the interests of secrecy, I shall be unable to show you the U. S. Pacific Fleet Operating Plan—Rainbow No. 5 (Navy Plan 0–1). Naturally, we would expect to exchange appropriate information of this nature were we both at war in the Pacific, but the Chief of Naval Operations believes, at present, that knowledge of the details of the Operation Plans should be held by a very small number of persons—a view which the British Chiefs of Staff apparently share, as we are never informed concerning the details of projected British operations.[50]

ADVICE DISREGARDED OR SOFTENED

The Director of War Plans, back on 19 July 1941, in a long memorandum to the Chief of Naval Operations had recommended that "trade with Japan not be embargoed at this time."[51] But, on 26 July 1941, just seven days later, the President announced an embargo on the export of petroleum and cotton products to Japan.

After the President had done what Rear Admiral Turner thoroughly believed would cause Japan to see war as the only solution open to her continued development of the Greater East Asia Co-Prosperity Sphere, he continued to advise his military senior to try to persuade the President not to take steps which would bring on that war in the near future. As late as 5 November 1941, in drafting a memorandum to the President for Admiral Stark to sign, commenting on a State Department proposal to send United States troops to China, he warned that:

> undertaking Military operations with U. S. forces against Japan to prevent her from severing the Burma Road . . . would lead to war.

---

[50] Rear Admiral Turner to Rear Admiral V. H. Danckwerts, RN, letter, A16–1/EPB/Ser 011512072 of Oct. 1941, Strategic Plans, ABDA–ANZAC File 1941–1942.

[51] (a) DWP to CNO, memorandum, 19 Jul. 1941; (b) U.S. Department of State, *Foreign Relations of the United States,* 1941 (publication No. 6325), Vol. IV, pp. 839–40.

He urged

> that the despatch of United States armed forces for intervention against Japan in China be disapproved, [and] that no ultimatum be delivered to Japan.[52]

On 25 November 1941, Turner drafted a despatch to the Commander in Chief of the Asiatic Fleet for release by the CNO, which contained the words:

> I consider it probable that this next Japanese aggression may cause an outbreak of hostilities between the U.S. and Japan.

Admiral Stark took this message to the President—who changed the releasor to himself—and softened the judgment words "probable" to "possible" and "may" to "might," and he added the bad guess: "Advance against Thailand seems the most probable."

A photostat of the original despatch appears on pages 178–9, together with a memorandum from the President's Naval Aide, which indicates that both the CNO and the Army Chief of Staff (COS) were willing to drop the statement that war with Japan was "probable."

The Beardall memorandum to the President showed the ever present reluctance of the military heads of the Armed Forces to accept the unwanted but logical conclusion of events, and a reluctance to tell appropriate responsible outpost officials of such a conclusion.

WILL JAPAN ATTACK THE UNITED STATES? THE SOVIET UNION?

The Director of War Plans drafted the 24 January 1941 letter, approved by the Chief of Naval Operations, and signed by the Secretary of the Navy to the Secretary of War, which said in the first paragraph:

> If war eventuates with Japan, it is believed easily possible that hostilities would be initiated by a surprise attack upon the Fleet or the Naval Base at Pearl Harbor.[53]

When the President made the decision that on 26 July 1941 the United States would impose economic sanctions against Japan, Rear Admiral Turner

---

[52] Gerow and Turner, Memo for President of 5 Nov. 1941, subj: Estimate Concerning Far Eastern Situation.

[53] *Hearings*, part 1, SECNAV to SECWAR, letter, 24 Jan. 1941, p. 279.

ROUGH DRAFT

DECLASSIFIED

November 25, 1941 President

FROM: ~~The Chief of Naval Operations~~   TO: ~~Commander in Chief, Asiatic Fleet.~~ High Commissioner

~~THE PRESIDENT DIRECTS THAT YOU DELIVER THE FOLLOWING PERSONAL MESSAGE FROM THE PRESIDENT TO THE US HIGH COMMISSIONER TO THE PHILIPPINES TOGETHER WITH A PARAPHRASED COPY OF MY 272005 QUOTE~~

~~I AM REQUESTING~~ ADMIRAL HART ~~TO~~ DELIVER TO YOU A COPY OF A DESPATCH WHICH WITH MY APPROVAL THE CNO AND THE COS ADDRESSED TO THE SENIOR ARMY AND NAVY COMMANDERS IN THE PHILIPPINES X IN ADDITION YOU ARE ADVISED THAT THE JAPANESE ARE STRONGLY REENFORCING THEIR GARRISONS AND NAVAL FORCES IN THE MANDATES IN A MANNER WHICH INDICATES THEY ARE PREPARING THIS REGION AS QUICKLY AS POSSIBLE AGAINST A POSSIBLE ATTACK ON THEM BY US FORCES X HOWEVER I AM MORE PARTICULARLY CONCERNED OVER INCREASING ~~TRUCULENCE~~ OF JAPANESE LEADERS AND BY CURRENT SOUTHWARD TROOP MOVEMENTS FROM SHANGHAI AND JAPAN TO THE FORMOSA AREA X PREPARATIONS ARE BECOMING APPARENT IN CHINA FORMOSA AND INDO CHINA FOR AN EARLY AGGRESSIVE MOVEMENT OF SOME CHARACTER ALTHOUGH AS YET THERE ARE NO CLEAR INDICATIONS AS TO ITS STRENGTH OR WHETHER IT WILL BE DIRECTED AGAINST THE BURMA ROAD THAILAND MALAY PENINSULA NETHERLANDS EAST INDIES OR THE PHILIPPINES X I CONSIDER IT ~~POSSIBLE~~ THAT THIS NEXT JAPANESE AGGRESSION ~~MAY~~ CAUSE AN OUTBREAK OF HOSTILITIES BETWEEN THE US AND JAPAN XX I DESIRE THAT AFTER FURTHER INFORMING YOURSELF AS TO THE SITUATION AND THE GENERAL OUTLINES OF NAVAL AND MILITARY PLANS THROUGH CONSULTATION WITH ADMIRAL HART AND GENERAL MACARTHUR YOU SHALL PRESENT MY VIEWS TO THE PRESIDENT OF THE PHILIPPINE COMMONWEALTH AND INFORM HIM THAT AS ALWAYS I AM RELYING UPON THE FULL COOPERATION OF HIS GOVERNMENT AND HIS PEOPLE X PLEASE IMPRESS UPON HIM THE DESIRABILITY OF AVOIDING ~~ANY~~ PUBLIC PRONOUNCEMENT OR ACTION THAT MIGHT MAKE THE SITUATION MORE DIFFICULT XX ~~I WOULD APPRECIATE EXPRESSION OF YOUR VIEWS AS TO THE ATTITUDE OF THE PRESIDENT AND PEOPLE OF THE COMMONWEALTH AND AS TO OTHER~~

(page one of two)

Turner-drafted despatch to Commander in Chief of the Asiatic Fleet, with President Roosevelt's changes.

```
November 25, 1941
FROM: CNO                TO: CINCAF

CONT'D

~~XXXXXX PERTINENT TO THE PRESENT CIRCUMSTANCES XX MIGHT ASSIST
ME IN THE FORMULATION OF FUTURE POLICY X PLEASE TRANSMIT THESE
VIEWS THROUGH ADMIRAL HART AS I CONSIDER THE NAVY CIPHER IS BROKEN
XXX XX SECURE THOUGHT~~
```

[signature]

Copy to: Op 12
          War Plans Division, U. S. Army
          (no other persons to receive copies)

(page two of two)

> THE WHITE HOUSE
> WASHINGTON
>
> November 25, 1941.
>
> SECRET
>
> MEMORANDUM FOR THE PRESIDENT:
>
> Admiral Stark suggests that if you wish only a short dispatch it can stop after the word "PHILIPPINES" in the 6th line (where the red dot and doubled pencilled lines are).
>
> Both Admiral Stark and General Marshall agree that the portion between the double pencilled lines might better be left out in order to avoid stirring people up, if you desire.
>
> Both Admiral Stark and General Marshall think that you may not wish to use the sentence, "I consider it probable that this next Japanese agression may cause an outbreak of hostilities between the United States and Japan."
>
> In the fourth line from the bottom General Marshall suggests deleting the word "ANY", to which Admiral Stark agrees, and in the 3rd line from the bottom, the word "SINCE" seems to add clarity.
>
> BEARDALL

Beardall memorandum to the President.

moved from agreeing with the Director of Naval Intelligence that Japan would not attack the United States to the following position:

> I believed it would make war certain between the United States and Japan.[54]

This 1945 testimony was in full agreement with the written forecast which Turner and McNarney had jointly made in December 1940.

The Director of Naval Intelligence (Wilkinson) with quite contrary

---
[54] *Ibid.*, part 4, p. 1945.

opinions to those of Rear Admiral Turner, in late 1945 testified and manfully and honestly stuck to what his December 1941 opinions had been:

> In fact, I did not think an attack would be made on any United States objective, but I thought that the Japanese would pursue a course of successive movements, infiltration, trying the patience and temper of the Anglo-Saxon nations without actually urging them into war.[55]

On 11 July 1941, about three weeks after Germany had attacked the Soviet Union, the Director of War Plans wrote a memorandum to the Chief of Naval Operations in which he recommended precautionary measures against Japan, saying it was his conclusion that:

> During July or August, the Japanese will occupy important points in Indo-China, and will adopt an opportunistic attitude towards the Siberian Maritime Provinces. Japanese action against the Russians may be expected if the Stalin regime collapses, and Russian resistance to Germany is overcome.
> Since it is inexcusable for military forces to be unprepared for an attack, even if the chances for an attack appear small, it is recommended that steps be taken to place our Army and Navy forces in the Far East in an alert status to be achieved as far as practicable within about two weeks.[56]

From this date on Admiral Turner stated that his belief and expressed advice to Admiral Stark was that Japan would attack in Siberia only if Germany defeated the Soviet Union. Up until June 1941, he had believed that Japan might well attack the Soviet Union, without the assistance of Germany.

On 31 July 1941, Admiral Stark had written to the Captain of the Fleet Flagship, Captain C. M. Cooke, U.S. Navy:

> As you probably know from our despatches, and from my letters, we have felt that the Maritime Provinces are now definitely Japanese objectives. Turner thinks Japan will go up there in August. He may be right. He usually is. My thought has been that while Japan would ultimately go to Siberia, she would delay . . . until there is some clarification of the Russian-German clash.

Admiral Turner's later reaction to Stark's letter was that when the Germans had just started into the Soviet Union on 22 June 1941, and carried all before them, he had expressed the opinion that Japan would move against the Soviets in August. But as the Soviets slowed the Germans, and as the Japanese started funneling troops southward toward Indo China, he backed away from this belief. This is supported by his written rebuttal of a contrary prognosis made by Commander Walter Ansel in the War Plans daily summary on 22 September 1941, and quoted later.

---
[55] *Ibid.*, p. 1776.
[56] DWP to CNO, OP–12–CTB, memorandum, 11 Jul. 1941.

The Army G-2 (Chief of Intelligence) had written, as late as 1 November 1941, that Japan would attack Siberia when the ratio of Japanese troops in Kwantung Province, Manchuria, to Soviet Union troops in Siberia reached 3 to 1, and suggested steps to help China and the Soviet Union.[57] It is believed correct to say that, at this time, the Director of War Plans thought the attack would not take place unless Germany defeated the Soviets in the West. Such a defeat was in the really questionable stage by 1 November 1941.

By 27 November 1941, when Rear Admiral Turner participated with many others in the drafting of the memorandum for the President to be signed by General Marshall and Admiral Stark, he found no problem in concurring with the statement:

> There is little probability of an immediate Japanese attack on the Maritime Provinces. . . .

WHO HAS THE BALL? INTELLIGENCE OR WAR PLANS?

Over the years, and occasionally in print, there has been much made of the fact that the Director of Naval Intelligence had to work through the Director of War Plans in sending out to the Commander in Chief of the Pacific Fleet:

> specific information, which information might require action by our Fleet or by our naval forces.

The Director of Naval Intelligence said this system was required so that this information

> would not be in conflict with his [the DWP's] understanding of the naval situation, and the operations for which he was responsible.[58]

This requirement irritated greatly some of the second echelon officers in the Office of Naval Intelligence. They objected both to the Navy system which channeled political action initiating intelligence through the War Plans Office, and to the strong-minded officer who occupied the billet of Director of War Plans.

As for the Navy system, Admiral Ingersoll pointed out:

> Our organization was not like Military Intelligence and that the estimate of the situation should be prepared by the War Plans Division, although the data

---

[57] *Hearings*, part 14, p. 1361.
[58] (a) A. A. Hoehling, *The Week Before Pearl Harbor* (New York: W. W. Norton & Co., 1963), p. 64; (b) *Pearl Harbor Hearings*, part 11, p. 5364.

for the part 'Enemy Intentions' naturally would have to be based on data and information gathered by 'Naval Intelligence.' [59]

Or to state the case as Admiral Turner saw it while testifying at the Congressional Pearl Harbor Hearings:

> VICE CHAIRMAN: Now, would it be fair to assume that from the standpoint of the real effect on operations that the War Plans Division had the highest responsibility for the advice given to the Chief of Naval Operations?
>
> ADMIRAL TURNER: That is correct.
>
> VICE CHAIRMAN: The Office of Naval Intelligence was largely charged with the responsibility of disseminating information?
>
> ADMIRAL TURNER: That is correct.[60]

Following the Pearl Harbor Attack, there were those who felt that this "system" had let the Navy down. The critics claimed a prescient ability for the Office of Naval Intelligence. There were also some who remembered various unsuccessful bouts with Rear Admiral Turner, and claimed that his mid-1941 belief that Japan would attack the Soviets in Siberia had diverted his attention away from alerting the Fleet in regard to an attack on Pearl Harbor.

It is worth a brief look to see if the administrative arrangements had not been as they were, whether ONI would have alerted CINCUS late on 6 December when the decoded version of 13 parts of the 14-part final Japanese diplomatic communication before committing the Pearl Harbor Attack became available.

It is well to remember that this long-winded final statement of Japanese diplomatic position created a communication problem for the Japanese, as well as a decoding problem for the cryptographers in Washington.

The extensive Japanese point of view of the deteriorating Japanese-United States relations was crammed into 13 despatches. The 14th despatch stated what the United States must do to meet Japanese conditions and ended up by breaking off the current negotiations. The 15th despatch directed that the contents of the prior 14 despatches should be delivered to the United States State Department at exactly 1 p.m. on Sunday, 7 December 1941. The 15th despatch acquired public identification as the "One o'clock despatch" during the Congressional investigation into the Pearl Harbor attack.

In Washington, the first 13 parts of the Japanese despatch were crypto-

---
[59] *Ibid.*
[60] *Ibid.*, part 4, p. 1983.

graphically decoded, and their translations circulated all together, during the evening of 6 December.

The 14th Japanese despatch was decoded and circulated routinely during the forenoon of 7 December, the limited list of viewers seeing it at various times. Many, including Rear Admiral Turner, saw it subsequent to the 15th despatch.

The 15th despatch received special expeditious delivery service, when it had been cryptographically decoded and translated. It was available to Admiral Stark around 9:30 a.m. the morning of 7 December 1941.

FIRST, THE DIRECTOR OF NAVAL INTELLIGENCE

Actually, the Director of Naval Intelligence, Rear Admiral Wilkinson, was not uneasy or agitated by the first 13 parts of the decoded Japanese despatch. He testified that he

> did not consider it a military paper . . . and there was nothing particularly alarming in those [13] parts. . . . The fact that [in the 15th part] there was a certain time for the delivery was not significant to me. . . . I thought that the message was primarily of concern to the State Department rather than the Navy and the Army.[61]

There is nothing, absolutely nothing in these statements or available elsewhere from testimony of the DNI (Director of Naval Intelligence) that he had any desire to send this Japanese summation of position, a Japanese white paper, on to Pearl Harbor to Admiral Kimmel.

When Rear Admiral Wilkinson saw the 14th part of the Japanese diplomatic message on Sunday morning, his reaction, as he remembered it, was:

> They were fighting words, so to speak, and I was more impressed by that language than by the breaking off of negotiations, which of itself might be only temporary.[62]

The DNI, being physically present in the Office of the CNO, on the morning of 7 December 1941 said:

> I believe that I advised that the Fleet should be notified, not with any question of attack on Hawaii in mind, but with the question of imminence of hostilities in the South China Sea.[63]

At this hour, the Japanese message (the 15th part) telling the Japanese

---

[61] *Ibid.*, pp. 1874–75.
[62] *Ibid.*, p. 1766.
[63] *Ibid.*, p. 1766.

Ambassador in Washington to present the message to the Department of State exactly at 1 p.m. Sunday, 7 December, had not been circulated.

NEXT, THE DIRECTOR OF WAR PLANS

When the Director of War Plans saw the first 13 parts of the diplomatic end of negotiations despatch, he

> considered the despatch very important but as long as those officers [Ingersoll and Wilkinson] had seen it, I did not believe it was my function to take any action.[64]

When Rear Admiral Turner was shown the one o'clock message in Admiral Stark's office about noon, he

> recognized its very great importance and asked him [Stark] if anything had been done about it. He told me General Marshall was sending a dispatch, and I did nothing further about it because I considered that would cover the situation.[65]

Even had he seen the 14th part at this time or prior thereto, the Director of War Plans thought:

> It was not my business to send that dispatch out. I consider that that was entirely the province of the Office of Naval Intelligence. . . . It was no evaluation whatsoever. My office never sent out information.[66]

In summary:

The first 13 parts of the Japanese despatch inspired neither the DNI nor the DWP to believe it should go to the Fleet.

The 14th part inspired the DNI with a belief that it should go to the Fleet. The CNO did not carry through on the recommendation. The DWP did not receive the 14th part of the "end of negotiation" despatch in his own office until after the attack.

The "one o'clock" despatch inspired both the DNI and the DWP to make recommendations for the CNO to send an advisory to the Fleet. The delay in sending this advisory, in part at least, was due to a reluctance of Admiral Stark to accept and immediately act personally and dramatically on the recommendation of these two of his subordinates, both united and voicing the same opinions by calling Admiral Kimmel on the voice-scramble telephone which was on his desk.

---

[64] *Ibid.*, p. 1924.
[65] *Ibid.*, p. 1924.
[66] *Ibid.*, p. 2025.

The "system" had no effect on the failure to alert the Fleet on Pearl Harbor Day, or the day before, insofar as the decoded Japanese diplomatic dispatches are concerned.

The reflections of nearly 20 years that had passed since Rear Admiral Turner had dominated War Plans and looked down his nose at the Office of Naval Intelligence, and most of its minions, had not changed the man's conviction that the 1941 division of responsibilities within the Office of the Chief of Naval Operations for advising the Chief of Naval Operations (and preparing papers or despatches for dissemination) in regard to the over-all international situation which might involve the United States in war, and thus bring War Plans into effect, was properly a duty of the Director of War Plans rather than the duty of the Director of Naval Intelligence.

The decision that this was the way it would be was made by Admiral Stark upon the official appeal of Rear Admiral Alan G. Kirk, the Director of Naval Intelligence prior to Wilkinson. The Vice Chief of Naval Operations and the Director of War Plans were also present in his office and participated with Kirk in the discussion.[67]

Rear Admiral Turner's belief that Admiral Stark's decision was an "interpretation" of the written instructions for the conduct of business in Naval Operations rather than a marked qualification or change of the written instructions was largely confined to himself and his immediate seniors.

The Director of Naval Intelligence interpreted the decision to be that ONI was not to disseminate to the Operating Forces any estimates of enemy, or prospective enemy, intentions the natural reaction to which would seem to call for immediate acts of war on the part of our Operating Forces, and so passed this interpretation on to his relief, Rear Admiral Wilkinson. The following testimony during the Pearl Harbor hearing bears this out:

> GESELL: In other words, you had the responsibility to disseminate, but where you reached a situation which led you to feel that the information disseminated might approach the area of a directive, or an order to take some specific action to the recipient; then you felt you were required to consult War Plans, or the Chief of Naval Operations?
> WILKINSON: Exactly.[68]

The belief of one of Rear Admiral Wilkinson's best subordinates, Commander Arthur H. McCollum, the Head of the Far Eastern Section in the

---

[67] *Ibid.*, pp. 1730, 1834–39, 1865, 1924–27.
[68] *Ibid.*, p. 1731.

Foreign Intelligence Division of ONI, was that the change was very much broader in effect, if not intent, and that

> the function of evaluation of Intelligence, that is, the drawing of inferences therefrom, had been transferred over to be a function of the War Plans Division.[69]

It is apparent from the above quotes that the policy decision of the Chief of Naval Operations created a gap between what the Director of War Plans thought ONI should and would send to the Operating Forces and what the most important intelligence subordinate of the Director of Naval Intelligence actually felt that the Office of Naval Intelligence was responsible for distributing to the Fleet. The McCollum interpretation of the decision was widely held at the second and third levels in ONI and since they believed that they had been robbed of one of their main functions, evaluation, they sulked in their tents. The essential close cooperation between War Plans and Intelligence suffered.

This War Plans-Intelligence gap was indirectly widened by the special handling of decoded enemy despatches called "magic" and later "ultra." These despatches were handled, and were known to be handled, in a completely separate and distinct manner from routine secret information. By and large, second echelon War Plans officers received more of the droppings from these despatches than second echelon ONI officers, except for the Far Eastern Section of ONI.

There also was a direct wedge widening the War Plans-Intelligence gap, which was the security precaution exercised by limiting strictly the distribution, within the Office of Naval Operations, of secret despatches relative to preparations or readiness of the Operating Forces for war. Such secret despatches were generally limited in their distribution to the head of each major subdivision of the Office of the Chief of Naval Operations and his immediate subordinate. This left out many, many seasoned officers at the working levels. Again second and third echelon officers in ONI were less likely to learn of these despatches than similar officers in War Plans.

It is suggested by this scribe that Admiral Stark's decision in this Intelligence-War Plans dispute, not only was based upon what he considered the correct channel of advice to him regarding "enemy intentions," but from whom, in this difficult and touchy area, he would be apt to receive the sounder advice.

It is also suggested that there undoubtedly was an administrative error

---

[69] *Ibid.*, p. 3388.

by both Turner and Kirk in failing to reduce to writing the CNO policy decision in regard to advising the CNO and the Operating Forces of political action initiating intelligence, so that the dividing line between the duties and procedures of Naval Intelligence and War Plans in this area was clearly etched. It is only necessary to state that on 12 December 1941 War Plans proposed such an arrangement.[70] This is described in some detail later on.

Although markedly different in personality, there was a complete rapport between the CNO and his Director of War Plans.

Admiral Stark said:

> Every time I think of Kelly Turner, or anyone mentions his name, I warm a little about the heart. . . .
>
> Probably nobody in Washington had a better understanding of the Japanese situation than Kelly did.[71]

Vice Admiral Turner testified in 1944:

> Admiral Stark's opinion and mine on the situation were very close together from the spring of 1941 on.[72]

Admiral Turner later added:

> The Navy was lucky to have as CNO a man as knowledgeable in world politico-military matters, and who had the ear of the President, the State Department and the Congress at the same time. His *Plan Dog*—which became *Rainbow Five*—showed his great perception. . . .
>
> He was a wonderful senior to me.[73]

War Plans issued strategic summaries every other day. ONI made daily strategic estimates, at least up until 24 October 1941, when for reasons never pinpointed, they were voluntarily discontinued. The probable reason can only be guessed, but it could be hazarded that they were dropped because they required a very considerable effort and ONI became aware that they were not heeded in the councils of the great.

Both ONI and War Plans evaluated the semi-raw "magic." But neither the Director of Naval Intelligence nor the Director of War Plans evaluated the bitter end Japanese diplomatic messages as presaging an attack on United States Territory at the "directed" delivery hour of the diplomatic despatch.

The Director of War Plans was not shown the 14th part, "the end of negotiations" despatch, until after the attack, so he in no way controverted

---

[70] DWP to CNO, memorandum, OP–12–VDS(SC)A8–1 of 12 Dec. 1941.
[71] Stark.
[72] Pearl Harbor *Hearings*, part 26, p. 84.
[73] Turner.

the recommendation of the Director of Naval Intelligence to the Chief of Naval Operations in this regard.

It can be said quite objectively that Admiral Stark did not receive the best of advice (that is advice so strongly and cogently expressed that he, following the advice, did in fact alert Admiral Kimmel) from either of these two major intelligence evaluating subordinates in the immediate hours prior to the Pearl Harbor Attack.

Rear Admiral Wilkinson, right up until 7 December 1941, did not think the Japanese would attack any United States Territory. On 6 December 1941 he had informed Turner that Turner was "mistaken in the belief that Japan would attack a United States objective." [74]

> QUESTION: Did you ever talk to Admiral Turner as to whether or not he thought of an attack upon Hawaii?
> WILKINSON: No, sir.
> QUESTION: But at least you had no thought of an attack upon Hawaii?
> WILKINSON: No, sir.
> QUESTION: And that continued on until after the attack?
> WILKINSON: Yes, sir.

Rear Admiral Turner thought the chances of a raid in Hawaii were about 50–50, but no specific mention of this belief appeared in the final version of any despatch which he drafted for the CNO to send to CINCPAC, although it has been asserted such a warning was in one of the preliminary drafts.[75]

And when Admiral Stark, on three different occasions, sought assurances that CINCPAC did in fact have decryption facilities, and the despatches available to him so he could read the Japanese diplomatic traffic, Rear Admiral Turner brought back the wrong information from the Director of Naval Communications. This was either through poorly phrased inquiries to Rear Admiral Noyes, since Noyes stated that he thought Turner was talking about traffic analysis (called radio intelligence), or through ignorance of Noyes in regard to what the decryption capabilities were at Pearl Harbor. The latter has been generally suspected, since (1) the Pearl Harbor Naval Radio Station routinely did not even copy Japanese diplomatic traffic, because there was no decoding machine in Pearl Harbor essential to change the coded Japanese diplomatic message into Japanese language, even if it was copied, and (2) because Rear Admiral Noyes's testimony showed ignorance of

---

[74] *Pearl Harbor Hearings*, part 4, pp. 1776, 1869, 1984.
[75] Hoehling, *The Week*, p. 55.

several other aspects of Pearl Harbor's decryption capabilities and systems. For example, he stated:

> . . . and as I learned from listening to Commander Rochefort's testimony, they [Pearl Harbor] could not read another code, which was necessary.

And:

> In listening to Commander Rochefort's testimony, I was surprised that there would have been anything intercepted in Hawaii [by the Army] that the Navy could translate that was not immediately passed to the Navy.[76]

As 7 December 1941 drew closer, a special despatch from Naval Communications on 28 November 1941 directing the cryptanalysis unit at Pearl, in addition to its normal tasks in regard to Japanese naval traffic, to undertake certain specific copying and decryption of lower echelon despatches in the diplomatic field, made clear that someone in the Office of Naval Communications was in no doubt as to the normal scope of activities of its Pearl Harbor unit regardless of what the Director of Naval Communications, Rear Admiral Leigh Noyes, knew or didn't know.

WARNINGS TO THE OUTPOSTS SOFTENED

Admiral Turner remembered, with some pride and much regret, that when he drafted the 16 October 1941 despatch directing CINCPAC, CINCAF, and CINCLANT to take preparatory deployments, his original wording had included the phrase that there "was a distinct probability Japan will attack Britain and the United States in the near future." He regretted that this wording had been toned down by his Joint Board seniors to "there is a possibility that Japan may attack these two powers." [77]

Admiral Turner also was proud of his authorship of "This is a war warning," in the 27 November 1941 despatch and regretted that his wording "war within the next few days" was changed to "an aggressive move by Japan is expected within the next few days." [78]

> There was discussion as to whether or not the opening sentence should be included in this despatch. I recall that Vice Admiral Turner was firmly of the opinion that it should be included.[79]

---

[76] (a) Pearl Harbor *Hearings*, part 4, pp. 1975–76; part 10, pp. 4714–15, 4722–23; (b) Wohlstetter, *Warning and Decision*, pp. 172, 173, 179, 181, 182.

[77] (a) Turner; (b) *Hearings*, part 26, p. 277.

[78] Turner.

[79] *Hearings*, part 26, p. 295. Testimony of Captain John L. McCrea, Special Assistant to Admiral Stark.

Planning for War, 1940-1941

The phrase "This is a war warning" was under attack from below as well as from above. Admiral Turner also regretted that the phrase "in any direction" included in the draft of the 24 November 1941 despatch was left off the sentence "an aggressive move by Japan is expected within the next few days" of the War Warning Despatch three days later.[80]

TURNER'S OPINIONS REGARDING PEARL HARBOR ATTACK

No real purpose can be served by a detailed rehashing of Admiral Turner's testimony before the Congressional Inquiry into the Pearl Harbor Attack, which extended from Wednesday, 19 December 1945, through Friday, 21 December 1945. Upon the conclusion of this testimony, the Vice Chairman wished All Hands a "Merry Christmas" and adjourned the hearings for ten days over the Holidays. Turner had already testified before the Roberts Commission, the Hart Inquiry, and the Navy Court of Inquiry. Despite a sharp examination by Admiral Hart during his inquiry and again by several Congressmen and the Committee Counsel during the Congressional Inquiry, a reading indicates no substantive change in the Turner testimony.

The Vice Chairman Representative Jere Cooper, Democrat of Tennessee, noted:

> My impression is that much of the information you have given us is somewhat in conflict with other information we have received during the hearing.[81]

However, since these conflicts were never pin-pointed by Congressman Cooper, this appears to have been a thrust in the dark. Admiral Turner was only the eighth military witness of over 240 to testify. From a close reading of the previous seven military witnesses' testimony, the basis of Congressman Cooper's statement is not readily apparent.

The only major differences of testimony on matters of substance between Admiral Turner and any of the more than two hundred succeeding military witnesses were (1) in the testimony of Rear Admiral Leigh Noyes, former Director of Naval Communications, on the question as to whether CINCUS was receiving the same decrypted information as was being received by the CNO, and (2) in the testimony of Captain McCollum that he took away from the office of the Director of War Plans, sometime between 1 December and 4 December 1941, his much marked up draft of an ONI message to alert CINCUS to the danger of imminent war.

---

[80] Turner.
[81] *Hearings*, part 4, p. 1982.

Admiral Turner testified that the Director of Naval Communications stated that CINCUS had the same decrypted information as the CNO. Rear Admiral Noyes, however, testified that he did not remember making any statement to the Director of War Plans that would imply that Admiral Kimmel had the means of decrypting "purple" (diplomatic) traffic and that he believed that Rear Admiral Turner had "traffic analysis" and "decrypted traffic" confused in his mind.[82]

Admiral Turner testified that Captain McCollum had torn up his own draft despatch. Captain McCollum testified that the marked up draft message was returned by him to the desk of the Director of Naval Intelligence and there it lay, until it disappeared into the circular file.[83]

WHERE WILL JAPAN ATTACK THE UNITED STATES?

Admiral Turner testified:

> I was satisfied in July that we would be at war with Japan certainly within the next few months. I believed during the first part of December that the probability of a raid on Hawaii was 50–50. . . . I felt that there were two methods, two strategic methods that the Japanese Fleet would pursue. One was to go down and base their fleet in the Mandates with the hope that our fleet would go after them, and they would be in a good position. The other was to make a raid on Hawaii. There were two major methods and without evaluating it too much, too greatly, I thought it was about a 50-50 chance of the raid on Hawaii.[84]

SUNDAY MORNING REACTIONS

Rear Admiral Turner's normal reaction to a real crisis was never frenzied, never violent. It was a rapid fire, clear, logical mental application to the problem at hand and rapid fire, clear, logical dictum of things to be done by those surrounding him, at either higher or lower levels. This did not happen on Sunday morning, 7 December 1941, in the Office of the Chief of Naval Operations.

Had Rear Admiral Turner viewed the situation in the true light of a real crisis, Admiral Turner says that he would have immediately urged Admiral

---

[82] *Ibid.*, part 4, pp. 1975–77, 2029; part 10, pp. 4714–15.
[83] *Ibid.*, part 4, pp. 1975, 2029; part 8, pp. 3388–90.
[84] *Ibid.*, part 4, p. 2007.

Stark to pick up the scramble telephone used for classified messages and call Admiral Kimmel.

> It wouldn't have done much real good at that late hour, but we might have had the ships buttoned up tight, all the guns manned and ready and a few planes in the air. . . . There would have been a lot of satisfaction from the Navy's point of view in that, and some lives might have been saved.[85]

But this did not happen. The only conclusion to be drawn is that Turner did not appreciate the reality of the time crisis.

When Admiral Turner was asked why he did not urge Admiral Stark to grab the scramble telephone and wake up Admiral Kimmel, he said:

> Why weren't I and a lot of others smarter than we were? I didn't put all the Two's and Two's together before Savo to get four. Maybe I didn't before Pearl, but damned if I know just where. If Noyes had only known that Kimmel couldn't read the diplomatic Magic. If Kimmel had only sent out a few search planes. If the words 'Pearl Harbor' had only survived the redrafting of the warning messages. . . . You find out the answers and let me know.[86]

OP-12 DAILY SUMMARIES

The fact that there were "Daily Summaries" and evaluations of information being prepared in various offices of the Navy Department was looked into by the Congressional Committee for the Pearl Harbor Attack.

A check of the Daily Summaries and evaluations prepared in the War Plans Division indicates that these were read by the Director of War Plans. Filed next to the 22 September 1941 summary, there is an undated RKT handwritten note addressed to Commander Walter Ansel, who was the actual drafter in OP-12.

> These are getting too long. You have drawn some premature and unwarranted conclusions, I believe. RKT

Another summary is marked in RKT's handwriting:

> "Bad History" and again I can't see this at all.

These comments lend credence to the thought that the evaluations appearing in other summaries were fairly close to RKT's opinions or they would have been marked up.

---

[85] Turner.
[86] Turner.

If the Director of War Plans was "obsessed" about Siberia and, if his subordinates could only "reflect his views," there is little in the OP-12 Daily Summary to support the charge. During September, October, November, and up to 7 December 1941 there are only three direct mentions of Siberia in the OP-12 Daily Summary and Evaluations. These are:

On 22 September 1941:

Far East

Japanese forces available for action against Siberia now number close to 500,000. She is *reaching a concentration of strength that would permit action there.*

On 24 October 1941:

Siberia

Neither side has the superiority to warrant an offensive—but this may change if Siberia forces are moved west to re-enforce European Russia.

On 14 November 1941:

Siberia

Japanese strength may be equal to the task, although the profit is small. Japanese better course is to await further developments in the Russian-German campaign with the ensuing possibility of Russian deterioration. Probability: awaiting opportunity.

Whether the comment of the RKT note quoted above and found filed next to the 22 September summary, referred to Commander Ansel's underlined prognosis of action in Siberia is unknown, since the 22 September 1941 summary bears no other mark. But the RKT comment is at least a logical one from his known position at this time.

A reading of the summaries and evaluations indicate that in fact they appeared less than every other day, to be specific on 3, 5, 7, 10, 12, 14, 17, 19, 21, 24, 26, and 28 November and 1, 3, and 5 December. They appear to be 80 percent a compilation of information with a limited ration of prognosis of the future.

POST PEARL STRATEGIC SUMMARIES

Those senior officers in Naval Operations who had had a responsibility in the matter, all felt that they had given CINCPAC adequate general alerts to ensure the Pacific Fleet's state of advanced readiness for actual war. It probably was a natural reaction to the real failure of the Office of the Chief

Planning for War, 1940–1941

of Naval Operations to, in fact, alert CINCPAC to be ready to meet a time crisis on 7 December 1941, that an effort was made in December 1941 to delineate more clearly, and in writing, the duties of the various divisions of Naval Operations in relation to alerting Commanders in Chief Afloat.

Rear Admiral Turner had his way for a short time, and on 12 December 1941, the following procedure was approved for the War Plans Division. It would issue as of 0800 daily:

> 1. 'The Naval Situation' for the President, giving all operational and related information affecting the United States Navy.
> 2. 'Bulletin for Naval Commanders,' giving a short summary of the 'The Naval Situation' and deleting information which should not go out of Washington.
> 3. 'A Daily Navy Department Situation Communique' . . . giving such information as should be made public.

Fortunately, Rear Admiral Turner's seniors did not buy for long this proposed diversion of effort by the War Plans Division from its primary business. The Secretary of the Navy put the Office of Public Relations back into the press release business, and the Director of Naval Intelligence, by 15 December 1941, was:

> endeavoring to collect, collate, and reconcile all enemy information in the Department, whether directly by despatch or whether obtained by other means (including Magic) and to send "out this information to the Commanders-in-Chief." [87]

The memorandum of 12 December 1941 is important only to show Rear Admiral Turner had a blind spot in regard to the duties of the Office of Naval Intelligence and that he believed the War Plans Division should transmit:

> To the principal naval commanders periodic secret bulletins giving information designed to keep these commanders up to date with regard to essential secret information in order that they can take appropriate military measures.[88]

This was bound to include information of the enemy, a proper chore for ONI.

By 28 January 1942, Rear Admiral Turner recommended in writing that the Joint Intelligence Committee should "put out a daily paper that meets

---

[87] (a) CNO to all Divisions of Operations, memorandum, OPBC Ser 604913 of 18 Dec. 1941, subj: Information for Release to Press; (b) DNI to DWP, OP–16, memorandum, Ser 91163416 of 15 Dec. 1941, subj: Dispatches concerning Intelligence of Enemy Activities.

[88] DWP to CNO, memorandum, OP–12–VDS(SC)A8–1(A&N), 12 Dec. 1941.

the President's needs," [89] and that the President should receive neither Army nor Navy individual situation reports. This was a long step forward.

1941 JITTERS

The state of jitters in Washington among Army and Naval officers after the Pearl Harbor attack is now hard to appreciate. On 12 December 1941, the Director of War Plans recommended to the Chief of Naval Operations that he inform the President in writing that

> the Chief of Naval Operations expects a raid on either Puget Sound or Mare Island Navy Yard today between 9 and 11 a.m. Washington time.[90]

And on the previous day the Joint Intelligence Committee, being far removed from the British cross channel weather in the winter months, had informed the President:

> Because of initial reverses received by the United States in Hawaii, the probability that Germany may be seriously considering an early invasion of the British Isles must be borne in mind.[91]

STATE OF FEMALE MIND—DECEMBER 1941

In a letter to her sister-in-law, written the Tuesday before Pearl Harbor, Mrs. Turner gave interesting insight as to the state of her mind at this time:

> The Japanese situation looks terrible. Kelly had to stay on the phone all day Sunday [30 November 1941] but wasn't called to the office. . . . Kelly feels fine and is still keeping up his morning walks, and it is dark when he starts out.[92]

In Mrs. Turner's next letter of Sunday, 7 December she wrote:

> Well, war has come and though we feared it, we all hoped Japan would not have the nerve. They phoned Kelly to come to the Department a little before eleven. He had no idea, because he was very calm. Said he knew what it was about and would be back before long. We were to have dinner at the Chevy Chase Club, so I had let Sadie go. He phoned we were at war before the radio broadcast it, and didn't know when he would get home. . . .

---

[89] DWP to CNO, memorandum, 28 Jan. 1942.
[90] DWP to CNO, memorandum, OP–12–VDS(SC)A8–1(A&N) of 12 Dec. 1941, encl. (B).
[91] JIC Daily Summary, Noon Thursday, 11 Dec. 1941.
[92] Mrs. RKT to Miss LLT, letter, 2 Dec. 1941.

I hate to be selfish, but for once, I am glad he is in Washington.
I sit here surrounded by Japanese things plus dogs.[93]

DISCLOSURE OF THE VICTORY PROGRAM

Just two days prior to the Pearl Harbor Attack, the Director of War Plans was busy writing a long four-page letter to the Chief of Naval Operations giving available information in regard to the apparent disclosure to the Chicago *Tribune* and the Washington *Times Herald* of the United States' "Victory Program."[94] The letter had to be personally written, because the Director of War Plans was the actual custodian of the only copy of the "Victory Program" in the War Plans office. The "Victory Program" was a Joint Board paper with individually prepared logistics requirements for the Army and Navy.

This investigation, called a witch hunt by some, and regarding which Turner disclaimed all responsibility for himself and his subordinates of disclosure to the press, had considerable influence in strengthening the belief in the Navy Department of the correctness of limiting secret information to those "who need to know."

Kelly Turner had long been an advocate of this "need to know" policy. Admiral King, when Commander in Chief of the Atlantic Fleet, had not been privy to the ABC-1 Staff agreements of 27 March 1941 which provided for American-British collaboration short of war and for full scale military cooperation in time of war. In Admiral King's opinion, Turner guarded his secret knowledge "with supererogatory zeal."[95]

JOINT CHIEFS OF STAFF

Before entering into the amphibious phases of World War II and the part played in the amphibious Pacific campaigns by Richmond Kelly Turner, a brief record of his influence on the overall United States military command structure for the war seems appropriate.

On 28 January 1942, the Joint Board discussed the creation of a Super Joint General Staff, which had been recommended in broad terms by the

---
[93] Mrs. R.KT to Miss LLT, letter, 7 Dec. 1941.
[94] RKT to CNO, OP-12-CTB, letter, Ser 0140112 of 5 Dec. 1941.
[95] *King's Record*, p. 328.

Navy's General Board. The Joint Board on this date had two planning agencies, the Joint Planning Committee, and a subsidiary, the Joint Strategic Committee.

As head of the Navy's War Plans Division, Rear Admiral Turner on 1 February 1942, was one of the two members of the Joint Planning Committee, the other representative being Brigadier General Dwight D. Eisenhower, of the War Department's War Plans Division. These two officers were handed the hot potato of determining what sort of a new military command organization should be established in the United States to provide direction and cohesion in running the United States military part of the war. The task was assigned on 28 January 1942, and the report of these two officers was submitted on 27 February 1942.

Brigadier General Eisenhower recommended that a Joint General Staff of fifteen members be created directly under the President and headed by a Chief of Staff who would be responsible only to the President. The General Staff would provide for coordination of both operations and logistic support, and be responsible for strategy and the employment of military forces, but would not command them. Command would be vested in Theater Commanders.

Rear Admiral Turner recommended the organization of:

1. A Joint Chiefs of Staff Committee, consisting of the Chief of Naval Operations, the Chief of Staff of the Army, the Commander in Chief of the U. S. Fleet, and the Commanding General, Army Field Forces.
2. A Joint training system for higher command levels of both Services, stating this to be an essential prior to the acceptance of Joint Annual Staff.

In order to obtain unity of command, he recommended

3. Assigning command responsibilities in campaign areas and on frontiers to an officer of the Service with primary interest and awareness of the anticipated problems.

The Joint Board did not accept either proposal when they were presented at the 16 March 1942 meeting and both proposals reached the President. The President, who perhaps was wary of Brigadier General Eisenhower's solution (which reflected General Marshall's desires), thinking it might dilute his own prerogatives as Commander in Chief to direct the war effort in some detail, eventually accepted what was in effect Rear Admiral Turner's proposal. All three of the Turner recommendations became realities during the war, two early in 1942, Joint Training in 1944. But President Roosevelt also accepted part of Brigadier General Eisenhower's proposal when Admiral William D. Leahy became Chief of Staff to the President in July 1942, although without command authority or responsibility, and without a staff.[96]

Thus Richmond Kelly Turner became the father of the Joint Chiefs of Staff.

---

[96] (a) Joint Board, meeting minutes, 28 Jan. 1942, 16 Mar. 1942; (b) JB, Ser 742; (c) Report, Joint Planning Committee to Joint Board, 27 Feb. 1942, encls. (A) and (B).

CHAPTER VI

1941 Naval Organization, Doctrine and Landing Craft Developments for Amphibious War

BACKGROUND

The *Ark* made the first recorded amphibious movement which is known to have had a deadline for both the building of the craft and for the departure of the passengers.

Those who have seriously studied the Books of the Old Testament of the Bible in an effort to determine the year date of the Flood, and the first peril-packed overwater movement to a distant shore, vary widely in their estimates of the exact Zero Hour and Zero Year of the Flood. A hundred years ago the Flood was guestimated by Biblical Scholars as between 2327 B.C. and 3155 B.C., a mere 800 year span.[1] Modern scholars and archeologists have been a bit more chary of naming years, but declare the Flood happened about 4000 B.C.[2]

In any case, this happened a long time ago. The *Ark's* building and departure was during a time of great stress, and the travelers embarked were a mixed lot generally unaccustomed to going to sea, and a bit untrained for foreign duty. They seem to have had only a hazy idea of where they were going and how they were going to get there. These characteristics almost seem inherent in amphibious operations and certainly were not unknown to our early amphibious operations in World War II.

As to the craft in which the first historically important overwater movement was made, the *Ark*, 525 feet long, 87½ feet abeam, and 52½ feet high, was a sizeable craft and far larger than the World War II LST (Landing Ship Tank), 327 x 50 x 40 feet. Its building probably was no less ex-

---
[1] Samuel W. Barnum, *A Comprehensive Dictionary of the Bible* (New York: D. Appleton & Co., 1868), p. 174.
[2] Werner Keller, *The Bible as History* (New York: William Morrow & Co., 1956), ch. 3.

pedited and its overwater movement no less surrounded by the perils of the deep than many a World War II amphibious craft.

But the *Ark* served its purpose well, and this without benefit of Congressional watch dog committees, expediters, super expediters, and public relations men, all of whom swarmed over the amphibious craft of the 1941–1945 era.

LANDING CRAFT

Since the man this study is about, Kelly Turner, played no personal part in the technical development of landing craft and landing boats until he arrived in the South Pacific, the interesting, colorful controversial pre-1942 development story of landing craft and landing boats will not be detailed herein. But some coverage is essential to understand World War II amphibious warfare.

The story of the development of landing boats during the pre-World War II period, and the early days of that war reads differently, depending upon which book is read.[3] Since most of the books devoting any large amount of space to this phase of the amphibious story have been sponsored by the Marine Corps or written by Marines, it is perhaps natural that the work and contributions of the Army and of various other parts of the Department of the Navy, as well as the contributions of some of our Allies, and the Japanese enemy, have not been stressed. And it is natural that the long years of trial and error before really usable landing craft were developed have been emphasized.

As Admiral Turner wrote to the Director of Naval History in 1950:

> I know that the Marines have engaged the 'Princeton History Group' to write a book about amphibious warfare as affecting the Marines, to cover the period from 1925 to 1945. I received the advance drafts of several chapters for comments. I spent 3 or 4 hours almost daily for several weeks in research

---

[3] (a) U.S. Congress, Senate, Special Committee Investigating the National Defense Program, 78th Cong., 2nd sess., Senate Report 10, part 16, March 4 [legislative day February 2], 1944; (b) Jeter A. Isely and Philip A. Crowl, *U. S. Marines and Amphibious War, Its Theory, and Its Practice in the Pacific* (Princeton: Princeton University Press, 1951), ch. 3, pp. 57–71; (c) Frank O. Hough, Verle E. Ludwig, and Henry I. Shaw, Jr., *Pearl Harbor to Guadalcanal*, HISTORY OF U.S. MARINE CORPS OPERATIONS IN WORLD WAR II (Washington: Historical Branch, Headquarters U.S. Marine Corps, 1958), ch. 3; (d) Lieutenant General Holland M. Smith, USMC, "Development of Amphibious Tactics in the U.S. Navy," *Marine Corps Gazette* (Jun. 1946–Mar, 1947), 5 parts; (e) General Holland M. Smith and Percy Fuch, *Coral and Brass* (New York: Charles Scribner's Sons, 1949).

and the preparation of corrections, but finally gave up. The work of the Princeton Group is so full of errors and generally so bad historically that I couldn't stand to work on it any longer. In my opinion, unless the book is changed entirely as to concept and material, it will be a very bad book. It may start serious controversies. Certainly, it will do the Marines no good in the long run, because it is so one-sided.

I believe it would be an equally bad thing for the Navy to publish a similar controversial book, written from the point of view of the Navy alone. No one Service invented amphibious warfare. The Marines contributed much (patterned on Japanese methods) to its development in recent years. But so also did the Navy, including Naval Aviation. Furthermore, beginning in 1940, the Army contributed a great deal. We should not forget that the biggest operation of all—Normandy—was very largely a U.S. Army and British affair. The Marines had nothing to do with the European and African landings, and the U. S. Navy was not the controlling element.[4]

To add a bit of balance to the story about landing craft, it is perhaps well to recall that in Fiscal 1935 the total research and development appropriation of the whole Department of the Navy, which included the Marine Corps, was only $2,544,000.00 of which two million dollars were for aviation. Even for Fiscal 1940, the Congress provided the Department of the Navy only $8,900,000.00 for research purposes.[5] The Bureau of Construction and Repair was only one among four technical bureaus in the Navy Department having significant research and development needs. Landing craft, controlled largely by the Bureau of Construction and Repair, was only one of the significant fields to need research funds.

Its successor, the Bureau of Ships, quite properly has not thought it a worthwhile effort to scour up a document which might show the actual dollars allocated to landing craft research and development in 1935 or 1940, or any intervening year. An informed, but completely unofficial and unsubstantiated estimate, by one who has researched this field in the records of Naval Operations during these years, is that $40,000 was available in 1935 and $400,000 in 1940.[6]

---

[4] RKT to Chief of the Division of Naval Records and History, letter, 20 Nov. 1950, subj: Isely-Crowl, *U.S. Marines in Amphibious War*.

[5] (a) Office of Naval Research, "U. S. Naval Research and Development in World War II," (manuscript) part I, pp. 100, 144; (b) Rear Admiral J. A. Furer, *Narrative History of Office of Coordinator of Research and Development*, 28 Jul. 1945, para. 47.

[6] (a) "History of Continuing Board for the Development of Landing Vehicles" (manuscript); (b) Rear Admiral J. A. Furer, USN, "Logistics of Fleet Readiness," The Fleet Maintenance Division (First Draft Narrative) in *United States Naval Administration in World War II;* (c) BUC&R to CNO, letter, 582-3(15)(DW), 6 Jan. 1937; (d) Lieutenant Colonel B. W. Gally, USMC, "A History of Fleet Landing Exercises" (manuscript), USS New York, 3 Jul. 1939; (e) Lieutenant

It is very difficult in the 1960s, with research and development money running out of everyone's ears, to recreate the parsimonious atmosphere of the 1920s and 1930s, when the research and development dollars available were exasperatingly few (and percentagewise of total naval appropriations only a shadow of today's percentage) and each development dollar was guarded as though it was the Navy's last.

NAVY RECOGNIZES LANDING CRAFT PROBLEM

Many have claimed to be responsible for the idea of a separate type of craft to land troops on a hostile shore. However, one of the earliest powerful and effective urges during the period between the World Wars for the Navy to develop a useful landing boat, to train personnel to man them, and to provide gunfire support for the Landing Force, came from Admiral Robert E. Coontz (Class of 1885), Commander in Chief of the United States Fleet, and later Chief of Naval Operations.

He wrote in 1925:

> In connection with landing operations, the Commander in Chief offers the following comments and suggestions:
>
> a. That the use of the regular ships' boats for the purpose of transporting landing parties ashore, when opposition is to be encountered, is a hazardous undertaking and little likely to succeed. He considers it of utmost importance that experiments be continued with a view to determine what type of boat is best for this purpose.
>
> b. Consideration of the necessity that ships detailed to cover and support landing operations be equipped with guns permitting high angle fire. This he believes is necessary in order that the Landing Force will not be denied artillery support at a time it is most essential.
>
> c. That a landing operation is likely to result in disaster if the officers in charge of the boats are not experienced in their duties.[7]

In regard to amphibious operations in the Fleet in 1924, Admiral Coontz wrote:

> The participation of the Marine Corps Expeditionary Force with the Fleet in the winter maneuvers of 1924 afforded the first real opportunity for determining the value of such a force to the Fleet.[8]

William F. Royall, USN, Landing Boat Officer, Atlantic Squadron, "Landing Operations and Equipment," *USS New York*, Aug. 1939. Contains 38 photographs of landing boats developed during 1936–1939 period.

[7] CINCUS, A.R., 1924, paras. 79, 114.
[8] CINCUS, A.R., 1924, para. 76.

The Advanced Base Defense Force became the Expeditionary Force in 1921 and then the Fleet Marine Force in 1933.

A plain recognition by the Navy of the need for action in the landing craft field was the creation, on 12 January 1937, by the Secretary of the Navy, acting upon recommendation of the Chief of Naval Operations, of the "Navy Department's Continuing Board for the Development of Landing Boats for Training in Landing Operations." Besides the Marine Corps, the Bureau of Construction and Repair, the Bureau of Engineering, and the Office of the Chief of Naval Operations supplied members; and the Assistant Director of the Fleet Maintenance Division in Naval Operations acted as the senior member of the Board. Captain (later Vice Admiral) W. S. Farber was a long-time senior member of this Board. His presence on it insured effective action at the OPNAV level.[9]

At the same time, the Commander in Chief, United States Fleet, was directed to organize a similar coordinating board to supervise and report, with recommendations, on actual landing boat experiments and tests which were conducted by the Fleet. The two Boards were to keep each other fully informed. A "Five Year Special Boat Plan" was drawn up in Naval Operations and on the premise that the Navy Budget Officer and the Federal Budget Officer, and the Congress would approve, the Navy hoped to spend a total of $1,264,000 in the fiscal years 1938, 1939, and 1940 on developing and procuring landing boats.[10]

Under this program, 18 different landing craft were designed and built by naval and civilian shipyards, and were ready to be Fleet tested during Fleet Landing Exercise Five in early 1939. On 27 September 1940 and again on 25 July 1941, the Chief of Naval Operations directed the inauguration in the Fleet of large-scale training programs for landing craft boat crews on board transports and cargo ships.[11]

The creation of these Boards, ashore and afloat, the assignment by the Bureau of Construction and Repair to its War Plans Desk of the duty of handling all landing craft matters at the working level, and the orders to the Fleet for training programs for landing craft boat crews indicate a basic

---

[9] Office of the Chief of Naval Operations, Naval History Division, *United States Naval Administration in World War II*, "Fleet Maintenance Division." p. 93.

[10] (a) SECNAV to CINCUS, letter, Ser 370112 of 12 Jan. 1937; (b) CINCUS to Commander Training Squadron, Scouting Force, letter, Ser 421 of 4 Feb. 1937.

[11] (a) CNO to Commander Transport Train, Atlantic, letter, OP–22–A, P16-3/S82-3/Ser 86622 of 27 Sep. 1940, subj: Landing Boat Crews; (b) CNO to Commander Train Atlantic and Commander Base Force Pacific, letter, OP–22–A(SC)P16-3, Ser 074422 of 25 Jul. 1941, subj: Boat Crews for Special Landing Boats.

appreciation and proper placement of the landing craft problem during the pre-World War II period.

LANDING CRAFT TANK (LCT)

A further small bit of history about the tank lighter is added by Captain Roswell B. Daggett, USN (Retired), who as a lieutenant commander to captain headed up the Bureau of Construction and Repairs (later the Bureau of Ships) "Small Boat" desk in the Design Division from 1937–1943. He was the designated relief for the War Plans officer when that officer was absent, as he was, in the hospital, in January 1939. From this date until 1943, Daggett's assignment and efforts were in the landing craft field.

He writes the following:

> We [Bureau of Ships] had a flush deck tank lighter building which had freeing ports and was the prototype of the larger lighters which held 5 tanks and proved very successful during the war. But none of the small ones had neared completion, when one day, I would say in the late Spring of 1941, I was called to Marine Headquarters and told the President had told the Marines to be ready to take the Azores by 1 July, and what could be done to get them tank lighters and landing boats. At that time, I was on excellent working terms with Higgins and knew him to be a 'Go-Getter.' I telephoned Higgins. He said he had a lighter built for South American use, and they wanted him to take his pay in bananas. He was not disposed to do so. Higgins suggested that I come down to New Orleans, and see, if together, we could work something out with the lighter he had.
>
> I flew down that night and remained a few days. We designed a ramp for the bow and Higgins proceeded to alter the lighter. We named the lighter 'Patches' because he did not have enough steel to alter it without using many small scrap pieces. He did the work in the middle of a roped off New Orleans street next to his shop, as he had no available working space under cover.
>
> In a short time, I returned and we tested the lighter on Lake Pontchartrain. The ramp leaked like a sieve and required modification.
>
> That was the story of the birth of the Higgins lighter.
>
> Higgins produced this one and a few more, and some landing boats (many without engines) which were shipped to Norfolk by rail to meet the Marines' date, and then not used for the operation planned.[12]

AMPHIBIOUS DOCTRINE

In the long history of maritime warfare, the navies of the world considered water movement of troops to a foreign shore one of their regular wartime

---
[12] Captain Roswell B. Daggett, USN (Ret.), to GCD, letter, 8 Jan. 1960.

tasks, but one for which up until the early years of the Twentieth Century, they made minimal advance preparations until the event was upon them.

The thought that this problem of overwater movement of troops and then assault on a foreign shore would be with our Navy in a large way in any war with Japan started to percolate through the Navy in the immediate post-Spanish American War era. Advance Base work was studied at Newport, Rhode Island, in 1901 and a permanent Advanced Base School was established at New London, Connecticut, in 1910—and moved to Philadelphia in 1911.

Starting in 1902–1903, Marines became occasional to frequent participants in the annual winter Fleet cruises as the backbone and sinew, first of an Advanced Base Defense Force, then of an Expeditionary Force, and finally of a Fleet Marine Force.

After the British-French unhappy experience at Gallipoli, Turkey, the study of that World War I amphibious campaign became a regular part of the Naval War College course at Newport.[13] In the early 1930s students at the Naval War College were taught that the lessons of Gallipoli to remember included:

    1. Do not fail to provide for clear command channels to all forces of all Services and arms involved, and for a single forceful overall commander.

    2. Be sure, by detailed orders, properly distributed at all echelons, that All Hands' know what the objectives are, who does what when, and where the coordinating levels of command are located.

    3. Do not attack prematurely with insufficient forces.

    4. Provide for supplies and equipment to be stowed aboard ship in reasonable proximity to the order in which they will be used or needed ashore, i.e., later called combat loading.

It can be presumed that Captain Turner learned these and other amphibious lessons during his three years at the Naval War College, and that their possible violation in the Guadalcanal campaign bothered him. It may be that Commander Nimitz and Captain King, who attended the Naval War College in 1923 and 1932, respectively, paid particular attention to the above first lesson of Gallipoli, for they implemented the principle of clear command channels and forceful commanders during World War II.

It also can be presumed that in addition to these "do's and don'ts," Captain

---

[13] (a) Captain W. D. Puleston, USN, *The Dardanelles Campaign* (Annapolis: U. S. Naval Institute, 1926). (b) Lieutenant General Holland M. Smith, USMC "The Development of Amphibious Tactics in the U.S. Navy," *Marine Corp Gazette* (July 1946–February 1947).

Turner learned that there were two prerequisites for a successful amphibious operation:

1. Secure lines of communications to the area of conflict.
2. Command of the sea and air around the objective.

If these two basic conditions could be satisfied, then it was essential to:

   a. select landing areas with both hydrographic conditions favorable to the Navy and terrain conditions favorable to the Marines or Army troops.
   b. deceive the enemy as to the chosen areas of debarkation as long as possible.
   c. by air bomb and naval gun fire prepare the landing area, so the troops could prepare to seize them with confidence.

Once the troops landed and seized the beachhead it would be necessary to:

   a. land artillery rapidly, and to secure any high ground commanding the beachheads so as to permit a quick shore-side build up of logistic support.

And one could then look forward to:

   b. an early transfer of the conflict from amphibious to land warfare.

All this and much more was set forth in Fleet Tactical Publication No. 167, the Bible of Landing Operations Doctrine published by the United States Navy in 1941.

THE NAVY ORGANIZES SHORESIDE FOR THE AMPHIBIOUS TASK AHEAD

Prior to June 1942, there were no distinctive "amphibious ships and craft" sub-sections in the various divisions of Naval Operations, except in the Fleet Training Division. Up to that time, amphibious matters were handled by the various "Auxiliary vessels" sub-sections.[14]

On 24 February 1940, there were only 35 personnel landing boats in the whole Navy built for that purpose and these were of the 30-foot type. On this same date there were 5 tank lighters and 6 artillery lighters. However, the following extract from a report from the Joint Planning Committee to the Joint Board and jointly signed by R. K. Turner and L. T. Gerow showed the vastly improved status on 30 September 1941:

---

[14] CNO Organizational Rosters, 1941–1942.

4. *a.* The Navy procurement situation is as follows:

Type	Delivered	Under Construction	Funds Available; Awaiting Contract	Total Authorized
Landing Boats				
Regular 36 ft.	400	197	367	964
Ramp 36 ft.	88	100	0	188
Tank 45 ft.	20	30	0	50
Regular 30 ft.	133	0	0	133
45 ft. Tank Lighters	26	71	0	97
47 ft. Tank Lighters	0	0	131	131
45 ft. Artillery Lighters	13	12	0	25
Rubber Boats	0	898	496	1394
Amphibian Tractors	0	300	188	488

b. The Army has procured 80 36-ft. landing boats and 8 45-ft. tank lighters.

c. A triangular division, Army or Marine Corps, should be prepared to land nine combat teams from combat unit loaded transports. Thirty-nine (39) 36-ft. landing boats (or the equivalent in other types to provide 1350 boat spaces) and seven (7) tank lighters are required per combat team. Hence the above program is sufficient for three triangular divisions, as shown in the following table:

	Available or Under Procurement			Maximum Requirements	
	Navy Total	Army Total	Grand Total	for 3 Triangle Divisions	Reserve
Landing Boats					
Regular 36'	964	80	1044	1044*	0*
Ramp 36'	188	0	188	9*	179*
Tank 45'	50	0	50	0	50
45' Tank Lighters	97	8	236	189	47
47' Tank Lighters	131				
Landing Boats					
Regular 30'	133	0	133	0	133
45' Artillery Lighters	25	0	25	0	25
Amphibian Tractors	488	0	488	300	188
Rubber Boats	1394	0	1394	0	1394

* The employment in varying combinations of the 36' ramp boats, the 30' boats, and the placing of troops in Amphibian Tractors or Rubber Boats will change these figures and correspondingly alter other figures in these columns.

> 6. The Navy Department has also initiated steps to procure an appropriate number of Support Landing Craft, patterned after a British design, and whose purpose is to furnish fire support against beach defenses and aircraft during landing operations."

By 23 October 1941 there were 30 large transports, needing 816 landing boats, and 11 AKs needing 80 landing boats, in commission, being procured or converted.[15]

By 30 September 1941, the 36-foot landing craft had been adopted as standard, but their availability had not caught up with the demand.

When the Fleet Training Division was transferred from Naval Operations to the Headquarters of the Commander in Chief on 20 January 1942, there was only an "Amphibious Warfare" desk in the "Instruction" subsection, with a major in the Marine Corps assigned.[16] As the tempo of preparations for amphibious warfare speeded up in the spring of 1942, the need for a large division in COMINCH Headquarters which would draw together and deal with all the operational elements concerned with amphibious warfare became apparent to Rear Admiral Turner.

On 18 April 1942, there was a conference, in COMINCH Headquarters, of the Commanders of the newly established Amphibious Force of the Atlantic Fleet (Rear Admiral Roland M. Brainard) and of the Pacific Fleet (Vice Admiral Wilson Brown). These officers came up with a number of agreed upon principles relating to amphibious organization and amphibious training, and made a number of recommendations which could be summarized in the words "more of everything is needed."

In giving Admiral King his generally favorable endorsement to these principles and recommendations, Rear Admiral Turner added a new and strong recommendation that

> a Joint Army, Navy and Marine section under a Flag Officer, be established in COMINCH Headquarters with specific responsibility to develop material and methods for amphibious forces. These matters are handled by a number of agencies throughout the Department and should be coordinated under one head. This is a large project and requires specialized handling here, as well as in the field. Until such action is taken, it is not believed that we will make satisfactory progress.[17]

---

[15] (a) CNO, OP–12, memorandum, 24 Feb. 1940; (b) DWP to Continuing Board for Developments of Landing Boats, memorandum, 23 Sep. 1941; (c) Joint Planning Committee to Joint Board, JB No. 355, Ser 687 of 30 Sep. 1941, approved by SECNAV, 3 Oct. 1941.

[16] (a) CNO Organizational Roster, Sep. 1941; (b) COMINCH Roster, 27 Jan. 1942.

[17] Turner to Admiral King, memorandum, 22 Apr. 1942 with endorsements thereon.

Rear Admiral Richard S. Edwards, Deputy Chief of Staff, in forwarding Rear Admiral Turner's memorandum wrote:

> The amphibious problem is assuming large proportions. Control is badly scattered in the Department. It should be centralized as Turner suggests. . . .
> I concur that an Assistant Chief of Staff be appointed for this purpose. . . .

Rear Admiral Turner and Rear Admiral Edwards well knew that there was no surer way to arouse Admiral King's wrath than to recommend an increase in officers on his staff or in those "attached to Headquarters." He had forcefully stated in early January 1942, that his staff would be "under 20" and the officers "attached to Headquarters," not more than 200. His personal approval of all new male officer billets was required.[18] So it is not surprising to find that Admiral King on 30 April 1942 vetoed the addition of a Flag officer and a new major subdivision for his staff and wrote on the memorandum:

> O.K. for section under a/CofS/Readiness, but first wish to get concurrence of Gen. Marshall.

It evidently took weeks to get General Marshall's concurrence, for the section (F-26) to handle Amphibious Warfare was not established until 4 June 1942, and then with a complement of only six officers. Several captains, who after detachment became Flag officers with advanced rank, headed up this undermanned and overworked amphibious section in Fleet Readiness (F-46). They included D. E. Barbey and I. N. Kiland. But amphibious problems continued to be handled at a lower level than Rear Admiral Turner considered desirable, or their mushrooming importance warranted.

AFLOAT

On 1 October 1939, when World War II was getting underway in Europe, the Navy had only two large transports (APs) in commission. They operated directly under the Chief of Naval Operations in logistic support of overseas commands, largely in the personnel area. By 15 October 1940, there were two additional large amphibious transports (APs) in commission in the Fleet, the *Barnett* (AP-11) and the *McCawley* (AP-10), and four fast destroyer-type transports.

---

[18] The number of officers on the Staff was 20 from 1 March 1942 until the end of the war. The number of male officers attached to Headquarters reached 181 on 1 January 1943, and was 193 on 1 October 1945, having touched 226 on 1 January 1944. Furer, p. 25.

As late as 22 October 1941, Rear Admiral Turner stated to the Joint Board that the number of large amphibious transports (APs) required by the Navy under the War Plans was only 36.[19] At this time the Navy had only 16 APs, all in the Atlantic Fleet. In addition there were five large amphibious cargo ships (AKs) and six destroyer hull transports (APDs) in the Atlantic Fleet, but only two AKs in the Pacific Fleet, making a total of 29 amphibious ships.[20]

In the immediate pre-December 1941 Navy, the amphibious ships, limited in number, were organized administratively into divisions and/or squadrons and assigned to the lowly Train Squadrons, whose primary mission was the logistical support of the Atlantic and Pacific Fleets. As the number of amphibious ships and landing craft grew phenomenally, and as the number of prospective tasks for them multiplied, it was obvious that the amphibious ships should be placed in a separate Type command within the major Fleets, such as had long existed in the Fleets for the aircraft carriers, destroyers, submarines and other ships of a particular character or classification. The Type commander handled matters dealing with personnel, materiel, and basic training.

On 14 March 1942, and 10 April 1942 respectively, the Amphibious Forces of the Atlantic and Pacific Fleets were created in accordance with instructions from COMINCH and in due time all amphibious units within the two Fleets were assigned to them. Organizational rosters issued close to these dates show that there were 12 APs, four AKs and two APDs in the Atlantic Fleet and six APs, two AKs and three APDs in the Pacific Fleet, when the Amphibious Forces were established as separate entities. And this was only four to five months before Guadalcanal.

The designation of the major amphibious types as APs, AKs, and APDs warrants a word of explanation. In the Dark Ages, when the standard nomenclature for the classification of naval ships was first promulgated by the Secretary of the Navy, the Navy had numerous colliers and tugs, but very few cargo ships and no transports. So the basic letter C was assigned to colliers and T to tugs. Later, such other obvious assignments as D to destroyer, H to hospital ship, N to net layer and R for repair ship were made. With the obvious coincident letters all assigned, transports drew P and cargo ships K from the remaining available letters of the alphabet.

---

[19] Joint Board, minutes of meeting, 22 Oct. 1941.
[20] (a) Pacific Fleet Confidential Notice 13CN–41, 1 Oct. 1941; (b) Atlantic Fleet Confidential Memo 10CM–41, 6 Oct. 1941.

At the time of the designating letter assignment, transports and cargo ships were auxiliaries to the combatant ships of the Fighting Fleets and so they also carried the basic A for auxiliary in front of their class-type designation. Thus, an AP was a naval auxiliary and a transport and AK was a naval auxiliary and a cargo ship. Since it became apparent in 1942 that the transports and cargo ships of the Amphibious Forces were anything but auxiliary in carrying the war to the enemy, the A in their designation galled those who served in these ships. The hurt was only partially relieved when early in the war, their designations were changed to APA and AKA and they became Attack Transports and Attack Cargo ships. Few old sailormen could forget that before the war APA officially designated an auxiliary, and an animal transport, while now it still designated an auxiliary, although an "attack transport." As late as 28 February 1944 in his report on GALVANIC, the operation to seize the Gilberts, CINCPAC stated that the operation "involved some 116 combatant vessels and 75 auxiliaries" and listed the larger transports among the auxiliaries.[21]

RESPONSIBILITY FOR AMPHIBIOUS OPERATIONS

It is important to remember that in pre-World War II days and for many months after 7 December 1941, both the United States Army and the United States Navy had overlapping functions in both the overseas movement and assault phases of Joint Overseas Expeditions. Joint Overseas Expeditions included (1) Joint overseas movements and (2) landing attacks against shore objectives. These functions which bore the approval of the Secretary of War and the Secretary of the Navy were set forth in *Joint Action of the Army and the Navy* prepared by the Joint Board in 1927 and revised in 1935.[22]

The general principle which frequently overrode the detailed Service assignment of tasks was known to all. It read:

> Neither Service will attempt to restrict in any way the means and weapons used by the other Service in carrying out its functions.[23]

---

[21] (a) *Ships Data Book*, 1938; (b) CINCPAC, Operations in Pacific Ocean Area, Annex E, para. 2.
[22] *Joint Action of the Army and the Navy*, 1935, para. 18. Hereafter *Joint Action*, 1935.
[23] *Joint Action*, 1935, para. 4(c)(1).

The Army was specifically charged, in connection with Joint overseas movements:

> To provide and operate all vessels for the Army, except when Naval opposition by the enemy is to be expected, in which case they are provided and operated by the Navy.[24]

In October 1940, the Army Transportation Service had fifteen ocean-going vessels, including eight combination troop transports, which carried some cargo, and seven freighters. In mid-December 1940, the War Department received authority to acquire seventeen additional vessels.[25] This addition made the Army's Transport fleet larger than the Navy's Amphibious Force which numbered only 14 transports and eight cargo ships on 18 January 1941 and in late April 1942 had but 18 regular transports attached to the Fleets, 13 working up to join, and seven more projected.[26]

Under War Plan *Rainbow Five,* the Navy was assigned responsibility to

> Provide sea transportation for the initial movement and continued support of Army and Navy forces overseas. Man and operate the Army Transportation Service.[27]

The Navy plans and projects underway in 1941 hopefully provided the first installment of personnel and ships for its assigned tasks in Joint overseas movements, but it had no personnel earmarked or available for the very considerable chore of "Man and operate the Army Transportation Service." Nor, as long as Army troops moved overseas in Army transports, were there naval personnel available or trained to perform the duty set forth in connection with "landing attacks against shore objectives," where the Army was given the task:

> The deployment into boats used for landing, these boats being operated by the Navy [28]

The Navy failed either to adequately plan for or, on the outbreak of war, to adequately undertake these two responsibilities [29] despite the fact that in 1941 "Admiral Turner, Director of War Plans, advocated making the

---

[24] *Joint Action,* 1935, para. 18(b)(1).

[25] Robert W. Coakley and Richard M. Leighton, *Global Logistics and Strategy 1940–1943,* Vol. VIII in subseries *The War Department* of series UNITED STATES ARMY IN WORLD WAR II (Washington: Office of the Chief of Military History, Department of the Army, 1955), p. 62.

[26] Revised U. S. Navy Operating Force Plan Fiscal 1941, dated 18 January 1941, CNO–OP–38– Serial 13738.

[27] WPL 46, May 1941, War Plan, Naval Transportation Service, 8 Jul. 1941.

[28] *Joint Action,* 1935, para. 18c(1)(a).

[29] Julius A. Furer, *Administration of the Navy Department in World War II* (Washington: Government Printing Office, 1959), pp. 718–19.

Naval Transportation Service a going concern" and ready and able to take over the logistic and amphibious duties of the Army Transportation Service.[30]

Consequently, the Navy was in no position to criticize the Army in the early days of the war for moving ahead rapidly in expanding its amphibious capabilities, because it appeared that the Army would not only have to provide the amphibious transports by which it might journey to foreign shores, but the boats and boat crews needed to make the actual landings during European amphibious operations.

The Army and the Navy proceeded as they did because each had primary authority and responsibility in certain areas relating to amphibious operations. However, coordination and standardization of procedures in training for amphibious warfare in the United States was provided for and effected by the Commanders of the Amphibious Forces, Atlantic and Pacific Fleets, and in overseas areas by the Theater Commanders.

This situation promoted competition, basically friendly though knife-edge keen between the two Services. It resulted in rapid progress, some wasteful duplication of effort and spending of money, and tremendous confusion at the soldier and sailorman level, who could not understand, for example, the why of Engineer Amphibian Commands which trained Army boat regiments and soldier "coxswains".

Admiral King, who as Commander in Chief of the Atlantic Fleet was bossman for Fleet Landing Exercise Seven in February 1941, reported on one aspect of this rivalry as follows:

> Two combat teams of the First Division, United States Army, commanded by Brigadier General J. G. Ord, USA, arrived in the Army Transports *Hunter Liggett* and *Chateau Thierry* to take part in the exercise. . . .
>
> . . . [King] soon discovered that they [three Army General Staff Officers] regarded themselves as in a position to criticize the amphibious techniques of the far more experienced Marines. Creeping and walking normally precede an ability to run, and as it seemed to King, that so far as amphibious landings were concerned, the Marines had learned to walk and were beginning to get up speed, while the Army still had to master the art of creeping, he was both amused and annoyed by the attitude of these observers.[31]

Despite this indication of a strong belief that the Marines would function better than the Army in the amphibious arena, Admiral King kept a painfully

---

[30] (a) Charles Snow Alden, "Brief History of the Naval Transportation Service from 1937 to March 1942," 1943, para. 39; (b) R. M. Griffin, "Brief History of the Naval Transportation Service March 14, 1942 to January 12, 1943"; (c) Duncan S. Ballantine, *Naval Logistics in the Second World War* (Princeton: Princeton University Press, 1946), p. 78.

[31] *King's Record,* p. 320–21.

tight rein upon expansion of the personnel of the Navy. Admiral King was also the one who kept the personnel throttle of the amphibious Navy barely cracked in the early days of 1942, thus making impracticable the manning with naval personnel of needed transports, cargo ships and amphibious boats and craft.

Transports with their boat crews were expensive in personnel. Many officers had no great desire to see men who were desperately needed in the explosive expansion of patrol craft and destroyers fighting a seemingly losing battle against the German submarine, diverted into the amphibious arena. Many naval officers believed it would best serve the Navy's war capabilities to let the "expansion minded Army" take over certain amphibious duties and suffer the pains and penalties of that expansion.

When the question of who should be prepared to do what in amphibious warfare was raised in the early months of 1942, the Navy's official position was that amphibious operations in island warfare should be a function of the Navy, and that amphibious operations against a continent should be a function of the Army.[32] The assigned reasons were:

> In the one case, landings would be repeated many times, and continuous Naval support is essential; whereas, in the second case, after the initial landing, the Navy's chief interest would be protection of the line of sea communications.[33]

As late as 29 April 1942, the Army was still proposing that it should be responsible for all amphibious operations in the Atlantic area and the Marines in the Pacific area of operations.[34]

It was not until early February 1943 that the Navy agreed to undertake the amphibious training of boat operating and maintenance personnel to meet future Army requirements and, based on this promise, the Army agreed to discontinue all amphibious training activities in the United States. The control and assignment of amphibian units and amphibious training activities in overseas theaters were left to Theater Commanders to determine. This represented a major advance toward assuring that all amphibious troops and all amphibious craft would have the same fundamental indoctrination in amphibious operations. The historic memorandum providing for this change is reproduced below.[35]

---

[32] JPS 2/1; JPS 2/7 (Joint U. S. Strategic Committee Study on Strategic Employment of Amphibious Forces; JSSC Study No. 24, Organization of Amphibious Forces).
[33] RKT to COMINCH, memorandum, 15 Apr. 1942.
[34] JPS 24.
[35] COMINCH–C/S USA, memorandum, 8 Mar. 1943. See also COMINCH to General Marshall, memorandum, FF1/A16–3/Ser 00224 of 5 Feb. 1942 and C/S USA to Admiral King, 16 Feb. 1943, subj: Army and Navy Amphibious Boat Crews.

MEMORANDUM OF AGREEMENT OF THE CHIEF OF STAFF,
U. S. ARMY, AND THE COMMANDER IN CHIEF, U. S. FLEET AND
CHIEF OF NAVAL OPERATIONS.

This agreement between the Chief of Staff, U. S. Army, and the Commander in Chief, U. S. Fleet and Chief of Naval Operations, confirms and approves the agreement arrived at in conference on March 8, 1943, between representatives of the War Department and the Navy Department, as follows:

a. The Army will discontinue all amphibious training activities except as noted in c below. The Army will retain responsibility for all training, other than amphibious, of Army units designated to receive training under the Navy.

b. The Navy will continue amphibious training of boat operating and maintenance personnel to meet future Army requirements of this nature, and also will train at a later date Army replacements for existing amphibian units if this should become necessary.

c. The 3rd and 4th Engineer Amphibian Brigades (Army), which have been especially organized for shore-to-shore operations in the Southwest Pacific will be retained under Army control and their training completed by the Army pending their movement to that theatre.

d. The control and assignment of amphibian units and amphibious training activities in overseas theatres will be as determined by the theatre commander concerned.

e. Upon completion of the training of the 3rd and 4th Engineer Amphibian Brigades the boats, shops, spares, tools and other facilities, not part of the organizational equipment of these units, shall be transferred to the Navy when and if required by that Service and the Amphibian Training installations and facilities at Camp Edwards, Massachusetts, and Camp Gordon, Johnston, Florida (Carrabelle), will be made available to the Navy for its use. The actual transfer of land is not contemplated.

A survey party with representatives of the Navy Department and War Department (Services of Supply) will be appointed to arrange the details of the transfer.

JOSEPH T. McNARNEY
Lieut. General, U.S.A.
Acting Chief of Staff, U. S. Army

E. J. KING
Admiral, U. S. Navy
Commander-in-Chief, U. S. Fleet
and Chief of Naval Operations

AMPHIBIOUS FORCE COMMAND RELATIONS

When, on 29 April 1942, Admiral King issued his LONE WOLF Plan for the establishment of the South Pacific Amphibious Force, he laid the ground work for a lot of later Marine abuse of Richmond Kelly Turner. This extremely terse and stimulating order, which made possible the successful WATCHTOWER Operation, had this important paragraph:

IX. *Coordination of Command*

a. Under the Commander, South Pacific Force, the Commander of the South Pacific Amphibious Force will be in command of the naval, ground and air units assigned to the amphibious forces in the South Pacific area.

b. The New Zealand Chiefs of Staff are in command of any United Nations units assigned to New Zealand specifically for the land defense of the Commonwealth of New Zealand.[36]

The Commanding General, First Marine Division (Major General Alexander A. Vandegrift, USMC) received registered copy No. 35 of the order. The Commandant of the Marine Corps received five copies.

I have been unable to locate, in the files of COMINCH, any letter of protest or comment from Marine Corps sources in regard to this order. The specific requirements of the order assigning command of the ground and air units to Commander Amphibious Force South Pacific are not mentioned in any of the better known Marine Force accounts of the Marine Corps Operations at Guadalcanal.[37] And yet each of these accounts creates the impression that Rear Admiral Turner was exercising command responsibilities during the WATCHTOWER Operation when he should not have done so.

Rear Admiral Turner's position was that the directive was drafted in a section of the COMINCH Staff headed by a senior colonel in the Marine Corps (DeWitt Peck, later Major General). It was cleared with Marine officers in the Office of the Commandant of the Marine Corps before it was initialed by the top echelon of COMINCH Staff and signed by Admiral King. There were no questions raised in regard to the command relationships, although the draft went through several other changes.[38]

On 13 May 1942, Vice Admiral Wilson Brown, Commander Amphibious Force, Pacific Fleet raised the question of command relationships between his command and that of Commander Amphibious Corps, South Pacific

---

[36] COMINCH, letter, FF1/A3–1/A16–3(5), Ser 00322 of 29 Apr. 1942, subj: LONE WOLF Plan.

[37] (a) Hough, Ludwig, Shaw, *Pearl Harbor to Guadalcanal*, pp. 240, 241, 341–342; (b) John L. Zimmerman, *The Guadalcanal Campaign*, Marine Corps Monograph (Washington: Historical Branch, Headquarters U. S. Marine Corps, 1949), pp. 93, 128, 153, 154; (c) Isely and Crowl, *U.S. Marines and Amphibious War*, pp. 153–57.

[38] LONE WOLF drafted by F1232 (Capt. B. J. Rodgers) in COMINCH Pacific Section of the Plans Division. This section was headed by Colonel DeWitt Peck, USMC, who was F123.

Force. This letter, and the endorsements placed upon it, was sent to the Commandant of the Marine Corps for comment. The Commandant did not utilize this opportunity to mention the command relationship problem of Commander Amphibious Force, South Pacific Force, and his Marine subordinate, if it then existed in his mind.[39]

Once the COMINCH order had been issued, the responsibility for exercising the command lay with Commander Amphibious Force, South Pacific. Rear Admiral Turner exercised command of the Marines during the early months of the WATCHTOWER Operations because the Commander in Chief directed him to do so. There was nothing in either the then current version of the Landing Operations Doctrine, 1938 Revised Fleet Training Publication 167, nor in the operations orders or instructions issued by any senior in the chain of command for the WATCHTOWER Operation which watered down the COMINCH directive.

This directive was reaffirmed by the Joint Chiefs of Staff on 2 July 1942. It did not speak of broad strategical direction. It talked of "direct command of the tactical operations" as follows:

> Direct command of the tactical operations of the amphibious forces [of which the Marines were the major ingredient] will remain with the Naval Task Force Commander throughout the conduct of all three tasks.

The three tasks referred to were the amphibious operations designed to secure control of:

1. Santa Cruz Islands, Tulagi, and adjacent position.
2. Remainder of Solomon Islands, Northeast Coast of New Guinea.
3. Rabaul, and adjacent positions; New Guinea—New Ireland.[40]

When, on the occasion of his visit to the Amphibious Force, South Pacific Command in late October 1942, the Marine Commandant, Lieutenant General Thomas Holcomb, raised the question of command relationships in SOPAC's Amphibious Force, and suggested changes in organization and in command relationships, Rear Admiral Turner was not adverse thereto.[41] When Commander South Pacific sent to Turner for comment a despatch with the suggested organizational changes, it was acceptable to him, with very minor modifications (nit picks), and when these changes were made he so informed Commander South Pacific Force in writing of his approval.

---

[39] (a) COMPHIBFORPACFLT, letter, A16-1/11/Ser 938 of 13 May 1942; (b) COMDT Marine Corps, letter, A0-278 003B15542 of 5 Jun. 1942.
[40] JCS 00581 of 2 Jul. 1942.
[41] Turner.

The minor modifications in wording Rear Admiral Turner had suggested in the first draft were made by COMSOPAC and that was the form in which the recommended change was approved and sent up the chain of command.[42] These changes:

    a. detached the First Marine Corps from the Amphibious Force, SOPAC, and established the Corps Commander on the same echelon of command as Commander Amphibious Force, SOPAC.

    b. provided that joint planning in the future by COMGENPHIBCORPS and COMPHIBFORSOPAC would be conducted under the control of COMSOPAC.

    c. provided that after conclusion of the landing phase of an operation, during which Marine units from the Amphibious Force command landed, a task organization for the shore phase of the operation would be established, or the Marine Corps units would revert to Corps command, when and as directed by Commander South Pacific.

This established a pattern carried out with minor modifications, throughout the Pacific phase of World War II.

In order that Rear Admiral Turner's thinking in late October 1942 in regard to his command of the Marines can be set forth for all to read, and so inferences that he was bypassed when the matter was considered and then opposed any change thereto, as intimated in the official Marine history,[43] can be shown to be less than accurate, the official letter is quoted below:

                                                                                                         00/hw

File No.   AMPHIBIOUS FORCE
FE25/A3–1   SOUTH PACIFIC FORCE
                      OFFICE OF THE COMMANDER

Serial 00342

                                        U.S.S. McCAWLEY, Flagship,
                                                   October 29, 1942

SECRET

From: Commander Amphibious Force, South Pacific
To: Commander South Pacific Force.
Subject: Reorganization of Amphibious Force, South Pacific

---

[42] (a) COMSOPAC to CINCPAC, messages, 312126, Oct. 1942; COMINCH to CINCPAC, 091950 Nov. 1942; CINCPAC to COMINCH, 030201 Nov. 1942; COMSOPAC to TF Commanders, SOPAC, 161114 Nov. 1942; (b) Turner.

[43] Hough, Ludwig, Shaw, *Pearl Harbor to Guadalcanal*, p. 341.

References: (a) Second·draft of proposed secret despatch from Comsopac to Cincpac.
(b) Cominch secret letter FF1/A3–1 serial 00935 of September 7, 1942.

1. I am in entire sympathy with the purpose of reference (a). The rigid organization prescribed by reference (b), and now in effect, is cumbersome, results in a diffusion of responsibility and authority, and injects into the organization of the forces an echelon of command which, while possibly convenient for delegating authority for training (such as on the West Coast of the United States), is not likely to be effective for the many variations of offensive and defensive operations involved in warfare in the South Pacific.

2. However, the question of the organization and operations of the Amphibious Force is very closely tied up with the organization and operations of all parts of the South Pacific Force, to a degree that does not apply to other Task Forces. Furthermore, it is believed that the major lines of organization of the South Pacific Force require some clarification. For this reason, it is suggested that reference (a) would solve only one part of the problem. Furthermore, since it is in direct conflict with reference (b), it might not be looked upon with favor by higher authorities unless the entire picture is clarified.

3. It is, therefore, recommended that a despatch be sent to the Commander in Chief, U. S. Pacific Fleet, somewhat along the lines indicated in the following draft:

File No.　　　　　　　AMPHIBIOUS FORCE
FE25/A3–1　　　　　　SOUTH PACIFIC FORCE
　　　　　　　　　　OFFICE OF THE COMMANDER
Serial 00342
SECRET
Subject: Reorganization of Amphibious Force, South Pacific.

From: COMSOPAC
To: CINCPAC
EXPERIENCE IN SOPAC INDICATES PERMANENT ORGANIZATION OF AMPHIBIOUS FORCE AS NOW PRESCRIBED BY JCS EIGHT ONE SLANT ONE OF SEPTEMBER FIFTH FORWARDED BY COMINCH SECRET SERIAL ZERO ZERO NINE THREE FIVE OF SEPTEMBER SEVENTH LEADS TO UNDESIRABLE COMPLICATIONS IN ADMINISTRATION CMA AND TO DISPERSION OF RESPONSIBILITY AND AUTHORITY FOR NORMAL AND USUAL LAND SEA AND AIR OPERATIONS PARA SINCE THIS SUBJECT CMA DUE TO GEOGRAPHY AND THE VARIED NATURE OF THE FORCES ASSIGNED MY COMMAND CMA IS CLEARLY BOUND UP WITH OPERATIONS AND ADMINISTRATION OF THE ENTIRE SOUTH PACIFIC AREA CMA I RECOMMEND THAT THE SOUTH

PACIFIC FORCE BE ORGANIZED AS FOLLOWS COLON AFIRM PACIFIC FLEET OPERATIONAL COMBATANT TASK FORCES ASSIGNED PERMANENTLY OR TEMPORARILY WHOSE ADMINISTRATION GENERALLY UNDER TYPE COMMANDERS EITHER OF PACFLT OR SOPAC TEMPORARY CHANGES IN TASK FORCE WILL BE MADE AS REQUIRED WHILE IN SOPAC BAKER AIRCRAFT SOPAC WITH ADMINISTRATION OF ALL SHORE BASED NAVAL AIR UNITS CMA AND OPERATION CONTROL OF ALL ARMY NAVY AND MARINE AIR UNITS NOT ASSIGNED FOR LOCAL DEFENSE OR TEMPORARILY ASSIGNED OTHER TASK FORCES COMMANDERS FOR PARTICULAR TASKS CAST US ARMY FORCES SOPAC WITH ADMINISTRATION OF ALL US ARMY FORCES CMA AND OPERATIONAL CONTROL OF US AND ALLIED LAND FORCES ASSIGNED BY COMSOPAC DOG FIRST CORPS US MARINES WITH ADMINISTRATION OF ALL MARINE UNITS SOPAC LESS UNITS ASSIGNED TO SAMOAN AREA CMA AND OPERATIONAL CONTROL OF US AND ALLIED LAND FORCES ASSIGNED BY COMSOPAC EASY AMPHIBIOUS FORCE SOPAC WITH ADMINISTRATION AND OPERATION OF ALL COMBAT TRANSPORTS CARGO VESSELS AND ATTACHED UNITS IN SOPAC CMA AND OPERATIONAL CONTROL OF LAND SEA AND AIR FORCES TEMPORARILY ASSIGNED FROM OTHER FORCES FOR PARTICULAR TASKS FOX BASE FORCE SOPAC WITH ADMINISTRATION OF ALL NAVAL BASES IN THE AREA AND OPERATIONAL CONTROL OF ALL PORTS CMA EXCEPT AS TO MILITARY FEATURES CMA WHICH REMAIN UNDER THE MILITARY COMMANDERS OF BASES GEORGE SERVICE SQUADRON SOPAC ADMINISTRATION OF LOGISTICS AND SUPPLY BASES PAREN INCLUDING SHIP REPAIRS AND PERSONNEL REPLACEMENT PAREN CMA REQUIRED FOR SUPPORT OF NAVAL UNITS IN SOPAC CMA WHETHER LAND SEA OR AIR CMA PLUS LOGISTIC SUPPLY FOR MARINES ARMY AND ALLIED FORCES AND CIVIL POPULATIONS FOR PARTICULAR ITEMS WHICH MAY BE DECIDED ON AND OPERATIONAL CONTROL OF NTS UNITS PERMANENTLY OR TEMPORARILY IN SOPAC CMA PLUS ARMY ALLIED AND CHARTERED VESSELS ASSIGNED HYPO JOINT PURCHASING BOARD AS NOW ORGANIZED PARA IT IS TO BE UNDERSTOOD THAT OPERATIONAL CONTROL IS TO INCLUDE CONTROL OF SPECIAL TRAINING OF UNITS FOR THE PARTICULAR OPERATIONS IN PROSPECT CMA AND THAT COMSOPAC WILL ACTIVELY COORDINATE JOINT PLANNING TRAINING AND OPERATIONS AMONG TASK AND ADMINISTRATIVE AGENCIES PARA UNDER THE FOREGOING CONCEPT NORMAL AND USUAL OPERATIONS LAND SEA AND AIR WILL BE UNDER LAND SEA AND AIR COM-

MANDERS CMA MINOR AMPHIBIOUS OPERATIONS WILL CONVENIENTLY BE ARRANGED BY LOCAL COMMANDERS WITH THE FORCES NORMALLY ASSIGNED CMA AND MAJOR AMPHIBIOUS OPERATIONS WILL BE EXECUTED BY THE COMMANDER AMPHIBIOUS FORCE WITH TASK FORCES ADAPTED TO THE PURPOSE AND PLACED AT HIS DISPOSAL X DECISIONS AS TO THE TIMES FOR THE FORMATION AND DISSOLUTION OF AMPHIBIOUS TASK ORGANIZATIONS AND THE SCOPE OF THE TASK WILL VARY WITH PARTICULAR CIRCUMSTANCES AND SHOULD REMAIN AT THE DISCRETION OF COMSOPAC.

R. K. TURNER

And yet it has not been infrequent for this scribe to hear a First Division Marine who was on Guadalcanal in 1942 start off a comment on Admiral Turner by saying "That S.O.B. Turner, always interfering with the Marines." He was not interfering with them. He was performing an assigned command function.

DOCTRINE 1941

Amphibious Doctrine is a statement of the working principles of amphibious warfare. Just what our amphibious doctrine was when we entered World War II on 7 December 1941 is not always agreed upon, although in the *War Instructions* and in *Landing Operations Doctrine* of that period are two clear bench marks.[44]

In the 1934 edition of *War Instructions, United States Navy*, the subject "amphibious warfare" was not even listed in the index. In the actual textual matter, it was only indirectly referred to as one of the eight main tasks of the Navy in war in the following words:

> Escort of and cooperation with Expeditionary Forces in the seizure and defense of advanced bases and the invasion of enemy territory.[45]

In 1939, when *Joint Action of the Army and the Navy* was changed to deal in greater detail with Joint Operations, the Navy was assigned the following task which soon appeared in a change to the *War Instructions*.

> To seize, establish, and defend until relieved by Army forces, advanced naval bases, and to conduct such limited auxiliary land operations as are essential to the prosecution of the Naval Campaign.[46]

---

[44] *War Instructions, United States Navy,* 1934 (FTP 143) with changes to December 1941; Landing Operations Doctrine, 1938 (FTP 167) with change No. 1.
[45] *Ibid.,* 1934, Ch. III, para. 310e.
[46] *Ibid.,* 1934, Change No. 6a, RPM No. 1121 of 14 Sep. 1939.

In 1941, *War Instructions, United States Navy* was backed up in detail by a number of confidential publications titled *Tactical Instructions* each separately relating to the tactics of aircraft, submarines, battleships, destroyers, or other type ships in the support of the general doctrines stated in *War Instructions*. In the field of amphibious warfare the detailed publication was *Landing Operations Doctrine, United States Navy, 1938*. However, there was one great difference between amphibious warfare, and such areas as mine warfare, anti-submarine warfare, or air warfare. The backer-up publication was 99.44 percent of the whole.

It was not until late 1944 that amphibious operations were given a full chapter treatment in the 1944 *War Instructions*, which was a complete re-write of the 1934 edition. This edition noted that an "amphibious operation" was synonymous with a "Joint overseas expedition," a term frequently used by the Army and Navy during the previous 50 years.[47] It was Admiral Turner's belief that some of those who talked or wrote of vast changes which took place in amphibious doctrine during World War II tended to confuse the fast changing techniques which were used to implement the doctrine with changes in the basic doctrine itself.[48]

Admiral Turner, in 1960, recalled that during his three years at the Naval War College, the basic amphibious doctrine taught there from 1936 to 1938 related directly to the seizure of advanced bases which would facilitate the projection of the United States Fleet into the Western Pacific. The Admiral summarized the pre-World War II Amphibious Doctrine about as follows:

1. The place chosen for landing amphibious troops must be favorable from the naval point of view, so that the landing craft can land easily; and the terrain in the rear of the chosen beach must be favorable from the Landing Force point of view, so the attack can move away from the beach area.
2. The naval gun and the airplane must be used to control the sea and air at the objective area, to reduce or eliminate enemy resistance in the chosen landing beach area, and to assist the Landing Force in moving out of the beach area to its objectives.
3. The Landing Force early objectives must be far enough away from the chosen landing beach to remove the landing beach from the field of enemy artillery fire.
4. The logistic support of the Landing Force via a reasonably secure

---
[47] *Ibid.*, 1944.
[48] Turner.

line of communications must build up rapidly so as to free the Fleet for further movement.

5. As soon as the action ashore changes from amphibious warfare to land warfare, the Army relieves the Marines.

Admiral Turner added:

> All of these were of course subject to all the over-riding General Principles of War, such as surprise, landing where and when the enemy wasn't immediately expecting you, and the only part of this general doctrine which I would say that was changed markedly in the war was the fifth one. The Army got into amphibious warfare in a big way, and in the earliest stage—at Guadalcanal, they didn't relieve the Marines as soon as I thought the doctrine called for.
>
> Of course during Guadalcanal, I can't say we had a secure line of communications, or that at Okinawa we had control of the air all the time. But that didn't change the doctrine. We just were temporarily unable to carry it out.[49]

TRAINING

The question could be logically asked whether the future Commander Amphibious Force, Pacific Fleet received practical training as a lieutenant commander, commander or junior captain during the major Fleet Landing Exercises (FLEX 1 to FLEX 6) or the more elementary Landing Force exercises in 1922, 1923, 1924, 1925, 1931 or 1932?

With one exception, the answer is "No." As a lieutenant commander and Gunnery Officer on the Staff of Commander Scouting Fleet during Fleet Problem 3, in January 1924, he took part in planning that exercise. The 5th Marine Regiment of the Marine Expeditionary Force landed at the Atlantic end of the Panama Canal, and provided the diversion and holding effort during which the Atlantic locks were simulated to be blown up to prevent the passage of the Pacific Fleet. The balance of the Marine Expeditionary Force, the forerunner of the Fleet Marine Force, landed at Culebra, and prepared it as an island defense base.

Commander Turner missed the 1936, 1937, and 1938 amphibious exercises through being on duty at the Naval War College, and the 1931 and 1932 exercises when he was assigned to the Navy Department. He was in the *California* (BB-44) in 1922, and she did not participate in the Marine phases of the 1922 Fleet Problem, nor in the Marine landing exercises at

---
[49] Turner.

Panama in 1923. He was in the *Saratoga* in 1935, but she did not participate in FLEX 1.

Starting in late 1938 when Captain Turner was back afloat in command of the heavy cruiser *Astoria,* the Fleet Landing Exercises had become pretty much the property of the Atlantic Fleet and the *Astoria* was in the Pacific Fleet so he missed the experimental night landings of 1939 and 1940. By October 1940, Captain Turner was back in the Navy Department. He participated in planning Fleet Problems and Joint Exercises at the departmental level but again he missed both FLEX 7 which took place in the Atlantic and the Joint Landing Exercises in the Pacific in 1940 and 1941.

In his younger years, like all naval officers facing promotion examinations and annual inspections, he had studied the Navy's 1920 and the 1927 revised edition of the *Landing Force Manual.* At the Naval War College he studied the Joint Board pamphlet, titled *Joint Overseas Expeditions,* promulgated in 1933, as well as the Navy's 1935 *Tentative Landing Operations Manual* which, though based on the Joint Board text, was drafted at the Marine Corps Schools at Quantico.

Final reports on Fleet Problems and Fleet Landing Exercises were comprehensive documents circulated by the Navy Department and by Fleet Commanders to ships and stations. In this way, all officers were generally in touch with amphibious warfare techniques, lessons learned and suggestions made for improvement. Yet, Admiral Turner, an avid student of all that related to past and present naval operations, stated that he had nothing but "a highly theoretical knowledge of amphibious warfare" and a "willingness to learn" to take into the WATCHTOWER Operation.[50] It was the "willingness to learn" that paid such high dividends to the Navy.

THE AMPHIBIOUS OPERATION BIBLE

The 1938 edition of *Landing Operations Doctrine, United States Navy* (FTP-167) is a rare publication in its uncorrected and original condition, but a necessary bench mark for the status of United States amphibious techniques and material development before World War II started in Europe. It superseded the 1935 *Tentative Landing Operations Manual.* The 1935 Manual was very largely based on the *Tentative Manual for Landing Operations* drafted by four officers, including Lieutenant Walter C.

---
[50] *Ibid.*

1941 Developments for Amphibious War

Ansel, USN, of the Marine Corps Schools Staff and issued in January 1934, but retitled *Manual for Naval Overseas Operations* in August 1934. The January 1934 publication in turn superseded the *Landing Force Manuals* of the Navy of earlier years which were about 98 percent devoted to the "Manual of the Infantryman" and the parade, and were mostly non-amphibious in character despite their titles. The early Landing Force Manuals basically arose from the need to train sailormen as infantry for the countless Naval landings on foreign shores to protect American lives and property during the previous one hundred years, when the Marines had to be supplemented with sailormen.

In May 1941, Change No. 1 to the 1938 *Landing Operations Doctrine*, based on the more recent Fleet Landing Force Exercises, reports of observers overseas, and material developments of the 1938–1941 period, was issued. It was "a complete revision of FTP 167 except for the title page."[51] The WATCHTOWER Operation was based on this massive revision of FTP 167, although Change No. 2, with 60 new pages was issued in Washington on 1 August 1942, six days before the Tulagi-Guadalcanal landings.

The amphibious experience in the Solomons and in North Africa led to further revisions, and these came out in another fifty new pages of the *Landing Operations Doctrine* in August 1943. In these changes, Rear Admiral Turner not only had a hand; he many times called the tune.

---

[51] *Landing Operations Doctrine,* 1938, Change No. 1, p. III.

CHAPTER VII

WATCHTOWER;
One for Ernie King

THE DECISION TO OPEN THE OFFENSIVE-DEFENSIVE PHASE

To get the United States offensive-defensive phase in amphibious warfare started against the southward rolling Japanese, the military decision that this was a practicality, within United States amphibious resources, had to be taken.

Then the area of the counter-offensive had to be chosen, and specific amphibious operations within this area had to be conceived.

Note: The official U. S. Army history of the Guadalcanal Operation, written in 1948, states that the documents in the files of the Navy in regard thereto are "widely diffused." [1] This was the understatement of the year. Official War Diaries of ships and unit commands are available in quantity, but when it comes to locating background data in the files which individual ships and lower unit commands continuously maintained during World War II, it cannot be done, because these files are non-existent. They were officially destroyed and went up in smoke. The Directors of Naval Record Centers witnessed this great historical loss as they struggled to stay within available stowage space or below a set maximum cubic footage of record allowed by orders originating in the Executive Office of the Secretary of the Navy or in the Department of Defense.

Even the War Diaries were limited in scope and contents. In June 1942 the Assistant Chief of Staff to the Commander in Chief, Pacific Fleet addressed a letter to the Commander Amphibious Force, Pacific Fleet in which he said:

'To conserve paper and time, it is suggested that the reference report [War Diary] could be materially condensed.'

There was not much in the Amphibian War Diaries before this, and after the word got around, a whole month's War Diary appeared on two pages with nary a mention of policy, plans, or progress contained therein.

PESTILENCE was the code name assigned for the entire offensive operation in the South Pacific Area initiated in July 1942. WATCHTOWER was the code name for the Tulagi Phase. CINCPAC to COMSOPAC Ser 070231 of Jul. 42.

[1] (a) John Miller Jr., *Guadalcanal: The First Offensive*, Vol. 5 in subseries *The War in The Pacific* of series UNITED STATES ARMY IN WORLD WAR II (Washington: Historical Division, Department of the Army, 1949), p. xi. (b) CINCPACFLT to COMPHIBFORPACFLT, letter, A16-3/LE/A6-5(05)/Ser 01745, of 21 Jun. 1942. Signed by Capt. Irving D. Wiltsie, USN. (c) COMPHIBFORPACFLT, *War Diaries*, Jun.-Dec. 1942.

Next, the basic military decision and the specific operation had to be sold first at the highest Joint Military and then at the highest U.S. political level. Practical knowledge of amphibious operations was thinly held at both these levels.

And finally, the plan had to become a simple practical reality, with probable success lying within the hard framework of calculated risk.

Everything about the Watchtower Phase of the PESTILENCE Operation initiated by the Navy-Marine amphibious team against the fast moving and hard fighting Japanese Army and Navy was difficult. But the most difficult part was the taking of the military decision at the Joint Chiefs of Staff level to initiate the offensive-defensive phases of amphibious warfare in the Pacific War. It was Rear Admiral Turner who, at the working level, spearheaded Admiral King's drive to secure this decision at the Joint military level.

NAVY PLANNERS' POSITION

In accordance with the pre-World War II promulgated Joint Army-Navy War Plan, *Rainbow Five,* the United States Navy was under orders to commence an immediate amphibious offensive against the Japanese Central Pacific Islands, as soon as war with Japan was declared.[2] But, at the Joint Board Meeting of 8 December 1941, because eight battleships of the Pacific Fleet were out of action, the unhappy decision had to be taken by the Board "to postpone or abandon the task to capture and establish control over the Caroline Islands and Marshall Island Areas."[3]

Everyone who had read the *Rainbow Five* War Plan, and this included most mature officers in the Navy, knew that this amphibious task against these Japanese held islands was to be undertaken by the Navy despite the fact that *Rainbow Five* clearly stated that Europe was the principal theater of the war and Germany the major enemy. Hence, it was quite logical that naval officers would continue to expect that the early 1942 war effort in the Pacific would encompass amphibious action against Japanese outposts as part of the effort to strangle Japan, despite the postponement or cancellation of the particular pre-war planned offensive against the Caroline and Marshall Islands.

---

[2] Navy Basic War Plan, *Rainbow Five,* WPL–46, part III; ch. II; sec. 1; para. 3212, sub: Tasks of Pacific Fleet.
[3] Joint Board No. 325, Ser 738, 8 Dec. 1941.

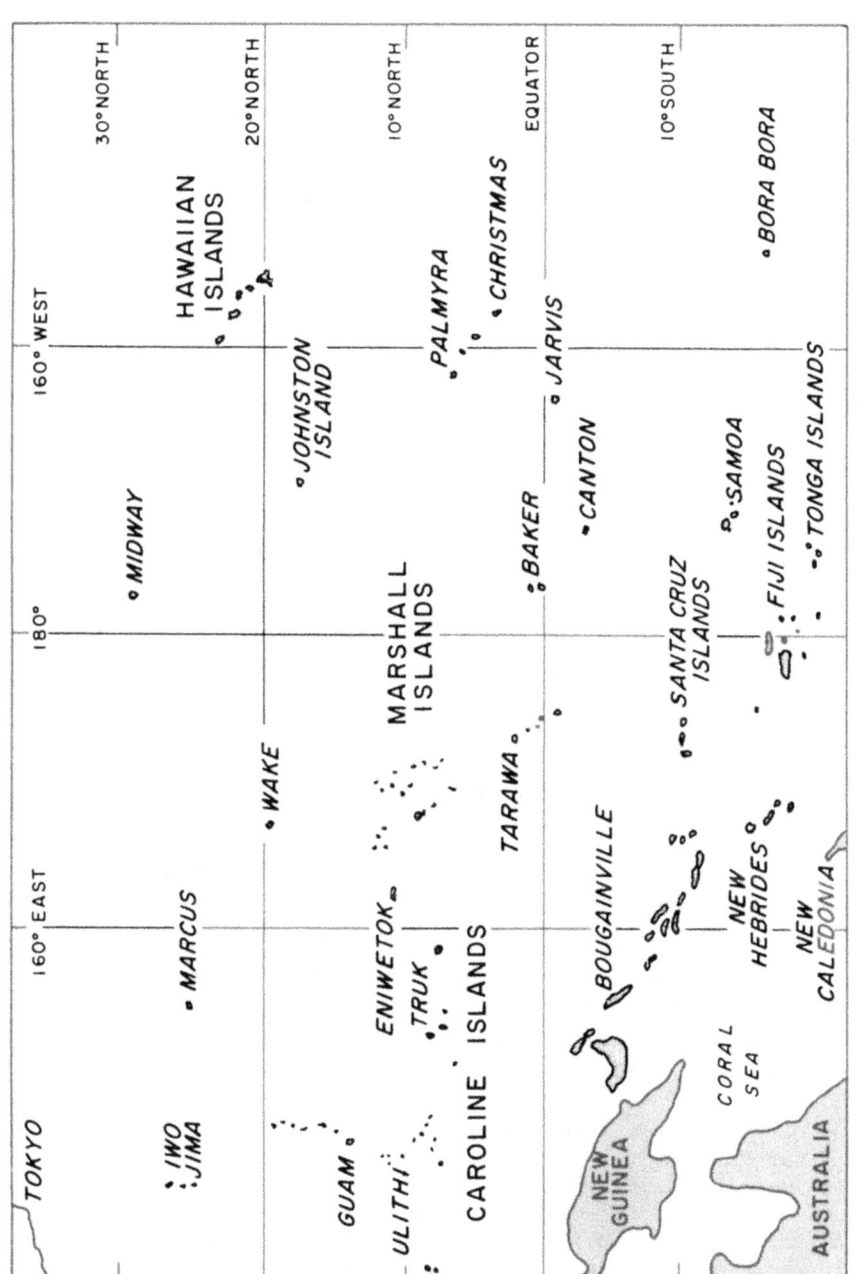

Central and South Pacific Area.

The author can record that the Naval War Planners, which Rear Admiral Turner headed (as F-1 on Admiral King's Staff), and of which the writer (as F-11 on the Plans Division for the first year of the war) was a very small cog, were under a great deal of professional pressure to make the concept of offensive amphibious action, as in the *Rainbow* Plan, live again.

ARMY PLANNERS POSITION

The United States Army Planners in Washington[4] in early 1942 took a dim view of any large scale diversion of Army resources for counter-offensive purposes in the Pacific Ocean Area, as long as the over-all direction for the conduct of the war stated that:

1. Germany is the predominant member of the Axis Powers,
2. The Atlantic and European Area is considered to be the decisive theater, and
3. "The principal United States military effort will be exerted in the decisive theater, and operations of United States forces in other theaters will be conducted in such a manner as to facilitate that effort."[5]

The Army's official history makes this position clear.

The basic Army position was:

> ... to emphasize the need for economy of effort in 'subsidiary' theaters. They classified as subsidiary theaters not only the Far East but also Africa, the Middle East, the Iberian Peninsula, and the Scandinavian Peninsula. ... to consider all other operations as strictly holding operations, and to regard with disfavor any proposal to establish and maintain in a 'subsidiary' theater the favorable ratio of Allied to enemy forces, that would be necessary in order to take the offensive there.[6]

---

[4] Senior Army War Planners in late 1941 and early 1942 included Major General L. T. Gerow, Chief of War Plans Division, General Staff; Major General Carl Spaatz, Army Air Force; Brigadier General D. D. Eisenhower, Deputy Chief, War Plans Division, General Staff; Brigadier General J. T. McNarney, War Plans Division, Army Air Force; Brigadier General R. W. Crawford, War Plans Division, General Staff; Colonel T. T. Handy, War Plans Division, General Staff. At this time there was no separate Air Force. The Air Force was created from the Army Air Force on 26 July 1947.

[5] Navy Basic War Plan, *Rainbow Five*, WPL-46, app. I, sec. IV, para. 13a, subj: Concept of the War.

[6] Maurice Matloff and Edwin M. Snell, *Strategic Planning for Coalition Warfare 1941–1942*, Vol. III in subseries *The War Department* of series UNITED STATES ARMY IN WORLD WAR II (Washington: Office of the Chief of Military History, Department of the Army, 1953), p. 101–02.

The Army Air Force History indicates the same position for the air arm:

> The prime factor affecting all Army air forces in the Pacific and Asiatic theaters was the pre-eminence accorded by the Combined Chiefs of Staff (CCS) to the war against Germany. Because of the paramount interests of the U.S. Navy in the Pacific, there was no stinting of naval forces there in favor of the Atlantic. But during the early part of the war, allocations for Army air (and ground) forces were strictly conditioned by the needs of the European Theater of Operations (ETO).[7]

There was no disagreement with the basic Joint *Rainbow* directive on the part of the high command of the Navy, or their supporting war planners.[8] In fact, the basic philosophy on the concept and conduct of the war, and its grand strategy, stated above, had been so phrased in the initial versions of the *Rainbow* War Plan, as drafted by the Navy War Plans Division. This particular wording had survived to the final document, and *Rainbow Five* had been placed in effect when the war started. Two weeks later, on 22 December 1941, this concept, and the Navy's overall support of *Rainbow Five,* was reaffirmed by Admiral H. R. Stark, Chief of Naval Operations.[9] It was in the interpretation of the phrase, "Operations in other theaters will be conducted in such a manner as to facilitate that effort," in the European theater, which brought forth a strong divergence of naval opinion from that held by many in Army Headquarters.

ARCADIA CONFERENCE

This basic philosophy of *Rainbow Five* on the grand strategy of the war was approved at the ARCADIA Conference, held in Washington, D. C., from 22 December 1941 to 14 January 1942, between Prime Minister Churchill, President Roosevelt and their principal military subordinates and supporting staffs.[10]

However, during the ARCADIA Conference, a "clarification," which

---

[7] U.S. Air Force Historical Division, *The Pacific: Guadalcanal to Saipan,* Vol. IV of THE ARMY AIR FORCES IN WORLD WAR II, eds. Wesley Frank Craven and James Lea Cate (Chicago: University of Chicago Press, 1950), p. x.

[8] Senior Naval War Planners included (roster of 27 January 1942) Rear Admiral R. K. Turner, Chief of War Plans Division; Captain Bernhard H. Bieri, Assistant Chief; Captain O. M. Read; Captain R. E. Davison; Captain B. J. Rodgers; Captain Forrest P. Sherman.

[9] *King's Record,* p. 361.

[10] Proceedings of ARCADIA Conference held in Washington, D.C., 24 Dec. 1941—14 Jan. 1942, Part II. Approved Documents, U.S. Ser ABC–4/CS–1, 31 Dec. 1941; subj: American-British Grand Strategy.

amounted to a modification, was given to the phrase in *Rainbow Five* which read:

> Operations of United States forces in other theaters [than the European theater] will be conducted in such a manner as to facilitate that [European] effort.

The clarification was accomplished despite the similarily strong statement in the British drafted paragraph in the ARCADIA document which read:

> . . . it should be a cardinal principle of American-British strategy that only the minimum of force necessary for the safeguarding of vital interests in other theaters should be diverted from operations against Germany.[11]

These two paragraphs might be literally interpreted to establish a barbed wire fence against any offensive efforts by the United States Navy in the Pacific.

Clarification was essential to make indisputable the Naval Planners' position that "facilitating operations against Germany" required that vital interests in the Far East Area must be safeguarded.

The Combined Chiefs of Staff, after stating the "cardinal principle" of their future strategy, set forth six essential features of this grand strategy. They then prescribed 18 supporting measures to be taken in 1942 to further its various aspects. Only the last of the six essential features and the last of the 18 supporting measures related exclusively to the Pacific.

The Combined Chiefs modified, in effect, their "cardinal principle" a bit by stating one subordinate task so that it was more to the liking of those in the United States Navy, who were anxious to try to stop the Japanese before they controlled the whole Pacific Ocean south of the equator. This modification was contained in subparagraph 4(f) of the Grand Strategy document, which read:

> Maintaining only such positions in the Eastern Theatre [British term for the Far East Area] as will safeguard vital interests (*See paragraph 18*) *and denying to Japan access to raw materials vital to her continuous war effort, while we are concentrating on the defeat of Germany.*

The "see paragraph 18" and the phrase following, italicized above, appear as additions to the original British draft. Paragraph 18 in the original draft, was important to the United States Navy point of view since it had the sentence: "Secondly, points of vantage from which an offensive against Japan can eventually be developed must be secured." [12]

---

[11] *Ibid.*, para. 3.
[12] *Ibid.*, para. 18.

The secret document containing this general statement of the American-British strategy was the only one of the 12 papers approved at the ARCADIA Conference carrying the eye-catching instructions that it was "to be kept under lock and key" and its circulation "restricted to the United States and British Chiefs of Staff and their immediate subordinates." This same document mentioned 1943 as the agreed upon year for a "return to the continent of Europe," which in effect meant no real counter-offensive against the Japanese until 1944 or later, since Germany had to be defeated on the continent of Europe first.[13] The restrictive instructions in regard to this document were closely observed in the Headquarters of Admiral King with the result that some echelons of the Staff were unaware for some weeks of this 1943 European invasion provision. Consequently, they kept up pressure for "seizing points of vantage" in 1942, to be used later in what they anticipated would be a 1943 offensive against the Japanese.

ADMIRAL KING PERSISTS

It was Admiral Turner's belief that Admiral King was the persistent influence at the Joint Staff and Presidential level, which resulted in the initiation of an amphibious counter-offensive in the Pacific Ocean Area during the late summer of 1942.[14] But Admiral King received welcome and somewhat unexpected help from the British, and the right nudge at the right time from the Japanese. Not until the British influence was made felt at the Presidential level did the Army Planners, in good conscience, wholeheartedly join in the vital start to eventual amphibious success in the Pacific.

There are many dates to record and events to recall in connection with the first counter-offensive operation against the Japanese. But the first date relating to PESTILENCE is 11 January 1942. On this date Admiral King figuratively stood on his feet at the ninth meeting of the ARCADIA Conference and talked not about Guadalcanal, but about New Caledonia, 800 miles to the southeast of Guadalcanal. Lieutenant General H. H. Arnold, Chief of Army Air Corps, had questioned the high priority assigned to the Army Air Force contingent of aircraft planned for New Caledonia whose defense was an accepted Australian responsibility, but one the Australians could not fulfill. The French had agreed, on 24 December 1941, to United

---

[13] *Ibid.*, para. 17.
[14] Turner.

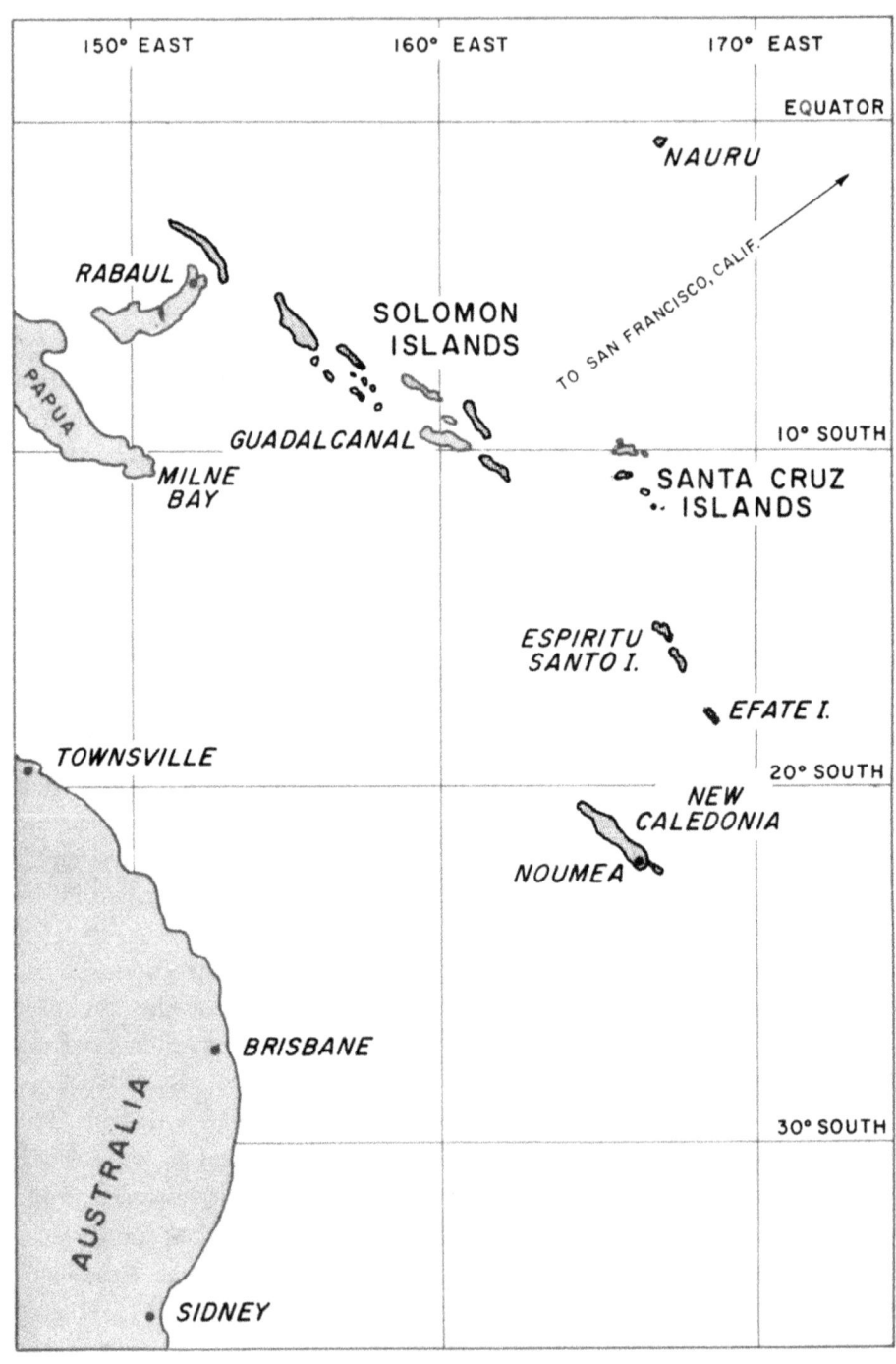

Solomon Islands, Santa Cruz Islands and New Caledonia.

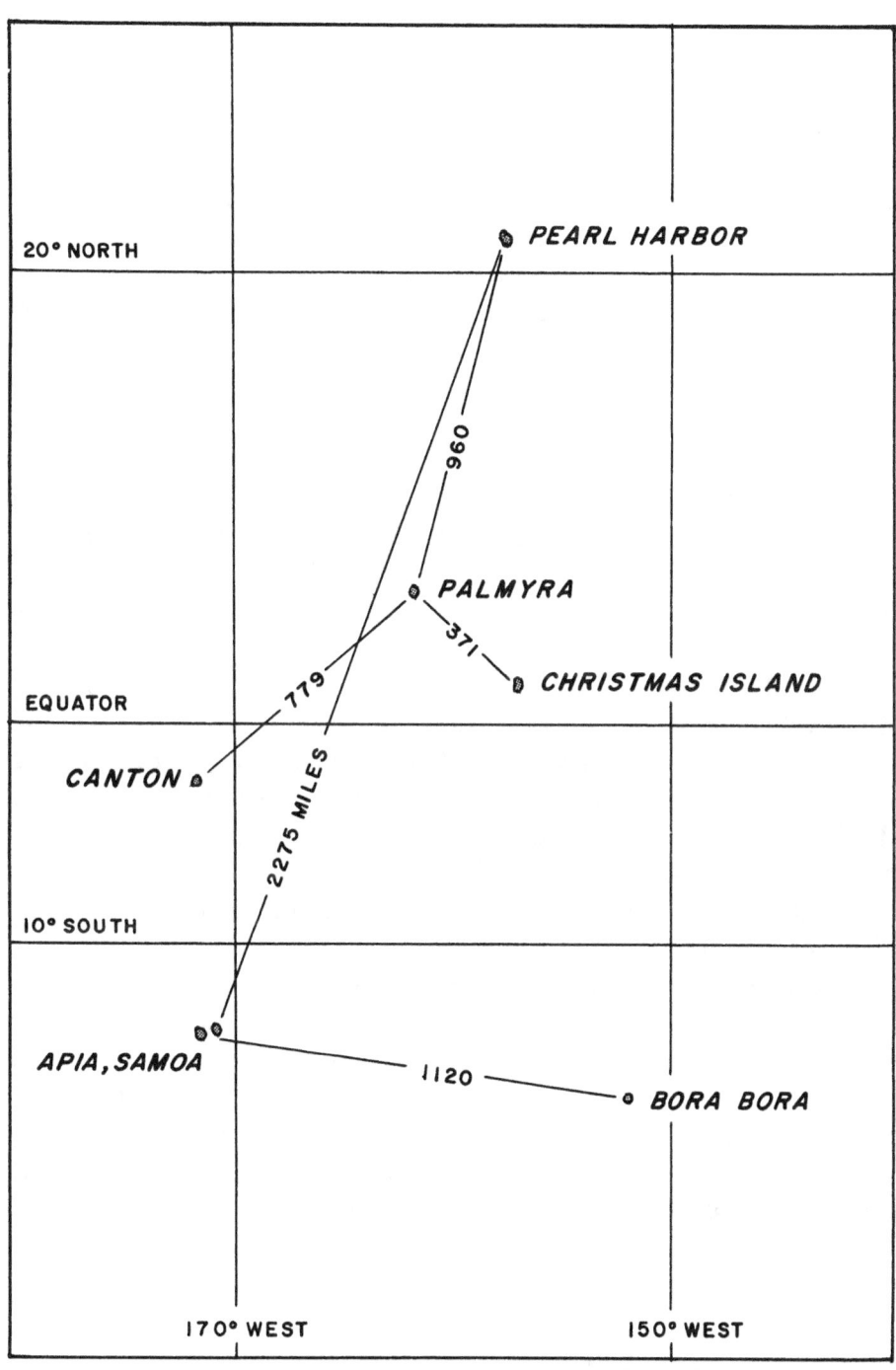

South Pacific Area island garrisons.

States Forces garrisoning New Caledonia, and Army planning for this was going forward.[15]

Believing that the 7,000-mile line of communications between San Francisco and eastern Australia must be held securely, and to do this the Japanese must be stopped well short of that line, Admiral King pointed out that New Caledonia was of great importance for this purpose. Not only were the nickel mines of New Caledonia a tempting bait for the Japanese, but also, if the island was in Japanese possession, all reinforcements to Singapore, the Dutch East Indies, and Australia would have to take the long sea route south past New Zealand.[16]

Admiral King's statement fitted neatly into three essential features of our pre-World War II naval strategy for fighting Japan. These held that it was important to deny Japan's access to raw materials vital to her continuous war effort, to hold points of advantage from which an amphibious offensive against Japan could be developed, and to maintain secure lines of air and sea communication. Admiral King's statement also fitted into his burgeoning interest in the Solomon Islands, 800 miles away to the northwest of New Caledonia.

A straight line on a mercator chart from San Francisco in California to Townsville, termed the capital of Australia's North,[17] passes just south of the island of Hawaii and just south of Guadalcanal Island in the Solomons. In Admiral King's belief, the Japanese should not be permitted to impinge on this line, if the line of communications from Hawaii to Australia through Samoa, Fiji, and the New Hebrides was to be secure.[18]

And there was no demonstrable reason at this time or for months thereafter why the Japanese would not impinge on it.

On the very day Admiral King addressed the ARCADIA Conference, a Japanese submarine was shelling Pago-Pago, Samoa, the eastern hinge of the line of communications to Australia, and 1,400 long sea miles to the eastward of New Caledonia. Twelve days after 11 January 1942, the Japanese were to land 1,100 miles to the northward of New Caledonia on Bougainville in the Solomon Islands, but only 300 miles north of a position (Tulagi) where their aircraft might begin to really threaten the line of communications to Australia.

Three days before this ARCADIA discussion, Admiral King, Admiral Stark

---

[15] SECNAV to SOP, Bora Bora, letter, Ser 05313 of 19 Jan. 1952, Encl. (A).
[16] ARCADIA Proceedings, 11 Jan. 1942, p. 9–6.
[17] *Encyclopaedia Britannica*, Vol. XXII, p. 336.
[18] *King's Record*, pp. 364, 381.

and General Marshall signed a Joint Basic Plan for the "Occupation and Defense of Bora Bora."[19] The purpose of this occupation was to provide in the Free French Society Islands a protected fueling station for short legged merchant ships, 4,500 miles along on the 7,500-mile run from the Panama Canal to eastern Australia. It also provided a fueling station on a direct run from California to New Zealand. 3,750 U. S. Army troops were to be employed to defend the 120,000-barrel naval fuel base projected for Bora Bora.

DEFENSIVE GARRISONS IN THE SOUTH PACIFIC

In the basic *Rainbow Five* Plan, the Navy had responsibility for the defense of Palmyra Island almost 1,000 miles south of Pearl Harbor and of American Samoa another 1,300 miles further on in the long voyage to New Zealand. Samoa was the hinge in the line of communications from both the West Coast and from Pearl Harbor where the line swung from southerly to westerly to reach the Southwest Pacific. Small Marine garrisons at Palmyra and American Samoa were considerably reinforced shortly after 7 December 1941 to make more secure the northern flange of the hinge.

The Army quickly promised, and provided, garrisons for the two atolls, Canton (1,500 troops) and Christmas (2,000 troops), located south of Palmyra on the route to Samoa.[20] The first big strains on available Army troop resources came when a 17,000-man defense force sailed from New York City on 22 January 1942 for New Caledonia, and a 4,000-troop garrison sailed from Charleston, South Carolina, on 27 January 1942 for Bora Bora.[21] The establishment of these two defense forces was the first of many forward steps taken for the "Defense for the Island bases along the Lines of Communications between Hawaii and Australia." This was the title of a Joint Planning Staff paper which brought forth much pointed, and at times unamiable, inter-Service discussion and underwent many, many changes.[22]

The Navy War Planners, from January through March 1942, continuously were pressing their opposite numbers in the Army for additional Pacific commitments, quoting again and again that "the main sea and air route from

---

[19] COMINCH, Joint Basic Plan for the Occupation and Defense of Bora Bora, Ser 0010 of 19 Jan. 1942.
[20] Sailed from San Francisco 31 January 1942.
[21] War Department, letters, AG 370.5(1-17-42)MSC-E and AG-381(1-22-42).
[22] JPS 21/5/D; JPS 21/7; JCS 48.

the United States to Australia via Hawaii, Palmyra, Christmas Island, Canton, Fiji and New Caledonia must be secured," and "points of advantage from which an offensive against Japan can eventually be developed must be secured." [23] The Army Planners, with whom Rear Admiral Turner was discussing the island garrison problem day in and day out, responded by stating again and again these principles:

> 1. Forces should not be committed to any more than the minimum number of islands necessary to secure the Hawaii-Australia lines of communications.
> 2. Forces committed to any one island should be the minimum needed to secure that particular island.

As stated in the Army History, General Marshall's position was:

> To set a limit to future movements of Army forces into the Pacific and find a basis for increasing the rate at which Army forces would be moved across the Atlantic became, during February and March, the chief concern of General Marshall and his advisors on the War Department staff, and the focus of their discussion of future plans with the Army Air Forces and the Navy.[24]

Yet, even as the Army troops sailed for Bora Bora and New Caledonia in late January 1942, Rear Admiral Turner pressed the Army Planners to provide garrisons in the New Hebrides, 300 miles north of New Caledonia and in the Tonga Islands, 400 miles south of Marine-held Samoa. It was a fundamental Navy Planners' position during this period that

> strong mutually supporting defensive positions in Samoa, Fiji, and New Caledonia are essential for the protection of the sea and air communications from the United States to Australia and for the defense of the island areas of the mid-Pacific, and for maintaining a base area for an eventual offensive against Japan.[25]

The reasons behind the Navy's position was the rapidity with which the Japanese were eating up Pacific Islands. Although the Japanese did not declare war on the Netherlands and invade the Netherlands East Indies until 11 January 1942, only 12 days later they were landing forces on Bougainville Island in the Solomons 2,500 miles further to the southeast. As the Japanese moved in at the head of the Solomon Islands, the chance of their making another big leap forward (900 to 1,100 miles) to seize one of the islands in

---

[23] ARCADIA Proceedings, DoC ABC–4/CS–1 paras. 10, 11, 18.
[24] Matloff and Snell, *Strategic Planning*, p. 147.
[25] COMINCH, letter, FF1/A16–3 Ser 00191 of 17 Mar. 1942; subj: Basic Plan for Occupation and Defense of Western Samoa and Wallis Island.

the New Hebrides or Ellice Island groups worried the Naval Planners. New Caledonia was well within air range from the New Hebrides, being only 300 to 400 miles away to the South. The Fijis were at the extreme air range from Funafuti in the Ellice Islands, 560 miles to the North.

Ten days before Singapore fell, Admiral King forwarded a Navy War Plans Division paper, drafted by Rear Admiral Turner, to the Joint Chiefs, recommending the establishment of an advance base at Funafuti in the Ellice Islands to provide:

a. an outpost coverage of Fiji—Samoa.
b. a linkage post toward the Solomon Islands.
c. support for future offensive operations in the Southwest Pacific.[26]

Three days after Singapore fell to the Japenese on 15 February 1942, Admiral King proposed to the Chief of Staff, U. S. Army, that the Tonga Islands, 200 miles southeast of the Fijis, and Efate, 500 miles to the west of the Fijis in the New Hebrides, be garrisoned. He asked that the Chief of Staff

> agree to this proposition, and immediately initiate planning and the assembly of troops and equipment, with a view to despatching these garrisons as soon as necessary shipping can be found.[27]

The day before Admiral King signed this letter, Brigadier General Eisenhower who was to fleet up to be Chief of the Army War Plans Division on 16 February 1942 was recording:

> The Navy wants to take all the islands in the Pacific—have them held by Army troops, to become bases for Army pursuit and bombers. Then! the Navy will have a safe place to sail its vessels. But they will not go further forward than our air (Army) can assure superiority.[28]

It was Admiral King's position that the vital line of communications through Samoa, Fiji, and New Caledonia was "too exposed" to air raids arising after the anticipated Japanese seizure of intermediate and nearby islands and that Tongatabu in the Tonga Islands would be the ideal location for "the principal operating [logistic support] naval base in the South Pacific."[29] The Tonga Islands were about 1,100 miles along the direct convoy

---

[26] JCS 5.
[27] COMINCH to C/S USA, letter, FF1/A16/c/F1, Ser 00105 of 18 Feb. 1942, and 00149 of 2 Mar. 1942.
[28] Quoted in Matloff and Snell, *Strategic Planning*, p. 154.
[29] *King's Record*, pp. 377, 383.

run from New Zealand to Samoa, Hawaii, and San Francisco. Since at that time the New Zealanders provided the air units for the Fiji Islands and a fair share of their logistic support, a through convoy could be regrouped at Tongatabu, and a small section sent to the Fiji Islands. Additionally, the Tonga Islands would provide a protected anchorage and make possible an air base, whose air contingent would provide mutual support for those on Fiji and Samoa, and which would serve as an alternate staging point on the South Pacific Air Ferry Route.

As for Efate in the New Hebrides, Admiral King opined "it will serve to deny a stepping stone to the Japanese if they moved South from Rabaul, New Britain," and provide a strong point "from which a step-by-step general advance could be made through the New Hebrides, Solomons and Bismarcks." [30]

The Chief of Staff of the U. S. Army was very reluctant to provide Army forces for more islands along the Pearl to Australia line of communications. In a memorandum to the Commander in Chief of the U. S. Fleet, dated 24 February 1942, he stated:

> It is my desire to do anything reasonable which will make offensive action by the Fleet practicable.

However, he wanted to know the answers to a lot of questions, including:

> What the general scheme or concept of operations that the occupation of these additional islands was designed to advance?
> Were the measures taken purely for protection of a line of communications or is a step by step general advance contemplated?

The Chief of Staff ended by writing:

> I therefore feel that, if a change in basic strategy, as already approved by the Combined Chief of Staff is involved, the entire situation must be reconsidered before we become more seriously involved in the build up of Army ground and air garrisons in the Pacific Islands.[31]

General Marshall further stated that

> Our effort in the Southwest Pacific must, for several reasons, be limited to the strategic defensive for air and ground troops,

supporting this with statements that:

---

[30] (a) COMINCH, letters, FF1/A16–3/F–1, Ser 00105 of 18 Feb. 1942; (b) Quoted in Samuel E. Morison, *Coral Sea, Midway and Submarine Actions, May 1942–Aug. 1942*, Vol. IV of HISTORY OF UNITED STATES NAVAL OPERATIONS IN WORLD WAR II (Boston: Little, Brown & Co., 1954), p. 246.

[31] C/S USA to CINCUS, memorandum, 24 Feb. 1942. Modern Military Records, National Archives.

a. the geography and communications of Australia impose serious limitations on offensive air and ground offensive actions.

b. limitations of tonnage for the long voyage restrict U. S. ground commitments.

c. requirements for U. S. air units in other theatres would seem definitely to limit for some time to come the extent to which we can provide for a further expansion in the Pacific-Australian theater.

In reply to General Marshall's letter, Admiral King stated that:

> The scheme or concept of operations is not only to protect the line of communications with Australia, but, in so doing, set up 'strong points' from which a step-by-step general advance can be made through the New Hebrides, Solomons, and the Bismarck Archipelago. It is expected that such a step-by-step general advance will draw Japanese forces to oppose it, thus relieving pressure in other parts of the Pacific and that the operation will of itself be good cover for the communications with Australia." [32]

Admiral King then answered each question of the Chief of Staff with his frankly more offensively minded concepts of our future Pacific endeavors:

> When the advance to the northwest begins, it is expected to use amphibious troops (chiefly from the Amphibious Corps, Pacific Fleet) to seize and occupy strong points under the cover of appropriate naval and air forces.
>
> I agree that the time is at hand when we must reach a decision—with the knowledge of the combined Chiefs of Staff—as to what endeavors the United States is to make in advance of the general Allied interest.

This difference of opinion at the highest military level led to much ruffling of feathers at the Joint Planners level. This ruffling was the more apparent because at the time when this question of essential "land forces required to hold base areas in the first defensive stage" was being hotly debated at the Joint Staff planning level, many of the planners who were assigned duty in both the Combined Staff as well as the Joint Staff were repeating the same arguments at the Combined Staff planning levels, since the Combined Chiefs of Staff had directed the Combined Staff Planners to come up with their recommendations to this same problem.[33]

All this talking and memorandum writing and planning took time. The Joint planning effort to provide major defensive positions of groups of islands along the line of communications to Australia was not even partially agreed upon until the end of March 1942, and it was early May before the

---

[32] COMINCH to C/S USA, memorandum, A16–3/1/00149 of 2 Mar. 1942.

[33] (a) Post ARCADIA Vol. 1, minutes of meeting; (b) CCS 4th Meeting. 10 Feb. 1942.

major part of the 56,000-man garrison force agreed upon (41,000 Army; 15,000 Marines) arrived at their islands.[34]

The basic disagreement separating the Army and the Navy Planners during this period was whether holding Australia was vital to the United States war effort. Rear Admiral Turner believed it was. As late as 28 February 1942, Brigadier General Eisenhower, did not agree. He advised General Marshall:

> The United States interest in maintaining contact with Australia and in preventing further Japanese expansion to the Southeastward is apparent . . . but . . . they are not immediately vital to the successful outcome of the war. The problem is one of determining what we can spare for the effort in that region, without seriously impairing performance of our mandatory tasks.[35]

Rear Admiral Turner believed that maintaining contact with Australia was a mandatory task in view of the deteriorating British, Dutch and American military situation in the Far East. This, fortunately, was also the view of President Roosevelt, who on 16 February 1942, advised Prime Minister Churchill: "We must at all costs maintain our two flanks—the right based on Australia and New Caledonia and the left on Burma, India and China." The President did not go along, however, with Rear Admiral Turner's thinking that "No further reenforcements [should] be sent to Iceland and the United Kingdom until Fall."[36]

Not only were Rear Admiral Turner and Admiral King pressuring the Army during February 1942 for more positive action in the Pacific, but they were also pressuring Admiral Nimitz, and through him, subordinate Naval commanders in the Pacific. On 12 February 1942, CINCPAC was told:

---

[34] (a)	Order Issued	Troops Sailed	Troops Arrived
American Samoa (Marine)	21 Dec. 41	6 Jan. 42	19 Jan. 42
Bora Bora, Society Islands	8 Jan. 42	27 Jan. 42	12 Mar. 42
Noumea, New Caledonia	17 Jan. 42	22 Jan. 42	12 Mar. 42
Tongatabu, Tonga Islands	12 Mar. 42	10 Apr. 42	9 May 42
Western Samoa (Marine)	17 Mar. 42	9 Apr. 42	8 May 42
Efate, New Hebrides	20 Mar. 42	12 Apr. 42	4 May 42
Viti Levi, Fiji Islands	28 Apr. 42	May 42	10 June 42

New Caledonia, 22,000; Bora Bora, 4,000; Christmas Island, 2,000; Canton, 1,100; Tongatabu, 7,200; Efate, 4,900; Samoa, 13,500 (Marines). 32,000 of the 41,000 Army were "ground troops"; (b) Matloff and Snell, *Strategic Planning*, pp. 147–54; Miller, *Guadalcanal: The First Offensive*, p. 24; (c) COMINCH, memorandum, FF1/A16-3/Ser 0019 of 17 Mar. 1942.

[35] Quoted in Matloff and Snell, *Strategic Planning*, p. 157.

[36] (a) Turner; (b) Roosevelt to Churchill, 16 Feb. 1942 in Robert E. Sherwood, *Roosevelt and Hopkins: An Intimate History* (New York: Harper & Bros., 1948), p. 508; (c) Turner to King, memorandum, 17 Feb. 1942; subj: Pacific Ocean Area.

My 062352 [February] is to be interpreted as requiring a strong and comprehensive offensive to be launched soon against exposed enemy naval forces and the positions he is now establishing in the Bismarks and Solomons.[37]

And again on 15 February:

Current operations of the Pacific Fleet, because of existing threat, should be directed toward preventing further advance of enemy land airplane base development in the direction of Suva and Noumea. . . .[38]

On 26 February CINCPAC was informed:

our current tasks are not merely protective, but also offensive where practicable. . . .[39]

THE BRITISH URGE ACTION IN PACIFIC

The British also were in agreement with United States naval opinion, and began to put political pressure on President Roosevelt and military pressure at the Combined Chiefs' level to give increasing protection to Australia and New Zealand, and to step up American naval action in the Pacific. Both of these were to be done at the expense of American Army action in the European Theater of Operations.

On 4 March 1942, Prime Minister Churchill advised President Roosevelt:

I think we must agree to recognize that Gymnast [the varying forms of intervention in French North Africa by Britain from the east and by the United States across the Atlantic] is out of the question for several months.[40]

This despatch gave the Navy Planners a talking point, since the GYMNAST Operation had a tentative date of 25 May 1942, and was responsible for overriding Army troop commitments to the European Theater.

On 5 March, Mr. Churchill advised the President:

. . . it should be possible to prevent oversea invasion of India unless the greater part of the Japanese Fleet is brought across from your side of the theater, and this again I hope the action and growing strength of the United States Navy will prevent.[41]

The word "action" was needling in effect, whatever its intent. And again in the same message:

---

[37] COMINCH to CINCPAC, 122200 Feb. 1942.
[38] COMINCH to CINCPAC, 151830 Feb. 1942.
[39] COMINCH to CINCPAC, 261630 Feb. 1942.
[40] Winston S. Churchill, *The Hinge of Fate*, Vol. IV of *The Second World War* (Boston: Houghton Mifflin Co., 1950), p. 190.
[41] *Ibid.*, p. 192.

> Japan is spreading itself over a very large number of vulnerable points and trying to link them together by air and sea. . . . Once several good outfits are prepared, any one of which can attack a Japanese-held base or island and beat the life out of the garrison, all their islands will become hostages to fortune. Even in this year, 1942, some severe examples might be made, causing great perturbation and drawing further upon Japanese resources to strengthen other points.[42]

This despatch seconded the Naval Planners' desire for a more positive policy towards the Pacific War.

The President replied on 8 March 1942:

> We have beeen in constant conference since receipt of your message of March 4.

The President pointed out, among other things, that using ships in the Pacific rather than in the Atlantic meant that "GYMNAST cannot be undertaken," and that

> American contribution to an air offensive against Germany in 1942 would be somewhat curtailed and any American contribution to land operations on the Continent of Europe in 1942 will be materially reduced.[43]

Moreover, he accepted the Prime Minister's urging for more action in the Pacific, and lower priority for Army troops for Europe. Essentially, this was a common sense decision to give higher immediate priority to defensive operations in the Pacific necessary to hold vital positions and to defend essential lines of communication, than to the initiation of early, but inadequately prepared, offensive operations in Africa. With the troops made available by this change in overall strategic policy, the Army members of the Joint Planners were happy to agree that the Army should provide the garrisons for Efate in the New Hebrides and for Tongatabu in the Tonga Islands.

On the very day, 5 March 1942, when the British Prime Minister was urging the United States Navy to "action" in the Pacific, Admiral King was advising the President by written memorandum that only when Samoa, Fiji and New Caledonia had been "made reasonably secure," and the requisite "naval forces, air units, and amphibious troops" were available, could the United States "drive northwestward from New Hebrides into the Solomons."[44] Since the United States Army garrison had not yet arrived at New Caledonia, and the others (Tonga, New Hebrides, and Fiji) were a

---
[42] *Ibid.*, p. 194.
[43] *Ibid.*, pp. 195–96.
[44] *King's Record*, pp. 384–85.

month away from even embarking in the United States, and the Marines were only in modest strength in American Samoa, it was obvious that nothing was going to happen soon to start the drive northward into the Solomons. Rear Admiral Turner was in full agreement with a stand-fast policy for the present, advising Admiral King on 26 March 1942 that if an attempt was made at that time to establish bases in the Solomons, "the ventures would be failures." [45]

But Efate was the camel's nose under the edges of the Army tent in getting to the Solomons and no one knew it better than Admiral King and his Chief Alligator and Head Planner, Richmond Kelly Turner.[46]

At this same time, Rear Admiral Turner and his boss were keeping pressure on the Navy's Pacific forces. Thus, Admiral Nimitz was given a vehicle to keep his subordinates "up on the step," when this Turner drafted despatch was sent off on 30 March.

> You are requested to read the article, 'There is only one Mistake; To do Nothing,' by Charles F. Kettering in the March 29th issue of *Saturday Evening Post* and to see to it that it is brought to the attention of all your principal subordinates and other key officers.[47]

Individual task force commanders were also occasionally jigged. One well-known incident in which Rear Admiral Turner played a part probably did not endear him to this particular officer, a Task Force Commander and his senior by six years, who reported to CINCPAC having been at sea for so long that stocks of provisions in his command were so reduced that meals would soon be on a "beans and hard tack basis." He requested CINCPAC authority to withdraw for provisioning. CINCPAC sent the message on to COMINCH for action. A reply which said simply "Eat beans and hard tack," was drafted by Rear Admiral Turner. However this was modified and softened by Admiral King to read:

> Noted that Brown has shown some concern about provisions during or after current operations. It is my feeling that he should return to Pearl on a "beans and hardtack" basis rather than deplete stocks now or soon to be south of equator.[48]

To make the point clearer, later in the same month, two other dispatches were sent out by COMINCH.

---

[45] ACofS(P) to COMINCH, memorandum, 26 Mar. 1942, subj: Strategic Deployment in the Pacific against Japan. Modern Military Records, National Archives.
[46] Turner.
[47] COMINCH to CINCPAC, 301320 Mar. 1942.
[48] COMINCH to CINCPAC, 071820 Mar. 1942.

a. Your 292346 not understood, if it means you are retiring from enemy vicinity in order to provision.

b. The situation in the area where you are now operating requires constant activity of a Task Force like yours to keep enemy occupied. Requirements for use of other Task Forces like yours make it necessary to continue your active operations South of equator until your Force can be relieved.[49]

GENERAL EISENHOWER PERSISTS

Despite the practical steps taken toward recognizing that Australia would be held and a real effort made to stop the Japanese short of the main line of communications from Hawaii through Samoa to Australia, and although President Roosevelt informed Prime Minister Churchill on 18 March 1942 that "Australia must be held" and "we are willing to undertake that." Brigadier General Eisenhower on 25 March 1942, in a memorandum to the Army Chief of Staff, still recommended that these objectives be placed "in the highly desirable rather than in the mandatory class."[50] This was a further indication that the thinking of the Army Plans Division was the antithesis of Rear Admiral Turner's.

At the London military conferences from 8 to 15 April 1942, the American plan for an emergency landing and establishment of a bridgehead at Cherbourg in the fall of 1942 (SLEDGEHAMMER) and a major invasion of Europe between Havre and Boulogne in April 1943 was proposed by General Marshall and accepted (with some mental reservations) by the British Chiefs of Staff and the British Government. Colonel Albert C. Wedemeyer of the Army Plans and Operations Division, who accompanied General Marshall, agreed that "Japanese successes should not be allowed to go so far as to prevent the defeat of Germany," but "he warned that the Allies must expect some loss of territory in the Pacific in order to concentrate on Germany."[51] Just which islands fitted into this "loss of territory" was not disclosed.

THE SOLOMONS GET INTO THE OFFICIAL PLANNING

On 17 March 1942 Admiral King sent one of his many official memoranda to General Marshall.

---
[49] COMINCH 301930 Mar. 1942; 311455 Mar. 1942.
[50] (a) JCS 23, 14 Mar. 1942; (b) Churchill, *The Hinge of Fate*, p. 200; (c) Matloff and Snell, *Strategic Planning*, p. 181.
[51] Matloff and Snell, p. 187. British Chiefs of Staff views 8 April 1942.

Because of the consequent urgency of the situation in the Pacific [the Japanese had just invaded New Guinea and occupied Rangoon, Burma] I assume that the War Department will give first priority to movement of troops and aircraft to Australia and the islands in the strength approximately as shown in the subject paper JCS 23 'Strategic Deployment of Land, Sea and Air Forces of the United States' as amended by action taken at the meeting held today.[52]

On 26 March 1942, Rear Admiral Turner in an official memorandum to COMINCH pointed out that the Army reply to Admiral King's memo of 17 March:

> . . . (1) made no commitments as to priority of the movement of Army forces to the islands of the Pacific; (2) markedly lowered the Army Air Corps strength to be supplied to the South Pacific Area islands (75 planes versus 242 planes) over that proposed by the approved JCS 23 as well as the total aircraft for the area (532 planes versus 746 planes).

Rear Admiral Turner further stated:

> It is a far different matter attempting to establish advance bases in the Solomons than in the islands heretofore occupied by the United States and New Zealand.[53]

This latter paragraph indicated that the Solomons venture was beginning to influence future planning—a landmark in the history of the Solomons operation.

Rear Admiral Turner in the same memorandum further recommended that the South Pacific Area be established "as soon as possible" and that COMINCH

> 1. appoint a naval commander of the South Pacific area. . . .
> 2. send amphibious troops. . . .
> 3. assign COMSOPAC tasks commensurate with his forces and require him to carry on a campaign of operations within his power.

DEMARCATION OF AREAS

On 4 April 1942, after discussion and agreement at the highest political and military levels, the whole Pacific Theater was divided into these areas:

Pacific Ocean Area (POA)
Southwest Pacific Area (SWPA)
Southeast Pacific Area (SEPA)

---

[52] Admiral King to General Marshall, memorandum M37/A16-3(4) of 17 Mar. 1942. Memo bears an ink note "General Eisenhower" with the initials GCM.
[53] DNP to COMINCH, memorandum, 26 Mar. 1942.

The Pacific Ocean Area was further divided into three subareas:

North Pacific Area
Central Pacific Area
South Pacific Area

The Pacific Ocean Area was established on 20 April 1942 and the Southwest Pacific Area on 18 April 1942.

The main difference of opinion between Rear Admiral Turner and the Army Planners in regard to the demarcation of areas and area responsibility was caused by the Army's desire to include New Zealand, New Caledonia, New Hebrides, and the Fijis in the Southwest Pacific Area command under General MacArthur, instead of in the Pacific Ocean Area command under Admiral Nimitz. The Fijis lie 1,500 miles east of Australia, and New Zealand lies 1,200 miles to the southeast.

The Navy Planners believed that the Fijis and New Caledonia were parts of the line of communications from Hawaii to Australia, and that the over-all defense of this line of communications should be under one commander. This commander should be a naval officer because it was primarily a sea area line of communications.

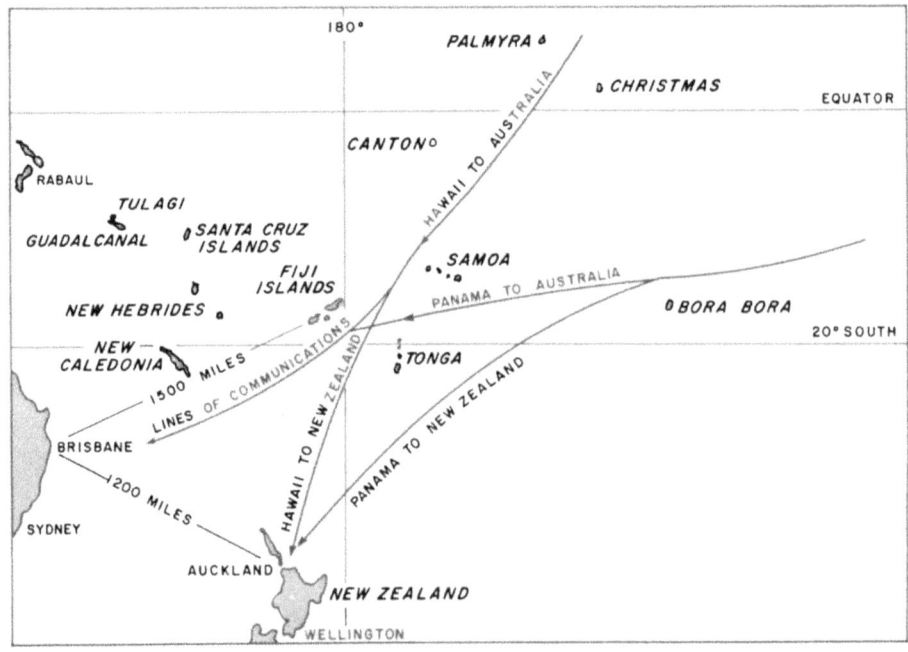

South Pacific lines of communication.

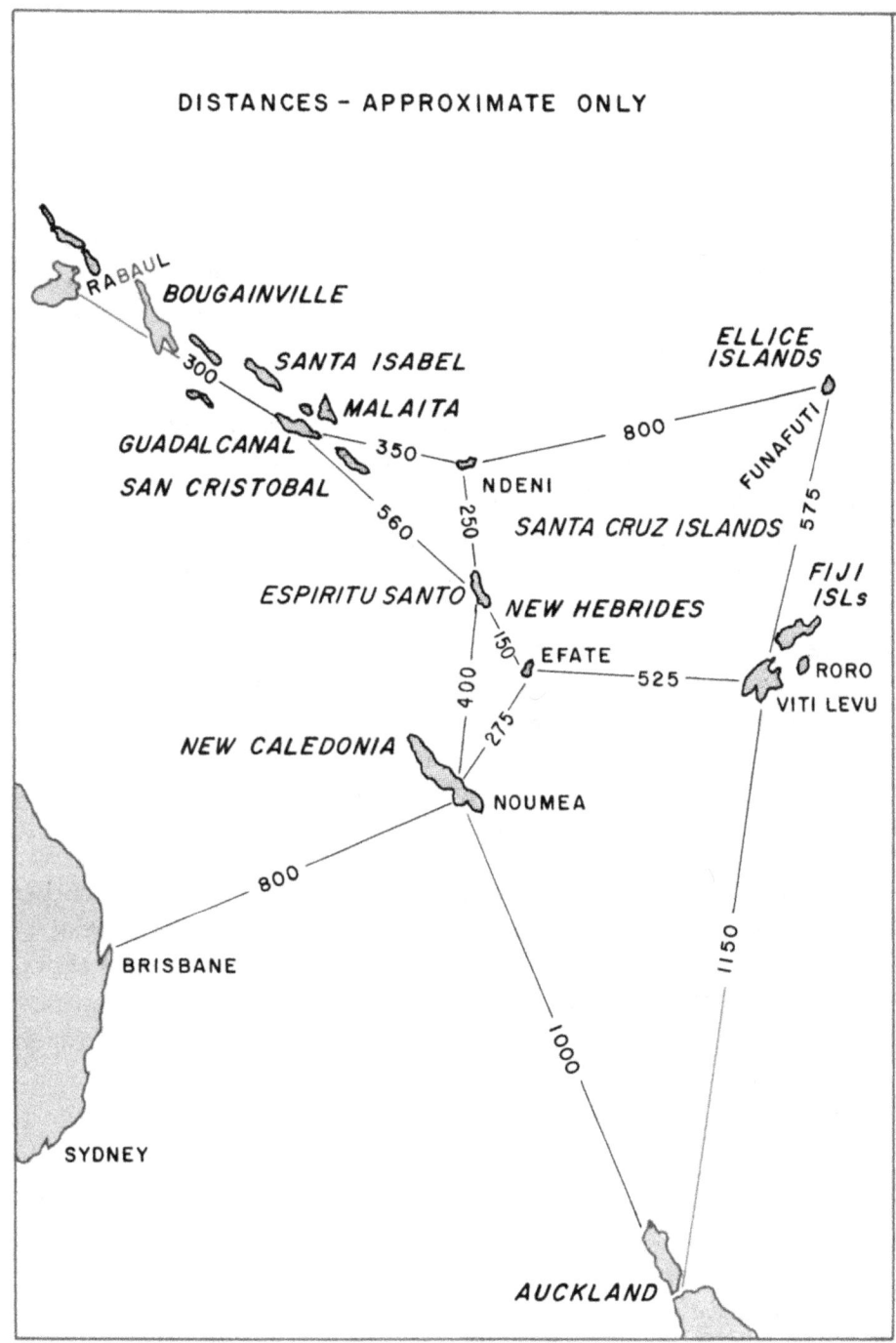

South Pacific distances.

It appeared also to the Navy Planners that if a Japanese Expeditionary Force moved towards either of these areas, it would have to do so under the close protection of the main Japanese Fleet. The defeat of the Japanese Fleet and the turning back of the Japanese Expeditionary Force would depend, as it did later at Coral Sea and Midway, primarily on the Navy, and therefore these areas should be within naval command. On the other hand, the movement of Japanese Expeditionary Forces over short distances of sea area, such as from Amboy in the Netherlands East Indies to Darwin, Australia (600 miles), might occur before the United States Navy could rise to its responsibility and intervene, and the defeat of the Japanese Expeditionary Force would be primarily a land-air task.[54]

The Army Planners and General Marshall eventually accepted this reasoning, and New Zealand, New Caledonia, the New Hebrides, and the Fijis were placed in the Pacific Ocean Area of responsibility. This was not a complete victory for the Naval Planning Staff, however. By agreeing to the 165° East Meridian as the borderline between the Southwest Pacific Area and the Pacific Ocean Area south of the equator to 10° South, the Navy Planners let themselves in for a very difficult negotiating period when a couple of months later they started to get the Navy-Marine amphibious team moving northward toward the Solomons in the South Pacific.

THE SCALES TIP AGAIN

Following General Marshall's return from London, the scales tipped markedly towards giving BOLERO priority over any further build-up of air units or ground strong points on the line of communications from Hawaii to Australia. BOLERO was the general operation of transferring American Armed Forces to the United Kingdom for future use in the European Theater.

However, the period was seized by Rear Admiral Turner to outline to Admiral King his concept of the future war to be waged against Japan in the 25 million square miles of the Western Pacific. This concept is well worth summarizing:

> a. The *FIRST STAGE* in which we are now engaged, envisages building up forces and positions in the Pacific Theater and particularly in the South Pacific and Southwest Pacific for the purpose of holding these areas, and in

---

[54] Admiral King, memorandum for the President, 5 Apr. 1942 (in CCS 57/2).

preparation for launching an ultimate offensive against the Japanese; and for supporting the Fleet forces operating there. During this stage the amphibious forces necessary to carry on this offensive will be assembled in the areas and trained . . . available air, amphibious and naval forces will make minor offensive actions against enemy advanced positions and against exposed naval forces for purposes of attrition. . . .

b. The *SECOND STAGE,* as now envisaged, involves a combined offensive by United States, New Zealand and Australian Amphibious, naval and air forces through the Solomons and New Guinea to capture the Bismarck Archipelago and the Admiralty Islands. Heavy attrition attacks would then be undertaken against the enemy forces and positions in the Caroline and Marshall Islands.

c. The *THIRD STAGE* involves seizure of the Caroline and Marshall Islands and the establishment of Fleet and air advanced bases.

d. The *FOURTH STAGE* involves an advance into the Netherlands East Indies, or alternately, into the Philippines whichever offers the more promising and enduring results.[55]

This memorandum of Real Admiral Turner had major significance for the future conduct of the war. Admiral King approved the memorandum, wholeheartedly. With the addition of annexes containing suitable reference data on Japanese dispositions and losses and copies of certain Joint Planning Staff papers and policy despatches, it became a directive to the Commander in Chief U. S. Pacific Fleet, titled "Information and Instructions Relative to the Pacific Campaign" and was keyed to specific paragraphs of the Navy Basic War Plan, *Rainbow Five,* WPL-46. The letter became a titled part of the War Plan.[56]

One of the annexes to this directive contained the first summary of information available to the Forces Afloat on the assembly of personnel and materiel for Main Fleet Advanced Naval Bases called LIONs, and Secondary Advanced Naval Bases called CUBs, two of the basic ingredients for the success formula in the Pacific. One could sense that the Navy was starting to move.

Despite Prime Minister Churchill's despatch on 17 April 1942, that "a proportion of our combined resources must, for the moment, be set aside to halt the Japanese advance," on 6 May 1942, the President wrote the Joint Chiefs: "I do not want BOLERO slowed down." The President was still hoping and pressing hard for action across the English Channel in 1942.

---

[55] ACofS(P) to COMINCH, memorandum, 16 Apr. 1942, subj: Pacific Ocean Campaign Plan. Modern Military Records, National Archives.
[56] COMINCH to CINCPAC, letter, FF1/A16-3(1) of 23 Apr. 1942, WPL-46-PC. Hereafter WPL-46-PC.

"The necessities of the case call for action in 1942—not 1943." This meant SLEDGEHAMMER.[57]

With this same point of view held strongly in the Army planning staff, it can be seen how difficult it was to take the Joint military decision that it was practical, within United States available resources, to start the offensive-defensive phase of amphibious warfare in the South Pacific. But this, both Admiral King, and his tireless subordinate, Rear Admiral Turner, were still hoping to do.

THE JAPANESE STIR UP THE EAGLE

The Joint Staff Planners, in late April 1942, moved to pass on to the Joint Chiefs their long standing deadlock in regard to "Defense for the Island Bases along the line of communication between Hawaii and Australia," when on 24 April 1942 they agreed that the Joint Staff Plans Committee would proceed as follows:

> Admiral Turner and General Handy will each prepare a memorandum setting forth their views on certain controversial points, these views to be incorporated in the paper when forwarded.[58]

The new draft was available in the early days of May, and Admiral King sought General Marshall's help to resolve the issue since any real acceptance of the Navy's position would require a more offensive minded Army Air Corps position, as well as the ground Army, toward the Pacific War.

However, at this point the Japanese came to the support of the Navy planners' desire for "action" in the Pacific, particularly a United States move into the Solomons. The 1938 Japanese Basic War Plan, in effect at the start of the Japanese-United States phase of World War II, called for the occupation of New Caledonia, Fiji, and Samoa, as a second phase task following conquest and consolidation in Malaya, Netherlands East Indies and the Philippines. These second phase occupations were judged necessary by the Japanese in order to cut the lines of communication between the United States and Australia and make feasible Japanese occupation of Australia.

As a start on these second phase tasks the Japanese, in April 1942, organized for seizing the first stepping-stone 350 miles southward toward New Caledonia. Their then current positions were at Rabaul in New Britain and

---

[57] (a) Churchill, *The Hinge of Fate,* pp. 320, 340; (b) Presidential Memoranda to General Marshall and JCS, 6 May 1942.

[58] Joint Planning Staff Meetings, minutes, 24 Apr. 1942.

at Bougainville in the Northern Solomons. A Tulagi Invasion Group equipped for setting up a seaplane base at Tulagi Island in the Southern Solomons landed there on 3 May 1942. This forward movement put the Japanese almost astride the direct sea route from Hawaii to northern Australia. It also put the planners on COMINCH Staff, who were particularly concerned with the SOPAC area, in the jumping up and down stage. But it was to be 60 days and 60 nights more before the Joint Chiefs could agree on a directive governing counter-offensive movements in the SOPAC-SOWESPAC Area.

And, Admiral King, on the day before the President said "I do not want BOLERO slowed down," was outlining to the Joint Chiefs the reasons for doing more to meet the vital military needs of the United States in the Pacific. He wrote:

MEMORANDUM TO JOINT U.S. CHIEFS OF STAFF
Subject: J.C.S. 48. Defense of Island Bases in the Pacific

1. In paragraph 5 of the memorandum from the Joint Planners forming a part of J.C.S. 48, the statement appears; 'The Army members of the J.P.S. are reluctant to recommend any increase in aviation in the Pacific Area at this time due to the fact that any increase in this area means not only a corresponding decrease in the main effort but also an inordinate delay in its initiation.' I agree that there must be no undue delay in the deployment of available forces in the main effort; but I am not in agreement with the recommendation that forces in the Pacific be kept at a bare minimum.

2. The Pacific Theater is an area for which the United States bears full strategic responsibility. The recent Japanese successes in Burma, added to previous successes, leave the Japanese free to choose any new line of action they see fit, including an attack in force on Australia, on the Australia-Hawaii line of communications, on Hawaii or on Alaska. Even now they are massing strong land, sea, and air forces in the Mandate Area beyond our range of observation.

3. The basic strategic plan on which we are now operating is to hold in the Pacific. I am not convinced that the forces now there or allocated to that theater are sufficient to "hold" against a determined attack in force by the Japanese, an attack which they can initiate very soon. The mounting of BOLERO must not be permitted to interfere with our vital needs in the Pacific. I am not convinced that the Japanese are going to allow us to 'hold' but are going to drive and drive hard.

4. The disastrous consequences which would result if we are unable to hold the present position in the Pacific Areas are self-evident. We have already seen, in the Far East and in Burma, the results of being 'spread out too thin;' we must not commit the same error in the Pacific Ocean Areas.

5. Important as the mounting of BOLERO may be, the Pacific problem is

no less so, and is certainly the more urgent—it must be faced *now*. Quite apart from any idea of future advance in this theater we must see to it that we are actually able to maintain our present positions. We must not permit diversion of our forces to any proposed operation in any other theater to the extent that we find ourselves unable to fulfill our obligation to implement our basic strategy plan in the Pacific theater, which is to hold what we have against any attack that the Japanese are capable of launching against us.[59]

E. J. KING

The Japanese occupation of the Southern Solomons had taken place during the same period when they made an unsuccessful attempt to occupy Port Moresby in Southeast New Guinea only 500 miles north of Townsville, Australia. Air reconnaissance units operating from Tulagi and Port Moresby would have brought all of the Coral Sea and northeastern Australia under their conquering eyes.

GENERAL MacARTHUR HELPS THE NAVAL PLANNERS

General MacArthur, after the 8 May 1942 Battle of the Coral Sea, which had luckily turned back the Japanese Port Moresby Invasion Group, joined forces with the Navy Planners in plugging for stronger action in the Pacific. His despatch of 23 May 1942 read in part:

> Lack of sea power in the Pacific is and has been the fatal weakness in our position since the beginning of the war.

Continuing, he was so bold as to suggest that the Indian and Atlantic Oceans be stripped of sea power so as to combine British and American naval strength and to overwhelm the Japanese Navy:

> Much more than the fate of Australia will be jeopardized if this is not done. The United States will face a series of such disasters.[60]

This despatch struck a responsive note with Admiral King since an appreciation of the realities of sea power was not always displayed by Army Planners at lower levels in Washington. The next day, 24 May 1942, Admiral King sent to General Marshall a paper which he proposed should be transmitted to the Combined Chiefs of Staff by the Joint Chiefs of Staff. In this paper, Admiral King stated that the Japanese were devoting "practically their entire naval strength, plus a great part of their air and army strength for offensive action against the Australia—Noumea—Fiji—Samoa

---

[59] COMINCH, memorandum, 5 May 1942.
[60] Australia Dispatch 199.

—Hawaii—Alaska line."⁶¹ Admiral King included among his recommendations that air strength in the Pacific be increased as rapidly as possible and that the British Eastern Fleet be moved to Colombo as soon as practicable, for concentration in the Fiji-Australian area by 1 July 1942.⁶²

Any time Admiral King felt it necessary to call in the British Navy to shore up the United States Navy in its own bailiwick, the long reaches of the Pacific, one could surmise that he considered the situation bordered on the desperate.

As May drew to a close and the coming battle for Midway Island became more imminent with every passing hour, Admiral Nimitz proposed to General MacArthur that the Pacific Ocean Area Marines try to knock out the seaplane base the Japanese were evolving at Tulagi in General MacArthur's domain. He suggested using the 1st Marine Raider Battalion based in Samoa, 1800 miles to the eastward of Tulagi. The object was to deny the Japanese seaplane reconnaissance south of Tulagi against the South Pacific major amphibious offensive, hopefully to be inaugurated in accordance with the COMINCH directive of 3 April.

Had the air base at Espiritu Santo in the New Hebrides been complete or just usable on the day this despatch was sent, 28 May 1942, the reaction to this offensive proposal in Admiral King's headquarters would have been more strongly favorable despite General MacArthur's negative reaction. However, the construction forces were just arriving. Tulagi was about equidistant from Rabaul and from Espiritu Santo, but the Japanese air base at Rabaul was operational and well manned by a Japnese air flotilla, while the Espiritu Santo air base was little more than a gleam in Vice Admiral Ghormley's eye. The Marines would be subject to air attack mounted from Rabaul and not under air protection mounted from Espiritu Santo. Therefore Admiral King's approval was limited to a "disabling or destroying raid," but no "permanent occupation." Admiral Nimitz said later this had been his intention in the first place.⁶³

THE BRITISH COOL OFF SLEDGEHAMMER

About this same time, the British again cooled off the United States Army Planners on the immediacy of the cross-channel operation. The Prime

---
⁶¹ Proposed JCS Memo to CCS, 24 May 1942.
⁶² COMINCH to COMNAVFOREUR Ser 100046 of Jun. 1942.
⁶³ COMINCH 031905 Apr. 1942; CINCPAC to COMSOWESPACFOR, 280351 May 1942; COMSOWESPACFOR 291335 May 1942; COMINCH 010100 Jun. 1942.

Minister, on 28 May 1942, in a despatch to the President stated that "certain difficulties had arisen in the planning," put in a plug for the occupation of North Africa and stated that Admiral Lord Louis Mountbatten was being sent to Washington to discuss "a landing in the North of Norway."[64] Lord Louis arrived on 3 June 1942, by which time the Army Air Force B-17s had already started making near-misses on Admiral Tanaka's Transport Group of the Japanese Midway Occupation Force.

However, on 1 June 1942, the President was telling Mr. Molotov, the Soviet Union's People's Commissar of Foreign Affairs, in Washington as a special representative of Commissar Stalin, that he expected to establish a Second Front in 1942, and giving him a strong commitment to do so.[65] If the President's word was to be his bond, it was apparent to the military planning staffs that the priority build-up in England of United States troops and landing craft must continue at maximum rate.

Elated by the Navy's victory at Midway, on 4 June 1942, the whole COMINCH Planning Staff was anxious that the United States seize the Pacific Ocean initiative from the Japanese. This could not be done by sitting back and congratulating each other on the first real major victory of the Pacific War. Midway had to be promptly followed by new initiatives in the Pacific Ocean, and this was the point Rear Admiral Turner stressed as in late May and early June he progressively handed over his Chief Planner's billet on Admiral King's staff to his relief, Rear Admiral Charles M. Cooke. The very minimum effort necessary to retain the intiative, he believed, would be to seize island positions essential for disrupting the flow of strategic materials within the Japanese Co-prosperity Sphere.[66]

By late June 1942, the British Prime Minister was in Washington again, depressed over the surrender of his 33,000-man garrison at Tobruk. He was anxious for American help nearly everywhere except on the continent of Europe. He was ready "to bury 'SLEDGEHAMMER,' which had been dead for some time."[67]

ADMIRAL KING STIRS UP A PESTILENCE—
LIGHTS UP A WATCHTOWER

Admiral King seized this moment, when it appeared that United States

---
[64] Churchill to Roosevelt, 28 May 1942, in Sherwood, *Roosevelt and Hopkins*, p. 556.
[65] Matloff and Snell, *Strategic Planning*, pp. 231–32.
[66] Turner.
[67] Churchill, *The Hinge of Fate*, pp. 382, 433.

Army and Navy forces being sent to England for SLEDGEHAMMER or BOLERO might be there a long time before facing combat, to direct CINCPAC and COMSOPAC to prepare for an offensive against the Lower Solomons, using United States Marines. He hoped the Santa Cruz Islands would be occupied before the Japanese got there and Tulagi would be taken from the Japanese before it could be built up to great defensive strength.[68]

Rear Admiral Turner prepared to undertake this considerable task and to bring it to consummation in just 35 days. Even though he was then on leave in California, the First Marine Division was on the high seas enroute to far away New Zealand and the essential amphibious ships were scattered all over the eastern and southern half of the Pacific Ocean Area. Only a leader like Admiral King with great knowledge and great faith in his organization and the subordinates who were to lead their parts of it, could have issued such a preparatory order.

When Admiral King's history-making despatch went out on 25 June 1942, the undertaking of offensive-defensive amphibious operations hadn't been approved by the Joint Chiefs, whose Army representative was the chief revivifier of SLEDGEHAMMER. Much less had it been approved by the President, who, at the moment, hankered for action on the continent of Europe and for nothing more than hanging on in the Pacific. How Admiral King decided he could overcome these two major obstacles, and a not so minor one of whether the Army or the Navy would command the first offensive amphibious operation, is not known. It is known, however, that when the Chief of Staff of the U. S. Army writes a letter to the Commander in Chief of the United States Fleet and gets an answer the same day, the question under discussion is hot. This happened on 26 June 1942.[69]

The subject in controversy was who was to command the first real offensive-defensive amphibious operation in the Pacific. The Army had the book partly on its side, since one of the objectives, Tulagi, lay in the area of the Army Commander of the Southwest Pacific, General Douglas MacArthur. However, the other objective, the Santa Cruz Islands, was in the area of the Naval Commander of the South Pacific area, Vice Admiral Robert Ghormley. The Navy thus had the book partly on its side and Admiral King wholly on its side, plus the logical military reasons that:

---

[68] COMINCH to CINCPAC, despatch 24 Jun. 1942. Info C/S USA, COMSOWESPACFOR, and COMSOPACFOR.
[69] (a) C/SA to CINCUS, memorandum, no ser of 26 Jun. 1942. Modern Military Records, National Archives; (b) COMINCH to C/S USA, letter, Ser 00555, 26 Jun. 1942.

1. nearly all the offensive forces directly involved were to be supplied by the naval Pacific Ocean Area.
2. the offensive forces must prepare for the operation while within the naval Pacific Ocean Area.
3. the offensive forces must be covered during the operation from the naval Pacific Ocean Area, and then supported logistically from the naval Pacific Ocean Area.

With this background Admiral King advised General Marshall that the offensive operation "must be conducted under the direction of the Commander in Chief, Pacific Fleet."

It is a tribute to General Marshall's military judgment that he saw the validity of the points made, particularly when he read the last sentence "I think it is important that this [the immediate initiation of these operations] be done, even if no support of Army Forces in the Southwest Pacific be made available." Admiral King made this point even clearer by informing CINCPAC on 27 June that the Navy might have to go it alone and planning should go forward on that basis.[70]

To preserve the validity of area command for posterity, the Joint Chiefs then agreed to a 60 to 360 mile westward shift of area boundaries between the Pacific Ocean Area and Southwest Pacific Area in the island cluttered expanse of the ocean south of the equator between 159° East Longitude and 165° East Longitude. Effective 1 August 1942, the new boundary would run south from the equator along 159° East Longitude. This shifted the boundary so that it was just 35 miles to the westward of Guadalcanal Island.[71]

After this westward shift, both of the proposed landings, Santa Cruz and Tulagi, would be in the Pacific Ocean Area.

With the command issue agreed upon, and without too much further discussion, the Joint Chiefs received Presidential approval to open the United States offensive-defensive phase of the amphibious war in the Pacific.

There are two amazing things about the first offensive amphibious operation insofar as the Joint Chiefs' 2 July 1942 directive is concerned.[72] This directive listed Task One, Task Two and Task Three objectives. The Task One invasion objectives were:

a. Santa Cruz Islands

---

[70] COMINCH 271414 Jun. 1944.
[71] COMINCH to C/SA, Ser 00555 of 26 Jun. 1942.
[72] JCS 00581 of 2 Jul. 1942, Joint Directive for Offensive Operations in the Southwest Pacific Area.

b. Tulagi
   c. Adjacent positions.

Yet, Santa Cruz, first on the list, was not even occupied for months, and Guadalcanal, where most of the fighting took place, was not even mentioned by name in the directive. It is a further anomaly that the code name for the whole Task One operation was PESTILENCE, and the subsidiary Tulagi operation was named WATCHTOWER and the repeatedly postponed Santa Cruz Islands operation was designated HUDDLE. The only one of these code words to survive at all is WATCHTOWER, while the code name for the island of Guadalcanal, CACTUS, is part of the folklore of all World War II American adults.

SOUTH PACIFIC AREA AND SOUTH PACIFIC FORCE

When Vice Admiral Robert L. Ghormley, the prospective Commander of the South Pacific and Kelly Turner's future boss, arrived in Washington from London on 17 April 1942 where he had been a highly successful Naval Observer, working with the British Admiralty, the determination to try for seizure of the Santa Cruz Islands and the lower Solomons was strong in COMINCH Plans Division. However, this was a period when SLEDGEHAMMER and BOLERO were riding high. Therefore, no agreement at the Joint planning level, or the Joint Chiefs' level, was practical for a definite amphibious operation in the South Pacific.

Despite this lack of a specific agreement at the Joint working level, COMINCH had directed CINCPAC on 3 April 1942 to

> prepare for execution of major amphibious offensive against frontiers held by Japan, initially to be launched from South Pacific and Southwest Pacific Areas.[73]

This dispatch would get the Planning Staff at Pearl up on the step.

Draft instructions for Commander South Pacific Area to be issued by CINCPAC were already in existence in COMINCH Headquarters during this mid-April period and Vice Admiral Ghormley contributed to their further development. On 23 April 1942, Admiral King from Washington and Admiral Nimitz from Pearl, officially proceeded under temporary additional duty orders to San Francisco for a conference. Out of this conference came the basic CINCPAC directive to Commander South Pacific which also con-

---

[73] COMINCH 031905 Apr. 1942.

tained the magic words; "Prepare to launch a major amphibious offensive against positions held by the Japanese." [74]

Meanwhile Vice Admiral Ghormley was briefed by Rear Admiral Turner back in Washington on the build-up of naval forces in the South Pacific which would permit this offensive. Dates and specific objectives were not only "iffy," they were in the realm of speculation. They depended specifically on obtaining approval from the Joint Chiefs, which depended, in turn, almost wholly on when the necessary resources could be made available, and where the greatest rewards would come from using them. The Fall of 1942 seemed to be the earliest possible date.[75]

However, to prevent the Japanese leap-frogging from the Solomons to New Caledonia via the Santa Cruz Islands and the New Hebrides, the necessity of early occupation of the Santa Cruz Islands and northern New Hebrides was pointed out to Vice Admiral Ghormley.

It was late in March or early April and weeks before Vice Admiral Ghormley's departure from Washington on 28 April 1942 that Rear Admiral Turner learned that he was to leave his planning assignment after being relieved by Captain Charles M. (Savvy) Cooke, U. S. Navy, Class of 1910, who was already slated to be promoted to rear admiral. Although he had specifically requested the amphibious detail, there was a long, difficult, worry-loaded two months, not ending until 3 June 1942, before Rear Admiral Turner knew definitely that he was to be lucky enough to serve under Ghormley in the South Pacific Area in the "opportunity packed billet" as Commander Amphibious Force South Pacific Force.[76]

The Chief of Naval Personnel signed Rear Admiral Turner's first set of orders on 20 May 1942. These orders directed him to report to the Commandant of the 12th Naval District for shore duty. The Commandant, 12th Naval District, operated a "Receiving ship for Admirals." On tap here for call up by CINCPAC were one or more Flag officers who could be used for new organizations or task forces as well as to replace any Flag officers killed or incapacitated for duty, or who did not meet their superiors' expectations.

---

[74] CINCPAC to Prospective Commander of South Pacific Area and South Pacific Force, letter, A16-3/P17 Ser 090W of 12 May 1942.

[75] Quoted in Morison, *Coral Sea, Midway and Submarine Actions, May 1942–August 1942* (Vol. IV), p. 251.

[76] (a) Turner; (b) RKT to Deputy CNO Administration, letter, 27 Sep. 1950; (c) Captain C. M. Cooke, USN, was detached from CO *Pennsylvania* by orders signed in BUPERS on 3 April and reported COMINCH on 18 April 1942; (d) "Propose employ Turner as Commander Amphibious Force, South Pacific." CINCPAC 020503 June 1942.

These rear admirals were available without the normal delay entailed in relieving them from a current job.

About 20 May 1942, the decision of Admiral King to make Rear Admiral Turner available, in the near future, to CINCPAC for duty afloat in the Pacific Fleet was passed to the Bureau of Naval Personnel. New orders were issued on 25 May appropriately modifying the original orders and directing Turner to report to CINCPAC at the end of his leave of absence. Then Admiral King decided he wanted Rear Admiral Turner at hand until after the Japanese attack on Midway had been met. So a third set of orders was issued.[77] Under this last set, Rear Admiral Turner departed Washington on 12 June 1942 by automobile for Pacific Grove, California, under proceed (four days' delay) orders, ten days' travel time, and ten days' delay to count as leave of absence.

Rear Admiral Turner was delighted to get to the business at hand, fighting the Japanese, and greatly concerned with his share of the responsibility for making the first amphibious operation a victory of which the Navy and Ernie King would be proud.[78]

Vice Admiral Ghormley had departed Washington on 1 May 1942 and assumed command of the South Pacific Area and South Pacific Force on 19 June some seven weeks later, although he was in the South Pacific Area for almost a month before assuming command. Rear Admiral Turner assumed command of the South Pacific Amphibious Force about a month later, 18 July 1942. This was just 14 days before the initial target date for the first major United States Navy amphibious landings in World War II, and 20 days before the actual landing.

ASSEMBLING THE STAFF OF COMPHIBFORSOPAC

The first business of a Flag officer upon being designated to a new command is to try to prevail upon the Bureau of Naval Personnel to order a few top flight officers—the real heavy cream of the crop—into key positions on his staff. Whether he succeeds or not depends on such factors as:

1. The Flag officer flies one, two, three, or four stars.
2. For whom the desired officer is currently working and how cooperative this officer may be in letting him go to another billet.

---

[77] BuPers Orders Pers 6312-38970, 20 May 1942, 25 May 1942, and 2 Jun. 1942; (b) Note, RKT on June 2nd Orders.
[78] Turner.

3. The actual availability of the desired officer from the viewpoint of the Bureau of Naval Personnel.
4. The officer's own personal assessments of the change, and how hard he tries for the staff billet.

If the Flag officer has worked his way up the ladder through billets in the Bureau of Personnel, he has a far wider knowledge of officers' records and reputations than if he has not, and generally a warmer friendship with those currently sitting at the detail desks. Rear Admiral Turner had not been a BUPERS bureaucrat. He had been a two-star Flag officer only seven months. And he had had a few stormy telephone conversations with detail desks in the process of assembling an adequate planning staff for COMINCH.

In any case, Admiral Turner remembered that he had had a "hell of a time" trying to get anyone whom he particularly wanted ordered to his first afloat staff. In fact, he "fired and fell back." He batted .000 on the names he submitted.[79]

The Bureau then suggested officers and he accepted them. In May 1942, there was a miniscule number of naval officers with a background of peacetime amphibious training and none with a background of wartime amphibious operations. Rear Admiral Turner had not touched stays often enough with any of the few peacetime amphibiously qualified officers to pinpoint them as desirable members of his staff. The Bureau had a thousand times more places to billet such officers in the explosively expanding amphibious forces than there were officers available.

Consequently, it is regrettable, but not surprising, that, except for the Flag Secretary, not a single naval officer selected by the Bureau and ordered to the staff of the Commander of the Amphibious Force South Pacific, which was our first amphibious command in World War II to enter into large scale combat with the enemy, had any special amphibious training, or any recent peacetime amphibious experience. Professional knowledge based on actual training in amphibious operations, had to come from the Marine officers on the staff. As might be expected, the Marines were a first-rate group.[80]

By 9 June 1942, Rear Admiral Turner knew which officers the Bureau of Personnel planned to order to his staff, for he drafted a four-page memorandum to the Assistant Chief of Staff, Colonel Linscott, on that date,

---

[79] Turner.
[80] Ibid.

listing them and all the existing COMINCH letters bearing on LONE WOLF or the establishment of PHIBFORSOPAC.[81]

> ... I believe that the most difficult and most important task of the Flag Officer is to select his chief assistant. More hinges on this decision than on any other.[82]

The most obvious shortcoming of the Bureau of Personnel was the failure to provide a Chief of Staff who could report before Rear Admiral Turner actually arrived in the South Pacific. At that time, Captain Thomas G. Peyton, U. S. Navy, who had only served a dog watch as Captain of the Port at Noumea, New Caledonia, reported for this important billet. Peyton did not seek the duty and was not a personal friend of Rear Admiral Turner.[83] Furthermore, Captain Peyton lacked two of the desirable attributes for measurable success under Turner. He was not "lightning fast on the uptake," and he was not given to fighting back with all his resources, when picked upon. But Peyton was a very capable naval officer of the highest moral character. He had a very real degree of humility among a breed of cats, where the humble were as scarce as typhoons in the Pacific in June.

The 11-man staff [84] listed below consisted of seven Naval officers and four Marine officers. All were of the regular service except the assistant communications officer. Only Linscott, Weir, and Harris made contact in Washington prior to Rear Admiral Turner's departure. Doyle and Bowling joined up in San Francisco. Hains joined in Pearl Harbor; Peyton reported in Auckland; and Lewis could not report until the Task Force was off the Fiji Islands, in late July. Baskin and Williams did not report in Noumea for another month, on 19 August 1942.

Captain Thomas G. Peyton   Chief of Staff [85]

---

[81] COMINCH, memorandum of 9 Jun. 1942.

[82] Lieutenant Commander H. H. Frost, "Letters on Staff Duty," *United States Naval Institute Proceedings*, Vol. 45 (August 1919), p. 1316.

[83] Interviews with Commodore Thomas G. Peyton, 22 and 29 May 1961. Hereafter Peyton. Captain Peyton reported as Captain of the Port, Noumea on 20 May 1942; ordered as Chief of Staff, COMPHIBFORSOPAC by BUPERS on 4 July 1942; detached as Captain of the Port on 14 July 1942; reported 18 July 1942.

[84] COMPHIBFORSOPAC, letter, 18 Jul. 1942, subj: Establishment of Amphibious Force South Pacific Force. Hereafter Establishment Letter, 1942.

[85] PEYTON (Commodore) (1915); Battleship duty in World War I, then destroyer duty and command and submarine duty and command; Flag Lieutenant Commander Battleship Division One; Prior World War II, Command Destroyer Divisions 18 and 60 and Destroyer Squadron 9; Six months Turner's staff; Distinguished service in command of battleship *Indiana* through New Georgia campaign and in command of a logistical task group supporting 3rd and 5th Fleets during Iwo Jima and Okinawa campaign; Commandant Naval Base Guam after World War II.

Colonel Henry D. Linscott, USMC	Assistant Chief of Staff [86]
Captain James H. Doyle	Operations Officer [87]
Lieutenant Colonel Frank E. Weir, USMC	Assistant Operations Officer (Air) [88]
Lieutenant Colonel Harold D. Harris, USMC	Intelligence Officer [89]
Lieutenant Commander Hamilton Hains	Aide and Flag Secretary [90]
Lieutenant Commander Selman S. Bowling	Communications Officer [91]
Lieutenant Commander Arthur C. W. Baskin	Assistant Intelligence, Aerologist [92]

---

[86] LINSCOTT (Lieutenant General) (Commissioned May 1917); Santo Domingo and France in World War I; 1927 Nicaraguan Campaign; postgraduate law 1930–33; Division Marine Officer BATDIVONE; Operations and Training Officer, Amphibious Corps, Atlantic Fleet 1941–1942; 12 months Turner's staff; distinguished duty staff 3rd Amphibious Force during Vella Lavella, Treasury-Bougainville, and Empress Augusta Bay operations; Command Amphibious Training Pacific Fleet; Director, Landing Force Development Center.

[87] DOYLE (Vice Admiral) (1920); Battleship, destroyer, tender duty 1919–1926; postgraduate law (with distinction) at George Washington University; destroyer duty and command; staff duty Commander Destroyers, and Aide Commandant 16th Naval District; Command *Regulus*, a 10,000-ton, 11.5-knot, 20-year-old non-amphibious cargo ship early 1942; 12 months Turner's staff; distinguished duty Amphibious Section Admiral King's Headquarters; distinguished duty in command light cruiser *Pasadena* during Okinawa campaign; again on Turner's staff at the United Nations; Korean War, Commander Amphibious Force Far East during the amphibious triumphs of the Inchon landing and the Hungnam evacuation.

[88] WEIR (Major General) (1923) (Aviator); amphibious exercises at Culebra 1924; flight training; Nicaraguan Campaign 1927; various Marine Squadron Air Billets; Marine Corps School, Chemical Warfare School 1934, Army Air Corps Tactical School 1938; tactical aviation instructor at Marine Corps School 1940–1942; 12 months Turner's staff; distinguished service Staff, Commander 3rd Amphibious Force, during Vella Lavella, Treasury-Bougainville, and Empress Augusta Bay Operations; Command Marine Aircraft Group 32 in China in immediate post-World War II period.

[89] HARRIS (Brigadier General) (1924); Ecole Superieure de guerre and Army Infantry Schools; Officer in Charge Intelligence Section of Plans and Policies, Marine Corps Headquarters 1941–42; five months Turner's staff; Distinguished duty with 1st Marines during the New Britain Campaign; Command 5th Marines at Peleliu; Again on Turner's staff at United Nations.

[90] HAINS (Rear Admiral) (1925); battleship and destroyer duty; postgraduate general line and junior course Marine Corps School 1933–36; destroyer and cruiser duty; 12 months Turner's staff; then distinguished duty as Commander Escort Division during Bismarck Archipelago Campaign and on Staff, Commander Amphibious Group Six, 7th Fleet, during five major landings.

[91] BOWLING (Rear Admiral) (1927); gunboat, destroyer, light and heavy cruiser duty 1927–1934; postgraduate applied communications, radio officer; Staff COMBATDIVTWO, then Battleship *Colorado*; four months on Turner's staff; two years distinguished duty in motor torpedo boats in 7th Fleet during New Guinea, Borneo, and Philippine Campaigns.

[92] BASKIN (Lieutenant Commander) (1927); battleship, destroyer, light cruiser duty 1927–1934; postgraduate general line, then lighter than air training and postgraduate in meteorology at California Institute of Technology; aircraft carrier *Ranger* and Naval Air Stations; eight months' duty Turner's staff; hospitalization and physical retirement 1 May 1944.

Lieutenant Commander John S. Lewis	Aide and Flag Lieutenant [93]
Lieutenant Robert A. Williams (SC)	Supply Officer [94]
Captain R. A. Nicholson, USMCR	Assistant Communications Officer [95]

This unmethodical and straggling forming up of the new PHIBFOR-SOPAC staff stretched over 10 weeks and 10,000 miles of ocean. Only the marked capabilities of the individual regular officers of that period, their resourcefulness and acceptance of the principle of doing the best they could with what was at hand provided a basis for the hope that our first large scale amphibious invasion of Japanese held positions would go off reasonably well.

AMPHIBIOUS PERSONNEL PROBLEMS

This is as good a time as any to discuss the officer personnel problem which lay like a heavy soaking blanket over the amphibious forces during the 1942 and 1943 period.

As a result of the 1938 Personnel Bill, which the old Bureau of Navigation urged the Congress to inflict on the Navy, the seagoing officers of the Navy, upon completing the required years of service in grade, became eligible for selection to commander and captain. The yearly selection board then divided them into four main categories:

1. Selected as best fitted for promotion.
2. Selected as fitted for promotion and retained on active duty.
3. Selected as fitted for promotion, but not retained on active duty.
4. Not qualified and not selected for promotion.

---

[93] LEWIS (Rear Admiral) (1932); battleships and destroyer duty 1932–1936; postgraduate general line, then heavy cruiser *Portland;* 23 months Turner's staff; then distinguished service command destroyer *Soley;* After World War II, duty on Turner's staff at United Nations; command light cruiser *Astoria,* duty with NATO, and Staff, Commander Amphibious Force, Pacific Fleet.

[94] WILLIAMS (Captain Supply Corps); Harvard, 1937; Supply School, shore assignments; five months Turner's staff; 23 months supply officer heavy cruiser *Vincennes* during Marianas, Philippine, and Okinawa Campaigns; post-World War II command Naval Supply Depot Guantanamo, duty with Bureau Supplies and Accounts and Defense Supply Agency.

[95] NICHOLSON (Marine Corps Reserve); Washington and Lee, 1939, Phi Beta Kappa; Marine Corps Schools; then 18 months Turner's staff.

Rank upon retirement and year of Naval Academy or other college graduation shown in brief summary of service.

The "best fitted" group averaged from 60–70 percent of each Naval Academy class. The two "fitted" groups totaling 25–30 percent contained many officers whose capabilities were judged to be only a small fraction below those of the "best fitted" group, plus a number who were not carrying a full head of steam as they moved into their early or late forties. Occasionally a personality idiosyncrasy of an extremely capable officer caused his name to appear in the "fitted" list, and from time to time a minor dereliction of duty after many years of highly satisfactory performance led to the same tagging, although generally such officers just were not deemed qualified and were not selected.

Fortunately for the Navy, the Congress, disturbed by the approach of war in Europe, soon authorized the Navy to order a considerable number of retired officers to active duty, and a little later to retain on active duty all officers who were slated to be retired upon completion of 21, 28, or 35 years of service after failure of selection to the next higher rank. These yearly bench marks were those set by law for automatic retirement of lieutenant commanders, commanders, and captains respectively when not selected to the next higher grade.

The Bureau of Naval Personnel rated command duty in large combatant ships—carriers, battleships, cruisers—and command of units of destroyers as requiring the service of the "best fitted" officers in the senior grades. For years and years, auxiliary ships and other minor commands had been rated more than a shade less desirable than large combatant commands. Amphibious ships started World War II officially titled "auxiliaries," although it soon became apparent that they were "the closest to the enemy the mostest" of any ships in the Navy. As these large made-over merchantmen came into commission in the Navy in 1941 and 1942, they received more than their share of Commanding Officers who

1. As it turned out, were not selected to rear admiral with their contemporaries,
2. Had lost station on their classmates as they battled up past the ever more critical selection boards, or
3. Had been designated as "fitted" for promotion to commander or captain but not as "best fitted."

The amphibious skipper was apt to think, or say, he was serving in "The Second Class Navy." This was a tremendous morale factor which had to be fought every step of the way by the Flag officers ordered to command amphibious groups or forces. It was not licked in a month or even in the first year of World War II. The prime billets for the BUPERS "hot shots" were the big carriers, and the new battleships, and Rear Admiral Turner's efforts to draft some of these "hot shot" officers into the amphibious ship commands were futile, even after he had acquired three stars on his shoulders. He was forever grateful to those officers in our Navy who had acquired less than an ultra plus ultra rating in the peacetime Navy, but who turned in a superb and winning performance in battling through to the beaches with their troops and long tons of logistic support.[96]

Rear Admiral Turner faced the following situation in July-August 1942. In the three transport divisions of transports and cargo ships (APs and AKs) in Amphibious Force South Pacific Force, on the day of its formal organization, 18 July 1942, there were nine captains and 10 commanders of the United States Navy either commanding one of the ships or having a division or squadron command.[97] At this time, the most recent rear admiral selection list extended down through the Class of 1915, and actual promotion to rear admiral had taken place recently down into the Class of 1913. The captain selection list extended down through the Class of 1920, and actual promotion had taken place recently down through three quarters of the Class of 1918.

Of the 19 naval officers in command in these transport divisions, only four were on station and had not missed either the recent selection to the next higher rank, or a previous one at some time in their naval career. Nevertheless, performance of duty of the very highest order in WATCHTOWER and in subsequent combat operations in the Pacific brought promotion to the great majority of these 19 officers. Three became commodores, one a rear admiral, and one a vice admiral on the active list of the Navy. Nine of the 10 commanders won promotion to captain on the active list during the war. Despite Rear Admiral Turner's strong and repeated recommendations to the Navy Department, supported by his seniors in the chain of command, he was unable to obtain promotion to rear admiral of several of the commodores who so ably served him, the Navy, and the nation.[98]

WHEN, WHERE, WITH WHAT?

Admiral King was pressing his naval subordinates to get on the counter-

---

[96] Turner.
[97] (a) N.R., 1938–43; (b) N.D., 1 Mar. 1942; (c) Establishment letter, 1942.
[98] (a) Turner; (b) N.R., 1942–45, 1947; (c) COMPHIBFORSOPAC to COMSOPAC 192350 Jul. 1942; COMSOPAC to CINCPAC 210050 Jul. 1942.

offensive all during the second half of June. At the same time, he was pressing his co-worker on the Joint Chiefs of Staff, General Marshall, for the same purpose:

> As you know, it has been my conviction that the Japanese will not stand still in the South Pacific and will not let us stand still. Either they will press us with an extension of their offensives, seeking weak spots in order to break our line of communications, or we will have to be pressing them. It is urgent, in my opinion, that we lose no time in taking the initiative ourselves.[99]

Although Rear Admiral Turner knew when he left Washington on 12 June 1942 that there were going to be combat operations in the South Pacific, he did not know WHEN the operation was to take place, nor exactly WHERE, though his personal choices of objectives were the lower Solomons and Santa Cruz Islands.

He enjoyed his leave of absence, as much as anyone could under the circumstances. Before his leave was up, he was ordered by a COMINCH telegram into San Francisco on 29 June 1942 to rendezvous with five of his staff officers (Linscott, Weir, Harris, Doyle, and Bowling). COMINCH and CINCPAC were also soon to head towards San Francisco.

Rear Admiral Turner wrote in regard to this period:

> I first knew definitely of the Operation on June thirtieth, when staff officers of mine flew from Washington and met me in San Francisco. I drew up a project and submitted it to Admiral King and Admiral Nimitz on July third. This project was approved in general terms. Then on July fourth, I flew to Honolulu; remained three days consulting with Admiral Nimitz, and his staff, and Admirals Fletcher, Kinkaid, and Admiral Fitch. Admiral Noyes was at sea, en route from San Diego to the South Pacific with some of the troops. On July eighth, I departed Honolulu, flew to Auckland, arriving on July fifteenth. Took command of the Amphibious Forces on July eighteenth and sailed from Wellington with part of the force on July twenty-second.[100]

It was the nation's and the Navy's great gain that CINCPAC survived a crash landing coming into San Francisco on 30 June 1942 for his conference with Admiral King of 3 July, when his big four-motor Sikorsky amphibian turned over on its back, killing the co-pilot. Admiral Nimitz had another

---

[99] COMINCH to C/SA, letter, FF1/A16-3(1), Ser 00544 of 25 Jun. 1942, subj: Offensive Operations in the South and Southwest Pacific Area, encl: draft directive for WATCHTOWER.

[100] RKT to Admiral Hepburn, memorandum, Mar. 1943; (b) Colonel Linscott in Washington telephoned Rear Admiral Turner the day the decision embodied in COMINCH 231255 June was taken, and in guarded language informed him that he would be going to work sooner than expected but in the general area previously discussed. (Despatch directed "Seizure and Occupation of Tulagi, Target Date 1 August.") Interview with Colonel Linscott, 10 Dec. 1962. Hereafter Linscott.

Captain James H. Doyle, USN, at Guadalcanal, 1942.

stroke of good fortune when he heard about the project which Rear Admiral Turner had spent three days cooking up with the intelligent help of Colonel Henry Linscott and Captain Jimmie Doyle who were to serve him extremely well throughout the next year in the South Pacific.

Rear Admiral Turner and his staff had the advantage of seeing General Marshall's despatch to General MacArthur which directed that despite any unhappiness over the command set up for PESTILENCE, "every available support both Army and Navy must be given to operations against the enemy," and of General MacArthur's reply:

You may rest assured that every possible resource under my control will be used to the maximum against the enemy at all times and under any circumstances.[101]

The project which Rear Admiral Turner submitted to Admiral Nimitz and then to Admiral King was titled a "Limited Amphibious Offensive in South and Southwest Pacific." [102] It called for:

a. The occupation of Ndeni Island, the largest and most western of the Santa Cruz Islands. (Ndeni lies about 250 miles north of Espiritu Santo in the New Hebrides and 300 miles east of Guadalcanal in the lower Solomon Islands.)

b. (1). The capture of tiny Tulagi and nearby Florida Island in the lower Solomons, some 560 miles northwest from Espiritu Santo,

(2). the occupation of an airfield (or airfield site) on the north coast of the 90-mile long and 25-mile wide island of Guadalcanal, and

(3). the establishment of an aircraft warning service on outlying islands in the lower Solomons (San Cristobal, Malaita, Santa Isabel, New Georgia, and Choiseul).

c. The occupation of Funafati in the Ellice Islands, 800 miles east of Ndeni, as an advanced base for temporary occupation of patrol planes. (Funafati was an atoll, 7 miles long and 150 yards wide.)

d. The reinforcement of the Espiritu Santo Army garrisons currently 500 strong and the construction of a landplane base there. Espiritu Santo was the northernmost and largest island in the New Hebrides. (It was 75 miles long and 45 miles wide and lay about 400 miles north of Noumea, New Caledonia.)

On New Caledonia was a strong army garrison numbering 22,000. New Caledonia was then the "furthest north" strong point of American arms in the South Pacific area.[103]

It should be recorded here that Rear Admiral Turner, ever the man to take the steps necessary to get the job done, even when entirely without command responsibility, reported at this time to COMINCH and CINCPAC,

that with respect to LIONs and CUBs, he had taken the liberty of advising the logistic people at San Francisco, that such units required for organized

---

[101] (a) General Marshall to Admiral King, memorandum, 29 Jun. 1962; (b) Turner.
[102] R. K. Turner, memorandum for CINCPACFLT, 3 Jul. 1942. Hereafter PESTILENCE Memo.
[103] Inspection Report by South Pacific Advanced Base Inspection Board on "State of South Pacific Area Bases—May-June 1942."

operations should take precedence over units being assembled for ROSES [EFATE, NEW HEBRIDES] and other localities.

As a forerunner of later difficulties with some of his logistic subordinates Rear Admiral Turner added this view:

> that with respect to captured islands, we should set a date of one week for the establishment of an airfield.[104]

It is also worth pointing out that Rear Admiral Turner picked Guadalcanal Island before it was known by the Navy or reported to the Navy by the Army Air Force that the Japanese had actually started construction of an airfield in its north central plain area. This was the reason for the parenthetical "or airfield site" in the plan submitted to CINCPAC and COMINCH in San Francisco. Definite information that an airfield had actually been started by the Japanese on Guadalcanal Island did not reach Rear Admiral Turner until after his arrival in New Zealand.[105]

As early as 22 May 1942, Army forces on New Caledonia had reported to the War Department a Japanese photo reconnaissance plane observed over Guadalcanal and suggested that the Japanese were "planning aerodrome construction there." This prophetic G-2 despatch was not given the normal routing to the Navy or special COMINCH routing which so many incoming Army informatory despatches were given.[106]

The following despatch from New Caledonia to the War Department's General Staff (Intelligence) on 25 June 1942 was circulated by G-2 to the Navy Department on 26 June 1942:

> There is no construction at Guadalcanal although the plain is burned off as if for an airdrome. There are tents and sea activity, and construction of a wharf at Lunga, but not cargo unloaded.[107]

A group of General Headquarters Southwest Pacific Area despatches originating from 22 through 26 June were handled similarly.[108] These despatches reported Japanese naval activity around Guadalcanal and, in bits and pieces, supplied the information summarized by G-2 in New Caledonia in their 25 June despatch. Several of the CINCSWPA despatches bear a *K* indicating Admiral King saw them and others bear a *C* indicating Rear Admiral Turner's relief, Rear Admiral Cooke, saw them.

---

[104] Notes on conversations between COMINCH and CINCPAC, 4 Jul. 1942.

[105] Turner.

[106] CM–IN–6593, 5/23/42. This and the following Army intelligence despatches are located in the Archives Branch of the Washington National Records Center, Suitland, Maryland.

[107] CM–IN–7326, 2/25/42.

[108] (a) CM–IN–7283, 6/22/42; (b) CM–IN–7850; 6/24/42; (c) CM–IN–8307, 6/25/42; (d) CM–IN–8416, 6/26/42; (e) CM–IN–8607, 6/26/42.

Presumably on the basis of these despatches, CINCPAC on the 26th of June asked COMSOWESPACFOR to arrange for photo reconnaissance of all Japanese airdromes in the Solomons. On 28 June and subsequent days, Army Air Force planes in General MacArthur's command made the requested flights. These were supplemented by reconnaissance planes from COMAIRSOPAC's command.[109] On 1 July, the Australian intelligence organization in the Solomon's titled FERDINAND was alerted to the presence of a good sized Japanese labor party on Guadalcanal Island, but this information indicated that actual work on the airfield awaited the arrival "within a week" of the "11th and 13th Pioneer Forces." [110]

According to Samuel E. Morison:

> On 5 July, Admiral Nimitz, received a bit of news that sparked off the whole operation. An American reconnaissance plane observed that the Japanese were starting to build an airfield—the future Henderson Field—on Guadalcanal.[111]

Actually the information did not come from either an American or an Allied reconnaissance plane. CINCPAC read a Japanese radio message stating that the "Guadalcanal landing was designated 'AN' operation, with 4 July as 'X' day. Force consisted of naval landing party, plus 11th and 13th Pioneer Forces." From this it was deduced that actual construction of the airfield would start soon after 4 July.[112]

The intelligence reports for 4 through 10 July from CINCSWPAC, COMSOPAC and New Caledonia contain no information in regard to the start of the building of an airdrome on Guadalcanal but tell of landing barges and pontoon landing jetties, and of cruisers, destroyers, and small craft near Lunga Point.[113] As late as 17 July, CINCSWPAC reported "no actual construction work on runway." [114]

---

[109] (a) CM-IN-9649 6/29/42; (b) Air Force, *Guadalcanal and Saipan*, p. 26.

[110] (a) Samuel B. Griffith, *The Battle for Guadalcanal* (New York: J. B. Lippincott Co., 1963), pp. 20–21; (b) Eric A. Feldt, *The Coast Watchers* (Melborne, Oxford University Press, 1946), p. 83.

[111] Morison, *Coral Sea, Midway and Submarine Actions* (Vol. IV), p. 261. On page 12 of Volume V, Morison states it a bit differently: "But on 4 July, an allied reconnaissance plane reported the Japanese were starting work on an airfield."

[112] COMSOPAC, Op Plan 1–42, 16 Jul. 1942, Appendix II, Intelligence Annex A, subj: Guadalcanal—Enemy information captured by CINCPAC.

[113] (a) CM-IN-0925 7/3/42; (b) CGSNPA Operations Report of 7/4/42 (without identifying numbers); (c) CM-IN-1742 7/5/42; (d) CM-IN-1761 7/5/42; (e) CM-IN-1988 7/6/42; (f) CM-IN-2068 7/6/42; (g) CM-IN-2264 7/7/42; (h) CM-IN-2309 7/7/42; (i) CM-IN-2861 7/9/42; (j) CM-IN-3038 7/9/42; (k) CM-IN-3094 7/9/42; (l) CM-IN-3439 7/10/42.

[114] CM-IN-5953 7/17/42.

The day previous, 16 July, when Vice Admiral Ghormley issued his Operation Plan for WATCHTOWER, the information in regard to the landing field near Lunga Point on Guadalcanal in the Intelligence Annex read as follows:

> Troops observed burning grass plains behind Lunga, Tenaru, and Kukoom on July 14, no actual work on runways was observed.

The plan further confirmed the lack of definite information on 16 July 1942 by ordering that:

> On Dog Day capture and occupy Tulagi and adjacent positions, including an adjoining portion of Guadalcanal suitable for the construction of landing fields. Initiate construction of landing fields without delay.

It was not until 25 July, as Rear Admiral Turner was worrying about the landings soon to be rehearsed in the Fijis, that CINCSWPAC reported

> large airdrome nearing completion eight miles east of TENARU.

The quite obvious error as to where the airdrome actually was located was corrected in due time to locate it two miles south of Lunga Point and on the east side of the Lunga River.[115]

The high powered and presumably all-seeing Joint Intelligence Committee (JIC) in Washington had no better information on this all important subject. The JIC Daily Summary of 10 July 1942 stated:

> *Guadalcanal Island.* There are indications of construction on an airfield.

Ten days later the JIC noted:

> *Guadalcanal.* Runway completed on 20 July 1942.

It might be noted as a lasting memorial to Rear Admiral Turner's mistaken desire to keep the Office of Naval Intelligence and all related Army intelligence activities ignorant of impending naval operations, that in the 28-day period between 10 July and 7 August, when WATCHTOWER was really being launched, there were only six mentions of Guadalcanal Island in the JIC Summaries. The only other one of particular moment was on 26 July when it was noted:

> An enemy airdrome appears to be nearing completion on Guadalcanal Island and another is under construction.[116]

The failure of both Naval and Army Air Force air reconnaissance to give to COMPHIBFORSOPAC a clear day-by-day report of progress on the

---

[115] CM–IN–8926 7/26/42; CM–IN–9973 7/29/42.
[116] JIC Intelligence Summaries, 16 Jun. 1942 to 8 Aug. 1942.

building of the airdrome between 17 July and 25 July has never been satisfactorily explained. But the word finally did get through and it was clearly stated in the Intelligence Annex of the PHIBSOPAC Operation Plan issued on 30 July that an "enemy landing field is known to exist in the Solomons at Guadalcanal."

In addition to believing that there had been some failure to get routine air reconnaissance intelligence through to him during a crucial period, it was Admiral Turner's strong belief that Morison's *History of Naval Operations in World War II* gave quite the wrong inference when it stated: "It was the start of airfield construction there [Guadalcanal], before the end of June, that sparked off the whole Guadalcanal operation." It was Admiral Turner's belief that it had been "sparked off" long before that.[117]

As to planning, the best testimony comes from Fleet Admiral King who wrote:

> The planning of the Solomons landings was done in COMINCH Headquarters by Rear Admiral Richmond Kelly Turner, who was then sent to the South Pacific in command of the amphibious force that was to carry them out.[118]

---

[117] (a) Turner; (b) Morison, *Coral Sea, Midway and Submarine Actions* (Vol. IV), p. 256.
[118] *King's Record*, p. 434. Reprinted by Permission of W.W. Norton & Co., Inc.

CHAPTER VIII

CACTUS Bound

THE JAPANESE SUBDUE OUR SERVICES' DIFFERENCES

By early July it was obvious to all the planning staffs in Washington that the time had arrived when something had to be done to really stop the southward extension of island control and daily air reconnaissance by the Japanese. Both the Army and the Navy, at long last, were agreed that offensive air-sea-ground action was the answer. Cooperation by all hands, at all levels, might lack from practice, but did not lack from willing effort.[1]

While Rear Admiral Turner was at Pearl Harbor (5–8 July 1942) radio intelligence made it clear that Japanese forces would be found in some strength on Guadalcanal. If the Japanese after local reconnaissance had chosen Guadalcanal as the best place to build an airfield, and moved their Pioneer Forces there to do this essential chore, and antiaircraft units to protect the site, then Rear Admiral Turner knew the Navy and Marines' first priority task must be Guadalcanal.

Since the available amphibious forces in the South Pacific were not adequate to land at Ndeni in the Santa Cruz Islands and at the islands, Tulagi, Gavutu, Florida, and Guadalcanal, in the Solomons all at the same time, the decision was made at CINCPAC Headquarters to postpone the occupation of Ndeni, where the enemy was not, until Tulagi and Guadalcanal, where the enemy was, were in hand. This was considered to be within both the spirit and letter of the Joint Chiefs of Staff directives, which directed the seizure of Tulagi and "adjacent positions."

PLANNING FOR PESTILENCE

The receipt of COMINCH despatch 031905 of April 1942 to prepare for the execution of major amphibious operations had oriented CINCPAC's

---

[1] (a) Air Force, *Guadalcanal to Saipan*, p. 6; (b) Turner.

planners toward offensive amphibious operations, in general, and particularly toward initiating these from the South Pacific and Southwest Pacific Areas. This planning assisted mightily in the development of a naval belief in the practicality of the over-all concept of PESTILENCE.

When Admiral Nimitz arrived back in Hawaii after his 23–24 April conference with Admiral King in San Francisco carrying the specific directive to COMSOPAC to "prepare to launch a major amphibious offensive against positions held by the Japanese," detailed staff studies were undertaken at CINCPAC Headquarters to carry out this broad task, starting in the Santa Cruz and lower Solomon Islands. These anticipatory staff studies together with subsequent CINCPAC and COMSOPAC lively actions, made possible the telescoping from three months to three weeks of the necessary operational planning at the amphibious level for the WATCHTOWER Operation. For four days, 5–8 July, the senior members of Rear Admiral Turner's staff, Linscott, Doyle, Weir and Harris, worked alongside members of CINCPAC staff in the CINCPAC Headquarters.

Turner Collection

Kelly Turner at Tongatabu, Tonga Islands with Brigadier General Benjamin C. Lockwood, AUS, and Commander Charles E. Olsen, USN, bound for Guadalcanal, 12 July 1942.

Fleet Admiral Nimitz, in recalling the occasion, said:

> This was my first opportunity to work closely with Kelly Turner. I never served in the same ship or organization with Kelly Turner. He was in War Plans when I was Chief of the Bureau of Navigation, and I used to see him in Stark's office.
>
> I once asked Kelly Turner: 'Could I look at our War Plans?'
> He said: 'We will tell you what you need to know.'
>
> As an aside, perhaps you would like to hear about my becoming CINCPAC [Commander in Chief Pacific Fleet].
>
> On 16 December, Colonel Knox sent for me and asked: 'How soon can you travel? The President and I have just decided that you are going out to take command of the Pacific Fleet. . . .' I asked for Russell Willson or Kelly Turner to be my Chief of Staff. Neither could be sprung. I decided it would be foolish of me to try to disrupt the Navy Department.
>
> Our PB2Y plane almost capsized on trying to take off. Finally got off on 24 December and arrived Pearl on Christmas morning.[2]

Rear Admiral Turner could not actually issue any orders until he took command of the South Pacific Amphibious Force, but he had the attentive ear of those who could issue orders.

With every day counting, and with Rear Admiral Turner's impatience mounting as a hound dog's scenting the fox, the flight from Pearl Harbor to Auckland in northern New Zealand was interminable. Bad weather delayed the Patrol Wing Two plane a day in Canton and a day in Tongatabu, Tonga Islands. But Rear Admiral Turner, ever the busy bee and top notch staff officer and making one hundred percent use of the time available while at Tongatabu, went "thoroughly into the status of the construction projects, as regards completion." He sent off his opinion that "most of the work can be done within the next four months," in a detailed four-page report to Rear Admiral Raymond A. Spruance, Chief of Staff to CINCPAC.[3]

Arrival at Auckland and reporting to Vice Admiral Ghormley did not take place until 15 July, a week out of Pearl, and four days later than Rear Admiral Turner had planned. The last leg had to be made via Fiji rather than direct because of a weather front.[4]

On Thursday, 16 July, after receiving a "Can do" from Rear Admiral Turner, COMSOPAC set the date for the landings as 7 August 1942.[5]

On Friday, 17 July 1942, Rear Admiral Turner flew south to Wellington,

---
[2] Interview with Fleet Admiral Chester W. Nimitz, USN, 19 Oct. 1961. Hereafter Nimitz.
[3] Turner to Spruance, letter, 13 Jul. 1942.
[4] Linscott.
[5] (a) Linscott; (b) COMSOPAC to CINCPAC, 160612 Jul. 1942.

ORGANIZATION OF SOUTH PACIFIC FORCE

```
                    CINCPAC
                    NIMITZ
                       |
                    COMSOPAC
                    GHORMLEY
    _____|_____
    |           |           |             |
AMPHIBIOUS    AIR         ARMY          NAVAL
 FORCES     FORCES       FORCES        FORCES
  TF 62      TF 63                      TF 61
  Turner    McCain       Harmon        Fletcher
               |                          
           SERVICE                     ISLAND
          SQUADRON                     BASES
           Bowman
```

Based on Pacific Fleet confidential notice of August 8, 1942 for Fleet Units.

New Zealand, and went aboard his flagship, the *USS McCawley*. Saturday morning he assumed command of Amphibious Force, South Pacific Force. The heat was on him, and he raised the operating temperature all around him, as he threw himself into detailed planning and last-minute training.

THE SOUTH PACIFIC AMPHIBIOUS FORCE

Rear Admiral Turner's amphibious command was the first balanced amphibious force assembled by the United States Navy in World War II. The backbone of its strength was a Marine Division, 13 transports, and five cargo ships. Temporarily assigned for the purpose of the particular operations ahead were two Marine Defense Battalions tailored for island occupation and defense, a Marine Barrage Balloon Squadron, four destroyer-type transports and five destroyer-type minesweepers.

Rear Admiral Turner viewed his own duties in the command as purely operational. Administrative command of the units of the force was vested by him in the following subordinate commanders: the Commanding General,

ORGANIZATION OF PERMANENT FORCES OF PHIBFORSOPAC

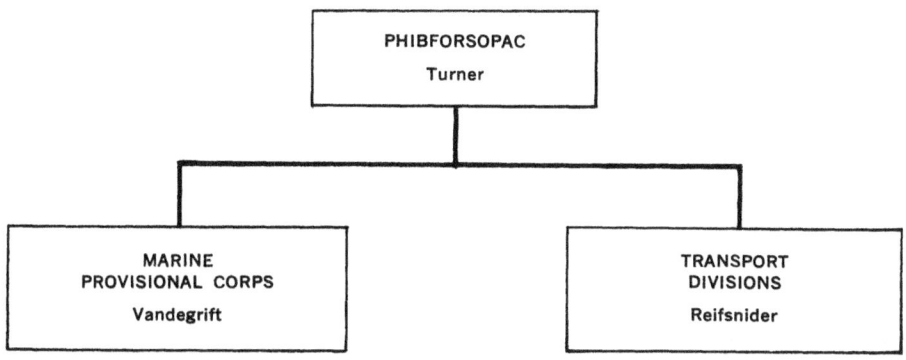

As given in establishment letter of July 18, 1942

South Pacific Marine Provisional Corps, Major General Alexander A. Vandegrift, USMC; Commander Transport Divisions, South Pacific Force, Captain Lawrence F. Reifsnider, U. S. Navy (Class of 1910); and Commander Minesweeper Group, Commander William H. Hartt, U. S. Navy (Class of 1918). Commander Naval Bases, South Pacific, a direct subordinate of COMSOPAC, had not been named. This command not yet fully activated was to administer and train the Amphibious Force Boat Pool, initially to be located at Wellington. Commander Service Squadron, SOPACFOR, Captain Mark C. Bowman, U. S. Navy (Class of 1909) another direct subordinate of COMSOPAC was responsible for logistic support of the Amphibious Force, South Pacific.[6]

Transport Division Eight and Transport Division Ten were regularly assigned to Transport Divisions South Pacific Force. Transport Divisions Two and Twelve were temporarily assigned. The individual transport divisions were organized as follows:

TRANSPORT DIVISIONS, SOUTH PACIFIC FORCE
Captain L. F. Reifsnider, U. S. Navy, Commanding (1910)

TRANSPORT DIVISION TWO
Captain Pat Buchanan, U. S. Navy, Division Commander (1911)

AP- 9	USS *Zeilin* (Flagship)	Captain Pat Buchanan (1911)
AP-40	USS *Crescent City*	Captain I. N. Kiland (1917)

---

[6] (a) COMPHIBFORSOPAC, letter, no Ser of 18 Jul. 1942, sub: Establishment of PHIBFOR, SOPAC; (b) The *Alchiba* (AK–23) (Commander James S. Freeman), which participated in the WATCHTOWER Operation was assigned administratively to Transport Division Six.

AP-39	USS President Hayes	Commander F. W. Benson (1917)
AP-38	USS President Adams	Commander C. W. Brewington (1917)
AP-37	USS President Jackson	Commander C. W. Weitzel (1917)
AK-26	USS Alhena	Commander C. B. Hunt (1919)
AK-28	USS Betelgeuse	Commander H. D. Power (1920)

TRANSPORT DIVISION EIGHT
Captain G. B. Ashe, U. S. Navy, Division Commander (1911)

AP-16	USS Neville (Flagship)	Captain C. A. Bailey (1911)
AP-14	USS Fuller	Captain P. S. Theiss (1912)
AP-12	USS Heywood	Captain H. B. Knowles (1917)
AP-13	USS George F. Elliott	Captain W. O. Bailey (1918)
AK-20	USS Bellatrix	Commander W. F. Dietrich (1917)
AK-22	USS Formalhaut	Commander J. D. Alvis (1918)

TRANSPORT DIVISION TEN
Captain L. F. Reifsnider, U. S. Navy, Division Commander (1910)

AP-10	USS McCawley (Force Flagship)	Captain C. P. McFeaters (1914)
AP-11	USS Barnett	Captain W. B. Phillips (1911)
AP-35	USS American Legion	Captain T. D. Warner (1919)
AP-27	USS Hunter Liggett (Flagship)	Commander L. W. Perkins, U. S. Coast Guard
AK-53	USS Libra	Commander W. B. Fletcher (1921)

TRANSPORT DIVISION TWELVE
Commander H. W. Hadley, Division Commander (1922)

APD-4	USS Little (Flagship)	Lieutenant Commander J. B. Loftberg (1927)
APD-5	USS McKean	Lieutenant Commander J. D. Sweeney (1926)
APD-3	USS Gregory	Lieutenant Commander H. F. Bauer (1927)
APD-2	USS Colhoun	Lieutenant Commander E. C. Loughead (1923)

It should be noted that Transport Division Two was shy a separately detailed division commander, and that Commander Transport Division Ten doubled in brass as Commander Transport Divisions.

The South Pacific Marine Provisional Corps had the First Marine Division regularly assigned. The First Division was organized around the 1st, 5th and 7th Regiments of Infantry and the 11th Regiment of Artillery. This division was without its 7th Marine Regiment reinforced, which was on base defense duty in Samoa. It was to receive from the Second Marine Division the 2nd Marine Regiment currently enroute from San Diego, and in addition the 251st Marine Observation Squadron.

The following Marine units were temporarily assigned to PHIBFOR-SOPAC:

1st Marine Raider Battalion—at Noumea, New Caledonia

3rd Marine Barrage Balloon Squadron
5th Marine Defense Battalion—under orders to reenforce the 2nd Regiment upon its arrival from the East Coast

The 3rd Marine Defense Battalion, to sail from Pearl Harbor on 22 July in the *Zeilin and Betelgeuse,* was due to be assigned to PHIBFORSOPAC upon arrival.

THE FLAGSHIP

The *McCawley,* named after the eighth Commandant of the Marine Corps, was a 13,000-ton, 17-knot diesel-engined merchant ship (*SS Santa Barbara*) designated AP-10 (later APA-4). She had been built by the Furness Ship Building Company in England in 1928. After purchase by the Navy Department from the Grace Steamship Line she was commissioned in the United States Navy in August 1940, after a 25-day "conversion" job. Needless to say, the *McCawley's* communication capabilities and staff accommodations were far from what the Solomon Islands' amphibious operations would show were needed in an amphibious flagship. At that time, she even lacked a regularly installed voice radio. But, based on the state of the amphibious art as it was known in June 1942, she was deemed adequate.[7] Furthermore, the *McCawley* was available in the South Pacific, having carried Marine Observation Squadron 251 to Pago Pago, Samoa, in early May. That neither Rear Admiral Turner, nor the drafter of the letter designating the *McCawley* as flagship, nor Admiral King who signed it 7 June 1942, had any idea at that time that COMPHIBFORSOPAC would be landing at Guadalcanal only 61 days later, on 7 August, is indicated by the fact that the letter prescribed "Flag Allowances of publications, personnel, and material . . . should be sent in time to arrive Wellington by 7 August 1942."

Her skipper, when Rear Admiral Turner broke his flag afloat for the first time, was Captain Charles P. McFeaters of the Class of 1913. The Executive Officer was Lieutenant Commander George K. G. Reilly. These two officers struggled constantly to meet the demanding requirements of a stern taskmaster and an eager beaver staff, but never quite made the grade.[8] An

---

[7] (a) *McCawley* designated as flagship by COMINCH on 7 June 1942. COMINCH letter FF1/A3/1/A16–3, ser 00468 of 7 Jun. 1942; (b) Defects of Conversion in CNO to CINCLANT, letter Ser 013423 of 15 Feb. 1941. Commander in Chief of the Atlantic Fleet stated that the *McCawley* was not equipped to conduct successful landings in Force.

[8] (a) Turner; (b) Interview with Rear Admiral John S. Lewis, USN (Ret.) (ex-Flag Lieutenant), 7 Nov. 1962. Hereafter Lewis.

indication of how very busy they were is that no July or August 1942 War Diary for the ship survives in any of the depositories, and it seems probable it never was forwarded.

Although the 13,000-ton *McCawley* had been the Grace Line's passenger ship *Santa Barbara* for some years, and presumably had more than adequate living accommodations for any naval purpose, this did not prove the case. Staff officers of the rank of lieutenant commander were crowded together three in a room, and the more junior ship and communication officers were stacked up in bunk rooms. The *McCawley*, as one of the 13 transports designated for WATCHTOWER, had to carry her share of troops and the boats to land them. This task absorbed communication facilities needed by the Amphibious Commander.

Of the PHIBFORSOPAC Staff, only the aerologist filed a "satisfactory" report on the particular flagship facilities needed for his efficient functioning.[9]

PUTTING THE PIECES TOGETHER

In his San Francisco Memorandum to CINCPAC, Rear Admiral Turner bluntly stated that "neither the troops, ships, nor aircraft assigned to this project are adequately trained in amphibious warfare." The Commanding General of the Amphibious Corps, Pacific Fleet, had reported recently:

> The state of readiness of the First Marine Aircraft Wing is such that it is considered imperative that steps be taken immediately to remedy the situation.

However, Rear Admiral Turner believed that "there is sufficient time to remedy training deficiencies provided corrective steps are taken at once."[10] To initiate the corrective steps, he attached to his memorandum to CINCPAC a prospective training schedule. This schedule included landing Marines during an actual gun and air bombardment, conducted by the aircraft, heavy cruisers, and destroyers slated to support the initial landings and controlled by air controllers and shore fire control parties from these ships.

---

[9] (a) Interviews and questionnaires from PHIBFORSOPAC Staff, 1961–1963. Hereafter PHIBFORSOPAC Staff Interviews; (b) A.C.W. Baskin, letter, 16 Nov. 1962.

[10] (a) PESTILENCE Memo, para. 2; (b) Commanding General, 1st Marine Aircraft Wing, Pacific Fleet, to Commander Amphibious Force, Pacific Fleet, letter, KV10/A16/CSN–082 of 11 May 1942 and First Endorsement thereon by Commanding General, Amphibious Corps, Pacific Fleet, 13 May 1942. This was the Wing whose forward echelon landed on Henderson Field, 20 August 1942.

CINCPAC directed this to be done insofar as ship availability made it practicable.

As soon as Rear Admiral Turner reached Pearl on 5 July 1942, the despatches started to fly from CINCPAC Headquarters.

1. The transport *Heywood* was directed to transfer the 1st Marine Raider Battalion from Tutuila, Samoa to Noumea, New Caledonia to arrive 10 July 1942.
2. Transport Division Twelve (composed of four fast destroyer-type transports) was ordered to Tutuila, to arrive 15 July 1942. It was slated to embark the 1st Raider Battalion at Noumea.
3. The *Zeilin* (AP-9) Flag of Transport Division Two, and the *Betelgeuse* (AK-28) of the same division, under orders to proceed to Pearl from San Diego, were ordered to sail from Pearl about 20 July 1942, to the South Pacific Area.
4. Air and ground reconnaissance of the Fiji Islands by Marines of the First Division was directed for selection of an appropriate site for rehearsal of the prospective amphibious operations.

PROPHETS OF GLOOM

On the same day that Rear Admiral Turner was leaving Pearl for New Zealand (8 July 1942), full of zest for the difficult fight ahead, Vice Admiral Ghormley, his prospective area boss, was leaving New Zealand for Melbourne, Australia, under order from COMINCH and CINCPAC to confer with General MacArthur.

Vice Admiral Ghormley had no taste for the conference.

> On account of early commencement of Task One and the great detail of planning necessary, will be accompanied by minimum officers and my stay must be as short as possible.[11]

Vice Admiral Ghormley and General MacArthur also had no taste for the operation, then scheduled to take place only three weeks later.

> The two commanders are of the opinion, arrived at independently, and confirmed after discussion, that the initiation of the operation at this time without a reasonable assurance of adequate air coverage would be attended with the gravest risk. . . . surprise is now improbable. . . . successful

---

[11] Ghormley to MacArthur, message 050011 Jul. 1942. He took only the Flag lieutenant and one other officer from his staff. Conference lasted 0800–1230, 1400–1450 on 8 July 1942.

accomplishment is open to the gravest doubts. . . . It is recommended that this operation be deferred.[12]

This gloomy and surprising despatch crossed one in which Admiral Nimitz told Vice Admiral Ghormley: "I have full confidence in your ability to carry this operation to a successful conclusion." [13]

Fortunately for Rear Admiral Turner's peace of mind during the next week, he did not see the pessimistic despatches until he arrived in Auckland, and by that time, General MacArthur's and Vice Admiral Ghormley's recommendation to their respective Chiefs of Service to defer the operation had been turned down, and the "Go" signal was resounding throughout the South Pacific.

At the same time that the tremendous difficulties of the WATCHTOWER Operation were being pinpointed to the Chiefs of Staff by two of the principal commanders concerned with its execution, the Imperial General Headquarters of the Japanese Navy was pulling in its horns and cancelling the Japanese plans to occupy strategic points in New Caledonia, Fiji, and Samoa. However, neither General MacArthur nor Vice Admiral Ghormley could have their hopes buoyed by this information, as the fact that the Japanese had cancelled out was not known to them until after the formal surrender of Japan.[14]

The pessimistic despatches of 8 July from General MacArthur and Vice Admiral Ghormley more than served a purpose in Army and Navy Headquarters at Washington. They caused the Army to get the Army Air Force to do what the Navy had been unsuccessful in pleading for it to do for many months, which was to increase markedly and soon the heavy bomber strength available in the South Pacific.

Vice Admiral Ghormley summarized the South Pacific air situation up to this time as follows:

> On the feature of Army aircraft based in the South Pacific, the Planners were in complete disagreement. The Army wanted to supply a limited number of aircraft to be based in the South Pacific Area and depend entirely on reinforcements from Hawaii or the Southwest Pacific in order to strengthen

---
[12] COMSOPAC to King, 081012, 081017, 081020 Jul. 1942.
[13] CINCPAC to COMSOPAC, 090633 Jul. 1942.
[14] On 5 May 1942, the Japanese occupations of New Caledonia, Fiji, and Samoa had been postponed "until after Midway and the Western Aleutians had been occupied." On 18 May 1942, the 17th Japanese Army had been established, and the Navy alerted to capture New Caledonia, the Fijis, and Samoa in early July. On 11 June these operations were postponed "for two months." IGHQ Navy Order #20, dated 11 July 1942, cancelled them, once and for all time.

our heavy bomber force, so necessary in this area of great distances between bases. The Navy Planners' stand that these heavy and medium bombers should be based in the South Pacific ready for action was sound. This was later demonstrated many times. The reason for the Army Planners' refusal to agree to the Navy's proposition was doubtless based on shortage of suitable aircraft; however this shortage was probably due to the following causes:

    a. The need for building up a plane reserve for the African invasion.

    b. Lend-lease Commitments to Great Britain and Russia.

    c. The unwillingness of the Army Air Corps to place their Squadrons and groups under naval control.[15]

It was the plan of the Chief of the Army Air Corps, General Arnold:

> To hold the bulk of his heavy bomber strength at each end of the Pacific line, ready for concentration at any intermediate base. One heavy group, then assigned to Hawaii, would be available outside the Central Pacific on orders from the Joint Chiefs of Staff.[16]

During early July 1942, the Chief of Staff, U. S. Army, had directed that the Hawaiian Mobile Air Force and the Australian Mobile Air Force be created. This took several weeks for the reluctant Army Air Force to implement. But, despite reluctance

> by July 15th, the 19th Bombardment Group (H) had been designated as a mobile force in the Southwest Pacific and on the following day the 11th Group . . . received its designation as Mobile Force, Central Pacific.

Four days later the 11th Group left Hickam Field for operations from Fiji, New Caledonia, Efate, and Espiritu Santo.[17]

The first B-17 from the Hawaiian Mobile Air Force (11th Group) landed on Espiritu Santo on 30 July 1942. However, the Australian Mobile Air Force was slow to gain its scheduled strength. It "was never called down [called over would be more accurate] as were the Hawaiian units." [18]

General Arnold's plan to hold the bulk of his heavy bomber strength at each end of the Pacific line was the one officially approved by the Joint Chiefs, but the Joint Chiefs implemented the plan by promptly ordering the Hawaiian Mobile Air Force to the South Pacific Area. This accomplished a fair share of the Navy's desire for more airplanes in the South Pacific Area, prior to the WATCHTOWER Operation.

---

[15] Vice Admiral R. L. Ghormley, manuscript covering the early history of the South Pacific Force and South Pacific Area, 22 Jan. 1943 pp. 34–35. Hereafter, Ghormley manuscript.

[16] Air Force, *Guadalcanal to Saipan*, p. 28.

[17] *Ibid.*, pp. 28–29. See also COMINCH to CINCPAC and COMSWPACFOR 032255 Jul. 1942; CM-0221-OUT-1 Jul. 1942; CM-0741-IN-2 Jul. 1942; CM-1100-OUT-4 Jul. 1942.

[18] Air Force, *Guadalcanal to Saipan*, p. 101.

The implemention of the Army Air Force plan in this manner did not mean that General Arnold had a change of opinion in regard to the desirability of increasing the land based air power in the South Pacific. As late as 29 July 1942, the Chief of the Army Air Forces was so little worried with the upcoming PESTILENCE operations that he strongly recommended that the nine heavy bombardment groups slated for the Southwest Pacific Area not be sent there until the requirements of the European Theater for the "modified BOLERO," the build-up of United States forces and supplies in the United Kingdom for its cross-channel attack, and for TORCH, the Allied invasion of North Africa, were "completely implemented." [19]

IN COMMAND AT LONG LAST

On the day that Rear Admiral Turner assumed command of the Amphibious Force South Pacific, the just published 174-page Operation Plan for WATCHTOWER from Commander South Pacific Force (No. 1-42 dated 16 July 1942) was flown in. This plan designated his command as "Task Force 62" for the WATCHTOWER Operation. The much shorter designation, TF 62, found greater favor and use than the longer administrative title, PHIBFORSOPAC.

During the four days between assuming command and sailing for the lower Solomons via the Fijis, where there would be a dress rehearsal, Rear Admiral Turner and his small staff ground out a large part of the 87-page Operation Plan (and its annexes) which were to govern in detail the first large-scale United States amphibious offensive operations of World War II. This was a large chore for a small staff inexperienced in amphibious warfare. It had to be driven through because radio silence would be an essential after sailing. Every word in it was checked and nit-picked by the Boss Man and a goodly share of the important parts written personally by him.[20]

Rear Admiral V. A. C. Crutchley, Royal Navy, arrived in Wellington on 19 July with Task Force 44, "General MacArthur's Navy," consisting of three Australian cruisers, two U.S. Navy heavy cruisers and seven 1,500-ton U.S. destroyers, with two more U.S. destroyers soon to join.

Major General Alexander Archer Vandegrift, U. S. Marine Corps, Commanding General First Marine Division, and the "South Pacific Marine

---

[19] Henry Harley Arnold, *Global Missions* (New York: Harper & Brothers, 1949) p. 335.

[20] (a) COMPHIBSOPAC (TF 62) Operation Plan, A3-42, Ser 0013 of 30 Jul. 1942; (b) Staff Interviews and questionnaires; (c) Turner.

Rear Admiral Turner with Major General Alexander Vandegrift, USMC, on the Flag Bridge of USS McCawley *(APA-4), July-August 1942.*

Provisional Corps" had been in New Zealand a month when Rear Admiral Turner arrived. He was tremendously helpful in the necessary orientation, and in having all ready a "Scheme of Maneuver" quite workable from the Navy's point of view.[21] Transport Division Ten under Captain Reifsnider, at Auckland since 25 May 1942, had carried out much needed boat training—while the Marine Corps gear was being unloaded from the transports and reloaded by the Marines specifically arranged for the WATCHTOWER combat operation.

The staff log of COMPHIBFORSOPAC, in the handwriting of the Chief of Staff, notes during this four-day period with monotonous regularity and marked simplicity:

> All ships of Transport Group, South Pacific Force, in company, engaged in reloading and rearranging cargo on basis of projected operations [and] in embarkation of troops. As these processes completed, ships anchored in the harbor in succession.

---

[21] *Ibid.* A Scheme of Maneuver is the tactical plan to be executed by a force in order to seize assigned objectives.

INTELLIGENCE CHILLS

One of the first things that Rear Admiral Turner was told upon his arrival in Wellington, New Zealand, was that Tulagi had already been named in the local papers as a probable amphibious assault objective. This perturbed him.[22]

A Wellington daily newspaper, *The Dominion,* on 4 July 1942 carried a long story with a New York City dateline quoting Major George Fielding Eliot as having said in the *New York Herald Tribune:*

> What is needed, is to drive the Japanese out of their positions and convert them to our own use. The only way to take positions such as Rabaul, Wake Island and Tulagi is to land troops to take physical possession of them.[23]

Observation of the amenities of military life seemed the best and simplest cover plan to disguise the imminence of the combat operation, if not its destination, so the Governor General of New Zealand, Marshal of the Royal Air Force, Sir Cyril Newall, E.C.B., O.M., G.C.M.B., C.B.E., kindly entertained the senior officers at dinner.

Despite the cover plan, on 21 July 1942, the day before sailing, Rear Admiral Turner, reported to the Area Commander, Vice Admiral Ghormley:

> A very disturbing circumstance is that a lot of New Zealand civilians in the government service seem to know the general features of our plans. We are having this investigated, but believe the leak occurred in the New Zealand Intelligence Office, which the Marines consulted in order to obtain information.

However, in a happier mood, he said:

> On the whole, I feel well satisfied with the plan, although there are one or two tough spots in it. I do not underestimate enemy reaction either in the air or on the surface. On the contrary, the arrangement of force proposed is designed to take care of these reactions as well as we can. I am trying to leave as little to chance as possible—but since the operation has been decided upon, the best thing to do is to assume it will be successful and to push it through as rapidly as possible.[24]

ORGANIZATION FOR WATCHTOWER

The command diagram in COMSOPAC's Operation Plan 1–42 for WATCHTOWER, dated 16 July 1942, was simplicity itself.

---

[22] Turner.

[23] Herbert L. Merillat, *The Island* (Boston: Houghton Mifflin Co., 1944), p. 11. Reprinted by permission of Harold Ober Associates Inc. Copyright 1944 H. L. Merillat.

[24] RKT to Ghormley, personal letter, 21 Jul. 1942.

CACTUS Bound 291

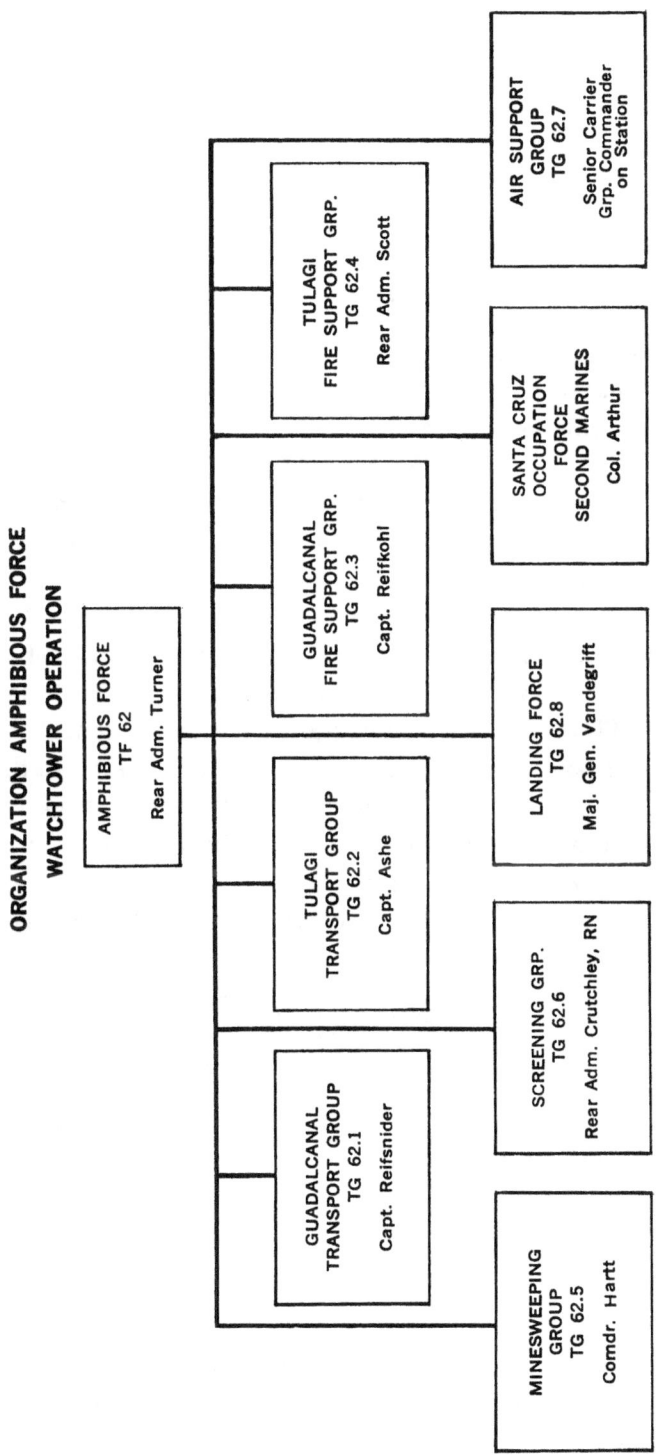

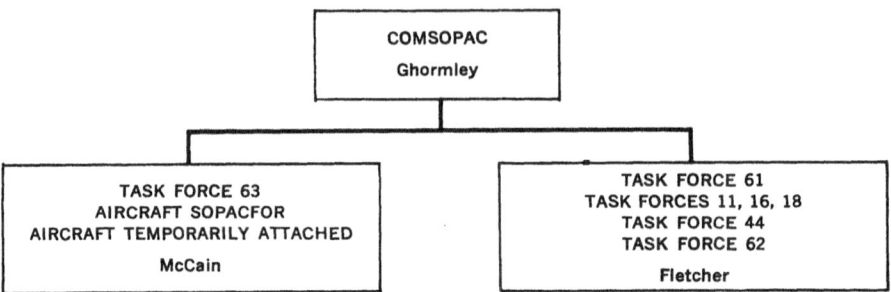

Vice Admiral Ghormley placed all his land and water-based aircraft in TF 63. All other seagoing units with a capability to carry out the operation, he put in TF 61, the Expeditionary Force.

Task Forces 11, 16, and 18 each were single carrier task forces with supporting cruisers and destroyers. Task Force 44 from General MacArthur's Navy contained four cruisers and nine destroyers. Task Force 62 was a beefed-up Amphibious Force South Pacific.

In 1942, *Joint Action of the Army and the Navy* governed all Joint Overseas Expeditions. This publication called for the appointment of a Commander Expeditionary Force and the naming of all forces assigned to his use. WATCHTOWER was an Overseas Expedition although not a Joint one, and it was both necessary and natural for COMSOPAC to designate an Expeditionary Force Commander and to name the forces assigned, with such broad organizational guide lines which he believed appropriate.

This left the detailed organizing of Task Force 61, the Expeditionary Force, up to Vice Admiral Fletcher, who organized it in his Operation Order 1–42, dated 28 July 1942, as follows:

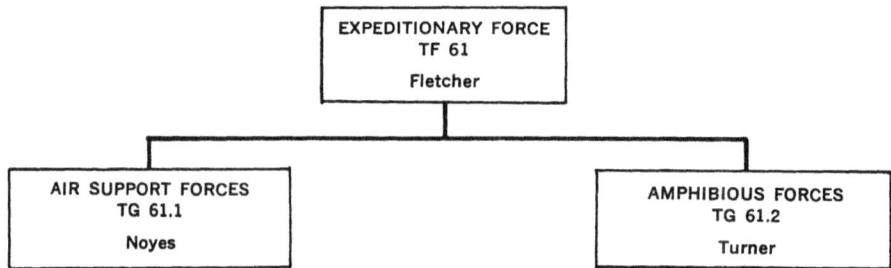

Vice Admiral Fletcher's Op Order for WATCHTOWER did not indicate when, nor under what circumstances, the amphibious forces command would shift from being TG 61.2 to TF 62. However, it made real progress in welding the amphibious force organizationally by not carrying forward as a separate entity a Task Group designation, 61.6, previously assigned to the naval command coming from the Southwest Pacific Area.

He thus made the basic naval organization for WATCHTOWER as follows:

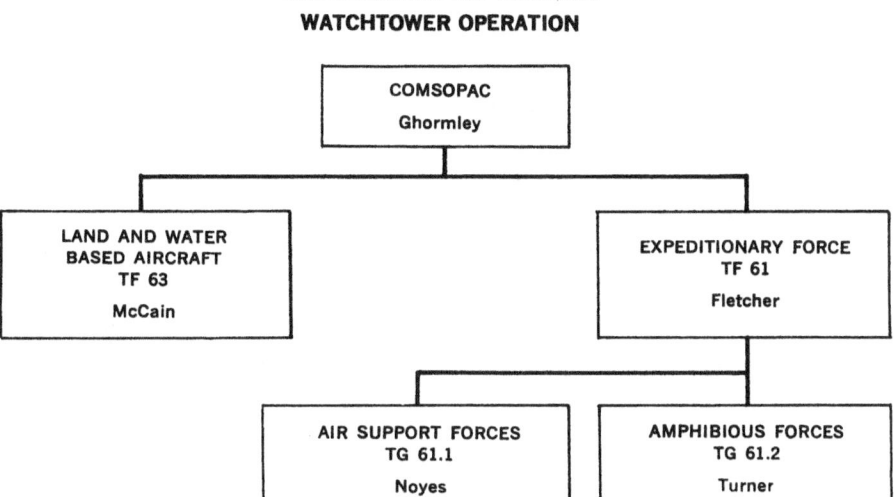

COMMAND PROBLEMS TF 61 AND TF 62

The command problem of the Expeditionary Force (TF 61) and its integral carrier task forces was complicated by the fact that Rear Admiral Leigh Noyes, Class of 1906, was the senior carrier task force commander, while Rear Admiral Frank Jack Fletcher, a classmate just three numbers his junior on the Navy List, was the far more war-experienced, having commanded naval task forces at the Battles of Coral Sea and of Midway. Noyes commanded Task Force 18 built around the *Wasp,* while Fletcher commanded Task Force 16 centered on the *Enterprise.* On 10 May 1942, and 21 June 1942, CINCPAC recommended to COMINCH that Fletcher be promoted to Vice Admiral. On 28 June he repeated this recommendation and added that Fletcher should be given the Expeditionary Force Command. CINCPAC renewed his recommendation personally on 4 July at the San Francisco Conference. As late as 14 July Admiral Nimitz, with the carrier task groups all at sea and headed for a rendezvous north of the Fijis, was still trying to get approval for the actual promotion or for his request that "Rear Admiral F. J. Fletcher be authorized to wear the uniform and assume the rank of Vice Admiral at once."

The first big hurdle to get by was Admiral King. After this, the promotion had to be approved by the President and by the Senate. On 15 July 1942, CINCPAC was notified that this had been accomplished and the promotion papers were in the mail. Soon thereafter Fletcher had his three star rank by radio dating back to 26 June 1942, the date the recommendation had finally cleared the Navy Department to the President. He became Commander Expeditionary Force, while Noyes was designated as Commander Carrier Aircraft of the Expeditionary Force.[25]

The command problem of Task Force 62 was complicated by the fact that the second senior officer in the force, Rear Admiral V.A.C. Crutchley, was from an Allied Navy, the British Navy, which of itself had no ships in the Task Force. The three Australian cruisers present therein had just come under the command of recently promoted Rear Admiral Crutchley, who, in June 1942, had been loaned by the British Admiralty to command the Australian Naval Squadron since the 30-year existence of the Australian Navy had not been long enough to mature many officers to Flag rank.

On 29 July 1942, Rear Admiral Turner notified Rear Admiral Crutchley that he would be designated as:

> Second–in–Command of the Operation. . . . The Third–in–Command will not be named, as the command will automatically pass by seniority in the case of the United States Service. It would be well for senior Captains to have an idea of their relative rank, whether British or United States.[26]

This did not please Rear Admiral Crutchley. He replied:

> I am very honoured to hear that you are contemplating nominating me as Second-in-Command of what amounts to a very considerable United States Expeditionary Force. I must say that I doubt the propriety or wisdom of this suggestion. It is mainly a U.S. Force and you have another U.S. Flag Officer on the scene [Rear Admiral Norman Scott]. I have not yet been able to ascertain his seniority, we are both too junior to appear in our respective Navy lists. . . . I feel that as long as there is a U. S. Flag Officer present, he should be in charge.[27]

Despite this reluctance, Rear Admiral Crutchley was designated as Second-in-Command, when the final draft of the operation order was distributed.[28]

TF 62's RUN TO THE RENDEZVOUS

There was no pain, no strain on the run to the rendezvous, except the hot bearings on the recently reduced allowance of typewriters and mimeograph

---

[25] (a) CINCPAC to COMINCH, 092219 May 1942, 202013 Jun. 1942, 272251 Jun. 1942, and 141027 Jul. 1942. COMINCH 151500 Jul. 1942; (b) King papers; (c) Notes on conversations between CINCPAC and COMINCH, 4 Jul. 1942.
[26] RKT to Crutchley, letter, 29 Jul. 1942.
[27] Rear Admiral Crutchley to RKT, personal letter, 30 Jul. 1942.
[28] PHIBSOPAC, Op Plan A3-42, 30 Jul. 1942, para 5(c).

machines, directed by Admiral King, as they were worked on a 24-hour basis, grinding out the last version of the rehearsal order. This was distributed the second and third days after departure from Wellington, together with the first version of the WATCHTOWER Operation Order.[29]

The Task Force sailed off from Wellington at 0800 on July 22nd to the southeast at speed 14 knots on course 140°. It did not take up northeasterly courses toward the rendezvous until late afternoon, in the hope of making useless to the enemy any intercepted sighting reports of the task force course by small fishing craft or off-course commercial aircraft.

The weather was ideal the first day but by Friday the 24th, the sea was really rough and the visibility was poor. The speed was reduced to 11 knots to reduce the seasickness factor and the steady pounding of the heavily laden ships. (Task Force 62 labeled the weather "quite heavy." Several ships termed the weather "a gale.")

Copies of the rehearsal plan and first draft copies of the WATCHTOWER Plan were sent on ahead to Task Force 61 and all others afloat and ashore in the Fiji area who needed to know, by the workhorse of the Navy, the destroyer.

Up to the time the ships coming from the north and east assembled at the rendezvous and received copies of the prospective operation order, most of the lower echelons did not know where the operation would take place. The War Diaries contain such entries as:

> Loading marine equipment and stores for destination unknown. . . .
> To transport marine personnel stores and equipment to destination unknown. . . .
> For operations in the South Pacific. . . .[30]

THE GATHERING OF THE CLAN AT FIJI

Rendezvous day was Saturday, 25 July 1942, 350 miles south of Suva in the Fijis. Seventy-six ships were directly involved in the rendezvous and 72 made it on time. Fourteen ships did this via a 1,250-mile detour to Wellington from Australia; 15 in Task Force 18 came 5,500 miles via Great Circle course from San Diego; 16 in Task Force 11 and 11 in Task Force 16 rolled down the 3,100 miles from Pearl Harbor, while Rear Admiral Turner and 26 ships, including 14 from Australia had the shortest run, 1,000 miles from New Zealand. The rest came from Pearl Harbor in small task units.

---

[29] (a) PHIBSOPAC, Op Plan A2–42, 22 Jul. 1942; Rehearsal Op Plan AR–42, 22 Jul. 1942; (b) COMPHIBSOPAC War Diary, Jul. 1942.
[30] USS *Betelgeuse* War Diary, 20–31 Jul. 1942; USS *Maury* War Diary, 15 Jul. 1942.

The 2nd Marine Regiment (Reinforced) (Colonel John M. Arthur, USMC, Commanding) from the Second Marine Division was in the transports loaded at San Diego, and escorted to the rendezvous, by Task Force 18, centered on the carrier *Wasp* (CV-7) (Captain Forrest Sherman). The *Wasp*, in company with the brand new battleship *North Carolina* (BB-55) (Captain George H. Fort) had departed Norfolk, Virginia, for transfer from the Atlantic to the Pacific Fleet two days prior to the sinking of the *Yorktown* (CV-5) at Midway (5 June 1942). It had been anticipated that this transfer would mean a highly desirable increase in carrier air power in the Pacific Ocean areas, but actually it only made good a severe loss. Departure of Task Force 18 from San Diego was on 1 July 1942.

Every responsible commander in the Navy thought highly of the Marines. Commander Task Force 18, Rear Admiral Leigh Noyes, thought so highly of them that he requested Colonel Arthur to submit a plan for the capture of the Guadalcanal-Tulagi area, with nothing more than the ground forces under his command plus one Marine raider battalion embarked in four destroyer transports.[31] Since the 2nd Marine Regiment had been aboard the transports since 1 June, and were going to be aboard more than another month, they probably would have been quite willing to undertake this considerable combat task just to get off the transports.

The 1st Marine Raider Battalion was in Samoa but was to be transported to Noumea by the *Heywood* and then picked up by the four fast destroyer transports in Transport Division 12 currently en route with Task Force 11 from Pearl Harbor.

The First Marine Division (Reinforced) included the 1st, 5th, and 7th Marine Regiments, but only the 1st and 5th were in the transports coming up from Wellington. The 7th Regiment was in Samoa to defend that island, and was not sprung until 20 August 1942.

The 3rd Defense Battalion (Colonel Robert H. Pepper, USMC) in the *Zeilin* (AP-9) (Captain Pat Buchanan) and *Betelgeuse* (AK-28) (Commander Harry D. Power) was the last Marine unit of the 19,000 Marines the Navy was scheduled to assemble. This essential event did not take place until 3 August, long days after the dress rehearsal had been completed.

These two ships had sailed from San Diego on 8 July, seven days later than Task Force 18 which was taking a far more direct Great Circle route for the rendezvous. They sailed from Pearl Harbor in a six-ship convoy on 21 July, six days after Task Force 16 departed for the rendezvous, and 13 days later than Task Force 11.

---

[31] *USS Wasp* War Diary, 6 Jul. 1942.

Convoy 4120 leaving Pearl had expected to make good 13 knots, but as luck would have it, one ship of the convoy, the *SS Nira Luckenback,* found it impossible to maintain the anticipated 13-knot speed, so the convoy was cut back to 12.5 knots, then to 12.25 knots, and even then the *Nira Luckenback* had "engine trouble." The convoy then ceased zigzagging, adding to the risk of submarine attack in order to gain greater advance towards its rendezvous.[32]

With everybody maintaining a strict radio silence, the heavy cruiser escort for the convoy, the *San Francisco* (CA-38) (Captain Charles H. McMorris), at 0430 in the morning of 1 August went darting over the horizon trying to locate Task Force 61 to effect the rendezvous. Two hours later she was back. She had not made contact. So the convoy went in to Suva Harbor arriving about 1800 and learned that Task Force 61 had departed westward about 1630 on the 31st, but that Commander Task Force 62 had left two destroyers behind for their escort.

Having missed their 30 and 31 July rendezvous with Task Force 61, the *Zeilin* and *Betelgeuse* took up the stern chase at 16 knots, escorted by the *Dewey* (DD-349) and the *Mugford* (DD-389). The *Betelgeuse,* pushing its top speed, had a fire in the exhaust trunk lagging of the engine room and had to stop for nearly three hours and put the exhaust trunk plates back together to stop the leak of carbon monoxide gas.

All this time Rear Admiral Turner was worried, darn worried, because an essential battalion of Marines was missing. The entries in the Staff Log reveal this:

August 1st *Zeilin, Betelgeuse,* not yet joined or reported. . . .
August 2nd All ships present except *Zeilin* and *Betelgeuse.* . . .

But on August 3rd, the log contained this entry:

August 3rd
 0555. Sighted ship bearing 110° true which proved to be *USS Zeilin* escorted by *USS Mugford. Betelgeuse-Dewey* still absent and unsighted. . . .
 1700. *Betelgeuse* and *Dewey* joined formation. . . .

AIRCRAFT FOR WATCHTOWER

About 635 aircraft participated in the WATCHTOWER Operation. These came from the United States Navy, Marine Corps, and Army Air Force, the Australian Air Force, and the New Zealand Air Force. Of the 635 aircraft, some 238 U.S. naval aircraft were on the three carriers in the air support

---

[32] (a) *USS Zeilin* War Diary, 21, 22, 27 Jul. 1942; (b) Hawaiian Sea Frontier Op Order 34–42, 19 Jul. 1942.

forces and under the control of Rear Admiral Leigh Noyes, CTG 61.1, and 45 in the 10 heavy combatant ships in the amphibious forces, CTG 61.2, under Rear Admiral R. K. Turner. Some 290 land and water based aircraft were in Task Force 63 under Rear Admiral John S. McCain's operational control, but of these, 145 were in the rear area of the South Pacific (Fiji, Tonga, and Samoan Islands) and were able to render support to WATCHTOWER only by air reconnaissance and by keeping the rear bases secure. They did not operate in the combat zone. The 145 aircraft under CTF 63 operational control which did participate in the early Tulagi-Guadalcanal combat phase of the operation consisted of 27 B-17s, 10 B-26s, and 38 P-39s from the Army Air Force; six Hudsons from the New Zealand Air Force; 24 Marine scout bombers (SBDs) at Efate, New Hebrides; 17 Marine SBDs at Espiritu Santo, New Hebrides; 22 seaplanes (PBYs) and three scouting planes (VSOs) operating from Seaplane tenders.[33]

From General MacArthur's command, about 20 B-17s of the 19th Bombing Group of the Army Air Force were to search the Solomon Sea and the northern Solomons area to the west of New Georgia (158° 15' E). About 40 reconnaissance aircraft of the 435th Reconnaissance Squadron, including Australian Air Force planes, assisted by searching the Coral Sea area, eastern New Guinea and New Britain area.

ADMIRAL TURNER AND THE MARINES

Admiral Turner remembered:

> During the first five months of the war in the Pacific our armed forces, and those of our Pacific Allies, were outfought as well as kept off balance by the Japanese. I believed then and said so that a realistic effort had to be made by United States forces, professionally well trained and mentally ready for battle, to jolt the Japanese off balance, and stop their island eating advance. The Japanese Army and Japanese Marines had been fighting in China for years. They were battle experienced, tough and capable.
>
> I had the greatest faith in our Marines. I believed that even with their disadvantage of not having fired any shots in anger for some years, they could stand up to the Japanese; and outwit them and outfight them.
>
> I thought it essential that a battle trial be held soon, or the millions of civilians we were training to be soldiers, sailors, airmen and marines would come into the Military Services with a defeatist attitude, which would be hard to cure.

---

[33] COMAIRSOPAC (CTF 63), Op Plan 1-42 of 25 Jul. 1942. Colonel Clyde Rich, Army Air Force, CTG 63.1, commanded the 69th Bombing Squadron at Espiritu Santo, along with the New Zealand Hudsons, the 67th Pursuit Squadron, and several PBYs. Colonel LaVerne G. Saunders, Army Air Force, CTG 63.2, commanded the 11th Bombardment Group of 16 B-17s at Efate.

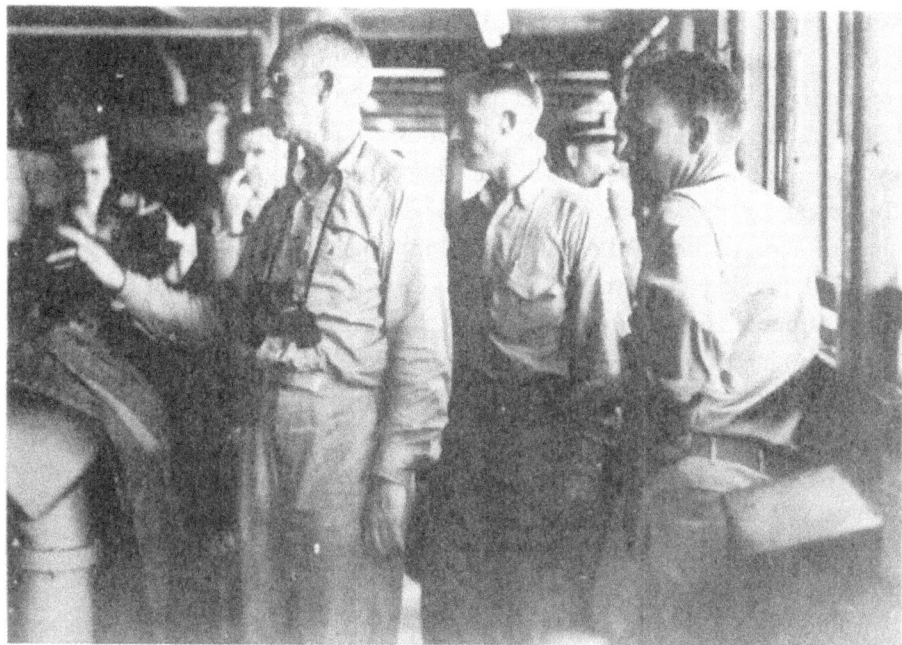

Turner Collection

On the bridge of USS McCawley, *Flagship of Commander Amphibious Force South Pacific. Left to right: Rear Admiral Turner; Lieutenant Colonel Harold D. Harris, USMC, Intelligence Officer; and Lieutenant Colonel Frank D. Weir, USMC, Assistant Operations Officer.*

As May turned into June, and June into July, I became more and more convinced that it was time for 'our turn at bat.'[34]

FIGHTING THE PROBLEM

On Sunday, 26 July 1942, Vice Admiral Fletcher held a conference of senior officers on board the Expeditionary Force flagship, the *Saratoga* (CV-3) near Koro Island about 100 miles south of Suva, Fiji Islands. It was not only a pre-rehearsal conference for DOVETAIL but the vital conference for WATCHTOWER. DOVETAIL was the code name assigned by CINCPAC for the rehearsal of the WATCHTOWER Operation.[35]

It was a large conference. The log of destroyer *Hull* (DD-350) that picked up and delivered the passengers to the *Saratoga* indicates that 17 went to the conference from Commander Task Force 62's flagship, the *McCawley*. These included Turner, Vandegrift, Peyton, Linscott, Doyle,

---
[34] Turner.
[35] CINCPAC to COMSOPAC, 070231 Jul. 1942.

Weir, Harris, and Bowling, and all the senior First Marine Division staff officers. The junior ones from both staffs attended subsidiary conferences of intelligence, communication, and Landing Force officers.

During the main conference, the most important decision announced by Vice Admiral Fletcher was that the carrier task groups built around the *Enterprise,* flagship of Rear Admiral Thomas G. Kinkaid; the *Wasp,* flagship of Rear Admiral Leigh Noyes; and the *Saratoga,* flagship of Vice Admiral Frank Jack Fletcher, would not be held in a position where they could support the Tulagi-Guadalcanal landings for more than two days; that is, no later than the morning of Sunday, 9 August 1942.

It is easy to say (but not yet proven) that this decision allowed the Japanese Navy to make an unhampered and largely undetected run at our seaborne forces gathered north of Guadalcanal Island the night of 8 August 1942. But there is no question that the carrier task force withdrawal provided the Japanese an unpunished retirement after their glorious victory at Savo Island.

The decision, proven later to have permitted a risky Japanese operation to thumb its nose at our carriers and escape the dangers of this thumbing, is not one that anyone present at the conference, with the exception of Admiral Fletcher and Admiral Kinkaid, still seeks to be associated with. These two still stated 20 years after the event that, based on our capabilities then and those of the Japanese, the arrangement was essential.[36]

The only contemporary written record of the conference now known to exist was prepared by Rear Admiral Daniel J. Callaghan, Vice Admiral Ghormley's Chief of Staff [37] and he apparently was not in sympathy with the announced decision in regard to the withdrawal of the carrier task groups, for in advising COMSOPAC of this decision, he wrote:

> Task Force must withdraw to South from objective area (i.e. general advanced position) within two days after D day![38]

This exclamation point and his dissatisfaction with the decision could be directly related to the suggestion made by COMSOPAC (Ghormley) to CTF 61 (Fletcher) several days later of an involved operational arrangement by which carrier aircraft equipped with special belly tanks would operate from Efate while the carriers huddled in a strip-tease condition

---

[36] Fletcher; Kinkaid.
[37] Callaghan was a fresh caught (three months to the day) and temporary rear admiral, but he had 32 years of naval service behind him, and according to three senior witnesses (Fletcher, Kinkaid, Peyton) very ably represented the strategic commander of the operation.
[38] Ghormley manuscript, p. 67.

several hundred miles south of Guadalcanal. CTF 61 did not buy this proposal and COMSOPAC later decided it was impractical.[39]

One of the participants interviewed labeled the *Saratoga* conference "stormy." Captain Peyton's (Chief of Staff to COMPHIBFORSOPAC) recollection of the conference ran as follows:

> The conference was one long bitter argument between Vice Admiral Fletcher and my new boss [Turner]. Fletcher questioned the whole upcoming operation. Since he kept implying that it was largely Turner's brainchild, and mentioning that those who planned it had no real fighting experience, he seemed to be doubting the competence of its parent.
>
> Fletcher's main point of view was the operation was too hurriedly and therefore not thoroughly planned, the Task Force not trained together; and the logistic support inadequate.
>
> My boss kept saying 'the decision has been made. It's up to us to make it a success.'
>
> I was amazed and disturbed by the way these two admirals talked to each other. I had never heard anything like it.
>
> In my opinion too much of the conference was devoted to 'fighting the problem,' as we used to say at the [Naval] War College, and too little time to trying to solve the problem.[40]

A more senior observer and one more used to the sharp give and take during the councils of the naval great, took a much calmer view of this conference.

> I would call the mood of the conference animated rather than stormy. Turner asked for a lot of things, much of which he didn't get, because they were not in the realm of the possible.
>
> The sharpest divergence of opinion was in regard to the length of time the carriers should be held in an area where they could support the landings. Fletcher insisted that two days was all that could be risked—because of both the submarine danger and the risk of Japanese shore based air attack.
>
> Other divergences of opinion related to air search and logistics.
>
> After the conference was over, I overheard Turner ask Vandegrift 'How did I do?' Vandegrift's answer was 'all right.' That also was my personal assessment.[41]

Vice Admiral Fletcher's remembrance of the conference was that:

> Kelly and I spent most of our time picking on Dan Callaghan because of the poor logistics situation. . . . Fuel was my main consideration.
>
> Kelly was no shrinking violet, and always spoke his piece in conferences.

---

[39] (a) COMSOPAC to CTF 61, 020240 Aug. 1942; (b) COMAIRSOPAC to COMSOPAC, 041436 Aug. 1942; (c) CINCPAC to COMAIRSOPAC, 022115 Aug. 1942.
[40] Peyton.
[41] Interview with Admiral Thomas C. Kinkaid, USN (Ret.), 20 May 1963. Hereafter Kinkaid.

> But there was no bitterness in the discussion. Plenty of opinions vigorously expressed as to what or could be done.
>   One thing I remember particularly well and have been telling it ever since the Battle of Savo Island. I said: 'Now Kelly, you are making plans to take that island from the Japs and the Japs may turn on you and wallop the hell out of you. What are you going to do then?' Kelly said: 'I am just going to stay there and take my licking.'
>   Kelly was tough, a brain, and a son-of-a-bitch, and that's just what he did.[42]

Vice Admiral Fletcher's appraisal of the logistical aspects of the conference is borne out by Rear Admiral Callaghan's notes. Fourteen of his 23 numbered paragraphs of notes were under the heading of "Logistics."

In Admiral Ghormley's "The Tide Turns" he states:

> I was desirous of attending this conference, but found it impossible to give the time necessary for travel with possible attendant delays. I, therefore, sent my Chief of Staff, Rear Admiral Callaghan and my Communication Officer, Lieutenant Commander L. Hardy.[43]

There is always the possibility that had Vice Admiral Ghormley attended the conference, he would have sided with the Commander of the Amphibious Forces and overruled Vice Admiral Fletcher. But in view of Vice Admiral Ghormley's generally cautious approach to operational problems and operational commanders, this does not seem a likely possibility. In fact his absence from what should have been a "must" conference, dealing with the first major naval offensive of the war, and the first in his command area, is a straw in the wind of his stand-off approach to operations in the South Pacific Area.

And Rear Admiral Turner did not appeal the decision. When asked nearly 20 years after the event why he did not, his answer was:

> Whom to, and who was I to do so? Fletcher was my old boss, and at that moment the most battle experienced commander in our Navy. It was his judgment, and it was my job to live with it.[44]

Vice Admiral Fletcher had expected that Vice Admiral Ghormley would be with him in his flagship *Saratoga* during the operation.[45] This was in accordance with Admiral King's expressed desires in his message of 022100 July 1942, which stated:

> It is assumed Ghormley will be made Task Force Commander at least for

---
[42] Interview with Admiral Frank Jack Fletcher, USN (Ret.), 25 May 1963. Hereafter Fletcher.
[43] Ghormley manuscript, p. 64.
[44] Turner.
[45] Fletcher.

CACTUS Bound

Task 1 (WATCHTOWER) which he should command in person in operating area.

Admiral Nimitz's 0633 of 9 July 1942 followed this up by telling Vice Admiral Ghormley: "You will exercise strategic command in person."

Admiral Ghormley's reaction to the CINCPAC order, which did make him the commander for Task One and in "direct operational control of combined forces," from 10 July 1942 on, was to plan to move 1,000 miles north from Auckland to Noumea, five days before D-Day, but not to lend his person to the most important conference which took place prior to the WATCHTOWER Operation in the South Pacific.[46]

Rear Admiral Callaghan's notes of the 25 July 1942 conference in the *Saratoga* throw some further light on this matter:

> Admiral Fletcher called me aside and said that he was pleased that you [Admiral Ghormley] put him in tactical command of this operation. Thought you were going to exercise that function. Said he hoped you would not hesitate to change tactical disposition if you thought it necessary, and he would not take it amiss, as you might be in much better position to see the whole picture. Told him I thought you would not hesitate to do this if you found it necessary but hoped that need for such action would not arise. Pointed out that during radio silence our knowledge of his tactical disposition would have to be based solely on his operation order and some guessing, unless he could keep us informed by plane. He promised to do this at every opportunity.[47]

FUZZY COMMAND DIRECTIVES

To do justice to Vice Admiral Ghormley, it should be pointed out that when he was in Pearl Harbor in early May 1942, he had discussed with Admiral Nimitz a draft policy directive governing task forces of the Pacific Fleet entering the South Pacific Area prior to its issuance. When issued on 12 May 1942, Admiral Nimitz's directive read as follows:

> When Fleet Task Forces operate in the South and/or Southwest Pacific Area, my command of them will, unless otherwise specified, be exercised through you. Under some conditions these forces will be made available to you to accomplish such of your tasks as you see fit. At present, their tasks are being assigned by me in broad terms in order that sufficient initiative may be left to the Senior Task Force Commander, and ordinarily will require

---

[46] (a) CINCPAC Operation Order 34–42, 30 Jun. 1942; (b) COMSOPAC, 170602 Jul. 1942; COMSOPAC completed shift of headquarters to Noumea on 8 November 1942.

[47] Ghormley manuscript, p. 69.

little amplification by you. It is expected, however, that you will exercise such direction as you may consider necessary when changed or unforeseen situations arise. . . .[48]

Vice Admiral Ghormley, on 9 May 1942, spelled out his understanding of this directive in considerable detail in the very excellent COMSOPAC War Diary as follows:

> The Commander-in-Chief, Pacific Fleet would order Task Force Commanders to report to the Commander South Pacific Force for duty. The Commander South Pacific Force would direct the Task Force Commander to carry out his mission (as given by the Commander-in-Chief Pacific Fleet). The Commander South Pacific Force would not interfere in the Task Force Commander's mission unless circumstances, presumably not known to the Commander-in-Chief Pacific Fleet, indicated that specific measures were required to be performed by the Task Force Commander. The Commander South Pacific Force would then direct the Task Force Commanders to take such measures.[49]

It is certainly deducible from this, that if COMSOPAC felt he had only limited authority to interfere in the broad mission, then he had even less authority to interfere in how the mission was carried out tactically.

This CINCPAC directive apparently was so firmly in Vice Admiral Ghormley's mind that when the despatch version of the WATCHTOWER directive from the Joint Chiefs of Staff arrived on the Fourth of July 1942, stating that COMINCH assumed Ghormley would command in person in the operating area, he still did not visualize himself as an operational commander exercising the full range of command authority in an operating area. This was so even though the word "command" had been used by COMINCH without limiting adjectives and therefore included "the direction, coordination, and control of military forces." [50]

Admiral Nimitz's despatch of 9 July that COMSOPAC would exercise "strategic command in person" was certainly a modification of the basic CINCPAC 9 May directive to COMSOPAC, but it was also a modification of the CINCPAC despatch of 27 June telling COMINCH that "Ghormley will be placed in full command of operation." [51] The use of the words "strategic command" by Admiral Nimitz could have been interpreted as a warning not to step into the immediate tactical field, and certainly left no

---

[48] CINCPAC, Instructions to Prospective COMSOPAC, Ser 09000 of 12 May 1942.
[49] COMSOPAC War Diary, 9 May 1942.
[50] Joint Chiefs of Staff, *Dictionary of United States Military Terms for Joint Usage* (Washington: Government Printing Office, 1960).
[51] CINCPAC to COMINCH, 272251 Jun. 1942.

question that Vice Admiral Ghormley would not be the tactical commander. COMSOPAC might well have assumed also that, if there was a difference of opinion between Admiral King and Admiral Nimitz as to where in the grey area between strategical and tactical command he should operate, then by notifying them both of his personal movement to on board the *Argonne* (AG-31), he had afforded them an opportunity to step in and clarify the situation.[52]

If anything further need to be said as to why Vice Admiral Ghormley should have attended the Koro Island conference in the *Saratoga* and been present "in the operating area" regardless of the side effects his absence would have had on the administrative command of the South Pacific Force, he has supplied the necessary quotation:

> I did not receive Fletcher's order for the operations until in September, a month after the operation had commenced. . . . The orders issued by Crutchley for the naval protection of our forces, I did not see until he and Turner returned to Noumea after the landing.[53]

THE UNSATISFACTORY REHEARSAL

The Fijis was the location recommended by Rear Admiral Turner to CINCPAC for the rehearsal. While not so judged by the military defenders of the islands, the Fijis were in the process of becoming a rear area (1,100 miles from Guadalcanal) from where it would be difficult for the Japanese or neutral nation agents to collect and transmit intelligence on a large gathering of U.S. Navy ships. Additionally the Fijis were a practical meeting point, based on availability and distances of the forces being assembled from San Diego, Hawaii, New Zealand, and Australia for the actual conduct of the WATCHTOWER Operation.

The period allocated for the rehearsal was 28 to 31 July. Upon recommendation of Rear Admiral Turner, as well as by the Navy Port Director at Suva, Commander F. S. Holmes, U.S. Navy, and the First Division Marines who actually reconnoitered the Fiji area, the rehearsal was held at Koro Island in reef-locked Koro Sea. Koro Island was not one of the

---

[52] (a) CINCPAC, 092001 Jul. 1942, 122359 Jul. 1942; (b) COMSOPAC, 311510 Jul. 1942.
[53] Ghormley manuscript, pp. 60–61. Fletcher's Op Order 1–42 was not issued until 28 July 1942. Crutchley Op Order does not bear a date but Turner in commenting on it, told him on 29 July, he "could issue it any time. . . ." COMSOPAC was not on Crutchley's distribution list for the order.

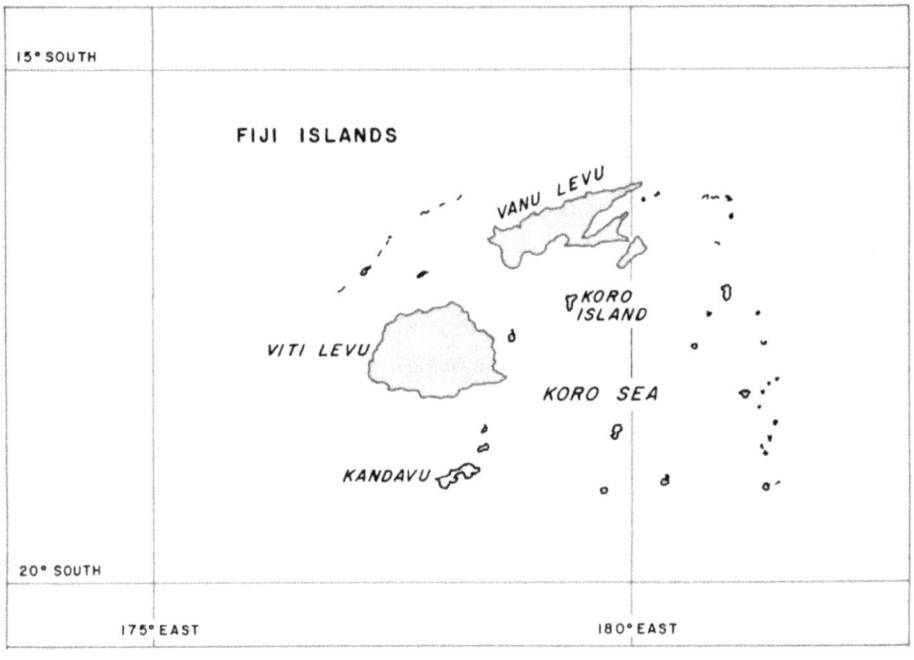

Fiji Islands.

three islands initially suggested as suitable by CINCPAC, and turned out on the days of the rehearsal to be quite unsuitable.[54]

The uncertainties involved in this rehearsal related not only to those always present when bringing together a large number of ships, aircraft, and men inexperienced in battle, but

> at the time the basic order was made out [for the rehearsal], there was some uncertainty as to the identity of all ships in Squadrons X-RAY and YOKE specifically [Transport Divisions Two and Twelve] and also uncertainty as to the identity of the squadron commanders.[55]

On 24 July, Rear Admiral Turner sent a personal letter to Rear Admiral V. A. C. Crutchley of the Royal Navy, then in the Australian cruiser *Australia* enroute to Koro Island. He commanded the Screening Group of four heavy and one light cruisers and nine destroyers. The letter reveals that at this late date, Rear Admiral Turner still did not know whether he would have any minesweepers for use in the operation or any tankers to provide

---

[54] (a) CINCPAC to COMSOPAC, 041844 Jul. 1942; (b) RKT to Deputy CNO Admin, letter, 27 Sep. 1950.

[55] RKT to Rear Admiral Norman Scott, prospective Commander Gunfire Support, 25 Jul. 1942.

continuing logistic support. It also made clear that the transport *Zeilin* and the cargo ship *Betelgeuse* carrying the 3rd Defense Battalion of Marines would not join "off KORO" until "about the 30th," and hence these Marines would not participate in the rehearsal everyone knew was essential.

Additionally, Rear Admiral Turner wrote:

> The thing which most concerns me at the moment is the prompt organization of the Attack Force, once we meet the other elements of the Pacific Fleet.
>
> I regret deeply that lack of time and ability to consult you require that I myself make the assignment of vessels to stations in Squadrons X-RAY and YOKE. [Which Admiral Crutchley's Screening Force was to protect from air and submarine attack, as well as from enemy surface force attack.] However, I believe this is necessary if we are to obtain a prompt organization of the squadrons on the 26th and 27th.[56]

Since Rear Admiral Turner was dealing with a particularly distinguished and particularly brave British Naval Officer, it probably was especially hard to decide that circumstances required him to take over a task properly belonging to this subordinate.

In a much longer letter [57] to Vice Admiral Fletcher the next day, 25 July 1942, Rear Admiral Turner reported:

    a. Encountering 'quite heavy weather,' and being four hours late for the rendezvous.

    b. The cargo ship *Fomalhaut* (AK-22) Commander John D. Alvis, U. S. Navy, Commanding, being a 'lame duck.'

    c. Refueling and refilling with ammunition used in the rehearsal would be necessary for the destroyers, and refueling for three transports.

    d. A conference after the rehearsal was essential.

    e. The *Australia* aircraft warning radar 'has a consistent working range of only fifteen miles,' and that he believed Admiral Crutchley should shift his flag to the *Chicago*.

    f. If things go well, it seems likely we may be able to send Transport Division Two (Captain I. N. Kiland, U. S. Navy) to the rear on the night of D-Day, and probably send the rest of the transports out on the night of D plus one Day. The great difficulty is going to be with the five cargo vessels left. Estimates for unloading vary all the way from three to six days, but you can rest assured that we will get this done as soon as possible. We will need air protection during this entire period, but will be able to send out about all the Pacific Fleet combatant ships with the Second Group of transports.

---

[56] RKT to Rear Admiral Crutchley, letter, 24 Jul. 1942.
[57] RKT to Vice Admiral Fletcher, letter, 25 Jul. 1942.

g. 'There is plenty more to talk about when we meet.'

It should be noted that Vice Admiral Fletcher apparently did not agree with Rear Admiral Turner in three important respects:

1. No general conference was held after the rehearsal by Commander Expeditionary Force, CTF 61, a *sine qua non* for amphibious operations. Since Commander Expeditionary Force did not call such a meeting, a conference of most of the group and unit commanders of Task Force 62 was held in the H.M.S. *Australia* on 31 July.[58]
2. Air protection was not provided during the "three to six days" of the unloading period.
3. Vice Admiral Fletcher did not direct Rear Admiral Crutchley to shift his Flag to the *Chicago,* nor regrettably did Rear Admiral Turner, who could have done so, but probably encountered reluctance by that officer to shift to an American ship.

In his letter to Rear Admiral Norman Scott, Rear Admiral Turner had said:

> I foresee considerable difficulty, particularly in the rehearsal, in keeping the transports in the same locality all day long while loading and unloading. The water is too deep to anchor, of course, and I hope we don't have a lot of collisions. However, there will be more important difficulties in the combat operations, so we can't worry about these.

The rehearsal, from 28 through 31 July, was less than full blown. The original plan had been to conduct landing exercises on 28 July, re-embark the Marines on 29 July, and then conduct further landing exercises on the 30th, with accompanying air bombings and ship gunfire support fire, and again re-embark the troops on the 31st.

Despite the fact that the sea was smooth, COMPHIBFORSOPAC Staff Log for 28 July 1942 reads as follows:

> 0900. Began rehearsal exercises on Koro Island. Beach conditions very inadequate and hazardous for boats. Landing conducted on beaches Blue and Green in accordance with plan, but incomplete on beach Red.

The COMPHIBFORSOPAC order had said:

> Care will be taken to avoid damage to boats, as they cannot be replaced before being required for combat.

This explains why COMPHIBFORSOPAC's War Diary records that:

---

[58] PHIBSOPAC (TF 62), Rehearsal Operation Plan AR–42, 22 Jul. 1942. Paragraph X (6) directed his subordinates to hold conferences on 1 August 1942 prior to issuing their final operation plans.

Beach condition proved hazardous and endangered future employment of ship's boats and tank lighters. Troops not ashore were recalled. Boats were hoisted in and troops not landed were re-embarked.

The personal notes of Rear Admiral Turner on the first day of the rehearsal are limited to a page and a half, and mainly directed towards the planned rewrite of the PHIBFORSOPAC Operation Plan A2–42. They included such items as:

   a. All personnel not required on upper decks must remain below decks as long as possible, until immediately before debarking.
   b. Change task of gunfire support ships to include covering of transports while unloading.
   c. Indicate type number alongside names of ship in Task Organization, thus *Fuller* (AP-14).

On Affirm plus one day, there was much concern about the boats, while the troops on Beach Blue and Beach Green were re-embarked. This was done successfully. On the last two days of the rehearsal, the previously designated units of troops were put into the boats, but not put on to the beaches.

Revealing an unanticipated liberty attraction ashore, the COMPHIB-FORSOPAC Staff Log records for 30 July that:

   Three Marine Corps stragglers from *American Legion* [APA-17] were apparently left on Koro Island.

A more serious worry:

   Fleet tanker USS *Kaskaskia* failed to keep appointed rendezvous with the force.

And on 31 July and 1 August:

   USS *Kaskaskia* still unaccounted for. . . . USS *Kaskaskia* still missing.

There is an old Navy saying that:

   In every task force there is always some so and so ship that doesn't get the word.

On 1 August 1942, it was the *Kaskaskia*.

The *Kaskaskia* (AO-27), Commander Walter L. Taylor, had been in the same convoy as the radarless *Zeilin* and *Betelgeuse* and had arrived Suva, Fiji, the late afternoon of 1 August. She turned to and fueled 15 small harbor craft in the next two days, but she did not sail. Her onward orders from Commander South Pacific did not arrive until 3 August. The initial words of the despatch tell the story.

> This is a reencipherment of NPM Fox Number 710. Apparently bad set up. . . .[59]

In non-seagoing language this meant that the coding set up for the message had turned out a garbled product.

REHEARSAL TRIALS, TRIBULATIONS, AND BENEFITS

Only a little better than one-third of the Marines who were supposed to have had the benefit of an actual rehearsal for an amphibious landing had debarkation or shoreside training at Koro. On the other hand, gunfire support ships and the air support aircraft carried out the pre-landing shelling and bombings of the rehearsals as planned and derived benefit therefrom. For the amphibious ship the rehearsal was the cornerstone of later successes. As related by the Commanding Officer *Alhena*:

> We had hoisted our wooden-hulled Higgins boats [before leaving San Diego] in and out for so long that we thought that we knew all there was to know; but always in harbor and never in any sort of landing exercise. Off Onslow Beach in the early days I had acted as a spare parts supply ship, doling out engines and propellers as they were burned or beaten up. How well the others had been trained I do not know, but we all certainly heard from U-NO-HOO after the first rehearsal in the Fijis. Kelly sounded off in no uncertain terms and no one was spared. We hoisted the boats in and did it again. Times were cut about fifty percent but still it was not good enough. The third time we all thought that we did a real bang up job, but not so, according to the Boss. And he was right. After a conference aboard his ship that night we went out to sea, came in and did it again in about one third the time of our first try and with ten times the precision. Here again Kelly was the perfectionist—not the sundowner—and his driving was certainly needed and paid off.[60]

In May 1943, in making his official report on the WATCHTOWER Operation, Major General Vandegrift informed the Commandant of the Marine Corps:

> Rendezvous was effected on 26 July and from 28 July until 31 July rehearsals for the forthcoming operation were conducted at Koro. Coral conditions on the island beaches rendered them impractical for actual landing operations and to that extent the rehearsal period was unsatisfactory. It proved invaluable, however, in providing an opportunity for familiarization

---
[59] COMSOPAC, 022340 Aug. 1942.
[60] Hunt.

with debarking procedure, ascertaining debarkation intervals and the conduct and timing of large scale boat movements. . . .

It also permitted the necessary exchange of staff visits and conferences. . . . during which further details of execution of the attack were agreed upon and minor changes carried into effect. . . .

In the light of this experience an effective and workable boat pool was established. . . .

General Vandegrift on 12 March 1948, in talking with the Marine Corps History Group at Princeton, described the Koro rehearsal as a "complete bust," and this terse description caught fire and has been carried forward into the Official Marine Corps History as well as most unofficial writings on Guadalcanal.

Rear Admiral Turner was unhappy about the selection of the Koro beaches and thought the partial rehearsal "unsatisfactory" but he thought it far, far from being "a complete bust."

In retrospect, General Vandegrift agreed with him, writing in 1964:

Although I later described the rehearsal as 'a complete bust,' in retrospect it probably was not that bad. At the very least, it got the boats off the transports, and the men down the nets and away. It uncovered deficiencies such as defective boat engines in time to have them repaired and gave both Turner and me a chance to take important corrective measures in other spheres.

This confirmed again what the General had written officially way back in March 1943:

The 'unusually successful landings' reflected the benefits to be obtained from a period of rehearsals of the precise operation immediately prior to its execution.[61]

1100 MILES OF WORRY

Admiral Fletcher remembered:

Fuel was my main consideration during the run from the Fijis to the Solomons.[62]

And it was a major consideration for all his subordinate naval commanders.

On Thursday, 29 July, CTF 61 (Fletcher) advised COMSOPAC (Ghormley) and his subordinate commanders that TF 61 would be short

---

[61] (a) Commanding General, First Marine Division, WATCHTOWER Operation, Ser 00204, Phases I-IV; (b) Alexander A. Vandegrift, *Once a Marine* (New York: W.W. Norton, 1964), p. 122; (c) PHIBFORSOPAC Staff Interviews; (d) RRT to DCNO (Admin), letter, 20 Aug. 1950.
[62] Fletcher.

2.1 million gallons of fuel oil on departure from the Fijis for the Solomons. CTF 61 considered it "imperative" that his force should be fully fueled on departure and topped off en route to the landings.[63]

The *Ranier* (AE-5), *Platte* (AO-24), and the *Kanawha* (AO-1) worked at rearming and refueling the fast carrier task forces on 30 and 31 July, but when, at 1630 on the 31st, the Expeditionary Force started its decoy course to the southward before turning westward to the Coral Sea and Guadalcanal, three heavy cruisers and seven destroyers of the fast carrier task forces still were not fueled. These were temporarily detached and worked at their task throughout the night. All heavy combatant ships and three transports were fueled by 1000 on 1 August 1942, but some of the destroyers had not fueled to capacity.[64]

On 31 July, Task Group 61.2, the designation of the amphibious forces while part of the Expeditionary Force, also fueled from our oldest tanker, the 28-year-old *Kanawha* (Commander Kendall S. Reed), and from the *Platte* (Captain Ralph H. Henkle) and replenished the ammunition expended in the rehearsal from the *Ranier* (Captain W. W. Meek).

The logistical support forces were inadequate, and the problem was only beginning to be handled at the highest operational level in the task forces of the Navy. According to the official history of naval logistics:

> The vital importance of an adequate supply of fuel, and its timely and properly allocated delivery to the vessels of the South Pacific for the campaign about to begin, was clearly recognized by Admiral Ghormley. The distances involved, the scarcity of tankers, and the consumption of oil by task forces operating at high speeds made the solution of this logistic problem difficult enough if the normal operating consumption was used for estimates. But what would constitute 'normal' when the offensive was underway? . . . Furthermore, though Ghormley foresaw the situation, and tried to anticipate it, his logistic planners were too few and had too little experience.[65]

At the late date, 31 July, the *Zeilin* and *Betelgeuse,* carrying essential Marines and Marine equipment, had not joined and no one in TF 61 knew where they were, so CTG 61.2 (Turner) directed the heavy cruiser *Chicago* (CA-29) (Captain Howard D. Bode) to fly two planes northeast to Suva to: "ascertain if the *Zeilin* and *Betelgeuse* are in Suva; if not, does the Director of the Port know where they are?"[66]

---

[63] CTF 61 to COMSOPAC, 280201 Jul. 1942.
[64] COMPHIBSOPAC Staff Log.
[65] Worrall Reed Carter, *Beans, Bullets and Black Oil* (Washington: Government Printing Office, 1951), p. 24.
[66] RKT to Captain Bode, letter, 31 Jul. 1942.

Another letter from Rear Admiral Turner carried by these planes was addressed to the Director of the Port, Suva, and contained the following:

> The *Kaskaskia, Zeilin* and *Betelgeuse* did not show up. I am much afraid that they have gone to Koro and are awaiting there for me, in which case they are sure to be too late to join me. . . . The *Dewey* (DD-352) and *Mugford* (DD-389) have orders to wait at Suva until nightfall (or longer if they get orders from COMSOPAC), in order to escort the *Zeilin* and *Betelgeuse* to join me.[67]

The reply via the *Chicago*'s plane brought good news.

> A plane took off at about 1015 to Koro to order the *Zeilin* and *Betelgeuse* to the rendezvous off Suva as directed. . . .[68]

Rear Admiral Turner made every effort to top off his fuel enroute to the Solomons. On Sunday, 2 August, he sent the Australian light cruiser, *Hobart* (Captain H. A. Showers, R.A.N.), six destroyers of Destroyer Squadron Four, and five destroyer-type minesweepers, Mine Squadron Two, to top off at Efate in the Southern New Hebrides.

They were to obtain oil from shore facilities, if they existed, or from the chartered Merchant Tanker SS *Esso Little Rock*. The latter presumably had been diverted by COMSOPAC to Efate in the New Hebrides on her run from the Fijis. However, by mischance the USS *Wilson* (DD-408) (Lieutenant Commander Walter H. Price), on the northern flank of the circular cruising disposition of TG 61.2, had contacted the *Esso Little Rock* during the early morning hours (0200) and seeking to keep the ship clear of the formation, had directed her to steam north for one and a half hours before resuming her course for Efate. This unhappy and too extended diversion ordered by an officer not knowing the urgency of the timing in *Esso Little Rock's* mission delayed the arrival of the tanker well past the hour when Commander Destroyer Squadron Four (Captain Cornelius W. Flynn) and his flock arrived at Efate. The non-exsitence of other oil resources at Efate made the visit fruitless, and, of course, further deteriorated the oil situation of the 12 ships involved.

Since no other fuel was available, on 4 August, all 24 of TG 61.2 (Amphibious Forces) destroyer and destroyer-types and the Australian *Hobart*, a short-legged cruiser by American standards, were fueled from the transports and cargo ships of the task group. The exception was three destroyers which completed the emptying of the fleet tanker *Cimarron*

---

[67] RKT to Commander F. S. Holmes, Director of the Port, Suva, letter, 31 Jul. 1942.
[68] Commander Holmes to RKT, letter, 31 Jul. 1942.

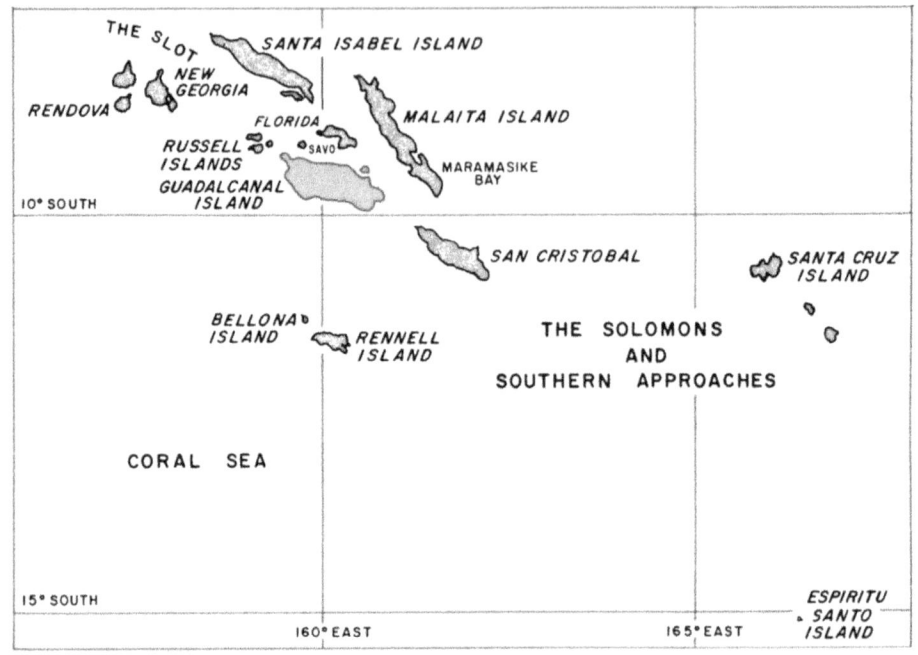

The Solomons and Southern Approaches.

(Commander Russell M. Ihrig), which had fueled TG 61.1 (Air Support Forces) the same day.

On 5 August, Rear Admiral Turner brought his task group to a halt to transfer 17 newly and prematurely graduated ensigns from the Naval Academy Class of 1943 and their monumental baggage to their assigned ships via ship boats, instead of by high line transfers from the *Zeilin*, the ship which brought them out from the States. This stopping of the task group observed from afar disturbed Vice Admiral Fletcher and while Task Group 61.1 and 61.2 were not cruising together, he stepped in and sent a message to CTG 61.1 to get underway immediately.

> I just figured that Kelly was punch drunk and my short despatch would snap him out of it. When I next saw him, which was in Noumea, we laughed together about the incident, and he admitted he might not have been very bright. But he still said there were no Jap submarines anywhere around.[69]

On the morning of 6 August, the day before the landings, the weather was hazy, visibility was four miles, and later became even less. COMPHIB-FORSOPAC Staff Log stated the problem and the result:

---

[69] Fletcher.

No navigational sights possible. . . .
At 0800 reported positions [from ships of the force] differed by 27 miles in latitude and 15 miles in longitude. . . .
At 1200 despatched Comdesron Four in *Selfridge* (DD-357) to Bellona Island, about 60 miles to the northeast, with orders to fix navigational position, and rejoin disposition by 1800. . . .
Haze closed down, with some rain. . . . Still not zigzagging in order not to complicate navigational data.

GUESSING THE SUBMARINE MENACE

After deploying 27 submarines in direct connection with the Pearl Harbor attack, the Japanese Navy made minimal offensive use of their 60-ship submarine fleet during the first six months of the war.[70] But it was gloomily, and quite erroneously, anticipated by Rear Admiral Turner that as the United States Navy moved from the defensive to the offensive, the Japanese Navy would make much more effective use of their submarines. He thought the Japanese submarines would orient their attacks away from the fast-moving well-compartmented combatant ships which were fully destroyer-protected to the far slower and far less watertight compartmented transport and logistic support ships of the amphibious forces.[71]

During this July-August 1942 stage of the Pacific War, the Japanese had the capability to assign 20 submarines in the Solomon Island area, and in September they reached this standard.[72] However, in July and up until 7 August, the best evidence available is that there were only three Japanese submarines (I-123, I-169, I-172) actually operating in the almost million square miles encompassed by the Fiji-New Caledonia-Solomon Island, South Pacific Area.[73]

But Rear Admiral Turner did not think that Task Force 62 had much to worry about from submarines, until after the Japanese had felt the initial weight of its amphibious attack, and had time to make the command decision to orient their submarine fleet toward the Solomons and the

---
[70] E. B. Potter and Chester W. Nimitz, *Sea Power, A Naval History* (Englewood Cliffs: Prentice Hall, 1960), pp. 796–800.
[71] Turner.
[72] (a) Mochitsura Hashimoto, *Sunk; The Story of the Japanese Submarine Fleet, 1941–1945*. trans. E.H.M. Colegrave (New York: Henry Holt & Co, 1954), pp. 2, 48, 70, 90, 91, 238. (b) Morison, *The Struggle for Guadalcanal* (Vol. V), p. 130. (c) Emanuel Andrieu d'Albas, *Death of a Navy; Japanese Naval Action in World War II* (New York: Devin-Adair Co., 1957), p. 173.
[73] Hashimoto, p. 258.

United States Amphibious Forces therein. So on the 800-mile run from Auckland to the Fiji Island rendezvous, his 26-ship task force zigzagged during daylight, but not during dark.

On 29 July 1942, Rear Admiral Turner wrote to Rear Admiral Crutchley, who was concerned over the task force not zigzagging at night and possible submarine attacks:

> I agree that submarines are a menace in this operation, but not very much so. The Japs have few submarines down here, and it is a very large ocean, so these few cannot cover much of it. I do not believe we are likely to find any in this immediate vicinity, though of course, I may be surprised. Ordinarily we will zigzag during daylight.
>
> I have considerably greater concern over the dangers of an air attack, than over the dangers of a submarine attack, particularly in the early stages of the action after arrival in the Tulagi Area.[74]

However, Rear Admiral Crutchley was not dissuaded. On the next day he replied:

> As regards the 2nd paragraph, your intelligence is probably much more complete than mine, but we have had persistent reports of growing numbers of submarines in the Rabaul area as well as reports of large and small (R.O. Class or even Midget) submarines in the Solomons.
>
> I regard the former as a menace at sea and the latter as a great menace after we have arrived for their small size makes them very difficult to detect by ASDIC. I hope that I shall prove wrong.[75]

Rear Admiral Crutchley very politely did not add that a Japanese submarine, later learned to be I-169, had just sunk the Dutch Ship *Tjingara* close to New Caledonia. The survivors had been picked up by the USS *Platte* on 27 July 1942. Nor did he add that the Army Air Force had reported the presence of midget submarines in the Solomons just as the task force left Auckland, and regular-sized submarines off Santa Isabel Island only 60 miles from Guadalcanal as Task Force 62 moved towards Koro Island in the Fijis.[76]

The Japanese Navy reacted with their submarines to the 7 August landings by ordering seven additional submarines from Truk to the lower Solomons, and by concentrating in Indispensable Strait, which separates Guadalcanal Island from Malaita Island to the northeast, those submarines

---

[74] RKT to Rear Admiral Crutchley, RN, personal letter, 29 Jul. 1942.
[75] Crutchley to RKT, personal letter, 30 Jul. 1942.
[76] (a) USS *Platte* to COMAIRSOPAC 262010 Jul. 1942; (b) Hashimoto, p. 258; (c) CM–IN–7335, 7/21/42, CM–IN–7634, 7/22/42, CM–IN–8247, 7/24/42. The Archives Branch of the Federal Records Center, Suitland, Md.

already in the South Pacific Area. The attack objective of their submarines was not changed to the amphibious and logistic support forces, as had been anticipated by Rear Admiral Turner.[77]

On the run from Wellington to Koro in the Fijis, there were only two submarine alarms, but as the COMPHIBFORSOPAC Staff Log indicates "contact could not be developed, presumed non-submarine."

On the first days of the six-day run from the Fijis to Guadalcanal, there were no submarine alerts within Task Force 62, a most unusual occurrence for a large task force at sea, and indicative that the submarine menace in the South Pacific had a low evaluation in the minds of the hundreds of alert sailormen who manned the submarine detection gear.

A WORD OF CONFIDENCE

Just before dark, on the night before the assault landing, Rear Admiral Turner sent out the following personally written message to Task Force 62.

PUBLISH TO ALL HANDS.

On August seventh, this Force will recapture Tulagi and Guadalcanal Islands, which are now in the hands of the enemy.

In this first step forward toward clearing the Japanese out of conquered territory, we have strong support from the Pacific Fleet, and from the air, surface and submarine forces in the South Pacific and Australia.

It is significant of victory that we see here shoulder to shoulder, the U. S. Navy, Marines and Army, and the Australian and New Zealand Air, Naval and Army Services.

I have confidence that all elements of this armada will, in skill and courage, show themselves fit comrades of those brave men who already have dealt the enemy mighty blows for our great cause.

God bless you all.

R. K. TURNER, *Rear Admiral, U. S. Navy, Commanding*

Rear Admiral Turner thought enough of this message to retain it in his personal files. This was the only one of the many he sent prior to an operation that he so retained. It was neither a public relations office blurb, nor a football pep rally speech, but a subdued and serious statement by a very serious-minded man.

---

[77] From August through November 1942 in SOPAC Area two U.S. carriers, one battleship and one anti-aircraft cruiser were torpedoed: *Saratoga* (CV-3), 31 August by I-26; *Wasp* (CV-7), 15 September by I-19; *North Carolina* (BB-55) 15 September by I-15; *Juneau* (CL-119), 13 November by I-26. *Juneau* was sunk, and *Wasp* disabled was then actually sunk by U. S. forces. Others were damaged.

Compare it with the one sent out from Vice Admiral Ghormley's Headquarters:

> We look to you to electrify the world with news of a real offensive. Allied ships, planes and fighting men carry on from Midway. Sock 'Em in the Solomons.[78]

HISTORY FORETELLS

One of the better students of military history, Captain B. H. Liddell Hart, had written in 1939:

> A landing on a foreign coast in the face of hostile troops has always been one of the most difficult operations of war. It has now become almost impossible, because of the vulnerable target which a convoy of transports offers to the defender's air force as it approaches the shore. Even more vulnerable to air attack is the process of disembarkation in open boats.[79]

Admiral Turner later said:

> I had read Lidell Hart's book and that part of it kept coming back to my mind as we chugged around Guadalcanal in the haze on 6 August.[80]

"AT LAST WE HAVE STARTED"

With these words CINCPAC advised COMINCH that the WATCHTOWER Operation was underway. Where did Admiral Nimitz first learn of the start? From COMSOPAC or from Commander Expeditionary Force? Neither. He learned it from reading Japanese radio traffic.[81] Six hours later CINCPAC still had no report from COMSOPAC or Commander Expeditionary Force, but the Japanese were keeping him informed of the favorable progress of the WATCHTOWER Operation.[82]

The first detailed summary report of the operation was sent by COMPHIBFORSOPAC to all interested seniors as of 2000, local time on 7 August, a bit late for a good staff officer. In this summary report, COMSOPAC and CTF 61 were requested to provide "scouting against approach enemy forces from westward."[83] It was a wise but fruitless request.

---

[78] COMSOPAC to TF's 61, 62, 63, 061040 Aug. 1942.
[79] B. H. Liddell Hart, *The Defense of Britain* (New York: Random House, 1939), p. 130.
[80] Turner.
[81] CINCPAC to COMINCH, 062045 Aug. 1942.
[82] CINCPAC to COMINCH, 070231 Aug. 1942.
[83] CTG 61.2 to COMSOPAC and CTF 61, 071030 Aug. 1942.

CHAPTER IX

Success, Then Cliff Hanging

WHERE ARE WE HEADED?

In the first 42 years of the Twentieth Century, the United States Navy felt that it had visited a fair share of the Pacific Ocean, and its islands, and that it "knew the Pacific." But somehow the Solomon Islands, although in friendly British hands, were outside the Navy's wide ranging sweeps.

During 1941, this had been intentional. In a letter to Admiral Husband E. Kimmel, Commander in Chief of the Pacific Fleet, Admiral Harold R. Stark, Chief of Naval Operations, had written:

> We should not indicate the slightest interest in the Gilbert or Solomon or Fiji Islands at this time. If we do, our future use of them, might be compromised.[1]

Until the amphibians and their combatant escorts sailed from Wellington on 22 July 1942, the great majority of the officers and practically 100 percent of the sailormen in Task Force 62 did not even know where in the South Pacific they were to join with the enemy 16 days later. "When they were told that this event would take place in the Solomon Islands, they still didn't know anything but a name." [2]

Admiral Turner reminisced: "I think it can truthfully be said that our officers and men were ignorant of the Solomons." General Vandegrift has written that he did not even know the location of Guadalcanal when Vice Admiral Ghormley told him that he was to land there on 1 August 1942.[3]

And until Commander South Pacific Force and CTF 62's Operation Plans 1–42 and A3–42 with their informative Intelligence Annexes were received and distributed to all of Task Force 61 on 31 August 1942, the great majority of the officers and men in the carriers and destroyers of the Air

---

[1] Admiral Stark to Admiral Kimmel, letter, 11 Feb. 1941.
[2] Interview with Rear Admiral Herbert K. Knowles, USN (Ret.), 6 Jul. 1962. Hereafter Knowles.
[3] (a) Turner; (b) Vandegrift, *Once a Marine*, p. 110.

The Solomon Islands.

Support Force were in the same state of geographical ignorance. Ignorance was not limited to geography alone. When the *San Francisco* (CA-38) (Captain Charles H. McMorris) joined the Task Force less than a week before the landings, the captain was bold to officially say that he had "no orders, dispatches, and little information regarding operations."[4] Another officer recalled:

> When Admiral Turner talked of Tulagi, Guadalcanal or the Santa Cruz Islands, he talked knowledgeably, but the rest of us naval officers were just plain geographically ignorant; learning fast, but at the moment ignorant.[5]

SOLOMON ISLANDS

The whole Solomon Island Group stretches southeasterly 600 miles from Buka Island in the northwest to 300 miles south of the equator and San Cristobal Island in the southeast, located 1,200 miles due east of the northern

---
[4] (a) Fletcher; (b) Kinkaid; (c) *USS San Francisco* to CTF 61, 012115. Aug. 1942.
[5] Peyton.

Success, Then Cliff Hanging

tip of Australia. The Northern Solomons were under German control from 1899 until early in World War I, when in September 1914, they were captured by the Australians. This part of the Solomons, primarily the islands of Buka and Bougainville, became an Australian mandate in 1920, under the League of Nations.

All of the Solomons became an Australian defense responsibility with the outbreak of World War II. Great Britain had controlled the Southern Solomons since 1899, and the British resident commissioner resided on the island of Tulagi, a sliver of an island nestled under the hills of Florida Island, 20 miles north of Koli Point in the center of the North Coast of Guadalcanal.

The Australians had chosen the tiny island of Tulagi as their principal base for the discharge of their defense responsibilities, because between Tulagi and Florida Island, there was a good medium size ship anchorage (15–25 fathoms) and a sheltered seaplane operating area, a mile and a half long and a half mile wide. This was quite suitable for any concentration of ships of the Australian Navy. Nearby Gavutu Island was judged particularly suitable for a seaplane base—and just a few more miles away was Purvis Bay, banana-shaped but deep-watered and adequate for innumerable small ships.

From the operation orders, the amphibians learned some of these facts. They also learned from them the hazards of nature as well as the dangers of a skillful enemy, that had to be endured in the Solomons. The transports were to proceed to an anchorage area where: "uncharted reefs may be expected," and where "winds of sufficient velocity to drag anchor over coral patched holding ground may be expected any day of the year."

But come what may, the amphibians were told that they must land their Marines on the chosen coastal beaches which were "lined with coconut plantations."

Fortunately, the landings on this hostile shore about 600 miles south of the equator were to take place during the "fine weather season." Only eight inches of rain generally fell in all of August, and while humidity might be expected to average an unpleasant 80 percent, temperatures ordinarily ranged only from a moderate 75 degrees to a somewhat uncomfortable or hot 85 degrees.[6]

Rear Admiral Turner's desire was to keep his task groups in the open sea as long as possible, and out of sight of any Japanese lookout posts high up

---
[6] COMSOPAC Op Plan 1–42, 16 Jul. 1942, Intelligence Annex, pp. 14–20.

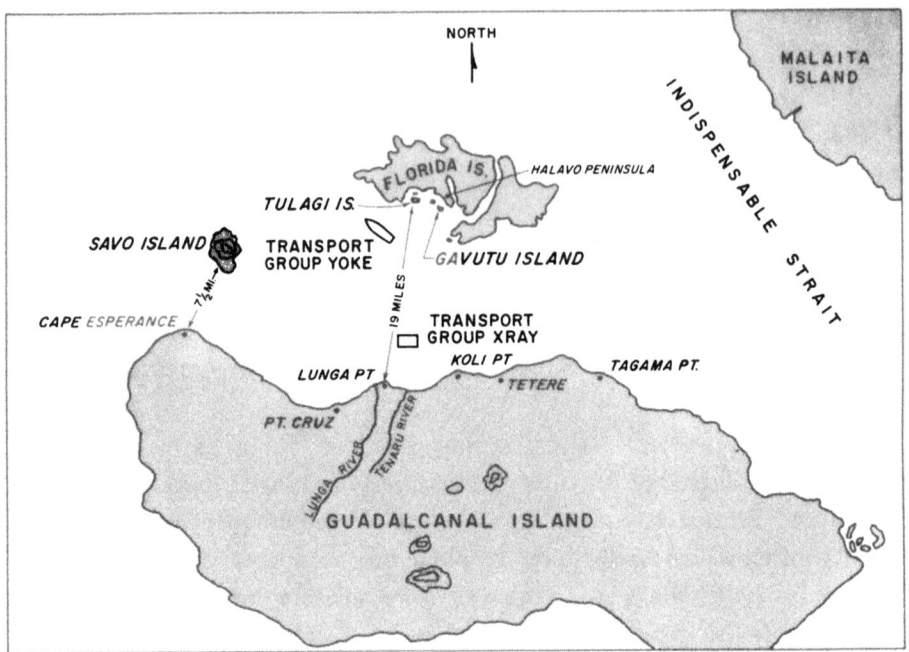

Guadalcanal-Tulagi.

on the 7,000–8,000 foot razorback mountain chain which ran from northwest to southeast along the middle of Guadalcanal. The shorter route through Indispensable Strait from the Fijis lying to the southeast could not be used because of this requirement and because:

> Two weeks observation of Japanese air scouting from Tulagi indicated that one or two seaplanes daily came down the New Hebrides Chain to the vicinity of Efate; and apparently on alternate days, at least, one seaplane came about the same distance on a direct line toward the Fijis. . . . The Task Force 62 approach route was laid out to pass to the south and west of known or estimated plane searches.

So Rear Admiral Turner planned to make the approach from the Coral Sea to Florida Island and to Lunga Point around the western end of Guadalcanal and through the 12-mile wide channel separating that island and the Russell Islands.[7]

The amphibians and their escort had made the 1,000-mile westward passage from Koro Island in the Fijis to a position (16°34′ S, 159°00′ E)

---

[7] (a) COMPHIBFORSOPAC Staff Interviews; (b) RKT to DCNO (Admin), letter, 27 Sep. 1950.

400 miles directly south of the Russell Islands without sighting an enemy plane or submarine, although the *Enterprise* (CV-6) (Captain Arthur C. Davis) had reported a torpedo wake crossing her bow 50 yards ahead, a little after 2200 on the night before the landing and the *Chicago* had reported a submarine contact on 3 August, later evaluated as a large fish. Army Air Force bombers and COMAIRSOPAC PBYs had flown over the force from time to time to protect it and to familiarize lookouts and gun and director crews with the B-17, but the voyage still had had its alarms. The amphibians had been forcibly reminded that the hazards of mine warfare were not too far removed when radio reports were received, on 4 August, that the destroyer *Tucker* (DD-374) had had her back broken by a mine only 150 miles north of their track, at Espiritu Santo in the New Hebrides.

The Task Force was in a circular cruising disposition maintaining radio and radar silence and, at night, visual silence. Seventeen destroyers and fast minesweepers were equally spaced on the three-mile circle from the formation guide in the center; the cruisers and remaining destroyers were on or near the two-mile circle; and the 19 transports and cargo ships were in a line of five divisions spaced one-half mile apart in the center of the disposition. The destroyer-type transports were in line abreast a thousand yards ahead of the Formation Guide, the *Hunter Liggett* (AP-27), flagship of Captain Reifsnider, Commander Transport Divisions, South Pacific Force. Five of the eight protecting cruisers were in division columns in the bow quadrants at 40 degrees relative, right and left, between the one and two-mile circle. The other three cruisers were astern of the guide, between the two and three-mile circle.

This formation was well balanced against both submarine attack and surprise air attack, as it was shepherded along in unfamiliar waters by the Air Support Force at 13½ knots.

The Escort Commander, Rear Admiral Crutchley, R.N., was:

> responsible for the safety of the Force against enemy action and for maneuvering the Escort for action against the enemy.[8]

All ships of Task Force 62, except the transports, were placed under the command of the Escort Commander for this purpose.

THE DARK OF THE NIGHT

At noon on 5 August, the formation course was changed to North and

---

[8] COMPHIBSOPAC (CTF 62) Operation Order A5–42, 30 Jul. 1942, para. 3.

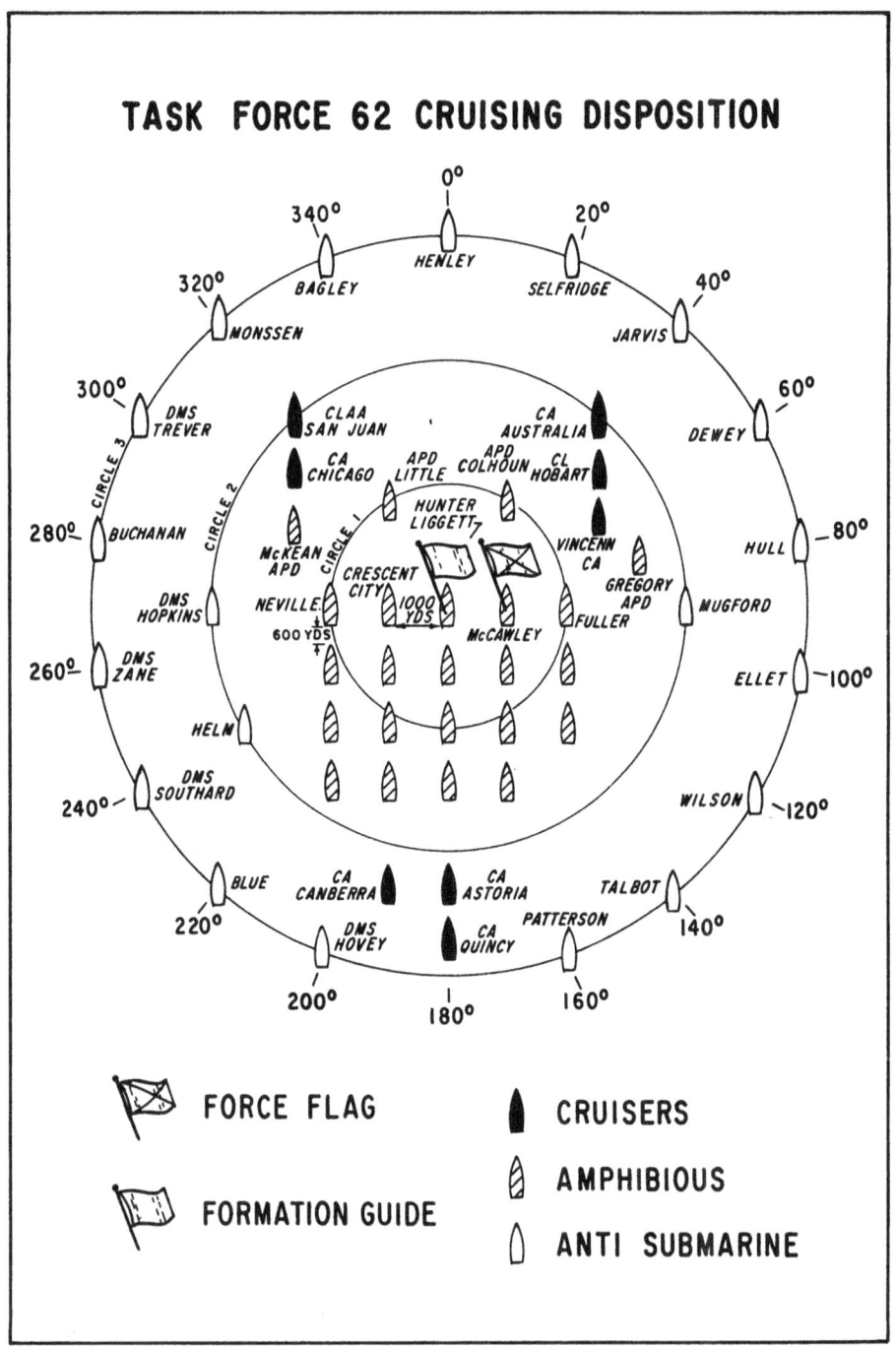

Task Force 62 Cruising Disposition.

Success, Then Cliff Hanging

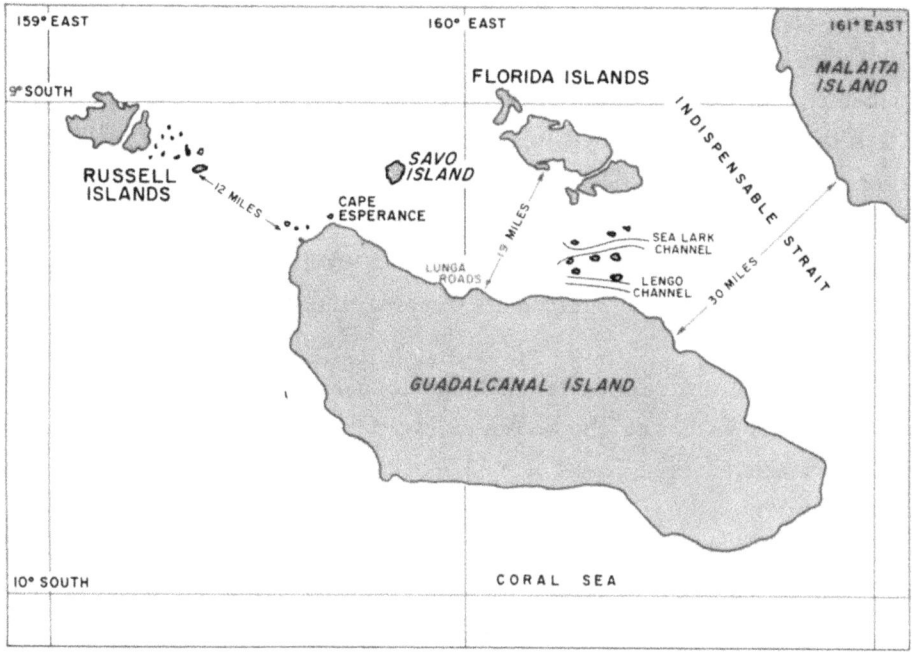

Guadalcanal and the Russell Islands.

the run in to the Russell Islands was started at 13 knots. The weather turned hazy and there were rain squalls.

A 12-mile clearance from outreaching and dangerous Russell Island rocks on the port hand to outreaching and dangerous Guadalcanal Island rocks on the starboard hand had looked most adequate on the charts, particularly as the approach disposition into which the formation would be shifted in late afternoon narrowed the front of the Task Force from 12,000 yards to 3,500 yards.

However, the Russell Islands had been reported by "pilots familiar with these waters" and "information sources in New Zealand" to be four to five miles eastward of their charted position. If this was true, and acceptance of the report as valid was sufficient to write it in on the Attack Force Approach Plan, then the navigational channel between Guadalcanal and the Russells was only seven miles and the clear and safe channel for night navigation considering the quirks of current, markedly less.[9]

It was also desirable to have the outboard ships far enough away from

---

[9] (a) RKT to Crutchley, letter, 29 Jul. 1942; (b) COMPHIBSOPAC Operation Plan A3–42, 30 Jul. 1942, Annex JIG; (c) Staff Interviews.

the beach on either side, so that an alert Japanese sentry would not spot the ships passing by and sound the alarm. This hazard dictated splitting the channel with exact midway piloting of the formation. To accomplish this task the staff navigator had to know exactly where the formation was by not later than 1600 on the 6th.[10]

But, as noted in the previous chapter, the 51 navigators of the 51 ships were all over the lot in their morning and noon position reports. It was as though they had all agreed to disagree and worry the Admiral and the staff navigator.

Perhaps the real reason was that the Coral Sea currents were tricky, the weather was hazy, and the Solomons were beyond the range of the few 1942 surface radars in Task Force 62. The Staff Log for 6 August 1942 tells the story:

> Last [good] sight about 1400, August 5, 1942. . .
> During forenoon obtained various sun lines of doubtful value. . .
> [No] zigzagging in order not to complicate navigational data. . .
> At 1730 *Selfridge* [DD-357, Lieutenant Commander Carroll D. Reynolds after sighting Bellona Island] rejoined disposition reporting position of *San Juan* [CL-54, Captain James E. Maher] at 1655 as Latitude 10–58 South, Longitude 159–01 East [115 miles due south of Russell Islands].[11]

With this firm position from *Selfridge* in hand, an exact approach through the shoal bound waters ahead was practicable at last for the 51-ship formation.

Later in the afternoon of 6 August, the carrier groups totaling 26 ships which had been hovering around and protecting the amphibians, broke off contact and disappeared to the southward. The amphibians were shifted into a column of squadrons of transports so as to narrow the front of the formation. Speed was changed to 12 knots and the final die cast.

The long day of 6 August and the one preceding it had had their blessings not known or directly recognized at the time. The rain squalls and the haze had been even heavier and thicker further north and closer to the equator in the area toward which the Expeditionary Force was moving. Thus Japanese Air reconnaissance flights from Rabaul and from the Tulagi-Gavutu air bases were either washed out, or the pilot's visibility was limited. The

---
[10] *Ibid.*
[11] COMPHIBFORSOPAC Staff Log.

Success, Then Cliff Hanging

Japanese land based planes were unequipped with radar. Neither the carriers nor the amphibians were sighted.[12]

At midnight on the sixth on board the flagship, it had been established that:

> The force is 3 miles southward or behind planned position with respect to time.[13]

The *Henley* (DD-391) (Commander Robert Hall Smith) and the *Bagley* (DD-386) (Lieutenant Commander George A. Sinclair) led the ships into what was later called "Iron Bottom Sound." The *Henley* early on 7 August had sighted the big high dark mass of Guadalcanal at 0133, less than an hour before the moon in its last quarter tried to break through the murk of the night at 0223. From the force flagship, *McCawley*, the sky at midnight on the sixth had appeared

> overcast, visibility poor. . . . ships in sight—one ahead, one astern, and in next adjacent columns, only one ship in sight.

However, at 0050 on the seventh, fortune had begun to shine on the amphibians:

> Stars out, visibility improving. . . .
> 0130. Counted eight ships in left-hand column and seven in right. . . . *Betelgeuse* and Transdiv Dog widely opened out. Directed these ships to close up, using blinker tube with reduced iris. . . .
> 0440. The moon after disclosing Guadalcanal and Savo Island became obscure. . . .[14]

For the day of the landing, the seventh, the weather was about all that could be hoped for at Guadalcanal. The sky was mostly cloudy and the average temperature was 80°F.[15]

Off Cape Esperance, the northwest cape of Guadalcanal, Task Force 62 had been split, with the lead transports bound for Florida Islands (Group YOKE, Captain George B. Ashe) passing north of Savo Island and the much larger Group XRAY (Captain Lawrence F. Reifsnider) bound for Lunga Point, taking the channel to the southward. Savo Island was abeam just before 0500, with sunrise due about 0633.

---

[12] (a) Samuel B. Griffith, *The Battle for Guadalcanal*, p. 40; (b) U.S. Naval War College, *The Battle of Savo Island August 9, 1942* (1950), pp. 9–10. Hereafter War College, *Savo Island*.
[13] Staff Log.
[14] *Ibid.*
[15] *USS Hull* War Diary, 7 Aug. 1942.

A BEAUTIFUL ISLAND

As darkness turned to light on 7 August 1942, the Lower Solomons came into view of Task Force 62. The sailorman's first impression on the morning of 7 August turned out to be so different from that carried in most literature on Guadalcanal, that this first impression should be noted. A Marine combat correspondent making the initial landing aptly put this impression in these words:

> . . . Guadalcanal is an island of striking beauty. Blue-green mountains, towering into a brilliant tropical sky or crowned with cloud masses, dominate the island. The dark green of jungle growth blends into the softer greens and browns of coconut groves and grassy plains and ridges.[16]

Admiral Turner put it more briefly:

> A truly beautiful sight that morning.[17]

Although Task Force 62 at 1600 the previous afternoon had been only 125 miles from the south coast of Guadalcanal, and presumably within the range of a late afternoon seaplane reconnaissance from both distant Rabaul or close Tulagi, the first enemy knowledge of the approach of the amphibians could have come from a routine early morning 7 August Japanese aircraft search. At 0600 the Staff Log noted:

> Observed lights of two planes taking off the water in vicinity of Lunga Point.
> At 0609, red flare dropped over [HMAS] *Australia*.[18]

Two minutes before schedule:

> At 0613 *Quincy* [CA-39, Captain Samuel N. Moore] opened fire on the beaches at Guadalcanal.
> At 0615 destroyers opened fire.
> At 0616 ships commenced firing on the Tulagi side.[19]

* * * *

It appeared that the approach of Task Force 62 and the subsequent attack took the Japanese by surprise as no shots were fired, no patrol boats [were] encountered, no signs of life were evident until Group XRAY opened fire on Guadalcanal Island objectives across the channel, about twenty miles away. Then a cluster of red rockets went up from the direction of Tulagi Island.[20]

---

[16] Merillat, *The Island*, p. 20. Reprinted by permission of Harold Ober Associates, Inc. Copyright 1944 by H. L. Merillat.
[17] Turner.
[18] Staff Log. *Alchiba* (AK-23) also reported plane with running lights at 0600.
[19] Staff Log. War College, *Savo Island*, gives one minute later for each of these events.
[20] *USS Neville* War Diary, 7 Aug. 1942.

FIRST BLOOD

First blood on the hostile shore was "a large oil fire" at the small village of Kukum, just to the westward from Lunga Point.

First seagoing blood was drawn at sea by two destroyers in the van of Squadron XRAY where the *Dewey* (DD-349) and *Hull* (DD-350) were on the starboard bow and the *Selfridge* (DD-357) and *Jarvis* (DD-393) were on the port bow. At 0620, the *Dewey* and the *Selfridge* opened fire on a Japanese schooner. The *Selfridge* reported that

> *Selfridge* fired 26 rounds 5"/38 common on a small vessel loaded with gasoline.

The *Dewey* made a low key report:

> *Dewey* expended 20 rounds. . . .

Her consort, the *Hull* logged

> *Dewey* sank small Japanese schooner.

The Transport Group Commander recorded:

> At 0630 a destroyer of the screen concentrated gunfire on a small 80-foot craft directly ahead of the formation. The vessel was carrying a deck load of gasoline in drums and was quickly enveloped in flames.

The flagship briefed the action:

> Two masted schooner sunk by leading destroyer.

And finally, one of the cargo ships, the *Alchiba* reported:

> After four salvos from a destroyer in the van at 0630, the small craft ahead was hit and burst into flame. . . .[21]

However, the *Dewey* (Lieutenant Commander Charles F. Chillingsworth) magnanimously reported "checked fire when aircraft attacked" and "one small schooner sunk by own aircraft."[22]

From the reports of all the witnesses present, it appears that the aircraft bomb brought a quick end to a schooner already in extremities from the gunfire of the destroyers despite the *Ellet's* (DD-398) opinion that one destroyer's shooting was "ragged."[23]

The long drawn-out anti-aircraft battle in the Solomons was soon to

---

[21] Quotations from Action Reports or Logs of USS *Selfridge, Dewey, Hull, Alchiba*, CTG 62.1, and *McCawley*.
[22] *Dewey*, Action Report, 16 Aug. 1942.
[23] *Ellet* War Diary, 7 Aug. 1942.

start, at least in the minds of those having their first brush with the Japanese. According to the Staff Log and the final Marine report:

> 0618. sighted unidentified plane on port bow.
> 0620. AA fire on plane ahead.[24]
> .... only one aircraft got into the air and it was destroyed immediately after takeoff by cruiser anti-aircraft fire, off Lunga Point.[24]

A tiresome check of the war diaries, action reports, and logs of surviving ships does not reveal which cruiser or destroyer fired anti-aircraft fire at this hour of the morning. The haze of the Solomons was beginning.

THE JAPANESE FIRST REPORT THE ALLIGATOR

Although U.S. ships must have been visible by 0600 and had commenced firing by 0613, Japanese records indicate that it was not until nearly 40 minutes later, 0652 on 7 August, that Commander Air Base Tulagi got off a report to Commander 25th Air Flotilla, his senior at Rabaul, that "enemy task force sighted."

This message was not nearly so succinct or so immediate as that of Commander Logan Ramsey, U. S. Navy, Operations Officer on the staff of Patrol Wing Two at the Naval Air Station, Pearl Harbor. His 0758 message reporting the 0755 attack by the Japanese on December 7, 1941 read:

> Air Raid Pearl. This is not a drill.

It was another 13 minutes before the report of Commander Air Base, Tulagi was amplified:

> Enemy task force of twenty ships attacking Tulagi, undergoing severe bombings, landing preparations underway; help requested.[25]

"Enemy has commenced landing" was reported at 0715.

TULAGI—GAVUTU—FLORIDA

The Japanese forces in the Southern Solomons had moved initially onto Tulagi Island, primarily because they needed a seaplane base in that area for aerial reconnaissance in connection with "and subsequent to" Operation

---

[24] (a) Staff Log; (b) Commanding General, First Marine Division, Final Report on Guadalcanal Operation, Phase 1 of 24 May 1943.
[25] Japanese CRUDIV 6, Battle Report.

"M-O," the May 1942 Japanese forward movement which had brought on the Battle of the Coral Sea.

Prior to May 1942, the British controlled the Solomon Islands protectorate from Government House on the northeast side of Tulagi, and the Australians provided the minor defense forces and "Ferdinand," the highly effective coast watcher's organization.[26] On 7 August 1942, "Ferdinand" began paying extra intelligence dividends. Based on their information and aerial photographs, Vice Admiral Ghormley had estimated in his Operation Plan No. 1–42, that some 3,100 Japanese were to be reckoned with at the Marine objectives. Interrogation after the war of senior Japanese Army officers directly concerned with the Lower Solomons indicates this estimate was excellent and that there were about 780 Japanese including labor troops in the Tulagi-Gavutu-Tanambogo area and 2,230 on Guadalcanal. Some 1,700 of the Guadalcanal contingent were labor troops and the rest largely were Japanese Marines.

Since their initial landings, the Japanese had spread out from Tulagi, which was only about one-half mile wide and two miles long, to the much

---

[26] Buka and Bougainville Islands were part of the Australian Mandated Territory of New Guinea.

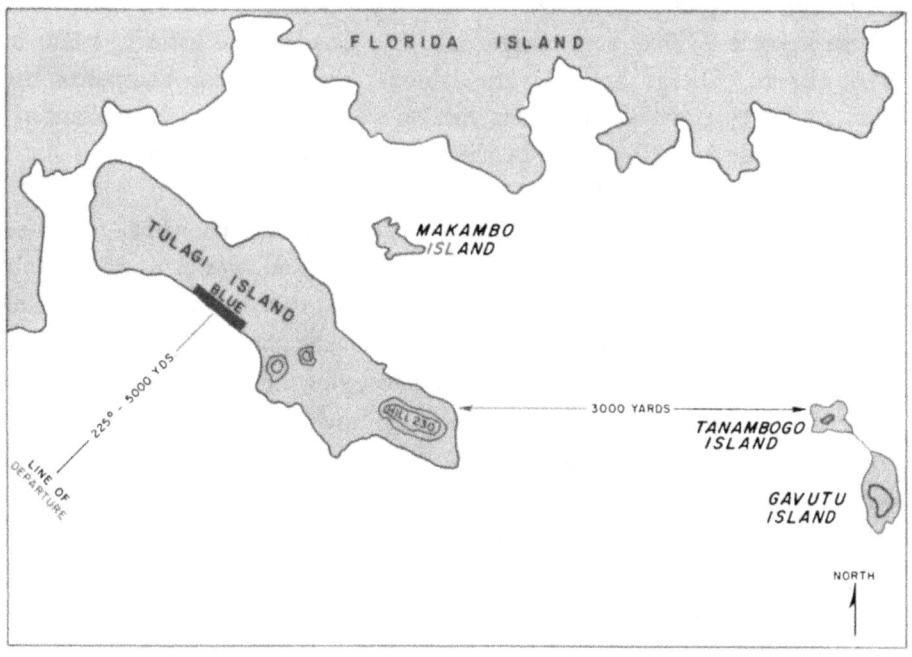

Landing Objectives in Tulagi-Gavutu Area.

larger island of Florida to the immediate north, and to the small hillish islands of Gavutu and Tanambogo some 3,000 yards to the eastward of Tulagi. The Japanese had established their seaplane base at Gavutu Island, which was reef ringed.

All this dispersion complicated mightily the Scheme of Maneuver, and the gunfire support plan for the attacking forces in the Tulagi area.

Aerial photographs had shown the Japanese defenses were strongest on the northeast and southeast beaches of Tulagi. So the southwest beach area was chosen for the initial main landing. This gave the landing craft for the main Blue Beach landing a rudimentary straight approach from the transport area and a real break.

To take Gavutu Island, and to land at Halavo Peninsula, Florida Island, to the eastward of Gavutu, a difficult turning operation was required of the landing craft, in addition to picking a circuitous path through a heavily reefed area.

SCHEME OF MANEUVER

During the planning phases, of the approximately 19,500 embarked Marines, some 11,000 were assigned to the Guadalcanal assault, 4,000 to take Florida, Tulagi and Gavutu Islands, and the rest composed the Division Reserve, whose secondary mission was to act as the Ndeni Landing Force in Phase 3 of Task One of the PESTILENCE Operation, the second phase of which was WATCHTOWER.

The agreed upon Scheme of Maneuver for Guadalcanal which governed the amphibians' approach to that enemy-held island was a comparatively simple one for the untested seagoing amphibians to execute their part. The Scheme of Maneuver for Tulagi, Gavutu, Makambo, and Florida was considerably more complicated from the naval viewpoint, although markedly fewer large transports and cargo ships were involved.

The assault beach on Guadalcanal was 1,600 yards of the 2,000-yard wide Red Beach. It lay just to the east of the mouth of the Tenaru River and five miles east of Lunga Point, a good landmark on the north central coastline. The Japanese air strip was inland a mile, and about half way between Tenaru and Lunga.

Nine transports and six cargo ships, Transport Group XRAY, under the command of the second senior naval officer regularly detailed in the

Amphibious Force South Pacific, Captain Reifsnider, in the *Hunter Liggett* (AP-27) were assigned to the Guadalcanal task. They were to initially anchor in two lines, 1,500 yards apart, with the inshore line just outside the hundred fathom curve, four and a half miles north of the mouth of the Tenaru River. As soon as the fast minesweepers could sweep the area between the initial transport area and the 10 fathom line the transports and cargo ships were to move closer to the beach.

The main assault beach on Tulagi was 500 yards of the 600-yard wide Blue Beach. It lay in the west central sector of the south coast of Tulagi. An additional landing was to be made on the east coast of Gavutu Island, and two small landings at areas five miles apart on Florida Island—Haleta Harbor to the west and Halavo Peninsula to the east of Tulagi.

Three transports, four destroyer-type transports and one cargo ship, Transport Group YOKE, under the command of Captain George B. Ashe, the third senior officer regularly detailed in the Amphibious Force South Pacific and in the *Neville* (AP-16), were assigned to this more complicated task. They were to initially anchor southwest of Blue Beach, with the inshore line just outside the hundred fathom curve which in this case again was about five miles from the beach.

Groups XRAY and YOKE were initially anchored about 11 miles apart.

The Lines of Departure from where the assault landing craft were to initiate their run for the shore in formal formation were two and a half miles from the designated beaches, both Red and Blue. About two-thirds of the Marines were embarked in the 36-foot Higgins boat, the LCP(L) (Landing Craft, Personnel without ramp) and about one-third in the newer LCV or LCPR with the highly desirable ramp. Tanks and trucks were to be ferried ashore in medium-sized landing craft, the 45-foot LCMs.

After the first two days of rehearsal at Koro Island, and its accompanying routine landing mishaps and engine failures, the large transports and cargo ships of Task Force 62 had been told to signal the number of landing craft each would have available and ready for the WATCHTOWER landing. To this was added the number anticipated to be available from the *Zeilin* and *Betelgeuse* and the four LCP(L)s in each of the four destroyer transports. The grand total listed was 475 consisting of:

    (a) 8 "X" Type (30-foot personnel craft without ramp).
    (b) 303 LCP(L) (36-foot Landing Craft, Personnel, without ramp).
    (c) 116 LCV or LCPR (36-foot Landing Craft Vehicle, Personnel, with ramp).

Turner Collection

Landing craft from the Hunter Liggett *(AP–27), later APA–14, lands its last Marines at Tonga Island in October 1942. Note the lack of landing ramps.*

(d) 48 LCM (45-foot Landing Craft, Medium, for tanks and trucks, with ramp).[27]

None of the landing craft were really old and most had been built within the year. The eight oldest type landing craft in the WATCHTOWER Operation were the 30-foot "X boats," four in the flagship *McCawley* and four in the *Barnett* (AP-11). The LVTs (amtracs) of the Amphibian Tractor Battalion of the First Marine Division were in addition to the craft listed above.

On 22 June 1942, COMINCH had changed the designations of many of the landing boats, but his written order was circulated by slow sea mail to the South Pacific, and was not passed on to Task Force 62 until mid-August, so that the official reports of this period all use the earlier designa-

---

[27] Annex George to COMPHIBSOPAC Op Plan A3–42, 30 Jul. 1942, listed the craft anticipated to be available 8/7/42. Up until 22 June 1942, the LCPR had been designated "TR boats," the LCP(L) "T boats," and the LCM were "WL lighters."

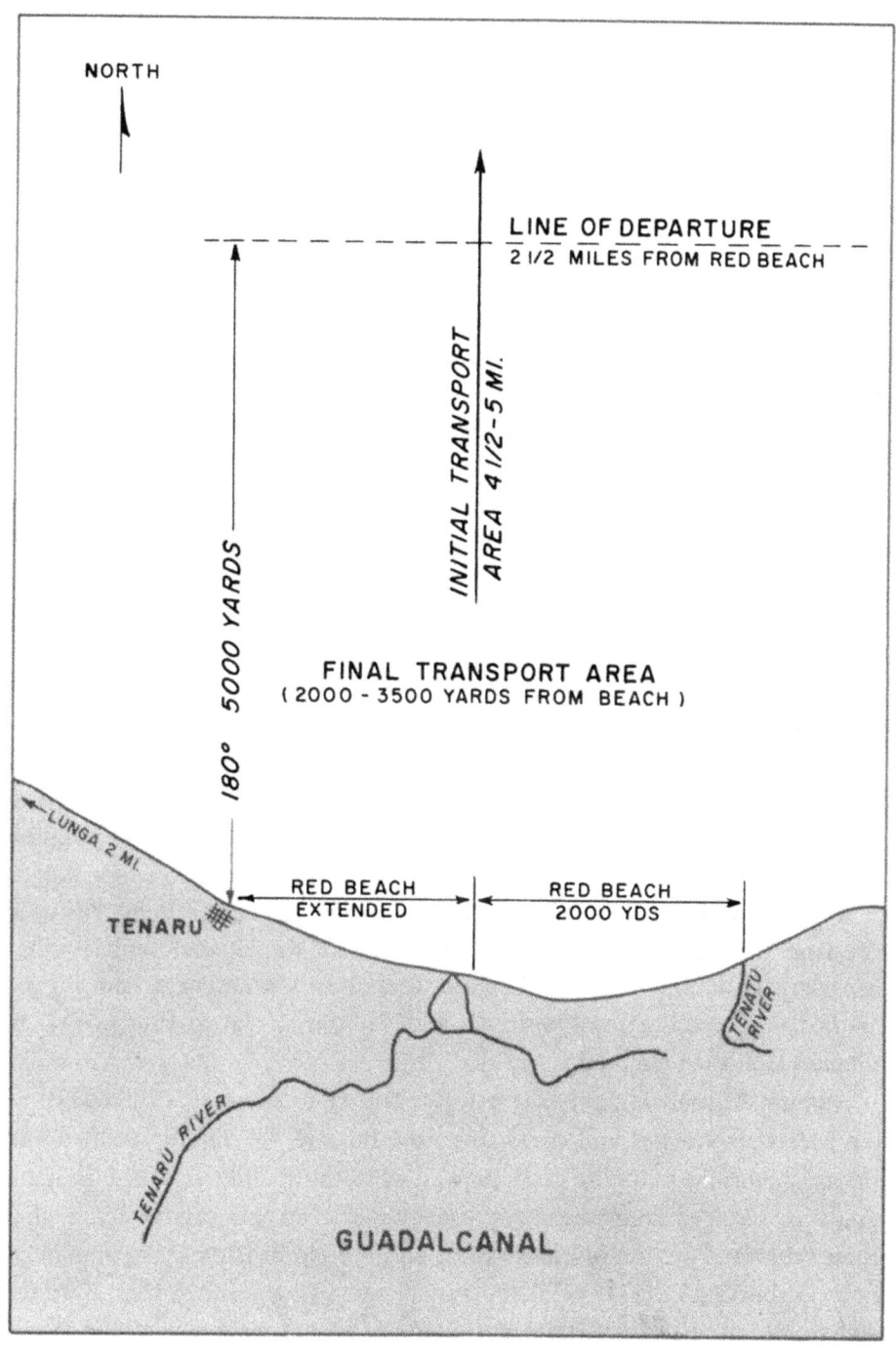

Transport Area, Guadalcanal.

tions. The 36-foot "TR boats" with ramp, officially became LCV, but popularly known as LCPR; "T boats" without ramp became LCP(L); and the 45-foot "WL lighters" became LCM. The LCP(L) had diesel engines, but all the LCV or LCPR in WATCHTOWER were gas engine craft, as were part of the LCM.[28]

AWAY ALL BOATS

It was 0615 on 7 August 1942 and time for the landing craft to go to work. The boatswain's mates' shrill pipes and the crane operator's skillful control would soon fill the warm, calm and apathetic anchorage areas with landing craft. It had taken the Navy a very long eight months since 7 December 1941 to put a full Marine division into position before enemy held islands. It was the first time in the war that the confident Marines were in a position to make the Japanese start looking over their shoulders to note how far they had to retreat to reach either their ancestors or their homeland in Honshu or Kyushu. It was a moment of pride for the amphibians.

At 0637, CTF 62.2 (Captain Ashe) on the Tulagi side had really sent the amphibians to their tasks when he executed the General Signal "Land Landing Force, Zero Hour is 0800." Since the Marines wished one rifle company, reinforced by one machine gun platoon, landed on Florida Island at Haleta to the westward of Blue Beach on Tulagi at H minus 20 minutes, or at 0740, Captain Ashe's landing schedule was barely off to a good start. It was not until 0652 that Rear Admiral Turner off Lunga Point executed the same General Signal, but set Hypo Hour for the Guadalcanal landings considerably later, at 0910. Captain Reifsnider's transports had lagged markedly in coming into position, and H-hour at Guadalcanal was 40 minutes later than planned.

Admiral Turner thought that it was a tribute to the basic competence of the boatswain's mates and coxswains manning the 475 rapidly trained and partially rehearsed landing craft, as well as to the soundness of the training guidance received from the many echelons of command above them, that these sailormen put the Marines ashore on the right beaches at the appointed hour in the WATCHTOWER Operation. His hat was off to the sailormen and young officers of his command, many of whom were new to the Navy.

---

[28] COMINCH, memorandum, FF–1/S28–1, Ser 01170 of 22 Jun. 1942, subj: Designation of Landing Craft Ships and Vehicles, with endorsement of 18 August 1942 distributing to TF 62.

One ship reported that over 90 percent of the officers and 42 percent of the men were members of the Naval Reserve.[29]

Admiral Turner remembered that he was incredudous that at Guadalcanal the initial landing at Red Beach was unopposed and it added to his pleasure that on the Tulagi side, the initial landings at Haleta and Halavo were unopposed, and at Blue Beach unopposed except for a limited number of snipers.[30]

Not that everything at either landing had gone perfectly.

> . . . the *Neville* experienced a period of waiting of 41 minutes between the time all boats were in the water and time to commence loading troops. The APDs were idle 15 minutes. . . .[31]

The seven-mile approach to the Line of Departure for Gavutu "in a choppy head sea thoroughly drenched all personnel and equipment."[32]

MINESWEEPING

Since there had been many aerial photographs taken of Japanese naval and merchant ships in various anchorages off Lunga Point and off Tulagi in the weeks before the landings, it was known that there were generous unmined areas in these waters. So despite the fact that the operation order read "Water less than 100 fathoms in depth must be presumed to be mined," it was just a question of determining the exact boundaries of any mined areas that existed.[33]

The five fast minesweepers of Mine Squadron Two, *Hopkins, Southard, Hovey, Trever, Zane*, were under orders to sweep in from the 100 fathom curve toward Port Purves in the Gavutu Island area first, then, dividing into two groups, simultaneously sweep from the 100 fathom curve in toward Beach Red on Guadalcanal and a thousand yard wide passage through Lengo Channel leading to Indispensable Strait.

In order not to alert the Japanese, and not to interfere with the early waves of landing craft, sweeping was not to start until 90 minutes after zero hour at Tulagi (0930) and not required by the operation orders to be completed off the Tenaru and Beach Red until 1800 on the 7th.[34]

---

[29] (a) Turner; (b) USS *President Adams,* Action Report, 15 Aug. 1942.
[30] Turner.
[31] COMTRANSDIV Eight Action Report, 12 Aug. 1942.
[32] *Heywood* Action Report, 12 Aug. 1942.
[33] Staff Interviews.
[34] COMPHIBSOPAC Op Plan A3–42, 30 Jul. 1942, Annex Baker.

The minesweeping was actually completed, with no mines swept, at 1550, except for the area immediately off Beach Red which could not all be done because the transports had moved into the area.

Well before the start of minesweeping, two of these converted destroyers were to fire concentrated fire on Bungana Island for five minutes and three ships were to concentrate on Gavutu Island for five minutes. Then they were to act as control ships at the Line of Departure and as salvage ships for the Halavao, Florida Island landing.

While the minesweepers were proceeding to their initial stations, the Japanese gunners manning the 3-inch and smaller guns on or near the top of Gavutu decided the destroyer minesweepers at 4,000 yards were worthwhile targets and opened up with a straddle on the flagship, *Hopkins* (DMS-13), and erratic fire on the others. The *Hovey* (DMS-11) which "had 30 brand new men aboard who had never heard gunfire" reported:

> During the bombardment directed against Gavutu Island by the ship . . . enemy AA guns fired AA shells with fuses set to explode short and above the ship. . . .[35]

There was much counterbattery fire from the fast minesweepers, and some air bombing of Gavutu before the DMS left to proceed to their initial minesweeping stations.

The sweeping schedule meant that during the initial hours of the landing, the transports and cargo ships, in Group **XRAY**, would be discharging Marines and cargo into boats from four and a half to five miles from the assault beaches if the ships were to await the completion of sweeping before moving in. This was a serious weakness in Rear Admiral Turner's plans, not to be repeated willingly in later operations, and remedied before the morning was out by prompt action of Captain Reifsnider in the Red Beach area, whose War Diary noted:

> Debarkation positions were 4½ miles from BEACH RED. Half an hour after the initial waves had landed, the transports moved 3½ miles closer to the beach to reduce the long water ride for the Marines.[36]

Commander Transport's summation was on the optimistic side. The detailed record shows that the transport squadron's movement closer inshore was individualistic. The *Hunter Liggett* moved in at 0942. The *McCawley* logged: "1045, commenced closing beach, 1121 anchor in 23 fathoms." The *President Adams* (AP-38) "shifted inshore and anchored BEACH RED

---

[35] *Hovey*, Action Report, 11 Aug. 1942.
[36] CTG 62.1 War Diary, 23 Sept. 1942.

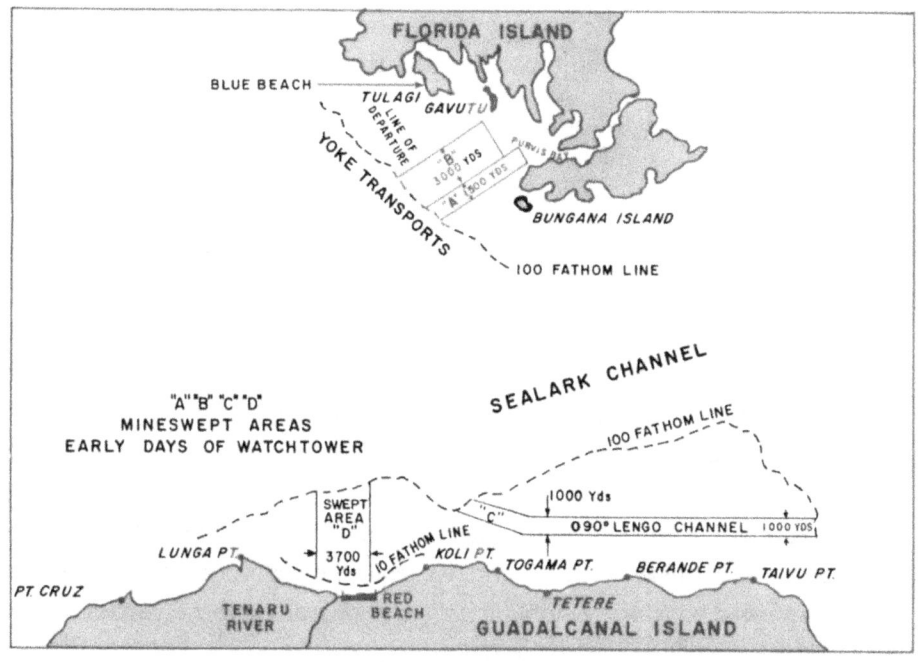

Mineswept Areas, WATCHTOWER.

1201." The *Barnett* "at 1045 completed debarkation and proceeded to anchorage off RED BEACH." *Alchiba* (AK-23) "anchored at 1055." *Betelgeuse* "anchored in 27 fathoms about one mile off RED BEACH at 1108." *USS Libra* (AK-53) logged: "0950. On despatch from OTC started maneuvering inshore to 100 fathoms curve. 1125. In compliance with signal from OCT, moved to anchorage 2000 yards off and parallel to Beach 'Red'." *Alhena* (AK-26) "at 1130, Moved in to 3,500 yards from the beach and anchored." The *Bellatrix* logged: "1029. On signal that the intended anchorage off RED BEACH was not mined, crossed slowly inside the 100 fathom curve. 1123 anchored." [37] But by and large, the transports and cargo ships moved cautiously to ease the boating problem.

Insofar as the destroyer minesweepers were concerned, their action reports and other correspondence do not contain any world shaking "lessons learned" or "changes recommended" for future operations. They had done all the chores requested in an effective manner with no fuss or feathers. Besides being jacks of many trades, gunfire support, control and salvage,

---

[37] Ships' Logs and War Diaries.

antisubmarine, antiaircraft, and despatch ship, they had been masters at their basic trade, minesweeping, at least in this area of no Japanese mines.

STATE OF THE ART

Gunfire support and air support are two of the essential ingredients of any amphibious landing on a hostile shore.

The elementary Japanese air and ground defenses in the Guadalcanal-Tulagi area closely matched the elementary state of the gunfire support art in the U. S. Navy on 7 August 1942. And the air bombing art was judged not too much better than elementary by some, including Rear Admiral Turner.[38]

Rear Admiral Turner had been in Washington when the Battles of the Coral Sea and Midway were fought. He read the reports of our Army Air Force and naval aviators' bombings in some phases of those battles. Then he read the decoded damage reports of Japanese commanders to their superiors. "The difference was so great that it wasn't even understandable." [39] Admiral Turner thought this point could, and should, be illustrated in this book.

An excellent example involves the Japanese "Tulagi Invasion Group" which consisted of two minelayers, one transport, two destroyers, two subchasers and four minesweepers.[40] The transport unloaded and departed. The rest of the force was attacked by carrier aircraft from the *Yorktown* on 4 May 1942. They reported having sunk seven ships (two destroyers, one cargo ship, and four gunboats), forced a light cruiser to beach itself, severely damaged both a third destroyer and a seaplane tender, which "may have been a heavy cruiser" and damaged an 8–10,000 ton freighter. As a matter of record, however, no destroyers and only a total of three very small ships were sunk. The "light cruiser" beached, in fact, was a modest sized 1,320-ton destroyer, the 17-year-old *Kikuzuki* of the 1925 class. Her beaching was fortunately permanent. The "cargo ship" sunk was the 264-ton converted minesweeper, the *Tama Maru*. The four "gunboats" sunk were not four

---
[38] (a) Turner; (b) Staff Interviews.
[39] Turner.
[40] d'Albas, *Death of a Navy*, p. 110. One of the minesweepers initially listed for Tulagi was shifted to the Port Moresby invasion group.

but two small 215-ton coastal minesweepers. The damaged "seaplane tender" or "heavy cruiser" was the 4,400-ton minelayer *Okinoshima*.[41]

SHIPS GUNFIRE SUPPORT

The amphibian gunfire support organization provided five fire support sections at Guadalcanal to make up the Fire Support Group Love, and one Fire Support Group designated Mike at Tulagi-Gavutu. On the Guadalcanal side, three of the fire support sections were single ships—a heavy cruiser with two of its observation planes; the other two sections consisted of two destroyers each. On the Tulagi side, there were a light anti-aircraft cruiser and two destroyers, with two observation planes from a heavy cruiser assigned to work with Commander Landing Force, Tulagi and this gunfire support group.

Each of the three United States heavy cruisers assigned fire support chores had five seaplanes. Eight of the aircraft were allocated to control by the Marine commanders for liaison and shore artillery observation. One was allocated to Commander Screening Group for anti-submarine patrol.

There was a naval gunfire liaison party from each cruiser sent ashore with the early landing craft boat waves. The observation seaplanes were required to look for and report enemy troop movements or targets, as well as to spot the gunfire of Marine artillery and supporting ships.

Gunfire was to start at daylight.

GUNFIRE—GUADALCANAL

The naval gunfire problem on the Guadalcanal side was the simple one of destroying the anti-aircraft and coast defense guns, all above ground, in the Kukum, Lunga, and Tetere areas. These had been reported by the Army Air Force B-17s flying out of the New Hebrides or Australia. Twelve anti-aircraft guns were reported in the Kukum area. These had been bombed numerous times by the B-17s during the past fortnight and they were to be

---

[41] CO *Yorktown* Action Report, 11 May 1942; (b) U.S. Army, Far East Command, Military History Section, "The Imperial Japanese Navy in World War II" (Japanese Monograph No. 116) (1952), pp. 176, 251, 265; (c) Joint Army-Navy Assessment Committee, *Japanese Naval and Merchant Shipping Losses during World War II by All Causes* (NAVEXOS P–468) (Washington: Government Printing Office, 1947).

further attacked by naval dive bombers from Rear Admiral Noyes's Task Group 61.1 at 15 minutes before sunrise, occurring at 0633.[42]

The locations of these anti-aircraft and coast defense guns were not accurately known to the fire support ships primarily because of the absence of good photographs and secondarily because the dissemination of photographic interpretation had not been developed in the amphibious forces to the necessary extent. So all that the ships were told was that there were "shore batteries from Lunga Point westward," or "AA guns reported vicinity Tetere," or "AA guns near Tenaru." But it was presumed the coast defense guns and the anti-aircraft guns, if dual-purpose, would open fire on the ships, and that the spotters in the cruisers' sea planes would coach the fire support ships' guns on to them. This contingency did not arise.

The initial gunfire and air strikes brought these results according to the logs being written on the flagship:

> 0635. A large fire on Kekum, bearing 214. . . .
> Heavy smoke bearing 210°. . . .
> Enemy ammunition dump at Lunga Point and supply depot at Kukum ablaze.[43]

Despite these early successes, Japanese anti-aircraft fire from the beach areas continued.

> 0643. AA fire from beach bearing 196° T.[44]

However, after another seven minutes of gunfire attention, the Flag Log noted:

> 0650. No gunfire from beaches.[45]

In addition to destroying any hidden larger guns which might take the amphibious ships under fire while they were disembarking troops and equipment, 135 8-inch shells and 1,400 5-inch rounds were to be put on the 1,600-yard assault area on Red Beach to a depth of 200 yards, and extending 800 yards on both sides. This shelling was to take place during the period Zero Hour minus 10 minutes to Zero Hour minus five minutes, to prevent the beaches from being taken under fire by Japanese defenders.

Three heavy cruisers and four destroyers began this concentrated firing at 0900, as the landing craft moved smartly from the Line of Departure

---

[42] (a) COMAIRSOPAC War Diary, Vol. I, 23, 31 Jul. 1942, 1, 2, 4, 5 Aug. 1942; (b) COMAIRSOPAC to COMSOPAC, 060313 Aug. 1942.
[43] (a) *McCawley* Log; (b) Staff Log.
[44] Staff Log.
[45] Ibid.

toward Red Beach. They ceased fire about 0907, and the first LCVP touched the beach at about 0910.

Since there was no hostile fire against the landing troops in the Red Beach area at Guadalcanal, the second part of the close support fire plan to put 800 rounds of 5-inch supporting fire to the east and west of Red Beach at Guadalcanal, starting at plus five minutes after the first wave landed, was cancelled.

GUNFIRE—TULAGI

The naval gunfire problem in the Tulagi area was complicated by the lay of the land, the multiplicity and strength of known Japanese defense positions, and the fact that the islands of Tulagi, Tanambogo, and Gavutu lay beneath promontories of the larger Florida Island just to the north and east, where Japanese guns could be advantageously located.[46]

It was known from photographic data, that the southeast end of Tulagi was more heavily defended than other Tulagi areas. However, to prepare for and cover all the actual Marine landings on Florida and Tulagi Islands, it was necessary to divide the modest early morning gunfire effort between preparatory fire on the Blue Beach and the Haleta area, and the southeast end of Tulagi where the known defenses, including antiaircraft guns, were located.

Preparatory gunfire was also supplied for steep hilled Gavutu and Tanambogo, with 92 rounds of close fire support from 500 yards by the destroyer *Monssen* (DD-436). This gunfire was particularly effective at Tanambogo the second day after a 200-round five-minute bombardment from a respectable 4,000 yards had proven ineffective the first day.[47] This close fire support by the *Monssen* was the first really "close up" use of the 5-inch naval gun from a thin shelled naval ship to blast Japanese defenders from caves and well-prepared defense positions.

LESSONS LEARNED

Not too much was said about ship gunfire support in the reports on the WATCHTOWER Operation. All three of the 8-inch gun ships which had

---

[46] Staff Interviews.
[47] *USS Monssen* War Diary, 7 Aug. 1942.

specific heavy gunfire support tasks were sunk within 48 hours of the landings. The only remaining United States Navy heavy cruiser, the *Chicago*, did not have a specific gunfire support task. So gunfire support was not even mentioned in her WATCHTOWER action report. The *Vincennes* (CA-44) skipper, in a report written from memory after his ship sank, wrote that the ship had bombarded only native villages where "possible presence of enemy had been previously reported." [48]

The *Buchanan* (DD-484) reported that her preparatory and covering fire on Blue Beach, Tulagi, was carried out at ranges of 6,000 to 7,000 yards, but by afternoon the *Buchanan* had moved in to a range of 1,100 yards in delivering call fire on Tanambogo. The *Helm* (DD-388) delivered 5-inch fire support at 9,000 yards on Tulagi. [49]

The other destroyers and destroyer-types were equally reticent in commenting on their firing although the *Hovey* (DMS-11) remarked that the bombardment carried out by the high speed minesweepers was "at times, erratic."

The 5-inch anti-aircraft cruiser *San Juan* (CL-54), that fired preparatory fire on Tulagi, Tanambogo, Gavutu, and Florida Island, did so from outside the 100 fathom curve and therefore at ranges of 9,000 yards or more in order to keep clear of possibly mined areas. She fired 3,231 rounds of 5-inch ammunition between 7 and 9 August, of which 3,005 rounds were against shore targets. Due to her northerly position this anti-aircraft cruiser did not participate in the defensive fire against any of the Japanese air attacks on 7 August and fired only 226 rounds on the 8th during air attacks. [50]

The marriage of gunfire support duties with control of boat waves by destroyers had been both short and generally unhappy. A position near one extremity of a Line of Departure is not always compatible with the maneuvering necessary to pinpoint gunfire support, and a World War II destroyer was just too large a craft to function smartly in control of boat waves.

High-capacity, thin-shelled ammunition had been used by the ships, and while these were effective against exposed troops or lightly sheltered ones, the shells were not rugged enough to pierce strong defensive structures. Time fuses for firing against shore targets had been forbidden, although it was known and stated in the Gunfire Support Plan that "5-inch 25-caliber projectiles without base fuses will not detonate satisfactorily on impact."

---

[48] *USS Chicago* Action Report, 19 Aug. 1942; *Vincennes* Action Report, 15 Aug. 1942.
[49] *USS Buchanan* Action Report, 13 Aug. 1942; *USS Helm* Action Report, 14 Aug. 1942.
[50] *USS San Juan* Action Report, 15 Aug. 1942; *USS Hovey* Action Report, 11 Aug. 1942.

Success, Then Cliff Hanging

Unfortunately, the initial WATCHTOWER landings provided no real test of either ships gunfire or the methods of controlling ships gunfire by shore based fire control parties. The lack of response to the ships gunfire in the WATCHTOWER Operation was a dangerous precedent for Tarawa.

CLOSE AIR SUPPORT

Carrier Air Group Three was in the *Saratoga,* Carrier Air Group Six was in the *Enterprise,* and Carrier Air Group Seven was in the *Wasp.* On D-Day, the *Wasp* Air Group was assigned to the Tulagi-Gavutu area, and the *Saratoga* Air Group to the Guadalcanal area. Four squadrons of aircraft (one VF and three VSB) were assigned to close air support and two additional squadrons (one VF and one VSB) were assigned for the initial attack sweeps.

In the early hours of the operation, Commander Air Group Three and Commander Air Group Six alternated in command of aircraft in the Guadalcanal area. Commander Air Group Seven initially was over Tulagi.

Sunrise on D-Day was at 0633 and at 15 minutes before sunrise, while the transports were coming up to position, one fighter squadron was to drop in on the Japanese seaplane base at Tulagi-Gavutu-Tanambogo. At the same minute, a second fighter squadron was to sweep over the Point Cruz-Kukum-Lunga-Koli-Togama Point area, striking any Japanese aircraft, motor torpedo boats, or submarines.

Two dive bombing squadrons were ordered to attack at the same early hour, with the tasks of destroying anti-aircraft and coastal defense guns in or near the two Marine assault areas, and any aircraft on airdromes, fuel and ammunition dumps, or concentration of vehicles. One dive bombing squadron was assigned to blast the Tulagi hills from minus 10 minutes to H-hour.

Air Group Six provided a half squadron of fighters for follow through of the "15 minutes before sunrise" attack on Guadalcanal airdromes and AA installations, and a half squadron of dive bombers for follow through of the Tulagi initial sweep. Forty-four planes comprised the initial sweep at Guadalcanal and 41 planes struck at Tulagi-Gavutu.

The Air Support Group polished off the 18 Japanese seaplanes in the Tulagi area with its first attack. There were no seaplanes sighted on the Guadalcanal side and no Japanese land planes on the airstrip.

Subsequent thereto, during daylight, the Air Support Group provided one and a half squadrons (18 planes) of dive bombers continuously for striking gun positions in the assault areas and a varying number of fighters, normally one-half squadron (6 planes), continuously for air cover. Additionally, the Air Support Group provided one plane over Guadalcanal and one over Tulagi for air ground liaison with the forces in those areas, as well as an artillery spotting plane over Guadalcanal, until it was known that the Marine artillery was not to be used. Both the fighters and dive bombers carried out close air support of the Marines or dropped their bombs on targets of opportunity before returning to land on the carriers.

The basic plan provided that air support for the Marines during the amphibious assault phase would be controlled by an air support group temporarily attached to the staff of the amphibious force commander. Fighter cover over the assault area was to be controlled by a fighter director group attached to the staff of the Second-in-Command to the Amphibious Force Commander. Specifically this meant that control and coordination of air units in the assault area was exercised by the Air Support Director Group in the *McCawley*, working through the Senior Carrier Air Group Commander on station over the assault area, who was in airborne command of the aircraft from the Air Support Group.

The Air Controller of the Fighter Director Group from the Air Support Director Group, at the last moment, had to be stationed in the heavy cruiser *Chicago* rather than in Rear Admiral Crutchley's flagship, the *Australia*, because the *Australia* had a completely inadequate aircraft radar with a working range of 15 miles. The *McCawley* could not pick up this additional chore because of inadequate aircraft radio communication channels.

The Air Controller in the *McCawley* had radio communication with the home base—the carriers—and up and down the naval chain of command in the combat area, as well as with the Marine chain of command, and with the Senior Carrier Air Group Commander and the liaison planes in the air, but in part it was step by step communication. He did not have direct voice communication with all ships nor with lower echelon Marine units. These Marine ground units did not have direct communication with the individual planes circling overhead.

All scheduled air strikes were delivered on time and largely on target. Some targets had not been minutely described or pin-pointed and so were not recognized. The carrier pilots, not specially trained for this exacting and difficult air support chore, did not always come up to the expectations of the Marines, their own desires, or the desires of the top command.

Success, Then Cliff Hanging

Turner Collection

Japanese bombing attacks at Guadalcanal, 7–8 August 1942.

The Fighter Director Group aboard the *Chicago* did not function up to par on 8 August, after having done well the morning before, and the heaviest enemy air attack of 45 Bettys and escorting Zekes was not intercepted by our fighters prior to the delivery of torpedo attacks on Task Force 62, despite an hour's advance warning from a coast watcher.

The lack of separate radio frequencies for the Tulagi and the Guadalcanal Air Support Groups caused much radio interference at times. Admiral Turner wrote:

> . . . there was a partial ground or short on the antenna of the *McCawley's* TBS, which was not discovered and remedied until about November, 1942. The effects of the ground were to cause a rough tone to both reception and transmission, and to reduce the range of incoming and outgoing messages from the usual 20 miles to about 8 miles. For example, TBS exchanges between the *McCawley* and ships off Tulagi, 15 miles away, had to be relayed through a DD of the outer screen of the XRAY Group.[51]

The most important lesson learned in close air support in the first two days of the WATCHTOWER Operation was that it was

---

[51] RKT to DCNO Admin, enclosure to letter of 20 Aug. 1950, p. 18.

essential that ground forces in an operation of this type have radio communication directly with the liaison planes or Air Group Commander in order that maximum support may be afforded ground personnel.[52]

The second most important lesson learned was that the Air Support Director Group should not be positioned at limit of voice radio range from any part of the forces being supported, or there will be constant delays or failures in air support operations.

THE TRANSPORT NAVY LEARNS ITS LESSONS

The first lesson the amphibians learned at Guadalcanal was that they were going to have to get used to being shot at. One coxswain reported:

> After getting the ramp up, we backed down as far as we could so as to keep the ramp between us and the line of fire. When we started around a little knoll, which was lined with trees, we were fired at from these trees. We spotted the flash from a gun up in one of these trees. I picked up the Marine's Risen gun and blasted the flash and the Jap fired again and I got a better bead on him, and fired again and he came tumbling down like a bird.[53]

Another coxswain reported:

> The Japs were firing at the four of us as we were cranking up the ramp and one bullet hit the winch and splattered little pieces of lead in Morgan's side along his ribs under the skin but didn't hurt him much.[54]

The *President Adams* related that

> The boat course from the ship to shore was like the letter U. . . . boats were under sniper fire during about the latter fourth of the trip. The final boat course was opposite to the original, this fact by itself shows the difficulty with which our boats were faced.[55]

The 19 large transports and cargo ships of Task Force 62 that arrived at Guadalcanal-Tulagi on 7 August were not newly built ships, although most of them were relatively new to the Navy. All of the large transports and cargo ships had participated previously in some amphibious exercises with troops, equipment, and cargo to be unloaded, and a number had participated in landing the Marines in Iceland, the August 1941 New River

---

[52] *USS Wasp* Action Report, 14 Aug. 1942, encl. (B), p .4.
[53] *USS President Adams* Action Report, 25 Aug. 1942, Encl. (A), Report of G.L.D. Sporhase, BM2c.
[54] *Ibid.*, Encl. (B), Report of B. W. Hensen, BM2c.
[55] *Ibid.*, CO's Report, 15 Aug. 1942.

Turner Collection

Japanese high-level bombing attacks at Guadalcanal, 7 August 1942.

and the January 1942 Lynnhaven Roads Training Exercises. Several, including the *McCawley* and *Hunter Liggett,* were veterans of Fleet Landing Exercise Number 7 in early 1941.

But, by and large, these amphibious ships did not have enough officers and men to continuously unload over a 72-hour period. It was both good and bad fortune that the Japanese made three air raids and threatened another during the first 48 hours of unloading. For these gave many of the boat crews a breathing spell, and also supplied an urgency to the need to get the unloading job done.

The second lesson the amphibians learned at Guadalcanal was they just had to have more people in their ships and craft.

LINE OFFICERS

To indicate the scarcity of seagoing Line officers in the transports at this period, it is only necessary to record that a dentist, in the *President Adams* (AP-38), was Commander Boat Division Seven in that ship. Lieutenant

R. E. Schaeffer (DC), U.S. Navy, in a surf boat, a relic of the *President Adams* merchant ship days, made a night landing on Gavutu "in pitch darkness and heavy rain," leading in three loaded Amtracs via a circuitous, unmarked and reef studded approach. Doctor Schaeffer had his reward after three groundings enroute, when our Marines fired at him, being unable to tell friend from foe in the darkness. He salvaged a stranded and abandoned jeep lighter from *Neville* (AP-16) on the way back to the ship. A reserve supply officer had also been trained as boat division officer in the same transport.[56]

Other transports were equally undermanned and short of personnel, as *Neville's* and *Alchiba's* reports indicate:

> Due to the physical exhaustive nature of the work on transports during unloading it is essential that transports be fully manned for an operation of this kind.[57]

* * * * *

> This vessel, at present, has insufficient personnel to run boats continuously for any protracted period.[58]

The skipper of the *McCawley,* several months later summed up the personnel situation in his ship succinctly.

> The Commanding Officer particularly desires to pay the highest tribute to an undersized crew who performed a superhuman task of completely unloading this vessel. It really has been a pleasure to serve with such a splendid crew. Previous recommendations to fill this vessel to a complement of 490 men should be accomplished. . . . At present no reliefs are possible and all men are served meals on station and in the boats.[59]

BEACH TROUBLES—GUADALCANAL

The third lesson the amphibians learned at Guadalcanal was that the logistic support of the troops over the beaches in the first 24 hours had to be both beefed up and streamlined.

In WATCHTOWER, the Marine plans provided that about half the 1st Pioneer Battalion which totaled about 660 men would be attached to the Support Group which was assigned the task of close-in ground defense of the beachhead area at Red Beach at Guadalcanal. One platoon of 52 men went

---
[56] *Ibid.,* 15 Aug. 1942.
[57] *Neville* Action Report, 13 Aug. 1942.
[58] *Alchiba* Action Report, 16 Aug. 1942.
[59] *McCawley* Action Report, 23 Nov. 1942.

to Tulagi. According to the Marine Corps Monograph: "The rest of the battalion had been parceled out to various regiments as reinforcing elements."

With this disposition of Marine labor resources specially trained and needed for the unloading of logistic support from ship's boats, it is not surprising that logistic chaos took over at the beachhead. This was only partially alleviated when Captain Reifsnider ordered each transport and cargo ship to land 15 sailormen to assist in handling supplies at the beachhead.[60]

Commander Transports summarized one aspect of the problem:

> The statement of the Assistant Beachmaster from the *George F. Elliott* that literally hundreds of Marines were sitting on the beach watching the confusion mount, while hundreds of others were roaming through the cocoanut groves etc., is confirmed by reports of officers sent ashore by me to investigate.[61]

The Boat Group Commander, *USS Barnett* wrote:

> There were approximately fifteen or twenty men unloading boats and about fifty others in swimming. I beached my boat and started looking for the Beachmaster who could not be found. While looking for the Beachmaster, I saw about one hundred men lounging around under the palm trees eating cocoanuts, lying down shooting cocoanuts from the trees; also playing around and paddling about in rubber boats. All of these men were Marines that should have been unloading boats.
>
> * * * * *
>
> About 0600 August 8, commenced to notice canned rations floating around about one mile off the beach. Upon approaching the beach I found that most of the supplies which had been unloaded during the night had been dumped at the low water mark, and as the tide came in, these supplies, which consisted of many items such as sugar, coffee, beans, cheese and lard which were all over the sides of the boats lying on the beach, were being ruined.[62]

The Captain of the *Hunter Liggett* reported:

> After dark conditions reached a complete impasse. It is estimated that nearly one hundred boats lay gunwale to gunwale on the beach, while another fifty boats waited, some of these, up to six hours for a chance to land. . . .
>
> No small share of the blame for this delay, which prolonged by nearly twenty-four hours the period when the ships lay in these dangerous waters, would seem to rest with the Marine Corps personnel and organization. The

---

[60] (a) First Marine Division Operation Order 7–42 of 20 Jul. 1942; (b) First Marine Division Operation Order 5–42 of 29 Jun. 1942; (c) Commanding General, First Marine Division, Final Report on Guadalcanal Operation, Phase 1 of 24 May 1942 Annex K (3); (d) Zimmerman, *Guadalcanal Campaign* (Marine Corps Monograph), p. 46.

[61] COMTRANSDIV to SOPACFOR report, FB7–10/A16–3/Ser 063 of 19 Aug. 1942.

[62] Report of Boat Group Commander, *USS Barnett*, 13 Aug. 1942.

Pioneers, whose function it was to unload the boats and keep the beach clear, were far too few in numbers. As a result much of this work was accomplished by boat crews, and stores which they landed at low water were frequently damaged or destroyed by the rising tide before the Pioneers removed them to safety. Meanwhile hundreds of Marines, many of them truck drivers, tank crews, special weapons and support groups, whose equipment had not been landed, lounged around the beach in undisciplined idleness, shooting down coconuts or going swimming. There was no apparent reason why these men could not have rendered valuable assistance in unloading the boats.[63]

Commander Transport Group XRAY, discussing the delays in unloading caused by the Japanese air attacks, stated:

Notwithstanding the foregoing interruptions, supplies were piling up on the beach faster than could be moved and by dark there were about 100 loaded boats at the beach and 50 more lying off waiting. It finally became necessary to discontinue unloading for the remainder of the night.[64]

The skipper of the *Heywood* wrote:

At 0200, 8 August, unloading stopped because of lack of boats, and at 0400 all ships were ordered to stop sending in loaded boats due to great congestion on beach. After daylight, as boats became available, they were loaded and kept at ship until about 0930, when orders were received to commence unloading.[65]

The Captain of the cargo ship *Formalhaut* stated:

Discharging cargo on twenty-four hour basis—but very slow procedure due to shortage of transportation. . . .

. . . unable to have boats unloaded at beach due to working parties there being engaged in repelling enemy snipers.[66]

During the night of 7–8 August, the *Hunter Liggett* reported:

Despite the quiet night, the Marines had failed to clear the beach and very little cargo was worked prior to the air alarm at 1043 [on 8 August].

And when some fancy cheese broke out of a melted carton, the thought was expressed:

Weapons, ammunition prime movers, and canned rations are more worthwhile than fancy groceries during the first days or even weeks of such an operation.[67]

---

[63] *Hunter Liggett* War Diary, 7 Aug. 1942.
[64] Commander Transport Divisions, SOPAC (CTG 62.1) Action Report, 23 Sep. 1942.
[65] *Heywood* Action Report, Ser 18, 12 Aug. 1942.
[66] *Formalhaut* War Diary, 8 and 9 Aug. 1942.
[67] *Hunter Liggett* War Diary, 8 Aug. 1942.

BEACH TROUBLES—TULAGI

Over at Tulagi, according to the transport *Neville*'s War Diary

> It was not until about midnight that the first word had been received to send the important food rations and ammunition ashore and from then till daylight it went slowly due to insufficient personnel to unload and conflicting orders as to where to land the stores.[68]

Not all the beach trouble was caused by inadequate Pioneer parties. Often the transports and cargo ships overloaded the landing craft.

> A considerable number of landing boats, chiefly ramp lighters, were stranded on the beach, adding to the confusion. These ramps had been loaded too deeply by the head, and could not be driven far enough up on their particular beach to keep from filling and drowning the engine when the ramp was lowered.[69]

Rear Admiral Turner after the landing wrote:

> There were two primary reasons for failure to completely unload. First the vast amount of unnecessary impediments taken, and second a failure on the part of the 1st Division to provide adequate and well organized unloading details at the beach.

Rear Admiral Turner summed up his attitude on all these unloading problems in this way:

> The Marine officers on my staff feel very strongly on these matters—as strongly as I do.[70]

When all was said and done, however, the amphibians in 26 actual hours of unloading had gotten a very large percentage of the Marines logistic support out of the holds and on to the beaches. This was accomplished despite three Japanese air raids, one of 45 planes, and another of 43, and rumors of other raids which had caused the amphibians to stop unloading and get underway. But the transports and cargo ships did not get 100 percent of the logistic support ashore and that was the least that they would have to do to accomplish their mission and satisfy the Marines.

---

[68] *Neville* War Diary, 9 Aug. 1942.
[69] *Hunter Liggett* War Diary, 8 Aug. 1942.
[70] RKT to Colonel James W. Webb, USMC, CO 7th Marines, letter, 20 Aug. 1942.

CHAPTER X

Savo—The Galling Defeat

THE BATTLE OF SAVO ISLAND

When the *Astoria* visited Japan in 1939, with Captain Richmond Kelly Turner commanding, a Japanese poet drew on the muses for the following words:

> The spirit, incarnate, of friendship and love
> Deep in the Heart of history.
> The record of the human world, full of changes and vicissitudes.
> The people of Japan, where cherries bloom,
> In the future far away
> Will never forget their gratitude to the *Astoria*.
>
> 20 April 1939   Bansui Doi

The "changes and vicissitudes" led the Japanese to "forget their gratitude to the *Astoria*" on 9 August 1942.

Commander Expeditionary Force (CTF 61) set the radio call authenticator for 9 August 1942, to be used on that same day by all ships in his command to verify their messages, as "Wages of Victory." It was a prophetic choice, for the "Wages of Victory" at Tulagi and Guadalcanal was Savo Island.

No American can be happy about the Battle of Savo Island. A good many professional United States naval officers feel a stinging sense of shame every time the words "Savo Island" are uttered.

A distinguished former Commander in Chief of the United States Fleet, and, in 1942, Chairman of the General Board of the Navy, Admiral Arthur J. Hepburn, U. S. Navy (Retired),[1] mentally active and physically vigorous, spent over four months between 23 December 1942 and 13 May 1943 inquiring into the Savo Island disaster, personally questioning the principal commanders in the South Pacific and Southwest Pacific Areas, and the

---

[1] Admiral Hepburn, Class of 1897, alive at age 87 at time this chapter written.

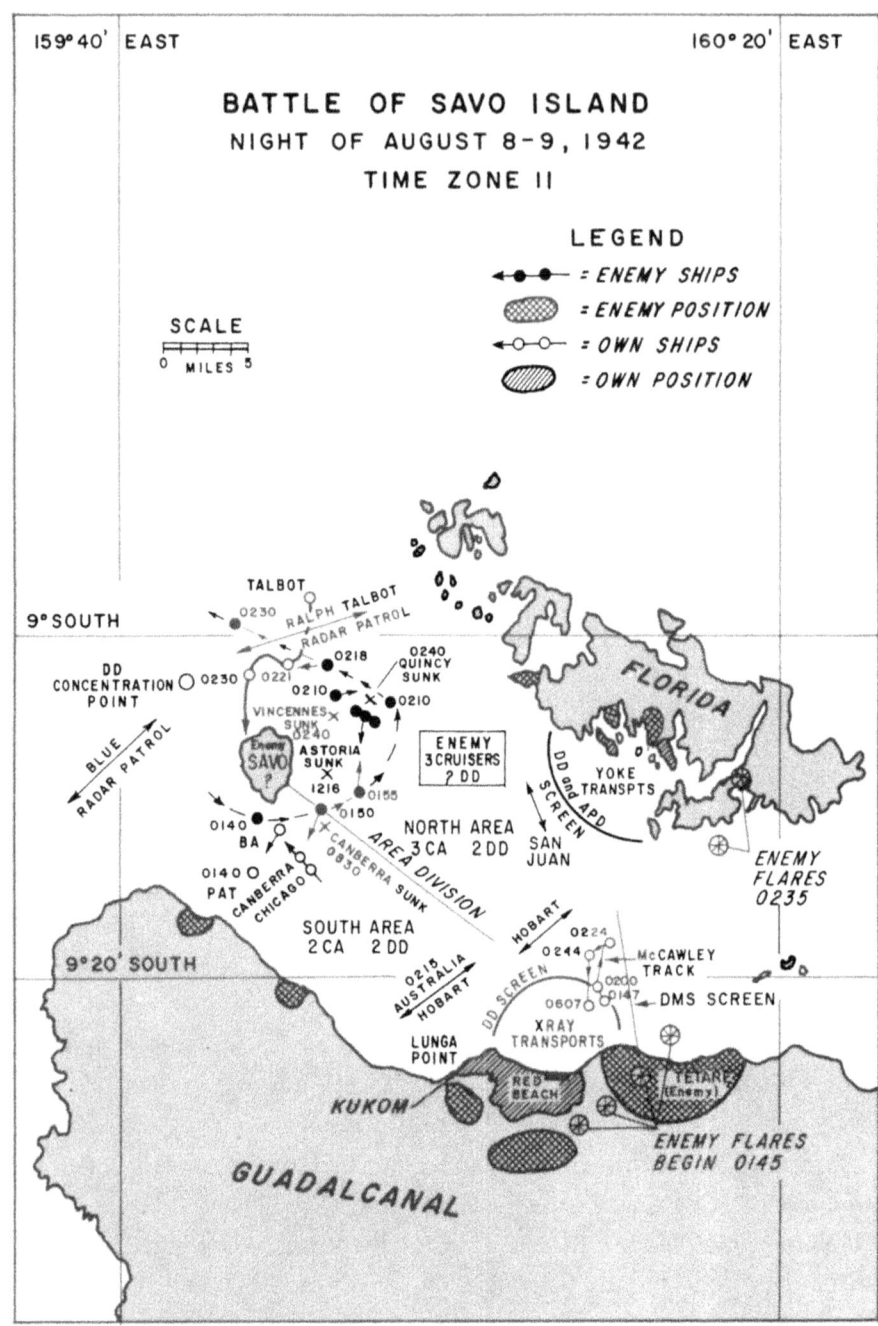

Battle Area Dispositions, Savo Island.

Commanding Officers still alive, as well as gathering a large amount of documentary evidence.

A two-volume *Strategical and Tactical Analysis of the Battle of Savo Island* has been published by the U.S. Naval War College at Newport, Rhode Island.[2] Several full-length books on the battle, one labeling Admiral Turner "a blacksmith's son," have been written for popular consumption.[3] Morison devotes a lengthy chapter to the subject in his 15-volume history of *United States Naval Operations in World War II* and much space in his other writings about that war.[4]

It is not the intention to rehash in detail here this sad story of the U.S. Navy in its first night heavy surface ship fight with the Japanese Navy. If there are any readers who are not familiar with this night battle, such readers should consult Morison before going further in this Chapter. Suffice it to record here that it occurred at the Savo Island terminus of a skillfully concealed Japanese dash south from Rabaul. It was carried through by a hastily gathered eight ship cruiser-destroyer force, which in the early hours of 9 August effected complete surprise and one-sided damage in turn to two different five-ship Allied cruiser-destroyer units patrolling to protect our transports at Tulagi and Guadalcanal.

The Japanese Navy achieved a stunning victory. It was aggressive in the planning concept of this operation and it was equally aggressive in carrying it out. Their night-time operational ability was far superior to that of the U.S. Navy ships companies which they encountered. They cleared from the roster three United States heavy cruisers and one Australian heavy cruiser with minor damage to their own ships. They placed the waters lying between the islands of Guadalcanal and Tulagi on the books as "Iron Bottom Sound" and manned it with an initial complement of United States Navy and Australian Navy ships.

Admiral Turner's comment in 1960 on the 1942 battle was as follows:

Whatever responsibility for the defeat is mine, I accept.

Admiral Hepburn, who, in 1942 investigated the defeat for Admiral King did a first-rate job. The Naval War College in 1950, did the most thorough analysis possible. I had my chance to comment on the Hepburn report to

---

[2] Naval War College, *Savo Island*, Vols. I and II.
[3] (a) Richard F. Newcomb, *Savo The Incredible Naval Debacle off Guadalcanal* (New York: Holt, Rinehart and Winston, 1961); (b) Stan Smith, *The Battle of Savo* (New York: McFadden-Bartell Corp., 1962).
[4] (a) Morison, *Struggle for Guadalcanal* (Vol V), ch. 2; (b) Samuel E. Morison "Guadalcanal-1942" *Saturday Evening Post*, vol. 235 (July 28–August 4, 1962), pp. 22–23, 63–65; (c) Samuel E. Morison, *Two Ocean War* (Boston: Little Brown and Co., 1963), pp. 167–77.

Admiral Nimitz, before he placed his comments thereon. My comments contained the following:

'I desire to express myself as entirely satisfied with this admirable report. It is accurate, fair, logical, and intuitive.'

We took one hell of a beating. The Japs sank four cruisers, but missed their greatest opportunity during the war to sink a large number of our transports with surface ship gunfire. This was at a time when it would have really hurt, because we didn't have 50 big transports in our whole Navy. We got up off the deck and gave the Japs one hell of a beating, and the so and so critics can't laugh that off.

For a long time after the ninth of August, I kept trying to fit the pieces together to change our defeat into a victory. It all boiled down to needing better air reconnaissance, better communications, better radar, a more combative reaction, and a greater respect for Jap capabilities.[5]

In response to a question, if he expected to be relieved of command because of the disaster, Admiral Turner commented:

Only if the Navy found it necessary to satisfy the desire of the American people for a goat. Fortunately for me, the Navy resisted any pressure there might have been for this end.[6]

In this connection, Admiral Nimitz was asked the question by this writer: "Did you contemplate having Admiral Turner relieved after the defeat at Savo Island?"

He replied, "No, I never did, not for an instant. I thought he did very well."[7]

This decision not to relieve Rear Admiral Turner was labeled by Samuel Eliot Morison in 1954 "wise and just."[8]

However, Morison's 1954 appraisal of this decision is hardly supported by his later writings. In 1962, Morison wrote that Turner made a "bad guess" that the Japanese were not coming through that night, and that:

This was not Turner's only mistake that fatal night. He allowed his fighting ships to be divided into three separate groups to guard against three possible sea approaches by the enemy. . . . Turner was so certain that the enemy would not attack that night that he made the further mistake of summoning Crutchley in *Australia* to a conference on board his flagship, *McCawley*, twenty miles away, in Lunga Roads, Guadalcanal . . . [for a consultation]

---
[5] Turner. Actually only a total of 41 APs were in commission on 8 August 1942. 16 APs were assigned to the Pacific Fleet on 8 August 1942. (PACFLT Fleet Notices 18CN-42 of that date).
[6] Turner.
[7] Nimitz.
[8] Morison, *Struggle for Guadalcanal*, p. 63.

Savo—The Galling Defeat

to decide whether the partly unloaded transports should depart that night or risk repeated Japanese air attacks without air protection [the next day].[9]

In 1963, Morison, the great and good god of World War II Naval History, wrote:

> Dogmatically deciding what the enemy would do, instead of considering what he could or might do, was not Turner's only mistake on that fatal night. He allowed his fighting ships to be divided into three separate forces to guard three possible sea approaches by the enemy.[10]

THE HEPBURN INVESTIGATION

The reason that Admiral Turner applauded the Hepburn Investigation is not difficult to find. In it there was no direct or implied criticism of Rear Admiral Turner's action or decisions.

One can take his pick—either (1) the ever changing appraisals of the semi-official naval historian; (2) the inordinately biased hocus-pocus of the popular fiction writer; (3) the analysis of the Naval War College as to why Savo Island happened and what was the degree of responsibility of the various seniors present, including Commanding Officers of the various ships; or (4) make up his own mind from the existing official record.

Admiral King, never one to flinch from damning an officer whom he believed to have erred badly, in his endorsement on Admiral Hepburn's Investigation Report said:

> I deem it appropriate and necessary to record my approval of the decisions of and conduct of Rear Admiral R. K. Turner, U. S. Navy, and Rear Admiral V. A. Crutchley, Royal Navy. In my judgment, those two officers were in no way inefficient, much less at fault, in executing their parts of the operations. Both found themselves in awkward positions, and both did their best with the means at their disposal.

Admiral King was thoughtful enough to provide a copy of his endorsement to Rear Admiral Turner and Rear Admiral Crutchley.

To complete the picture, the following should also be quoted from the King endorsement:

> 5. . . . Adequate administrative action has been taken with respect to those individuals whose performance of duty was not up to expectations.

Captain George L. Russell, at that time Flag Secretary to Admiral King,

---
[9] Morison, "Guadalcanal—1942," *Saturday Evening Post.*
[10] Morison, *The Two-Ocean War* p. 169.

and the reviewing officer on the staff of the Commander in Chief, U. S. Fleet, for the Admiral Hepburn Investigative Report gave more detail on the administrative action. He later was Judge Advocate General of the Navy and then a Vice Admiral, U. S. Navy. His review was passed on and concurred in by the Deputy Chief of Staff, Rear Admiral W. R. Purnell, later Vice Admiral, U. S. Navy, and the Chief of Staff, Vice Admiral R. S. Edwards, later Admiral, U. S. Navy.

In this review, Captain Russell pointed out that:

> (a) Vice Admiral Ghormley, who was head man in the area, and therefore answerable for the operation, was relieved not long afterward. Regardless of the fact that no reason for his change of duty was announced, there was a stigma attached to it, with everything indicating that he was relieved because of this defeat. . . .
>
> (b) Admiral Hepburn mentions the failure of Rear Admiral McCain to search out the area in which the Japs must have been, after Rear Admiral Turner, in effect, asked him to do so, but apparently does not feel that he should be called to account for it. . . .
>
> (c) Admiral Hepburn gives Admiral Turner pretty much a clean bill of health.
>
> (d) Vice Admiral Fletcher and Rear Admiral Noyes have been relieved of their commands. Again no reason has been assigned, but the inference is that the latter, at least, has been tried and found wanting. In other words, something has already been done, administratively.
>
> * * * * *
>
> It does not necessarily follow that because we took a beating somebody must be the goat. . . to me it is more of an object lesson in how not to fight, than it is a failure for which someone should hang. . . .[11]

The two-volume Naval War College analysis, in its 23 pages of "Battle Lessons," mentions no personalities, but some of the biting "Lessons" apply directly to specific actions of specific command personalities. There are 26 Lessons. One of these was pertinent to Rear Admiral Turner personally. Nearly all of them are pertinent to every naval officer exercising command in the nuclear age, as well as in World War II, and several will be mentioned later in the chapter.

THE PRIMARY CAUSE—INADEQUATE AND FAULTY AIR RECONNAISSANCE

Admiral Turner, when asked, in 1960, if he would name "the primary

---
[11] Hepburn Report Vol. I, no ser of 13 May 1943, Memorandum for Admiral, 31 Jul. 1943, attached by Reviewing Officer.

cause of his defeat at Savo Islands, and the thing about this primary cause which stuck in his craw the hardest," said: "Inadequate and faulty air reconnaissance and more faulty than inadequate." [12]

Before making this particular answer, he carefully considered a list drafted by this author and discarded the following as not being the primary cause:

- a. Lack of respect for Japanese aggressiveness.
- b. Lack of a specific night action battle plan in the Screening Group in event of an undetected surprise raid.
- c. Lack of combat reaction at the command level in the cruisers and destroyers of the Screening Group, or lack of a specific night action plan for these units.
- d. Delay of Screening Group Commander in rejoining his command.
- e. Withdrawal of Air Support Force.
- f. Command organization.
- g. Personnel fatigue.
- h. Lack of night battle training.
- i. Lack of appreciation of the limitations of radar, or radar failures.
- j. Communication delays, or failures.
- k. Failure to have more picket destroyers.
- l. Division of heavy ships (CA and CLAA) of Screening Force into three groups.
- m. Failure to maintain the prescribed condition of ship readiness in the heavy cruisers.
- n. The United States Navy's obsession with a strong feeling of technical and mental superiority over the enemy.

The official history of the Army and the monographs of the Marine Corps as well as Newcombs popular *The Incredible Naval Debacle,* all give the impression that air reconnaissance, or perhaps osmosis, furnished information of such a nature that Rear Admiral Turner *knew* that a Japanese Naval Force was *approaching* the lower Solomons. These are the words these books use:

> Word of this approaching force reached Admiral Turner at 1800, and when Admiral Fletcher notified him shortly thereafter that the carrier force was to be withdrawn, Turner called Vandegrift to the flagship, *McCawley,* and informed the general that, deprived of carrier protection, the transports must leave at 0600 the next day.[13]

---

[12] Turner.
[13] Zimmerman, *Guadalcanal Campaign* (Marine Monograph) p. 259.

At 1800 on 8 August, Admiral Turner received word that the Japanese Force was approaching.[14]

Turner had it [the despatch] too, and he knew he was in trouble.

Later, they could not say for sure when they first knew it, but for certain the fleet knew by midafternoon that the Japanese were coming.

Japanese surface forces were heading his way; everybody knew that.[15]

The Army history and the Marine monograph cite as their authority the following entry in the 8 August 1942 War Diary of Rear Admiral Turner as Commander Amphibious Force South Pacific Force.

> About 1800 information was received that two enemy destroyers, three cruisers, and two gun boats or seaplane tenders were sighted at 1025Z at 5° 49′ S, 156° 07′ E course 120, speed 15 knots.

This entry, except for the first six words and the zone time of the sighting, was almost a Chinese copy of the first part of a dispatch originated at General MacArthur's Combined Headquarters at Townsville, Australia, at 1817 that evening which read:

> Aircraft reports at 2325Z/7Z 3 cruisers 3 destroyers 2 seaplane tenders or gunboats. 05–49 S 156–07 E course 120 true speed 15 knots. At 0027/8Z 2 subs 07–35 S 154–07 E course 150 true.[16]

This information was not in fact passed on by the aviator who made the actual sighting for seven hours and 42 minutes after the sighting, when a despatch was originated at his home base, after his return thereto, and time dated in New Guinea at 1807. The despatch was then

> passed over the Australian Air Force circuit from Fall River to Port Moresby and thence to Townsville . . . . [and thence to Brisbane and thence] over the Navy land-line circuit to Canberra in COMSOWESPACFOR 081817 [only ten minutes later] for transmission over the air on the Canberra BELLS broadcast schedule. Canberra then transmitted on the BELLS [broadcast] schedule to the Australian Forces, and to Pearl Harbor for transmission on the HOW FOX schedule to the U. S. Forces.[17]

Canberra completed its transmission at 081837, and Pearl Harbor completed its transmission on the Fleet (or FOX) broadcast schedules at 081843.

It was received in the *McCawley* via the FOX broadcast schedule, as the

---

[14] Miller, *Guadalcanal: The First Offensive* (Army), p. 78.

[15] Newcomb, *Savo*, pp. 80, 82, 86.

[16] COMSOWESPACFOR to All Task Force Commanders, Pacific Fleet, 080717 Aug. 1942. Cited in Hepburn Report, Annex T.

[17] (a) Naval War College *Savo Island*, Vol. I, p. 101; (b) COMSOWESPACFOR Communication Officer to Commander D. J. Ramsey, memorandum, 19 Feb. 1943. Cited in Hepburn Report, Annex T.

Savo—The Galling Defeat

Plane sightings of Vice Admiral Mikawa's Cruiser Force. Vice Admiral Gunichi Mikawa, IJN.

McCawley had only two transmitters and five radio receivers, and could not spare one of the receivers to guard the Australian BELLS circuit.[18] The message, not in the air until 1843, was decoded and available on the Flag Bridge of the *McCawley* about 1900, and not about 1800 as the War Diary entry would indicate.[19] Rear Admiral Crutchley in the *Australia* received the message via the Australian BELLS broadcast circuit at 1837, since the Australian ship guarded this circuit in lieu of the American FOX schedule. He did not pass it to Rear Admiral Turner in the *McCawley*. This factual difference of one hour between the times many have assumed the message was available, and the time it was actually available to Rear Admiral Turner is important.

The sighting of the Japanese task force was some eight and a half hours old. The Japanese ships were 40 miles east of the town of Kieta situated on the east central shore of the island of Bougainville as shown in the map on page 363. They were not "In the Slot" but well east of it. Their reported course was not the course "Down the Slot," nor a course that would put them "In the Slot." Their reported speed was far from the 22–26 knots necessary to get them the 340 miles to Guadalcanal Island the night of 8–9 August.

Instructions governing Army Air Force reconnaissance missions stipulated that:

> A plane making contact at sea is to remain in the vicinity of the sighted target until recalled or forced to retire.[20]

The pilot of the Royal Australian Air Force Hudson Plane A16/218 on Search Mission FR623, originating at Fall River Field at Milne Bay, New Guinea, who sighted Vice Admiral Gunichi Mikawa's Cruiser Force headed south, shall remain unidentified, and alone with his own conscience, as far as this writer is concerned.[21]

He quite erroneously identified the seven cruisers and one destroyer that were in the waters below him. According to Morison:

---

[18] Note: The five receivers were on circuits of
1. Pearl Harbor FOX (CINCPAC broadcast to all ships)
2. CTF 61 Group Commanders Circuit
3. CTF 62 Immediate Subordinate Commanders who were CTG 62.1, CTG 62.2, 62. 3 etc.
4. TF 62 All units tactical circuit
5. Aircraft Warning Circuit.

[19] Hepburn Report, Vol. 3, Communication Log.

[20] General Headquarters Southwest Pacific Area, Signal Annex to Operation Instruction Number Two, 25 Apr. 1942.

[21] COMSOWESPACFOR Communication officer, memorandum, 19 Feb. 1943.

Instead of breaking radio silence to report as he had orders to do in an urgent case, or returning to base which he could have done in two hours, [he] spent most of the afternoon completing his search mission, came down at Milne Bay [tip of Papua] had his tea, and then reported his contact.[22]

He not only failed to identify what he saw, but he failed to trail his contact, and he failed to report promptly. Four of the five Japanese heavy cruisers were sister ships, alike as peas in a pod from a distance.

After the war, an examination of Japanese action reports revealed that this plane was in sight from various Japanese cruisers of Vice Admiral Mikawa's force from 1020 to 1036, certainly long enough for the Hudson crew to get a good look at the formation.[23]

A later sighting of Vice Admiral Mikawa's Cruiser Force was made at 1101 by another of General MacArthur's Hudsons on Flight A16/185. This 1101 sighting suffered an even longer delay before reaching the officers who needed the information. The aviator did not get this sighting on the air for nine hours and 46 minutes after the occurrence. This 080947 report, when considered alongside the previous one, further confused the picture as seen by Rear Admiral Turner.

The second despatch read:

> Air sighting 0001Z/8 Position 05–42 South 156–05 East. Two Cast Affirm Two Cast Love one small unidentified. One cruiser similar Southampton class. When plane attempted correct approach ships opened fire. At zero one two zero slant eight sighted small merchant vessel in 07–02 South 156–25 East course 290 speed 10.[24]

The Naval War College version of this despatch places an "or" between the two CAs and two CLs.[25]

The fact that the Australian plane attempted a "correct approach" on what to the aviator looked like a British heavy cruiser indicated that there was a question in the aviator's mind as to whether or not these were Allied ships. The fact that he was fired at probably riveted his attention on the ship immediately before him rather than the six other cruisers and one destroyer in the immediate area "and within visual signal distance."[26] It should be

---

[22] Morison, *Struggle for Guadalcanal*, p. 25.
[23] Naval War College, *Savo Island*, Vol. II, p. 383.
[24] COMSOWESPACFOR to all Task Force Commanders, 080947 Aug. 1942.
[25] Naval War College, *Savo Island*, Vol. I, pp. 101, 383 (18). The quoted version is found in both COMSOPAC War Diary and the Hepburn Report, as well as the Plotting Room Officer, COMSOPAC, to Admiral Ghormley, memorandum 14 Aug. 1942.
[26] *Ibid.*, pp. 73–74.

Vice Admiral Gunichi Makawa, IJN.
Victor at Savo

noted that the Japanese Flagship *Chokai* sighted this aircraft, immediately after four of the five Japanese heavy cruisers had finished recovering their seaplanes at 1050, and while the seven large ships were forming up into a single column. The *Chokai* opened fire on the plane at 1100. The plane retreated and disappeared from sight of the *Chokai* at 1113. Vice Admiral Mikawa reported that his ships were on the northwesterly course of 300° and that the plane was in sight for 13 minutes.[27]

How the Japanese ships all in sight of each other sighted the plane, and the plane did not correctly count the number of ships below it, lacks a ready explanation, except for the "fog of war."

This second sighting report added perplexity to the mystification already existing on the *McCawley's* Flag Bridge. The position reported indicated the Japanese force, if it was the same force as reported some 35 minutes previously, had moved northward and westward 7.5 miles. Since the Australian aviator, in this second sighting report, had not included a course and speed of the ships below him and since a plot of the two positions checked out the previous report by the pilot of A16/218 of a leisurely speed of 15 knots, Admiral Turner guessed that the seaplane part of the force as first reported was proceeding on to Rekata Bay and that part of the covering force was returning to Rabaul.[28]

It is an amazing fact, but one showing the vagaries of radio communications, that Vice Admiral Ghormley apparently was not cognizant of the 1025 sighting of the Japanese Cruiser Force until after Rear Admiral Turner arrived back in Noumea and told him of it.

A "Memorandum for Admiral Ghormley" prepared jointly on 14 August 1942 by his Staff Aviation Officer and his War Plotting Room Officer, while listing the 1101 sighting report, does not list the 1025 sighting despatch among the despatches received by COMSOPACFOR from COMSOWES-PACFOR relating to enemy surface units on 7 August and 8 August 1942.[29]

No record of the time of receipt of the second Australian plane's report survived the flagship *McCawley's* torpedoing and sinking 10 months later. COMSOPAC radio watch finished copying the second sighting message at 2136, and it still had to be decoded. On 21 February 1943, six months after Savo Island, Rear Admiral Crutchley in an official report on Savo Island

---

[27] (a) *Chokai* War Diary; (b) Japanese Eighth Fleet War Diary, CIG 74633, USSBS Interrogation.

[28] (a) Turner; (b) Staff Interviews.

[29] Copy of Memorandum supplied by Captain Charles W. Weaver USNR and original then located in Comsopac files.

did not list this message as having been received at all by his flagship, the *Australia*. In 1960, Admiral Turner and one member of his staff reasoned that the second sighting report was not available on the Flag Bridge when CTF 62 (Turner) drafted and sent out his 081055 just before 10 p.m., or it would have been referenced in that despatch just as the initial sighting report was referenced. The only possible reference in the TF 62 official record currently available in regard to this second despatch is found in Rear Admiral Turner's statement:

> All or at least some of these [four highly important] despatches [from COMSOWESPACFOR] were brought into my cabin during my conference with Admiral Crutchley and General Vandegrift.[30]

General MacArthur's Combined Headquarters at Townsville drew the inference from these two aircraft sighting reports of

> a possible occupation of Bougainville and Buka Islands in strength . . . [and] possible use of Kieta aerodrome.[31]

Rear Admiral Turner had gotten into the guesstimating act at 082155—35 minutes before General MacArthur's guesstimating despatch sought the air. Rear Admiral Turner's guess, influenced by the fact that a *Wasp* scout had shot down a seaplane north of Rekata Bay, was quite as wrong as General MacArthur's. He opined:

> Estimate from NPM 706 that Force named may operate torpedo planes from Santa Isabel possibly Rekata Bay. Recommend strong air detachments arrive Rekata Bay early forenoon. Bomb tenders in manner to ensure destruction.[32]

When Rear Admiral Turner sent this despatch, he did not know that CTF 63's (Rear Admiral McCain) search planes on the eighth of August, had not covered the Slot areas which TF 63 had been requested to cover. CTF 63's report of his air searches for the 8th was not time dated in his New Caledonia Headquarters on that day until 2333—27 minutes before midnight.[33]

The special air reconnaissance in the Choisel-Bougainville Slot Area requested by CTF 62 (Turner) of CTF 63 [34] failed to provide a contact

---

[30] (a) COMSOPAC Action Report; (b) Turner; (c) Staff Interview (d) Undated, but probably June 1943 Official Statement of Rear Admiral Turner on Admiral Hepburn's Report. Made prior to submission of CINCPAC's 28 June 1943 endorsement on that Report.
[31] COMSOWESPACFOR to CINCPAC and All Task Force Commanders, Pacific Fleet, 081130 Aug. 1942. Hepburn Report, Annex T.
[32] CTF 62 to COMAIRSOPAC, 081055 Aug. 1942. Hepburn Report, Annex T.
[33] CTF 63 to CTF 61 into CTF 62, 081233 Aug. 1942 in Hepburn Report, Annex T.
[34] CTF 62 to CTF 63, 070642 Aug. 1942. Hepburn Report, Annex T.

Savo—The Galling Defeat

with the Japanese cruisers, when the TF 63 Army Air Force planes turned back at 1215 some 60 miles south of the Japanese cruisers and far, far short of the 750-mile search which had been expected and of which the B-17s were capable.

Admiral Hepburn commented:

> ... this important negative information did not become known to Rear Admiral Turner until the next day....
>
> It is not unreasonable to suppose that timely information of the failure of the search plan might at least have resulted in a precautionary order to the Screening Force to maintain the highest degree of readiness....[35]

TF 63 AIR RECONNAISSANCE

The problem of the undetected approach of the Japanese cruiser squadron to Guadalcanal was one which could have been solved but was not.

While it is the inadequate performance of the individual Australian pilots which is more often publicized when pre-Savo Island air reconnaissance is mentioned, there is also to be considered the record of inadequate search plans by CTF 63. These plans were a real help to the Japanese cruiser force.

CTF 61 (Vice Admiral Fletcher) had alerted CTF 63 (Rear Admiral McCain) to the problem of the undetected approach as early as 29 July in a message to Rear Admiral McCain in connection with Dog Day and Dog Day minus one.

> [In accordance] Your Operation Plan 1–42, assume planes searching sectors 3 and 5 will arrive at outer limit search at sunset searching return leg by radar. Note that enemy striking group could approach undetected ... by being to the northwest of sector 5 and north of sector 3.[36]

The capabilities of the aircraft and air crews for night flying weighted CTF 63's reply:

> If weather forecast indicates favorable navigation conditions will comply your 290857. Otherwise daylight search will be made....[37]

The Operation Order as issued initially by COMSOPAC on 16 July called for air reconnaissance by AIRSOPAC to

> cover the approach to, and the operation within, the TULAGI-GUADAL-CANAL Area by search

---

[35] Hepburn Report, 13 May 1943, paras. 85, 87.
[36] CTF 61 to CTF 63, 290857 Jul. 1942, Hepburn Report despatches.
[37] CTF 63 to CTF 61, 300820 Jul. 1942, Hepburn Report despatches.

with

> scouting from NDENI by about 12 VPB not later than Dog minus 2 Day,

and

> from east coast MALAITA with about 12 VPB beginning Dog Day.[38]

As the result of a recommendation from Rear Admiral McCain, Vice Admiral Ghormley changed his directive so as to reduce the requirement of 12 planes at Ndeni and Malaita to half that number and to delay the commencement of the search 24 hours at each place.[39]

In view of the decreased number and the later initiation of air reconnaissance by Rear Admiral McCain's forces, Rear Admiral Turner sought to better the air reconnaissance by having six VO planes placed directly under his command. He requested them from COMSOPAC.

As late as the conference in the *USS Saratoga* on 26 July, he was still trying to get some VO (observation) aircraft directly under his command. Rear Admiral Turner wanted these VO planes based at Tulagi under his immediate control for local search purposes against Japanese surface forces known to be in the Rabaul area.[40]

Rear Admiral Callaghan noted this in his post-26 July conference memo to Vice Admiral Ghormley.

> 6. 6 VO planes Turner wanted. Desired them from BLEACHER. [Tongatabu, Tonga Island.] . . . Much argument how to get them to TULAGI-AREA. No conclusions. I said, at the moment, could see no ship in sight to make this move.[41]

In 1960, Admiral Turner was convinced that if Rear Admiral McCain had appreciated the problem of the undetected Japanese surface ship approach more than apparently he did, that initially he would have made more airtight search plans for his aircraft in TG 63.2 and TG 63.6, and that had he been more flexible, he would have undertaken late afternoon search efforts on 8 August by the TF 63 PBY planes tender-based at Maramsike Estuary, Malaita, only 83 short air miles from Lunga Point.[42]

There is no operational or action report for the WATCHTOWER Operation by COMAIRSOPAC (McCain) in any of the record centers of the Navy. Nor is there a special COMAIRSOPAC report telling why he or his

---

[38] COMSOPAC Op Plan 1–42, Ser. 0017 of 16 Jul. 1942, para. 3, Annex Baker.
[39] COMAIRSOPAC to COMSOPAC, 190646, 201300 Jul. 1942. Hepburn Report dispatches.
[40] Turner.
[41] Ghormley manuscript, p. 68.
[42] Turner.

subordinates did or did not do certain things, filed with Admiral Hepburn's investigation of this 7–10 August 1942 period. CTF 63's story just is not currently available. The War Diaries of COMAIRSOPAC and the *USS McFarland,* seaplane tender at Maramsike Estuary, Malaita, record only the incomplete nature of the planned searches.

Admiral Turner desired that the air reconnaissance matter be thoroughly researched in available records and then presented to him again. He died before this was done.

In 1960, he believed that CTF 63's air search despatch report for the eighth of August was unjustifiably tardy, and that it was inexcusable not to have told him earlier in the day of the TF 63 failure to search because of weather, or the extent and results of the special search he had requested. Because of the tardiness or omission of the air search reports, he did not know that TF 63 planes had not searched the Slot areas to the north of New Georgia. Since no positive sighting reports by the TF 63 planes in this area were made during the day, and no report of inability to search was made by Rear Admiral McCain, Rear Admiral Turner watched the clock on the Flag Bridge move from 8 to 9 August believing that it was a reasonable deduction that no enemy surface forces were in the area.[43]

CTF 63's (McCain's) failure to tell CTF 61 (Fletcher) and CTF 62 (Turner) that his planes were carrying through their assigned searches in a very limited way because of weather problems or other reasons vitiated the agreement made by CTF 63 on the *Saratoga* on 26 July 1942. As related in the Hepburn Inquiry:

> It was specifically arranged by the Commanders Task Force Sixty-One, Sixty-Two, and Sixty-Three, that if the air scouting could not be made in any sector, Task Force Sixty-One would fill in for short range scouting, both morning and late afternoon, to protect against the approach of surface forces.[44]

TURNER VERSUS THE FIELD OF HISTORIANS

Admiral Turner's reaction in 1960 to the official histories or monographs stating that he was advised of an "Approaching Force" is informative:

> I have been accused of being and doing many things but nobody before ever accused me of sitting on my awrse and doing nothing. If I had known

---
[43] Turner.
[44] CINCPAC, letter, PAC–11–SN–A17, Ser. 00888 of 28 Jun. 1943, subj: Comments on Hepburn Report, Annex F to encl. (A), p. 2.

of any 'approaching' Jap force, I would have done something—maybe the wrong thing, but I would have done something. What they wrote is just a g.d. distortion, and that sort of thing is why I want you to be g.d. certain that you don't distort in what you write.

What I failed to do was to assume that the g.d. pilots couldn't count and couldn't identify and wouldn't do their job and stick around and trail the Japs and send through a later report. And I failed to assume that McCain wouldn't keep me informed of what his pilots were or weren't doing. And I failed to guess that despite the reported composition of the force, and the reported course, and the reported speed, the Japs were headed for me via a detour, just like we arrived at Guadalcanal via a detour.

I wouldn't mind if they said I was too g.d. dumb to have crystal-balled these things, but to write that I was told of an 'approaching force' and then didn't do anything, that's an *unprintable, unprintable, unprintable* lie.

Nobody reported an 'approaching force' to me. They reported a force which could and did approach, but they reported another kind of a force headed another kind of way.

It was a masterful failure of air reconnaissance and my fellow aviators.[45]

BRINGING REAR ADMIRAL CRUTCHLEY TO THE FLAGSHIP

In regard to Morison's labeling as a "mistake" the summoning of Rear Admiral Crutchley in the *Australia* to the *McCawley*, the fact is that Rear Admiral Crutchley had sent the following despatch to his immediate senior shortly after nine o'clock the morning of 8 August:

> As Second-in-Command when you have time could I have rough outline of present situation and future intentions.[46]

This was a request not lightly to be disregarded or denied. It was received before the message reporting 40 heavy Japanese bombers heading toward the Tulagi-Guadalcanal area, which required all the transports, including the *McCawley* to get underway.

The COMPHIBFORSOPAC Staff members interviewed could not remember why their Admiral had put off Rear Admiral Crutchley until evening. In 1961–1962 they rationalized that it was probable that CTF 62 (Turner) felt, at that mid-morning hour, and with no favorable reports in from Tulagi where the Marines had been held up, that he did not know enough more than CTF 62.6 (Crutchley) did about the "present situation and future in-

---
[45] Turner.
[46] CTF 62.6 to CTF 62, 072211 Aug. 1942, Hepburn Report, Annex T.

tentions" to justify the conference. In any case, CTF 62 made the decision to bring CTG 62.6 aboard later.[47]

Soon thereafter the transports all were underway because of a Japanese air attack. The transports remained underway until just before 5 p.m.

The problem of bringing CTG 62.6 aboard before dark was discussed again by CTF 62 with the Staff.[48]

Just after 6 p.m. (1807) the message came in wherein Vice Admiral Fletcher recommended to Vice Admiral Ghormley the immediate withdrawal of all carriers. Rear Admiral Turner hoped that Vice Admiral Ghormley, looking at the larger picture and attaching more importance to the success of the whole operation than to the safety of the carriers, would turn Vice Admiral Fletcher down. However, now it was essential that the Second-in-Command be called aboard and the changed situation be discussed. This was done at 2037 in the evening.[49] One specific question asked Rear Admiral Crutchley during his 70-minute stay in the *McCawley* was whether he "considered the screening ships could stick it out for one or two more days without carrier air support." [50]

Neither the Hepburn Investigative Report, the Naval War College, nor this writer think it was a mistake for Rear Admiral Crutchley, the Second-in-Command, to want a conference with his Commander, nor a mistake for his Commander to grant such a request. It was a necessity. As Admiral Hepburn stated: "CTF 62's need to confer with his senior commanders cannot be questioned." [51]

The Naval War College stated: "This action of CTF 62 in calling this conference was sound." [52]

ENEMY'S CAPABILITIES
THE NAVAL WAR COLLEGE SUGGESTS

1. The enemy's capabilities, as well as the enemy's intentions must be considered. The highest priority must be given by a commander to those enemy courses of action considered more dangerous to his own force.[53]

By inference, Commander Task Force 62 did not give adequate weight to the capabilities of the enemy "cruiser-destroyer-seaplane force" sighted at

---

[47] Staff Interview.
[48] *Ibid.*
[49] (a) Staff Interview; (b) CTF 62 to CTG 62.6, 080937, Aug. 1942, Hepburn Report, Annex T.
[50] RKT to Director Naval History, letter, 1948.
[51] Hepburn Report, para. 84.
[52] Naval War College, *Savo Island*, Vol. I, p. 90.
[53] *Ibid.*, p. 48.

1025 on 8 August, 340 miles northwest of Guadalcanal, on course 120°, speed 15 knots.

When Admiral Turner had this read to him and was asked to comment thereon, he said:

> It was the inclusion of the words '2 seaplane tenders' in that aviator's despatch which threw me for a loss. A seaplane tender—except for the seaplanes on its elevator platform—looks like a merchant ship. It is a merchant ship with special seaplane handling gear and stowage space. It doesn't look like a cruiser, or a destroyer or a gunboat. We didn't have very many in our Navy. By looking at *Jane's Fighting Ships* we learned the Japs had about ten—more or less—basically the same design as ours. Top speed for our seaplane tenders was about 16 knots. The new Jap seaplane tenders were supposed to be a bit faster. [*Jane's* 1942 gives 3 of them credit for 20 knots, others top speed of 17 knots.] I didn't think 3 Jap cruisers and 3 destroyers would come to Guadalcanal and attack our 7 cruisers and 25 destroyers and I didn't think any seaplane tenders would be sticking their nose up close to our carriers, when they couldn't run any faster than 17 to 20 knots.
>
> I did consider the capabilities of the reported enemy, but I didn't take these capabilities and multiply them by three or four and then dirty my trousers. If every time that a report had come in to Ghormley or Halsey or me during the next six months that some part of the Jap Navy was at sea 350 miles from Guadalcanal and their capabilities had been multiplied three or four times, we would have all died of fright and never would have licked them.
>
> My error was one of judgment, putting faith in the contact report. General MacArthur's staff which had, or could have had, the opportunity to talk with the pilots made the same error.[54]

WAS IT A MISTAKE TO DIVIDE THE SCREENING GROUP?

In regard to Morison's opinion that Rear Admiral Turner made the mistake of dividing the Screening Group, the following information and opinions have a bearing on this matter.

The Naval War College in commenting on the division of the Screening Group, said:

> While a flat statement that it is unwise to divide a force may contain a sound element of caution, it is not necessarily unwise to do so for a division of forces may be necessary or desirable. Such axiomatic advice to be adequate should indicate when and in what measure such division may or may not be necessary or desirable.[55]

---

[54] Turner.
[55] Naval War College, *Savo Island*, Vol. I, p. 348.

The primary reason for the division of screening forces into two main units and one lesser unit on the nights of 7–8 and 8–9 August was the geographical lay of the land and the required positioning of the two transport groups to accomplish the basic TF 62 mission.

A two-ship light cruiser unit, one Australian and one United States, was stationed in the sector east of the meridian of Lunga (160° 04'E) to cover an unlikely Japanese cruiser approach but possible enemy destroyer or PT boat approach through the restrictive waters in and surrounding Lengo Channel or Sealark Channel.

To the westward past Savo Island, there were two entrances to block. The northern was 12 miles wide, the southern seven and a half miles wide. These distances were such that the six heavy cruisers in one station keeping formation could not accomplish this blocking objective by withdrawing far enough to the eastward of Savo Island to obtain safe night maneuvering room without coming up against the northern Transport Area. Here it would be highly undesirable to fight a night battle, since it would put the transports within range of the enemy guns and torpedoes. If the heavy cruisers were projected to the westward and immediately beyond Savo Island, having the six heavy cruisers in one column formation at a practical night cruising speed in limited waters, 18 knots, would open up one entrance for the enemy to slip through when the formation was reaching the extremity of the other entrance.

It was as simple as that.

A secondary reason for the division of the Screening Group was that Rear Admiral Crutchley, as Commander Task Force 44, a Combined Force, during the months prior to WATCHTOWER, had issued special instructions "covering communications, tactics, including the use of searchlights" to Task Force 44 containing both Australian and United States Ships "to cover various points of doctrine and procedure." He did not issue these special instructions to *Astoria, Vincennes,* or *Quincy,* when these United States ships and numerous destroyers came under his temporary command off Koro Island and he became CTG 62.6. This difference of detailed instructions influenced him, in part at least, to think it wise to employ the *Vincennes* group, from the Combined United States-Australian ship group "with only general direction as to cooperation, rather than try to incorporate them within a single tactical unit." [56]

---
[56] Hepburn Report, para. 92.

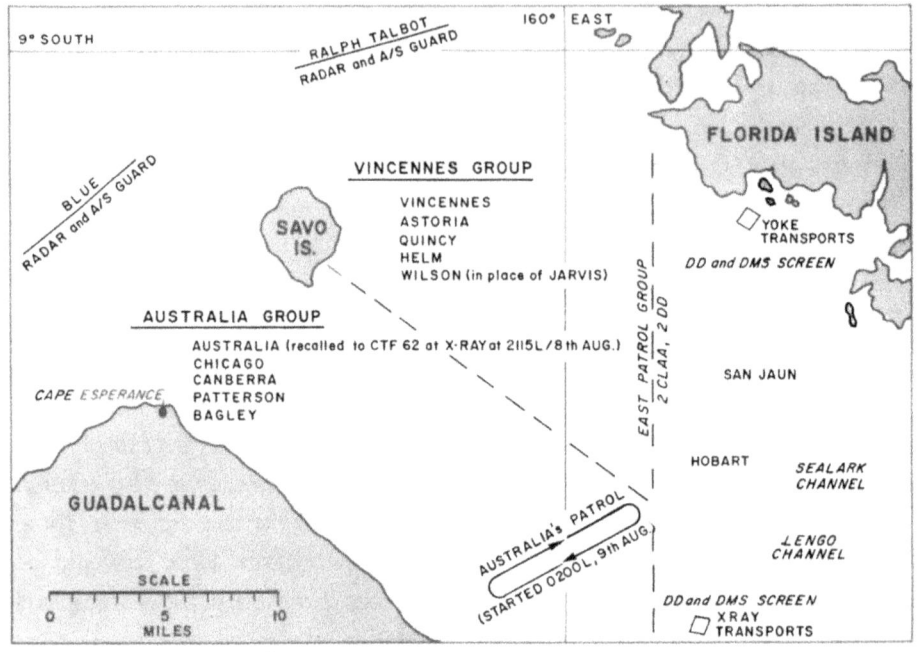

Ships disposition prior Savo Island Battle.

Rear Admiral Crutchley stated his case as follows:

> I would point out that neither *Australia* nor *Canberra* were fitted with T.B.S. [Voice radio] and they had done some night training with *Chicago* and Desron 4, but none with the other cruisers, thus it was my firm intention to avoid handling a mixed force at night.
>
> Speaking generally, I consider heavy ships in groups of more than 4 to be unwieldy at night.
>
> * * * * *
>
> ... I therefore decided to block one SAVO entrance with the three CAs I knew I could command, and leave the other SAVO entrance to the three U. S. vessels.[57]

Rear Admiral Turner may be charged by historical theorists with a mistake in approving this procedure, whereby the *Vincennes* group operated under one set of detailed instructions and the *Australia* group under another, instead of demanding Combined night training on the way to the battlefield under the Australian set of instructions. But few salt water sailormen of the pre-radar, pre-voice radio eras will so charge either him or Rear Admiral Crutchley who sponsored the procedure.

---

[57] CTG 62.6 to Admiral Hepburn, memorandum, 21 Feb. 1943. Hepburn Report, Annex B.

The basic task was protection of the transports and cargo ships by the Screening Group irrespective of the approach route of a Japanese surface force. A plan which protected only against the particular approach chosen by the Japanese would not have passed muster.

In this connection, it is worth noting that the Japanese battle plan called for a division of their attack force into two attack groups and that they did so divide. As the Japanese stated it:

> Crudiv 6 was to attack the transports at GUADALCANAL, while Crudiv 18 was to attack the TULAGI transports.
>
> * * * *
>
> It was the original plan for the FURATAKA group [Crudiv 6] to take the outer course, but they took the inner course. I do not know why. I was with the inner group on the TENRYU [Crudiv 18].[58]

In March 1943, in response to a long questionnaire from Admiral Hepburn, Rear Admiral Turner wrote:

> The difficulty of having two national services in one organization is recognized. It is believed that this was a mistake, although it was felt at the time that Admiral Crutchley's force [Task Force 44] probably was a more effective tactical unit than the remainder of the force [Task Force 62], which had never operated together, and whose vessels were from several task forces in both the Atlantic and Pacific Fleets. In connection with the matter of employing Admiral Crutchley's force in Task Force Sixty-Two, I made the specific recommendation to Admiral Fletcher that all units assigned to me should be from the U. S. Navy. See my despatch 200135 of July. This recommendation was not approved.[59]

Until someone comes forward with a workable alternate plan whereby the three approaches to the two groups of unloading transports could all be covered by an undivided Screening Group, labeling the division of the Screening Group a mistake is an opinion of one uninformed (a) of the seagoing standards and procedures of the Australian and United States Navy in August 1942, or (b) that all the cruisers in TF 62 had not been trained together, or (c) that all the ships of the United States and Australian Navies in TF 62 were not fitted with both radar and voice radio, or more probably, (d) of the lay of the land and depths of water in the Savo area.

Admiral Turner's reaction to Morison's comment that Rear Admiral Scott

---

[58] USSBS, *Interrogations of Japanese Officials,* USSBS Interrogation No. 255, Vol. I, p. 255. (Rear Admiral M. Matsuyama). Hereafter only the USSBS Interrogation No. and the page from *Interrogations of Japanese Officials* will be cited.
[59] RKT, Memorandum for Admiral Hepburn, Mar. 1943, p. 10, Hepburn Report, Annex F.

should have been shifted to the *Vincennes* and placed in command of the North Area Force was:

> TF 62 during the night of August 8 was divided into three important and valuable task groups: the XRAY (Guadalcanal) Group; the YOKE (Tulagi) Group; and the Screening Group. These three major groups were tactically separated by from 15 to 20 miles. All were prosecuting important operations throughout the night. Three Flag officers were available; Turner, Scott, and Crutchley. I considered then, and consider now, that the best command arrangement was for one Flag officer to command each of these major groups. (Until after the battle, I believed that Crutchley in *Australia* had rejoined his cruiser unit instead of displacing the Hobart in the latter's assigned position near the XRAY Group.)
>
> There was another important reason which would have made me reject the idea, had it occurred to me, of transferring Scott to the *Vincennes*. Scott had been a Flag officer a very short time, and on this expedition was exercising his first semi-independent Flag command. He and Riefkohl of the *Vincennes* were Naval Academy classmates, and, until his promotion, Scott had been the junior. Riefkohl was considered a good officer and apparently was performing his tasks satisfactorily. To have superseded Riefkohl on his own ship by a classmate recently promoted over him would have been a heavy blow to general morale, and would have gone far toward destroying all prospects of Riefkohl's future usefulness and chances of promotion. Furthermore, a Flag officer's effectiveness is temporarily impaired when suddenly transferred to a strange flagship.
>
> To my mind, the reasoning that led to the formulation of this criticism is entirely faulty.[60]

As Admiral Hepburn wrote:

> The one outstanding consideration was that an enemy approaching the transport group through either of the passages around SAVO ISLAND should be certainly intercepted and brought to action, and this object was in fact achieved.[61]

But, one may add, at the price of a galling defeat.

The error in judgment in regard to the Screening Group would not appear to have been in dividing it into three fighting groups; more realistically the judgment error was in the split of the destroyer types between picket duty and anti-submarine duty. This division of strength resulted in an inadequate assignment of only two destroyer-types to picket duty to the west of Savo Island.

---

[60] Admiral Turner to DCNO (Admin), official letter, 20 Aug. 1950, sub: Comments on Morison's Vol. V, pp. 10–11. Note Admiral Turner's statement that *Hobart* was near XRAY Group.

[61] Hepburn Report, para. 95.

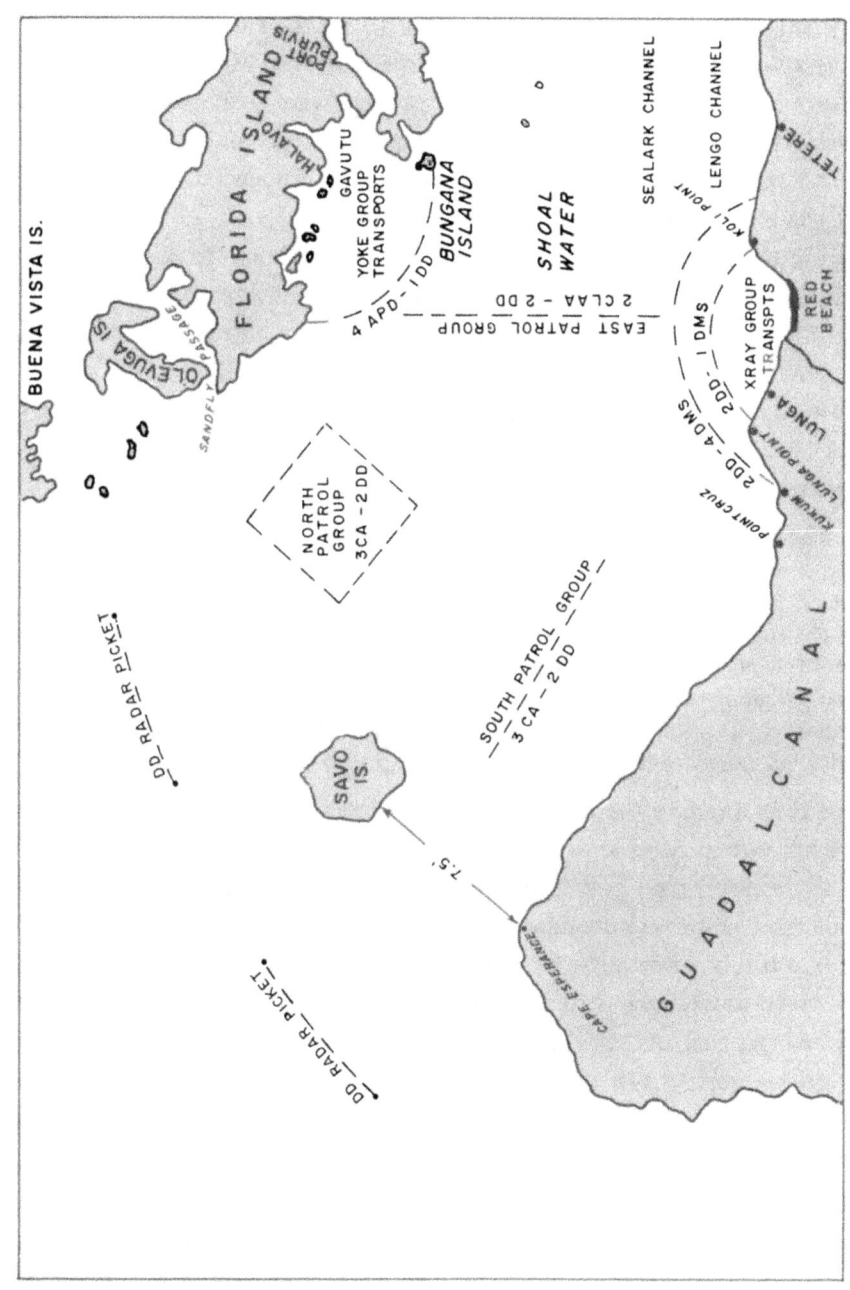

Disposition of Patrol and Screening Groups prior to the Battle of Savo Island.

380 *Amphibians Came To Conquer*

Two destroyers, a minimum, were assigned to anti-submarine duty around each of the three cruiser forces in the North, South, and East. Two other destroyers were assigned to picket duty. Five destroyers, four destroyer-type transports and five destroyer-type minesweepers were assigned to anti-submarine duty around the two transport groups (XRAY and YOKE), in an outer and an inner anti-submarine patrol. This was somewhat more than the limited sea room called for.

Shifting of the two destroyers in the outer anti-submarine patrol around the XRAY group of transports to picket duty could have paid big dividends on the night of 8 August 1942, and still left a strong anti-submarine patrol of seven anti-submarine craft for XRAY and five for YOKE.

Knowledge in regard to the capabilities and limitations of radar in early August 1942 was limited.

Rear Admiral Turner, in March 1943, recalled:

> The only point about which I was uncertain was the use of only two screening destroyers to the west of SAVO, employing radar. The number seemed small, but after some inquiry, I received assurances that these two vessels ought surely to detect the approach of any enemy vessels up to twelve to fourteen miles. Knowledge possessed by me and the staff concerning radar was practically non-existent. Admiral Crutchley had an officer who was considered well qualified in radar. I consulted some other officers with experience. All seemed to think this team was satisfactory.[62]

Some may question the desirability of leaving only fast minesweepers in the XRAY Group outer anti-submarine screen, but it should be remembered that the destroyer-type fast minesweepers, minelayers, and transports had retained their destroyer anti-submarine equipment upon conversion and were used for anti-submarine missions during this and many subsequent operations. One of these converted destroyers, the *Colhoun* (APD-2), made a submarine attack on 7 August 1942 and claimed in its special report on the action, that "numerous observers saw the bow of the submarine *keel up,* break water at an angle of 40° to the horizon." No Japanese record supports this kill. However, the *Southard* (DMS-10) was credited, post-war, with a firm submarine kill on the I-172 on 10 November 1942 and a converted destroyer, the *Gamble* (DM-15), was similarly credited on 29 August 1942 with sinking the I-123. So during this period, these old converted destroyers were capable of effective anti-submarine action.[63]

---

[62] RKT, Memorandum for Admiral Hepburn, Mar. 1943, pp. 4–5.
[63] *Colhoun* Anti-submarine Action Report, 7 Aug. 1942.

Rear Admiral Turner had these comments on destroyer deployments:

> Without question, subsequent events have shown that it was a grave military error not to have had more destroyer pickets. However, the picket line could not have been advanced very far to the front and still have given effective protection because then they would have uncovered the pass between FLORIDA and SANTA ISABEL ISLANDS, and the pass between GUADALCANAL and the RUSSELLS.[64]

The problem of Commander Screening Group was to provide protection to Transport Group XRAY and to Transport Group YOKE against air, submarine, and surface ship attack. Each of these enemy elements required diversion from giving fully adequate attention to the others. Enemy air attack required that the anti-aircraft guns of the whole Screening Group be positioned close to the transports at least at dawn and dusk as well as throughout the day. Enemy submarine attack required the 24 hour diversion of adequate destroyer-types to anti-submarine patrolling close around the transports as well as in the avenues of submarine approach. The threat of surface ship attack required principally the ready availability of the main and secondary

---

[64] Rear Admiral Turner to CINCPAC, official comment on Hepburn Report, 8 Jun. 1943.

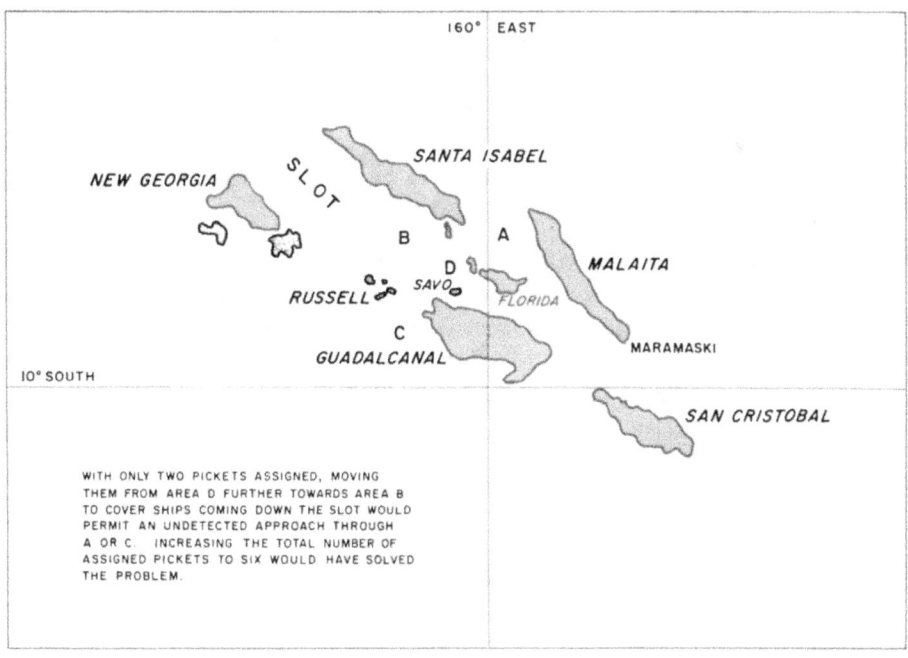

Multiple Approach routes; inadequate radar pickets, prior to the Battle of Savo Island.

batteries of the cruisers, and an early alert to the presence of the enemy ships.

In his 21 February 1943 report on the defeat of his forces, Rear Admiral Crutchley listed four radio message alerts from higher authority in regard to submarines in the area prior to 7 August, three more alerts on 7 August, and three further alerts on 8 August.[65]

That those on the spot were convinced of an increasing submarine menace is indicated by CTF 62's first post-Savo report in which, based on a *Monssen* report, he reported that one enemy submarine was probably sunk.[66] Rear Admiral Crutchley in his report to Admiral Hepburn wrote:

> . . . from information available, submarines appeared the greater menace [than a surface ship attack].[67]
>
> * * * * *
>
> . . . The submarine menace was considered so serious that, by order of Admiral Turner, all cruiser planes except those assigned to liaison duties with troops were used on the 8th for A/S screen and search for submarines.[68]

A survey of all TF 62 action reports indicates that four submarine contact reports were made in TF 62 on 7 August and six on 8 August 1942.[69]

FIRST REACTION TO DEFEAT

Sometimes first reactions are bitter but truthful. In Rear Admiral Turner's files, there is the first letter to his immediate senior following the defeat, written by the Rear Admiral Commanding H. M. Australian Squadron which contains this paragraph:

> Having been placed in charge of the screening forces by you, I have naturally been searching for my mistakes which may have led to, or contributed to, this great loss. I feel that undoubtedly there must be some, but there are to my mind two main points that stand out—one is that fatigue to personnel caused lack of warning. In an operation of this kind, this is almost inevitable. The other is, that we, U. S. and British, must have practice in night fighting

---

[65] (a) Crutchley to Turner, report, 21 Feb. 1943, pp. 4, 5, Hepburn Report, Annex B; (b) COMSOPAC 071142 Aug. 1942; CINCPAC 062336, 080141 Aug. 1942, Hepburn Report, Annex C.

[66] (a) CTF 62 to COMSOPAC, 090815 Aug. 1942, Hepburn Report, Annex T; (b) *Monssen* and *San Juan*. Action Reports.

[67] Hepburn Report, para. 82.

[68] Hepburn Report, para. 89.

[69] Action Reports of *Colhoun, Monssen, San Juan, Mugford, Wilson, Crescent City, President Adams, Little, Neville.*

for we cannot prosecute the kind of offensive required, without welcoming a night engagement.[70]

DEFENSIVE DECISIONS

At 1807 local time 8 August, 1942, Vice Admiral Fletcher (CTF 61) sent this message to COMSOPAC (Ghormley).

> Fighter plane strength reduced from 99 to 78. In view of large number of enemy torpedo planes and bombers in this area, I recommend the immediate withdrawal of my carriers. Request tankers be sent forward immediately as fuel running low.

Vice Admiral Ghormley approved this request, thus setting the stage for the withdrawal of the air support for the amphibians and for the Battle of Savo Island. The background for this crucial withdrawal follows:

(A) The Prediction

In the despatch which Vice Admiral Ghormley and General MacArthur sent on 8 July to their respective Chiefs of Staff opposing the launching of WATCHTOWER in early August, they said:

> The Carrier Task Groups will be themselves exposed to attack by land based air while unprotected by our land based aviation and it is extremely doubtful that they will be able to retain fighter escort to the transport area, especially should hostile naval forces approach.[71]

(B) The Basic Problem

Again on 11 July, Vice Admiral Ghormley had advised his seniors:

> I wish to emphasize that the basic problem of this operation is the protection of surface ships against land based aircraft attack during the approach, the landing attacks, and the unloading.[72]

---

[70] V. Crutchley to RKT, letter, 13 Aug. 1942.
[71] COMSOPAC to COMINCH, 081012 Jul. 1942.
[72] COMSOPAC to COMINCH, 112000 Jul. 1942.

(C) Carrier Strength and Husbanding by Non-Aviator Commanders

Vice Admiral Fletcher was a distinguished Line officer, a wearer of the Medal of Honor, but not an aviator. He was serving as the commander of an Expeditionary Force containing 75 percent of the battle line carriers in the United States Navy, the *Saratoga*, the *Enterprise*, and the *Wasp*.[73]

The United States Navy had started the war with six battle line carriers and the slower and much smaller *Ranger* of only 16,000 tons. The latter could not be and was not used as a battle line carrier during World War II. No new carriers were due to reach the Fleet for another nine months, until the spring of 1943. One-third of the large carriers had been lost in action. The *Lexington* had been sunk on 8 May 1942, at the Battle of the Coral Sea. The *Yorktown* went down not quite a month later at the Battle of Midway. Both of these losses occurred in task forces under Vice Admiral Fletcher's immediate command. Naval aviators could be heard to say that the losses would not have occurred, had the Task Force Commander been a naval aviator. Vice Admiral Fletcher was conscious of these criticisms and determined that in all future operations full weight would be given to sound aviation points of view.[74]

This was one reason he flew his flag in the *Saratoga*, whose Commanding Officer, Captain DeWitt C. Ramsay (later Vice Chief of Naval Operations and then Commander in Chief, Pacific) was known to be up on the step and rising fast.

(D) Over-Riding Instructions

Admiral Nimitz's special instructions governing future combat operations, and issued prior to the Battle of Midway, contained these controlling words:

> You will be governed by the principle of calculated risks which you shall interpret to mean the avoidance of your force to attack by superior force without good prospect of inflicting, as a result of such exposure, greater damage to the enemy. This applies to a landing phase as well as during preliminary air attacks.[75]

---

[73] The *Hornet*, which on 7 July CINCPAC (CINCPAC 070125 July) had indicated to COMSOPAC might participate in WATCHTOWER, was being held in the Hawaiian Area for defensive and training purposes.

[74] Interview with Admiral Frank J. Fletcher, USN (Ret.), 25 May 1963. Hereafter Fletcher.

[75] CINCPAC to Commander Striking Force, Letter of Instructions, A16–3/A14–3 GG13(12) (16), Ser. 0115 of 28 May 1942.

Savo—The Galling Defeat

It was Vice Admiral Fletcher's belief that with only Japanese shore facilities to attack and only Japanese shore based air to fight, there was no prospect of inflicting *greater* damage on the enemy than the Navy's three precious carriers could receive. Additional Japanese submarines had been reported by CINCPAC enroute to the Guadalcanal area. Japanese land-based aircraft were active in the area and he had been informed by General MacArthur that "the Air Force now in sight for the Southwest Pacific Area is not adequate to interdict hostile air or naval operations against the Tulagi Area." [76]

Vice Admiral Fletcher felt that he had no choice but to obey his instructions.[77]

(E) The Immediate Problems—Enemy Carriers and Fuel Shortages

(1) Enemy carriers

Despite the loss of four carriers at the Battle of Midway, the Japanese Navy in August 1942, still had as many battle line carriers (*Junyo, Shokaku, Zuiho, Zuikaku*) as the United States Navy.

From the middle of the afternoon of Friday, 7 August, when Japanese dive bombers hit destroyer *Mugford,* Vice Admiral Fletcher had been keenly alert to the possibility of Japanese carriers being in the vicinity. These dive bombers were from the 25th Air Flotilla land based on Rabaul, but Vice Admiral Fletcher was not sure of this and they were a type of aircraft which could have been flown off carriers.

Soon after this dive bomber attack, he suggested to Rear Admiral Noyes, Commander Air Support Group, that the Saturday morning air search be toward Rabaul.

Rear Admiral Noyes replied:

> ART [code name for *Enterprise*] has already been told to search. My information dive bombers probably land based from Rabaul via Buka or Kieta.[78]

Despite this reply containing a very sound deduction as to the source of the dive bombers, CTF 61 remained unconvinced that there were no carriers moving in on him. He told CTG 61.1 that "Bombers last seen leaving

---

[76] CINCSOWESPACAREA, COMSOWESPACFOR 081012, Jul. 1942.
[77] Fletcher.
[78] CTF 61 (Fletcher) to CTF 61.1 (Noyes), 070357 Aug. 1437 (local time). CTF 18 (Noyes) to CTF 61, 070527 Aug. 1942.

Tulagi on westerly course," instead of the northwesterly course that they would have taken if returning directly to Rabaul.[79]

This northwesterly direction tied in with a practical position of the carrier which had been reported (erroneously) by General MacArthur's reconnaissance planes on the day before the landing. These Southwest Pacific planes, on 6 August, in error had reported an enemy carrier (15,000 tons) and three destroyers 32 miles south southwest of Kavieng in latitude 03°22' South, longitude 150°30' East, roughly. One hundred twenty miles west of Rabaul and 660 miles northwest of Guadalcanal, and to compound the error the carrier sighting had been "confirmed by photographs," with full data.[80] Actually only Japanese destroyers were sighted.

Commander Air Support Group in his Operation Order for Saturday, 8 August, issued a few minutes later to the three carriers, directed:

> Operations tomorrow Saturday forenoon, *Wasp* search toward Rabaul primarily for reported Cast Victor [carrier]. . . . Afternoon same, but *Enterprise* replaces *Wasp*.[81]

The possibility of Japanese carriers being in the Solomons area continued to affect the disposition of aircraft all during Saturday, the 8th of August. Commander Air Support Group continued to refuse requests to divert the *Saratoga's* fighters to provide additional combat air patrol over the amphibious forces even when it was known as early as 0957 that "40 large twin engined planes" were enroute south to attack and that the first United States ships they would meet would be the transports.

When this large scale torpedo plane attack on the 8th of August was detected heading southeast, the Fighter Director for the carriers recommended to Fletcher, the Task Force Commander, the following disposition of aircraft.

> All *Saratoga* available fighters Tulagi at 1100 plus one half *Wasp* fighters.
> Over carriers all *Enterprise* plus one half *Wasp*.

However, the Fighter Director ran into a stone wall, either at the Air Support Group Commander (Noyes) level or at the Task Force (Fletcher) level.

The following despatches give the questions and the answers.

> Fighter Director requests *Saratoga* launch 8 VF Combat air Patrol for carriers at 0830. And at 1030.

* * * * *

---
[79] (a) Fletcher; (b) CTF 61 to CTG 61.1, 070500 Aug. 1942.
[80] ONI Summary Information, 8 Aug. 1942, (CINCSOWESPACAREA, COMSOWESPACFOR C-127, 7 Aug. 1942).
[81] CTF 18 to *Saratoga, Enterprise, Wasp*, 070510 Aug. 1942.

Savo—The Galling Defeat

> Your . . . not approved. *Saratoga* must be ready to launch for or in case of attack. Please carry out my _____.
>
> * * * * *
>
> *Saratoga* does not appear to be complying with my orders for today's operations which require her until noon to maintain fighters and attack group ready for launching at all times in case of bombing attack or locating of enemy CV. Please refer conflicting requests to me.
>
> * * * * *
>
> Red Base again requests eight VF for combat patrol from me. Advise.
>
> * * * * *
>
> Your . . . negative. Invite your attention to present situation if enemy CV should be located and I ordered your attack group launched. Your fighters should also be ready for launching for actual bombing attack until noon.[82]

After the large scale Japanese morning torpedo plane attack against the amphibious forces on 8 August had been completed, having been met with devastating surface ship anti-aircraft fire—but a minimum of fighter opposition—and the results reported to the Expeditionary Force Commander (Fletcher), he had difficulty being convinced that the Japanese had carried out such a large scale torpedo plane attack.

He signalled:

> Request any information about attack this morning. Were planes actually carrying torpedoes?

When assured of the actuality and multiplicity of the torpedoes, including one that had missed the *McCawley's* stern by "about 40 feet," the Expeditionary Force Commander made his decision to recommend withdrawal of the carriers because of the possibility of new torpedo plane attacks.

If the Expeditionary Force Commander (Fletcher) had not been worried greatly about there being a Japanese carrier over the horizon, it seems quite logical that he would have stepped in earlier and suggested to his senior subordinate (Noyes), the Air Support Commander, that 40 Japanese large twin engine planes were a sufficiently worthy target to justify diversion of defensive fighters to offensive use.

This Japanese torpedo plane attack was the one which torpedoed the *Jarvis* and directly led to her being sunk the next day, 9 August, by the Japanese 25th Air Flotilla, with the loss of all hands.

(2) The Fuel Problem—Strawman or Real.

Admiral Turner recalled

> Enroute from Koro to the Solomons my big worry was OIL, OIL, OIL.[83]

---

[82] (a) CTF 61.1 to CTF 16,070120, Aug. 1942; (b) CTF 61.1 to *Saratoga*, 072225, Aug. 1942; (c) CTF 61.1 to CTU 61.1.1, 072315 Aug. 1942.

[83] Turner.

At 1200, local time, 8 August, Rear Admiral Kinkaid, Commander Task Unit 61.1.2 in the *Enterprise* made an entry in his War Diary reading as follows:

> Fuel situation this Force becoming critical. It is estimated the destroyers have fuel for about three days at 15 knots, and the heavy ships have little more.

Every naval commander at sea in Word War II suffered from that strange logistical disease of AFFAG, and the malady affected some officers much more than others. For AFFAG related to the amount of Ammunition, Fuel Oil, Food and Aviation Gas, in each of the ships of his command at any given hour of the day.

On 29 July, Commander Task Force 61 (Fletcher) had reported that his force would be short over two million gallons of fuel oil after the scheduled Task Force fueling on that day.[84]

On 3 August CTF 61 notified COMSOPAC:

> If no tankers Efate for Task Force 62, top off situation may be serious.[85]

And COMSOPAC knew the Tanker *Esso Little Rock* had missed her rendezvous with Task Force 61 at Efate.

Every effort was being made to keep the ships of Task Force 61 full. To illustrate, the *Enterprise* fueled on 24 July in Tongatabu Harbor taking about 12,000 barrels of fuel oil (504,000 gallons) and 61,900 gallons of aviation gasoline, again at sea on 29th July taking 4,000 barrels of fuel oil (168,000 gallons) and 34,000 gallons of aviation gas, and again on 10 August from the *Kaskaskia* (AO-27) taking 20,000 barrels of fuel oil (840,000 gallons) and 120,000 gallons of aviation gas.[86]

On as important and busy a day as 7 August, D-Day, the destroyer *Gwin* (DD-433) in Rear Admiral Kinkaid's task unit was fueled by the battleship *North Carolina* (BB-55). The fueling was conducted during darkness, which required a new skill for the 1942 United States Navy.[87]

The actual fuel situation on 8–9 August 1942 for all 16 destroyers in the Air Support Group and some of the heavier ships, was as follows:

---

[84] CTF 61 to COMSOPACFOR, 280201 Jul. 1942.
[85] CTF 61 to COMSOPAC, 030150 Aug. 1942.
[86] Ships' Logs.
[87] (a) Kinkaid; (b) Ships' Logs.

NOON FUEL REPORT AS INDICATED FOR

TU 61.1.1		Received	Expended	On Hand
Dale	SAT 8– 8–42	0	3693	164456
	SUN 8– 9–42	0	4619	159037
Farragut	SAT 8– 8–42	0	19835	84696
	SUN 8– 9–42	0	16638	68058
MacDonough	SAT 8– 8–42	0	16315	70213#
	MON 8–10–42	0	11832	44568
Phelps	SAT 8– 8–42	0	19193	96382
	SUN 8– 9–42	0	14263	82119
Worden	SAT 8– 8–42	0	18011	72850
	SUN 8– 9–42	0	13975	58875

TU 61.1.2				
Enterprise	FRI 8– 7–42	0	61656	760116
	SUN 8– 9–42	0	77826	616602
North Carolina	SAT 8– 8–42	0	68966	877570
	MON 8–10–42	0	56745	739774
Portland	SAT 8– 8–42	0	60948	395328
	SUN 8– 9–42	0	41131	354294
Atlanta	SAT 8– 8–42	0	26297	199556
	SUN 8– 9–42	0	28290	171266
Balch	FRI 8– 7–42	0	24980	98227
	SUN 8– 9–42	0	19824	54271
Maury	SAT 8– 8–42	0	21951	69814
	MON 8–10–42	117760	16418	155806
Gwin	SAT 8– 8–42	0	23530	87660
	SUN 8– 9–42	0	16475	71185
Benham	SAT 8– 8–42	0	18925	67872
	SUN 8– 9–42	0	20496	46872
Grayson	SAT 8– 8–42	0	18925	39520#
	SUN 8– 9–42	0	15695	23825

Low Ship in Group on 8 August, the day the withdrawal recommendation was made.

NOON FUEL REPORT AS INDICATED FOR

TU 61.1.3		Received	Expended	On Hand
Aaron Ward	FRI 8– 7–42	0	12200	128252
	SUN 8– 9–42	35481	8309	141801
Farenholt	SAT 8– 8–42	0	16104	68050
	SUN 8– 9–42	0	18280	49770
Laffey	SAT 8– 8–42	0	13750	93564
	SUN 8– 9–42	0	12370	81194
Lang	SAT 8– 8–42	0	18371	71553
	SUN 8– 9–42	0	15292	56261
Stack	FRI 8– 7–42	0	15088	78676
	SAT 8– 8–42	0	14703	63973
Sterrett	SAT 8– 8–42	0	19509	59497#
	MON 8–10–42	0	12649	32691 [88]

[88] Data taken from ships' logs. When data for 8 or 9 August does not appear in log, data from 7 or 10 August is listed. Not all the arithmetic checks, but that is the way the logs record the data.

Low Ship in Group on 8 August, the day the withdrawal recommendation was made.

With these data in hand, it is appropriate to consider:

THE FIRST DEFENSIVE DECISION—FLETCHER'S DECISION TO WITHDRAW

At 2330 local time on 8 August, Commander Task Force 16 (Kinkaid) entered in his War Diary:

> Due to enemy air attacks and reduction of fighters in our forces due to losses, together with critical fuel situation, has caused CTF 61 [Fletcher] to recommend to COMSOPAC [Ghormley] that carriers be withdrawn.

The English in this entry was as questionable as the decision it noted. The reduction in number of fighters had been caused by operational losses, as well as by enemy action.

Indicative of the communication time delays directly affecting operations is the delay surrounding the CTF 61 despatch requesting retirement. It went off a few minutes after 6:00 p.m. (081807). It was five and a half hours before a reply was originated by COMSOPAC and more than nine hours elapsed before COMSOPAC's 081144 reply was received in Turner's flagship, the *McCawley*, and it surely took another half hour to decode, write up, and deliver to Turner's Flag Bridge (090330).

In the meantime between 7 p.m. and 4 a.m., many decisions had to be on a tentative basis, depending upon what turned out to be the final COMSOPAC decision.

The fundamentals of the withdrawal as Admiral Fletcher recalled them in 1963 were:

> a. United States over-all carrier strength was at low ebb—four.
> b. No carrier replacements were in sight for another nine months.[89]
> c. The Japanese Navy could put more carriers in the area than TF 61 had in the area (4 vs 3).
> d. Japanese land based air (high level bombers, dive bombers and torpedo planes) was present and offensively active.
> e. CTF 61's instructions from CINCPAC were positive and limiting in regard to risking the carriers in the command.
> f. COMSOPAC had informed CTF 61 on 16 July that from 'captured documents,' the early arrival of a submarine division in the New Britain Area was predicted. 'Captured documents' was the euphemism used to obviate the non-permitted words 'decoded radio despatches.' The COMSOPAC submarine information of 16 July in regard to submarines in the general area had been followed up by a warning from CINCPAC of submarines moving south closer to the carrier operating area on 7 August:
> Enemy subs are on move to attack Tulagi occupation forces at Tulagi.[90]

This in turn had been followed by another despatch from CINCPAC on the eighth.

> One division SUBRON Seven and units SUBRON Three en route Florida Area.[91]

On top of these fundamentals was one factor that Admiral Fletcher could not remember having seen discussed in public print since his 8 August 1942 decision, but which was much in his mind at that time. This factor was that the Japanese Zero plane and its pilot were given a very high rating in August 1942.

> Nobody mentions the matter, for fear of bringing down the wrath of the aviators upon him, [but at that time] the Japanese Zero's all wore Seven League Boots [and] our aviators gave them a lot of g.d. respect.[92]

---

[89] The *Essex*, the next carrier to come into service was not commissioned until 31 December 1942 and joined the Fleet in May 1943.

[90] (a) Fletcher; (b) CINCPAC despatch, 062336 Aug. 1942, COMSOPAC despatch, 071142 Aug. 1942, Hepburn Report despatches; (c) COMSOPAC, Op Plan 1–42, Annex A, para. 1.

[91] CINCPAC, despatch, 080141 Aug. 1942.

[92] Fletcher.

Support for the existence of this factor at this 1942 date is found in the following passage by a historian of Marine Corps Aviation:

> ... It is necessary to remember that the Japanese Zero at this stage of the war was regarded with some of the awe in which the atomic bomb came to be held later. U. S. fighter pilots were apt to go into combat with a distinct inferiority complex. Tales from the Pacific had filtered back to the U. S. . . . which attributed to the Zero (and the Japanese pilots) a sort of malevolent perfection. . . . The Japanese fighter plane had not been mastered at Coral Sea nor Midway . . . and the Zero certainly lost none of its prowess there.[93]

Lieutenant Commander John S. Thach, USN, Commanding Fighting Squadron Three in the *Saratoga* on 6–7 August 1942 and a veteran of Midway, as well as the Marshall Islands and Salamaua-Lae attacks, said in "large attendance" interview at the Bureau of Aeronautics on 26 August 1942:

> In connection with the performance of the Zero fighter, any success we have had against the Zero is not due to performance of the airplane we fly but is the result of the comparatively poor marksmanship on the part of the Japanese, stupid mistakes made by a few of their pilots, and superior marksmanship and teamwork on the part of some of our pilots. . . .
>
> This deficiency not only prevents our fighter from properly carrying out its mission but it has had an alarming effect on the morale of the fighter pilots in the Fleet at this time and on those who are going to be sent to the Fleet.[94]

Admiral Fletcher also wanted the record to show:

> My despatch didn't say anything about needing to withdraw to fuel. If my recommendation to withdraw was approved, then I wanted to fuel as soon as tankers could reach me, as my staff had told me fuel was running low on some of the shortlegged destroyers and Task Force Sixty One had never been belly full since its formation.[95]

It is worth noting that when COMSOPAC passed to CINCPAC the information of the 8 August withdrawal of the carriers on the next day, he did not mention the presence of large numbers of torpedo planes and dive bombers in the area or the 20 percent reduction in fighter aircraft to oppose

---

[93] Robert Sherrod, *History of Marine Corps Aviation in World War II* (Washington: Combat Forces Press, 1952), p. 81.

[94] BUAER Intelligence Interview, 26 Aug. 1942. Lieutenant Commander John S. Thach later became Deputy Chief of Naval Operations (Air) and then Commander U.S. Naval Forces, Europe. The Zero was more maneuverable but the United States Navy's fighters with their good pilots were "more fightable." The Zero out performed but did not have the survivability that the armor and self-sealing fuel tanks gave American planes. Nor did it have as heavy armament. Hence the ratio of losses in combat strongly favored the United States Navy.

[95] Fletcher.

them as the reason for the withdrawal. He just said, "Carriers short of fuel proceeding to fueling rendezvous." [96]

This is the despatch which Admiral Fletcher believes has brought unwarranted censure on him because it assigned a reason for the withdrawal he had not used. The basic decision he considers was justified.[97]

It should be noted in this connection that on 9 September 1942, Vice Admiral Fletcher replied to COMSOPAC's request to supply supporting evidence for the latter's use in answering CINCPAC's questions about the Air Support Force withdrawal, avowedly due to a low fuel situation. Extracts from the reply follow:

> On 7 August, CTF 16 [Kinkaid] sent a despatch saying his destroyers, except *Gwin,* had fuel remaining for two days at a speed of 15 knots.
>
> * * * * *
>
> At noon 8 August CTF 18 [Noyes] reported his destroyers had fuel remaining for only 31 hours at 25 knots.
>
> * * * * *
>
> At noon 8 August destroyers of Task Force 11 [Fletcher] had fuel remaining for only 35 hours at 25 knots.
>
> * * * * *
>
> It was not practicable to fuel destroyers from cruisers as the latter only had fuel available for 50 hours at 25 knots.

It is apparent that the virus of AFFAG was virulent in the Air Support Force on 7 and 8 August and that the CTF 16 (Kinkaid) despatch, if quoted correctly by CTF 61, was downright misleading, since TF 16 did not actually fuel until 1700 on 10 August and the destroyers of TF 16 did steam at speeds of 15 knots or higher in the meanwhile.

In connection with CINCPAC's question as to why the Air Support Force did not proceed post haste to a position where it could launch a dawn air attack on the retiring Japanese cruiser force, the Commander Expeditionary Force (Fletcher) stated that he was too far south by that time and that

> the first indication of any night attack on Tulagi-Guadalcanal Area was received by this force at 0400 local time.[98]

The first record of the Savo battle in the Air Support Force War Diaries and Action Reports is at 0300 on 9 August by CTF 16 (Kinkaid) in the *Enterprise,* but all indications are that it was not until an hour later that

---

[96] COMSOPAC to CINCPAC, 090830, 090834 Aug. 1942, Hepburn Report despatches.
[97] Fletcher.
[98] CTF 61 to COMSOPAC, letter A16–3 (0039N), subj: Preliminary Report Solomon Islands Operation.

the Expeditionary Force Commander's Staff in *Saratoga* got the word and Admiral Fletcher insists it was between 0500 and 0600 when he was awakened and given the word. He was awakened shortly after 0330 on the 9th and told that COMSOPAC had approved the withdrawal of the Air Support Force. He then approved the change to the previously decided upon withdrawal course which was to be made at 0400. It was quite obvious that had the word on Savo been available to the TF 61 Duty Officer in the *Saratoga* at that time, it would have been given at that time to the Admiral. He later said:

> Had I known of the attack then, since we were on a northerly course, I might well have continued on it. But it wasn't until much later that I was awakened and given the first indication of Savo.[99]

Admiral Kinkaid when asked about the decision of CTF 61 to withdraw the carriers on 8 August said that it was "a valid decision at the time, but wouldn't have been valid later in the war.[100]

Scanning the figures in the fuel table given in detail before, from the safe distance of 25 years, might lead one to observe that on the 8th of August 1942 when Rear Admiral Kinkaid was making the entry in his War Diary, only the *Grayson* (DD-435) (Lieutenant Commander Frederick J. Bell) justified the critical stage of worry about fuel which undoubtedly existed in TG 61.1.

Even though not critical, the fuel situation in the Expeditionary Force was a problem as indicated in the report of the transport *President Jackson* which was landing troops at Tulagi the morning of 7 August.

> At 0759 rigged ship for fueling destroyers of TRANSDIV 12 (APDs).

At this time fire support groups and planes were shelling and bombing Tulagi, and

> between 1004 and 1239, APDs *McKean* and *Little* were fueled. At 1304 APD *Colhoun* prepared to fuel alongside but numerous enemy plane radar contacts received during the afternoon prevented, so that it was not until the third attempt that fueling was completed at 1750.[101]

In 1963, Admiral Kinkaid could not remember whether he was asked for a recommendation by CTF 61, before that officer (Fletcher) went to COMSOPAC with his recommendation to withdraw the carriers from the support area, but he did not believe that he was consulted. He knows that he raised no

---

[99] (a) Fletcher; (b) Rear Admiral Harry Smith, a lieutenant commander in 1942 and the Flag Lieutenant to Vice Admiral Fletcher, related the same story in an interview on 17 May 1963.
[100] Kinkaid.
[101] *President Jackson* Action Report, 19 Aug. 1942.

question at the time in regard to the decision, which in view of the necessity of conserving our carrier strength he viewed then and continues to view as sound.[102]

However, had information become available to the Commander Task Force 61 (Fletcher) during the night of the Japanese success at Savo Island, Admiral Kinkaid thinks that the task Force should have been turned north and every effort made to make air attacks on the retreating Japanese ships the next morning.[103]

Admiral Fletcher was told by this scribe:

> Forrest Sherman, Commanding Officer of the *Wasp*, tried to persuade Admiral Noyes to recommend to you to turn north after the first word was received of the Japanese surface ships being in the Guadalcanal Area.

The author then asked:

> Did anyone try to persuade you to do this? Did this thought occur to you?

Admiral Fletcher's answer was:

> I didn't know anything about Savo Island happening until about five to six the next morning, and I couldn't get through to Kelly Turner by radio and get details in regard to the Japs. One or two of my staff recommended that we go back. I said if I was a Jap, I would have planned on all our carriers coming back and would hit them with all my land based air.
>
> If I had it all to do over again that morning and know about our losses, I would leave one carrier group behind to fuel, and would move two carrier groups up to attack and to continue to provide air support to Kelly Turner. This did not occur to me at the time as being sound.[104]

Rear Admiral Harry Smith, USN, Fletcher's Flag Lieutenant and Signal Officer in August 1942, stated in May 1963:

> For some reason the *Saratoga* did not or could not copy CTF 62's blind despatches sent that night, and it wasn't until other ships sent us the news by blinker or infrared that we started to get the word about the Battle of Savo.

SUMMARY

Considering all these fundamentals, and particularly Admiral Nimitz's instructions, Admiral Fletcher, in 1963, still thought:

> A defensive decision was in order on 8 August although perhaps not exactly the one I made at the time.[105]

---

[102] Kinkaid.
[103] *Ibid.*
[104] Fletcher.
[105] Fletcher.

THE SECOND DEFENSIVE DECISION—VANDEGRIFT'S— PERIMETER DEFENSE

Admiral Turner recalled that the defensive type naval decision made by Vice Admiral Fletcher to withdraw the carrier Air Support Forces (CTG 61.1) from an area where they might soon be subject to concentrated and coordinated submarine and land based air attacks was followed the next morning, Sunday, 9 August, by a defensive Marine decision made by Major General Vandegrift, which was equally decisive on the flow of the war in the Lower Solomons during the next four months.[106]

Major General Vandegrift at his 0900 conference of regimental commanders on the 9th directed that the planned ground offensive operations cease, that "further ground operations be restricted to vigorous patrolling," and that "defenses be immediately organized to repel attack from the sea." [107]

On Guadalcanal Island there were nearly 11,000 Marines stranded but intact. The first day on Guadalcanal, as the Army history relates it:

> the Guadalcanal forces had landed unopposed and captured the airfield without casualties.[108]

Or as the Marine history puts it:

> . . . the lack of opposition (on the Guadalcanal side only) gave it somewhat the characteristics of a training maneuver. . . .[109]

Contact with the enemy on Guadalcanal the first and second day was nominal. As the Army history states it:

> The enemy garrison, composed of 430 sailors and 1,700 laborers, had fled westward without attempting to defend or destroy their installations. . . .[110]

The Marine Corps history states:

> There were hardly enough Japanese fighting men ashore on the island to bother the Vandegrift force. . . .[111]

But,

> if the Japanese struck hard while the landing force was abandoned and without air support, the precarious first step to Rabaul might well have to be taken all over again.[112]

---

[106] Turner.
[107] Griffith, *The Battle for Guadalcanal*, p. 68.
[108] Miller, *Guadalcanal: The First Offensive* (Army), p. 75.
[109] Hough, Ludwig, and Shaw, *Pearl Harbor to Guadalcanal* (Marine), p. 257.
[110] Miller, p. 73.
[111] Hough, Ludwig, and Shaw, p. 257.
[112] *Ibid.*, p. 274.

Savo—The Galling Defeat

So,

> estimating a counter landing to be the most probable course of Japanese action, General Vandegrift placed his MRL [Main Line of Resistance] at the beach. . . . The bulk of the combat forces remained in assembly area inland as a ready reserve to check attacks or penetrations from any sector.[113]

Admiral Turner summarized his current thoughts on this second major defensive decision of the WATCHTOWER Operation in this way:

> It's at least an 'iffy matter', as FDR used to characterize tough posers, whether a hard driving Marine offensive against the Guadalcanal Japanese starting on the 9th wouldn't have destroyed or completely dispersed the nucleus of Japanese forces on Guadalcanal Island. This would have permitted an adequate shore welcoming reception party for the first Japanese re-enforcements [5th Sasebo Special Naval Landing Force] whose advance elements of about 200 men aboard a single Jap destroyer [the *Otie*] arrived a week later— 16 August—and made an unsupported daylight landing of troops and supplies.
>
> After all, the 6000 Marines on Tulagi captured that island and a couple of others from some 750 well dug in and well organized Japanese with the moderate loss of about 150 killed and 200 wounded.
>
> It's certainly a question whether if the Marines had been on the offensive, instead of dug in on the defensive, the Japanese were in enough strength to fight their way ashore even when on August 18th some 900 Army troops of the famous Ichiki Midway Landing Force of the 17th Army arrived.
>
> A proper Marine reception committee at appropriate beaches around Lunga Point would have made the Japanese think more than once about 'reinforcing Guadalcanal' particularly if there had been no one to reinforce.[114]

In a memorandum to COMPHIBFORSOPAC on 2 August 1942, the Commanding General First Marine Division had written:

> Operations against outlying Japanese detachments on GUADALCANAL and the smaller islands will be commenced without delay. . . . The 1st RAIDERS BATTALION will be employed for this purpose. That Battalion has been ordered to reembark following seizure of TULAGI. . . . This reembarkation was ordered for a dual purpose; namely, to have the Raiders available for operations against outlying detachments but primarily to have them available as a highly mobile rapidly striking reserve which could be landed on GUADALCANAL at some point in rear of hostile forces and thus greatly speed the conclusion of the attack on Japanese forces on that island.[115]

---

[113] *Ibid.*, p. 275.
[114] Turner.
[115] COMGENFIRSTMARDIV to COMPHIBFORSOPAC, Memorandum, A6-3(4)076/222 AE-0020 of 2 Aug. 1942.

Admiral Turner opined:

> The Navy made a defensive decision; the Marines made a defensive decision. Each one helped to bring on months of hard and costly defensive and then offensive fighting. In the long run, both fights were won.[116]

SAVO—RETROSPECT

Considering the number of rear admirals whose performance in action during World War II failed to reach the high standards set by Admiral King and Admiral Nimitz and who were peremptorily removed from command or gently eased into non-battle assignments, it is quite apparent that had Rear Admiral Turner actually made a major mistake on that fateful evening of 8 July 1942, that Admiral King or Admiral Nimitz would not have kept him at sea in one of the more important combat assignments throughout the war.

When the captains of opposing football teams meet in the center of the field before the game starts, the referee tosses a coin, the designated captain calls "heads" and the coin turns up "tails." This captain has made a bad guess but not a culpable mistake in judgment. The coach doesn't bench him because of his bad guess.

The Battle of Savo Island was primarily a United States Navy defeat. All of the dozen "causes" listed earlier contributed to this defeat. Beyond the U.S. Navy, the Australian Navy and Air Force and the United States Army Air Force also contributed to setting the stage of the defeat.

As Commander of Task Force 61, under the Navy code, Rear Admiral Turner bore a command responsibility for whatever success was attained or failure suffered. He did not shrink from his command responsibility. He vigorously set about correcting those matters of operations, training, materiel and personnel which were within his purview, and recommending action in other areas.

> Savo Island was a defeat. Guadalcanal was a victory. The important thing was to learn and apply every possible lesson from both.[117]

---

[116] Turner.
[117] Turner.

THE MISSING FINAL REPORT

In writing about Savo Island, Morison says:

> Every ship in this battle except *Jarvis* submitted an Action Report. Admiral Turner made none. . . .[118]

To begin with, it should be noted that upper echelon commanders generally made operation reports on whole operations such as WATCHTOWER, and group, unit, and ship commanders made action reports on battles occurring during the operation. So it could as logically be said that Admiral Turner made no action report on the campaign in the Gilberts, the Marshalls, or the Marianas, omitting to state that he made operational reports.

Rear Admiral Turner, as Commander Task Force 62, or as Commander Amphibious Forces South Pacific originated three written official reports concerning the WATCHTOWER Operation which included the Battle of Savo Island. The first report, three pages in length plus a track chart, reproduced on page 356 was dated 12 August 1942 and titled "Night Action of Savo Island, August 8–9, 1942." It described and summarized the action as known at that early date by CTF 62. It included a "sketch chart, Battle of Savo Island" and requested any additional information that the Second-in-Command could furnish. It was addressed to the Second-in-Command, TF 62. A copy was given by hand by COMPHIBFORSOPAC (Turner) to COMSOPAC (Ghormley) together with 67 pages of reports from subordinate unit commanders. COMSOPAC sent all of this on to COMINCH via CINCPAC on 16 August 1942, as part of COMSOPAC's "Preliminary Report—WATCHTOWER OPERATION." The initial document penned by Rear Admiral Turner, together with the track chart and other reports, was described officially by COMPHIBFORSOPAC as a "fairly comprehensive preliminary report," and is just that.

The second Amphibious Force, South Pacific report was dated 29 August 1942, and forwarded reports from eleven ships regarding the first three days of the amphibious landings as well as the night battle off Savo Island, and stated that "comment on tactical features of the night battle of Savo Island" will be submitted by the Commander Amphibious Force, South Pacific in his report of the WATCHTOWER Operation."

The third report, made on George Washington's birthday in 1943, by COMPHIBFORSOPAC was titled "Solomon's Operations, August 7–8 and

---
[118] Morison, *The Struggle for Guadalcanal*, p. 17.

9, 1942" and was nothing more than a blanket forwarding of reports slowly extracted from 36 subordinate units and commanders regarding the first three days of the WATCHTOWER Operation plus a statement that "pressure of operations has, so far, prevented completion of the final report" and "in view of the forthcoming operations, it seems likely that a final report will be further delayed." One could read between the lines that COMPHIBFORSOPAC would never get time to make a WATCHTOWER final report. This was an excellent prognostication. A final comprehensive report on WATCHTOWER or the Savo Island Battle was never originated by COMPHIBFORSOPAC (CTF 62).[119]

In addition to these reports originated by Rear Admiral Turner, on 15 October 1942, COMSOPAC addressed to CINCPAC a supplementary report to his preliminary report on "Operations in Solomons, 7–9 August 1942." This comprehensive report was forwarded to CTF 62 for comment before forwarding to CINCPAC and COMINCH, and thus gave Rear Admiral Turner a chance to provide any additional facts, and to express any differences of opinion that he might have had with COMSOPAC in regard to the known events or COMSOPAC's interpretation of them during the operations covered.

So it is hardly the correct story to say that "Admiral Turner made none," when writing about official reports on the Savo Island battle.

RETROSPECT

Admiral Turner was quite prepared to admit that he had not turned in a flawless performance in WATCHTOWER or "any other big operation."

> I could always find things I didn't do or could have done better in any big operation.
> Late on August 8th, and long after Vandegrift and Crutchley had left the *McCawley*, I was still waiting for Ghormley's reply to Fletcher. I was hoping

---

[119] (a) CTF 62 to CTG 62.6, letter, FE25/A16/Ser 0034 of 12 Aug. 1942 included in COMSOPAC Ser 0053 of 16 Aug. 1942; (b) COMPHIBFORSOPAC to COMINCH, letter, FE25/A16-3(3) Ser 0092 of 29 Aug. 1942 with 11 enclosures; (c) COMSOPAC to COMINCH, letter, A16-3(1)/, Ser 00171 of 15 Oct. 1942 with endorsements, including COMPHIBFORSOPAC, A16-3/, Ser 00317 of 24 Oct. 1942; (d) COMPHIBFORSOPAC to COMSOPAC and CINCPAC, letter, A16-3(3)/, Ser 00126 of 22 Feb. 1943 with 36 enclosures; (e) COMPHIBFOR, SOPAC, letter, A16-3(3)/, Ser 231 of 6 Apr. 1943. Forwarding copy of lost report of CTG 62.6 dated 13 Aug. 1942 re First Battle of Savo Island; (f) COMSOPAC to CTF 62, letter, A16-3/, Ser 0058 of 30 Aug. 1942 relating to CINCPAC's Ser 02576 of 23 Aug. 1942, re Preliminary Report, Solomon Islands Operations.

against hope that Ghormley would say 'No' to Fletcher and tell him to stay around for another 24 hours. I had no idea that Fletcher had been heading southeast all late afternoon and evening and was well south of San Cristobal by 2300. That information would have been most valuable to me and to all the Screening Group. But Fletcher didn't send it to me. Ghormley's reply approving Fletcher's withdrawal didn't come in until about 0330, and by that time Iron Bottom Sound had its first contingent [of our ships].[120]

Admiral Turner believed that the major effect of Vice Admiral Fletcher's announced intention of withdrawal on the actual Battle of Savo Island was that it resulted in Rear Admiral Crutchley not being with his Screening Group at the particular time the Japanese struck. It was his opinion that this was a serious loss of command ability, command cohesion, command knowledge of the situation, and command offensive response.

As for the effect after the Battle of Savo Island, Rear Admiral Turner had said frequently during the war, and the man continued to say in 1960, that the withdrawal permitted Mikawa's Cruiser Force "to live and enjoy their victory."[121]

Admiral Turner thought that there were a number of major lessons which he had learned out of the WATCHTOWER Operation, but that not everybody would agree with him. His key thoughts in 1960 related to organization. The basic task force organization established by COMSOPAC placed Commander Expeditionary Force and the Commander Aircraft Force, South Pacific at the same level in the command echelon. At the next lower level were Commander Air Support Force and the Commander Amphibious Force.

Over the years, Admiral Turner came to believe that the basic task organization established by COMSOPAC was faulty in at least one respect and that was:

> at the top level, where the major element of air reconnaissance in the SOPAC area was not under the operational control of the Commander Expeditionary Force.

To this was added a grasping at might-have-been straws:

> Had TF 63 [the air reconnaissance force] been included in the Expeditionary Force, perhaps Frank Jack [Fletcher] would have felt more like an Expeditionary Force commander and assumed a greater responsibility for sticking with the whole Force through to a success.

Finally, Admiral Turner commented:

> Unity of command increases the chances for victory. The shore-based aircraft under General MacArthur's command was a large percentage of the total

---
[120] Turner.
[121] Turner.

reconnaissance aircraft searching the operational area. In WATCHTOWER, unity of operational command might have produced a greater feeling of responsibility on the part of the individual reconnaissance aircraft pilot to get his intelligence of enemy forces through to his top operational commanders promptly, as well as more direct communication channels. [Between air reconnaissance and the top operational commanders.] [122]

The lesson to be drawn from these remarks is that defeat in battle early in a war can quickly gain adherents to sound principles which will produce future victories.

---

[122] Turner.

CHAPTER XI

Logistics:
The Heart of the Six Months Battle
August 1942–February 1943

The two sectors of the Navy which were quite inadequately developed on 7 December 1941 were logistics and intelligence.

The primary reason for the logistical deficiency was that the officers of the Line of the Navy had taken only a cursory interest in logistics in the years just before World War II. This occurred because in the day by day peacetime Fleet operations, there were few really large difficult logistical problems demanding command decisions.

Consequently, logistical matters were handled mainly by officers of the various excellent Staff corps, particularly the Supply Corps. So the command corps, the Line, lacked skill and experience in handling logistical matters on a large scale.

The secondary reason for the logistical deficiency in the Navy was that no one had ever been able to free the seagoing Navy from the thinking that its operations should be on an austere basis in the field of logistics. It was quite unprepared mentally for wartime operations with their tremendous actual expenditures and waste, or to use the cover-up word for waste, "slippage."

Both the intelligence and logistical sectors received a great war influx of citizen sailors. These citizen sailors soon found that their sectors were rated by the professional officers of the Line as markedly less important than the command and operational sectors of the naval effort.

The penalty for the failure of the professional officer to adequately evaluate intelligence and logistics in pre-World War II days was a massive take over of these important wartime functions by officers with little or no naval knowledge or experience in the vast waterlands of the world to provide balance to their technical judgments.

GUADALCANAL LOGISTICS

It was Admiral Turner's belief that:

a. The United States Navy's concept of logistics broadened mightily during the early months of World War II.
b. In no part of naval combat operations did logistics require a larger part of a commander's attention than in our early amphibious operations.[1]

The pre-World War II experience in logistical austerity, combined with the multiple handlings arising from the nature of amphibious operations and the juxtaposition of waves, coral, sand and hot sun, provided the pertinent background for the Navy's initial logistical inadequacies in the Lower Solomons.

In the early amphibian operations, there were no LSTs or LCTs and very few DUKWs.[2] The guts of logistical support for the first phase of WATCHTOWER had to be winch-lifted out of the deep, deep holds of large transports and cargo ships, and loaded like sardines into small landing craft dancing on the undulating seas, and then hand-lifted and piled at a snail's pace onto the beaches by tired sailormen or by combat oriented Marines who, with rifle in hand, might better have been pressuring the retreating and scattered Japanese.

Admiral Turner said:

> Eighty percent of my time was given to logistics during the first four months of the WATCHTOWER operation [because] we were living from one logistic crisis to another.[3]

Many of the transport Captains in the WATCHTOWER Operation became distressingly familiar with one phase of the complex logistics problem when their ships in July had to unload all Marine supplies and equipment in New Zealand and then load them right back aboard so that they would be available in the order in which they would be needed when the Marines hit the beach. This "combat loading" was never quite so efficient

---

[1] Turner.

[2] LST—Landing Ship Tank; LCT—Landing Craft Tank. In the 1943 operations these landing ships and craft ran directly up onto the beach and waterproofed wheeled vehicles or tanks unloaded through bow doors. When depth of water or beach gradient did not permit this type of unloading, they ran up onto hastily constructed "hard" ramps or dropped their nose doors onto beach grounded pontoon barges. DUKWs. These amphibious trucks could be loaded aboard ship, unloaded by winch or launched out of bow doors and move through the water up onto the beach and inland surmounting the surf and riding over reefs or through swamps.

[3] Turner.

in the utilization of all available cargo space as "commercial loading" but was essential. And the transport Captains learned a second phase of the complex problem at Guadalcanal and Tulagi. For no matter how hard the planners had planned and how skillfully the Transport Quartermaster had loaded, it was almost inevitable that actual operations would turn out to be different than planned operations, and real and pressing needs would arise for changes in the Marines' priorities for unloading the logistical support.

LOGISTICS—THE BUGBEAR

Admiral Kinkaid, when asked if he had talked with Rear Admiral Turner during the August to November 1942 period during which Kinkaid was CTF 16, replied:

> Only once. That was after the Battle of Santa Cruz. [26–27 October 1942] He was mainly concerned with logistical matters at Guadalcanal then.[4]

Logistics got off to a bad start in the South Pacific and in WATCHTOWER, the area's first operational venture. This occurred because of several questionable logistical decisions made outside the South Pacific Area, relating to time and distance, as well as because of an inadequate appreciation of logistical problems by those within the SOPAC Area. A particular problem was the need to move logistical support bases forward as operations were undertaken to halt the enemy and, if possible, move him backward toward Japan.

During the early months of 1942, the naval activities of South Pacific island bases, even though they fell within the CINCPAC command area, generally made direct application to the logistic agencies in the United States for their support. They did this rather than apply to Pearl Harbor since Pearl Harbor did not have material resources to spare or even personnel to handle the heavy logistical communication load.

In April 1942, the Army directed that its forces in the South Pacific Area should be supplied directly by the Port of Embarkation, San Francisco. At the same time the Commander Service Force Pacific Fleet indicated a willingness to handle logistic requests from all bases—Army or Navy—in the South Pacific Area. Since both Army and Navy bases and their com-

---

[4] Kinkaid.

manders were on the same island, these differing instructions from the higher echelons were confusing.

At the Navy Department end:

> The various Joint plans [for the establishment of defense and logistic support of island bases] did not, however, constitute a general supply procedure, nor did they stipulate in any detail the channels through which supply would be furnished.[5]

In other words the assigned Army, Army Air Corps, Naval, Marine, and New Zealand Forces for these island bases did not have Unified, or Joint, logistic support. Each Service at each island base had individual procedures for its logistic support.

> In general, the Army will furnish and transport its own logistic support, plus rations for Navy personnel, and the Navy its own, plus fuel, diesel and aviation gasoline.[6]

At Pearl, before WATCHTOWER was much more than a gleam in Admiral King's eye, CINCPAC recommended to COMINCH a definite division of responsibility between the Army and the Navy for logistic support of each individual base in SOPAC by categories of supply.[7] In other words, he wanted a system wherein every island base received its bailing wire from the Navy and every island base received its coffee from the Army.

From SOPAC, Vice Admiral Ghormley, came the recommendation in late July 1942 that Auckland, New Zealand, be used for unloading and resorting material for all Advanced Bases in the SOPAC Area.[8] Admiral King, in February 1942, had said that Tongatabu in the Tonga Islands would serve for this purpose.[9]

It is presumed the SOPAC recommendation was made because COMSOPAC as well as his senior logistical commander, COMSERVRONSOPAC, and a Joint Purchasing Board were all physically located in Auckland at the time. It apparently was approved by higher echelons because Auckland was the only SOPAC base considered safe from Japanese attacks at that date. But Auckland was 1,100 miles further from San Francisco than Tongatabu; it was 1,825 miles from Guadalcanal and 250 miles farther from Guadalcanal than the Tonga Islands.

Commencing in mid-April 1942, the South Pacific Service Squadron under

---

[5] Ballentine, *U. S. Naval Logistics in the Second World War*, p. 99.
[6] COMSOPAC Op Plan 1–42, Logistic Annex.
[7] CINCPAC to COMINCH, 250225 Jun. 1942.
[8] COMSOPAC to CINCPAC, 260551 Jul. 1942.
[9] COMINCH to C/S USA, letter, FF1 A16/CF1 Ser 00105 of 18 Feb. 1942.

Captain Mark C. Bowman, U. S. Navy (1909), had been established with its headquarters at Auckland, New Zealand. When COMSOPAC's recommendation making Auckland the Supply Center for SOPAC was approved, requests from the island bases, which were all north and northeast of Auckland, had to be sent, most by airmail, the thousand or more miles south to Auckland where they were coordinated and sent on north again, many via airmail, past the various bases on to Subordinate Command, Service Force, U. S. Pacific Fleet in San Francisco.

When the request could be filled, the supplies then moved (the bulk of them at 10 or 12 knots) in the same perverse and time consuming manner, southwest the entire 5,680 miles down to Auckland from San Francisco and then back north and northeast 1,000 or more miles to the island bases. This was the roundabout way by which the Marines on Guadalcanal received their rations as late as October 1942.[10]

In mid-July 1942, the Army and Navy in Washington agreed upon and promulgated a "Joint Logistic Plan for the Support of United States Bases in the South Pacific Area." This Joint Plan, which followed CINCPAC's recommendations in general, stipulated which Service would be responsible for furnishing items common to both the Army and the Navy. It was just coming into effect when WATCHTOWER suddenly imposed its logistical burdens upon the SOPAC island bases. The new Joint Plan was similar to its predecessor in calling for the screening of all requests from island bases by the Joint Purchasing Board in New Zealand to see if they could be fulfilled from local SOPAC resources. Thus it retained the potential for long shipping delays in SOPAC logistical support.

Superimposed upon the logistical tasks of carrying through WATCHTOWER was the problem of logistic planning and preparing for the operations to follow WATCHTOWER.

Rear Admiral Turner had always had the comprehensive mind and the talent for remembering a million details which together are the earmarks of the first flight working logistician.

When he "hauled awrse" from Guadalcanal-Tulagi on the afternoon of 9 August 1942, he was saddled with a hundred worries about ships and sailormen lost—by what, if any, dereliction of his own self he was not clear—and with a thousand worries about the 10,000 good Marines for whom he could no longer provide minute by minute logistic or other direct support.

At the late conference with Major General Vandegrift aboard the

---

[10] COMSERVRONPAC to COMSOPAC, 220655 Aug. 1942.

McCawley on the 8th of August, it was decided that the latter, with Captain Peyton and Colonel Linscott of the TF 62 Staff, would visit Tulagi, ascertain the situation there militarily and logistically and then CTF 62 would confirm or change the departure hour for the transports already tentatively set for 0600 of the 9th.

Major General Vandegrift did not get back aboard the *McCawley* until 0908 on August 9th at which time it was mutually agreed that the transports would depart about 1330. This was only the first of many difficult operational decisions based on logistical factors which Rear Admiral Turner would make in the next six months.

Not knowing that Rear Admiral Turner, his senior subordinate at Guadalcanal, had already started TF 62 forces south toward Noumea, Vice Admiral Ghormley had ordered the withdrawal of all surface ships at Guadalcanal by 1830 local time on the 9th,[11] and informed his subordinates and superiors that there were indications Japanese Landing Forces were proceeding toward Guadalcanal on 9 August.[12] This latter despatch, it is believed, did nothing to ease the mental strain on the amphibians, or to quiet the mind of the Commanding General of the First Marine Division.

Despite the fact that the transports had done a commendable job within the limited hours of unloading available, Rear Admiral Turner knew that the Marines would be unhappy that they were not getting 100 percent of the logistic support which had arrived for them off Red Beach and Blue Beach.[13] It was apparent that the problem of getting to the Marines the supplies not landed would be the first order of business.

The first entry in the TF 62 Staff Log on 14 August after recording arrival at Noumea reads:

> Commenced preparation for the hospitalization of wounded, transferring and equipping of survivors, and logistics plans for supply of forces in the CACTUS-RINGBOLT [Guadalcanal-Tulagi] Area. Transports and AKs proceeding with unloading and rearrangement of cargo in order that essential supplies may be forwarded to CACTUS [Guadalcanal] for quick unloading.

It was not until six days after the *McCawley* arrived in Noumea on 13 August that the only Supply Corps Officer on the PHIBFORSOPAC Staff, a senior lieutenant, reported for duty, and thus made available on the staff of Rear Admiral Turner an officer trained in the techniques and techni-

---
[11] COMSOPAC to CINCPAC, 090830 Aug. 1942.
[12] COMSOPAC to CTF 62, 090551 Aug. 1942.
[13] Turner.

Rear Admiral Richmond Kelly Turner, USN, taken at sea, 1942.

calities of logistics support.[14] The lack of such a logistically trained officer during the previous month was another contributory factor to the inadequate logistic plans for WATCHTOWER.

The first letters in Rear Admiral Turner's personal file after his arrival at Noumea, New Caledonia, deal with logistics—and the great majority of letters in this file dated during the next four months deal with the same subject. According to the Staff, they worked at and slept with and dreamed logistics. Even the Flag Lieutenant grew out of being a Flag Lieutenant and became a Logistics Officer in all but title.[15]

Major General Vandegrift's first post-Guadalcanal landing letter to his immediate Naval Commander, sent to Noumea by the first plane, a Navy PBY-5A, to land on Guadalcanal, reported, as of 12 August 1942: "We are all well and happy." But it mainly dealt with the priority of a number of logistic support items needed. In addition he suggested: "That if we are to hold this place that the 7th [Regiment] be sent up." [16]

THE BEST LAID PLANS OF MEN AND MICE

Rear Admiral Turner had planned tentatively to shift his flag ashore at Guadalcanal, when the *McCawley* was withdrawn to Noumea, after unloading during WATCHTOWER.

> ... Command of this Force shall be shifted to a land base in the Tulagi-Guadalcanal area, after establishment ashore by the Marine forces. All Staff functions will be conducted from this land base until such time as the permanent garrison is established and the Amphibious Force is released to proceed with further operations.

A partial draft order in pencil, from which the above is quoted, is contained in the files of Commander Amphibious Force, SOPAC.[17]

At the time this draft was written, it was assumed that the communication facilities of the *McCawley* would be available at Guadalcanal long enough for CTF 62 to conduct the initial stages of the HUDDLE (Santa Cruz) Operation as well as to follow through on the anticipated initial surge of despatches regarding logistic support of WATCHTOWER.

---

[14] (a) *McCawley* Ship's Log; (b) Staff Log, 19 Aug. 1942.
[15] Staff Interviews.
[16] Commanding General First Marine Division (Vandegrift) to RKT, letter, 12 Aug. 1942.
[17] (a) COMPHIBFORSOPAC, Tentative Command Order, no date; (b) CTF 62, Op Plan A3–42, para. 5(c); Annex K, para. 2.

The CTF 62 Op Plan stated:

> The [TF 62] HEADQUARTERS radio station will be established using the FIRST MARINE DIVISION TBW radio equipment.

The *McCawley's* communication facilities were meager enough, but they were several times larger than the two TBW's which would be available on Guadalcanal for use by CTF 62 if he went ashore and the *McCawley* departed. So at the same time the decision was made to withdraw all surface amphibious forces from Guadalcanal, Rear Admiral Turner made the hard decision to withdraw himself and TF 62 Staff.[18]

Support that this 'second guess' decision was correct and that the radio facilities being taken into Guadalcanal were inadequate, even without CTF 62's communication load, is found in the extracts below from a four-page mailgram picture of the Guadalcanal communication situation on 28 August 1942.

> From RDO Guadalcanal
> To   COMAMPHIBFORSOPAC
>   220400
>
> Naval communication facilities available in the Solomons on 20 August 1942.
>
> * * * * *
>
> Radio facilities are daily becoming more inadequate.
>
> * * * * *
>
> Captured Jap receiver utilized to copy FOX.
>
> * * * * *
>
> We hope to improve our situation somewhat by the repair of a Japanese 2 kilowatt transmitter.

Rear Admiral Turner was grateful thereafter that he had withdrawn because he was able to do a far more comprehensive job of logistic support from Noumea than he could have done from Guadalcanal, although he knew that some Marines thought and said he had run away.[19]

Guadalcanal logistics over the long haul centered on troops, planes, food, ammunition, and aviation gas, but during the first two weeks, getting the airfield into condition to operate aircraft received highest priority. This latter chore the Japanese had not quite accomplished.

From the aerial photographs, an estimate had been made that the airfield being built by the Japanese would be ready to operate aircraft on 15 August 1942. This was an excellent estimate and does some unknown photographic

---
[18] (a) Turner; (b) Staff Interviews.
[19] Turner.

intelligence officer great credit. But to make ready the airfield by this date certainly put the heat on the Marines who landed on Guadalcanal-Tulagi on 7 August. By 12 August the landing strip was usable and by 20 August, Henderson Field with two squadrons of operating Marine aircraft was in business and would remain so throughout the war.

AUGUST–SEPTEMBER 1942

The days and nights of August and September 1942 were full of TF 62 logistics and of fighting to permit the flow of TF 62 logistics through to its most important element—the Marines on Guadalcanal.

It is necessary to recount just a few of the main events for background.

Task Force 61, under Vice Admiral Fletcher, acting as a Covering Force for the cargo ships *Formalhaut* and *Alhena* carrying the first large load of logistic support to Guadalcanal, fought the indecisive Battle of the Eastern Solomons on 24 August 1942, which resulted in the *Enterprise* being bomb-damaged. The *Saratoga* unfortunately was damaged by a submarine torpedo on 31 August.

The Marines, within their perimeter on Guadalcanal, were placed under heavy attack at the Battle of the Bloody Ridge on 12–14 September. Task Force 65 under Rear Admiral Turner's command with 4,000 Marine reinforcements, the 7th Marine Regiment, made a delayed landing on 18 September on Guadalcanal, but battleship *North Carolina,* carrier *Wasp* and destroyer *O'Brien* from the Covering Force all were torpedoed by submarines on 15 September. The *Wasp* was lost, and the *O'Brien* went down more than a month later while enroute to the United States for battle repairs.

The delivery of the 4,000 Marines and the logistic support that went ashore with them on 18 September were a real satisfaction to Rear Admiral Turner, CTF 65.[20]

The worry and concern over the logistical situation at Guadalcanal and the heavy naval losses sustained in maintaining the flow of logistic support extended up and down the command chain of the Navy, and to the Army and its air arm.

On 16 September 1942, Admiral King was reported as having told the Joint Chiefs of Staff that "the Navy is in a bad way at this particular moment." [21]

---

[20] Turner.
[21] Henry Harley Arnold, *Global Mission*, p. 338.

One of the many high ranking visitors to the SOPAC Area, Lieutenant General Henry H. Arnold, U. S. Army, Chief of the Army Air Corps, and a single-minded advocate of using the resources of the Army Air Corps to "exert direct pressure against Germany," appraised the SOPAC situation in late September 1942 with pithy comments as follows:

> . . . The Navy was hard-pressed at Guadalcanal. They needed a 'shot in the arm'—and needed it badly; but I was not sure that the way to give it to them was by sending airplanes that might better be used against the Germans from England.[22]
>
> * * * * *
>
> It was obvious to me that the Naval Officers in this area were under a terrific strain. It was also obvious that they had chips on their shoulders.[23]
>
> * * * * *
>
> . . . Ghormley and other Naval officers in that area—Admiral John ('Slew') McCain and Admiral Daniel Callaghan—were very worried about the situation there.
>
> * * * * *
>
> It was obvious the Navy could not hold Guadalcanal if they could not get supplies in, and they could not get supplies in if the Japanese bombers continued to come down and bomb the ships unloading supplies.
>
> * * * * *
>
> . . . General Patch [Commanding General Americal Division at Noumea] was very insistent that the Navy had no plan of logistics; that the Marines and the Navy would both have been in one hell of a fix had he not dug into his reserve stock and furnished them with supplies.[24]
>
> * * * * *
>
> My estimate, upon leaving Admiral Ghormley's headquarters, was this: So far, the Navy had taken one hell of a beating and at that time was hanging on by a shoestring. They did not have a logistic setup efficient enough to insure success.[25]

But fortunately one of the chips on the shoulders of Uncle Sam's Navy was to get at the Japanese and pay them back for Savo Island. As General Arnold put it, although he (as did others from far, far away Washington) misidentified the SOPAC area through which he was traveling:

> As I traveled through the Southwest Pacific, it was impossible not to get the impression that the Navy was determined to carry on the campaign in that theater, and determined to do it with as little help from the Army as possible.

---

[22] *Ibid.*, p. 337.
[23] *Ibid.*, p. 340.
[24] *Ibid.*, p. 341.
[25] *Ibid.*, p. 342.

It was their fight, the Navy's fight; it was their war against the Japanese; and they were going to clean it up if they could.[26]

The Chief of the Army Air Corps carried news of the worried state of the naval commanders in the South Pacific Force back to Washington, where he arrived on 2 October 1942, having covered 21,000 miles in 12 days. While his solution to the Admirals' problems was far from being similar to theirs, he served a most valuable purpose in alerting the home folks in Washington that there were SOPAC and Pacific problems crying for early assistance.

Lieutenant General Arnold's appraisal of the state of the logistic art in the Navy was conveyed in a memorandum to General Marshall which said:

> Naval planning and operations to date have demonstrated a definite lack of appreciation of the logistic factor, and as a consequence, operations to date have lacked continuity by reason of the shortage of essential supplies and installations to support military operations.[27]

And to this statement many naval logisticians would say "amen."

Lieutenant General Arnold's round of briefings of important people in Washington included the President, which probably played a real part in the President's memorandum to the "Eyes Only of the Joint Chiefs" on 24 October 1942, which in turn played such a vital part in the Guadalcanal victory. The President wrote:

> My anxiety about the Southwest Pacific is to make sure that every possible weapon gets into the area to hold Guadalcanal, and that having held in this crisis, munitions, planes and crews are on the way to take advantage of our success.

This memorandum came just 12–13 days after the Battle of Cape Esperance during which the surface combatant forces of the Japanese Navy and the United States Navy had traded punches and losses in the Iron Bottom Sound area, and just nine days after Admiral Nimitz was recording in his 15 October Daily Command Summary:

> It now appears that we are unable to control the sea area in the Guadalcanal Area. Thus our supply of the positions will only be done at great expense to us. The situation is not hopeless, but it is certainly critical.

---

[26] *Ibid.*, p. 348. Time late September 1942.
[27] C/S AAF to C/S USA, memorandum, 6 Oct. 1942. OPD 384. Modern Military Records Division, National Archives.

IMPROVING THE LOGISTICAL SUPPORT SYSTEM

It did not take the stress and strain of active operations very long after 9 August 1942 to demonstrate that the naval logistical organization in the South Pacific was inadequate both in concepts and in capabilities.

On 23 August, Rear Admiral Turner in a long six-page letter to Major General Vandegrift wrote:

> This whole Marine and Navy supply system down here seems to be bad, and I am trying to get them to reorganize it so it will function.[28]

By 30 August 1942, COMSOPAC accepted this estimate of the logistic situation and was convinced that:

> Our supply set up is not right under present conditions. For operations such as this, logistics and operations must go hand in hand.[29]

This last statement is a basic logistical principle and it actually took only three weeks to have it fully accepted by all echelons in SOPAC which could be some kind of a record. However, accepting the principle in a command 9,000 miles from Washington, and actually applying it to logistic support largely under the control of other naval commands or to logistic support on a Joint or Combined basis, were quite different things.

And the fact was that logistics had not gone hand in hand with operations; the WATCHTOWER Operation had gone ahead with logistical support hurrying along well behind. For logistical support in the South Pacific to flow evenly and adequately, the Navy needed Advanced Bases that were reasonably stocked. These did not exist on 7 August 1942.

The Advanced Base at Efate, 285 miles north-northeast of Noumea, started on 4 May 1942, had gotten a good head start on Noumea and a two months' head start on Espiritu Santo—but it was 700 miles from Guadalcanal. Efate was a small but going concern in early August 1942, the airfield having been used since 28 May 1942, and its underground aviation gas tanks shortly thereafter, but it could not begin to support WATCHTOWER all by itself.

The Advanced Base at Espiritu Santo, started on 8 July 1942, was in early August 1942, a small shadow of its later size, although commencing 30 July bombers operated from the first airstrip built there. It was not until 14 August, when with the approval of COMSOPAC, COMPHIBFORSO-

---
[28] RKT to Major General Vandegrift, letter, 23 Aug. 1942, p. 2.
[29] COMSOPAC to COMSERVRONSOPAC, 301110 Aug. 1942.

PAC directed the establishment of a branch of the First Marine Division Base Depot at Espiritu Santo, utilizing the services of the Quartermaster of the 2nd Marine Regiment, that the Marines on Guadalcanal could begin to plan on having at some long-distant date back-up logistical support only 500 to 600 miles away. It was not until LION One arrived on 10 February 1943 that major realistic steps were underway to make Espiritu Santo into a full-fledged Advanced Base Supply Depot.

From May through July 1942, Noumea functioned as a logistical staging area for Efate and Espiritu Santo after making a false start as a fuel depot for an Advanced Naval Base in late June 1942. Beginning in mid-August, it then grew like Topsy. On 11 November 1942 the Navy started major construction of an Advanced Base Construction Depot at Noumea and the necessary port development to permit the proper functioning of the nearly all-inclusive logistic support facilities projected.

In summary it can be said that, in mid-August 1942, logistic support of Guadalcanal from naval sources had to be provided through:

1. The established, but largely not built and not stocked, main Supply Base at Auckland, New Zealand, 1,825 miles to the south.
2. A small Advanced Air Base without supply support facilities at Efate in the New Hebrides, 700 miles southeast of Guadalcanal.
3. A considerably larger Advanced Naval Air Base at Espiritu Santo 560 miles southeast of Guadalcanal in the earliest throes of being built and stocked.
4. Direct shipment from continental United States.

Shortly after mid-August, on 20 August 1942 to be exact, CTF 62 (Rear Admiral Turner), an operational commander, acting with the oral authority of COMSOPAC, directed the establishment of Marine Advanced Supply Depots at Noumea and at Espiritu Santo even though this was an administrative act.[30]

No one denied that the rear area logistic effort for support of the fighting Marines was strenuous, not only by the amphibious command, but by all the logistic support forces of both the Services. Yet despite this effort, the tall tale carried back to the United States was that the Marines were hungry and that:

> For three months the Marines fought without substantial supplies or reenforcements and cursed the Navy.[31]

---

[30] CTF 62 to TF 62, letter, FE 25/NT6/A4–2/Ser 0056 of 20 Aug. 1942. Subj: Establishment of Marine Advanced Supply Depots.
[31] *Time Magazine*, 7 February 1944.

Logistics: August 1942–February 1943 417

The facts were a bit different at least in one respect.

On 15 August a week after landing, the Landing Force had 17 days of regular field rations available in addition to three days of Type C rations and 10 days of captured Japanese rations.[32]

By the second half of September, according to General Vandegrifts' report:

> During this period, six weeks after the initial attack, rations were adequate and three full meals were served daily. . . .[33]

Actually, then, it took only half of three months, until September 18th, before the Marines were placed on full U. S. rations. No Marine or Army soldier ever seemed to have quite enough logistic support during WATCHTOWER, but the major essentials of battle—adequate men, rations, aircraft, bullets, bombs and aviation gasoline—were always present on Guadalcanal although the reserve stocks rode the sine curve roller coaster with distressing speed.

Noumea was a logistical bottle neck. It lacked berthing space, storage space, unloading equipment and adequate numbers of skilled or unskilled longshoremen. The port was not organized on a Joint basis, and until this was done in November 1942, each Service competed at Noumea for use of each ingredient of logistical support.

Cargo ships to make the run to Guadalcanal were another bottleneck. This was true from Dog Day on, and to make matters worse, on 9 September 1942 the word came in from CINCPAC that COMINCH desired a regiment of experienced amphibious troops and a division of transports and cargo ships made ready for transfer to General MacArthur's command in the Southwest Pacific Area for his use in forthcoming offensive operations. This led to some soul searching at the SOPAC level, and when passed down to Rear Admiral Turner for a recommendation, he came up with a long-winded despatch which, in effect, said:

> No ships available now or later, and no Marines until 1 October, and then only the 8th Regiment of Marines, who aren't combat trained.[34]

At the same time, the Pacific Fleet was meeting an earlier call on its inadequate resources to provide amphibious ships for the TORCH November 1942 landings in North Africa. CINCPAC looked to the SOPAC Area for replacements. COMPHIBFORSOPAC pleaded his case noting that his

---

[32] COMGENFIRSTMARDIV Final Report on Guadalcanal Operation, Phase III, Annex C.
[33] (a) *Ibid.,* Phase V, Annex T; (b) Hough, Ludwig, Shaw, *Pearl Harbor to Guadalcanal* (Marines), pp. 311–13.
[34] COMPHIBFORSOPAC to COMSOPAC, 092300 Sep. 1942 and referenced despatches.

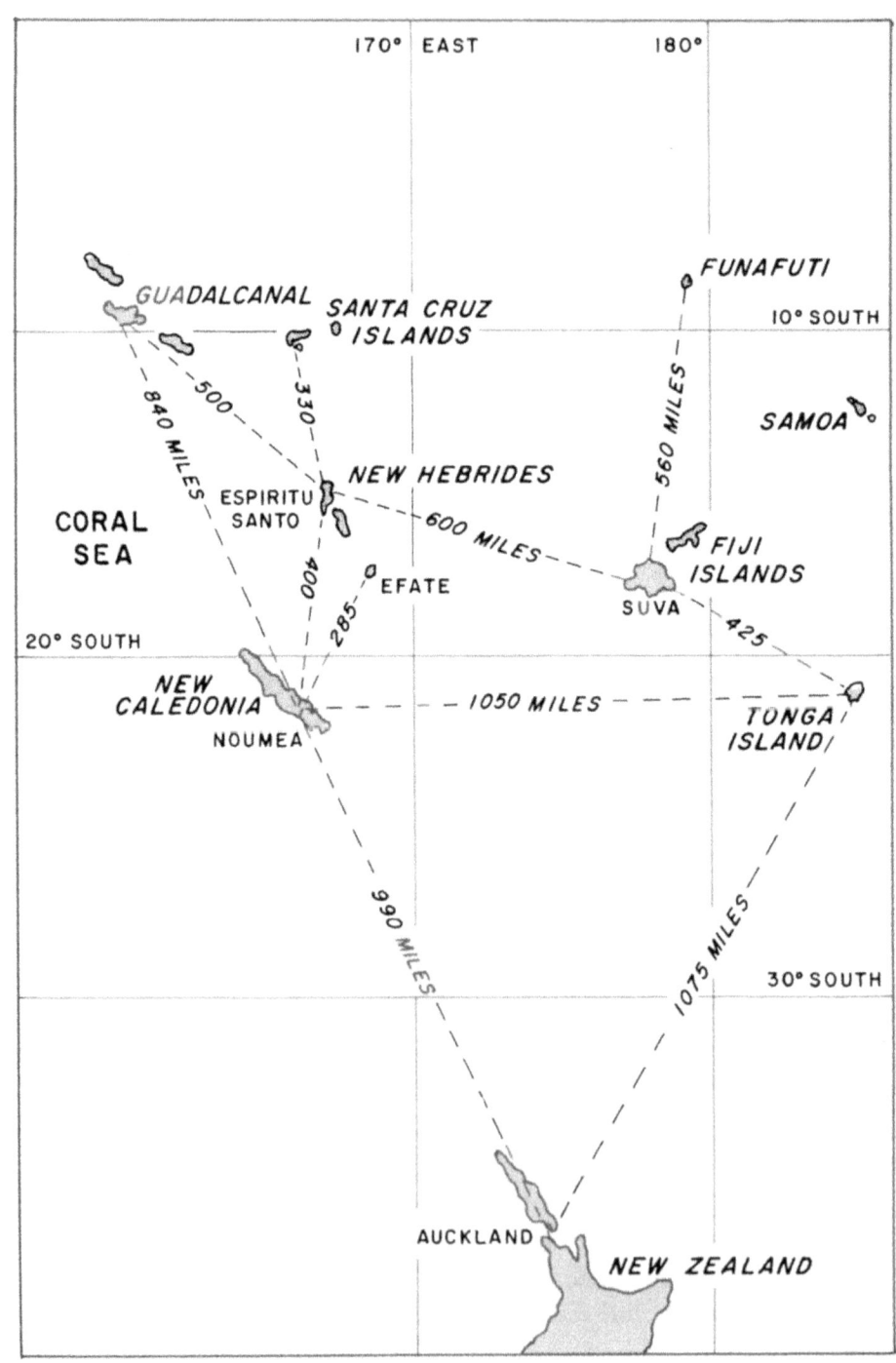

Guadalcanal supply lines.

cargo ships finally were down to four in number through losses from Japanese submarines and air attacks.[35]

The lack of unloading facilities at Guadalcanal Island was one more logistical problem. All logistic support had to be lightered to the beaches, where it was painfully and slowly unloaded, then reloaded on to some type of moving vehicle, and moved to the Marine or Army Supply dumps.

But the biggest logistic bottleneck, in this scribe's opinion, was the basic lack of know-how by the Navy concerning logistical support for a big operation six thousand miles away from a United States source of supply. The only consolation to be derived from this is that, had the logistical problem been fully appreciated, it is doubtful whether the WATCHTOWER Operation would have been undertaken when it was, which was just in time to obtain success.

When discussing the problem of logistic support on Guadalcanal, it is worth mentioning that both the United States Navy and the Japanese Navy had problems in providing it from their nearest advanced base area. To accomplish this support the United States Navy had about a 50 percent longer sea run than the Japanese Navy until, after long months, a supporting base was created and stocked at Espiritu Santo.

During the first week of the WATCHTOWER Operation, the Japanese Forces on Guadalcanal were without logistic support, since the Marines had captured the Japanese living and supply areas. The United States Navy provided the first of many, many contingents of men and supply support the early evening of 15 August—only six days after TF 62 had left—using four destroyer transports, carrying a total of 120 tons of aviation gasoline, lubricating oil, bombs, spare parts, and 120 aviation ground personnel mostly from CUB One.[36]

The Japanese Navy on the same day provided supplies in woven baskets to both the United States Marines and to the Japanese, the Marines getting four out of six air drops. It was the next day before the Japanese landed 200 troops and their logistic support from a single destroyer.

Broad scale but irregular logistic support for the Marines commenced

---

[35] (a) COMSOPAC to COMPHIBFORSOPAC 082140 Sep. 1942 and related despatches; (b) COMINCH, letter, FF1/A3-1, Ser 001006 of 18 Sep. 1942; COMINCH 261302 Sep. 1942; CINCPAC 120635 Nov. 1942; (c) COMPHIBFORSOPAC, letter, A3-1 Ser 00394 of 17 Nov. 1942, subj: Proposed return to Pacific Coast of AP's and AK's temporarily assigned the South Pacific Force.

[36] (a) COMAIRSOPAC to COMGENGUADALCANAL, 130623 Aug. 1942; (b) RDO Tulagi to RDO Auckland, 150459 Aug. 1942; (c) COMSOPAC to CINCPAC, 231301 Aug. 1942.

when the store ships *Albena* (AK-26) and *Formalhaut* (AK-22), the *McFarland* (AVD-14) loaded with aviation gasoline drums, and six APDs loaded with rations arrived at Guadalcanal on 21-22 August 1942, and landed over 2,000 tons of logistic support including 200 tons of rations, some personnel of the 2nd Marine Regiment, and their equipment and supplies.

During October 1942 logistic support ships were unloading at Guadalcanal-Tulagi on 13 days of the month. By December there were one or more support ships unloading on 31 days of the 31-day month. But during the last 20 days of August, the Marines had seen this pleasant sight only on six days.

It is a logistic truism that there is nearly always a conflict between those who ship and those who ask for the shipment, and this was re-emphasized at Guadalcanal.

In war, logistics is always a worry factor. Many times it is the chief worry factor and at times it is the only worry factor. Quotes from Rear Admiral Turner's letters support this truth.

In a letter to Captain W. G. Greenman in early November dealing with the logistic situation, Rear Admiral Turner wrote:

> All the Amphibious Force ships, all my staff, and I myself are working our hearts out to keep you going, and to try to get men and supplies to you. One of our troubles is to get decisions on matters I do not have under my control, and to get material to you which is available, but for which we have no transportation.[37]

In a letter to Major General Vandegrift:

> Your situation as regards food, fuel, and ammunition as you well know, gives me the greatest anxiety. This is still a hand-to-mouth existence. By now, I had hoped that you would have some reasonable reserves. However, the enemy has held up our deliveries so continuously that our cash-in-bank is very low. You can rest assured that every ship I can get my hands on will be used to relieve this critical situation.[38]

No longer than ten days after arrival at Noumea, recommendations for improvement in the logistic area of amphibious operations were sought from all commands in TF 62, and a proposed reorganization of the Shore Party and Beach Party drafted by the Staff of CTF 62 was forwarded for comment by the amphibians. It was on the basis of the recommendations

---
[37] RKT to Captain W. G. Greenman, letter, 7 Nov. 1942.
[38] RKT to General Vandegrift, letter, 16 Nov. 1942.

received from this letter that Commander Amphibious Forces SOPAC made proposals for revision in the Amphibian Bible, FTP 167.[39]

When Vice Admiral Halsey made the decision, shortly after assuming command of SOPAC, to shift the building up of a Main Fleet Base in the South Pacific from Auckland, New Zealand, to Noumea, New Caledonia, he accomplished more in cutting the Gordian Knot of the SOPAC logistical problem, than any of the many of hundreds of other actions taken for this purpose. His recommendation to this end went forward on 21 October 1942.[40] While negotiations to obtain buildings and area for this purpose had to be carried out with the Free French via General De Gaulle in London who controlled New Caledonia, the approval for the move was not too long in arriving.

On 8 November 1942, SOPAC Headquarters was established ashore, and Noumea commenced striving to fulfill the logistical mission and functions previously assigned to Auckland.

Espiritu Santo and Efate in the New Hebrides were rapidly built up as Advanced Bases and depots of material. An Advance Base Construction Depot was established at Noumea. By December 1942, Noumea was becoming a Main Fleet Base in the South Pacific in more than name. Support ships were daily landing the requirements of the Army and Marines at Guadalcanal, and the troops were eating some refrigerated food. Logistical support was largely in hand.[41]

BUILDING UP THE GUADALCANAL BASE

The saga of the building of the Guadalcanal-Tulagi base area has yet to be written, but this base area played a vital role in the logistic support furnished by COMPHIBFORSOPAC to the Marines and Army troops on Guadalcanal and to the later operations in the middle and upper Solomon Islands. So, because of the importance of bases in connection with amphibious operations, the story of its early trials and tribulations should be told in some detail.

Plans for an Advanced Naval Base in the Tulagi-Guadalcanal area to

---

[39] (a) CTF 62, letter, FE 25/A16/Ser 029 of 23 Aug. 1942 and replies thereto from transports and cargo ships and commands; (b) COMSOPAC, letter, A16-3/(00) Ser 00936 of 4 Dec. 1942; (c) TU 66.3 Op Orders J-1, K-1, K-2, H-1, incorporating trial revisions.

[40] COMSOPAC to CINCPAC, 210517 Oct. 1942.

[41] FIRSTMARDIV Final Report on Guadalcanal Operations, Phase V, Annex T, p. 2.

contain units to meet aviation, hospital, and minor supply needs were part and parcel of the short hectic advance planning for WATCHTOWER.[42]

Way back on 15 January 1942, when Rear Admiral Turner was in the War Plans Division, he had initiated a plan calling for the establishment of Advanced Base units to build and operate four Main Fleet bases (LIONs) and 12 secondary bases (CUBs).[43]

Despite this advance planning, neither COMSOPAC nor COMPHIBFORSOPAC mentioned a prospective Advanced Naval Base at Guadalcanal-Tulagi in their WATCHTOWER Operation Orders. COMSOPAC's Op Order had no section on logistics. COMPHIBFORSOPAC Op Order had a Logistic Section, but did not include any information about an Advanced Base. The nearest mention was when COMPHIBFORSOPAC provided for a Naval Local Defense Force with a lieutenant commander of the Coast Guard in command at a headquarters ashore. Lieutenant Commander D. H. Dexter, USCG, actually did go ashore with the Marines, but his command included only picket boats (landing craft), a harbor signal station and a small landing craft repair crew.

COMSOPAC rectified the omission in his Operation Order on the day after the initial landings by directing:

> For construction and administration and operation of Advance Air Base Guadalcanal-Tulagi, COMAMPHIBFORSOPAC initially in charge.[44]

This created the certainty that Rear Admiral Turner would step on the toes of the Marines.

CUB One, containing the essential units from which an Advanced Base could be built, left San Francisco on the day before Rear Admiral Turner left Pearl Harbor. Its orders were to report to Commander South Pacific and its destination was New Caledonia, but enroute the four ships carrying CUB One were diverted to Espiritu Santo Island in the New Hebrides.

According to the Chief of Naval Operations' directive:

> CUB bases are to be equipped to care for the logistic support of a small Task Group of Light Forces with no repair facilities on shore. Aviation repair, operation and maintenance facilities for 105 planes are included. [Personnel requirements are 138 officers and 3,200 men, of which 59 officers and 1,528 men are in the aviation service unit].[45]

---

[42] CINCPAC Basic Supporting Plan for Advanced Air Bases Santa Cruz Island and Tulagi-Guadalcanal, Ser 09910 of 8 Jul. 1942.
[43] Ballentine, p. 57.
[44] COMSOPAC to COMPHIBFORSOPAC, 080826 Aug. 1942.
[45] CNO letter, Ser 018753 of 25 Aug. 1942, subj: LION and CUB bases.

Commander James P. Compton (1916), who had served with Vice Admiral Ghormley in the Naval Observer Unit in London, England, was the Commanding Officer of CUB One. He took command on 8 July 1942 at Moffett Field in California, the day the unit sailed for the South Pacific in two transports and two merchant ships via Pago Pago, Samoa. It arrived at Espiritu Santo on 11 August 1942.

When he departed San Francisco, Commander Compton had no knowledge that the WATCHTOWER Operation was immediately pending. He had been shown, but did not have a copy of an order from CNO directing that CUB One and CUB 13 (just being formed up) were to build three bases in the South Pacific, including one on the Santa Cruz Islands at Ndeni.[46]

Compton's story runs as follows:

> Upon arrival at BUTTON [Espiritu Santo] I reported by despatch to COMSOPAC. No immediate orders from him. After I had been there a couple of days, I was ordered by COMSOPAC to fly to Noumea. He was aboard ship. I talked to Ghormley and his C/S Callaghan and to Colonel Peck on the Staff. I was told the base was to be built at Guadalcanal-Tulagi— no instructions as to when to go forward. . . . I did not even know that I was to work for Kelly Turner. He was in the harbor when I was there, about 14–15 August, and had I known I was to work for him, I would have gone to see him. I did not then or later receive any orders to report to COMPHIBFORSOPAC. I did not know anything about Savo happening and I was not told when I got back to Espiritu Santo.
>
> I assumed that I was sent out with the CUB-One equipment so as to help any way I could in the South Pacific. I had some aviation equipment so I landed gasoline trucks etc., to help out at BUTTON, plus gasoline drums. My arrival at Espiritu Santo resembled the arrival of Santa Claus on a playground with a full bag. The staff of General Rose [commanding at Espiritu Santo] assembled in my tent daily to determine the items they wanted.
>
> The primary purpose of CUB One, as I understood it, was to establish air bases and supporting facilities. This was in accordance with CINCPAC's supporting plan, which was about the one piece of official paper I received upon arrival at BUTTON. First people in CUB One to go to Guadalcanal—an Ensign George Washington Polk—two Seabee warrant officers and a 100 plus men—arrived on 15 August 1942.
>
> After a short time in Espiritu Santo (observing the complete lack of personnel at the Air Base there from which Colonel Saunders' B-17s were operating), I originated a despatch to CNO recommending that the full aviation complement of CUB One be sent as soon as possible. Apparently this caused consternation in OPNAV because despatches received indicated that to pro-

---

[46] (a) Interview with Captain James P. Compton, 1 Feb. 1962; Memorandum from Captain Compton, 17 Jun. 1969. Hereafter Compton; (b) COMSOPAC, 022310 Aug. 1942.

vide CUB One with the aviation personnel set up in the allowance list would have required stripping personnel from all available sources. It was the first indication to me that I had command of a paper tiger.

At about this time a radio order from COMSOPAC was received to establish a base at Espiritu Santo. COMCUBONE was an action addressee.

I got a despatch from Kelly Turner to go up to Guadalcanal on the fast transports—Hugh Hadley's ships [Transport Division 12]. I gave him machine guns from CUB One to mount on his ships. I took some doctors . . . communicators and pay clerk and the CO of Seabee Battalion Six [Lieutenant Commander Paul Blundon (CEC)USNR]. On 27 August 1942, I embarked for Guadalcanal and arrived 29 August. . . . My people were scared. Everybody was scared. I set up my headquarters near Henderson Field where the earlier elements of CUB One had been established.

We moved our camp after the shelling of the airfield, toward the beach. [Later to be at Lever Brothers plantation house on the coastal lagoon between Lunga Point and Kukum.]

The Seabees had most of their equipment on a civilian ship, the *Santa Ana*, a Grace Line Ship. I sent a despatch to Kelly Turner to have the *SS Santa Ana*, the ship I thought best suited for the Guadalcanal situation, to come to Guadalcanal but he thought no civilian manned ships should go up at that time.

The Seabees aided the building and repair work at Henderson Field and my aviation personnel acted as ground crews and fueled the planes. Aviation gas drum storage records were kept and with this information, I was the only one in Guadalcanal that really knew [the amount of] gasoline available.

My unit gradually took over Island Communications. We, plus Dexter's original outfit, operated landing craft, housed units such as Black Cats, transients, and maintained a base at Tulagi.

My job personally as I saw it when I first arrived was to be useful around the airfield. The overriding mission was the defense of CACTUS [Guadalcanal].[47]

Rear Admiral Turner expected the skipper of CUB One to start building an Advanced Naval Base as soon as possible and this required him to develop a specific plan for the Guadalcanal-Tulagi area soon after his arrival.

On 23 August 1942 Rear Admiral Turner wrote to Major General Vandegrift:

Commander Compton, who is the Commanding Officer of CUB One, will probably move into CACTUS within a few days on the *William Ward Burrows* [AP-6]. If you and he will plan the development which is needed there, and send out your recommendations, we will do the best we can to

---

[47] (a) Compton; (b) C/S COMPHIBFORSOPAC to RKT, Memorandum of 26 Aug. 1942.

support your plans. Just as soon as possible, I will fly in to see you in order to be able better to help you out. Up to the present I have not been able to come, since we have all been working night and day to get things moving toward you and I have thought it better for me to stay here in charge.[48]

However, Commander Compton's written orders from CINCPAC centered around an air base, and Compton had landed during a period when the airfield had no steel matting and hence was vulnerable to rain, as well as to bombing and shelling. Keeping the airstrip in shape and building up communications took Compton's time. Although requested by despatch on a number of occasions and by letter on 15 September, his first plan for development of an Advanced Naval Base in the Guadalcanal-Tulagi area went forward about 28 September 1942.[49] In a subsequent letter Commander Compton stated:

> My main difficulty has been the lack of qualified officers to whom I could turn over details so that I would be free to proceed with more general plans.[50]

Captain Compton's present remembrance is supported by the few official documents located. On 27 September 1942, as Commanding Officer of CUB One, he wrote to COMAIRSOPAC:

> I have, in the employment of CUB One, endeavored to carry out the spirit of CINCPAC serial 09910 [supporting plan] for which CUB One and Thirteen were sent out. This involved the construction, operation, administration and maintenance of a land plane base at CACTUS, seaplane base at RINGBOLT; radio, harbor defense, hospital and other facilities. I consider that still my mission.[51]

His remembrance of his aspects of the logistic support problem on Guadalcanal was:

> The basic difference between Kelly Turner and me was: Why were the CUBS in SOPAC—to build bases or to support troops?[52]

Rear Admiral Turner, upset by the supply support difficulties of the first month of improvised logistic support of the Marines and the lack of any real start toward the development of bases in the Guadalcanal-Tulagi area, became convinced in early September 1942, that there had to be a Flag officer whose primary duty was the planning, the development, and the perform-

---
[48] RKT to AAV, letter, 23 Aug. 1942.
[49] (a) C/S COMPHIBFORSOPAC to RKT, memorandum of 26 Aug. 1942; (b) COMSOPAC, despatches 072206, 231326 Sep. 1943; (c) COMPHIBFORSOPAC to COMADVBASE CACTUS-RINGBOLT, letter, 15 Sep. 1942.
[50] JPC to RKT, letter, 8 Oct. 1942.
[51] COMCUBO to COMAIRSOPAC, letter, 27 Sep. 1942.
[52] Compton.

ance of the Advanced Naval Bases of the forward areas in the South Pacific. This officer would be a subordinate to the officer who had these tasks in addition to many other logistic tasks for the whole SOPAC area, the Commander Service Squadron, South Pacific Force.

Besides the pre-WATCHTOWER bases of SOPAC started in the Society, Samoan, Fiji and Tonga Islands, there were the newer Advanced Naval Bases at Efate and Espiritu Santo in the New Hebrides and now bases at Tulagi and Guadalcanal physically separated but working together in the Southern Solomons. In early September 1942, Commander Service Squadron SOPACFOR, Rear Admiral Calvin H. Cobb (1911), had just been given the over-all task of building up and supporting all bases in the SOPAC Area. Vigorous discussion in Noumea also centered around the need to stop building a major base way down south in Auckland and to start to build up a main base at Noumea.[53]

Rear Admiral Turner also became convinced that there should be established an Advanced Naval Base at Guadalcanal-Tulagi, not just an Advanced Air Base, and that an officer with some seniority should be ordered to it.

On 5 September 1942, he committed his views to paper,[54] including recommendations that Commander James P. Compton, U. S. Navy, the Commanding Officer of CUB One, be ordered as Commander Advance Bases CACTUS-RINGBOLT (Guadalcanal-Tulagi) and that an officer of appropriate rank be ordered to command each of the two bases in this base complex. Both of these recommendations were carried into effect by COMSOPAC, Commander Compton being ordered as Commander Advanced Bases CACTUS-RINGBOLT on 11 September 1942 and to the command of all Naval Activities in the area on 13 September 1942. It was more than another two months, however, before Commander H. L. Maples (1917) arrived, in December 1942, to command Naval Base, Lunga, which by May 1943 grew into the Advanced Naval Base—Guadalcanal.

In early August 1942 when Lieutenant Commander D. H. Dexter of the Coast Guard went ashore at Guadalcanal to head up the Local Defense Force, and become Port Director, Guadalcanal, Lieutenant R. W. Pinger, D-V, USNR, was ordered to take charge of the Gavutu-Tulagi Sub Base Local Defense Force.[55] Dexter was Port Director Tulagi-Gavutu. Under the principle of unity of command, he reported to Major General Vandegrift

---

[53] Staff Interviews.
[54] COMPHIBFORSOPAC to COMSOPAC, letter, Ser 00116 of 5 Sep. 1942.
[55] CTF 62, letters, P16–4/00, Ser 0027 of 5 Aug. 1942; and P16–4/00, Ser 0023 of 5 Aug. 1942, subj: Lieutenant Pinger's orders to the Local Defense Force, Sub-Area.

for duty. This sound principle was extended to Gavutu-Tulagi on 28 October 1942 when Pinger's relief, Lieutenant Commander John C. Alderman (1928), was given orders to report to Brigadier General William H. Rupertus, USMC, the senior officer present on Tulagi. On 27 November 1942, Commander William G. Fewell (1921) took over the Advanced Base at Tulagi from Alderman and only a month later, on 26 December 1942, he, in turn, was relieved by Commander Oliver O. Kessing (1914), soon to be promoted to captain.

Thus at the Gavutu-Tulagi Base, there were four different guiding influences in less than five months. At Guadalcanal, where the commander of the two bases in the area had his headquarters, there were three changes of command at this level in the same period. There were also three changes at the Lunga Base command level since the first two over-all commanders also commanded what in effect was the Lunga Base.

It was two months more and then after another plea from COMSOPAC that "planning and development bases this area is a major problem," before Captain Worrall R. Carter (1908) was ordered as Commander Naval Bases, South Pacific Force, and only after COMINCH had added his approval to the creation of this echelon of command. In January 1943, Captain Carter issued a Basic Organization of Naval Bases SOPAC.[56]

Rear Admiral Turner proceeded by air on 11 September to Guadalcanal, together with Rear Admiral McCain (COMAIRSOPAC) and the Commanding Officer 7th Marine Regiment and members of their staffs. The group returned to Espiritu Santo on 13 September and CTF 62 departed by transport on 14 September for Guadalcanal with the 7th Marine Regiment.

Captain Compton recalled:

> In September, Turner came to Guadalcanal. I was asked to have dinner by General Vandegrift together with General Geiger, Jock McCain and Colonel Wood. Kelly broke out a bottle of bourbon. During the evening General Vandegrift suggested that Turner was giving me a hard time. Kelly said:
> 'If I kick him around a bit, he will do a better job.'
> The second night Kelly was on Guadalcanal we took a big pasting. That morning we had a big bombing. Our radio shack was hit. Kelly drove up in a jeep. I tried to explain that I was taking care of things like that [getting the communications flowing again].[57]

An examination of the Marines' log of events at Guadalcanal shows that

---

[56] (a) COMSOPAC 072206 Sep., 061345 Nov. 1942; (b) COMGENCACTUS, letter, 13 Sep. 1942; (c) CNO, OP-30-B3, letter Ser 0291930 of 7 Nov. 1943, 1942 and references.
[57] Compton.

a 42-plane Japanese air strike occurred at 1150, 12 September, and put the main radio receivers on Guadalcanal out of commission for 32 hours. The night of 12 September, Guadalcanal was shelled by a Japanese light cruiser and three destroyers, and the first probing actions of the Battle of the Ridge occurred. On the 13th of September, Japanese planes made passes at Henderson Field just before and after Rear Admiral Turner departed Guadalcanal.

CUB ONE MOVES FORWARD SLOWLY

On 29 August, 357 officers and men of the Sixth Naval Construction Battalion (part of CUB One) embarked in the cargo ship *Betelgeuse* for Guadalcanal. This meant that two weeks after the initial landings about 480 personnel of CUB One had been started forward.

On 28 September 1942, in a letter to Major General Vandegrift, Rear Admiral Turner wrote in regard to preparing Guadalcanal as "our Major invasion base:"

> I am not satisfied with the number of men Compton has taken in there. He should have all of the CUB One and the Sixth Construction personnel, except a very small contingent at BUTTON [Espiritu Santo, New Hebrides] to act as a forwarding agency.[58]

On 30 September 1942, Commander Compton reported that 47 officers and 878 men of CUB One were still in Espiritu Santo, and he furnished a list of the tasks they were engaged in.[59] On 5 August 1942, CUB One had reported a strength of 139 officers and 1,828 men.

On 24 October 1942, Rear Admiral Turner sent to COMSOPAC an eight-page letter dealing with the "Development of Advanced Naval Base Solomons." This letter enclosed a four-page undated letter originated by Commander Compton as Commander Advanced Naval Base CACTUS-RINGBOLT, dealing with the organization and future development of the base area for which he was then primarily responsible. From its contents, it is believed this letter was originated about 28 September 1942.[60]

As background for several of the recommendations set forth therein by

---

[58] RKT to AAG, letter, 28 Sep. 1942.
[59] (a) AC/S to CTF 62, memorandum, 27 Aug. 1942; (b) COMADBASE CACTUS-RINGBOLT to COMAIRSOPAC and COMPHIBFORSOPAC, letters of 27 and 30 Sep. 1942.
[60] COMPHIBFORSOPAC to COMSOPAC, letter, FE25/A3–1/0032 24 Oct. 1942, with enclosure from COMADVBASE CACTUS, no ser, undated.

Rear Admiral Turner, it is pointed out that in his letter of about 28 September 1942 Commander Compton had stated:

> Much of CUB One material is already installed at BUTTON [Espiritu Santo, New Hebrides]. . . . Unless material of CUB 13 at WHITE POPPY [Noumea, New Caledonia] is carefully preserved for such use it will be difficult if not impossible to properly fit out RINGBOLT [Tulagi].[61]

Commander Compton also stated that his activities on Guadalcanal were divided into two classes:

 a. Services and operations immediately required by the current tactical situation.
 b. Development of naval facilities as required by CINCPAC Secret Serial 09910 of 8 July 1942.

In other words, Commander Compton, for what he believed made very good reasons, still was not moving towards the building of an Advanced Naval Base, but rather toward an Advanced Air Base.

In his letter of 24 October, COMPHIBFORSOPAC recommended that a new title, Commander Advanced Naval Bases, Solomons, be given to Commander Compton and that he be provided with a six-man staff. COMSOPAC agreed that a new title was desirable but decided that the new title should be Commander Naval Bases, Forward Area. This got away from the limited concept of an Air Base.

COMPHIBFORSOPAC felt that leaving approximately 40 percent of the total number of officers and men in CUB One at Espiritu Santo for over two months was a diversion of effort from the main task at hand. In his mind, Commander Compton had not acquired a clear idea of the very large naval base needed at Guadalcanal-Tulagi to serve for the future assembling of large invasion forces and their logistic support which would be needed to move into the Middle and Upper Solomons. He decided that a new and more senior officer was needed for the job.[62]

While Rear Admiral Turner was unhappy with results achieved up to that time, it is most evident that Commander Compton well pleased his Marine Seniors. The Commanding General, First Marine Air Wing, Brigadier General Roy S. Geiger, who arrived on Guadalcanal on 3 September 1942, wrote of Captain Compton:

> His wholehearted cooperation in placing all the facilities of his command at

---
[61] *Ibid.*
[62] Turner.

the disposal of the Commanding General, First Marine Air Wing aided the aviation units in repelling air and surface attacks.

And Major General Vandegrift wrote:

> You took over immediately the multiplicity of duties connected with the preparation and maintenance of the Naval and Air facilities at this station. These duties you have discharged in an outstanding manner. By your unceasing efforts, complete cooperation and willingness, you have made an invaluable contribution to the success of operations in this area.

In early November 1942, Rear Admiral Turner applied to COMSOPAC for the services of Captain W. G. Greenman (1912), the Captain of the ill-fated *Astoria* (sunk at Savo Island) who was still in the SOPAC area. COMSOPAC ordered Captain Greenman as Commander Naval Bases, Forward Area, and Commander Compton as his Chief Staff Officer.

Rear Admiral Turner sat down and wrote Captain Greenman a long letter:

> Congratulations on being assigned to your new job. You may or may not like it—so you should know that I recommended you for it, worked like hell before we got you, and am now trying to have you made a Flag officer so you have appropriate rank as Commander Advanced Naval Base, CACTUS-RINGBOLT. 'Advanced Naval Bases Solomons' does not seem to be acceptable to the boss, nor does 'Commander Naval Activities, Solomons' fit the bill. . . .
>
> I personally drafted the plan for the development of the SOLOMON base . . . because I was unable to get a satisfactory program from Compton, and not even any member of my staff really knew the story.[63]

Captain Greenman lasted but a month (7 November–12 December 1942) as he developed pneumonia and had to be shipped back to Pearl Harbor. Personal letters indicated that Captain Greenman was trying hard to get officers of appropriate seniority ordered in as Commanding Officers RINGBOLT and CACTUS.

The next over-all commander of these two Advanced Bases started out as Commander Advanced Naval Base CACTUS, but soon had a new title—Commander Naval Bases Solomons. He was Captain Thomas M. Shock (1913), who well satisfied his Boss and the Army who awarded him a Distinguished Service Medal, but in the spring of 1943, after serving from 12 December 1942 to 11 May 1943, he had to be invalided home.[64]

---

[63] RKT to Captain W. G. Greenman, letter, 7 Nov. 1942.
[64] (a) Commander Naval Bases South Solomons Sub-Area, *Command History*, p. 79; (b) Personal letters COMSOPAC to CINCPAC.

Your interesting letter of December twentieth has been received. It is just the kind of letter I would have expected you to write, and if any proof were needed, proves that we now have the right man in the very difficult position of Commander Advanced Naval Base, CACTUS.[65]

Captain William M. Quigley (1911), the next Commander Naval Bases, Solomons, did not arrive until 12 May 1943, and eventually received the promotion to Commodore which had been urged but never approved for his predecessors. Under his able command, the Naval Bases of the Southern Solomons further developed and provided highly effective support, both operational and logistic, for the New Georgia Campaign.[66]

Guadalcanal was a tough area for the health of oldsters. Captain Greenman was 54, and Captain Shock, 50. Commander Compton was only a bit younger, at 47.

In comparison with the speed and efficiency with which the Navy built many other Advanced Bases during its sweep up the Solomons and across the Pacific, it cannot be denied that the building of the CACTUS-RINGBOLT Base suffers badly. In second guessing the reasons for the slowness with which the Advanced Base CACTUS-RINGBOLT took shape, the four most apparent reasons are:

1. There was no adequate Base Plan developed by higher echelons of command prior to the assault landing.
2. The Base Area was under Japanese gunfire or air attack a far greater number of times during the first four months of building than other bases. There was a definite lack of appreciation by the officer in over-all charge, Rear Admiral Turner, of the part that defensive tasks were playing in absorbing the time and energies of the Base Commander.
3. The lack of a clear mission at the Base Commander's level, with the immediate senior in command (Major General Vandegrift) being primarily concerned with work which would contribute promptly or directly to his offensive or defensive potentialities, and the next senior in the chain of command (Rear Admiral Turner) keeping a constant eye to the future use of the Base.
4. A large amount of fuzziness in command lines with five seniors (COMSOPAC, COMGENFIRSTMARDIV, COMAIRSOPAC,

---

[65] RKT to Captain T. M. Shock, letter, 24 Dec. 1942.
[66] South Solomons Sub-Area, *Command History*.

COMPHIBFORSOPAC, COMSERONSOPAC) all sending despatches and letters direct to the Base Commander.

Rear Admiral Turner, far from seeking to enlarge his area of responsibility, or believing in the desirability of his being the appropriate responsible senior, or enjoying his responsibility to build up the Advanced Base at Guadalcanal-Tulagi, was anxious to transfer the responsibility to a more appropriate commander. Less than a month after he had been handed the hot potato, he felt strongly enough in the matter to seek a change.

On 5 September 1942, COMPHIBFORSOPAC recommended to his immediate seniors

> that Commander Amphibious Force South Pacific be relieved of his present responsibilities in connection with the upbuilding of this base, at a time deemed appropriate by the Commander South Pacific Force; and that the administration of the base be handled in a manner similar to the administration of the other Naval Advanced Bases in the Pacific Ocean.[67]

OPINIONS ON THE COURSE OF THE LOGISTIC DIFFICULTIES

After Vice Admiral Ghormley had left his SOPAC command, and had time to consider the broader aspects of his duty in that area, he wrote that he believed that there was in the Navy Department

> a marked failure in appreciation of the time element necessary for transportation to the South Pacific, for base construction and for airfield construction.[68]

Vice Admiral Halsey soon learned, as he told his seniors in a message of November 1942:

> Planning and development bases this area is a major problem.[69]

In June 1943, when Major General Vandegrift moved up to command of the Amphibious Corps South Pacific with Headquarters in Noumea, he opined:

> My biggest problem concerned supply, a field in which, at this point, the Navy did not excel.[70]

A fighting Marine and a keen observer who served throughout this period of logistic difficulties in the Southern Solomons thought that:

---

[67] COMPHIBFORSOPAC to COMSOPAC, letter, Ser 00116 of 5 Sep. 1942.
[68] Ghormley manuscript, p. 13.
[69] COMSOPAC, 061345 Nov. 1942.
[70] Vandegrift, p. 221. Reprinted from *Once a Marine* with permission of W.W. Norton & Co., Inc.

The guilty parties were behind snug desks in their Department in Washington.[71]

Commodore Peyton, the Chief of Staff TF 62, observed:

> The Navy was unprepared logistically to conduct operations at the end of a 6,000 mile pipe line. The logistic pipe line existed, but it was largely empty. Great effort was devoted to such commonplace items as oil and ammunition. To illustrate—we never were really full of fuel for the Guadalcanal Operation. We were supposed to fill up at the Fijis, but there wasn't enough fuel for all ships to fill full. We were supposed to top off at Efate. There was no fuel there.[72]

From the safe distance of 27 years, it may be pointed out that none of the operation orders dealing with WATCHTOWER issued by naval command echelons prior to the landing provided for scheduled or automatic resupply over the first 30 to 60 days of the operation. These orders contained no particular details regarding the follow-up movements for the tremendous logistic support which would be involved in building an Advanced Air Base, or the other essential facilities of a small Naval Operating Base at an overseas location. CINCPAC issued his orders for building the Advanced Air Base by CUB One on 8 July 1942 but the Commanding Officer of CUB One did not receive a copy of it until after the landings of 7 August 1942. This is logistics at its very worst, when the support forces are a month late in getting the word about the operations.

That the Line of the Navy, even those at the top echelon, learned fast about logistics is evidenced by this testimony of its senior officer in 1944:

> This war has been variously termed a war of production and a war of machines. Whatever else it is, so far as the United States is concerned, it is a war of logistics . . . The profound effect of logistics problems on our strategic decision are not likely to have full significance to those who did not have to traverse the tremendous distances in the Pacific.[73]

That the Marines occasionally contributed to the logistics problem at Guadalcanal is indicated by the following extract from an official report dated Christmas Day 1942 and covering the support operation of 17–18 December 1942:

> The straw that nearly tipped the balance was the box of cargo that broke

---

[71] Griffith, p. 138.

[72] Interview with Commodore Thomas G. Peyton, USN (Ret.), 22 May 1961. Hereafter Peyton.

[73] Admiral Ernest J. King to SECNAV, 23 Apr. 1944.

open in #3 hold and displayed the contents as tennis rackets and tennis balls. Of all items to waste ship space on in transport to CACTUS, this seems to be near the top.[74]

---

[74] Commander Transport Division Eight (Captain George B. Ashe) Report of Operations, 17–18 Dec. 1942.

CHAPTER XII

HUDDLE Slowly Scuttled

SANTA CRUZ ISLANDS (HUDDLE)

One of the factors influencing the 'when' and 'where to' United States forces would move from Guadalcanal, was the Santa Cruz Island operation, code named HUDDLE.

It is customary these days to beat Admiral Turner about the head because he did not chuck the HUDDLE Operation the day the Marines ran into their first real opposition on Tulagi—Guadalcanal. These critics blame him for not committing, with finality, the 2nd Marine Regiment resources, designated for occupying and defending Ndeni in the Santa Cruz Islands, to augment those on Guadalcanal.

His reasons for delaying sending off a recommendation to scuttle HUDDLE to his many seniors, all the way up to the Joint Chiefs of Staff, all of whom had directed the occupation and defense of the Santa Cruz Islands, were three in number. Rear Admiral Turner believed that:

1. The Japanese reaction to the loss of the lower Solomons as a base for air reconnaissance of the Coral Sea and air attacks on New Caledonia, could well be a try at outflanking the lower Solomons, and reducing their usefulness in United States hands by a seizure of the Santa Cruz Islands, and the building of airfields thereon. In other words, the Santa Cruz Islands offered an alternative route to the New Hebrides and New Caledonia which should be denied to the offensive-minded Japanese. It was learned from the natives that the Japanese had built a temporary air base on the Santa Cruz Islands and conducted a war game therefrom in 1940.[1]

2. In the early days of the WATCHTOWER Operation a despatch had come in from COMSOPAC on 28 July 1942 indicating that from cryptographic sources, it had been learned that the Japanese were planning to commence an operation on 29 July from the New Britain Area. Rear Admiral Turner thought that whatever objective this Japanese operation had been planned for, that it might well be diverted to the Santa Cruz Islands to balance off, in Japanese eyes, the American movements into the Southern Solomons.

---
[1] *See* CO 2nd Marines to COMSOPAC 140148 Aug. 1942.

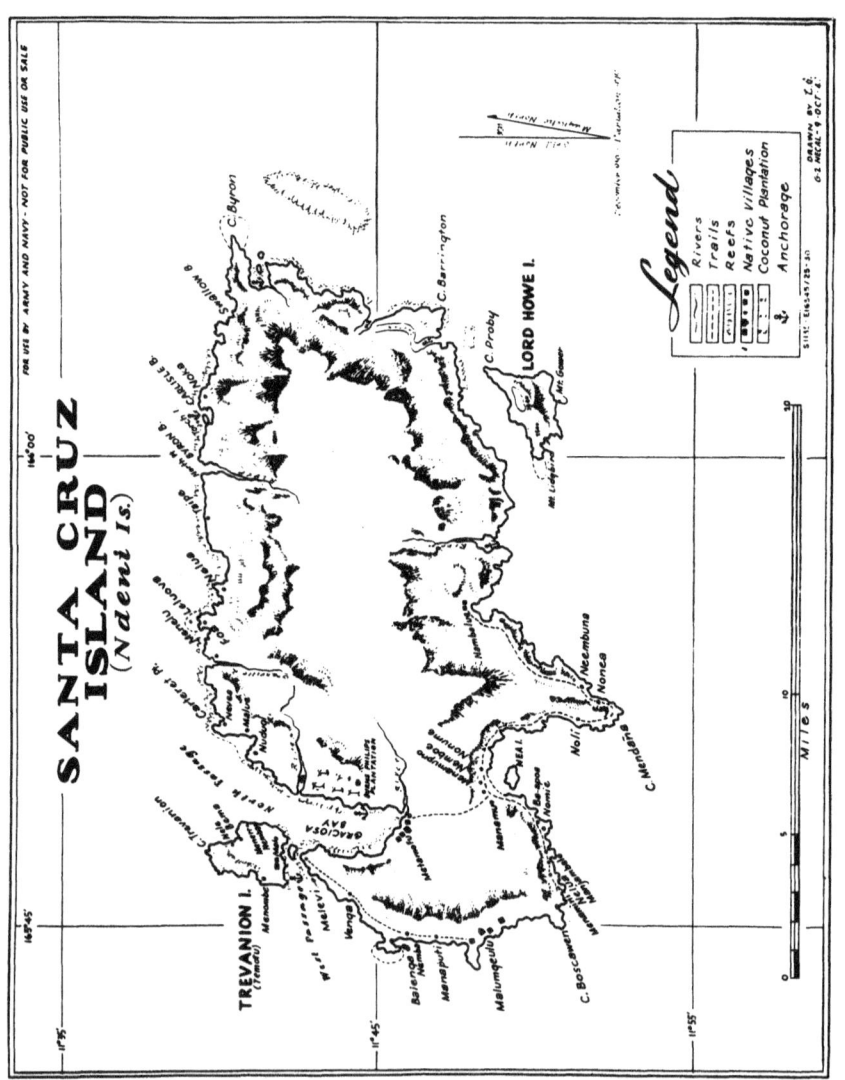

Santa Cruz and Trevanion Islands—the HUDDLE Objective.

HUDDLE Slowly Scuttled

3. There was a very real positive value to be obtained from the establishment of United States air bases in the Santa Cruz Islands and their use for air search to locate any Japanese Expeditionary Force movements from the Marshall Islands southeastward towards the Fiji and Samoan Islands.[2]

It is interesting that COMSOPAC's reaction to this cryptographic information seemingly was the same, since based on this despatch he told CTF 61 (Fletcher) to give consideration to an early end of Phase One and the commencing of Phase Two (HUDDLE) of Operation Plan 1–42.[3]

As early as 14 June, Vice Admiral Ghormley had advised COMINCH that he desired "to initiate an advance through New Hebrides, Santa Cruz and Ellice Island." He was still of the opinion that the Santa Cruz Islands were important when Rear Admiral Turner talked with him in Auckland in mid-July 1942 and he remained convinced of it up to the day of his detachment as COMSOPAC.[4]

At the 26 July conference regarding WATCHTOWER which Fletcher (1906), Noyes (1906), McCain (1906), Turner (1908), Kinkaid (1908), Vandegrift, USMC, Crutchley (Royal Navy), and Callaghan (1911) held at sea off Koro on 26 July, the questions of the forces to be finally assigned HUDDLE and the D-Day for the HUDDLE Operation were discussed. Callaghan's notes to the Area Commander in regard to these points were as follows:

> Movement to Ndeni to be started night of D-Day if possible. Much argument about need of whole 2nd Marines. Brought up Peck's point of using one battalion for this purpose—was voted down as all agreed that this must be held strongly account of its position and probability of major attack on it.[5]

This planning in regard to Ndeni had gone forward despite the fact that on 6 July 1942 COMAIRSOPAC had reported that actual reconaissance of the Santa Cruz Islands and the islands to the south had disclosed that airfield sites were going to be hard to come by. Only two heavily wooded areas, one on Ndeni and one on Trevanion Island, were possibilities.[6]

When the Marines were having real difficulties at Tulagi-Gavutu on D-Day, Major General Vandegrift requested from CTF 62 (Turner) the release of one battalion from the Force Reserve, the 2nd Marine Regiment,

---

[2] Turner.
[3] COMSOPAC to CTF 61, 272211 Jul. 1942.
[4] (a) COMSOPAC to COMINCH, 140614 Jun. 1942; (b) Turner.
[5] Ghormley manuscript, p. 67.
[6] COMAIRSOPAC to COMSOPAC, 060145 Jul. 1942.

to reinforce the Assault Force. He got not only one battalion, but two—all the battalions there were in the Force Reserve.[7]

On 10 August and after having received the first reports of the Savo disaster, COMSOPAC stated that he intended to use Espiritu Santo as a strong point for the "occupation [of] Santa Cruz Islands."[8] This despatch indicated that Vice Admiral Ghormley was still bent on carrying out the Joint Chiefs of Staff directive. Therefore his subordinate, Rear Admiral Turner, should be planning and moving toward this end.

It was not within CTF 62's area of authority to tell the Marines that they could forget about his seniors' plans for the use of the 2nd Regiment of Marines, nor could he personally forget about these plans. The Marines, the Amphibious Forces, and the South Pacific Force Commander all had protested setting D-Day for WATCHTOWER on August 1st, and had said it could not be done. The JCS acting through Admiral King had then tinkered with August 4th and when that day appeared impracticable and further protests and pleas against it had been sent all the way to Washington, August 7th had been set as D-Day with the understanding of no further delay, no matter what.

It would appear that Rear Admiral Turner was wise in not rushing into another exchange of pungent despatches asking for a further modification of COMSOPAC's, CINCPAC's, COMINCH's, and the Joint Chiefs' orders regarding HUDDLE, when the practicalities and necessities would settle the issue.

Back in early June, COMINCH had planned for the 7th Regiment of the First Marine Division, temporarily in Samoa, to rejoin its division.[9] The relief for the 7th Regiment, the 22nd Marine Regiment, was to leave San Diego as soon after 10 July 1942 as they were loaded aboard transports. There was a reasonable possibility that the 7th Regiment might be available to rejoin the First Marine Division by mid-August. In this case, the 7th Regiment could either undertake the Ndeni task or relieve the 2nd Regiment on Tulagi-Guadalcanal. Both arrangements would leave the First Division at full strength.

On 14 August, the Commanding Officer of the 2nd Regiment, after a visit to Ndeni, reported that the Jap airfield on Ndeni was overgrown but that Ndeni could be occupied.[10]

---
[7] Vandegrift, pp. 125, 126.
[8] COMSOPAC to COMAIRSOPAC, 092120 Aug. 1942.
[9] COMINCH Picador Plan, FF1/A16–3(15), Ser 00464 of 6 Jun. 1942.
[10] CO 2nd Marines to COMSOPAC, 140148 Aug. 1942.

On 15 August COMINCH transmitted a despatch from the Joint Chiefs to COMSOPAC (which COMPHIBFORSOPAC also received) containing these words:

> based upon the successful progress of Task One, it should be practicable to mount immediately that part of Task Two. . . . CINCPAC urges such actions. . . .[11]

It was apparent from this despatch that at the JCS, COMINCH, and CINCPAC level, it was anticipated that Task One, a major part of which was HUDDLE, would be successfully completed.

On 17 August COMSOPAC informed CINCPAC and COMINCH that Ndeni "will be occupied as soon as practicable." [12]

On 20 August 1942, Rear Admiral Turner at Noumea, issued his second Op Plan for the occupation and defense of Ndeni in the Santa Cruz Islands.[13]

He was in a vise. His immediate seniors, Nimitz and Ghormley, were urging him to get on with HUDDLE. His immediate Marine junior (Vandegrift) was urging him to scuttle HUDDLE.

That, at this date, Turner was just a bit on the fence is apparent from the fact that his Op Plan A9-42 was delivered to those who had tasks to plan and to do if the operation was carried out, but the copies for COMINCH, Naval Operations, the Commanding General First Marine Division, and others were marked: "Deferred Distribution (After execution of Plan)."

The deferred distribution of Op Plan A9-42 was never made.

On 23 August, Rear Admiral Turner informed Major General Vandegrift:

> The present plan is to send this regiment (7th) plus Fifth Defense Battalion (less your share) to Ndeni as a garrison, but of course that will be changed, if it becomes necessary.[14]

On 28 August 1942, by agreement between Rear Admirals McCain and Turner, Lieutenant Colonel Weir, the Assistant Operations Officer (Air) on the Amphibious Staff, flew up to Ndeni Island and made a ground reconnaissance of nearby Trevanion Island, our proposed airfield site.

> . . . What may not be so well known is the fact that the project was opposed with equal violence by COMAIRSOPAC (Rear Admiral McCain). He objected to the diversion of aircraft and construction forces. . . . I reported that the maximum runway which could be built was about 4000 feet. Also that because of irregular terrain and heavy woods, the project was impossible

---
[11] COMINCH to CINCPAC, COMSOPACFOR, 151951 Aug. 1942.
[12] COMSOPAC to CINCPAC, 170230 Aug. 1942.
[13] CTF 62 Op Plan A9-42, 20 Aug. 1942.
[14] RKT to Vandegrift, letter, 23 Aug. 1942.

with construction troops and equipment available in the foreseeable future. . . . No one in SOPAC had then seen a Seabee Battalion. . . .[15]

On 29 August, COMSOPAC informed CINCPAC and COMINCH:

> When the 7th Marines are embarked and if the situation then permits, I intend to seize Ndeni, the occupation of which and the establishment of an airfield thereon will greatly strengthen my position. . . .[16]

The actual deferment of HUDDLE became possible at the COMPHIBFORSOPAC level only after the Joint Chiefs of Staff approved CINCPAC's recommendation of 3 September that the JCS Directive of 2 July

> be modified to permit occupation Santa Cruz Islands to a later phase [of PESTILENCE] at discretion of COMSOPAC.[17]

On 9 September 1942, the modification having come through from the Joint Chiefs, COMSOPAC, in his Op Plan 3–42, took cognizance of this new authority and directed CTF 62 to "prepare to occupy Ndeni Island on further directive." [18] This was at least a step towards cancellation of the operation.

On the same day, with the 7th Regiment of the First Marine Division enroute from Samoa to a rendezvous with a detachment of Marines from New Caledonia, the needs of Guadalcanal rose up and demanded that the 7th Regiment proceed to Guadalcanal and that the 2nd Regiment remain there.

Also on 9 September, Rear Admiral Turner wrote Rear Admiral Leigh Noyes, Commander Task Force 18 in the *Wasp:*

> We have pending a decision as to whether or not to undertake an operation for the reinforcement of the Marine garrison at CACTUS. . . .
>
> * * * * *
>
> Final decision as to whether or not to make this landing at Taivu Point, will depend on Ghormley's decision after Vandegrift and I have had a conference within the next two or three days. . . .
>
> * * * * *
>
> I expect to go up to CACTUS the eleventh, return to BUTTON the thirteenth, and remain there until the move forward.[19]

---

[15] Major General F. D. Weir, USMC (Ret.) to GCD, letter, 14 May 1969.
[16] COMSOPAC to CINCPAC, 290310 Aug. 1942.
[17] CINCPAC to COMINCH, 032013 Sep. 1942.
[18] (a) COMSOPAC Op Plan 3–42; (b) COMSOPAC, 091016 Sep. 1942.
[19] RKT to Rear Admiral Leigh Noyes, letter, 9 Sep. 1942.

HUDDLE Slowly Scuttled

On 11 September Rear Admiral Turner informed COMSOPAC that he hoped availability of forces in SOPAC would be such as to permit an allocation of forces for the HUDDLE Operation because

> It is essential that we occupy Ndeni as soon as possible.[20]

But that did not necessarily mean now, nor necessarily with the 7th Regiment. It did mean that the JCS directive and the CINCPAC directive still contemplated the occupation of Ndeni.

On 12 September, and after a personal visit to Guadalcanal, Rear Admiral Turner definitely swung to the priority of Guadalcanal over Ndeni as the objective for the 7th Marine Regiment, and wrote:

> Personal reconnaissance and a careful review of the situation with COMGEN 1st MARDIV confirms opinion . . . one more regiment is essential to defense CACTUS now. . . . Recommend approval my departure from Espiritu Santo for Guadalcanal, morning 14th . . . with 7th Marines. . . .[21]

The COMPHIBFORSOPAC Staff Log tells the story of the next few days:

> *13 September.* [At Espiritu Santo] 0015. Received secret despatch from Adm. Turner [who was on Guadalcanal] to COMSOPAC recommending immediate reinforcement of CACTUS [Guadalcanal] by the 7th Marines.
>
> * * * * *
>
> 0400. Anchored as before, standing by to get underway on half hour's notice. AA Battery in Condition TWO.
>
> * * * * *
>
> 0800: COMAIRSOPAC reported morning search failed to reveal presence enemy ships this area and indicates no immediate threat to BUTTON [Espiritu Santo] today.
>
> * * * * *
>
> 1130. CTF 62, Assistant Chief of Staff, and the Staff Aviation Officer returned from a conference at CACTUS with Commanding General First Marine Division, and COMAIRSOPAC.
>
> * * * * *
>
> *14 September*
> 0048. Radio Guadalcanal reported in plain language being shelled by at least one cruiser and two destroyers.
> 0515. Units of Task Force 62 underway.
>
> * * * * *
>
> 0800. CACTUS garrison engaged all night at rear and right flank. Now [0800] engaged left flank. Bringing over one battalion 2nd Marines from RINGBOLT [Tulagi].

---

[20] COMPHIBFORSOPAC to COMSOPACFOR, 092300 Sep. 1942.
[21] COMPHIBFORSOPAC to COMSOPAC, 120530 Sep. 1942.

The Staff Log for the afternoon watch on 15 September 1942 contains the following entry in the Chief of Staff's handwriting:

15 September
Information of enemy shows strong concentration of Japanese Naval strength within 300 mile radius of CACTUS. One group of 3 BB, 4 CA, 4 DD at 7-50Z, 164E bombed by B-17s, 2 possible hits. 1 CV, 3 cruisers, 4 DD at 06-30S, 164-17E, another carrier group North of Kolombangara Island [180 miles NW from Guadalcanal.] Enemy attacks, land and naval forces throughout the night at CACTUS. . . . All factors of situation caused a decision on the part of CTF 65 [Turner] temporarily to withdraw in hopes of more favorable opportunity for reinforcement and also in order to rendezvous *Bellatrix* to take in [to Guadalcanal] large quantity AV Gas. . . .

The Staff Log continues:
16 September

* * * * *

1818: The strategical situation is doubtful. Practically no plane contacts today and practically no information of enemy. Covering Force of carriers, our Task Force 61, has withdrawn to BUTTON. Task Force 65 maintaining itself in vicinity of CINCPAC grid position 4794 in order to be prepared to take advantage of any favorable opportunity to enter CACTUS either east or west of San Cristobal. . . .

17 September
0000: En route to CACTUS.
1200: Visibility reduced by haze. Nothing sighted.

* * * * *

Considerable concentration of [Japanese] naval escort force, transport and landing craft at Faisi [250 miles NW Guadalcanal] indicates that a major effort will soon be made by enemy, either as direct landing attack or in building up Faisi as a base from which future operations may be projected.
Decision was made to proceed with plan for reinforcement of CACTUS.

18 September

* * * * *

0625: First Marine troops landed.[22]

The reinforcement moved forward, although the second try cost us the carrier *Wasp* and the destroyer *O'Brien*. But the 7th Regiment was successfully landed.

However, putting the 7th Regiment on Guadalcanal did not mean that COMSOPAC was relieved of his responsibility for carrying out his directive to occupy Ndeni in the Santa Cruz Islands "as soon as possible." The desira-

---

[22] COMPHIBFORSOPAC Staff Log.

bility of the operation was noted, on 22 September, by CINCPAC who in a despatch to COMINCH referred to the "necessity to occupy Ndeni." [23]

Various alternative forces in the rear areas were suggested by COMSOPAC and COMPHIBFORSOPAC as possible forces for the task, including one battalion of the 2nd Regiment on Guadalcanal, the 8th Regiment of the Second Marine Division in Samoa, and the 147th Regiment of the U. S. Army in the Tonga Islands.[24]

When COMPHIBFORSOPAC suggested as a possibility including the Armys' 147th Regiment in the required troops for the Ndeni Mission, COMGEN, SOPAC (Major General Millard F. Harmon, U. S. Army) stepped in, and on 6 October 1942 recommended strongly against HUDDLE being undertaken until "the Southern Solomon's were secured." [25]

Vice Admiral Ghormley was still intent on HUDDLE and turned down the recommendation of his senior Army advisor to cancel. The Marines on Guadalcanal went through another crisis in early October, and all troop resources in SOPAC were pointed towards our holding operation there. Rear Admiral Turner landed 2,850 Army troops from the 164th Infantry Regiment on 13 October along with 3,200 tons of cargo.

Shortly after Vice Admiral William F. Halsey took over command in SOPAC on 18 October 1942, the heat came off Rear Admiral Turner to undertake HUDDLE, although the operation was not actually dead until March 1943 when the Joint Chiefs of Staff cancelled their 2 July 1942 PESTILENCE Plan and issued their new plan of operations for the seizure of the Solomon Islands-New Guinea-New Britain-New Ireland areas to make possible the "ultimate seizure of the Bismarck Archipelago." [26]

It was Admiral Turner's belief that it was quite natural for the Marines, as long as they were maintaining a perimeter defensive position on Guadalcanal, to want every Marine in the South Pacific within that perimeter; but that he had to view the situation in a broader spectrum, and that he naturally was more responsive than the Marines to the overriding JCS directives and his immediate senior's requirements.[27]

Probably the root of the difference of opinion between COMSOPAC and

---

[23] CINCPAC to COMINCH, 222327 Sep. 1942.
[24] (a) RKT to AAG, letter, 28 Sep. 1942; (b) COMSOPAC to COMPHIBFORSOPAC, 290206 Sep. 1942; (c) COMPHIBFORSOPAC to COMSOPAC, 010430 Oct. 1942.
[25] (a) COMSOPAC to COMPHIBFORSOPAC, 290206 Sep. 1942; (b) Miller, *Guadalcanal* (Army), p. 141 and Appendix A; (c) COMPHIBFORSOPAC to COMSOPAC, 010430 Oct. 1942.
[26] JCS 238/5/D of 23 Mar. 1943.
[27] Turner.

COMPHIBFORPAC with the Commanding General First Marine Division was that Vice Admiral Ghormley and Rear Admiral Turner could not get out of their minds that all the early directives from higher authority listed taking the Santa Cruz Islands ahead of the Solomon Islands in the missions to be accomplished, and it had only been the imperatives resulting from the Japanese fast progress in building an airfield on Guadalcanal which had shifted the Santa Cruz Islands from number 1 to number 2 on the JCS chore list.

The original despatch to COMSOPAC gave him tasks having the:

> Immediate objective of seizing and occupying Santa Cruz Islands and positions in the Solomon Islands, with the ultimate objective of occupying Eastern New Guinea and New Britain.

Vice Admiral Halsey came into command of SOPAC without the background of a chore long assigned and not discharged, and, making an on the spot estimate of the situation, decided that HUDDLE could stand aside.

Admiral Turner's belief was that the HUDDLE planning had served a very useful purpose throughout, and that it had helped the Marines on Guadalcanal, rather than hindered them, in that it provided a hook upon which to hang urgent requests for additional troops in the SOPAC area.[28]

RELIEF OF MARINES BY ARMY TROOPS

The major problem of the Marines on Guadalcanal was the Japanese. There were two other Marine problems toward whose solution Rear Admiral Turner was working, although not always to the satisfaction of the Marines.

The first was support of the Marines, both combat and logistic, and the second was their relief by Army troops.

Admiral Turner felt that he had incurred the displeasure of his comrades in arms over the relief of the Marines by the Army on Guadalcanal. He thought that:

> The Marines were unhappy because they weren't relieved sooner, and the Army was unhappy because they were thrown on to Guadalcanal before they were fully ready.[29]

JCS 23, approved by the Joint Chiefs on 16 March 1942, had lumped the South Pacific and Southwest Pacific into one area and provided for 416,000

---

[28] *Ibid.*
[29] Turner.

United States troops to be stationed there by the end of 1942, and had stated that 225,000 were already so positioned. This figure of 225,000 troops possibly plagued all the Washington planners' memories, for it was a major factor influencing when and where United States forces would move on from Guadalcanal, and constantly was brought up at the COMINCH level as an ingredient of the relief of the Marines on Guadalcanal by Army troops. For the Navy planners believed that if the Army could relieve the Marines from land warfare on Guadalcanal, the Marines could carry out an amphibious operation directed by the Joint Chiefs against the Santa Cruz Islands.

When General MacArthur's area boundary was shifted westward of Guadalcanal on 1 August 1942, his pain was eased by telling him that the boundary shift was made so that COMSOPAC would be required to furnish garrison forces for the Solomons.[30] This represented a change from the initial draft directive which had provided:

> permanent occupation of Islands seized on the Solomons—New Guinea Area will be accomplished by the movement of garrisons from Australia under the direction of COMSOWESPACAREA.

The 2 July PESTILENCE three-phase directive issued by Joint Chiefs of Staff accordingly had provided that Army troops presently in the SOPAC area

> would be used to garrison Tulagi and adjacent island positions.[31]

Actually, there were only 32,000 United States Army troops in the SOPAC area at this time.[32] In Washington that number still seemed like a great many troops. In SOPAC, that number seemed quite inadequate to permit any enlargement of current responsibilities to garrison islands protecting the line of communications from Samoa to Australia.

Vice Admiral Ghormley raised the question of obtaining additional Army troops from the United States or from New Zealand on 13 July.[33] He was immediately informed:

> It is not the intention of the Army to provide garrison troops from the United States for Santa Cruz-Tulagi-Guadalcanal.[34]

---

[30] C/S USA to CINCSWPA, Msg. 334, 3 Jul. 1942. OPD 381, SWPA #85. Modern Military Records Division, National Archives.
[31] COMINCH to CINCPAC, COMSOPAC, 022100 Jul. 1942.
[32] Miller, *Guadalcanal* (Army), p. 24.
[33] COMSOPAC to CINCPAC, 190414 Jul. 1942.
[34] COMINCH to COMSOPAC, 142226 Jul. 1942.

In regard to obtaining New Zealand troops, COMINCH flashed a caution light:

> only if you believe you can handle without upsetting arrangements made re Fiji.

Admiral King referred to the prospective New Zealand take over in Fiji of troop defense responsibilities from the United States.

Vice Admiral Ghormley was upset also by a directive [35] from CINCPAC which required that authority be obtained from the Joint Chiefs of Staff for any plan involving the shift of Army troops in his area to relieve the Marines. He asked for "full authority to employ the forces in this area in accordance with his judgment in furtherance of the directives he has received." [36]

Since the governing publication *Joint Action of the Army and the Navy* provided that Army troops would relieve the Marines, as soon as there was judged to have occurred a change from amphibious warfare to land warfare, it was obvious to COMSOPAC that this particular decision was one which properly could and should be made in the immediate operational area and not in Pearl Harbor or Washington.

Both Vice Admiral Ghormley and Major General M. F. Harmon, the Commanding General, United States Army Forces, South Pacific Area were strongly convinced that they could not move forward forces recently arrived as island defense forces in the Fiji and New Caledonia Area to become garrison forces on the Solomons. The prowess of the Japanese in amphibious operations, and their ability to overcome locally superior United States and British Forces in the Philippines and in the Malay Peninsula, was too fresh in the minds of these commanders to permit them to take an offensive attitude. As Vice Admiral Ghormley wrote:

> The Japs might break through any minute and these ground forces were necessary to defend our bases which were supporting and controlling the line of communications.[37]

Starting in early September 1942, Commanding General First Division Marines kept pressing his immediate naval senior for relief of his Marines by Army troops, and in almost every letter there is some reference to it.

Rear Admiral Turner in replying to one letter in late September wrote:

> The question of the relief of Marine troops by the Army is a very large one; as is also the question of where you would go for reorganization when

---
[35] CINCPAC to COMSOPAC, letter, A4–3/FF12/A16–(6) Ser 01994 of 8 Jul. 1942.
[36] COMSOPAC to CINCPAC, 222245 Jul. 1942.
[37] Ghormley manuscript, p. 76.

relieved. I have given it a great deal of thought; the only conclusion I have come to is that we cannot, at present, reach a decision on that point. I sympathize entirely with your point of view and hope we can do the job the way you wish.[38]

According to the Chief of the Army Air Force, in late September 1942:

. . . The Marines on Guadalcanal wanted to know when the Army was going to relieve them. The Marines had understood they were to be there for a few days only, and then were to be relieved. Where was the Army?[39]

It was not until 6 October 1942 that the Army Commander in the South Pacific offered Army troops for Guadalcanal. They were not offered as a relief for part of the Marines on Guadalcanal but as an augmentation in time of need and as a far more desirable use of Army resources than on Ndeni.

The 164th Infantry Regiment of the Americal Division was landed by Rear Admiral Turner from the *McCawley* and *Zeilin,* commencing 13 October 1942, with their 3,200 tons of logistic support, bringing the total strength on Guadalcanal to over 23,000. Some 4,500 more troops were still on the Tulagi side. At the same time the Marine 1st Raider Battalion departed Guadalcanal for the rear area and this movement reaffirmed the principle of Marine relief by Army troops. And it was on 13 October, that the Japanese surprise bombed Henderson Field from the comparatively safe height of 30,000 feet, where our fighters could not reach them at all or else (F–4F) so slowly that the attackers were gone when the fighters reached that altitude. The same day the Japanese took the Marine-Army defensive forces under fire with their 15 long range 105-millimeter howitzers, which were positioned out of retaliatory range.

The success of the 164th Infantry Regiment in meeting the heavy Japanese attacks on 24–25 October, and the repeated pleas of Major General Vandegrift for more and more reinforcements to be followed by the relief of his Marines, made at the Noumea conferences of this same October period, led to an early decision for the landing of a battery of 155 guns from the 244th Coast Artillery Battalion, which was accomplished on 2 November 1942. This was followed by movement of the 147th Infantry Regiment which landed at Aola Bay on 4 November. From 12 November 1942 on there was a planned flow of relieving Army Troops, initially from the Americal Division.

---

[38] RKT to AAG, letter 28 Sep. 1942.
[39] Arnold, *Global Mission,* p. 348.

It was not only Vice Admiral Ghormley and Rear Admiral Turner who found it difficult to produce Army troops to relieve the Marines as soon as the official prescribed instructions and sound doctrine called for them to be produced, or when the Marines desired them. Vice Admiral Halsey, a month after he became COMSOPAC, wrote:

> It is not practical at this time to definitely settle the question of promptly relieving amphibious forces after a landing operation. It is a principle that should be followed, but the question is one hinging on the availability of troops and the practicality of the relief under varying situations which cannot be foreseen.[40]

On 7 December 1942 COMPHIBFORSOPAC was relieved of his operational command responsibility for the defense of Tulagi-Guadalcanal. Admiral Turner was delighted that by this date all the arrangements had been completed for the personnel of the First Marine Division who had landed on 7 August to depart for other shores.[41]

On 9 December 1942, the ground command at Guadalcanal changed from a Marine to an Army commander and the First Marine Division commenced its movement to Australia.

MARINE CRITICISM

Admiral Turner's reaction to the written post-war Marine criticism of his command activities during the early August to early November 1942 period was mild:

> The written record will show that I was charged with operational command. No officer fulfills his duty, if he doesn't exercise his command responsibilities. If you are in command, and do your job under difficult circumstances, you are bound to break a few eggs, even if they are good Marine eggs.[42]

Admiral Turner felt that any argument over the basic command question would be enlightened by quoting the documents in regard to the operational command set-up established for WATCHTOWER by the Joint Chiefs of Staff and reaffirmed by COMINCH and COMSOPAC (see Chapter VI).

When the Joint Chiefs of Staff directed that

> direct command of the tactical operations of the amphibious forces will remain with the Naval Task Force Commander throughout the conduct of all three tasks,

---

[40] COMSOPAC to COMGENFIRSTMARDIV, PHIBFOR. letter, P16–3(16), Ser 00106b of 22 Nov. 1942.
[41] Turner.
[42] Ibid.

the naval chain of command assumed that "direct command of tactical operations" meant just that, and when on 18 August 1942 COMSOPAC issued his post-WATCHTOWER landing Op Order 2–42, CTF 62 (Turner) was assigned tasks as follows:

> Defend seized areas with Marine Expeditionary Force. Expedite movement food and ammunition Guadalcanal-Tulagi Area.[43]

When COMSOPAC issued a further directive on 9 September 1942, he assigned the following specific tasks to CTF 62.

> Defend and strengthen Guadalcanal-Tulagi positions and expedite development of airfield CACTUS [Guadalcanal]. Mop up adjacent enemy outposts. Prepare to occupy Ndeni on further directive. Maintain the flow of supplies.[44]

It was not until the First Anniversary of Pearl Harbor on 7 December 1942, that COMSOPAC informed Rear Admiral Turner:

> COMAMPHIBFORSOPAC relieved responsibility [for] defense [Guadalcanal] but retains responsibility for transportation of reenforcements, relief units, supplies and equipment. . . .[45]

This same despatch established a Commanding General, Guadalcanal and assigned him command of the base and all troops and installations in the Guadalcanal-Tulagi Area.

Admiral Turner's view was:

> I exercised command of the Marines, when I had orders to do so. When they asked for my opinion regarding a change, I recommended a change. When I was no longer their commander, I so acted.[46]

There were several minor matters which Admiral Turner felt might be "cleared up" by presenting the record in some detail. One of these related to the Marines who did not get landed in the early echelons of the assault forces at Guadalcanal-Tulagi.

In the Marine monograph and the later history of the Guadalcanal Operation, the story of the Marines who did not get ashore at Tulagi or Guadalcanal on D-Day through D plus two is told in these words:

> The sudden withdrawal of the transports carried these units, which totaled about 1,400 officers and men, back to Espiritu Santo when they were used to 'reinforce the garrison there,' according to the reports of Admiral

---
[43] COMSOPAC to CTF 61, 62, 63, 64, 180916 Aug. 1942; COMSOPAC Op Order 2–42.
[44] (a) COMSOPAC to CTF 61, 62, 64, 091016 Sep. 1942; COMSOPAC Op Order 3–42.
[45] COMSOPAC to CTF 62, 070446 Dec. 1942.
[46] Turner.

Turner. On 14 August Turner ordered Colonel Arthur to report for duty with the Commanding General, Espiritu Santo. . . .

There seemed no question in Turner's mind about his unrestricted claim of 'possession' of the Marines in his area. . . .[47]

The fact of the matter, readily available to all in COMSOPAC's War Diary, was that COMSOPAC had directed CTF 62 late on 9 August after the disastrous battle of Savo Island, to

Divert 2nd Marines to Espiritu Santo to land and reinforce the garrison there.[48]

COMSOPAC followed this up in a memo to COMPHIBFORSOPAC on 14 August which directed:

All 2nd Marines now at Espiritu Santo to disembark and reinforce garrison.[49]

Thus, Rear Admiral Turner ordered Colonel Arthur, Commanding the 2nd Marines, to report for duty with the Commanding General Espiritu Santo, because the boss man of the area had made that decision and told him to do so.

When Brigadier General Rupertus sent on Colonel J. M. Arthur's request for the urgent return of this part of his command—800 men of the 2nd Marine Regiment—to Tulagi, Admiral Turner wrote on his Assistant Chief of Staff's memo:

Col. Linscott.
For the time being, this is out of our hands, as COMSOPAC ordered these units ashore in BUTTON. Keep in mind pending further developments.

The other matter which Admiral Turner thought needed a bit of "clearing up" related to HUDDLE (the Ndeni Operation), and that has been covered earlier in Chapter XII.

MARINE RAIDER BATTALIONS

In the early days of the Guadalcanal Operation, Rear Admiral Turner had been most anxious to get at the scattered Japanese detachments in the Lower Solomons, and visualized Marine Raider Battalions as the proper instruments to accomplish this. He visualized that each Marine Regiment would have a Raider Battalion as part of its permanent organization and recommended this organization up the chain of command. In order to obtain

---
[47] Hough, Ludwig, and Shaw, *Pearl Harbor to Guadalcanal* (Marines), p. 261.
[48] COMSOPAC to CTF 62, 091000 Aug. 1942.
[49] COMSOPAC to COMPHIBFORSOPAC, memorandum, 14 Aug. 1942.

the benefits sought with the Marines currently available in the South Pacific Area but not on Guadalcanal, he reported to COMSOPAC:

> . . . In order to prosecute promptly the operations required by prospective tactical situations, the Commander Amphibious Force South Pacific, will, unless directed to contrary, proceed with the organization of Provisional Raider Battalions in the Second, Seventh and Eighth Marines, and give these already trained troops such additional specialized training as seems appropriate.[50]

The Marine Officer on COMSOPAC Staff took a whack at the recommendation and at its originator. The Marines had their eyes set not only on divisions of Marines, but on corps of Marines, and Rear Admiral Turner had really stuck his hand in the vice when he wrote:

> The employment of divisions [in future operations] as a landing unit seems less likely.

This was more than an overstatement in support of the proposal being made. It was a poor judgment of the future, and few Marines forget to mention a distortion of the statement when Admiral Turner's name is brought up.

The other error in connection with Admiral Turner's proposal regarding Raider Battalions was that COMPHIBFORSOPAC failed to consult the Commanding General, First Marine Division, in the matter before going to higher authority. But he did not, as General Vandegrift recalled that he was later informed by the Commandant of the Marine Corps, seek to limit Marines to Raider Battalion-sized units. According to General Vandegrift:

> . . . Turner's attempts to break up certain regiments into battalion-size raider units, recommending to Nimitz and King in the process that Marines be limited to such size units in the future. . . .[51]

The official letter from Rear Admiral Turner, in fact, reads quite differently.

> [The originator] . . . recommends that Marine Corps Headquarters issue directions for the permanent organization of Raider Battalions as integral units of all the Marine Regiments now attached to, or ultimately destined for the Amphibious Force, South Pacific. . . .[52]

The letter was addressed to COMSOPAC, who readdressed it and sent it to CINCPAC, who sent it direct to the Commandant of the Marine Corps.

---

[50] COMPHIBFORSOPAC to COMSOPAC, letter, FE25/A16-3(5) Ser 0093 of 29 Aug. 1942.
[51] Vandegrift, p. 183. Reprinted from *Once a Marine* with permission of W.W. Norton & Co., Inc.
[52] COMPHIBFORSOPACFOR to COMSOPAC, letter, 29 Aug. 1942.

The Commandant returned it to CINCPAC and sent COMINCH a copy of his reply and of the basic letter and previous endorsements.

COMSOPAC approved the organization of a provisional Raider Battalion from the 2nd Marines, but disapproved it for the 7th and 8th Marines.

CINCPAC disapproved the basic recommendation that Raider Battalions be integral units of Marine Regiments, and indicated that the organization of a provisional Raider Battalion should be undertaken only in case of "due necessity."

The Commandant of the Marine Corps agreed with CINCPAC. He reported that as a result of recommendations from the Naval forces in the field, two additional Raider Battalions were being organized and added that:

> Steps have been taken to intensify training of all units destined for the South Pacific for the type of operations being conducted there.

The Commandant noted, with regret, that the basic letter did

> not contain the views of the Commanding General 1st Marine Division in a matter in which he is particularly qualified, and concerned.[53]

Without ever having discussed this matter with Admiral Turner, since he died before it was researched, the author can only guess as to whether there was any background reason for this unsuccessful foray into Marine organizational matters. But an earnest belief that the Japanese could be dislodged from their various placements in the Lower Solomons by landings in their rear, perhaps played a part. Before the initial WATCHTOWER landings, Major General Vandegrift had concurred in such a plan.

Rear Admiral Turner received strong support in his concept of using Marines in flanking operations or taking the enemy in the rear, rather than in frontal attacks when, in November 1942, Admiral King addressed a message to COMSOPAC which contained the following:

> The final decision cancelling the Aola Bay project brings to climax my uneasiness lest we continue to use up our strength in virtual frontal attacks such as now involved in expulsion of enemy from Guadalcanal.

Admiral King suggested that the Marines could be more profitably employed in a flanking operation in which the Marines would seize the base, where the enemy had an airfield, and from where he was currently operating in support of Guadalcanal.[54]

---

[53] (a) Commandant, Marine Corps, letter, 003A/27642, 3 Oct. 1942; (b) COMSOPAC, letter, Ser 0094b, 6 Sep. 1942; (c) CINCPAC, letter, Ser 0208 of 24 Sep. 1942.
[54] COMINCH to COMSOPAC, CINCPAC, 301915 Nov. 1942.

DIVERSIONARY EFFECT

Available personal RKT letters of this period are few in number. One addressed to the editor of the *Call Bulletin* of San Francisco, acknowledging receipt of a letter two months old which had just arrived by sea mail, included the comments:

> . . . Ever since I came into the Navy, I have always wanted to campaign in the tropics in an elephant hat, and now at last, it has to be in one made of tin.
>
> We are not having a particularly easy time down here. Starting from scratch; fighting in the jungle using boys that never saw jungle; our ships lying in ports that never saw ships; creating bases and facilities out of nothing; drawing our supplies from six thousand miles away. These are our problems, and they are difficult. But we hope to solve them. From the way our boys are acting, nothing will ever be too much for them.[55]

NEW CHIEF OF STAFF

When Captain Peyton, the Chief of Staff, pressed Rear Admiral Turner to be relieved, setting forth the COMINCH and BUPERS policy that all captains must have a successful big ship command under their belts before being eligible for selection to Flag rank, Rear Admiral Turner sought to obtain for Captain Peyton a first-rate command and luckily did so. This was the big and new battleship, the *USS Indiana* (BB-58), whose first Commanding Officer, Captain A. Stanton (Tip) Merrill, had just been promoted to command a cruiser division operating in the Solomons.

Commodore Peyton opined:

> Kelly Turner was an officer with the highest mental capacity. He was a tireless worker and had tremendous drive. His mental capabilities were such that he did all the brain work for the Staff. The Staff carried out the mechanics of operations and filled in all the details of the operation orders. He was a one-man staff.
>
> I was not qualified to be his Chief of Staff, as I was not on the same intellectual level with him.

Commodore Peyton also remembered:

> Admiral Spruance visited the Amphibious Force several times between July and December 1942. Turner used to go ashore about six and hoist a couple. Spruance did not participate nor concur. Turner would return, have dinner and work half the night or all the night. The cocktail hour seemed

---
[55] RKT to Edmond D. Coblentz, letter, 23 Dec. 1942.

to sharpen his mind and give him his second wind, if in fact he needed any second wind.[56]

Peyton's relief was Captain Anton Bennett Anderson, Class of 1912, a graduate of the logistically oriented Army Industrial College, and "as nice a guy as one could wish to serve with" according to staff members of the PHIBFORSOPAC.

Captain Anderson came from duty on Vice Admiral Halsey's Staff, where he had served very, very briefly as Head of the Board of Awards, COMSOPAC. This followed a tour of shore duty in the Office of the Chief of Naval Operations, primarily as Head of the War Plans section of the Fleet Maintenance Division, and as the senior working Navy member of the Army-Navy Munitions Board. Rear Admiral Anderson recalled:

> . . . The day after I took over [on SOPAC Staff] Admiral Turner dropped into my office and asked me if I would like to be C/S on his Staff. I was elated to get into a more active job and said that I would. He told me that his C/S Peyton had the opportunity of getting command of the *USS Indiana* (then in the harbor) and he didn't want to stand in his way and had let him go a day or two previously. He also told me that he had gotten Rear Admiral George Fort to take command of the Landing Craft Flotillas of the Amphibious Force, then being organized. . . .
>
> I went out to the *USS McCawley* flagship that same afternoon, January 21, 1943 and reported to Admiral Turner as C/S.

Prior to his becoming Chief of Staff, Anderson

> had never served with Admiral Turner and seldom saw him when he was in War Plans in OPNAV. The day after I reported for duty, Admiral Turner and I went over to visit Peyton aboard his new command. We stayed for about an hour. This is the only time I saw Captain Peyton.

In answer to the author's question of whether he functioned primarily in the logistic field or in the operational field as Kelly Turner's Chief of Staff, COMSOPAC AMPHIBIOUS FORCE, Rear Admiral Anderson answered:

> Mostly I was learning my job. However, I did work a little in both fields. I would say my work was more of an administrative nature.[57]

Captain Anderson, like his Admiral, prior to reporting to the Amphibious Force, SOPAC, "had no up-to-date amphibious training or experience," although he had observed various tests of amphibious craft at Cape Henry and worked with the board which had come up with the nomenclature for various types of amphibious craft.

---
[56] Interview with Commodore Thomas G. Peyton, USN, 22 May 1961. Hereafter Peyton.
[57] Interview with Rear Admiral Anton B. Anderson, USN (Ret.), Mar. 1962.

Rear Admiral Anderson opined:

> In general, I think my services were satisfactory to Turner most of the time, but in retrospect, I realize that during the six months I was with him, was for him an uncertain, unhappy and trying time.
>
> First, he had to remain in his flagship at anchor in Noumea harbor most of the time while some of his force made only the necessary trips to Guadalcanal.
>
> And again, I believe that it rankled him in that he thought some officers (higher-ups) believed that he was somewhat responsible for the loss of the three cruisers around Savo Island during the initial landing at Guadalcanal in August 1942.
>
> I also believe that he foresaw that the days of the Amphibious Force SOPAC were coming to an end, and he wanted new fields to work in. He often told me that an advance through the Central Pacific should be started soon.
>
> I really think that he was tired and somewhat bored. He didn't have any contemporaries to go around with and seldom saw Admiral Halsey outside of the 9 a.m. conferences. . . .[58]

The members of the PHIBFORSOPAC Staff were all of a mind that Captain Anderson was a very pleasant individual to have on the Staff, but he was not cut from the same tempered steel as Richmond Kelly Turner.

> In any case, he was in completely over his head. His mind was too slow to follow Admiral Turner whose mind turned over on the step at about 1000 RPM, while Andy was airborne at about 100 RPM.
>
> * * * * *
>
> Tom Peyton was unable to keep up with the Admiral's thinking. Andy Anderson was even slower.[59]

Rear Admiral Turner was just too damned impatient to deal with his staff through his Chief of Staff. He wanted to tend to the matter and get it over with and then get on to something else. When the Chief of Staff was unacquainted with operational matters, which the Admiral already was 98 percent up on, he just wouldn't wait. Thus,

> by the time Andy joined the Staff, the Admiral was as familiar with amphibious operations as any one who had spent six months working twenty hours a day on the subject could be. Andy just never could catch up to be on a par operationally with the Admiral.[60]

Commodore Peyton remembered that

> Turner was not a well man and during this period was always on edge for

---
[58] Rear Admiral Anderson to GCD, letter, 2 May 1962.
[59] Staff Interviews.
[60] *Ibid.*

fear his enemies would get him relieved during a spell of illness. . . . It was not possible for him to have a proper day-to-day diet.[61]

In support of this opinion in regard to the health of Rear Admiral Turner, during this 1942–43 period, the following extracts from a recent letter by the Medical Officer of the PHIBFORSOPAC Staff, Rear Admiral Ralph E. Fielding (Medical Corps), U. S. Navy, Retired, are pertinent:

> Before leaving Noumea for Guadalcanal (and prior to the Rendova landing) Admiral Turner had a recurrence of malaria and presumably an attack of dengue. He finally consented (with an affirmative from Jack Lewis) to go to the hospital ship. Commodore Reifsnider had command of the flotilla going to Guadalcanal. Admiral Turner told me I could shoot anyone who was caught without clothing coverage over his entire body [Because of the incidence of malaria among the troops taken into Guadalcanal, who did not observe antimalaria discipline].
>
> Admiral Turner had a mild coronary attack at Camp Crocodile. He wouldn't be transferred to Mobile 8 hospital, so we got a hospital bed moved from a nearby Station Hospital, and put it in his tent. But he insisted on seeing every incoming despatch while being treated.[62]

---

[61] Peyton.
[62] Rear Admiral Ralph E. Fielding (MC), USN (Ret.) to GCD, letter, 28 Mar. 1969.

CHAPTER XIII

Polishing Skills in the Russells

MOVING UP THE SOLOMONS

The first real move north was to Rendova Island in the New Georgia Group about 180 miles northwest of Lunga Point, but this most worthwhile step was preceded by an advance a stone's throw away to the Russell Islands lying only 30 miles northwest of Guadalcanal Island.

It was more than several months after Rear Admiral Turner arrived at Noumea from Guadalcanal for the first time, on 13 August 1942, before he started to think about, and his staff started to plan, the first offensive step forward from Guadalcanal to Rabaul.

The Amphibians had learned a good deal from the August landings at Tulagi and Guadalcanal, and they continued to learn a great deal during the long, hard five months' struggle to maintain logistic support for these two important toe holds in the Southern Solomons. By January 1943, marked changes had occurred in their thinking about the techniques of support through and over a beachhead, and new amphibious craft were just becoming available. They were anxious to test these changes and the new craft on a strange shore.

Ten days after the 13th of August arrival at Noumea, recommendations for improvement in the logistic area of the landing phases of amphibious operations had been sought from all commands in TF 62 by Rear Admiral Turner. It was on the basis of the recommendations received, that Commander Amphibious Forces SOPAC made proposals for revisions in Fleet Training Publication (FTP) 167, the Amphibians' Bible, and it was on the basis of these recommendations and those coming in from the Atlantic

---

Note: With the close of Chapter XII, Admiral Turner disappears, with very minor exceptions duly noted, as a direct source of information, comment and opinions not only of this work, but of the events related.

The author, due to Admiral Turner's sudden death, did not have the opportunity to discuss with him, in detail, any of the later operations of the World War II amphibious campaigns of the Pacific.

Fleet after the North African Landings that COMINCH issued on 18 January 1943, *Ship to Shore Movement U. S. Fleet* FTP 211.

This new publication brought into step the differing procedures used by amphibious ships trained separately in the Atlantic and the Pacific Fleet. It expanded markedly the Naval Platoon of the Shore Party, and more clearly defined its duties during the crucial early hours of logistic support of an assault landing.[1]

THE RUSSELLS

The last of the Japanese troops evacuated Guadalcanal on 7–8 February 1943, at which time WATCHTOWER could be marked in the books as completed. The pressure was immediately on the amphibians to get moving.

Thirteen days later the amphibious forces of the South Pacific Area landed in major strength on the Russell Islands.

This landing, on 21 February 1943, if it did not do anything else, fulfilled Major General Vandegrift's requirement that

> . . . landings should not be attempted in the face of organized resistance if, by any combination of march or maneuver, it is possible to land unopposed and undetected. . . .[2]

The Russell Islands landings were made unopposed and undetected. Since there was no blood and gore associated with the operation, it has been brushed off lightly in most historical accounts of the period.

THE PLANNING STAGE

Admiral Nimitz visited the South Pacific in late January 1943 in company with Secretary of the Navy Frank Knox. At a COMSOPAC conference of principal commanders and their planning officers on 23 January 1943, COMSOPAC had Brigadier General Peck of his staff present to Admiral Nimitz a concept for a Russell Islands operation. COMSOPAC received from CINCPAC a tentative and unofficial approval, tempered by a cautionary "No

---

[1] (a) Staff Interviews; (b) CTF 62 letter, Ser 029 of 23 Aug. 1942, and replies thereto; (c) COMSOPAC, letter, A16-3/(00) Ser 00936 of 4 Dec. 1942; (d) TU 66.3 Op Orders H-1, J-1, K-1, K-2.

[2] COMGENFIRSTMARDIV, Final Report on Guadalcanal Operation, Phase V, 1 Jul. 1943, p. 6.

Polishing Skills in the Russells

decision will be reached" which really meant "go ahead with the planning while my staff back in Pearl takes a hard look at the proposition." [3]

In this connection, the memory of the COMPHIBFORSOPAC's Chief of Staff at the time is that:

> ... Admiral Turner conceived the idea of taking over the Russell Islands, some 60 or 70 miles N.W. of Henderson Field, and up towards 'The Slot.' Admiral Halsey was lukewarm on the idea—he wanted something on a larger scale. However, he said 'go ahead, as some kind of action is better than none.' [4]

Shortly thereafter, on 28 January, COMSOPAC informed CINCPAC that if the reconnaissance then underway indicated the Russell Islands were undefended, he planned immediate occupation. After CINCPAC gave his formal approval (29 January) and despite somewhat misleading information received from the coastwatcher intelligence organization about "enemy activity Russell Islands increasing," COMSOPAC issued his preliminary operational warning order to the prospective commanders involved on 7 February 1943. COMSOPAC issued his despatch Operation Order first and then his Plan

---

[3] (a) Staff Interviews; (b) CINCPAC, *Command Summary*, Book Three, 23 Jan. 1943, p. 1342.
[4] Anderson.

Turner Collection

The Staff Allowance, Commander Amphibious Force South Pacific: Rear Admiral Kelly Turner in center with Colonel Henry D. Linscott, USMC, Assistant Chief of Staff, on his right and Captain James H. Doyle, USN, Operations Officer, on his left.

5-43 for the landings, code named CLEANSLATE, on 12 and 15 February 1942.[5]

The Russell Islands are 60 miles west-northwest of Henderson Field on Guadalcanal. The two main islands of the Russells are Pavuvu and Banika, the former being about twice the size of the latter which is nearest Guadalcanal. The first named island, mainly a 1,500-foot jungled foothill in 1943, is fanged in shape and about eight miles north and south by seven miles east and west. The latter island is about eight miles by two miles and is slotted by two comfortable inlets, one on its east coast, the other on its west coast. While there is a 400-foot high knob in the southern part of Banika, the rest of the island is low and in 1943 was clear of jungle although with many beautiful coconut trees. It was judged suitable for an airfield.

These two main islands, separated by Sunlight Channel half a mile wide, are surrounded by dozens of small islands extending to ten to twelve miles off shore, particularly to the eastward. The most vivid remembrances of those who touched stays with the Russells were of "rain, mud, and magnificent coconuts."

When Commander South Pacific Area issued his final CLEANSLATE Operation Plan, he initiated an action with a major resemblance to its predecessor, the WATCHTOWER Operation, in that there was to be no long planning period available to Rear Admiral Turner's staff prior to the actual landing just nine days away.

The major purposes assigned by COMSOPAC for the operation were:

1. to strengthen the defense of Guadalcanal, and
2. to establish a staging point for landing craft preliminary to further forward movement.

The mission also included establishing an advanced motor torpedo base, an advanced air base, and radar installations.[6]

Rear Admiral Turner, COMPHIBSOPAC, was named as the Commander of the Joint Force designated Task Force 61, with the Commanding General 43rd Division, Major General John H. Hester, U. S. Army, being the Commander Landing Force.

Despite the fact that in February 1943 none of the Landing Force troops were in the Guadalcanal area except the Army Regiment designated as Troop Reserve, and the anti-aircraft contingent of the 11th Marine Defense Battalion, Task Force 61 was tailored for a "shore to shore" amphibious task.

---

[5] COMSOPAC, 282239 Jan; 060636, 070506, 112230, 150247, Feb. 1943.
[6] COMSOPAC, 070506, 112230 Feb. 1943.

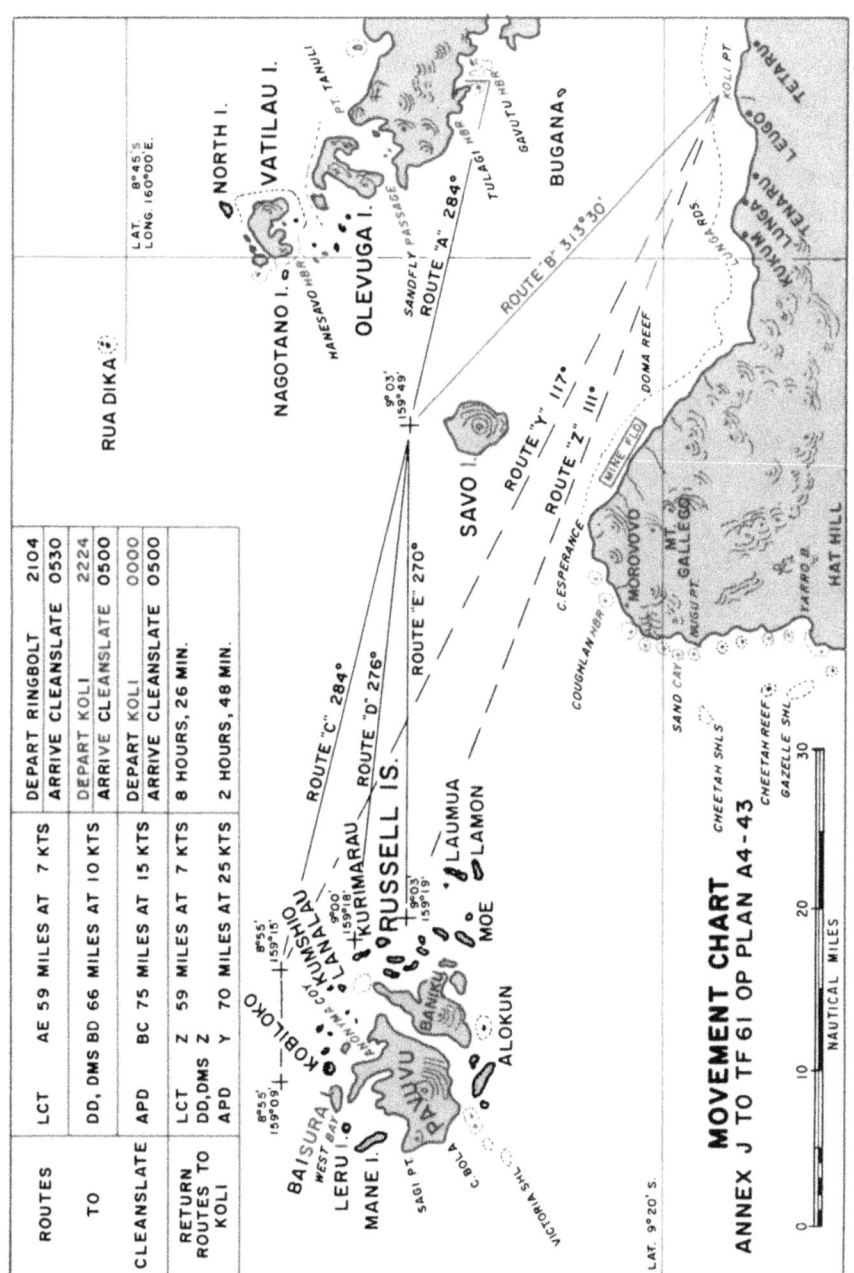

Movement Chart, CLEANSLATE.

In the language of the amphibians this meant that the assault movement of personnel and materiel would move direct from a shore staging area to the landing beaches of the assault objective, involving no further transfers between types of landing craft or into landing boats during the assault movement. The shore staging area designated for CLEANSLATE was Koli Point, Guadalcanal. Gavutu Island in Purvis Bay would handle the overflow.

Such a "shore to shore movement" meant that the long distance overwater movement to Guadalcanal of the amphibious troops participating in the D-Day initial landings of the CLEANSLATE Operation had to be carried out prior to the final embarkation at Guadalcanal for the assault.

A desire to effect complete surprise if the Japanese were still in the Russells, or if they were not, a desire to deny the Japanese knowledge of the occupation of the Russells for as long as possible, prompted the decision to carry out a shore-to-shore-type operation.[7]

The TF 61 organization for CLEANSLATE was as follows:

CLEANSLATE ORGANIZATION—TF 61

(a) *TG 61.1 Transport Group*—Rear Admiral Turner (1908)
   TU 61.1.1 TRANSDIV Twelve—Commander John D. Sweeney (1926)
   Stringham (APD-6) Lieutenant Commander Adolphe Wildner (1932)
   Manley (APD-1) Lieutenant Otto C. Schatz (1934)
   Humphreys (APD-14) Lieutenant Commander Maurice J. Carley, USNR
   Sands (APD-13) Lieutenant Commander John J. Branson (1927)
   Each with 4 LCP(L) and 15 LCR(L) on board.
   TU 61.1.2 Mine Group—Commander Stanley Leith (1923)
   Hopkins (DMS-13) Lieutenant Commander Francis M. Peters, Jr. (1931)
   Trever (DMS-16) Lieutenant Commander Joseph C. Wylie (1932)
   Southard (DMS-10) Lieutenant Commander John G. Tennent, III (1932)
   Maury (DD-401) Commander Gelzer L. Sims (1925)
   McCall (DD-400) Commander William S. Veeder (1925)
   TU 61.1.3 TRANSDIV Dog—Commander Wilfrid Nyquist (1921)
   Saufley (DD-465) Commander Bert F. Brown (1926)
   Craven (DD-382) Lieutenant Commander Francis T. Williamson (1931)

---

[7] Staff Interviews.

Hovey (DMS-11) Lieutenant Commander Edwin A. McDonald (1931)

Gridley (DD-380) Commander Fred R. Stickney (1925)

Zane (DMS-14) Lieutenant Commander Peyton L. Wirtz (1931)

TU 61.1.4 TRANSDIV *Easy*—Commander Thomas J. Ryan (1921)

    Wilson (DD-408) Lieutenant Commander Walter H. Price (1927)

    Lansdowne (DD-486) Lieutenant Commander Francis J. Foley (1931)

    LCT-158 Lieutenant Edgar M. Jaeger, USNR, LCT–58, LCT–60

    LCT-159 Lieutenant (jg) Frank M. Wiseman, USNR, LCT 156, LCT 369

    LCT-181 Lieutenant Ashton L. Jones, USNR, LCT-62, LCT-322

    LCT-63 Lieutenant (jg) Ameel Z. Kouri, USNR, LCT-323, LCT-367

Each destroyer type except *Hopkins, Wilson,* and *Lansdowne* towing 1 LCM, 1 LCV and 2 LCP.

(b) TU 61.1.5 *Service Group*—Lieutenant James L. Foley (1929)

    Bobolink (AT-131) with 1000-ton flat top lighter in tow.

TG 61.2 *Attack Group*—Lieutenant Allen H. Harris, USNR

    Motor Torpedo Boat Squadron TWO (THREE)

PT-36	PT-144
PT-40	PT-145
PT-42	PT-146
PT-48	PT-147
PT-109	PT-148
PT-110	

    8 of the 11 boats in the Squadron were to be picked for the operation.

(c) TG 61.3 *Occupation Force*—Major General Hester

    TU 61.3.1 *Landing Force*—Major General Hester

        43rd Infantry Division (less 172nd Combat Team)

        3rd Marine Raider Battalion (temporarily attached)

        one-third 11th Marine Defense Battalion

        one platoon of Company B, 579th Aircraft Warning Battalion (Radar)

        one regiment from CACTUS Force (when assigned)

    TU 61.3.2 *Naval Base*—Commander Charles E. Olsen (1919)

        Naval Advance Base Force

        ACORN Three

        one-half 35th Construction Battalion

        Naval Communication Units

        CLEANSLATE Boat Pool (50 boats)

---

* *Gridley* substituted for *Hovey* in initial movement.

AT THE LANDING CRAFT LEVEL

The Landing Craft, Tank (LCT) of 1942–43 was 112 feet over-all, had a 32-foot beam, and a draft of a little over three feet. It was normally expected to carry four 40-ton tanks or to load 150 to 180 tons or about 5,760 cubic feet of cargo. Its actual speed, loaded and in a smooth sea, was a bit more than six knots, although it had a designed speed of ten knots. These large tank landing craft, which shipyards in the United States started to deliver in large numbers in September and October of 1942, were the first of their kind to be used offensively in the South Pacific.

The LCT had but one commissioned officer and 12 to 14 men aboard them when they arrived in the South Pacific. The LCTs were not commissioned ships of the Navy, the one officer being designated as the Officer in Charge. They had insufficient personnel to keep a ship's log, much less a war diary, and by and large they passed in and out of their service in the Navy leaving no individual record, except in the memories of those who served in them or had some service performed by them. Presumably, the LCT Flotilla and LCT Group Commanders kept a log and a war diary, but if they did so, by and large they have not survived to reach the normal repositories of such documents.

The first mention of the LCT in Rear Admiral Turner's Staff Log occurs on 19 December 1942, when 6 LCT (5) were reported at Noumea loading for Guadalcanal. Presumably the LCT arrived on station earlier that month.

Through the leadership efforts of Rear Admiral George H. Fort (1912), his Chief of Staff, Captain Benton W. Decker (1920), and after arrival in SOPAC his senior landing craft subordinate, Captain Grayson B. Carter (1919), the Landing Craft Flotillas, PHIBFORSOPAC, were trained under forced draft. After only 12 months of war, the landing craft were manned to a marked extent with officers and men who had entered the Navy after the attack on Pearl Harbor. To assist in the training, Commander Landing Craft Flotillas in due time issued a comprehensive Doctrine full of instructions and information for the dozens of landing craft moving into the SOPAC command during the January to June period in 1943.[8] The LCT "Veterans" of CLEANSLATE became the nuclei for this massive training effort.

As a matter of record, the first 12 LCTs to get their bottoms crinkled in war operations in the South Pacific were LCT-58, 60, 62, 63, 156, 158, 159, 181, 322, 323, 367, 369, organized administratively as follows:

---
[8] Commander Landing Craft Flotillas, PHIBFORSOPAC Doctrine, May 1943.

LCT Flotilla Five—Lieutenant Edgar M. Jaeger, USNR
  LCT Group 13—Lieutenant Ashton L. Jones, USNR
    LCT Division 25—Lieutenant Ashton L. Jones, USNR
      LCT-58—Ensign Edward H. Burtt, USNR
      LCT-60—Ensign Austin H. Volk, USNR
      LCT-156—Ensign Richard T. Eastin, Jr., USNR
      LCT-158—Ensign Edward J. Ruschmann, USNR
      LCT-159—Ensign John A. McNiel
    LCT Division 26—Lieutenant (jg) Ameel Z. Kouri, USNR
      LCT-62—Ensign Robert T. Capeless, USNR
      LCT-63—Ensign Lunsford L. Shelton, USNR
  LCT Group 14—Lieutenant Decatur Jones, USNR
    LCT Division 27—Lieutenant Decatur Jones, USNR
      LCT-322—Ensign Carl M. Barrett, USNR
      LCT-323—Ensign Carl T. Geisler, USNR
    LCT Division 28—
      LCT-367—Ensign Robert Carr, USNR
      LCT-369—Ensign Walter B. Gillette, USNR
  LCT Group 15—Lieutenant Laurence C. Lisle, USNR
    LCT Division 29—Lieutenant Laurence C. Lisle, USNR
      LCT-181—Ensign Herbert D. Solomon
    LCT Division 30—Lieutenant (jg) Frank M. Wiseman, USNR

Most of the senior officers in this organization (Jaeger, A. L. Jones, Kouri, and Wiseman) participated in CLEANSLATE. They got the LCTs off to a good start in the South Pacific.

The largest landing craft carried by the amphibious transports and cargo ships was the Landing Craft, Medium (LCM). The LCM could carry 30 tons or 2,200 cubic feet of cargo. Amongst the smaller shipborne landing craft, both the Higgins Landing Craft, Personnel (LCP) and the ramp LCV could transport 36 men or one medium tank. The destroyers which had been converted into fast transports could carry 200 troops and limited amounts of these troops' equipment. The converted fast minesweepers could carry somewhat fewer troops.

THE SPIT KIT EXPEDITIONARY FORCE

Task Force 61, in effect the Joint Expeditionary Force, consisted of the Army troops and Marines in the 9,000 Landing Force, seven destroyers (*Craven, Gridley, Landsdowne, Maury, McCall, Saufley, Wilson*), four fast destroyer-type transports (*Stringham, Manley, Humphreys, Sands*), four fast minesweepers, the logistic service ship *Bobolink,* eight motor torpedo boats

(PTs) of Torpedo Boat Squadron Two, and twelve LCTs of Landing Craft Tank Flotilla Five.

The TF 61 Operation order for CLEANSLATE indicates that the 12 LCTs were from LCT Group 13, but as a matter of fact there were seven LCTs from Group 13, four LCTs from Group 14, and one from Group 15, all temporarily assigned to LCT Group 13 for operational control.

Of the 16 ships, 108 large and small landing craft and 8 motor torpedo boats in the spit kit amphibious force and CLEANSLATE, only the fast minesweepers *Hopkins, Trever, Southward,* and *Zane,* and the destroyer *Wilson* of the ships in the original WATCHTOWER invasion task force shared with Rear Admiral Turner the satisfaction of participating in the initial phase of the first forward island jumping movement of the South Pacific Area. The *Hovey* (DMS-11) lost out on this high honor when she did not arrive at Guadalcanal in time to load and the *Gridley* (DD-380) was substituted for her in the initial phase of CLEANSLATE.

In addition to the 43rd Infantry Division (less its 172nd Regimental Combat Team) the major units named to participate in the operation were the Marine 3rd Raider Battalion, anti-aircraft elements of the Marine 11th Defense Battalion, half of the 35th Naval Construction Battalion and ACORN Three, and the naval unit designated to construct, operate, and maintain the planned aircraft facilities on Banika Island. An ACORN was an airfield assembly designed to construct, operate, and maintain an advanced land plane and seaplane base and provide facilities for operation. Marine Air Group 21 and the 10th Marine Defense Battalion were enroute to the South Pacific Area and were to be assigned to the Russells upon arrival.

CLEANSLATE was the first major amphibious island jumping operation where radar-equipped planes, "Black Cats," were used to cover all of the night movements of our own ship and craft against the approach of enemy surface and air forces.

SUPPORTING FORCES

CTF 63, COMAIRSOPACFOR, Vice Admiral Fitch, was ordered to provide long-range air search, anti-aircraft cover, anti-submarine screen and air strikes. If needed, he would supply direct air support during the landing and advance from the beaches.

Cruiser Division 12, at the moment commanded by Captain Aaron S. (Tip) Merrill, about to be elevated to Flag rank, was ordered to provide immediate support to TF 61, and the fast carrier task forces were ordered to be within supporting distance of the Russells on D-Day to deal with any major Japanese Naval Forces entering the lower Solomons.

When COMSOPAC issued his despatch Operation Order for CLEANSLATE on Lincoln's birthday, 1943, the 43rd Division troops, ACORN Three, and the naval base personnel were in New Caledonia 840 miles south of Guadalcanal, while the Marine raiders and the construction battalion were in Espiritu Santo 560 miles to the south.

By the time the unanticipated needs and expressed desires of the Commander Landing Force, who doubled as Commander Occupation Force, had been met, the Landing Force totaled over 15,000. CINCPAC's Staff, after receiving COMSOPAC's list of CLEANSLATE participating forces, noted in their Daily Command Summary:

> The forces planned for this operation are greatly in excess of those mentioned in the recent conference between Admirals Nimitz and Halsey. [i.e. one Raider Battalion and part of a Defense Battalion] [9]

The staging movement of Army troops and Marines, Seabees, and other naval personnel into Guadalcanal and Gavutu was accomplished in large transports and cargo ships, six echelons arriving before D-Day, 21 February, and four follow-up echelons moving through after the 21st.

PRELIMINARIES

During the nine-day period between the issuance of COMSOPAC's CLEANSLATE Operation Order and the actual landing, two groups of observers from TF 61 visited the Russells and reported that the islands had recently been evacuated by the Japanese. These parties obtained detailed information in regard to landing beaches and selected camp locations and anti-aircraft gun sites. The second group remained to welcome the Task Force, and marked the landing beaches to be used. This was a task later to be taken over under more difficult and dangerous conditions by the Underwater Demolition Teams.

The main movement of the amphibians from the staging areas to the Russells was planned and completed in four major echelons. Over 4,000 of these were landed in the Russells from the first echelon ships and craft on the first day.

---

[9] CINCPAC, *Command Summary*, Book Three, 8 Feb. 1943, p. 1390.

The over-water movement from Koli Point, Guadalcanal, to the Russells for the initial landings was planned and largely carried out as shown on the accompanying movement chart.

During the preliminary movement when the first echelon of the 43rd Division was being staged the 840 miles from New Caledonia to Koli Point, Rear Admiral Turner moved with them in the *McCawley* which carried part of the amphibian troops. On 16 February 1943, he shifted his operational staff ashore to Koli Point from the *McCawley*. During the first phase of the CLEANSLATE landing operations he flew his flag in the fast minesweeper *Hopkins*, and commanded the Transport Group, TG 61.1.

On 19 February 1943, one task group (4 APA, 1 AO, 6 DD) carrying the second echelon of the amphibians and their logistic support from Noumea to the Koli staging area on Guadalcanal was subjected to a seven aircraft Japanese torpedo plane attack when about 20 miles east of the southern tip of San Cristobal Island. By radical maneuver, the transports and their destroyer escorts escaped damage, and by spirited anti-aircraft fire accounted for five Japanese aircraft lost. Otherwise, the ten-day preparation period was largely unhampered by the Japanese.

THE LANDINGS

Rear Admiral Turner's (CTF 61) and Commander Landing Force's orders called for three simultaneous landing at dawn on 21 February 1943. These were (1) on the north of Pavuvu Island at Pepesala Bay, (2) at Renard Sound on the east coast of Banika Island, and (3) at Wernham Cove on the southwest coast of Banika Island. According to Rear Admiral Turner's Operation Order:

> The landing beaches in the Russells are bad, with much coral. *Every precaution will be taken to prevent damage to boats, particularly propellers.*[10]

For the initial landings totaling 4,030 officers and enlisted [11] on Pavuvu and Banika, more than 200 men were ferried on each of the seven destroyers, four destroyer transports, and four fast minesweepers. Additionally, all the destroyers except the *Wilson* (DD-408) and the *Lansdowne* (DD-486), which were designated for anti-submarine patrolling around the task units, and all the fast minesweepers (less the *Hopkins*, designated both as Flagship

---
[10] CTF 61 Op Order Plan A4-43, 15 Feb. 1943, p. 6.
[11] CTF 61 to COMSOPAC, 210551 Feb. 1943.

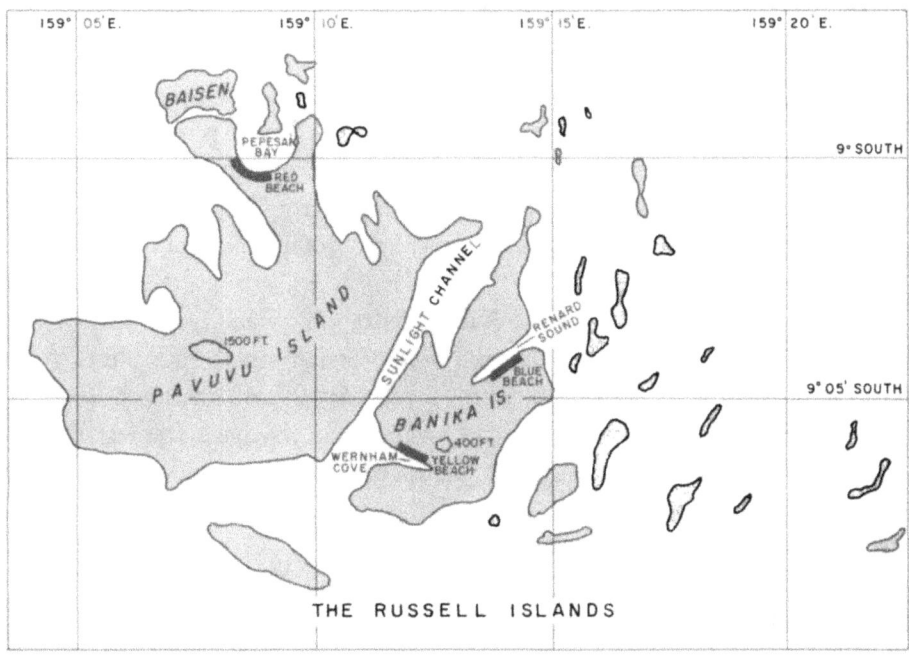

The CLEANSLATE Objective.

and for anti-submarine patrolling) towed four landing craft: two Landing Craft, Personnel (LCP) and two Landing Craft, Vehicle (1 LCV and 1 LCM). The four fast transports each carried, in addition to troops, four LCVPs and 15 rubber landing boats. The mighty *Bobolink* (AT-121) towed a 1,000-ton flat top lighter for use at Wernham Cove.

For the initial landings:

> The plan was for destroyers carrying a naval base unit and a certain number of troops to tow LCVs and LCVPs from naval bases at Guadalcanal and Gavutu (near Tulagi). . . . I can remember the Operations Officer, Captain Doyle, designing towing bridles for these small craft and ordering several of our vessels to make up a number of them.[12]

* * * * *

During three nights prior to the first movement, special pains were taken to obtain radar information as to the detailed night movement of enemy planes near GUADALCANAL and especially along the route from there to the RUSSELLS. The radar showed enemy planes were operating every night in areas to the westward of SAVO ISLAND from shortly after dark until about an hour before midnight. Consequently, movements of the CLEANSLATE force to the westward of SAVO were withheld until after that hour on

---

[12] Anderson.

February 20th, and [after final] decision was made to effect the first landing at daybreak the 21st.[18]

CLEANSLATE went off with precision, but without fanfare or publicity since it was believed that the Japanese were unaware of the preparations for the operation or its execution. So besides radio silence, there was press and public relations silence. All the ships and landing craft, except one LCT with engine trouble, departed for their return passages to Guadalcanal by 1230 on D-Day.

The 800 men of the 3rd Marine Raider Battalion, which had missed out on the WATCHTOWER Operation, were loaded onto four destroyer transports at Koli Point and at 0600 on 21 February landed on Beach Red in Pepesala (Paddy) Bay, Pavuvu Island, where the Japanese formerly had their main strength and where Major General Hester, Commander Landing Force, in his Operation Order expressed the opinion "definite possibilities exist that enemy patrols and small units may be located."

Rear Admiral Turner, Major General Hester, and their operational staffs went ashore from the *Hopkins* onto Beach Yellow in Wernham Cove, Banika Island. They landed just after 800 troops from two DDs and two DMSs and additional troops ferried in by eight LCTs had landed. The Naval Base Headquarters was established on the north side of Wernham Cove.

Another 800 troops from three DDs and one DMS and additional troops aboard four LCTs landed at Beach Blue, Renard South. Most of the Banika Island troops came from the 103rd Regimental Combat Team of the 43rd Infantry Division.

A follow-up landing of 800 troops from the 169th Infantry Regiment of the 43rd Division, U. S. Army, took place on the sandy beaches of Pepesala (Paddy) Bay in northern Pavuvu Island, early on the morning of 22 February, the day after the Marines had landed in this area. At the same time 1,400 more troops landed at Beach Yellow in Wernham Cove.

The second to fourth follow-up echelons moved on D plus 2, D plus 3, and D plus 4. The ships and craft continued to make most all their movements between Guadalcanal and the Russells at night, so as not to alert the Japanese to the operation. The destroyer-types made a complete round trip at night, while the LCTs largely made one-way passage each night. No public disclosure of the landing was immediately made and the base at CLEANSLATE maintained radio silence.

---

[18] COMPHIBFORSOPAC, Report of Occupation of Russell Islands (CLEANSLATE Operation), 21 Apr. 1943, para. 19. Hereafter CLEANSLATE Report.

In two days 7,000 troops were landed. By 15 March, 15,500 troops were in the Russells and by 18 April when, at long last, command passed to the Commanding General, Guadalcanal, 16,000 men were busy there and no less than 48,517 tons of supplies had arrived there by amphibious effort. The Japanese did not react to the occupation for 15 days. On 6 March 1943, they made the first of a series of air raids.

Commander Charles Eugene Olsen (1919), who had successfully skippered the early base building efforts at Tongatabu, and who had impressed Rear Admiral Turner when he had flown through the Tonga Islands in July 1942, was brought down and given the task of building the Advanced Naval Base in the Russell Islands. By the end of March, on Banika Island, there was a good airfield with three fighter squadrons on Marine Air Group 21, a motor torpedo base (at Renard Sound) and a growing supply activity.

Old Man Weather and his twin, navigational hazard, unhappily put three destroyer-types (*Lansdowne, Stringham, Sands*) on the beach on February 26th. The landing craft had a normal ration of unintentional groundings and breakdowns, but none of the destroyer-types became permanent additions to the Russells.

Airfield on Banika Island in the Russells.

COMPHIBFORSOPAC report of the operation stated that:

> As soon as all forces had landed, the airfield constructed, and stocks of ten units of fire and sixty days supplies built up, command was to pass to the Commanding General at Guadalcanal.

Long before this blessed event occurred, Rear Admiral George H. Fort relieved Rear Admiral Turner as Commander Task Force 61 (on 3 March 1943) and Rear Admiral Turner returned to Noumea to continue his favorite chore of planning the next operation.

RESULTS ACHIEVED

This CLEANSLATE Operation, with its most appropriate code name for the Southern Solomons, has been both praised and superciliously sneered at. *Time Magazine,* for example, said the

> operation went more smoothly [than Guadalcanal]. The Japs had evacuated.[14]

A week after the initial landings in the Russells, CTF 61 (Turner) sent out a routine logistical support despatch report to his superiors. Rear Admiral Turner listed the considerable number of troops and quantities of material already in the Russells and the extensive logistic support movements planned for the Russells during the next weeks. The sending of the despatch was prompted by COMSOPAC's urgent desires to begin to get ready to move further up the Solomon Islands chain toward Rabaul, and by the desire of one of his subordinates (Turner) to give him some heartening news of logistic readiness.[15]

This despatch came into COMINCH's Headquarters at a time when the question of Phase Two operations following Phase One of PESTILENCE operations was under daily review. Admiral King, as always, was against diversionary use of limited resources. So he reacted sharply. And while he very possibly set COMSOPAC and CINCPAC back on their heels for an instant, he also gave them an opportunity to enlighten the big boss on what they were hoping and planning to do reasonably soon.[16]

Although it has been inferred by several authors that Admiral King questioned the worth of the CLEANSLATE Operation by this despatch, this is

---
[14] *Time Magazine,* 31 Jan. 1944.
[15] Staff Interviews.
[16] CTF 61, 270628 Feb. 1943, and related COMINCH, CINCPAC, and COMSOPAC despatches.

not so.[17] What Admiral King questioned was the extent and purpose of the build-up in the Russell Islands following CLEANSLATE. His despatch contained these questioning words:

> What useful purpose is being served by operations on scale indicated by CTF 61's 270628? . . .

Admiral Nimitz and Vice Admiral Halsey supplied these satisfying answers to Admiral King:

> Halsey is planning to take Vila-Munda with target date April 10.
>
> Troops and material [are] headed in proper direction and thus completing first stage of next movement.

In June 1943, Rear Admiral Turner made a simple exposition to newspaper correspondents as to why we needed the Russells, before moving into the central Solomons:

> . . . It was simply because we must have fighter coverage for Rendova. . . . We couldn't have fighters from Guadal [canal]. It's that extra little distance west that makes coverage possible for Rendova [from the Russells].
>
> * * * * *
>
> . . . From Rendova to the Russells is 125 miles, from Guadal to the Russells 60 miles.[18]

When the Russell Islands logistical support movements were completed, COMSOPAC took note of this and smartly changed the code name of the Russells to EMERITUS.

SUMMARY

From the point of view of both COMSOPAC and COMPHIBFORSOPAC, the Russells had two great advantages over any and all other immediately possible objectives necessary to carry out the 2 July 1942 Joint Chiefs of Staff directive. The Russells (1) were on the direct line from Guadalcanal to Rabaul and (2) they lay within COMSOPAC's command area, so that high level arrangements in regard to command did not have to be negotiated, a process taking weeks or months. It is merely a guess but the latter reason surely carried the greater weight with COMSOPAC in choosing a spot where a quick operation could be carried out when WATCHTOWER was completed.

---

[17] (a) Morison, *Breaking the Bismarcks Barrier* (Vol. V), p. 98; (b) Henry I. Shaw and Douglas T. Kane, *Isolation of Rabaul*, Vol. II of HISTORY OF U.S. MARINE CORPS OPERATIONS IN WORLD WAR II (Washington: Government Printing Office, 1963), p. 26.

[18] Joseph Driscoll, *Pacific Victory 1945* (Philadelphia: J. B. Lippincott Co., 1944), p. 66.

A complementary benefit, however, was operational. The amphibians had an excellent opportunity to put together the dozens of suggestions arising out of WATCHTOWER for the improvement of amphibious operations and test them under conditions far more rugged than any rear area rehearsal could provide. The Russells added not only skill but confidence to the amphibians. As Rear Admiral Turner pointed out:

> During the course of the operation a technique was developed for the movement of troops and cargo from a forward base to a nearby objective without the use of APAs and AKAs. It is expected that the experience of this operation will prove useful in planning future offensives.
>
> The CLEANSLATE Operation again demonstrated that the overwater movement and landing of the first echelon of troops is only the initial step in a continuous amphibious series, all of which are integral parts of the same venture. Success of the venture depends upon the ability to deliver safely not only the first, but also the succeeding echelons of troops, engineers, ancillary units, equipment and operating and upkeep supplies and replacements. The aggregate of personnel and cargo for the later movements is far greater than that carried initially. Each movement requires protection, and losses in transit from the logistic bases to the combat position must be kept low enough to be acceptable. It is particularly when small vessels are used that an uninterrupted stream of them must be maintained.
>
> The first movement for the seizure of a position; the exploitation on shore of that position; the long series of succeeding movements of troops and material, together form a single operation. All parts must be accomplished, under satisfactory security conditions if the whole operation is to be successful.[19]

INTERLUDE

From the period of its activation in July 1942 to the completion of its first major tasks in January 1943, the Amphibious Force, South Pacific had about the same number of ships and landing craft assigned with replacements being supplied for ships sunk or worn out in war service. But there was a steadily growing prospect of a real increase in size when the coastal transports and larger landing craft, building or training on the East and West Coasts of the United States, were finally cut loose and sailed to the South Pacific to fulfill their war assignment.

By late January 1943, the ships and landing craft assigned to the Amphibious Force South Pacific had grown sufficiently so that a new organization was established as follows:

---

[19] COMPHIBFORSOPAC CLEANSLATE Report, 21 Apr. 1943, p. 14.

USS *McCawley* (APA-4) FORCE FLAGSHIP
Commander R. H. Rodgers (1923)

TRANSPORT GROUP, SOUTH PACIFIC AMPHIBIOUS FORCE
Captain L. F. Reifsnider (1910)

COMTRANSDIV Two
  Captain I. N. Kiland (1917)
    APA-18 *President Jackson* (F)
      Commander C. W. Weitzel (1917)
    APA-20 *President Hayes*
      Commander F. W. Benson (1917)
    APA-19 *President Adams*
      Captain Frank H. Dean (1917)
    AKA-8 *Algorab*
      Captain J. R. Lannon (1919)

COMTRANSDIV Eight
  Captain G. B. Ashe (1911)
    APA-17 *American Legion* (F)
      Commander R. C. Welles (1919)
    APA-27 *George Clymer*
      Captain A. T. Moen (1918)
    APA-21 *Crescent City*
      Captain J. R. Sullivan (1918)
    AKA-12 *Libra*
      Commander W. B. Fletcher (1920)
    AKA-6 *Alchiba*
      Commander H. R. Shaw (1929)

COMTRANSDIV Ten
  Captain Lawrence F. Reifsnider (1910)
    APA-14 *Hunter Liggett* (F)
      Captain L. W. Perkins, USCG
    APA-23 *John Penn*
      Captain Harry W. Need (1918)
    AKA-9 *Alhena*
      Commander Howard W. Bradbury (1920)
    AKA-5 *Formalhaut*
      Commander Henry C. Flanagan (1919)

COMTRANSDIV 12
  Commander John D. Sweeney (1926)
    APD-6 *Stringham* (F)
      Lieutenant Commander Adolphe Wildner (1932)
    APD-1 *Manley*
      Lieutenant Otto C. Schatz (1934)
    APD-5 *McKean*
      Lieutenant Ralph L. Ramey (1935)

APD-7 *Talbot*
  Lieutenant Commander Charles C. Morgan, USNR
APD-8 *Waters*
  Lieutenant Charles J. McWhinnie, USNR
APD-9 *Dent*
  Lieutenant Commander Ralph A. Wilhelm, USNR

COMTRANSDIV 14
  Captain Paul S. Theiss (1912)
    APA-15 *Henry T. Allen* (F)
      Captain Paul A. Stevens (1913)
    APA-7 *Fuller*
      Captain Henry E. Thornhill (1921)
    APA-4 *McCawley* (FF)
      Commander Robert H. Rodgers (1923)
    AKA-13 *Titania*
      Commander Victor C. Barringer (1918)

COMTRANSDIV-16
  Lieutenant Commander James S. Willis (1927)
    APD-10 *Brooks* (F)
      Lieutenant Commander John W. Ramey (1932)
    APD-11 *Gilmer*
      Lieutenant Commander John S. Horner, USNR
    APD-14 *Humphreys*
      Lieutenant Commander Maurice J. Carley, USNR
    APD-13 *Sands*
      Lieutenant Commander John J. Branson (1927)

LANDING CRAFT FLOTILLAS
Rear Admiral George H. Fort (1912)

LST Flotilla Five
  Captain Grayson B. Carter (1919)
  LST Groups 13, 14, 15

LST GROUP 13

Commander LST Group 13   Commander Roger W. Cutler, USNR

LST Division 25
  LST-446   Lieutenant William A. Small
  LST-447(FF)   Lieutenant Frank H. Storms, USNR
  LST-448   Ensign Charles E. Roeschke
  LST-449   Lieutenant Carlton Livingston
  LST-460   Lieutenant Everett Weire
  LST-472   Lieutenant William O. Talley
LST Division 26
  LST-339   Lieutenant John H. Fulweiller, USNR
  LST-340(FF)   Lieutenant William Villella

Polishing Skills in the Russells 477

    LST-395   Lieutenant Alexander C. Forbes, USNR
    LST-396   Lieutenant Eric W. White
    LST-397   Lieutenant Nathaniel L. Lewis, USNR
    LST-398(F)   Lieutenant Boyd E. Blanchard, USNR

LST GROUP 14

Commander LST Group 14   Commander Paul S. Slawson (1920)

LST Division 27	*LST Division 28*
LST-166	LST-71
LST-167	LST-172
LST-334	LST-203
LST-341	LST-207
LST-342(GF)	LST-353
LST-390	LST-354

LCI Flotilla Five
  Commander Chester L. Walton (1920)
  LCI Groups 13, 14, 15

LCI GROUP 13 (LCI–67 Flag)

Commander LCI Group 13   Lieutenant Commander Marion M. Byrd (1927)

LCI Division 25

    LCI-61(F)   Lieutenant John P. Moore, USNR
    LCI-62   Lieutenant (jg)) William C. Lyons (12570)
    LCI-63   Lieutenant (jg) John H. McCarthy, USNR
    LCI-64   Lieutenant Herbert L. Kelley, USNR
    LCI-65   Lieutenant (jg) Christopher R. Tompkins, USNR
    LCI-66   Lieutenant Charles F. Houston, Jr., USNR

LCI Division 26

    LCI(L)-21   Ensign Marshall M. Cook, USNR
    LCI(L)-22   Lieutenant (jg) Spencer V. Hinckley, USNR
    LCI-67(F)   Lieutenant (jg) Ernest E. Tucker, USNR
    LCI-68   Lieutenant Clifford D. Older, USNR
    LCI-69   Lieutenant Frazier L. O'Leary, USNR
    LCI-70   Lieutenant (jg) Harry W. Frey, USNR

LCI GROUP 14 (LCI–327 Flag)

Commander LCI Group 14
                Lieutenant Commander Alfred V. Janotta, USNR

LCI Division 27

    LCI-327(F)   Lieutenant (jg) North H. Newton, USNR
    LCI-328   Lieutenant Joseph D. Kerr, USNR
    LCI-329   Lieutenant William A. Illing, USNR
    LCI-330   Lieutenant (jg) Homer G. Maxey, USNR
    LCI-331   Lieutenant Richard O. Shelton, USNR
    LCI-332   Lieutenant William A. Neilson, USNR

LCI Division 28
  LCI(L)-23 Lieutenant Ben A. Thirkfield, USNR
  LCI(L)-24 Lieutenant (jg) Raymond E. Ward (12444)
  LCI-333   Lieutenant Horace Townsend, USNR
  LCI-334   Lieutenant (jg) Alfred J. Ormston, USNR
  LCI-335   Lieutenant (jg) John R. Powers, USNR
  LCI-336   Lieutenant (jg) Thomas A. McCoy, USNR

LCI GROUP 15

Commander LCI Group 15 Commander J. McDonald Smith (1925)

LCI Division 29   *LCI Division 30*
  LCI-222 Ensign Clarence M. Reese, USNR
  LCI-223 Lieutenant Frank P. Stone, USNR

LCT Flotilla Five
  Lieutenant Edgar Jaeger, USN
  LCT Groups 13, 14, 15

LCT GROUP 13

Commander of LCT Group 13 Lieutenant Ashton L. Jones, USNR
LCT Division 25
  Lieutenant A. L. Jones, USNR
LCT Division 26
  Lieutenant (jg) Ameel Z. Kouri, USNR

LCT GROUP 14

Commander of LCT Group 14 Lieutenant Decatur Jones, USNR
LCT Division 27
  Lieutenant Decatur Jones, USNR
LCT Division 28
  Lieutenant (jg) Thomas B. Willard, USNR

LCT GROUP 15

Commander of LCT Group 15 Lieutenant Laurence C. Lisle, USNR
LCT Division 29
  Lieutenant Laurence C. Lisle, USNR
LCT Division 30
  Lieutenant (jg) Frank M. Wiseman, USNR
LCT Flotilla Six
  LCT Groups 16, 17, 18

  By counting on one's fingers, it is obvious that among the large work horses of PHIBFORSOPAC there were now 18 ships (11 APAs and 7 AKAs) against 19 ships (14 APAs and 5 AKAs) six months earlier. However, there were 11 destroyer transports versus four at the earlier date and a definite promise of 127 landing ships and craft versus none at the earlier date.

  Eventually, it was planned that the Landing Craft Flotillas, SOPAC, would include 127 large landing ships and craft, i.e. 37 LSTs, 36 LCIs, and 54

LCTs. However, in late January 1943, only a few of the early birds had been formed up organizationally in the United States, much less trained in amphibious operations and pushed at speeds of eight knots or less across the wide spaces of the Central Pacific to the South Pacific.

Additional to the ships and craft listed above, four more APDs and 50 coastal transports (APCs) were under order to report to COMPHIBFORSOPAC, but they had not even reached the stage of paper organization into divisions and squadrons. When they reported, the force would consist of more than 200 ships and large landing craft.[20]

It is interesting to note from this roster list that the fast learning officers of the Naval Reserve had learned enough by January 1943 to take over command of some of the destroyer transports. And it is a commentary on how slowly the sky rocketing wartime promotion system spread to the Amphibious Force SOPAC, to note that a year after the Pacific War started, a fair number of the captains of the large and important transports of PHIBFORSOPAC had 23–25 years of commissioned service but were still wearing the three stripes of a commander.

---

[20] COMPHIBFORSOPAC letter, FE25/A3–1/Ser 007 of 20 Jan. 1943, subj: Organization and Staff of Amphibious Force, South Pacific, FE25/A3–1/Ser of 20 Jan. 1943, and CINCPAC's Organizational Roster dated 29 Jan. 1943.

CHAPTER XIV

Planning for Paring the Japanese Toenails in New Georgia

NEW GEORGIA—TOENAILS

TOENAILS was the code name given to the New Georgia Operation. The New Georgia landings in the Central Solomons commenced on 30 June 1943. Rear Admiral Turner was relieved of command of the Amphibious Forces, Third Fleet (South Pacific) by Rear Admiral Theodore S. Wilkinson (1909), on 15 July 1943. The New Georgia operation was completed on 25 August 1943. This chapter will deal with the planning phase and the chapter following will deal with the amphibious operations occurring prior to 15 July 1943.

LONG RANGE PLANNING—BREAKING THE BISMARCK BARRIER

The thinking of most planners in late 1942 was that in order to break the Bismarck Barrier, Rabaul had to be seized. To seize Rabaul, the United States had to have airfields within fighter plane range of Rabaul. To get such airfields, the United States must seize central, then northern islands in the Solomon chain as well as a position at the western end of New Britain Island, at whose eastern extremity Rabaul was located.

On 8 December 1942 the Chief of Staff COMSOPAC (Captain M. R. Browning) sent a memorandum to Rear Admiral Turner and to the Commanding General Amphibious Corps directing:

> Planning Sections initiate a preliminary examination of the possibility of our seizing this area [Roviana Lagoon, New Georgia] in the near future.

On 16 January 1943, a large conference was held by COMSOPAC for:

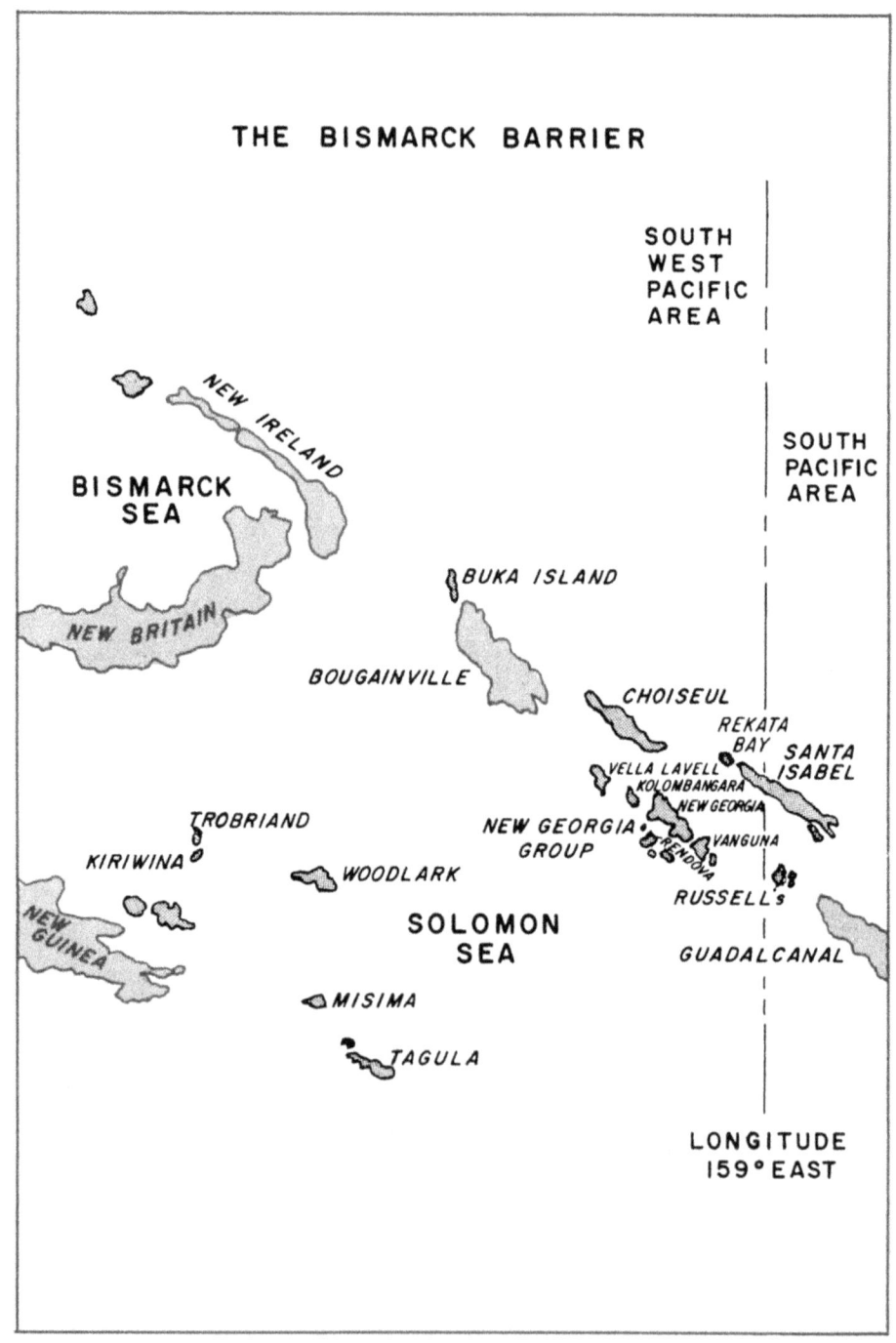

The Bismarck Barrier.

An informal discussion as to availability of units and supplies for offensive operations—objective Munda.[1]

In this latter memorandum it was assumed for "discussion purposes" that the movement would be a "shore to shore movement" from Guadalcanal to New Georgia of one Regimental Combat Team and two Raider Battalions.

At the same time that Rear Admiral Turner and COMSOPAC planners were focusing on Munda and New Georgia, CINCPAC planners were focusing on Rekata Bay and Santa Isabel Island. They opined:

> The choice between Munda and Rekata, for our next objective in the Solomons, is a close one, but hydrography makes the latter preferable—even though we have to build a field there ourselves.[2]

With the choice such a close one, and with SOPAC opting strongly for Munda, CINCPAC in due time gave his approval for this objective.[3]

OBJECTIVE—THE NEW GEORGIA GROUP

The New Georgia Group in the Middle Solomons covers an area 125 miles in length and 40 miles in width. It contains 12 large islands. COMSOPAC had a particular and immediate interest in four of the largest of these, New Georgia, Rendova, Kolombangara and Vangunu. Munda airfield located on New Georgia, the largest island in the group, was approximately 180 miles northwest from Guadalcanal and about 30 hours running time for an LCT. Thoughts of possession of Munda's 4,700-foot runway brought pleasant smiles to the planners' faces, for while the New Georgia Group was only a first step, one-third of the way to Rabaul, it was a step everyone at the time said was necessary.

All the charts of the pre-World War II period have all the larger islands in the New Georgia Group labeled "densely wooded." Those few who had visited them in pre-World War II days declared them heavily jungled. New Georgia Island was about 45 miles long and 30 miles wide, and the only really large low flat area on the island was around Munda airfield at the southern end of its northwest corner.

---

[1] COMSOPAC, memoranda, A1/A16–1/Ser 00121C of 8 Dec. 1942; A1/A16–3/00202 of 16 Jan. 1943.
[2] CINCPAC, *Command Summary,* Book Three, 15 Jan. 1943, subj: Estimate of the Situation, p. 1301.
[3] COMINCH 131250 Feb. 1943; CINCPAC 142357 Feb. 1943; COMSOPAC 161445, 250616 Feb. 1943.

Kolombangara across Kula Gulf to the northwest of New Georgia Island reached an elevation of 5,450 feet, while New Georgia Island itself topped out much lower at 2,690 feet. However, all the islands in the New Georgia Group were rugged with numerous peaks. There were no roads and few trails through the jungle growth. The islands were surrounded by an almost continuous outer circle of coral reefs and coral filled lagoons. The trees and undergrowth came right down to the beaches over a large part of the islands making it difficult to choose an area where it would be possible to move any logistic support inland.

It is desirable to recall that while the Joint Chiefs had prescribed that CINCPAC and COMSOPAC were to be the immediate commanders for Phase One (PESTILENCE) of the initial offensive move into the Solomon Islands, Phase Two which was the capture of the rest of Japanese-held Solomons and positions in New Guinea and Phase Three, the capture of Rabaul, were to be accomplished under the command of CINCSWPA, General Douglas MacArthur.[4]

On 6 January 1943, Admiral King had made a very definite attempt to have the naval tasks of these prospective Phase Two and Phase Three operations continue under the command of CINCPAC and his area subordinate, COMSOPAC, by limiting General MacArthur to the strategic direction of the campaigns. This did not evoke a favorable response from his opposite number in the Army, but it did stir the Joint Chiefs, on the 8th of January 1943, to ask General MacArthur how and when he was going to accomplish the unfinished task of Phase Two of PESTILENCE.[5]

At the Casablanca Conference, held from 14–23 January 1943, the Task Three decision in the 2 July 1942 Joint Chiefs PESTILENCE directive, which ordered the seizure of Rabaul in New Britain Island at the head of the Solomons, was reaffirmed. When this good news reached the South Pacific, where the concern was that the area might draw a later and lower priority than the Central Pacific, Vice Admiral Halsey on 11 February sent his Deputy Commander, Rear Admiral Theodore S. Wilkinson, to consult and advise with General MacArthur. Rear Admiral Wilkinson also carried COMSOPAC's comments on CINCSWPA's plans for Phase Two which were contained in CINCSWPA's despatches to the Joint Chiefs, information copies of which had been sent to CINCPAC and COMSOPAC.

---

[4] COMINCH, 022100 Jul. 1942.
[5] (a) CINCPAC to COMINCH, letter, A16-3/Ser 0259 W of 8 Dec. 1942; (b) COMINCH to C/S USA, memorandum, 6 Jan. 1943 and reply thereto; (c) JCS despatch 192 of 8 Jan. 1943.

Just a few days before Rear Admiral Wilkinson flew off to Australia, Admiral King on 8 February 1943 sent another memorandum to General Marshall, commenting on General MacArthur's reply to the Joint Chiefs of Staff despatch of 8 January 1943 and indirectly commenting on the command problem in his area.[6]

On the day before Lincoln's Birthday 1943, Vice Admiral Halsey informed COMINCH that the rapid consolidation of Japanese positions in the New Georgia Group emphasized the need for early United States seizure of these islands. He recommended that pressure on the Japanese be continued in the Southern Solomons, and that the occupation of the Gilbert and Ellice Islands (specifically Makin and Tarawa) in the Central Pacific, suggested by COMINCH as the next appropriate task after CLEANSLATE, be deferred until later.[7]

CINCPAC went along with this COMSOPAC recommendation.

On 14 February 1943, when there were many who believed the Japanese, now ousted from the Southern Solomons, would strike at some other island group in the South Pacific, Admiral Nimitz made the very shrewd estimate that the withdrawal of the Japanese from Guadalcanal probably indicated that the Japanese would shift to the strategical defensive in the South Pacific. Post-war Japanese records indicate that this is what happened.[8]

On 17 February 1943, the CINCPAC Staff Planners "assumed" that COMSOPAC "will attack Munda next and will employ one Marine Division." This represented some beefing up from the earlier concept of one Regimental Combat Team and two Raider Battalions, but still was a fair step away from the realities of the operation insofar as the landing forces are concerned. The planners reported to CINCPAC:

> It seems entirely feasible to make a simultaneous thrust up the Solomons, and in the Gilberts. Capture of objectives seems probable. Holding in Gilberts seems doubtful. . . . Because of preparation time required, May 15, 1943, is selected as the target date.[9]

The guestimate of a Dog Day of 15th of May by the CINCPAC Staff was missed by more than a long month, for it was the 21st of June before two companies of Marines were landed ahead of schedule at Segi Point, New

---

[6] (a) COMINCH to C/S USA, memoranda, Ser 0040 of 6 Jan. 1943; Ser 00195 of 8 Feb. 1943 and replies thereto; (b) JCS despatch 192 of 8 Jan.1943.

[7] (a) COMINCH to CINCPAC, 092200 Feb. 1943; (b) COMSOPAC to COMINCH, 110421 Feb. 1943; (c) CINCPAC to COMINCH, 112237 Feb. 1943.

[8] (a) CINCPAC to COMSOPAC, 142357 Feb. 1943; (b) Japanese Imperial General Headquarters (IGHQ), Army Directives, Vol. II, Agreement of 22 March 1943, p. 43.

[9] CINCPAC *Command Summary,* Book Three, 17 Feb. 1943, p. 1398.

New Georgia and Rendova Islands.

Georgia, and the 30th of June before Rendova and other islands in the New Georgia Group were invaded on schedule.

But in the four months from late February to late June 1943, much new meat was put in the grinder for future operations by the Joint Chiefs, only a small portion directly concerned with the South and Southwest Pacific. So it was not until the end of March 1943 that the Amphibious Force of the South Pacific, and other interested commands learned just what they were to do, although even then no definite time schedule was provided.

TALKING IT OVER AT A HIGH-LEVEL

On 12 March 1943, the Pacific Military Conference opened in Washington, D. C., with considerable talent present from the major commands of the Pacific. The chore was to examine, discuss, and if possible, decide upon ELKTON, which was General MacArthur's plan for carrying out Phase Two and Phase Three of the Joint Chiefs' 2 July 1942 directive for PESTILENCE.

The Navy planners sat back and drooled as General MacArthur's Chief of Staff set forth the considerable forces, particularly Army Air Forces, needed to carry out the ELKTON Plan. All during Phase One of the PESTILENCE Operation,[10] the SOPAC Navy felt that the Army Air Forces had short changed their needs in the South Pacific in favor of the bomber offensive against Germany. It was a distinct pleasure to hear the Army planners, in effect, saying that in order to move forward toward Rabaul, it would take about twice the then current allocation of air strength in the SOPAC-SOUWESPAC Areas.

Out of nearly ten days of proposal and counter-proposal and a meeting of some of the Pacific planners with the Joint Chiefs of Staff on 21 March 1943 came, in effect, a reaffirmation of Phase Two of the Joint Chiefs' PESTILENCE directive of 2 July 1942 and a requirement that it should be accomplished during 1943.

However, the Joint Chiefs made it clear that a new start was being made by cancelling the old 2 July 1942 directive. They issued a new directive for an operation labeled CARTWHEEL, an operation for (1) the seizure of the Solomon Islands up to the southern portion of Bougainville and (2) driving the Japanese out of certain specific areas in New Guinea and in Western New Britain. The Joint Chiefs made it equally clear that only a

---

[10] COMINCH, Memo for General Marshall, 2 Feb. 1943.

small proportion of the additional forces requested by General MacArthur would be supplied from the United States.

THE PROBLEM OF COMMAND SETTLED

The Joint Chiefs directed that the operations in the middle Solomons be conducted under the direct command of COMSOPAC, operating under the general (strategic) directives of CINCSWPA. Ships and aircraft from the Pacific Fleet, unless assigned by the Joint Chiefs to CARTWHEEL tasks, would remain under the control and allocation of the CINCPOA.[11]

It was a happy fact, from the Navy's viewpoint, that command during the CARTWHEEL Operation was to be exercised very much along the lines recommended by COMINCH to the Army Chief of Staff on 6 January 1943.

ON THE OTHER HAND—THE JAPANESE

The Japanese had largely by-passed the New Georgia Group in their giant strides towards New Caledonia until the struggle for Guadalcanal was in its later stages. Then they landed at Munda Point, New Georgia, on 14 November 1942 and, starting a week later, built a 4,700-foot airstrip during the next month. Following this, a Japanese airfield was built at Vila on Kolombangara Island just a scant 25 miles to the northwest of Munda. Two Special Naval Landing Forces (SNLF) were provided and the Japanese turned to and rapidly built up defenses around these two very usable and supporting airfields.

Further north up the Solomons, the Japanese also expanded their air facilities. There was an airfield at the south end of Vella Lavella Island, fifty miles to the northwest of Munda, and there were five airfields on Bougainville Island commencing with one 125 miles northwest of Munda. In addition, there was Ballale Island airfield in the Shortland Islands just south of Bougainville Island, and another airfield on Buka Island just north of Bougainville Island. All were backed up by the five airfields around Rabaul, 375 miles northwest of Munda. The Japanese worked diligently

---

[11] (a) JCS to CINCPAC, 232327 Mar. 1943; (b) JCS 5/9, 28 Mar. 1943; (c) JCS to CINCPAC-COMSOPAC, 291803 Mar. 1943; (d) CINCPAC to COMSOPAC, 302013 Mar. 1943 and reply thereto.

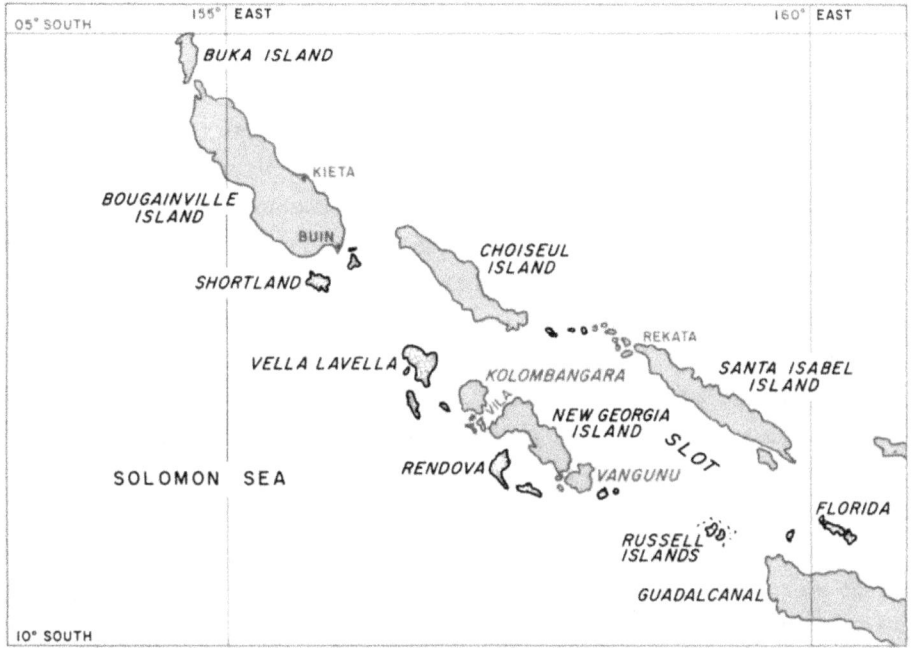

TOENAILS Operation Area.

for six months to perfect their defenses in the New Georgia Group. During a major part of these six months, the SOPAC forces planning to land in the New Georgia Group waited for the questions of high command and of concurrent operations in the Southwest Pacific Area to be settled before really being able to plan definite steps to push the Japanese out at a reasonably sure date.

Not that the problem of bringing available United States air power to bear in the Central Solomons was overlooked during this delay. Soon after capturing Henderson Field on Guadalcanal, a second airstrip on Guadalcanal had been started. Now there were four airstrips on Guadalcanal and two more in the Russells were being made ready. Planes from these fields, by regular bombing raids, kept the Japanese alert and particularly busy filling up holes on the Munda and Vila airfields. To show the extent of the air effort, CINCPAC reported that during June 1943, 1,455 SOPAC planes dropped 1,156,075 pounds of bombs on Japanese objectives in the Solomons.[12] Surface task groups had bombarded Munda and Vila on 6 March and again on 13 May 1943.

---

[12] CINCPAC, letter, A16–3, Ser 001100 of 6 Sep. 1943, subj: Operations in Pacific Ocean Areas, June 1943, encl. (A).

JAPANESE AREA COMMAND STRUCTURE

The Japanese Area Command structure was quite different from that of United States forces. However, just as the United States Joint Chiefs, in due time, recognized that for immediate command purposes the operations in the Buna-Gona area of New Guinea must be quite separate from those along the Solomons chain of islands, the Japanese high command recognized the same necessity. The Japanese met the problem in a different way than the United States. They assigned prime responsibility in the New Guinea-New Britain-New Ireland area of operations to their Eighth Area Army, and the prime responsibility for the Central Solomons Island Area to the Southeastern Fleet of their Navy, with command lines running in separate Service channels all the way back to Tokyo. No one Japanese military officer in the area of operations had overall strategic control.

The Japanese then threw in another hurdle to smooth command lines for their defense of the Solomons as a whole. The Commanding General 17th Army, a major command of the Eighth Area, was given the responsibility for defense in the Northern Solomons and his command lines flowed upward through his Army superior in Rabaul. So the Japanese Navy was responsible for the Middle Solomons, and the Japanese Army for the Northern Solomons.

The Navy Commander of the Japanese Southeastern Fleet and of the 11th Air Fleet, wearing the two hats, was Vice Admiral Jinichi Kusaka. Vice Admiral Kusaka's immediate superior was Admiral Mineichi Koga, Commander in Chief Combined Fleet, with headquarters in Truk. Kusaka's immediate junior was Vice Admiral Gunichi Mikawa who commanded the Eighth Fleet. Kusaka had orders to pursue an "active defense" in the Solomons. Mikawa's on the spot subordinate in the Central Solomons was Rear Admiral Minoru Ota, who with "primary responsibility" coordinated the efforts of the Joint Army-Navy Defense Force in the New Georgia Group. He did just that. He did not command. The Japanese Army Commander on New Georgia was Major General Noboru Sasaki, Commander New Georgia Detachment, Southeastern Army.

When Major General Noboru Sasaki in late June was directed to take over from Rear Admiral Ota the "primary responsibility" for the efforts of the Joint Army-Navy Defense Force in the New Georgia Group, he and Ota were continued on a "cooperation" basis rather than Sasaki being placed in "command." The only change was in the man who held the hot potato of "primary responsibility" in a cooperative effort.

JAPANESE ORGANIZATION FOR DEFENSE OF BISMARCK BARRIER

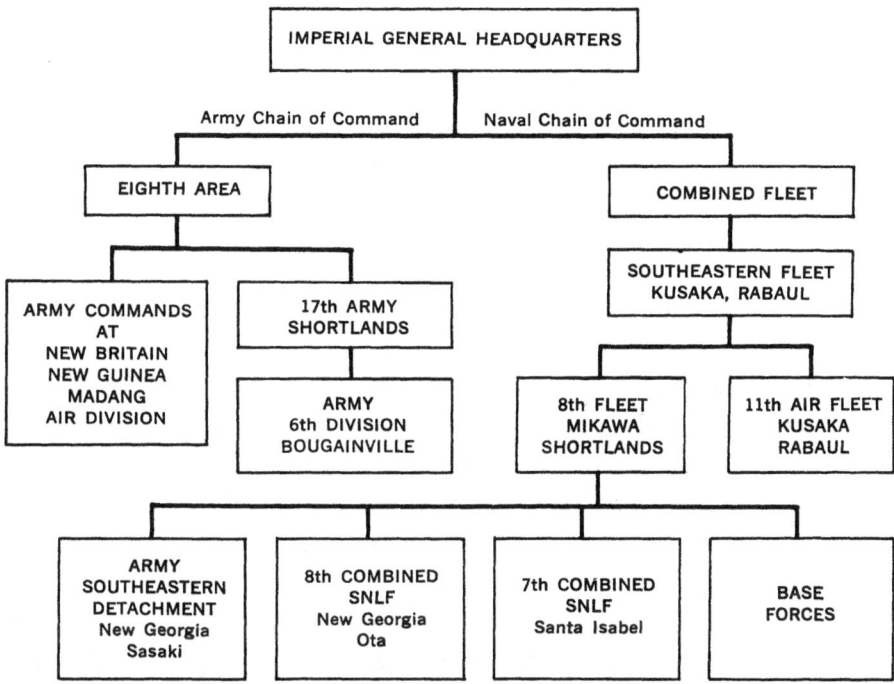

It would appear that the United States forces had a real command advantage in seeking to break through to the Bismarck Barrier over the Japanese seeking to defend its approaches, since one military officer, General MacArthur, who was actually in the area of operations, had over-all strategic control, and could time the movements of his subordinates in the two-pronged offensive.

The Japanese commanders, being on the strategic defensive, naturally had to react individually depending on the time and place they were attacked. But there was no Japanese area commander whose primary duty included the concentration of reserve forces prior to attack, and shifting these forces as the enemy attack developed.

JAPANESE DEFENSE PREPARATIONS

The New Georgia Group lay on the direct route from Guadalcanal to Rabaul, and had two good air bases, so the Japanese assigned to this group about 70 percent of their defensive troop strength available in the Central

Solomons. Their Navy sent the 7th Special Naval Landing Force (the Marines of the Japanese Navy) to Kolombangara and the 6th Special Naval Landing Force to New Georgia. Together these units formed the 8th Combined Special Naval Landing Force of about 4,000 men. These naval fighting units were gradually reinforced with Army troops of the Southeastern Army until the total strength in the New Georgia Group reached 10,500, about half of whom were on New Georgia Island. The Japanese also had the 7th Combined Special Naval Landing Force of about 3,000 men on Santa Isabel Island and 2,000 more on Choiseul in the Central Solomons. There also were about 10,000 Japanese Army troops in the Northern Solomons.

The Japanese had lookout stations scattered along the coasts of the islands of the New Georgia Group. Defensively, they had major subordinate commands and troops at Munda Point and Kolombangara, and minor troop units at Viru Harbor in southwest New Georgia, along eastern Vangunu Island opposite Wickham Anchorage and on Rendova Island. In trying to defend everywhere, there was some splintering of the forces available. The Japanese made it possible for Task Force 31 of the South Pacific Force to render ineffective a sizable proportion of the total Japanese defensive troop strength, by containing, scattering or capturing these various outpost contingents, which served no useful defensive purpose insofar as Munda and Vila airfields were concerned.

A professional post-war estimate based on available Japanese documents is that the Japanese had about 25,000 troops in all of the Solomons in June 1943 with larger contingents in both the Bismarck Archipelago (43,000) and in eastern New Guinea (55,000).[13] Presumably these allocations of troop strength roughly indicated how the Japanese evaluated the degree of danger to each area, and their own desires to retain them.

Just as the United States in the earlier days of the war did not know where the next enemy amphibious offensive might be headed or assault landed, the Japanese did not know where our offensive was headed nor where the assault stepping stones might be picked. With the Japanese in the middle Solomons, the immediate problem was whether United States eyes were lighting on the New Georgia Group of islands or on Santa Isabel, which the CINCPAC planners had favored. Santa Isabel contained the highly usable seaplane base at Rekata Bay, where unfortunately Rear Admiral

---

[13] John Miller, *CARTWHEEL: The Reduction of Rabaul*, Vol. VIII of subseries *The War in the Pacific* in Series UNITED STATES ARMY IN WORLD WAR II (Washington: Office of the Chief of Military History, Department of the Army, 1959), p. 47.

Turner had focused his eyes on the disaster-tinged evening of 8 August 1942. But Santa Isabel lay northeastward of the direct route to Rabaul from Guadalcanal and presumably so seemed to the Japanese a less likely objective for a United States attack than the New Georgia Group. In any case the Japanese had but 3,000 defenders on Santa Isabel compared to 10,500 in the New Georgia Group.

The Japanese in the Central Solomons pressed their defensive preparations with their typical military energy throughout the first six months of 1943, despite harassment from the air and sea. More particularly in the New Georgia Group, and in the Munda area, the Japanese believed that a major attack was most likely to come overland from Bairoko Harbor, seven miles to the north of Munda, and so a fair share of their defensive artillery was sited to meet an offensive from that direction.

They also knew that an attack on the Munda airstrip might come from the Roviana Lagoon which Vice Admiral Halsey's planners had named back in December 1942, or over the Munda Bar. But they knew that Roviana Lagoon was blocked from seaward by islands, coral reefs, and shallow surf-ridden entrances, suitable only for landing boats, or at best, an LCT. So they sited their seacoast guns to protect from an attack over Munda Bar, which to the United States Navy had looked like a near impossible obstacle.

That the degree of readiness of the Japanese in the Munda area to provide "an active defense" was high, is attested to by the length of the struggle before the Munda airstrip was captured on 5 August, and by the large reserve U.S. Army forces that had to be brought in to overwhelm the 5,000 defenders on New Georgia Island.

ORGANIZATIONAL CHANGES

Admiral King felt that part of the Navy's command difficulties with the Army arose from the fact that many of the organizational groupings of ships of the United States Fleet, called task forces, were identified by the areas where there were naval tasks to be accomplished on a continuing basis. Examples are: Panama Patrol Force, Northwest Africa Force, Southwest Pacific Force. Therefore, an officer of the Army exercising "area command" might logically expect to exercise direct control on a continuing basis over the ships carrying his area name tag. This led to area efforts to limit these task forces to minor offensive and defensive chores to the neglect of the broader, more important, and specific Naval and Fleet mission to "maintain control of the sea."

To alleviate this problem, on 15 March 1943, all the ships of the United States Fleet were changed from an area command nomenclature and put into numbered Fleets, the Fleets operating in the Pacific being allocated odd numbers. PHIBFORSOPAC became PHIBFORTHIRDFLT, or THIRDPHIBFOR. Rear Admiral Turner lost his well-known designation as CTF 62 and became CTF 32.[14] Despite this ordered change, for some months Vice Admiral Halsey, Commander Third Fleet, continued to use his COMSOPAC title.

DELAY AND MORE DELAY

On 3 March 1943 COMSOPAC informed COMINCH and CINCPAC that the tentative D-Day for the next offensive was April 10th.[15] The actual major movement of SOPAC forces into the Middle Solomons was 50 long days later. This delay beyond a date when the Area Commander reported his forces would be ready to move, marked the TOENAILS operations as different from all others in which the Turner staffs participated, since in previous and subsequent operations, the amphibious forces had great difficulty making the desired readiness date.[16]

On 28 March COMSOPAC dismounted from his galloping white charger long enough to tell the Joint Chiefs that he concurred with delaying major operations by SOPACFOR against New Georgia until the air base on Woodlark Island in SOWESPAC's domain was commissioned.[17]

It was quite obvious that since General MacArthur had been given the strategic direction of the operation, Vice Admiral Halsey could not move his invasion forces until General MacArthur approved. Admiral King was breathing hotly on the neck of COMSOPAC (later known as Commander Third Fleet) and Vice Admiral Halsey was breathing hotly on the neck of Rear Admiral Turner, but no final Dog Day could be set until after the staff representatives of Commander Third Fleet and CINCSWPA returned from Washington on 8 April 1943.[18]

On 15–16 April 1943, soon after the return of the Third Fleet representatives from Washington, Vice Admiral Halsey had a conference with Gen-

---

[14] COMSOPAC to SOPAC, 030407 Mar. 1943.
[15] COMSOPAC to COMINCH, CINCPAC 020450 Mar. 1943.
[16] (a) JCS 238/1, 18 Mar. 1943; (b) Staff Interviews.
[17] COMSOPAC to JCS, 280137 Mar. 1943.
[18] (a) COMINCH to COMSOPAC, 011810 Apr. 1943; (b) COMTHIRDFLT to COMINCH, 020720 Apr. 1943; (c) COMSOPAC to COMINCH, 142303 Apr. 1943.

NR & L (MOD) 31940

Training Seabees at Noumea, New Caledonia, for impending operations, April 1943. Rear Admiral Turner, Commander Third Amphibious Force, with his staff.

eral MacArthur. Vice Admiral Halsey happily agreed with General MacArthur's desire for setting Dog Day on 15 May in order that SOPAC Operations would start on the same day as the operations in the Southwest Pacific Area. These latter operations were for the seizure of Woodlark Island 210 miles west from the airfields in the south of Bougainville, as well as for the seizure of the Trobriand Islands further west. Soon General MacArthur delayed his readiness date to 1 June and eventually he said that his forces could not be ready before a 30th June date. When Commander Third Fleet was subjected to further Navy high command urging to get General MacArthur to set an earlier date, Vice Admiral Halsey responded by proposing that SOPACFOR charge up the Solomons and make a night landing on Rendova. However, he finally ended the high-level kibitzing by informing his superiors on 26 May that after much discussion and a reappraisal of the specific effort required by each subordinate command in the Third Fleet, a 30 June D-Day was agreeable to him also.[19]

---

[19] COMSOPAC to COMINCH, 160420, 260545 May 1943 and related despatches.

Rear Admiral Turner with Seabee officers after witnessing training operations.

Back on 9 March, the level of naval operations in the lower Solomons had so dropped off that COMSOPAC, upon Rear Admiral Turner's urging, directed the commencement of a three-week period of training of new units and of specific preparations for the next offensive.[20] With no specific Dog Day to plan for, this seemed a most desirable stopgap measure.

THE FIRST DEFINITE PLAN

About a month after the Third Fleet planners returned from General MacArthur's Headquarters, COMSOPAC issued his first definite planning directive for the TOENAILS Operation. This was on 17 May 1943 and he directed that:

> Forces of the South Pacific Area will seize and occupy simultaneously positions in the southern part of the NEW GEORGIA Group preparatory to a full scale offensive against MUNDA-VILA and later BUIN-FAISI [the southern end of Bougainville].[21]

---

[20] (a) COMSOPAC 080650 Mar. 1943; (b) COMPHIBFORSOPAC, letters, Ser 055 of 30 Jan. and 059 of 3 Feb. 1943, subj: Amphibious Training and Joint Training.

[21] COMSOPAC, Warning Instructions, Ser 00859 of 17 May 1943.

Planning for Paring the Japanese Toenails 497

The specific tasks were to seize, hold, and develop:

1. a staging point for small craft in:
   a. the Wickham Anchorage Area in the southeastern part of Vangunu Island and 50 miles from Munda airstrip.
   b. Viru Harbor on New Georgia Island 30 miles southeast of Munda airstrip.
2. a fighter airstrip at Segi, New Georgia, 40 miles from the Munda airstrip.
3. Rendova Island, whose northern harbor was just 10 short miles south of Munda, as a supply base, advanced PT Base, and an adequate support base to accommodate amphibians prior to their embarkation for an assault on Munda and/or Vila.

Dog Day was set for June 15th "or shortly thereafter." This date was in accordance with the good old Navy practice of getting everyone pressing to be ready ahead of the real date when they *had* to be ready.

Between the day when this order was issued and June 3rd when COMSOPAC issued his Operation Plan 14–43, there were several changes made in the planning, but the most important, at Rear Admiral Turner's working

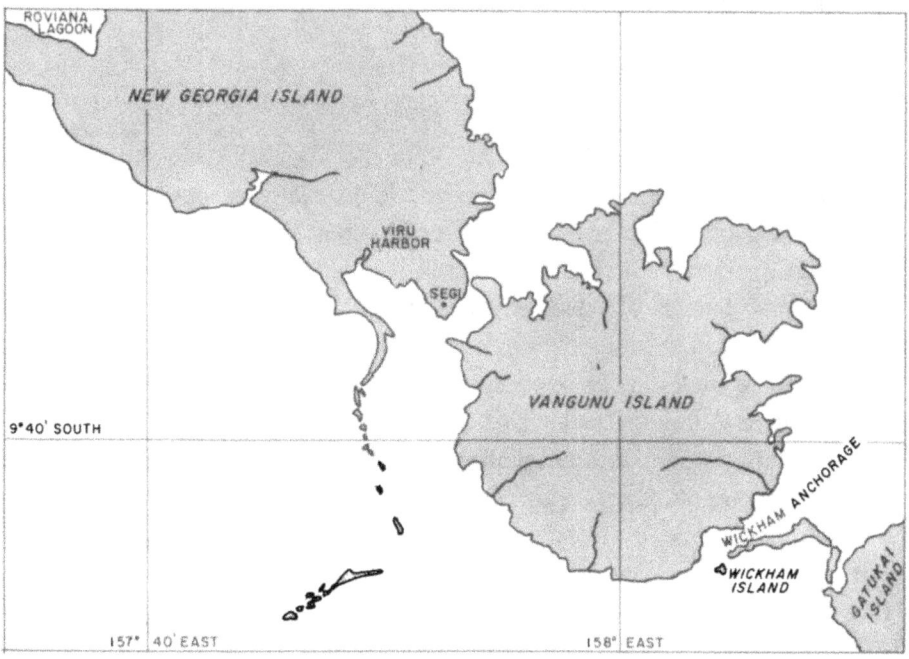

Eastern Force TOENAILS Objective.

level, was the change of Dog Day to 30 June 1943, and the change in Task Force designation for the Assault Force from Task Force 32 to Task Force 31.

COMSOPAC's Warning Instructions contained no information or instructions in regard to the components or the command of the New Georgia Occupation Force. Neither did his Operation Plan 14–43 issued two weeks later.

Rear Admiral Turner's (CTF 31) Operation Plan A8–43 gave the components of the New Georgia Occupation Force and indicated Major General Hester was the Commander, but stated in a separate subparagraph that command would pass from CTF 31 to other military authorities when so directed by Commander Third Fleet. Presumably, but not explicitly stated, this would occur when Major General Hester was established ashore on New Georgia Island and was ready to assume the command responsibility. Under these circumstances he would notify Commander Third Fleet and Rear Admiral Turner, CTF 31, would make his recommendation to Commander Third Fleet in the matter and the latter would decide whether, or when, the command should pass.

The failure of Vice Admiral Halsey's Operation Plan to spell out the command matter, after his experience in regard to the same problem in the latter phases of WATCHTOWER, is not understood.[22]

LOGISTICS COMES OF AGE IN SOPAC

In February 1943, COMSOPAC launched logistics operation DRYGOODS. This was the supply part of the logistic support needed to conduct the next big operation in the Middle Solomons. DRYGOODS called for building up on the Guadalcanal-Russell Islands some 50,000 tons of supplies, 80,000 barrels of gasoline (and storage tanks to hold this amount) and the tens of thousands of tons of equipment for the various units slated to participate in this next operation, which in due time was named TOENAILS. Rear Admiral Turner had drafted a memorandum to COMSOPAC on 14 January 1943, recommending this essential logistic step for future operational success. Despite all that could be said against the inadequacy of the unloading and storage facilities to be available at Guadalcanal in the spring of 1943, Vice Admiral Halsey gave the proposal a green light and thus made a major contribution to the success of TOENAILS. Since every-

---

[22] (a) COMSOPAC Op Plan 14–43, 3 Jun. 1943; (b) CTF 31 Op Plan A8–43, 4 Jun. 1943, para 5(b).

one in the United States with an alert ear knew by this time that Guadalcanal's code word was CACTUS, Guadalcanal received a change of code name from CACTUS to MAINYARD for the purpose of the DRYGOODS Operation.

On 20 May 1943, COMSOPAC created a Joint Logistic Board, composed of:

1. Commander Service Squadron, SOPAC,
2. Commanding General, Services of Supply, SOPAC, Army,
3. Commanding General, Supply Service, First Marine Amphibious Corps, and
4. Commander Aircraft, SOPAC (represented by COM Fleet Air, Noumea).

The Board was charged with keeping the appropriate departmental authorities in Washington informed of present and future Service requirements, with providing inter-change of emergency logistical support within SOPAC, and with recommending to Washington appropriate levels of supply within SOPAC.

THE LANDING CRAFT

SOPAC planning for TOENAILS was predicated upon the arrival in the South Pacific of an adequate number of LSTs (Landing Ship Tank), LCIs (Landing Craft Infantry) and LCTs (Landing Craft Tank). When delay succeeded delay in the delivery of these new landing craft, some being built by commercial shipyards themselves newly built, it became apparent that there would be little time to break them in to the hazards of the Solomons before they would have to load for TOENAILS. In this respect, it is obvious that Vice Admiral Halsey's desire for an April or May D-Day for TOENAILS was constantly tempered by the constant slippage of the arrival dates of the landing craft.

The first LSTs assigned to the South Pacific were built at three East Coast yards and were commissioned in December 1942 and January 1943. The LST used in the South Pacific had an overall length of nearly 328 feet, a 50-foot beam, and a draft of 14 feet when it displaced 3,776 tons fully loaded. Presumably when the LST blew its ballast tanks, its draft was 3 feet, 1 inch forward and 9 feet, 6 inches aft, but this desirable state for unloading Marine or Army tanks through the bow doors on the perfect beach gradient was rarely realized. All the large landing craft were diesel-engined.

The Landing Craft Infantry (LCI) was 157 feet overall, had a beam of 23 feet, and a displacement of 380 tons. The LCI was the fastest of the large landing craft with a designed maximum speed of 15 knots which permitted these craft to cruise at about 12 knots in a generally smooth sea. The LCI could carry 205 troops and 32 tons of cargo in addition to the ship's company and normal stores. The draft when loaded for landing was never less than 3 feet, 8 inches forward and 5 feet, 6 inches aft, but constant purges of stores and gear had to be held to even approach this desirable draft. The LCI discharged troops and equipment by means of gangways hinged to a platform on the bow, and lucky were the troops who got ashore in water less than shoulder high. The LCI complement was two officers and 22 men, but when they had that number they were equally fortunate.

The first LST which made news in the Landing Craft Flotillas, South Pacific Force was the LST-446 which arrived in the South Pacific about 6 March 1943. The Commanding Officer LST-446 in a loud howl sent off to OPNAV, CINCPAC, BUSHIPS, and half-a-dozen afloat commands, enumerated the trials and tribulations of a new type of ship operating in the Southern Solomons, and objected strenuously to his ship "being loaded" while the ship was beached.

The Commanding Officer continued:

> An LST is the only ship in the world of 4000 tons or over that is continuously rammed onto and off of coral, sand and mud.[23]

Despite this dim view of what became a very routine function, the arrival of LST-446 was a very real advance in the readiness of Rear Admiral Turner to conduct TOENAILS. Admiral Turner said:

> The LST was and is still a marvel, and the officers and men who manned them hold a high place in my affections.[24]

Captain G. B. Carter, Commander Landing Ship Flotilla Five, arrived in Noumea on 14 May 1943 with the first large group of the Landing Ship Tanks destined to see action in SOPAC. The officers and men of the 12 newly commissioned LSTs he brought with him, all carrying an LCT on board for launching upon arrival at destination, had learned "to go to sea" during their 67-day, 9,500-mile passage at 7 to 9 knots from the East Coast of

---

[23] (a) LST-446/L2–6 Ser No. 9 of 11 Mar. 1943; (b) Commander LST Group 13, letter, LST/A9/ Ser 10 of 22 Mar. 1943.
[24] Turner.

Planning for Paring the Japanese Toenails 501

the United States to Noumea. For many of them, this long cruise was also their first.

The LSTs in the South Pacific wore no halos. But, because these large and ungainly ships overcame dozens of engine and electrical casualties, and even ended up by towing their escorts and a coastal transport part way across the Pacific, they engendered a certain respect from the older units of the Fleet in that area.

Due to the almost complete absence of war diaries, the exact date of the arrival of the various units of LCI Flotilla Five in the South Pacific is unknown. LCI-328 arrived in Noumea from Panama on 2 April 1943. LCI-63 arrived in Noumea also from Panama on 14 April and went alongside LCI-64. On 14 April 1943 the TF 63 War Diary reported seven LCIs at Noumea. On 15 April it was noted that 23 LCIs of Flotilla Five (all except LCI-329) were present in SOPAC in an upkeep status.[25]

Both the LSTs and the LCIs, upon arrival in the South Pacific, were given a two-week period of upkeep and maintenance by Rear Admiral Turner to correct the many ailments arising during their arduous passage across the wide Pacific.

It can be observed that the written records located of LCTs and LCI(L)s of this period are few. The memories of the few seasoned officers who are still above ground and who made the passage aboard these landing craft are faint. Despite these handicaps, it can be written with certainty that the LCI's had less than eight weeks and the LSTs fewer than four weeks for the multiple tasks of operational amphibious training, movement to the staging areas 800 miles away, and then specific preparation and rehearsal loadings for TOENAILS.

ORGANIZATION—THIRD FLEET AMPHIBIOUS FORCE

On D-Day for TOENAILS Rear Admiral Turner, COMPHIBFOR, Third Fleet, still using his SOPAC title, issued an administrative organization chart, which showed that a considerable number of the more senior WATCHTOWER Commanding Officers were available to carry their acquired skills, burdens and satisfactions into the TOENAILS Operation. At long last their

---

[25] (a) CTF 32 *War Diary,* Apr. 1943; (b) Captain Chester L. Walton, U. S. Navy (Ret.) to GCD, letter, Apr. 1965; (c) LCI–63 and LCI–328 *War Diaries,* Apr. 1943.

Transport Commodore was a Commodore in fact.[26] The organization was as follows:

Amphibious Force, South Pacific

Commander Amphibious Force South Pacific
                Rear Admiral R. K. Turner (1908)
  Chief of Staff..................................Captain Anton B. Anderson (1912)
  APA-4 *McCawley* (Flagship)..........Commander Robert H. Rodgers (1923)

TRANSPORTS, SOUTH PACIFIC AMPHIBIOUS FORCE

Commander Transports, PHIBFORSOPAC
              Commodore Lawrence F. Reifsnider (1910)
  APA-14 *Hunter Liggett* (Flagship)
              Captain R. S. Patch, U.S. Coast Guard

Transport Division Two
Commander Transport Division Two
 Captain Paul S. Theiss (1912)
APA-18 *President Jackson* (F)
 Captain Charles W. Weitzel (1917)
APA-20 *President Hayes*
 Captain Francis W. Benson (1917)
APA-19 *President Adams*
 Captain Frank Dean (1917)
AKA-8 *Algorab*
 Captain Joseph R. Lannom (1919)

Transport Division Eight
Commander Transport Division Eight
 Captain George B. Ashe (1911)
APA-17 *American Legion* (F)
 Commander Ratcliffe C. Welles (1921)
APA-27 *George Clymer*
 Captain Arthur T. Moen (1918)
APA-21 *Crescent City*
 Captain John R. Sullivan (1918)
AKA-12 *Libra*
 Captain William B. Fletcher (1921)
AKA-6 *Alchiba*
 Commander Howard R. Shaw (1921)

Transport Division Ten
Commander Transport Division Ten
 Commodore Lawrence F. Reifsnider (1910)

---

[26] COMPHIBFORSOPAC, letter, Ser 0217 of 30 Jun. 1943, subj: Organization and Staff of Amphibious Force, South Pacific; (b) COMTHIRDPHIBFOR, letter, Ser 00256 of 29 May 1944, subj: Ships and Units of this Force participating in New Georgia Group Operations.

APA-14 *Hunter Liggett* (F)
   Captain R. S. Patch, USCG
APA-23 *John Penn*
   Captain Harry W. Need (1918)
AKA-9 *Alhena*
   Commander Howard W. Bradbury (1921)
AKA-5 *Formalhaut*
   Captain Henry C. Flanagan (1921)

Transport Division Twelve

Commander Transport Division Twelve
   Commander John D. Sweeney (1926)
APD-6 *Stringham* (F)
   Lieutenant Commander Joseph A. McGoldrick (1932)
APD-1 *Manley*
   Lieutenant Robert T. Newell, Jr. (USNR)
APD-5 *McKean*
   Lieutenant Commander Ralph L. Ramey (1935)
APD-7 *Talbot*
   Lieutenant Commander Charles C. Morgan (USNR)
APD-8 *Waters*
   Lieutenant Charles J. McWhinnie (USNR)
APD-9 *Dent*
   Lieutenant Commander Ralph A. Wilhelm (USNR)

Transport Division Fourteen

Commander Transport Division Fourteen
   Captain Henry E. Thornhill (1918)
APA-7 *Fuller*
   Captain Melville E. Eaton (1921)
APA-4 *McCawley* (FF)
   Commander Robert H. Rodgers (1923)
AKA-13 *Titania*
   Commander Herbert E. Berger (1922)

Transport Division Sixteen

Commander Transport Division Sixteen
   Lieutenant Commander James S. Willis (1927)
APD-10 *Brooks* (F)
   Lieutenant Commander John W. Ramey (1932)
APD-11 *Gilmer*
   Lieutenant Commander John S. Horner (USNR)
APD-12 *Humphreys*
   Lieutenant Commander Maurice J. Carley (USNR)
APD-13 *Sands*
   Lieutenant Commander John J. Branson (1927)

APD-18 *Kane*
   Lieutenant Commander Robert E. Gadrow (1931)

Transport Division Twenty-Two

Commander Transport Division Twenty-Two
   Lieutenant Commander Robert H. Wilkinson (1929)
APD-15 *Kilty* (F)
   Lieutenant Commander Dominic L. Mattie (1929)
APD-17 *Crosby*
   Lieutenant Commander Alan G. Grant (USNR)
APD-16 *Ward*
   Lieutenant Frederick W. Lemley (USNR)
APD-14 *Schley*
   Lieutenant Commander Horace Myers (1931)

MINESWEEPER GROUP, SOUTH PACIFIC FORCE
(TEMPORARY ASSIGNMENT)
Commander Stanley Leith, USN, Commanding (1923)

DMS-13 *Hopkins* (F)
   Lieutenant Commander Francis M. Peters, Jr. (1931)
DMS-10 *Southard*
   Lieutenant Commander Frederick R. Matthews (1935)
DMS-11 *Hovey*
   Lieutenant Commander Edwin A. McDonald (1931)
DMS-14 *Zane*
   Lieutenant Commander Peyton L. Wirtz (1931)
DMS-16 *Trever*
   Lieutenant Commander William H. Shea, Jr. (1936)

LANDING CRAFT FLOTILLAS, SOUTH PACIFIC FORCE

Commander Landing Craft Flotillas—Rear Admiral George H. Fort (1912)
   Chief of Staff..Captain Benton W. Decker (1920)
LST Flotilla Five—Captain Grayson B. Carter (1919)
   LST Group Thirteen—Commander Roger W. Cutler, USNR
     LST Division 25

        LST-446(GF)   Lieutenant Robert J. Mayer, USNR
        LST-447   Lieutenant Frank H. Storms, USNR
        LST-448   Ensign Charles E. Roeschke, USN
        LST-449   Lieutenant Laurence Lisle, USNR
        LST-460   Lieutenant Everett E. Weire, USN
        LST-472   Lieutenant William O. Talley, USN

     LST Division 26

        LST-339   Lieutenant John H. Fulweiler, USNR
        LST-340   Lieutenant William Villella, USN
        LST-395   Lieutenant Alexander C. Forbes, USNR
        LST-396   Lieutenant Eric W. White, USN

Planning for Paring the Japanese Toenails 505

        LST-397   Lieutenant Nathaniel L. Lewis, USNR
        LST-398   Lieutenant Boyd E. Blanchard, USNR
   LST Group Fourteen—Commander Paul S. Slawson (1920)
     LST Division 27
        LST-341   Lieutenant Floyd S. Barnett, USN
        LST-342   Lieutenant Edward S. McCluskey, USNR
     LST Division 28
        LST-353   Lieutenant Luther E. Reynolds, USNR
        LST-354   Lieutenant Bertram W. Robb, USNR
   LST Group Fifteen
     LST Division 29
        LST-343   Lieutenant Harry H. Rightmeyer, USN
        LST-399   Lieutenant George F. Baker, USN
LCI(L) Flotilla Five—Commander James McD. Smith (1925)
   LCI(L) Group Thirteen—Lieutenant Commander Marion M. Byrd (1927)
     LCI Division 25
        LCI-61   Lieutenant John P. Moore, USNR
        LCI-62   Lieutenant (jg) William C. Lyons, USN
        LCI-63   Lieutenant (jg) John H. McCarthy, USNR
        LCI-64   Lieutenant Herbert L. Kelly, USNR
        LCI-65   Lieutenant (jg) Christopher R. Tompkins, USNR
        LCI-66   Lieutenant Charles F. Houston, Jr., USNR
     LCI Division 26
        LCI-21   Ensign Marshall M. Cook, USNR
        LCI-22   Lieutenant (jg) Spencer V. Hinckley, USNR
        LCI-67   Lieutenant (jg) Ernest E. Tucker, USNR
        LCI-68   Lieutenant Clifford D. Older, USNR
        LCI-69   Lieutenant Frazier L. O'Leary, USNR
        LCI-70   Lieutenant (jg) Harry W. Frey, USNR
   LCI(L) Group Fourteen—Lieutenant Commander Alfred V. Jannotta, USNR
     LCI Division 27
        LCI-327   Lieutenant (jg) North W. Newton, USNR
        LCI-328   Lieutenant Joseph D. Kerr, USNR
        LCI-329   Lieutenant William A. Illing, USNR
        LCI-330   Lieutenant (jg) Homer G. Maxey, USNR
        LCI-331   Lieutenant Richard O. Shelton, USNR
        LCI-332   Lieutenant William A. Neilson, USNR
     LCI Division 28
        LCI-23   Lieutenant Ben A. Thirkfield, USNR
        LCI-24   Lieutenant (jg) Raymond E. Ward, USN
        LCI-333   Lieutenant Horace Townsend, USNR
        LCI-334   Lieutenant (jg) Alfred J. Ormston, USNR

LCI-335	Lieutenant (jg) John R. Powers, USNR
LCI-336	Lieutenant (jg) Thomas A. McCoy, USNR

LCI(L) Group Fifteen—Commander James McD. Smith (1925)
    LCI Division 29

LCI-222	Ensign Clarence M. Reese, USNR
LCI-223	Lieutenant Frank P. Stone, USNR

LCT (5) Flotilla Five—Lieutenant Commander Paul A. Wells, USNR
    LCT Group 13—Lieutenant Ashton L. Jones, USNR
        LCT Division 25—Lieutenant Ashton L. Jones, USNR

LCT-58	Ensign James E. Jones, USNR
LCT-60	Boatswain John S. Wolfe, USN
LCT-156	Ensign Harold Mantell, USNR
LCT-158	Ensign Edward J. Ruschmann, USNR
LCT-159	Ensign John A. McNiel, USNR
LCT-180	Ensign Sidney W. Orton, USNR

        LCT Division 26—Lieutenant Ameel Z. Kouri, USNR

LCT-62	Ensign Robert T. Capeless, USNR
LCT-63	Ensign Joseph R. Madura, USNR
LCT-64	Ensign Kermit J. Buckley, USNR
LCT-65	Ensign Grant L. Kimer, USNR
LCT-66	Ensign Charles A. Goddard, USNR
LCT-67	Ensign William H. Fitzgerald, USNR

    LCT Group 14—Lieutenant Decatur Jones, USNR
        LCT Division 27—Lieutenant Decatur Jones, USNR

LCT-321	Ensign Robert W. Willits, USNR
LCT-322	Ensign Frederick Altman, USNR
LCT-323	Ensign Carl T. Geisler, USNR
LCT-324	Ensign David C. Hawley, USNR
LCT-325	Ensign John J. Crim, USNR
LCT-326	Ensign Harvey A. Shuler, USNR

        LCT Division 28

LCT-367	Ensign Robert Carr, USNR
LCT-369	Ensign Walter B. Gillette, USNR
LCT-370	Ensign Leonard M. Bukstein, USNR
LCT-375	Ensign Richard I. Callomon, USNR
LCT-376	Lieutenant (jg) Francis J. Hoehn, USNR
LCT-377	Ensign Thomas J. McGann, USNR

    LCT Group 15—Lieutenant Frank M. Wiseman, USNR
        LCT Division 29—Lieutenant Frank M. Wiseman, USNR

LCT-181	Lieutenant (jg) Melvin H. Rosengard, USNR
LCT-182	Ensign Jack E. Johnson, USNR

Note: LCI-21 and LCI-22 at this time were temporarily attached to LCI Division 26 in lieu of LCI not yet reported. LCI-222 and LCI-223 were temporarily attached to LCI Division 25 and Division 26 respectively.

The LCT organization in the Third Fleet had filled out considerably since CLEANSLATE.

LCT-327	Ensign James L. Caraway, USNR
LCT-330	Ensign Leon B. Douglas, USNR
LCT-351	Ensign Robert R. Muehlback, USNR
LCT-352	Lieutenant (jg) Winston Broadfoot, USNR

LCT Division 30—Lieutenant (jg) Pickett Lumpkin, USNR

LCT-68	Ensign Edward H. Burtt, USNR
LCT-69	Ensign Austin N. Volk, USNR
LCT-70	Ensign C. M. Barrett, USNR
LCT-71	Ensign Richard T. Eastin, USNR
LCT-481	Ensign George W. Wagenhorst, USNR
LCT-482	Boatswain Herbert F. Dreher, USN

LCT (5) Flotilla Six—Lieutenant Edgar M. Jaeger, USN
LCT (5) Group 16—Lieutenant Wilfred C. Margetts, USNR
LCT Division 31—Ensign Robert A. Torkildson, USNR

LCT-126	Ensign Philip A. Waldron, USNR
LCT-127	Ensign Robert A. Torkildson, USNR
LCT-128	Ensign Joseph Joyce, USNR
LCT-129	Ensign Emery W. Graunke, USNR
LCT-132	Ensign Milton Paskin, USNR
LCT-133	Ensign Bertram Meyer, USNR

LCT Division 32—Lieutenant (jg) Donald O. Kringel, USNR

LCT-134	Ensign James W. Hunt, USNR
LCT-139	Ensign Ralph O. Taylor, USNR
LCT-141	Lieutenant (jg) Donald O. Kringel, USNR
LCT-144	Ensign E. B. Lerz, USNR
LCT-145	Ensign Willard E. Goyette, USNR
LCT-146	Ensign William W. Asper, USNR

Coastal Transport Flotilla Five—Lieutenant D. Mann, USNR
APC Division 25—Lieutenant Dennis Mann, USNR

APC-23(F)	Lieutenant Dennis Mann, USNR
APC-24	Lieutenant Bernard F. Seligman, USNR
APC-25	Lieutenant John D. Cartano, USNR
APC-26	Ensign James B. Dunigan, USNR
APC-27	Lieutenant Paul C. Smith, USNR
APC-28	Lieutenant (jg) Austin D. Shean, USNR

APC Division 26—(provisional) Lieutenant Arthur W. Bergstrom, USNR

APC-37(F)	Lieutenant James E. Locke, USNR
APC-29	Lieutenant (jg) Eugene H. George, USNR
APC-35	Lieutenant Robert F. Ruben, USNR
APC-36	Lieutenant (jg) Kermit L. Otto, USNR

All of the above amphibious units were in the initial echelons of TOE-NAILS except for LST Division 25 (minus LST-472, which did participate), LCI-32 and LCTs 68 through 71 and LCT-321. The latter arrived Tulagi

Courtesy of Major General Frank D. Weir, USMC (Ret.)

Colonel Henry D. Linscott, USMC, Assistant Chief of Staff, Commander Amphibious Force South Pacific, in front of his tent at Camp Crocodile, Guadalcanal, late Spring, 1943.

Harbor on 16 July 1943, and was logged in as "the newest arrival this area," and together with LST-475, LCTs 68, 69, 70, and a number of APCs participated in later phases of the South Georgia Group operations.

At the time the TOENAILS movement to the New Georgia Group began, there were 11 LSTs, 23 LCIs, 35 LCTs and 10 APCs (coastal transports) from Flotilla Five and Flotilla Six available in PHIBFORTHIRDFLT. On D-Day nearly all of these were either unloading in the Middle Solomons or loaded in the Guadalcanal-Russell Island area and waiting for orders.

During the month before TOENAILS was kicked off, the Landing Craft Flotillas were far from idle. They delivered 23,775 drums of lubricants and fuel, 13,088 tons of miscellaneous gear and 28 loaded vehicles to the Russell Islands alone. All cargo requirements for the TOENAILS Operation were loaded by 22 June 1943.

In this connection, Lieutenant General Linscott, who had been the very skillful and highly appreciated Assistant Chief of Staff for the Commander

Amphibious Force South Pacific during its very critical first year of existence, wrote:

> I feel that Commodore L. F. Reifsnider should receive some recognition for handling the 'Guadalcanal Freight Line' after Admiral Turner moved north from Noumea. These duties were in addition to his assignment as Commander Transport Group, South Pacific. His principal assistants were Commander John D. Hayes, Lieutenant Colonel W. B. McKean (who acted as Operations Officer) and Commander 'Red' [W. P.] Hepburn. All should be recognized for the effective manner in which they handled the task.[27]

FIRST MOVE ON THE TOENAILS CHECKERBOARD

As April inched into May, and D-Day for TOENAILS began to assume reality, it became apparent that Rear Admiral Turner would be on top of his job much better if he were personally located at Koli Point, Guadalcanal, where a large part of the Expeditionary Force was starting to gather, rather than at Noumea 840 miles to the southward and subject to all the delays and vagaries of encrypted radio communications.

The volume of radio traffic had steadily increased as the number of amphibious ships steadily increased, and traffic delays of 10, 12 and more hours for "operational" traffic were usual. Events were flowing far faster than the radio traffic.

In mid-May it was planned that on 27 May 1943, Rear Admiral Turner as CTF 32 and the *McCawley* as a unit of TU 32.8.2 which would consist of four transports, five merchant cargo ships, six motor torpedo boats, two small patrol craft and seven escorting destroyers, would depart from Noumea for Koli Point, Guadalcanal, which, with the Russell Islands, were to be used as staging points for TOENAILS. Task Unit 32.8.2 would carry a Marine Raider Battalion, three naval construction battalions, a coast artillery regiment and other smaller detachments. Upon arrival at Koli Point, Rear Admiral Turner and the operational staff would shift their headquarters ashore.[28]

However, as the 27 May departure date drew near, it was decided to sail the large Navy transports separately from the merchant ships, the latter sailing first. Thus, the date for the separation of Rear Admiral Turner from the ear of Vice Admiral Halsey was postponed until 7 June 1943.

---

[27] Lieutenant General Henry D. Linscott, USMC (Ret.) to GCD, letter, 18 Apr. 1969.
[28] (a) CTF 32 Movement Order A6–43, 23 May 1943; (b) CTF 32 Movement Order A7–43, 29 May 1943.

Courtesy of Capt. Charles Stein, USN (Ret.)

Officers' Quarters at Camp Crocodile, Guadalcanal, late Spring, 1943.

Just before departure on 7 June, Rear Admiral Turner came down with malaria, and the doctors insisted on transferring him to the hospital ship *Solace*. His temporary separation from active command of Task Force 32 and Task Unit 32.8.2 is referred to in the War Diary of his command only in these terms "Rear Admiral Turner was detained in Noumea." According to an author who was in the South Pacific at the time:

> Admiral Turner was a sick man before the New Georgia campaign started; he 'shoulda stood in bed,' as they say in the Bronx. A fortnight before D-Day, he was stricken with malaria and dengue fever and hoisted aboard the hospital ship *Solace*. . . .[29]

Rear Admiral Anderson, Turner's Chief of Staff at the time, remembered:

---

[29] Driscoll, *Pacific Victory*, p. 69.

Planning for Paring the Japanese Toenails

> Admiral Turner did not sail in the *McCawley* up to Guadalcanal . . . just prior to the New Georgia Operation. He became suddenly sick with both dengue fever and malaria and went aboard the hospital ship *Solace* then anchored in Noumea Harbor. He was a patient there for over a week. I went out to see him every forenoon and took him important despatches and correspondence for him to read. On several successive days he asked me to bring out to him a bottle of liquor. I wouldn't do it. Several times he really begged me to do it.[30]

Commander Landing Craft Flotillas recalls:

> [Turner's] health was apparently good until just before 'Toenails,' when he was at Noumea planning the operation with General Hester. I was in Guadalcanal . . . when I was informed that Turner was on the hospital ship in Noumea with both malaria and dengue fever. I was somewhat worried that I might be called upon to do that show, being No. 2 at that time, with no preparation at all. However, he bobbed up serenely and got up to Guadalcanal just in time. . . .[31]

Administration of Task Force 32 during this period when Rear Admiral Turner was busy in Guadalcanal was to be exercised by Captain A. B. Anderson, Chief of Staff, CTF 32, who with a small portion of the staff would remain in Noumea at the Administrative Headquarters of Commander Landing Craft Flotillas, Third Fleet (Rear Admiral George H. Fort).

Rear Admiral Anderson, in 1962, recalled:

> I set up the office in two quonset huts in the city. One was used to house part of the enlisted personnel. I, with Morck [Flag Secretary] moved into a house on the outskirts of Noumea formerly used by George Fort and Benny Decker [who] stayed with us for a couple of weeks, then went afloat.
>
> The *McCawley*, with other ships of the Force, was to pick up troops and train them in forward areas preparatory to the New Georgia Operation. Admiral Turner saw no reason for a number of officers and a large clerical force to be in the flagship when space was required for personnel of the Landing Force. Also, when the flagship was away, he wanted an office in Noumea to handle the day to day things that came up. Shipments of landing craft were arriving and he wanted them indoctrinated and trained before being sent forward. Admiral Fort had already gone forward with some of his Flotilla. Benny Decker (his C/S) was left in Noumea to train new additions. I was to work with him on this.[32]

While enroute to Guadalcanal on 10 June, 1943, TU 32.8.2 made up of five transports with six destroyers to guard them, and under the command

---
[30] ABA to GCD, letter, 2 May 1962.
[31] Vice Admiral George H. Fort, USN (Ret.) to GCD, letter, Apr. 1965. Hereafter Fort.
[32] Anderson.

of Captain Paul Theiss, Commander Transport Division 14 in the *President Jackson*, was harassed by Japanese snooper planes for six hours. It was attacked by seven Japanese bombing planes at deep dusk and again, after a half moon dark, with flares (luckily faulty) dropped to aid the planes. No ships were hit due to the well-timed and continuous radical maneuvering of the Task Unit, executed for two hours in the best Turner tradition, and by the heavy anti-aircraft fire of the destroyers.[33]

THE REHEARSAL

When Rear Admiral Turner arrived in Guadalcanal from the *Solace*, the day after a big Japanese air raid, Task Force 31 took over the TOENAILS invasion task from Task Force 32 and was promptly formed up at 1500 on 17 June 1943 with 12 LSTs, 12 LCIs, 28 LCTs, 10 APCs, three APDs, two DMs, and two ATs. The number of ships and landing craft assigned to Task Force 31 increased daily thereafter; Task Force 32 continued with shrinking strength to accomplish general administrative and support tasks.

The large majority of landing ships and landing craft for the TOENAILS Operation trained for their forthcoming operation in the Guadalcanal-Tulagi-Russell Islands area, but there was no overall dress rehearsal for TOENAILS with air support, gunfire support ships, and the large transports present. This omission of an overall dress rehearsal was a violation of the Amphibious Doctrine, as well as the lesson of WATCHTOWER which showed considerable advantage could be gained from a dress rehearsal. In trying to run down why there was no full-scale dress rehearsal for TOENAILS, the written record is scanty, and memories pretty dim. It seems that the Staff believed the danger from alerting the Japanese to the nearness of an invasion, should they detect the rehearsal from an unusually heavy volume of radio traffic, was greater than the danger from the loss of coordinated training.[34]

When Vice Admiral George H. Fort, USN (Retired), who was Second-in-Command of the Amphibious Forces in TOENAILS, was asked the question "Why didn't TOENAILS have a dress rehearsal?," his reply was, "Where would you have held it?" and later, "We seldom had a [full-scale] rehearsal in those days, having neither the ships or troops available until the last minute." [35]

---

[33] COMTRANSGRPSOPAC *Action Report*, Ser 0097 of 9 Jul. 1943.
[34] Staff Interviews.
[35] Fort.

Planning for Paring the Japanese Toenails 513

The rehearsal by the large transports for the TOENAILS Operation was held at Fila Harbor, Efate, in the New Hebrides, 560 miles to the southeast from Guadalcanal. This harbor area was quite acceptable since preparatory ships' gunfire was not required for the TOENAILS Operation. The large transports arrived at Efate on 16 June 1943, and remained there for ten days of training and rehearsal. This training was prescribed on 29 May 1943 when CTF 32 issued his Movement Order A7–43.

The large transports for the operation did not arrive up at Guadalcanal until 1000 on the 29th, when they were reassigned from Task Force 32 to Task Force 31.

The decision not to have the large transports in the Guadalcanal area in the first part of June proved an extremely wise one when the Japanese swept over the Iron Bottom Sound area, on 7, 12, and 16 June, with from 40 to 60 bombers and their escorting fighters. The last of these three raids hit and burned out the LST-340 and the *Celeno* (AK-76).

The War Diary of LST-340 for the 16 June incident included the following flesh and blood account by a newly trained amphibian:

> Another Condition Red came by radio. Each one scrambled into his life jacket and helmet and made for his battle station. Those were tense moments. The blood in one's very veins turned cold. There were many scared people. . . .
> In the evening to quiet the nerves of the bombed and fire weary sailors and officers, there was a beer party staged just off the ramp of the burned ship. It was for the personnel who participated in the disaster which befell the 340. . . .[36]

The Japanese surprisingly enough failed to pay a daily complimentary bombing visit to the staging areas of Guadalcanal and the Russells during the last two weeks before TOENAILS.

The late arrival at Guadalcanal of these large transports was purposeful even though it led to some grousing on the part of troops, Seabees and naval base personnel who had to be loaded aboard the transports with marked speed on Dog Day minus one. It was an effort to shorten the interval between the time Japanese air might sight and report these large transports, the Japanese high command might sense an invasion effort and start the Japanese Combined Fleet south from Truk, and when the transports would necessarily arrive in the New Georgia Group.[37]

By keeping the large transports out of the staging areas until the day

---
[36] LST Flotilla Five War Diary, 17, 18 Jun., 1943.
[37] Staff Interviews.

before the invasion, it is logical to assume that Rear Admiral Turner had deceived the Japanese of the imminence of the New Georgia effort, if not its immediate objectives. Conclusions in regard to the objective logically could have been drawn from our almost daily bombings of Munda and Vila airfields. (Munda was bombed on four out of five days and Vila on three out of five days beginning on 25 June, while no other base in the Central or Northern Solomons, i.e. Rekata Bay, Kahili, Ballale or Buka, was bombed more than twice.) [38]

THE SOPAC FINAL TOENAILS PLAN

The general concept of Vice Admiral Halsey's plan was that movements of the amphibians on 30 June 1943 into the New Georgia Group were the necessary prelude to capturing in succession Munda airfield on New Georgia, Vila airfield on Kolombangaru, and other enemy positions in the New Georgia Group.[39]

The only deadlines set by COMSOPAC were 30 June when the initial amphibious landings were to take place, and following which, at "any favorable opportunity," a flank assault on Munda airfield was to be launched, by landing at Zanana Beach on New Georgia, five miles east of Munda.

Vice Admiral Halsey's Operation Plan 14–43 divided the forces available to him for TOENAILS into four main segments and directed that the surface, air, and submarine elements would all support the amphibious element, which Rear Admiral Turner would command.

Specifically, the three elements supporting the amphibious forces were:

---
[38] COMAIRSOPAC *War Diary,* Jun. 1943.
[39] Commander Third Fleet Op Plan 14–43, 3 Jun. 1943.

THE OVERALL NAVAL ORGANIZATION FOR TOENAILS

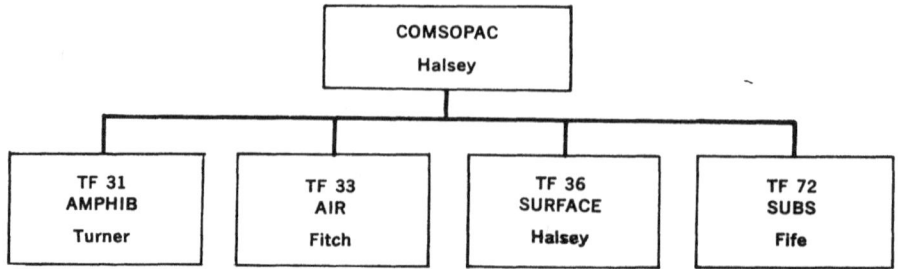

a. Task Force 33 which under Vice Admiral Aubrey Fitch controlled all the land based aircraft and tender based aircraft in the South Pacific Area.
b. Task Force 36 which under Vice Admiral Halsey's own command and coordination consisted of (1) two Carrier Task Groups, (2) three surface ship task groups, one including fast minelayers and (3) the Ground Force Reserve, and
c. Task Force 72 which under Captain James Fife, provided eleven submarines from the Seventh Fleet based on Australia.

Task Force 33, the SOPAC Air Force, was directed to:
a. Provide reconnaissance air cover and support.
b. Neutralize enemy air flying out from the New Georgia Group and Bougainville.
c. Arrange with and provide CTF 31 with air striking groups for use in the immediate vicinity of TF 31.

Task Force 36, the Covering Force, was directed to "destroy enemy forces threatening TOENAILS Operation."

Task Force 72, the Submarine Force, was directed to:
a. "Conduct offensive reconnaissance" near the equator and north of the Bismarck Archipelago, and
b. Cover the channels between Buka, New Ireland, and Bougainville.

Task Force 36 was divided into six Task Groups with a Flag or General officer heading up each group.

As CTG 36.1, Rear Admiral Walden L. Ainsworth (1910) in the *Honolulu* (CL-48) had CRUDIV Nine and five destroyers.

As CTG 36.2, Rear Admiral Aaron S. Merrill (1912) in the *Montpelier* (CL-57) had CRUDIV 12, five destroyers, and three fast minelayers.

As CTG 36.3, Rear Admiral DeWitt C. Ramsey (1912) in the *Saratoga* (CV-3) had three battleships, two anti-aircraft light cruisers, 14 destroyers and the British carrier *Victorious* as well as an oiler.

As CTG 36.4, Rear Admiral Harry W. Hill (1911) had two battleships from Battleship Division Four, and four destroyers.

As CTG 36.5, Rear Admiral Andrew C. McFall (1916) in the *Sangamon* (CVE-26) had Carrier Division 22 (three escort carriers) and six destroyers.

As CTG 36.6, Major General Robert S. Beightler, U. S. Army, had the 37th Division less two regimental combat teams.

Task Force 33 contained somewhere between 530 and 625 planes, the exact number on 30 June being difficult to determine. However, on 30 June,

Rear Admiral Marc A. Mitscher who under Vice Admiral Aubrey W. Fitch, Commander TF 33 and Air Force South Pacific, commanded the Solomon Islands Air Force, reported that 455 planes in his Force were ready to fly. These were 213 fighters, 170 light bombers and 72 heavy bombers. In contrast, the Japanese at Rabaul had but 66 bombers, and 83 fighter aircraft on this day, with an undetermined small number at Buka, Kahili, and Ballale, their three main operational airfields in the Northern Solomons.[40]

The main submarine unit of Task Force 72, commanded by Captain James Fife (1918), was Submarine Squadron Eight, commanded by Captain William N. Downes (1920). Captain Downes acted as Liaison Officer to Commander Third Fleet and was positioned in Noumea from the latter part of June until mid-July 1943. Six to eight submarines of this squadron were on station in the Solomons from mid-June to mid-July.

For Dog Day, the carrier task force was told to operate in an area nearly 500 miles south of Rendova—well out of range for any close air support and well clear of enemy shore based air.

One cruiser-destroyer force was assigned an operating area 300 miles south-southwest of Rendova, while another cruiser-destroyer-minelayer force was given the chore of laying a minefield 120 miles north of Rendova and bombarding various airfields north of New Georgia.

The planes from the escort aircraft carriers called "jeep" carriers,[41] were to be flown off to augment the shore-based aircraft of CTF 33, COMAIRSOPAC. One division of battleships was kept in a 2-hour ready status in far away Efate, 750 miles from the New Georgia objective.

AIRSOPAC would provide the aircraft umbrella, and the submarines would provide any unwelcome news of the approach of major units of the Japanese Fleet towards or past the Bismarck Barrier.

It should be noted that COMSOPAC's Plan:
1. provided that a shore-based commander, Vice Admiral Halsey, retained immediate personal control of the operation.
2. did not provide for the coordination of the various SOPAC task forces under one commander in the operating or objective area, should a Japanese surface or carrier task force show up to threaten

---

[40] James C. Shaw, "The Japanese Guessed Wrong at New Georgia," *The Marine Corps Gazette*, xxxiii (Dec. 1949), pp. 36–42.

[41] The escort aircraft carrier was a small carrier fashioned out of a merchant ship hull. It had low speed, modest plane carrying capacity and inadequate water-tight subdivision for a man-of-war. Like the Army jeep, it was called upon to do practically every type of task, hence its nickname "jeep."

Planning for Paring the Japanese Toenails

Courtesy of Capt. Charles Stein, USN (Ret.)

The Admiral's Head, Camp Crocodile, Guadalcanal Island.

or attack the amphibious force, i.e., did not provide an Expeditionary Force Commander.

3. Did not provide any aircraft under the control of the Amphibious Task Force Commander for dawn or dusk search of the sea approaches immediately controlling the landing areas.
4. Did not provide in advance the conditions for the essential change of command from the Amphibious Task Force Commander to the Landing Force Commander, merely stating: "The forces of occupa-

tion in New Georgia Island will pass from command of CTF 31 on orders from COMSOPAC."

COMSOPAC's Plan did provide for:
1. Air striking groups, under the control of the amphibious task force commander, for use in the immediate vicinity of that Force.
2. Commander Amphibious Force having the authority to ensure "coordination of detailed plans in connection with the amphibious movement and the immediate support thereof."
3. Broadcast of evaluated information on two circuits (SOPAC Love and NPM Fox).
4. An Air Operational Intelligence circuit to retransmit contact reports received from reconnaissance aircraft.
5. Stationing of submarine units to detect and report southward movement of Japanese surface forces from Truk or entering the northern waters of the Slot, in an effort to alert the amphibious forces to the approach of any heavy units from the Combined Fleet.

COMAIRSOPAC moved his operational headquarters to Guadalcanal on 25 June so that in the period immediately prior to the launching of the invasion forces he would be working in the same headquarters as the amphibious commander.

So at least some major steps were taken to prevent another Savo Island.

A LARGER STAFF

By the time of the TOENAILS Operation, the PHIBFORSOPAC Staff had expanded from 11 to 16 officers, and there were many new faces, including two majors from the United States Army. 21 additional officers were attached to the Staff in supporting roles mainly in the Communication and Intelligence areas.

On 8 May 1943, nine days before Vice Admiral Halsey issued his directive for the TOENAILS Operation, Rear Admiral Turner requested Lieutenant General Harmon to order five officers of the 43rd Division to report to COMPHIBFORTHIRDFLT for the preparation of the plans for TOENAILS, and suggested that these officers plan on living aboard the flagship *McCawley*.[42] This was done. The names of these officers are not shown below, as this was a temporary detail only.

---

[42] RKT to Harmon, letter, 8 May 1943.

Courtesy of Maj. Gen. F. D. Weir, USMC, (Ret.)

Lieutenant Colonel Frank D. Weir, USMC, Assistant Operations (Air), before his tent at Camp Crocodile, Guadalcanal.

STAFF OF COMMANDER AMPHIBIOUS FORCE, SOUTH PACIFIC

(COMPHIBFORTHIRDFLT)

Chief of Staff	Captain A. B. Anderson, USN (1912)
Assistant Chief of Staff	Colonel H. D. Linscott, USMC (1917)
Operations Officer	Captain J. H. Doyle, USN (1920)
Assistant Operations Officer (Air)	Colonel F. D. Weir, USMC (1923)
Communications Officer	Commander G. W. Welker, USN (1923)
Assistant Operations Officer (Aerologist)	Commander W. V. Deutermann, USN (1924)
Gunnery Officer	Commander D. M. Tyree, USN (1925)
Medical Officer	Commander R. E. Fielding (MC), USN (1928)
Aide and Flag Secretary	Commander Hamilton Hains, USN (1925)
Assistant Flag Secretary	Lieutenant Commander Carl E. Morck, USNR (1929)

Aide and Flag Lieutenant }	Lieutenant Commander J. S. Lewis, USN (1932)
Assistant Operations Officer }	
Intelligence Officer	Major F. A. Skow (CE), AUS
Transport Quartermaster	Major W. A. Neal, USMCR
Assistant Operations Officer	Major A. W. Bollard (GSC), USA
Assistant Communications Officer	Major R. A. Nicholson, USMCR
Supply Officer	Lieutenant C. Stein, Jr., (SC) USN (1937)

OFFICERS ATTACHED TO STAFF FOR SPECIAL DUTIES

Captain John E. Merrill, USMCR	Assistant Intelligence Officer
Captain Richard A. Gard, USMCR	Assistant Intelligence Officer
Lieutenant Leo M. Doody, USNR	Assistant Gunnery Officer
Lieutenant (jg) Leonard te Groen, USNR	Assistant Flag Secretary
Lieutenant (jg) Jeff N. Bell, USNR	Communication Watch Officer
Lieutenant (jg) August J. Garon, USNR	Assistant Intelligence Officer
Lieutenant (jg) George G. Gordon, USNR	Assistant Intelligence Officer
Lieutenant (jg) Clifford R. Humphreys, USNR	Assistant Operations Officer
Lieutenant (jg) Henry I. Cohen, USNR	Communication Watch Officer
Lieutenant (jg) Roger S. Henry, USNR	Communication Watch Officer
Lieutenant (jg) Howard H. Braun, USNR	Communication Watch Officer
Lieutenant (jg) Thomas A. Dromgool, USNR	Communication Watch Officer
Lieutenant (jg) William C. Powell, USNR	Communication Watch Officer
Ensign John P. Hart, USNR	Communication Watch Officer
Ensign Gordon N. Noland, USNR	Communication Watch Officer
Ensign Harry D. Smith, USNR	Communication Watch Officer
Ensign John G. Feeley, USNR	Communication Watch Officer
Radio Electrician Paul L. Frost, USN	Radio Electrician

Staff rosters available from March 1943 to July 1943 indicate that Captain Anderson, Lieutenant Commander Morck, Lieutenant (junior grade) John C. Weld, USNR and Acting Pay Clerk Melvin C. Amundsen were assigned with the Administrative Command at Noumea, New Caledonia, during this period. Lieutenant (junior grade) Henry D. Linscott, Jr., USNR, one of the Assistant Operations Officers, was temporarily with the Guadalcanal Freight Line on the Staff of Commodore Lawrence F. Reifsnider, and Lieutenant Leo W. Doody, USNR, was away on temporary duty in connection with gunfire support training. Consequently only 32 of the 38 officers (including Rear Admiral Turner) were available when the Staff picture was taken. 30 of these 32 appear in the picture.

All 15 members of the regular Staff quartered on Guadalcanal have been positively identified by three or more of its present living members. Of the

Planning for Paring the Japanese Toenails 521

Turner Collection

Front Row, Left to Right: (1) Lieutenant Colonel Frank D. Weir, USMC (2) Colonel Henry D. Linscott, USMC (3) Rear Admiral R. K. Turner, USN (4) Captain James H. Doyle, USN (5) Commander George W. Welker, USN.

Second Row, Left to Right: (6) Radio Electrician Paul L. Frost, USN (7) Commander William U. Deutermann, USN (8) Lieutenant Commander John S. Lewis, USN (9) unidentified (10) Major Robert A. Nicholson, USMCR (11) Lieutenant Charles Stein (SC) USN, (12) unidentified (13) Commander David M. Tyree, USN (14) Commander Ralph E. Fielding (MC) USN (15) Major Arthur W. Bollard, AUS (16) Captain J. C. Erskine, USMCR

Subsequent Rows, Left to Right: (17) Lieutenant (jg) George G. Gordon, USNR (18) Ensign Harry D. Smith, USNR (19) unidentified (20) Major Willis A. Neal, USNR (21) Ensign Thomas A. Dromgool, USNR (22) Commander Hamilton Hains, USN (23) Major Floyd Skow (GE) AUS (24) Lieutenant (jg) Howard H. Braun (?) (25) unidentified (26) Lieutenant (jg) Leonard te Groen (27) Lieutenant (jg) Jeff N. Bell, USNR (28) Captain Richard A. Gard (29) Captain John E. Merrill (30) Lieutenant (jg) Roger S. Henry (?)

15 other officers in the picture six: Captain John C. Erskine, USMCR, whom Merrill relieved, Gard, Gordon, Smith, Dromgrool, and Bell, have been identified by two or more members. Three more: Braun, te Groen, and Henry have been identified or guessed at by one or more members. Numbers 9, 12, 19, and 25 in the photograph have not been identified.

One Marine officer, Captain Gard, was placed in three different positions, before he was located in Hong Kong and identified himself.

AMPHIBIOUS FORCE GENERAL PLAN

The amphibious plan changed a number of times as the information or intelligence brought in by the reconnaissance patrols in regard to the New Georgia Group expanded or changed. To a marked extent, the Scheme of Maneuver agreed upon by Rear Admiral Turner and Major General Harmon and later by Major General Hester was determined by such hard physical facts as depth of water, reefs, beach gradients, numbers of troops or amounts of supplies which could be landed on narrow beaches, possible beach exits into dense jungle, jungle trails, jungle clearings, or possible bivouac areas.[43]

A major problem with the new large landing craft (LSTs and LCTs) was in finding beach gradients where they could land their cargo through the bow doors, and in finding breaks in the mile-long reefs. Munda Bar was another mental and physical hazard which tempered a desire to make a frontal attack on the airfield as had been done at Guadalcanal. Older British charts dating back to 1900 had shown three to seven fathoms over Munda Bar which would have permitted comfortable passage by destroyer-type fast transports and large landing craft, but more recent reports cast doubt on these depths and the best information was that there was only an unmarked 300-foot wide passage over the bar with 18 feet of water at high tide and 15 feet at low tide.[44]

Major discussion during the early part of the long planning period before Vice Admiral Halsey issued his Op Plan 14–43 centered on:

    a. whether a frontal assault on Munda could be attempted.

    b. the provision of close air and gun support during the first couple of days of an assault landing.

Close air support by land-based planes directly from Guadalcanal was

---
[43] CTF 31 Op Plan A8–43, 4 Jun. 1943; Op Order A9–43, 15 Jun. 1943; and Op Plan A11–43, 28 Jun. 1943 and all changes thereto.
[44] Intelligence Map, Munda Point, Sheet 2, H.O. 2907. Pack III. NHD.

difficult to impossible because of the distance—180 miles. Close air support from the Russells, 125 miles away, was limited by there being room for only two airstrips on Banika Island in the Russells.

The Third Fleet Commander, Vice Admiral Halsey, was reluctant to maintain carriers in a position to provide a major portion of such close air support over a period of more than two or three days. His position in this apparently was no different than Vice Admiral Fletcher's had been prior to and during the WATCHTOWER landings.

As the CINCPAC planners wrote in their estimate of the situation:

> A frontal landing from the south would require landing craft to approach through openings in the coral reef which can be covered easily from ashore, and which are narrow so as to prevent a broad approach.

The Amphibious Force Commander was reluctant to test his large landing craft over Munda Bar, in their first assault landing, and the Landing Force Commander was reluctant to give a firm guarantee of success for a frontal assault against Munda airfield within the short period of two to three days.

As soon as the decisions were made that neither the fast carrier task forces nor the jeep carriers would provide close air support for TOENAILS and that the amphibians would not risk an initial all out frontal assault over Munda Bar, an alternative plan was evolved and accepted by all hands.

This plan included making the major assault on Munda airfield from its eastern flank while simultaneously landing a holding assault against its seaward (southern) front and closing off its support lines to the north by a small landing on Kula Gulf. The plan also provided for building an airstrip at Segi Point, New Georgia, to provide close air support for the impending assault on Vila airstrip, and the making of Rendova Island into a combination staging point and artillery support position for the Munda assault.

Thus the Navy was relieved of the night time hazards of Munda Bar and the inhospitable coral-studded approaches to Munda Point beaches, and the Army of an assault without some semblance of its own artillery support. But the plan was not a prescription for quick victory.

The limited experience of CLEANSLATE had indicated that the tank landing craft, with their small crews, frequent breakdowns and slow speed in even moderate weather, required ports or protected anchorages at about 60-mile intervals where they could receive repairs and daytime rest, while they approached the landing beaches at night. This led to a search for protected harbors or anchorages in the Middle Solomons and to the selection of Viru Harbor, New Georgia, and Wickham Anchorage, at the eastern approaches to Vangunu Island, as areas to be seized.

Viru Harbor was, in the early planning, also a location where sizable forces could be profitably and safely disembarked from landing ships and then moved by small landing craft closer to Munda to assist in the flank assault on Munda airfield. Segi Point was selected because it was the only area where a fighter strip might be built to assist in the assault on Vila airfield or even on Munda, if success there was long delayed.

The small contingent of Japanese troops at Viru and Wickham, in each case, was a magnet as well. If the Japanese needed these locations to control and safeguard the islands, then we might need them also.

Rice Anchorage, upon Kula Gulf, almost directly north of Munda, was selected as the location where the troops whose task would be to seal off the northern flank of Munda would be landed.

ASSIGNING THE TASKS

The amphibians had one major task and four minor ones to accomplish the morning of 30 June, and a further task four or more days later.

Rear Admiral Turner divided the amphibious assault force of Task Force 31 into two major groupings for 30 June. The division was based on whether the tasks were to be accomplished in the eastern or western part of the New Georgia Group. Appropriately, he labeled them the Eastern Force and the Western Force.

The Rice Anchorage Landing Group was separately organized using the destroyer type transports and minesweepers assigned to the 30 June landings. It was called the Northern Landing Group.

CTF 31 (Rear Admiral Turner) retained immediate command of Task

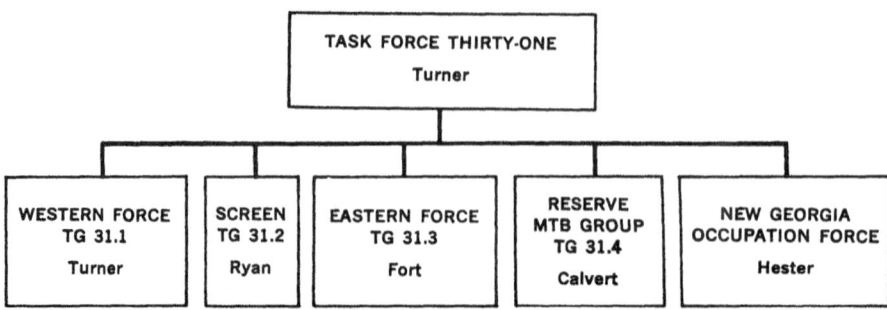

Group 31.1, an organization of all the large transports and cargo ships, part of the destroyer-type transports and minesweepers, most of the larger landing craft (LSTs) and the necessary protecting destroyers. Rear Admiral Turner assigned his senior subordinate, Commander Landing Craft Flotillas, Rear Admiral George H. Fort (1912), to command Task Group 31.3, an organization of destroyer-type transports and minesweepers, infantry and tank landing craft and coastal transports.

Task Group 31.1, which in violation of Naval War College doctrine for terminology, was named the Western Force instead of the Western Group, with Commander Transport Division Two, Captain Paul S. Theiss (1912), as Second in Command, was assigned the Rendova Island task.

Task Group 31.3 which was erroneously named the Eastern Force instead of the Eastern Group, with no designated Second-in-Command, was assigned the three assault chores at (1) Viru Harbor, New Georgia, (2) Segi Point, New Georgia, and (3) at Wickham Anchorage which lies between Vanguna and Gatukai Islands, the first two large islands to the southeast from New Georgia. These three places all could serve as first aid stations for tank landing craft or PT boats making the run from the Russells to Rendova or Munda.

The main Landing Force carried in the Western Force was to be put ashore in four echelons, the largest number of troops going in the first echelon aboard the transports and cargo ships. The second to fourth echelons were to be carried by the LSTs and LCIs.

The various occupation units carried in the Eastern Force were also to be landed in four echelons. The first echelons at Viru Harbor and Wickham Anchorage included destroyer transports, with coastal transports, LCIs, and LCTs making up the succeeding echelons at these points and the first echelon at Segi Point. Most landing craft had assigned tasks in more than one echelon.

There was to be a four-destroyer fire support unit and another four-destroyer anti-submarine unit in the Rendova area to keep down fire from Japanese shore batteries near Munda, to provide anti-aircraft protection and to keep submarines away from the unloading transports and cargo ships.

When CTF 31 departed Rendova to return to Guadalcanal at the end of D-Day, the 12 motor torpedo boats in the New Georgia MTB Squadron were to be under the immediate operational control of Commander Naval Base, Rendova. They had orders to set up their initial base on Lumbari Island in the western reaches of Rendova Harbor.

The New Georgia Occupation Force consisted of all the troops in the

Western Landing Force (mainly the 43rd Infantry Division), the Eastern Landing Force, the Reserve Force (mainly the 1st Marine Raider Regiment), the Naval Base Force, the New Georgia Air Force, and the Assault Flotillas (18 LCIs and boats from Boat Pool No. 8).

The Naval Base Force was a large force. It included one and one-half construction battalions, an ACORN, the boat pools, and the administrative and other units to operate the naval bases to be built as well as the New Georgia Motor Torpedo Boat Squadron. Altogether, it included over 250 officers and 4,000 men.

The 1st Echelon of the Western Force was organized as follows:

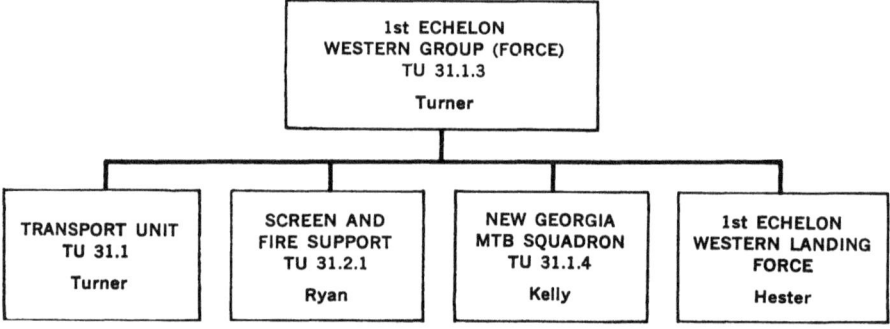

The Eastern Force task organization was:

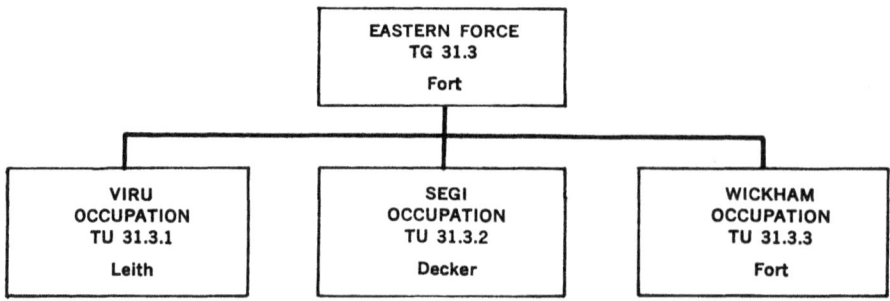

Captain Benton C. Decker's regular assignment was Chief of Staff to Commander Landing Craft Flotillas. Commander Stanley Leith's regular assignment was Commander Minesweeper Group.

The Army troops came from the 14th Corps, commanded by Major General Oscar W. Griswold, USA. Major General John H. Hester, USA, who commanded the 43rd Infantry Division, was the same officer Rear Admiral Turner worked with during CLEANSLATE.

OPERATIONAL FIRSTS

The TOENAILS Operation was the first major Pacific amphibious landing wherein (1) "transport planes were used to drop supplies and needed material, including shells and water to our combat troops" and (2) large tugs were available to salvage landing craft and landing boats.[45]

It also was the first amphibious operation where a Flag or General officer with a small staff was set up to control all aircraft in the objective area. In TOENAILS, Brigadier General Francis R. Mulcahy, USMC, Commander, Headquarters and Forward Echelon, 2nd Marine Aircraft Wing, was designated Commander Air New Georgia. He was positioned in the *McCawley* together with CTF 31 until the prospective Commander Occupation Force moved his command post ashore to Rendova Island. When that event occurred on D-Day, Mulcahy was to shift ashore to work under the command of that officer. Direction of fighters over Task Force 31 on D-Day initially was in the destroyer *Jenkins,* which had a fighter director group aboard. Close air support direction initially was in the *McCawley* which had a close air support group aboard. Both of these latter groups were under orders to shift ashore as soon as practical.[46]

INTELLIGENCE

The Intelligence Annexes of CTF 31's two Operation Plans (A8–43 and A9–43) for TOENAILS contained over 60 maps and drawings. Otherwise they were sketchy to an extreme. But even this was better intelligence than SOPAC'S Operation Plan 14–43 for TOENAILS which had no Intelligence Annex at all.

Despite the sketchiness of the intelligence data supplied, the overall guestimate of Japanese naval strength in the Solomons on 13 June 1943, by post-war Japanese account, was reasonably conservative: "6 destroyers and 5 submarines versus actually 1 cruiser, 8 destroyers and 8 submarines in the 8th Fleet with Headquarters in the Shortlands."

The 30 May 1943 estimate of Japanese air strength in the Solomons and at Kavieng and Rabaul—393 planes—also was low, on the date it was made,

---

[45] (a) CTF 31 Op Plan A8–43, Annexes (E) and (F); (b) CINCPAC Operations in the Pacific Ocean Areas, July 1943. P. 13.

[46] (a) CTF 33 Op Plan 7–43, 18 Jun. 1943; (b) Commander New Georgia Air Force (Brigadier General Mulcahy, USMC), Special Action Report covering the 1st phase of the New Georgia Operations, 29 Jun.–13 Aug. 1943. No ser, undated.

which was prior to the three Japanese air raids on Guadalcanal carried out on 7, 12, and 16 June 1943, which led to heavy air losses for the Japanese.

As to Japanese troops, it was estimated that there were 3,000 at Munda, 5,000 to 7,000 at Kolombangara across Kula Gulf to the north from Munda, 200 to 300 at Wickham Anchorage, and 30 to 100 at Viru Harbor. This was quite low for Munda, where there were probably 5,000 troops on 30 June.[47]

In February 1943, a small reconnaissance patrol of Marines visited the Roviana Lagoon area of New Georgia, and after that date other reconnaissance patrols had visited Segi, Viru Harbor, Wickham Anchorage areas and Rendova Island and brought back important intelligence and hydrographic information, including sketched shore lines. Air photographs were extensively taken and a major effort was made to improve the information available from British charts of the period 1912–1937. In May 1943, the Hydrographic Office in Washington ran off special reprints of charts of the New Georgia Group and they were carried by special messenger to the South Pacific. On 13 June, the last reconnaissance patrols were landed, some of whose members remained to guide or greet elements of the Landing Force.

LOGISTICS

The SOPAC's Operation Plan 14–43 covering the TOENAILS Operation had no logistic annex, but his amphibious subordinate again picked up some of the slack and at least issued a sparse logistic plan. Best of all, aided and abetted by Captain Charles E. Olsen, an informative "Naval Base Plan TOENAILS Operation" of 38 pages was issued. The Commander TOENAILS Naval Base Force rode up to Rendova with CTF 31 and Commander Occupation Force in the flagship to ensure close coordination up to the minute of the landings.

It is not believed that the lack of a logistics annex in COMSOPAC's Operation Plan indicated a lack of command attention in the logistic area, for certainly during the nine months since WATCHTOWER the logistic situation in the South Pacific Area had improved substantially. Much of this progress flowed directly from command decisions made by Vice Admiral Halsey. Probably the most important of these decisions was that all units of

---

[47] (a) CTF 31 Op Plan A8–43, Annex C paras. 1(b), (c), (d); (b) Miller, *Isolation of Rabaul* (Army), pp. 48–49.

Left: "Fish for Dinner." Results of dynamiting the river at a native village on Guadalcanal. Right: Lieutenant Charles Stein (SC), USN, gloats over the first well at Camp Crocodile, 13 July 1943.

all Services must consider themselves part and parcel of SOPAC forces and that there be communal use of all supplies and facilities. Additionally, the Army now placed in charge, and with time and more adequate personnel on its side, brought order out of chaos in the port at Noumea. The port at Espiritu Santo was also gradually beginning to function satisfactorily. On 23 June 1943, COMSOPAC advised the Vice Chief of Naval Operations that abnormal delays of shipping there were no longer anticipated.[48]

Commander Eastern Force was given the logistic responsibility for "embarking troops and supplies from the Russells destined for the support of TOENAILS" after the initial movement, and for all movements to Viru Harbor, Segi Point, and Wickham Anchorage. Commander Western Force controlled other logistic support movements into the objective area, and was responsible overall for the movement of troops and supplies to New Georgia Island. The Commanding General Guadalcanal was directed to support the operation by making available supplies in the Guadalcanal-Russell Islands area and furnishing the necessary labor details for loading or transshipment. And finally, in contradistinction to WATCHTOWER, there were 1st Echelon, 2nd Echelon, 3rd Echelon, and 4th Echelon logistic support movements set up for the TOENAILS Operation, prior to Dog Day.

THE JAPANESE CHANGE OUR PLANS

During the pre-invasion period, on 20 June, Rear Admiral Turner learned by radio from a coastwatcher that three barge loads of Japanese troops had landed at Segi Point and that the coastwatcher needed help to stay out of their clutches. In order to provide the help and ensure that the enemy would not have an opportunity to dig in, Rear Admiral Turner made the immediate decision to land Marines at Segi Point the next morning (21 June). This was nine days before D-Day for the main landings at Rendova. The change was considered necessary to ensure possession of this particularly desirable fighter-airstrip real estate and to be able to proceed promptly to build the airstrip to provide for close fighter aircraft air support during the landing operation against Munda or Vila.

The need for this close air support had to be balanced against the disadvantage of possibly tipping off the Japanese on the nearness of the impending Rendova attack. While the airstrips at the Russell Islands were

---

[48] COMSOPAC to VCNO, 230006 June 1943.

very helpful, they were 130 miles away from Munda and our fighter aircraft of that day could remain on station near Munda only a short time when taking off from the Russells.[49]

Much to the surprise of TF 31 Staff and others, the Japanese did not react to the landings on Segi Point. There did not seem to be any increase of air search nor any movement of the main Japanese Fleet out of Truk to the South. There were no more heavy air raids on the Guadalcanal area in the next nine days.

THE NIGHT BEFORE D-DAY

On the rainy and largely moonless night before D-Day, Cruiser Division 12 [*Montpelier* (CL-57), *Cleveland* (CL-55), *Columbia* (CL-56), and *Denver* (CL-58)] and Destroyer Division 43 [*Waller* (DD-466), *Saufley* (DD-465), *Philip* (DD-498), and *Renshaw* (DD-499)], led by Rear Admiral A. S. Merrill (1912), bombarded the Vila-Stanmore Area on the southeast coast of Kolombangara Island and the Buin Area at the southeast end of Bougainville Island, while three minelayers, *Gamble* (DM-15), *Breese* (DM-18), and *Preble* (DM-20), shepherded by the *Pringle* (DD-447), with Commander Destroyer Squadron 22 aboard, laid 336 mines off Shortland Harbor, 230 miles north of the Russell Islands.

The Task Units retired without loss, but without having inflicted any Savo Island in reverse. Still, they were on the flank of any Japanese surface force that might have been headed for the transports at Rendova on the night before D-Day.

The TF 33 aircraft which were due to bomb the Bougainville-Shortland airfields had their flights washed out on this rainy, stormy night but 99 other aircraft from TF 33 did bomb Munda and Vila on 29–30 June with more than 70 tons of bombs.[50]

Just as the tired and wet sea watch of TF 31 was being relieved at midnight of the 29th of June, Japanese submarine RO-103 guarding the channel between Gatukai Island and the Russells reported to headquarters in Rabaul that an enemy task force was headed northwest.[51]

---

[49] (a) CTF 31 Op Plan A8–43, 4 Jun. 1943; (b) COMSOPAC to COMINCH, 160420 May 1943; (c) COMSOPAC to COMSOWESPAC, 210942 Jun. 1943; (d) Staff Interviews.

[50] (a) CINCPAC, Operations in Pacific Ocean Areas, June 1943, Appendix I; (b) Staff Interviews.

[51] Japanese Monograph No. 99, Southeast Area Naval Operations, Part II, Feb.–Oct. 1943, p. 26.

OPERATIONAL READINESS OF AMPHIBIANS

Ten months had faded into the propeller wash since the SOPAC Amphibious Force landed at Tulagi and Guadalcanal. New types of landing craft had joined the amphibians with untried personnel manning them, but of the six big transports and cargo ships, only the *Algorab* (AK-12) was not a veteran of the initial landings of WATCHTOWER. Three of the WATCHTOWER destroyers, *Ralph Talbot* (DD-390), *Buchanan* (DD-484), and *Farenholt* (DD-491) had survived the holocaust of the Slot battles and were back to do their escorting, fire support and anti-aircraft chores.

There had been time to season under strong leadership since August 1942, and the naval amphibious forces of Rear Admiral Turner moving toward New Georgia were well trained and confident they would handle TOENAILS and the Japanese defenders.[52]

---
[52] (a) Fort; (b) Anderson; (c) Staff Interviews.

CHAPTER XV

Tough Toenails Paring
30 JUNE 1943 TO 15 JULY 1943

PROSPECTS

There were many in the TOENAILS Operation, who, having been told to be ready to commence the assault on Munda airfield on D plus four, hoped, like General Grant before Vicksburg to make a glorious announcement on the 4th of July. Their announcement would be that Munda airfield had been taken on that historic day. These optimists had not read carefully the operation orders nor heeded Commander Third Fleet despatches. The plans of the Landing Force Commander, Major General Hester, did not even contemplate an attack on Munda airfield until 8 July, when the supporting waterborne assault over Munda Bar was scheduled.[1]

Rear Admiral Turner carefully refrained from putting any such hope or prediction into print. His "Concept of Operation" in Op Plan 8-43 merely echoed Vice Admiral Halsey's directive which called for the initial movement of Marines and Army troops onto New Georgia Island "at the first favorable opportunity."

> Forces should be ready to initiate the movement against Munda by D plus Four Day, to take advantage of especially favorable opportunities. The date of the movement will depend upon circumstances.[2]

At a pre-invasion press conference, Rear Admiral Turner reputedly opined:

> . . . [Munda] is a most magnificent defensive area from the sea. There is a dense jungle behind. In front is the Munda Bar. . . . The water is chock full of reefs. . . .
>
> * * * * *
>
> Some people think Munda's not going to be tough. I think it's a very tough nut to crack. I know we can do it.[3]

---
[1] COMGEN New Georgia Occupation Force, Field Order 3-43, 28 Jun. 1943, para. 1 (b).
[2] CTF 31 Op Plan 8-43, Annex A, para. 5e.
[3] Quoted in Driscoll, *Pacific Victory*, pp. 66, 67.

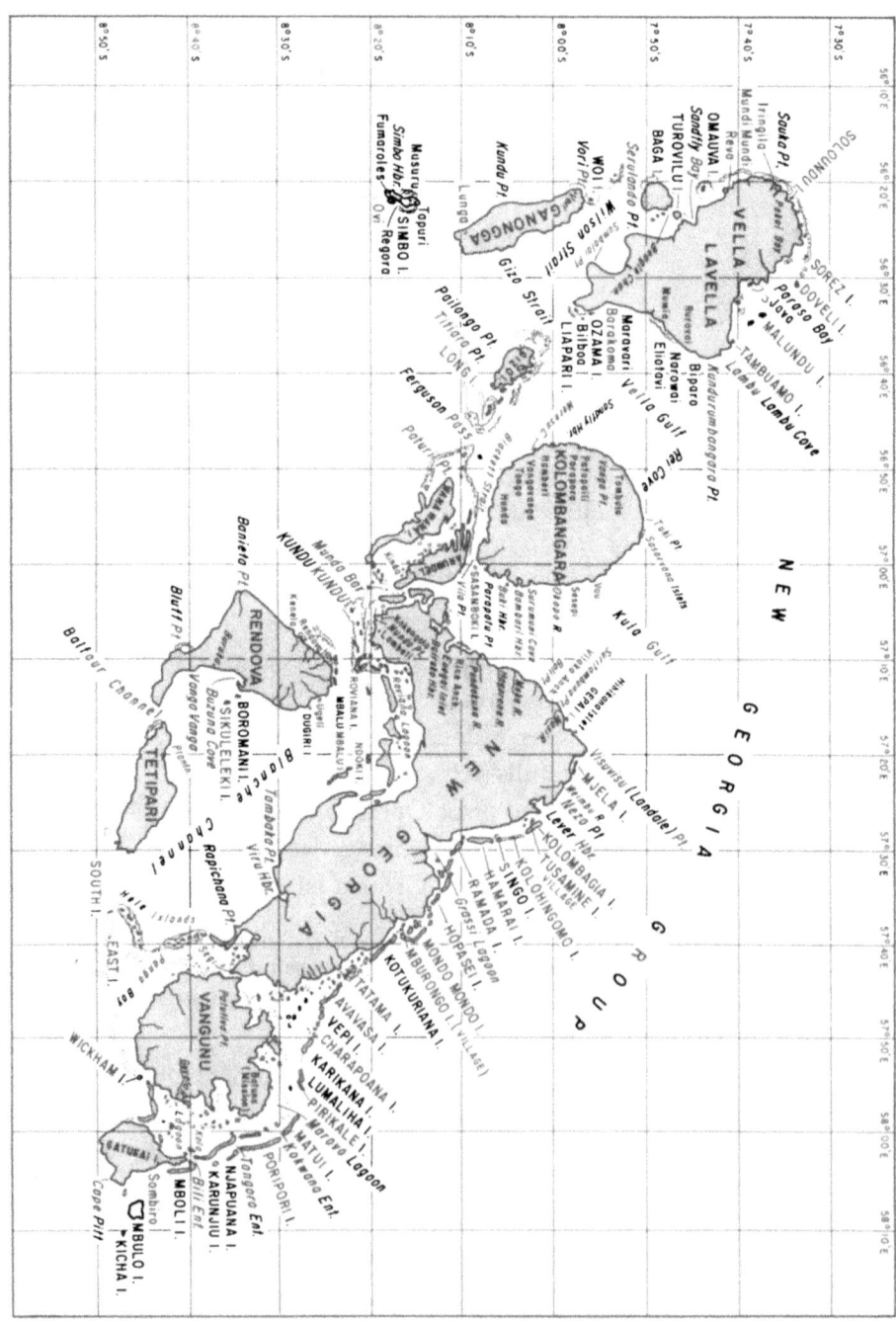

New Georgia Group.

Vice Admiral Halsey had directed that no assault landing on Munda airfield or surface ship bombardment of Munda airfield could be carried out without his personal permission prior to D plus nine (July 8). Then he had changed this restrictive date to D plus ten.[3a] This order was issued long days before the infiltrating troops on New Georgia Island started to run into major difficulties, but despite this the spirit of optimism for early major success pervaded the whole Task Force and its accompanying newspaper correspondents.

TOENAIL PARING

The operations of the Task Group designated the Western Force in TOENAILS during the first two weeks will be detailed first and then those of the Task Group designated Eastern Force. Following this, the landing operations of the Northern Landing Group will be told.

THE MAJOR ASSAULT FORCE ORGANIZATION

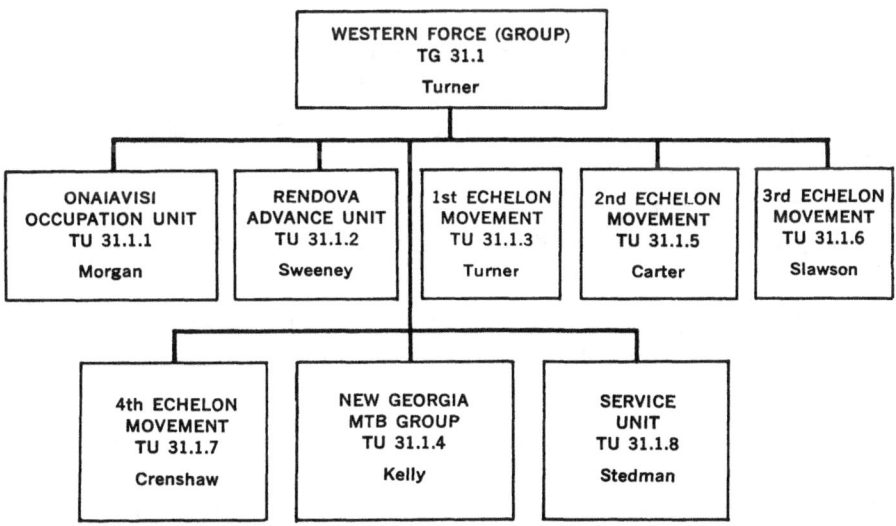

Since much has been made of the lack of a complete wrap-up operational report by COMPHIBFORSOPAC on the Guadalcanal Operation, let it be stated that also there was not a complete wrap-up operational report on TOENAILS by COMPHIBFORSOPAC, whose title had become COMPHIBFOR, Third Fleet. Neither Rear Admiral Turner, who left the area 15 July,

---
[3a] COMTHIRDFLT to CTF 31, 020050, 022300 Jul. 1943.

when TOENAILS was just hot on the griddle and half cooked, nor Rear Admiral Wilkinson, who, on the 15th of July, became the chief line backer rather than the quarterback for TOENAILS, ever submitted an Operational Report on TOENAILS. To polish off the report picture a final bit, Vice Admiral Ghormley, the immediate senior in command, did make an operational report on WATCHTOWER, but Vice Admiral Halsey, the immediate senior in command, made none on TOENAILS. So the top level reports and seasoned judgments regarding TOENAILS from the naval operational commanders at the time of the assault are more than a bit scanty. They are nonexistent.[4]

THE WEATHER

Bad weather was a major hindrance for military operations in the Central Solomons on 30 June 1943, D-Day for TOENAILS. Commander Aircraft Solomons (COMAIRSOLS) had reported late on the 29th that he could carry out no bombing operations on the 30th, "unless the weather clears," and that his information of enemy movements in the area was limited.[5] LCI(L)-333, the day before the actual landing, reported "sea rough; wind force 9" and that there were heavy swells, which would indicate that some young man was vastly underrating what a force 9 wind would and could do.

Rear Admiral Turner, in his War Diary, wrote:

> Weather enroute to Rendova—low ceilings, moderate showers, poor visibility in showers, surface wind SE, force four, shifting and gusty in showers, choppy seas.

Logs of the larger ships participating in the TOENAILS landings on 30 June show that it rained hard off and on during the night, then poured during the landings and on into the morning.

Stormy and rainy weather continued to plague the landing craft during the early days of TOENAILS. On July 1st, 2nd, and 3rd the seas were moderate to heavy with a force 4 wind. LCT-129 lost its ramp in the heavy seas and arrived back at the Russells with three feet of water on her tank deck. The LCIs had to reduce their speed from 12 knots to 8.5 knots due to head-on seas on the 2nd of July.

Task Unit 31.3.24, made up of LCIs and LCTs, was dispersed by the storm

---

[4] Commander Third Fleet, Narrative Account of the South Pacific Campaign, Ser 021 of 3 Sep. 1944.
[5] COMAIRSOLS to CTG 36.2, 290835 Jun. 1943.

on 3 July but all craft made it independently into Oleana Bay, New Georgia. LCT-322 broached and was carried high and dry on the beach, where she remained until 6 July when she was refloated by the aid of tugs.

On the 4th of July, seas started to moderate and by 6 July they were calm, but the heavens were not. "The second week of occupation brought torrential downpours that bemired virtually all mobile equipment, rendering doubly difficult the task of unloading the landing craft as they beached." [6]

THE WESTERN FORCE (GROUP) TASK

The basic plan (CTF 31 Op Order A8–31) contemplated putting ashore about 16,500 troops in the Rendova area in the first four days. To accomplish this task, the following organization was established:

Western Task Group Organization TG 31.1

(a) *Onaiavisi Occupation Unit* TU 31.1.1 Lieutenant Commander C. C. Morgan
 Talbot (APD-7) Lieutenant Commander C. C. Morgan
 Zane (DMS-14) Lieutenant Commander P. L. Wirtz
(b) *Rendova Advance Unit* TU 31.1.2 Commander J. D. Sweeney
 Waters (APD-8) Lieutenant Commander C. J. McWhinnie
 Dent (APD-9) Lieutenant Commander R. A. Wilhelm
(c) *1st Echelon Movement Western Group* TU 31.1.3 Rear Admiral Turner
 (1) *Transport Division* TU 31.1.31 Captain P. S. Theiss
  McCawley (APA-4) Commander R. H. Rodgers
  President Jackson (APA-18) Captain C. W. Weitzel
  President Adams (APA-19) Captain Frank Dean
  President Hayes (APA-20) Captain F. W. Benson
  Algorab (AKA-8) Captain J. R. Lannon
  Libra (AKA-12) Captain W. B. Fletcher
 (2) *Screening Group* TG 31.2 Captain T. J. Ryan, Jr.
  Fire Support Unit TU 31.2.1 Captain Ryan
   Ralph Talbot (DD-390) Commander J. W. Callahan
   Buchanan (DD-484) Lieutenant Commander F. B. T. Myhre
   McCalla (DD-488) Lieutenant Commander H. A. Knoertzer
   Farenholt (F) (DD-491) Lieutenant Commander A. G. Beckman

---

[6] (a) LCI Flotilla Five War Diary, 29 Jun. 1943; (b) Landing Craft Flotillas, SOPAC, War Diary Jul. 1943; (c) LCI Group 13 War Diary, Jul. 1943.

Anti-Submarine Unit TU 31.2.2. Commander J. M. Higgins
    Gwin (DD-433) Lieutenant Commander J. B. Fellows
    Radford (DD-446) Commander W. K. Romoser
    Jenkins (DD-447) Lieutenant Commander M. Hall
    Woodworth (DD-460) Commander V. F. Gordinier
(3) *Motor Torpedo Boat Squadron* TU 31.1.4 Lieutenant Commander R. B. Kelly
    MTBs 118, 151, 153, 154, 155, 156, 157, 158, 159, 160, 161, 162
(4) *1st Echelon Western Landing Force* Major General John W. Hester
    43rd Infantry Division (Designated units)
    9th Marine Defense Battalion
    1st Fiji Infantry (Designated unit)
    136th Field Artillery Battalion
    4th Marine Raider Battalion (Designated units)
    Naval Base Force Captain C. E. Olsen
        24th Construction Battalion (less designated units)
        Naval Base Units
    Headquarters, Assault Flotillas, Captain Paul S. Theiss
    Headquarters, New Georgia Air Force, Brigadier General Francis P. Mulcahy, USMC
(d) *2nd Echelon Movement Western Group* TU 31.1.5 Captain G. B. Carter
    LST Unit Captain G. B. Carter
        LST-354 (F) Lieutenant B. E. Robb, USNR
        LST-395 Lieutenant A. C. Forbes, USNR
        LST-396 Lieutenant E. W. White, USN
        LST-397 Lieutenant N. L. Lewis, USNR
    LCI Unit Commander J. MacDonald Smith
        LCI-61 Lieutenant J. P. Moore, USN
        LCI-64 Lieutenant H. L. Kelly, USNR
        LCI-66 Lieutenant C. F. Houston, USNR
        LCI-70 Lieutenant (jg) H. W. Frey, USNR
        LCI-222 (F) Ensign C. M. Freese, USNR
    2nd Echelon Western Landing Force Lieutenant Colonel Hill
        43rd Infantry (Designated units)
        9th Marine Defense Battalion (Designated units)
        192nd Field Artillery (Designated units)
(e) *3rd Echelon Movement Western Group* TU 31.1.6 Commander P. S. Slawson
    LST Unit Commander P. S. Slawson
        LST-342 (F) Lieutenant E. S. McClusky, USNR
        LST-353 Lieutenant L. E. Reynolds, USNR
        LST-398 Lieutenant B. E. Blanchard, USNR
        LST-399 Lieutenant J. W. Baker, USNR

3rd Echelon Western Landing Force
      24th Construction Battalion (Designated units)
      9th Marine Defense Battalion (Designated units)
(f) *4th Echelon Movement Western Group* TU 31.1.7 Captain J. S. Crenshaw
      LST Unit Lieutenant W. O. Talley
         LST-343 (F) Lieutenant H. H. Rightmeyer, USN
         LST-472 Lieutenant W. O. Talley, USN
      LCI Unit Lieutenant H. L. Kelly
         LCI-61 Lieutenant J. P. Moore, USNR
         LCI-62 Lieutenant (jg) W. C. Lyons, USNR
         LCI-64 Lieutenant H. L. Kelly, USNR
         LCI-65 Lieutenant (jg) C. R. Tompkins, USNR
         LCI-66 Lieutenant C. F. Houston, Jr., USNR
         LCI-222 Ensign C. M. Freese, USNR
(g) *Reserve MTB Group* TG 31.4 Commander Allen P. Calvert
      12 MTBs
(h) *Service Unit* TU 31.1.8 Lieutenant (jg) C. H. Stedman
      Vireo (AT-144) Lieutenant (jg) C. H. Stedman
      Rail (AT-139) Ensign L. C. Oaks
      PAB 4, PAB 8 (A PAB was a Pontoon Assembled Barge or lighter, a bit smaller than the "Rhino Barge" of the Normandy landings.)

Several differences will be noted between the amphibious ships and craft listed above and on later pages for the various tasks and echelons and those listed in Samuel E. Morison's account of the invasion of New Georgia. Morison's listings appear to have been taken from the basic operation orders, while the listings herein were made up from the issued revisions to the basic orders, war diaries, action reports, and despatches, and are believed far more accurate since last minute changes were made.[7]

TASKS

The major task of the amphibians of the Western Force was to get the 6,300 troops in the 1st Echelon ashore at Rendova Island on D-Day.

The minor task was to put ashore two companies of troops to seize the small islands guarding the most direct approach from Rendova Harbor to Zanana Beach on New Georgia Island. Zanana Beach was the spot where

---

[7] Morison, *Breaking the Bismarcks Barrier* (Vol. VI), pp. 144–46.

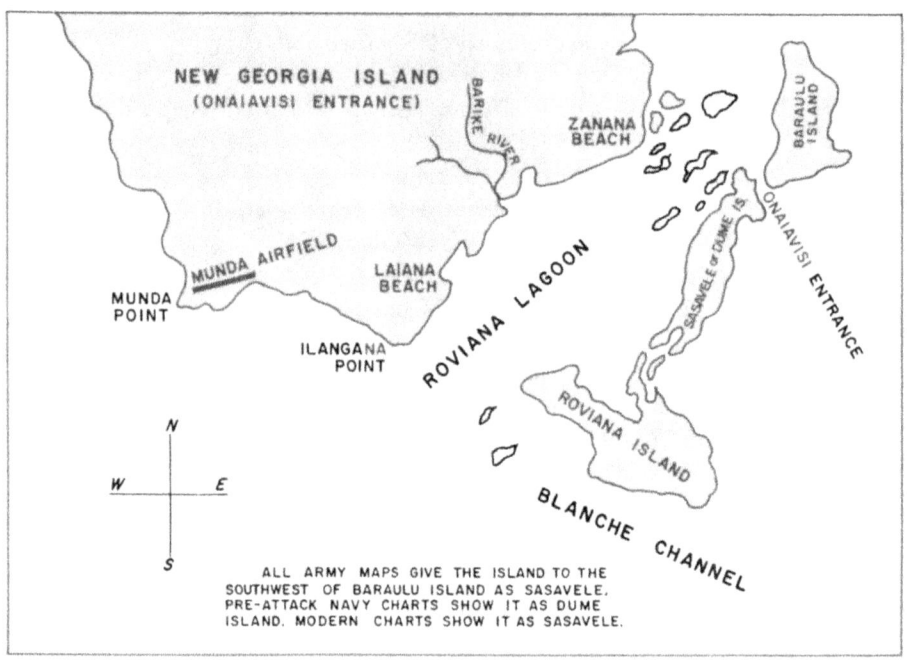

New Georgia Island, Onaiavisi Entrance.

the troops from Rendova were to land to commence their flank attack on Munda airfield.

Since the minor task was to be undertaken first, it is described here first.

ONAIAVISI ENTRANCE (TU 31.1.1)

Two miles east of the eastern end of the Munda airstrip on New Georgia Island is Ilangana Point, and the western end of the 25-mile long Roviana Lagoon. Onaiavisi Entrance, a block-busting name even for the South Pacific, separates Dume (Sasavele) Island and Baraulu Island, which together with Roviana Island and many smaller islands and long coral reefs, guard the western end of Roviana Lagoon and mark the northwestern boundary of Blanche Channel which separates Rendova and New Georgia Islands.

Laiana Beach, just north of Ilangana Point, was a fair beach and a logical place to land to start an assault on Munda airfield. However, Laiana Beach reportedly was defended, while equally good Zanana Beach, two and a half miles, several rivers and creeks and some densely jungled area to the eastward, was not defended.

So again following Major General Vandegrift's requirement that

> landings should not be attempted in the face of organized resistance, if, by any combination of march or maneuver, it is possible to land unopposed and undetected

the Scheme of Maneuver called for the ground attack on Munda airfield to be initiated following deployment to the westward after troop landings on Zanana Beach.[8]

Having accepted this Scheme of Maneuver, it was essential for the amphibians also to land troops on the islands controlling the direct approach to Zanana Beach.

The destroyer transport *Talbot* (APD 7) and the destroyer minesweeper *Zane* (DMS-14) each picked up a company of the 169th Infantry Regiment and an LCVP at the Russells on the 29th of June and landed their troops unopposed on Dume and Baraula Islands commencing about 0225 on the 30th. Each ship lost its landing craft tow before dark due to steaming at too high speed in the moderate swell. To top this off, the *Zane,* soon after arriving in the debarkation area, ran aground forward during the heavy rain squalls about 0257. After much effort she backed herself off with a final desperate four bells and a jingle about 0523, and almost immediately grounded again, this time aft. Despite her own and the *Talbot's* efforts she stayed aground until the tug *Rail* (AT-139) pulled her off nine hours later (1419). The *Rail* logged receipt of the order to go help at 0942. She was enroute at the rear of the amphibious movement, but bent on an extra knot. She passed her towline to the *Zane* at 1342. The *Zane* banged up her propellers when she grounded aft and ended up a sad sight by being towed to Tulagi.[9]

However, it can be said in behalf of these two ships that they landed their troops at the appointed hour and at the appointed beach. No alert Japanese artillery man hauled up a battery to take the *Zane* under fire when she was a stranded duck only five miles from Munda Airfield, and no alert Japanese pilot picked out the *Zane* for a bombing or strafing run when heckling the transports on the 30th of June. The troops of the 169th Infantry were in a position to hold Onaiavisi Entrance against the hour when Major General Hester would want to begin the shore to shore movement of the New Georgia Occupation Force to Zanana Beach.

---

[8] CGFIRSTMARDIV, Final Report on Guadalcanal Operation, Phase V, p. 6.
[9] *Talbot, Zane, Rail,* Ships' Logs.

RENDOVA ISLAND

Rendova Harbor was actually only a well-protected cove fronting about a mile and a half of beach area where the shoreline curved inland about three-quarters of a mile at the northwestern tip of Rendova Island. There were numerous unmarked shallow areas in the cove, and the beach gradient was very gentle. Bau Island and Kokurana Island guarded the principal narrow northern entrance to Rendova Harbor, and Lumbari Island guarded the harbor to the westward.

While Rendova Harbor did not have much to recommend it for large-scale naval use, Rendova Island had three advantages if a side door entrance was to be used by the troops bound for Munda airstrip:

1. The 3,400 feet at which the island peaked out would make a fine observation post for all activity within a range of 20 miles.
2. The short seven miles separating its outlying islands from Munda airfield would permit 155mm artillery emplaced on Kokurana Island just north of Rendova Harbor to deny the Japanese use of the airfield.
3. Lever Brothers' 584 acre plantation would provide a reasonably good staging area for the troops who would move by small landing craft and boats from Rendova to Zanana Beach on New Georgia Island to strike at Munda Airfield.

As late as 15 June it was planned to have two pre-dawn landings on Rendova Island by the following forces:

1. the Ugeli Attack Unit, which was to land its troops on the northeast coast near Ugeli Village and capture the 22-man Japanese garrison reported there in late May.
2. the Rendova Advance Unit, which was to land its troops on beaches southeasterly and southwesterly from the Renard Entrance to Rendova Harbor to act as a covering force for the major landing of the 43rd Division troops on these same beaches.

However, by 21 June it had been decided to use the Ugeli Attack Unit to seize both sides of Onaiavisi Entrance to Roviana Lagoon, since it was believed our unplanned for pre-D-Day landing on Segi Point at the eastern tip of New Georgia Island would lead the Japanese to build up their defenses along the coastline between Munda and Segi Point. This build-up would lead them to appreciate the importance of Onaiavisi Entrance for a landing on Zanana Beach, and to secure the islands guarding it.

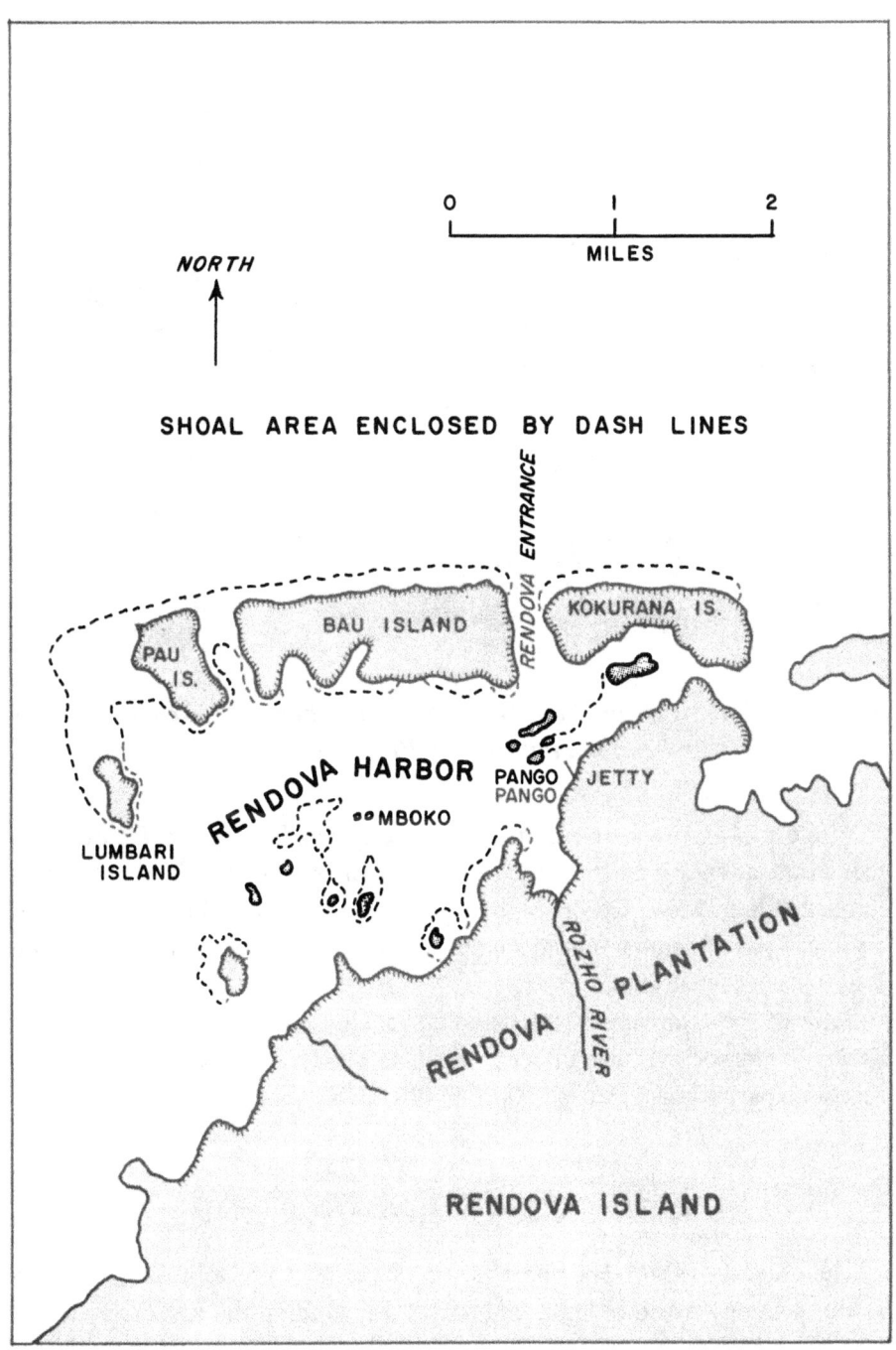

Rendova Harbor.

Turner Collection

Mud road leading from East Beach to West Beach at Rendova, British Solomon Islands, 30 June 1943.

While paying much attention to New Georgia Island, the Japanese had paid scant attention to the island of Rendova during the six months prior to our landings there. On 30 June they had only about 150 troops, including a signal detachment and some engineers on this heavily wooded 20-mile long squash-shaped island.

Some of these Japanese were manning lookout stations 8 to 12 miles from Rendova Harbor, but the majority formed a very surprised and ineffective reception party for the Army troops landing on Rendova.

THE RENDOVA ADVANCE UNIT

The *Dent* (APD-7) and the *Waters* (APD-9) were told off by CTF 31 as the Rendova Advance Unit, TU 31.1.2, for landing the first Army troops. These consisted of two jungle-trained and physically hardened companies of the 172nd Regiment, called Barracudas after the voracious pike-like fish dangerous to man.

Our reconnaissance party, on Rendova Island since 16 June, was to make navigation easier for the two destroyer-transports and their landing craft by placing on Bau Island a white light, showing to seaward and marking Renard Entrance. Each of these destroyer-transports had on board not only two members of the very valuable Australian coastwatchers organization, but also Solomon Islanders, all presumably knowledgeable or qualified as pilots for the Rendova area.

Despite all these assists, the Rendova Advance Unit managed to get started off on the wrong foot, and to stay on it.

The *Waters*, scheduled to have troops on the beach by 0540, logged her landing craft as just leaving her side at a very tardy 0606, and the *Dent* logged an even later departure of troops at 0615. Neither ship logged the fact that their presumably highly knowledgeable pilots did not guide their Barracudas in the landing craft to the correct beach areas on the first try.

The result of these nautical derelictions was that the specially trained Barracudas arrived at the specified assault beaches on Rendova Island after the regular troops from the large transports who were put ashore right on time and at the correct beaches.

Since neither the *Waters* nor the *Dent* submitted an action report on their performance in TOENAILS, the cause of the delay in getting their landing craft away or how they missed the correct beaches by miles is unrecorded in the official records. An excuse, which would be hard to accept, would be "low visibility and rain squalls."

When Rear Admiral Turner, in the *McCawley*, learned of the great delay of the destroyer-transports in getting their Barracudas away and to the correct beach areas, he immediately gave the troops in the leading landing craft from the large transports (by voice radio from the flagship at 0646) the surprising message:

You are the first to land, you are the first to land. Expect opposition.[10]

THE MAIN RENDOVA LANDINGS

The four large transports and two cargo ships, with the 6,300 embarked troops that made up the 1st Echelon Landing Force at Rendova, mostly had the benefit of a rehearsal period, although not of an over-all TF-31 dress rehearsal. They had had a rainy, gusty but uneventful passage from Guadal-

---

[10] CTF 31 War Diary, 30 Jun. 1943.

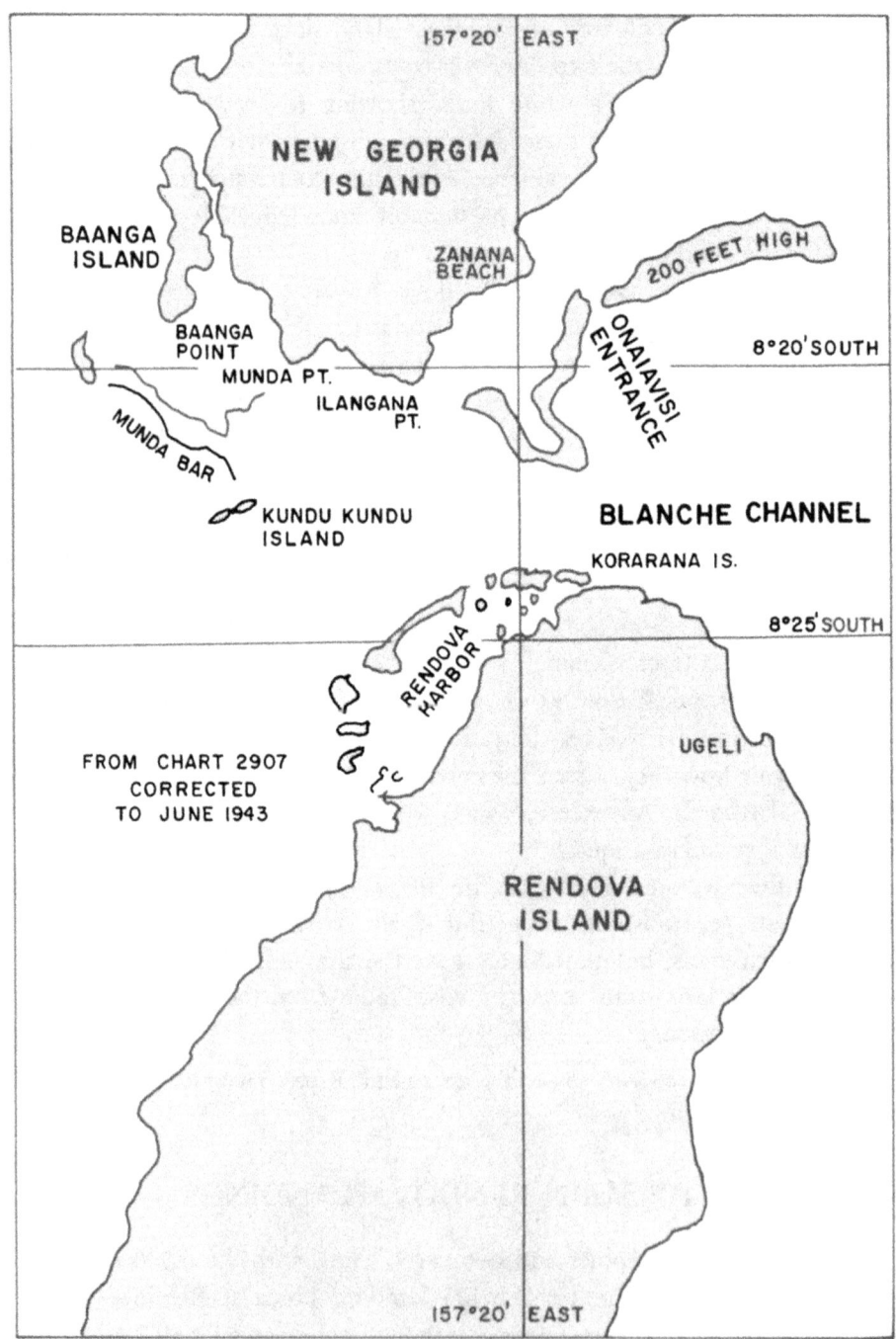

Rendova—New Georgia Area.

canal to Rendova, where they arrived on 30 June, hove-to close to Renard Entrance, and started to unload about 0640.

The transports *McCawley* and *President Adams* landed their troops at East Beach, and the *President Hayes* and *President Jackson* on West Beach. The cargo ships *Algorab* and *Libra* landed their troops and support on East Beach. The transport area was about one and a half miles from the prescribed landing beaches.

The *McCawley* logged her first troop landing at 0656, 16 minutes after the first boat left the side. The first boat was smartly back alongside to pick up logistic support at 0709, 13 minutes later.[11] "All troops, except working parties on board ship, were ashore within thirty minutes after the landing of the first wave." [12]

In this respect the large transports and cargo ships had done well. Lieutenant General Harmon sent a despatch to General Marshall saying:

> Nearly perfect was main convoy ship to shore operation.

The Army reported that:

> 105 Howitzers firing on Munda from Kokurana Island within two hours after initial debarkation.[13]

PROTECTING THE TRANSPORTS

During passage to Rendova, the eight destroyers assigned to Task Group 31.1 were in a circular anti-submarine, anti-aircraft defense screen around the six large transports and cargo ships which were in two columns of three ships each. Upon arrival at Rendova, the *Gwin* (DD-433), *Woodworth* (DD-460), *Jenkins* (DD-447) and *Radford* (DD-446) were placed in a Screening Unit and the other four destroyers in a Fire Support Unit, TU 31.2.1.

About 0708, half an hour after the transports reached their unloading stations to the eastward of Renard Entrance to Rendova Harbor, the Japanese shore batteries on Kundu Kundu Island, south of Munda Point, opened fire on two destroyers of the Fire Support Unit of *Buchanan* (DD-484) and *Farenholt* (DD-491) and two destroyers of the Anti-Submarine Unit, *Gwin* and *Jenkins*. These four ships were in the sea areas to the immediate west of the transports.

---
[11] *Ibid.*
[12] Miller, *The Reduction of Rabaul* (Army), p. 88.
[13] New Caledonia to War, No. 1133 of 1 Jul. 1943.

The *Buchanan* from the Fire Support Unit, which was designated by CTG 31.1 to silence the batteries so that the anti-submarine units could continue their patrol, reported:

> . . . there were six guns of 3" to 4.7" firing at this vessel. . . . 15 salvos were observed to be fired and as many splashes were observed close aboard. (50 to 300) yards. . . . A total of 223 rounds were fired in this first phase [by *Buchanan*]. The enemy appeared to fire an estimated 50 rounds. . . .
>
> At 0832 one gun of Baanga Point opened up on the *Buchanan* again. . . .
>
> At 1030 one shore battery on Baanga Point opened fire again using the *Buchanan* as target. . . .
>
> At 1315 single gun in Munda Point Area opened fire. . . . *Buchanan* . . . poured 64 rounds into the immediate area. No guns from any sector were heard thereafter.
>
> It is believed that a total of seven guns were silenced [by fire by *Buchanan*].[14]

The *Gwin* was hit in the engine room by a 4.7 inch projectile during the early Japanese salvos at about 0710. The *Farenholt* and the *Jenkins* in the Anti-Submarine Unit reported near-misses. The *Buchanan* continued to offer herself as a target until the troops were all landed.

Since Kundu Kundu Island is about two and a half miles south of Munda Point and only six miles from Renard Entrance to Rendova Harbor, the local Japanese officer controlling the guns rendered a major assist to TF 31 when he disclosed the presence of his guns to the destroyers. The 4.7-inch guns were silenced without taking real advantage of a good opportunity to shoot at much larger and nearly stationary targets—the large transports and cargo ships hove-to unloading off Renard Entrance to Rendova Harbor.

WESTERN FORCE AIR DEFENSE

On D-Day, aircraft from TF 33 had three clashes with Japanese aircraft during which the defensive effort of these United States planes made a major contribution to the successful landing. During the eight hours covering the period from 0645 to 1445 on 30 June when the large transports were unloading troops and impedimenta in the Rendova area, the Japanese mounted only one ineffective air attack on the large transports. However, they did delay the unloading.

Many bogies were reported to CTF 31 at 0856. TU 31.1.31 immediately

---

[14] *Buchanan* Action Report, Ser 00124 of 11 Jul. 1943, pp. 3–4.

got underway. The destroyers rejoined and assumed positions in an anti-aircraft cruising disposition. By the time the formation was formed up, the number of bogies reported had been reduced to one. The bogy continued to close until about 0908 and then gradually disappeared from the radar screens. By 0950 the transports and cargo ships were back in the Transport Area, and starting to unload again. TF 33 aircraft did not make contact with any Japanese planes at this time and post war Japanese records indicate that the Japanese aircraft were on a "look-see" mission.[15]

Another rash of bogies showed up at 1103. The transports got underway and formed up with the destroyers commencing at 1112. Twenty-seven Japanese bombing planes and their fighter escorts were reported. Dog fights were visible from the transports. The air defense was perfect and no planes came close to the transports. By 1214 the amphibians were back unloading again. Only a little over one hour's time had been lost in unloading because of this first attack, partially due to the fact that the ships had not anchored to unload, but just hove-to.

The Japanese aircraft did not return again until just after the large transports had completed their unloading chores about 1510 and headed for Guadalcanal. This time their attack was more damaging. They torpedoed the flagship of the Amphibious Force Commander, the *McCawley,* immobilized her, and left her a sitting duck for an unwitting coup de grace by our own PT boats. The third and last Japanese air attack of the day took place about 1715.

The Japanese aircraft were a bit late (1100) arriving for their first D-Day attacks on the transports. But the 1100 sweep probably contained over one hundred aircraft and was a very creditable Japanese effort. Nearly half as many aircraft made the sweep (1545) which started the *McCawley* towards the bottom. The late afternoon attack (1715) was a dog-tired and minor one of perhaps 15 aircraft.[16]

On 30 June 1943, the aviators on both sides gave glowing reports of their successes. The Japanese reports were particularly outlandish—claiming a cruiser and two destroyers sunk, and two destroyers and eight transports damaged, besides fifty planes destroyed, against an actual loss of one transport (the *McCawley*) sunk, none damaged and 17 aircraft shot down. Our aviators initially claimed 65 Japanese planes downed and the amphibious

---

[15] (a) COMAIRSOPAC War Diary, Apr.–Jun. 1943; (b) COMAIRSOLS 301252 Jun. 1943.

[16] (a) Shaw and Douglas, *Isolation of Rabaul* (Marine), pp. 82, 83; (b) *McCawley* War Diary; (c) CTF 31 War Diary.

ships claimed half as many more from their anti-aircraft fire. The Japanese, at the time, admitted to losing 30 planes and post-war accounts indicate a loss of 49.[17]

During the early days of TOENAILS, CTF 33 sought to keep 32 fighter aircraft (VF) on station over Rendova between 0700 and 1630 daily.[18] This was a real chore. Rendova was about equidistant from the Japanese air bases in Bougainville and our own air base in the Russells, so the defensive problem in the air was far more difficult than that of an air attacker, who could choose his own moment to strike. CTF 33 had only a remote chance of massing a larger number of defensive aircraft over Rendova than the Japanese could bring to bear against him.

Making the defensive problem of the naval aircraft even more difficult, in the five days prior to D-Day bad flying weather had reduced markedly the number of offensive flights from General MacArthur's Southwest Pacific Fifth Air Force. This command had the task of bombing the airfields at Rabaul and in the Bougainville-Shortlands Area prior to D-Day in order to reduce the number of Japanese aircraft available for attack in the New Georgia Group.

FIGHTER DIRECTION

On D-Day and D plus one the air cover missed intercepting the approaching Japanese aircraft several times, but generally only briefly. The amphibians fared well, losing only the *McCawley*.

The fighter direction team for the amphibious assault force was aboard the *USS Jenkins* during the approach and landing of 1st Echelon troops. The *Jenkins* reported that the team performed "remarkably well," but added the obvious remark that the "Fighters made interception a little too late on the group" which torpedoed the *McCawley*.[19]

On July 2nd, however, the fighter cover over the Rendova Area was withdrawn temporarily due to bad weather at home base. Shortly after this withdrawal, about 1330, some two dozen Japanese aircraft made an undetected and unopposed attack and caused considerable loss of shoreside personnel (64 killed, 89 wounded) and damage to supplies still jam-packed on the

---

[17] (a) CINCPAC Command Summary, Book Four, 1 Jul. 1943, p. 1613; (b) COMTHIRDFLT 010630 Jul. 1943; (c) *President Jackson, McCawley,* CTF 31, CTF 33 War Diaries, Jun. 1943.

[18] COMAIRSOPAC Op Plan 7–43, 18 Jun. 1943 and related despatches.

[19] *Jenkins* Action Report, Ser 0336 of 9 Jul. 1943.

Rendova beaches. Ammunition dumps and laboriously constructed fuel depots were blown up. In the morning before the attack, the Army radars were out of commission and the only Marine aircraft search radar set up ashore had stopped operating due to someone filling the motor generator's gas tank with diesel oil. These radar deficiencies combined with a lack of visual observation of the approaching aircraft permitted the attack to be a complete surprise.[20]

LOGISTICS AGAIN

The big problem at Rendova on the first day—as it had been at Guadalcanal—was not the enemy. It was logistics. This time the transports got the logistic support out of their holds and onto the beaches in double quick time, but Mr. Rain and Mr. Mud were the overseers on the Lever Brothers' Plantation where the landing was made that day. They really fouled up the logistic support for the troops. The heavy trucks and tanks soon were bogged down, and even hastily Seabee-built, coconut log roadbeds did not cure the logistical quagmire.

It was quite obvious to the amphibians that the marked changes and increases made since the Guadalcanal landings in the Shore Party, and in the Naval Platoon of the Shore Party, paid real dividends, even when they received no cooperation from unfriendly natural elements. The big transports left Rendova bragging about the high tons per hour they had unloaded on the beaches.[21]

By beefing up the unloading parties on each transport and cargo ship to 150 men—and by beefing up the Shore Party to 300 men—saving of time had been gained during the critical unloading period.

But it is quite apparent from reading the Action Reports of the transports and the reports of the observers on the beach, that the transports did not fully appreciate the logistical mess which they had left on the beaches, particularly when the rain continued to come down. The red clay mud was adequately stirred up and wheeled vehicles could not haul from the beaches to the supply dumps.[22]

Things became so bad in this respect that, on 3 July, Major General

---
[20] (a) Shaw and Douglas, *Isolation of Rabaul* (Marine), pp. 85, 87; (b) Miller, *Reduction of Rabaul* (Army), p. 91.
[21] McCawley, *President Jackson*, War Diaries.
[22] Shaw and Douglas, *Rabaul* (Marine), p. 82.

Hester requested that the 5th Echelon of heavy logistic support for Rendova be held up.[23]

SUPPORTING ECHELONS

While the large transports and their destroyer escorts were returning to Guadalcanal, the succeeding echelons of the Western Force were loading there and in the Russells.

As the LST-354 saw it on 1 July:

> Sky was overcast, low ceiling, with prolonged heavy rain showers throughout the day. . . . Embarkation of troops and cargo was handicapped by rains and heavy mud. . . .[24]

At 1800 on D-Day, the 2nd Echelon—Landing Ship Tanks and Landing Craft Infantry under the command of Captain Carter—departed for Rendova Harbor, which was something less than an amphibian's dream of the perfect landing place, as the following report shows:

> East beach [Rendova Harbor] was extremely unsatisfactory. The approach involved a very narrow, tortuous channel with a sharp, short turn to the beach behind Pago Pago Island. The beaching had to be made at dead slow speed and vessels were unable to plow their way through the mud to the beach proper. Vehicles could be operated only with difficulty because of deep mud and many had to be abandoned. . . .
>
> Discharge of cargo . . . was accomplished under extreme difficulties . . . with the men wading through water and mud knee deep. . . . Discharge . . . was accomplished by dark by virtue of back-breaking, exhaustive, and almost super-human efforts of all the men involved.[25]

Besides the unmarked channels, the sharp turns required to miss coral heads and the mud just back of the beaches, the landing craft had to contend with the Japanese, who mounted a number of air attacks on the amphibians during the days ahead.

The 2nd Echelon beached at Poko Plantation, Rendova Island, about 0735 on July 1st. They learned years later that five Japanese destroyers on a mission to locate them during the night, had failed to push into Blanche Channel. By 1015 the LSTs and LCIs had been properly greeted by several small strafing waves of Japanese aircraft which did no important damage.

---

[23] CTF 31 to CTG 31.3, 022150 Jul. 1943.
[24] LST Flotilla Five War Diary, 1 Jul. 1943.
[25] *Ibid.*

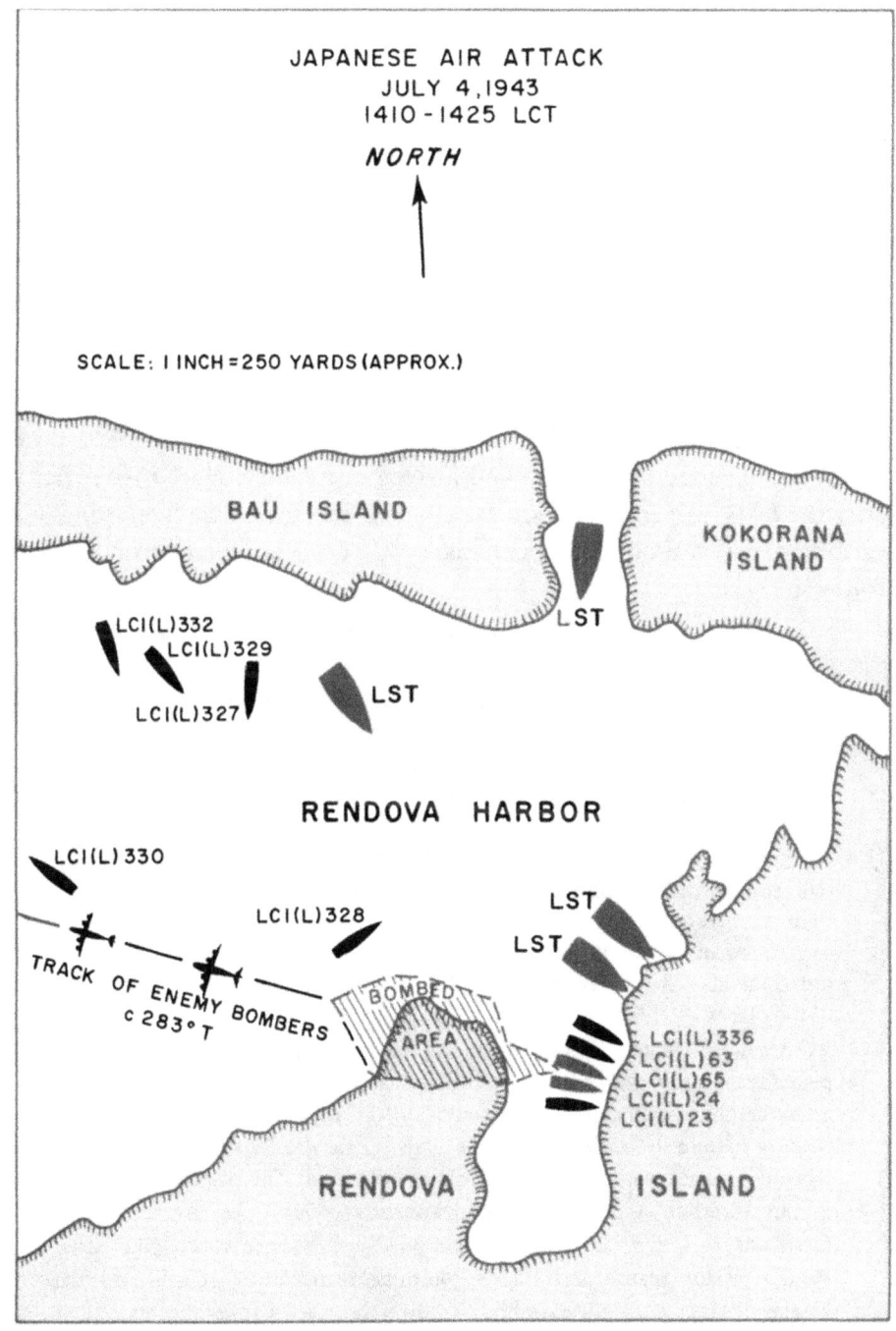

Location of LCI(L) Group 14 landing craft participating in anti-aircraft action, 4 July 1943, Rendova Harbor.

The 4th Echelon was not quite so fortunate as the 2nd. While it was enroute to Rendova, the LCI-66 and LCI-70 had a bow-on collision during execution of change of course, and there was the usual rash of bogies, which sent them to their guns. These amphibians beached about 0730 on the 4th of July.

Before the 4th Echelon completed their unloading, sixteen Japanese bombing planes, in tight formation, swept low over the beached landing craft dropping their bombs. On Independence Day 1943, LCIs 23, 24 and 65 picked up their war wounds, but the landing ships and craft had the satisfaction of assisting in putting no less than ten Japanese aircraft to final rest.

TU 31.3.12, the 2nd Echelon for Viru Harbor, with one APC and three LCTs, was diverted to Rendova and arrived in Rendova Harbor four hours after the LCIs, as part of the 4th Echelon for Rendova. The interesting and exciting experience of these amphibians was described by one of them as follows:

> At about 1413, although no warning had been received over the only frequency we were guarding, 3000 KCS, it was seen that the guns of the two LSTs near us were being put on battery. Our guns were on battery and had been from before daylight so it was only necessary to warn the gun crews that there might be a condition red. General quarters was called and the ammunition passers and reloaders hurried to their stations, when some bombers were sighted.
>
> As the planes approached, they could be identified as Japanese, probably twin-engine heavy bombers of the Mitsubishi 96 type. The planes were in a tight V, flying at from 2500 feet to 3000 feet. Staff Sergeant Biggerstaff, correspondent of the News Service Division of the Marine Corps, who had just come aboard for passage to the Russell Islands, agrees about the height of the planes.
>
> They were coming almost out of the sun which bore about 115°T. The planes were coming directly at us a little off our starboard bow. They dropped a few bombs, which as far as we could tell did little damage, most of them striking harmlessly in the water. The guns on the USS APC-24 opened fire when the planes were at a range of about 4000 feet. The planes approached in our direction and passed almost overhead. Our guns, four 20 MM Oerlikons and two 50 caliber Browning Navy type machine guns fired steadily at the planes and tracers could be seen hitting squarely in the fuselage, wings and tail assembly. Some of the tracers from the 50 caliber could be seen passing through the wings.
>
> The lead ship in the formation which took the fire from three 20 MM machine guns and one 50 caliber machine gun was fatally hit by our guns.

The plane burst into flames near the right engine, the tail assembly and main fuselage were blown off by an explosion, and the wings and forward cockpit with one side flaming fluttered like a leaf down toward us. Our gunners, in the meantime, shifted their attention to the second plane from the outside on the left of the V. Our other 20 MM and 50 caliber machine guns had been concentrating their fire on this plane and had it already limping when the additional fire was turned toward it. One motor was smoking. With all six guns riddling it back and forth, the plane suddenly exploded and fell in many blazing pieces into the harbor. In the meantime, the first plane we hit fell into the water about two or three hundred yards astern of us. By then it was impossible to direct the guns to fire at any individual plane. Our tracers could be seen going into several other planes and undoubtedly they assisted in the destruction of some more of the enemy bombers. By this time planes were falling so fast it was hard to keep track of them. A number of the enemy bombers fell in the direction of Bau Island and Pau Island. Some seemed to fall in the direction of the northeastern corner of Bau Island or in the sea on the other side.

It was impossible, in the short period of the action to count the number of bombers that fell. We believe we saw nine, but it may have been more. Only three out of the original sixteen returned in a tight formation and passed to the south of us out of range. Although out of range by then of anything but 40 MM and 90 MM, all ships in the harbor fired in their direction. We saw no other signs of the sixteen, and as there were so many being knocked out of the air, we figured on a possible thirteen of sixteen planes knocked down.

It is my personal opinion and the opinion of my other officers, and the Marine Correspondent Staff Sergeant Biggerstaff, that all of the planes knocked down were hit by the fire of various Landing Craft Flotilla vessels in the harbor. As far as we could determine, the shore batteries were not responsible for the downing of one plane.

This vessel ceased firing at 1425.

The surprising thing was the tight formation and low altitude the Japanese were using. It was as if they expected no opposition from anti-aircraft fire. Even though planes were being knocked out of their tight formation they held right on with it until they themselves were knocked out of the air.

In reporting on his gun crew, the Commanding Officer said:

Previous to this action, they had never fired their guns on enemy planes. Their entire experience being a four day course of 20 MM practice at Point Montara, California, where they were unable to fire because of fog, a four day course at Noumea and a practice firing at a sleeve on the first day out of Noumea.[26]

---

[26] APC-24 Action Report, 15 Jul. 1943.

Commander LCI Group 15 gleefully recorded for his War Diary subsequent to the heavy attack, the spirited antiaircraft fire, and the efforts of our fighters, which left

> pyres of burning Mitsubishis visible on the surface of harbor.[27]

Between building a temporary caisson needed to make possible replacement of a lost propeller on the LCI-223 and firing their guns in anger for the first time, the LCI amphibians of the 4th Echelon had a busy and glorious Fouth of July.

Unloading parties of 150 men on each LST, 50 men on each LCT and 25 men for each LCI absorbed a lot of men but numbers worked marvels in getting cargo out of the ships onto the beaches and then inland to the supply dumps, and speeded the amphibians away to calmer areas.

The story of the Western Force would not be complete without detailing the major happenings of the return to base of the large transports and cargo ships.

RETURN TO BASE

As has been mentioned before, the amphibian ships at Rendova had only two welcome hours to land their troops and equipment before radar contacts with an unidentified aircraft about 0900 on 30 June sent the crews hurrying to their anti-aircraft batteries, and the ships scurrying to their positions in a protective anti-aircraft cruising disposition. An actual attack did not develop, nor did actual bombing of the transports develop from a further radar alert about 1100, but in each case there was a period of about an hour of cruising about near the transport area when no unloading could be accomplished.

After these two interruptions, and having smartly completed the lion's share of their unloading and established new records of tons per hour winched out of their holds, the transports and cargo ships were underway in an anti-aircraft defensive formation about 1510 to withdraw to base. There were eight destroyers in the circular screen, the six large amphibians being in division columns abreast.

Shortly after 1545, there commenced a large scale "do or die" Japanese torpedo bombing attack on the formation, which washed out a fair share of the office files of the Commander Amphibious Force Third Fleet on the *McCawley* and about 20 of the 23 attacking planes.

---

[27] LCI Group 15 War Diary, 4 Jul. 1943.

Turner Collection

Men of the 24th Construction Battalion sawing coconut logs into proper lengths for road construction, Rendova, July 1943.

The *McCawley* was torpedoed about 1553 when in Blanche Channel about 12 miles east by south from Rendova Harbor. At that time, she was steaming at 14 knots and was the lead ship in the left-hand column with the *President Hayes* and the *President Jackson* astern. There was a rabbit's foot in the pocket of the Captain of the escorting *Farenholt*. The torpedo which hit the destroyer was a dud.

An hour and a quarter later, with the *McCawley* making heavy weather from her hit, her port engine room flooded and the rudder still jammed hard right, and while being taken under tow by the *Libra* (AK-53), the Japanese came back with eight dive bombers and some fighter escorts. They scored no hits on their wounded victim nor on the two escorting destroyers nor on the *Libra*.

In the WATCHTOWER Operation the large transport *George F. Elliott* (AP-13) had been sunk off Guadalcanal. The South Pacific amphibians were about to offer their TOENAIL sacrifice, and this time it was to be their flagship.

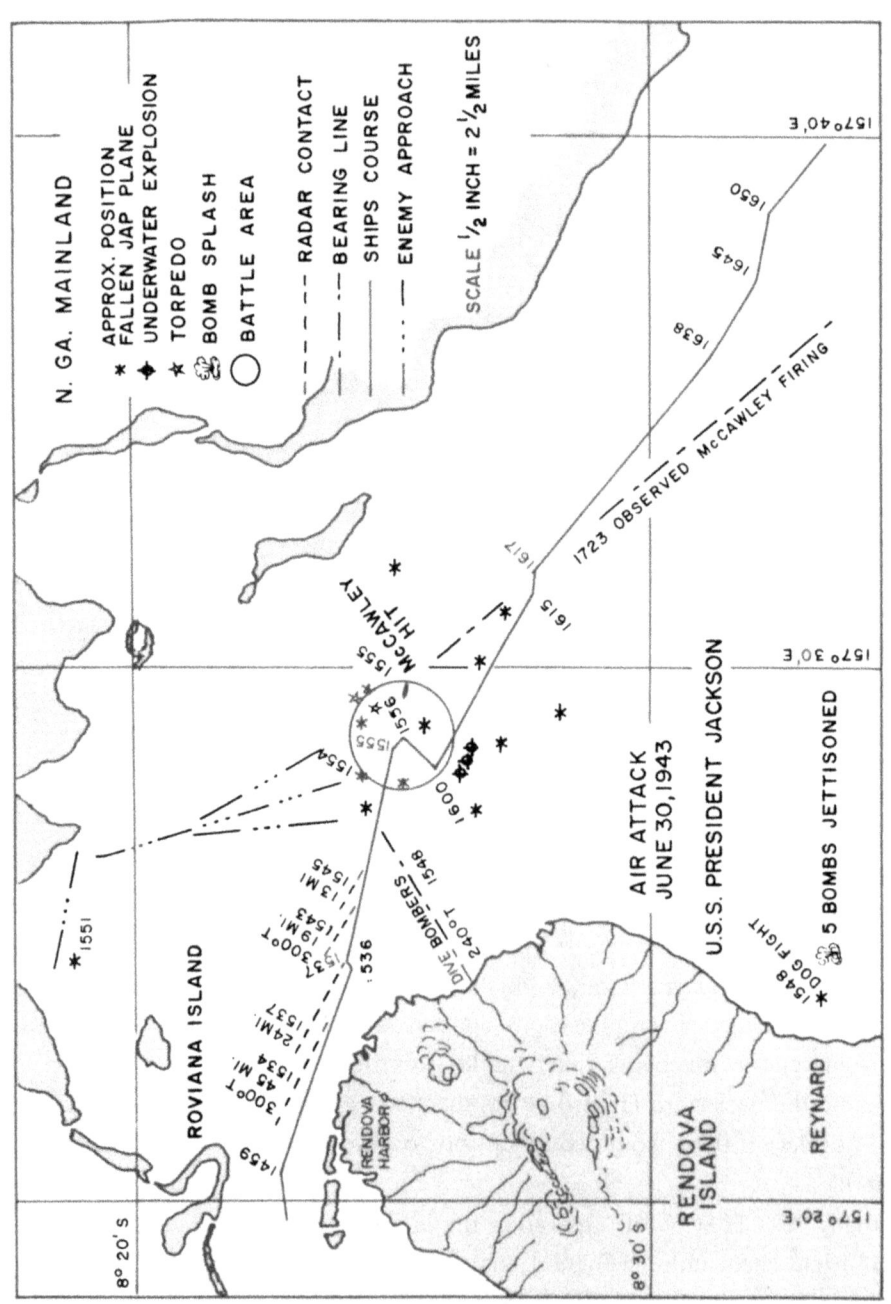

Japanese Air Attack, 30 June 1943.

THE END OF THE WACKY MAC

For the Rendova landings of TOENAILS, the *McCawley*, Commander Robert H. Rodgers (1923), commanding, carried 1,100 troops and 604 tons of equipment as well as the senior Army and Navy commanders in the Amphibious Force and their staffs.

The *McCawley* did not survive the day, and since the story of her demise has been variously reported, the official reports of her Commanding Officer and others are of interest, indicating, at least, that both information of our own forces and intelligence of enemy forces carry a premium value in wartime:

> After the completion of the unloading which was accomplished by the *McCawley* in record-breaking time, the task force got underway and proceeded for Guadalcanal.
>
> While entering Blanche Channel Task Force 31.1 was attacked by about twenty-three Mitsubishi '01' torpedo bombers. The Task Force had just executed a ninety degree turn to the right and opened fire when a torpedo was seen approaching *McCawley's* port side on a collision course. The rudder was put hard right. . . . This torpedo hit [at 1553] port side amidships in the engine room spaces, track angle about one hundred ninety degrees [one hundred and eighty would be from dead stern]. *McCawley* took a violent port list, but righting immediately still swinging right with rudder jammed hard over, all engines stopped, ship having lost all power. Two torpedoes then passed down the starboard side very close aboard, track angle one hundred eighty degrees.
>
> The attack ended with all enemy planes shot down by AA fire of Task Force 31.1, *McCawley* claiming four planes. Rear Admiral Turner ordered the *USS Libra* (AK-53) to take *McCawley* in tow and *Ralph Talbot* (DD-390) and *McCalla* (DD-488) to stand by to assist. Admiral Turner and staff then at (1625) shifted to the *USS Farenholt* (DD-491) and proceeded with remainder of Task Force, leaving Rear Admiral Wilkinson in *McCawley* as OTC [Officer in Tactical Command] of salvage group.
>
> At 1640, upon orders of Admiral Turner, *Ralph Talbot* came alongside and removed all personnel from *McCawley* except for a salvage crew. . . .
>
> [at 1717] *McCawley* was heavily strafed by attacking planes.
>
> At 1722 *Libra* swung clear and proceeded at five knots with *McCawley* in tow. The draft of the *McCawley* was then 21'06" forward, 35'00" aft. . . . At 1850, the draft aft was reported as thirty eight feet. Admiral Wilkinson then ordered *McCalla* alongside and gave the order for "all hands" to abandon ship. At 1920, *McCalla* came alongside and the entire salvage crew had left the ship by 1930 when *McCalla* pulled clear. At 2023 *McCawley*

was struck by three torpedoes fired by enemy submarine and sank stern first in thirty seconds in 340 fathoms of water. . . .[28]

This report is dated 4 July 1943. Commander Rodgers reported:

> If requisitioned damage control materiel had been delivered, damage control might have been accomplished. However, due to low priority, delay up to 18 months has been experienced.

In the last sentence of this report, "Speed" Rodgers added a spirited plea that there be:

> Full realization that attack transports are combat ships and they should be so classified.

A senior Army observer of the torpedoing of the *McCawley*, Lieutenant General M. F. Harmon, officially reported his observances to COMSOPAC as follows:

> I was standing on the port wing of the bridge and at about this time (1555–1600) observed torpedo release against the AP just astern of *McCawley* in our column. It looked like a perfect attack and I was anxiously awaiting the subsequent detonation when someone said 'Here it comes.' I glanced out to port, saw the approaching track and soon realized that it was going to be a hit—I thought just aft of the bridge. Glancing back at the next ship in line, I saw she had apparently not been hit, ducked away from the rail, crouched down with a yeoman-like grip on a stanchion and awaited the explosion. It came after a longer interval than I had anticipated; the ship gave quite a lurch, something big went over the port side from high above (maybe the top of the funnel) together with some odd bits and pieces and we listed quickly and sharply to port. Instinctively I moved starboard direction and heard the command 'Trim Ship.' On reaching the starboard rail a torpedo track was running about forty feet out at a slight converging angle to our bow and across our bow. It cleared us handily and missed the ship ahead though it looked bad for a moment or two.[29]

On the day before the *McCawley* report was written, Rear Admiral Wilkinson submitted his official report to COMPHIBFOR, Third Fleet:

> At 1900 I concluded that the chances of *McCawley* surviving the night were slim, that I would remove the remaining personnel, but that I would tow until she actually sank. . . . Unfortunately the *Pawnee* lost the tow at 2000. . . . At 2023 the *McCawley* was struck by two torpedoes. . . . She was seen to sink by the stern shortly thereafter.
>
> The source of the torpedoes was not seen, but within a few seconds after *McCawley* was struck, two torpedo wakes were seen approaching *McCalla*.

---

[28] *McCawley* Action Report, Ser 002a of 4 Jul. 1943.
[29] COMGENSOPAC to COMSOPAC, memorandum, 11 Jul. 1943.

By turning to parallel, both torpedoes were avoided, one passing ahead, one astern.

Since we had DF [Direction Finder] reports of a Japanese submarine generally off the sourthern entrance to BLANCHE CHANNEL, I concluded that the torpedoing was done by a submarine, and after the *McCalla* had dodged the torpedoes, I directed the Commanding Officer to turn to their apparent reverse course and attack the submarine. . . . A number of boats, apparently PT boats were then sighted well ahead and, to avoid fouling them, although not suspecting any of them had fired the torpedoes, I abandoned further search for the submarine, and directed *McCalla* to overtake the *Pawnee* and *Libra*. . . . I have, of course, since learned that PT boats made the attack.[30]

In these days when every naval craft larger than a rowboat seems to have one or more radars, it is perhaps well to record that eighteen months after the United States entered World War II that the *McCawley* was the only transport equipped with radar and when she was sunk, the large transports necessarily depended upon the destroyers for their radar information.

The Commander Motor Torpedo Boat Squadron Nine, Lieutenant Commander Robert B. Kelly (1935), in PT-153 during the night of 30 June 1943, reported on 1 July 1943 to the Commander Naval Base, Rendova Island:

At 2014 PT 153's radar detected a very large target distance 800 yards surrounded by eight smaller targets, apparently landing craft. The first section closed range to about 600 yards. Targets appeared to be a large destroyer, a 7000–10,000 ton transport and a small destroyer or transport. [They] were seen to have converged. The large transport was lying to, and the other ships were slowly circling behind it. At 2016, PT 153 fired four torpedoes at the transport and radioed for all boats in the first and second sections to press home the attack. PT 153 continued on same course and at same speed to allow other boats to fire undetected. When PT 153 was 300–400 yards from the transport, four torpedoes were seen to strike it in succession; one forward, two amidships and one aft. PT 153 then reversed course to the left and retired at slow speed. The first two torpedoes hit 4–5 seconds apart; the last two simultaneously. . . .

PT 118 on the starboard quarter of PT 153 fired two torpedoes at a small transport or destroyer and observed two direct hits. As the PT 118 retired following PT 153, her target appeared to be sinking by the stern.

PT 158 . . . fired two torpedoes . . . . no hits observed . . . changed her course . . . and fired her last two torpedoes . . . . these torpedoes were seen to straddle the target. PT 160 . . . fired one torpedo . . . but it missed. PT 159 . . . fired two torpedoes . . . both of which missed.[31]

---

[30] Rear Admiral T. S. Wilkinson, USN, to CTF 31, Report on loss of *McCawley*, 3 Jul. 1943.
[31] COMMTBRON Nine to Commander Naval Base, Rendova, Action Report, Ser 001 of 1 Jul. 1943.

Fortunately for the United States Navy, the motor torpedo boats of Topedo Boat Squadron Nine were poor shots, and they did not cause the carnage amongst the amphibious ships and escorts of the Third Fleet which they so earnestly, unwisely, and unskillfully attempted.

The *McCalla* (DD-488), and the target for one of the salvos of torpedoes (the torpedoes passed ahead and astern) reported that the PT boats did not respond to blinker tube challenge, which was made at 2043 just before one of them fired torpedoes.[32]

When Rear Admiral Turner's Flag Captain was asked what Kelly Turner's immediate reaction was when his flagship was torpedoed, he wrote:

> To get the Brass [his staff] and himself to a ship where he could continue to command the Assault Force. I put his LCVP barge in the water, and ten minutes after the torpedo hit, they were being transferred.
>
> I saw him the next morning at his headquarters in Guadalcanal. He gave me a bottle of 'Old Granddad,' said he would get me another command, and praised my work in not losing any more than the 14 original casualties. He never told me that Bull Kelly's PT boats gave the coupe de grace to the *McCawley*. I didn't know about this until 3½ months later. The *McCawley* was down to 12 inches of freeboard, all holds astern flooding and was sinking slowly at the time the PT torpedoes were fired.[33]

WESTERN FORCE (GROUP) TG 31.1 SUMMARY

Despite the loss of the amphibious flagship, and despite the logistical difficulties, the major mission of the Western Force had been accomplished. The Landing Force Commander, his initial echelon of troops and their impedimenta had been established ashore on D-Day. They were pretty wet and a bit unhappy about the rain and the mud, but they were where they had asked to be put.

EASTERN FORCE (GROUP) TG 31.3

The basic CTF 31 Op Order A9–31 contemplated the Eastern Group putting ashore about 7,700 troops from the first four echelons of amphibious movements at three widely separated landing beaches: Viru Harbor, Segi Point and Wickham Anchorage.

---

[32] *McCalla* Action Report, Ser 33 of 2 Jul. 1943.
[33] Rear Admiral Robert H. Rodgers, USN (Ret.) to GCD, letter, 29 Nov. 1965. Hereafter Rodgers.

Rear Admiral Fort retained direct command of the Wickham Occupation Group, and flew his flag in the destroyer-type minesweeper *Trever*. He withdrew his two senior subordinates from their normal assignments and placed one of them in command of the task units carrying troops to Viru Harbor and the other in command of the follow-up landing at Segi Point. His Chief of Staff, Captain Benton W. Decker (1920), commanded the Segi Occupation Group and Commander Stanley L. Leith (1923), Commander Minesweeper Group, drew the more interesting Viru Harbor assignment.

No one of these three task units polished off its operational tasks exactly "according to plan." Their trials, tribulations and eventual success will be related in some detail in the following pages.

The over-all task organization established was as follows:

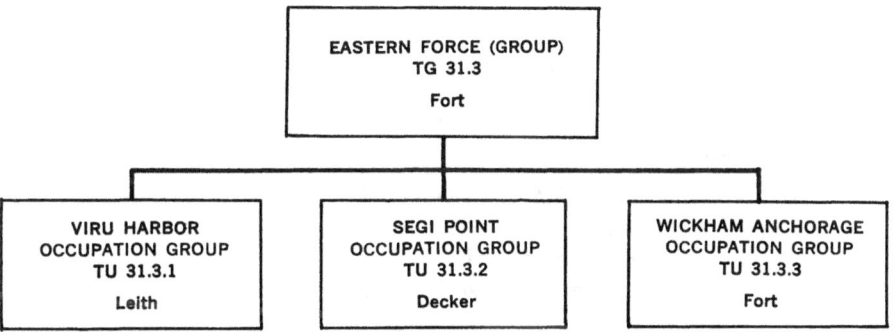

The detailed composition of the task units was as follows:

EASTERN TASK GROUP ORGANIZATION TG 31.3
VIRU HARBOR, SEGI, WICKHAM ANCHORAGE

(a) *VIRU HARBOR OCCUPATION GROUP* TU 31.3.1 Commander Leith
  (1) *Advance Unit,* Lieutenant Colonel Michael S. Currin, USMC
      4th Marine Raider Battalion (Designated companies)
  (2) *1st Echelon* TU 31.3.11 Commander Leith
      Hopkins (DMS-13) (F) Lieutenant Commander F. M. Peters USN
      Kilty (APD-15) Lieutenant Commander D. L. Mattie, USN
      Crosby (APD-17) Lieutenant Commander A. G. Grant, USNR
  (3) *2nd Echelon*—TU 32.3.12 Lieutenant B. F. Seligman, USNR
      APC-24 Lieutenant B. F. Seligman, USNR
      LCT-134 Ensign J. W. Hunt, USNR

LCT-330 Ensign L. B. Douglas, USNR
LCT-369 Ensign W. F. Gillette, USNR
- (4) *3rd Echelon* TU 31.3.13 Lieutenant D. Mann, USNR
  APC-23 Lieutenant Dennis Mann, USNR
  APC-25 Lieutenant J. D. Cartano, USNR
  LCT-139 Ensign Ralph Taylor, USNR
  LCT-180 Ensign S. W. Orton, USNR
  LCT-326 Ensign H. A. Shuler, USNR
  LCT-327 Ensign J. L. Caraway, USNR
  LCT-351 Ensign R. R. Muelhback, USNR
- (5) *4th Echelon* TU 31.3.14
  1 APC and 2 LCTs combined and sailed with the 3rd ECHELON, and are listed in (4) above.
- (6) *Landing Force*
  103rd Infantry Regiment (designated company)
  20th Construction Battalion (designated company)
  70th Coast Artillery (designated battery)
  Naval Base Units

(b) *SEGI POINT OCCUPATION GROUP* TU 31.3.2 Captain B. W. Decker
- (1) *1st Echelon* TU 31.3.21 Captain Decker
  First Section
    APC-23(F) Lieutenant D. Mann, USNR
    LCI-21 Ensign M. M. Cook, USNR
    LCI-22 Lieutenant (jg) S. V. Hinckley, USNR
    LCI-67 Lieutenant (jg) E. E. Tucker, USNR
    LCI-68 Lieutenant C. D. Older, USNR
    LCI-69 Lieutenant F. L. O'Leary, USNR
  Second Section
    LST-339 Lieutenant J. H. Fulweiller, USNR
    LST-341 Lieutenant F. S. Barnett, USNR
- (2) *2nd Echelon* TU 31.3.22 Lieutenant W. C. Margetts, USNR
  APC-27 Lieutenant P. C. Smith, USNR
  LCT-58 Lieutenant (jg) Pickett Lumpkin, USNR
  LCT-62 Ensign R. T. Capeless, USNR
  LCT-129 Ensign E. W. Graunke, USNR
  LCT-323 Ensign C. T. Geisler, USNR

  The LCT-129 lost her ramp, but did not founder.
- (3) *3rd Echelon* TU 31.3.23 Lieutenant E. M. Jaeger, USNR
  APC-28 Lieutenant (jg) A. D. Shean, USNR
  LCT-66 Ensign C. A. Goddard, USNR
  LCT-67 Ensign W. H. Fitzgerald, USNR
  LCT-128 Ensign Joseph Joyce, USNR
  LCT-324 Ensign D. C. Hawley, USNR

(4) *4th Echelon* TU 31.3.24 Lieutenant (jg) E. H. George, USNR
APC-29 Lieutenant (jg) E. H. George, USNR
LCT-146 Ensign W. W. Asper, USNR
LCT-156 Ensign Harold Mantell, USNR
LCT-159 Ensign J. A. McNeil, USNR
LCT-322 Ensign Frederick Altman, USNR
(5) *Landing Force*
103rd Regimental Combat Team (designated units)
ACORN Seven
70th Coast Artillery (designated units)
Naval Base Units
(c) *WICKHAM ANCHORAGE OCCUPATION GROUP* TU 31.3.31
Rear Admiral Fort
(1) *1st Echelon* TU 31.3.31 Rear Admiral Fort
First Section
Trever (DMS-16) (F) Lieutenant Commander W. H. Shea, USN
McKean (APD-5) Lieutenant Commander R. L. Ramey, USN
Schley (APD-14) Lieutenant Commander Horace Myers, USN
LCI-24 Lieutenant (jg) R. E. Ward, USN
LCI-223 Lieutenant F. P. Stone, USNR
LCI-332 Lieutenant W. A. Neilson, USNR
LCI-333 Lieutenant Horace Townsend, USNR
LCI-334 Lieutenant (jg) A. J. Ormston, USNR
LCI-335 Lieutenant (jg) J. R. Powers, USNR
LCI-336 Lieutenant (jg) T. A. McCoy, USNR
Second Section
APC-35 Lieutenant R. F. Ruben, USNR
LCT-63 Ensign J. R. Madura, USNR
LCT-133 Ensign Bertram Meyer, USNR
LCT-482 Boatswain H. F. Dreher, USN
(2) *2nd Echelon* TU 31.3.32 Lieutenant (jg) K. L. Otto, USNR
APC-36 Lieutenant (jg) K. L. Otto, USNR
LCT-60 Boatswain J. S. Wolfe, USN
LCT-127 Ensign R. A. Torkildson, USNR
LCT-144 Ensign E. B. Lerz, USNR
LCT-367 Ensign Robert Carr, USNR
LCT-367 developed engineering difficulties and turned back to Wernham Cove, Russell Islands, and became part of TU 31.3.33.
(3) *3rd Echelon* TU 31.3.33 Lieutenant A. W. Bergstrom, USNR
APC-37 Lieutenant J. E. Locke, USNR
LCT-132 Ensign M. Paskin, USNR
LCT-145 Ensign W. E. Goyette, USNR
LCT-325 Ensign J. H. Grim, USNR

LCT-367 Ensign Robert Carr, USNR
LCT-461 Ensign G. W. Wagenhorst, USNR
(4) *4th Echelon* TU 31.3.34 Lieutenant Parker
APC-26 Ensign J. B. Dunigan, USNR
LCT-158 Ensign E. J. Ruschmann, USNR
LCT-352 Lieutenant (jg) Winston Broadfoot, USNR
LCT-377 Ensign T. J. McGann, USNR
(5) *Landing Force*
103rd Regimental Combat Team (designated unit)
4th Marine Raider Battalion (designated unit)
20th Construction Battalion (designated unit)
70th Coast Artillery Battalion (designated anti-aircraft units)
152nd Field Artillery Battalion (designated unit)
(d) RUSSELL MTB SQUADRON—Lieutenant A. P. Cluster (1940)
12 MTBs

TOENAILS was the first major operation in the South Pacific in which the small coastal transport, the APC, participated. These small and slow wooden-hulled craft were 103 feet long, displaced 258 tons, and made 10 knots with a fair breeze at their sterns.

VIRU HARBOR TU 31.3.1

The commander of the small task unit assigned to the seizure and occupation of landlocked Viru Harbor on the southern side of New Georgia Island had the difficult chore of joining an overland movement with a sea movement at the scene of battle at a given hour of a given day.

The original assault plan was modified after the Marines from the 4th Marine Raider Battalion moved into Segi, ten air miles to the east of Viru Harbor, on 21 June 1943. This was done in an effort to take advantage of the Marines' position ashore and on the flank of Viru Harbor.

The revised plan called for a company of Marines in an Advance Unit to proceed from Segi by boat a mile and a half toward Viru Harbor, landing at Nono during darkness on 28 June. From this position, the Marines were to advance overland to a position from where, at about 0700 on D-Day, they could launch a grand assault on the Japanese troops guarding the entrance to Viru Harbor at the same time the Army troops in the Landing Force from the ships launched their water-borne assault.[34]

The Marine Raiders were to alert the ships when they were in position to launch their attack by firing a white parachute flare. When this was

---

[34] TG 31.3 Op Order AL10–43, 21 Jun. 1943, para 3.

seen, Commander Viru Harbor Occupation Group was to start the troops from the 103rd Infantry toward their landing beach.

The TF 31 reconnaissance patrols had reported, in early June, that there were 30 to 100 Japanese soldiers at Viru. An even smaller estimate of only 25 to 30 Japanese defenders at Viru Harbor was distributed by the prospective Commander New Georgia Occupation Force, Major General Hester, as late as 24 June.[35] But, in fact, during the last week of June, the Japanese were beefing up their troops in the southeastern end of New Georgia Island trying to run down a pesky Australian coastwatcher, Mr. Donald G. Kennedy, in the Segi Point Area. So perhaps the Japanese had as many as 300 defenders in this area on 30 June 1943. A reported 170 survived the Marine attack to participate in the defense of Munda.[36]

Information in detail about Viru Harbor was scarce, and available charts of the area were a bit sketchy and inaccurate in some details. This inaccuracy is illustrated by the difference between the upper and lower charts on the next page. The top one is taken from pre-invasion charts and the lower one from post-invasion maps.

However, there were some fine aerial photographs taken during the preparatory periods. These indicated that the small pier in Viru Harbor near which it was hoped to land the Army troops, could not be seen during a seaward approach until ships were right at the harbor entrance. This was true (1) because thousands of trees lined the high cliffs on either side of the harbor entrance, and (2) the 300-yard wide coral-studded channel veered steadily to the right for the better part of a mile before opening into the long narrow harbor.

On the western side of the harbor entrance, near Tetemara, the Japanese had mounted a 3-inch naval gun to protect the harbor approaches, together with four 80-millimeter anti-aircraft guns to protect the naval gun against air attack.

A late change of orders from CTG 31.3 directed the Marine Advance Unit to move from Segi westward during the night of 27 June, instead of 28 June, and to land at Regi, two miles nearer to Viru than Nono. This not only provided 24 additional hours for the Marines to get into position but shortened the overland march to less than seven miles by the map.

Commander Leith with the *Hopkins, Crosby* and *Kilty* arrived at a point

---

[35] COMGEN, New Georgia Occupation Force Field Order 3–43, 28 Jun. 1943, Annex 2.
[36] (a) Shaw and Douglas, *Isolation of Rabaul* (Marine), p. 72; (b) Miller, *Reduction of Rabaul* (Army), note 9, p. 137.

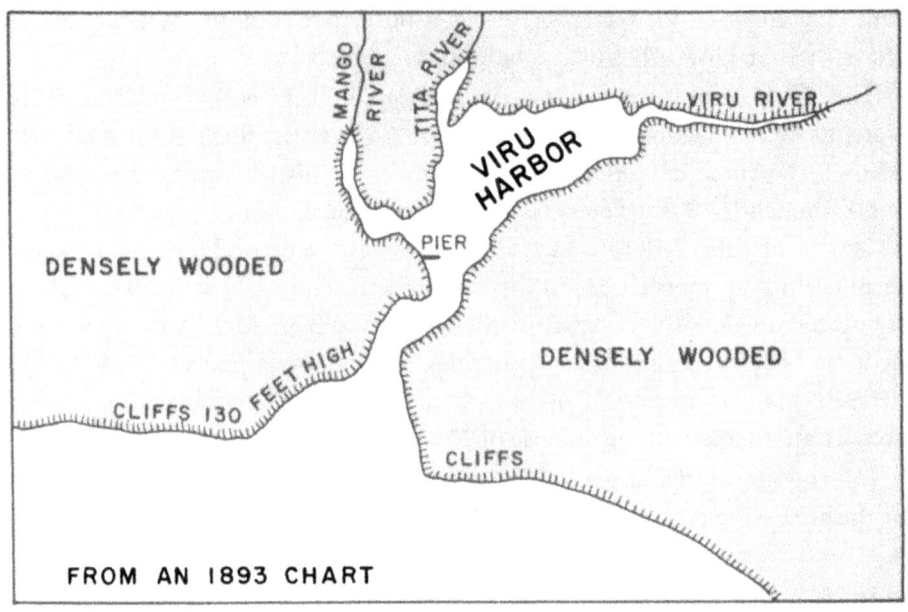

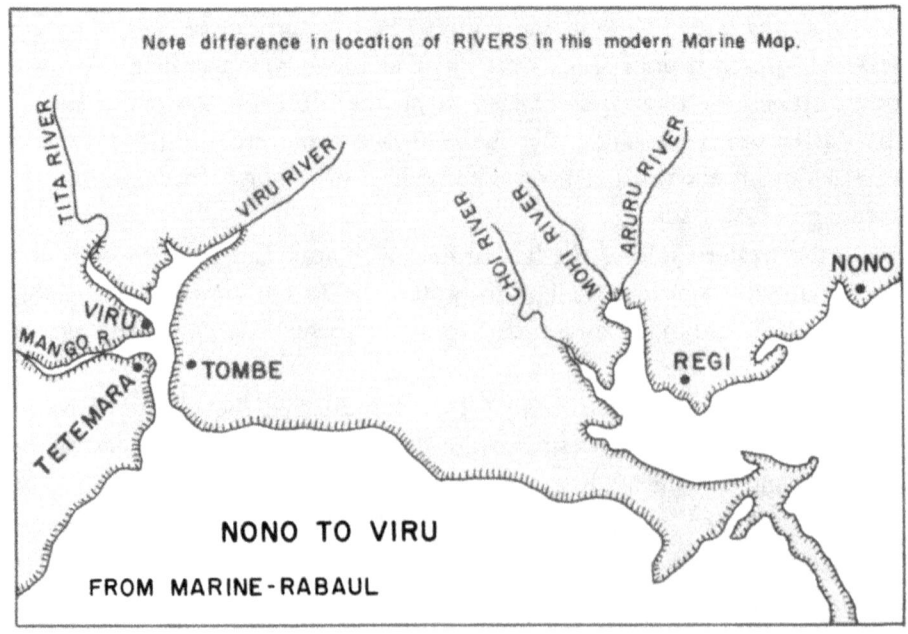

Above: Viru Harbor in 1893. Below: Viru Harbor in 1943.

two miles due south of the entrance to Viru Harbor at about 0610 on 30 June, and inched forward as the dawn brightened between showers.[37] The ships were unable to raise the Marine Advance Unit by radio. Nor did they raise the Japanese until about 15 minutes after sunrise when, at 0703, the Japanese opened fire with their single 3-inch gun. The *Kilty* and *Crosby* returned the fire with their 3-inch guns and skedaddled out of range. The *Crosby* reported that:

> After the 10th round, several stations reported seeing an explosion in the vicinity of the Japanese gun emplacement.[38]

In any case, the enemy ceased fire, and the ships did likewise as they moved out of range. The Japanese major commanding at Viru reported to his seniors at Munda that a landing attack had been repulsed, and in fact it had been.

In mid-morning, CTU 31.3.1 reported to TG 31.3 the lack of contact with the Advance Unit. He recommended against an assault landing from the sea because

> the entrance to Viru Harbor is through a narrow passage with sheer cliffs about 100 feet high.[39]

By early afternoon, approval had been received for landing designated units of the Army troops with their light equipment from the *Kilty* and *Crosby* back at the Choi River to the eastward. At 1630 the Army troops were put ashore not at the Choi River as ordered, but for some unknown reason four miles farther from Viru to the eastward, at Segi Point, and those two ships then returned to base, joining the *Hopkins* enroute.[40]

The Advance Unit of Marines had been delayed at the Choi River by the Japanese, and had been delayed by the very thick jungle covering the difficult terrain all the way between Regi and the two towns (Tombe and Tetemara) guarding the sea approaches to Viru. Part of the Advance Unit was headed for Tombe and part was headed for Tetemara. That part of the Advance Unit headed for Tetemara, the village on the west bank of Viru Harbor entrance, had three more rivers to cross after the Choi River before reaching the objective. These were the Viru, Tita and Mango rivers. In

---

[37] (a) Interview with Rear Admiral Stanley Leith, USN (Ret.), Jan. 1961. Hereafter Leith; (b) Deck Logs.

[38] *Crosby* Deck Log, 30 Jun. 1943.

[39] (a) Guadalcanal to COMINERON Two. 290805 Jun. 1943; (b) COMINERON Two, letter, Ser 00121 of 10 Jul. 1943, subj: Viru Occupation; (c) CTF 31 to COMSOPACFOR, 010035 Jul. 1943.

[40] *Crosby* Deck Log, 30 Jun. 1943.

addition there were mangrove swamps to overcome just outside of Regi and again on the far side of the Mango River. By great perseverance the Marines made it only a day late and captured the 3-inch naval gun guarding Viru Harbor, in mid-afternoon of 1 July.

Despite a CTF 31 operational priority despatch to hold the 2nd Echelon of the Viru Occupation Force at the Russells until informed that Viru Harbor had been captured, the heavy radio traffic of 30 June prevented the message getting through in time. This mighty force of one APC and four LCTs chugged along unaware that the port was still in enemy hands.

The LCTs in the 2nd Echelon for Viru Harbor arrived off the harbor entrance on schedule on 1 July, witnessed one mid-morning six plane air attack on Japanese-held Tetemara, then proceeded to land their supplies as soon as the Marine attack ended, with the surviving Japanese escaping toward Munda.

The *Hopkins* and *Crosby* arrived back at Viru Harbor at an early 0230 on 2 July but it was 0705 before they landed their Army troops, naval base units, Seabees, and logistic support for the Occupation Group, two days later than originally scheduled. The usual problems of the amphibians were present:

> Boats delayed in unloading because of small crowded beach. . . .
>
> * * * * *
>
> Boats reported being fired on by Japanese snipers.[41]

The *Hopkins* after completing its chores, picked up the Marine wounded and sped them back to the Russells.

Viru Harbor was indicative of what happened to operational time tables when land movements through the densely wooded areas of New Georgia were involved.

None of the ships made action reports. None of them kept war diaries. The logs of the Officers of the Deck and the report of Commander Leith were the only naval documents located. None of these documents explain why the Japanese gun positions were not worked over by the three destroyer-type ships on D-Day, using surface spot. None of them explain how one lone Japanese 3-inch gun chased away three destroyer-type ships that mounted a total of twelve 3-inch, albeit the ships were loaded with troops. And while the despatch instructions were for the troops to be landed at the Choi River, which would have given the troops a far shorter march, the

---

[41] (a) *Crosby* Deck Log, 2 Jul. 1943; (b) COMINERON to CTF 31, 012358 Jul. 1943.

ship's logs indicated the Army troops were disembarked at Segi Point on D-Day.

DIVIDENDS

The original plan for the establishment of a PT boat base at Viru Harbor was abandoned because the harbor was found unsuitable. The best dividend out of the occupation of Viru Harbor came from a small marine railway at Viru, built by the Seabees. It was useful in repairing the PT boats which all too frequently grounded in the months ahead while boiling along at high speed in poorly charted waters.

SEGI

Segi had been much in the planners' eyes. In the first place the planners knew something about the area because Segi home-ported a plantation and a coastwatcher. Reconnaissance patrols were frequently landed there. Very early planning at the SOPAC level had visualized landing the main body of troops for the flank assault on Munda at Segi and moving them through the dense woods to make the attack.

Second thoughts proved better. Marine troubles in getting two companies from Segi to Viru Harbor on 27, 28, 29, 30 June were harbingers of future difficulties when Marines and Army troops would attempt to move through the dense woods against Japanese-held positions around Munda air base.

Since Segi Point and its immediate surroundings had been taken by the Marines on 21 June, there was no problem for Commander Segi Occupation Group beyond piloting his 1st Echelon ships and craft, through largely unmarked channels to a specific beach area on a dark, rainy and windy night, and moving the troops into the boats and ashore in the choppy seas.

The problems of all the landing ships and craft are illustrated by the recorded experience of APC-27, which led the 2nd Echelon into Segi Point.

> 1 July 0030. In order to notify LCTs astern of change in convoy speed to five knots, swung out of lead position and notified first LCTs in column astern. Proceeded approximately one mile astern of these first three LCTs to notify the fourth which was straggling.
>
> 0946. Ran aground on reef in Panga Bay, said reef not charted on secret chart prepared from various sources for use in invasion operation. Unable to work free under own power.

1123. Came off reef with no apparent damage to ship.

2 July 0600. Making extremely slow headway due to slow speed maintained by reason of strong head winds and seas, coupled with fact that one LCT lost her ramp and was difficult to control.⁴²

APC-27 was not the only landing ship which unintentionally ran aground during TOENAILS. The LCT-322 in the 4th Echelon for Segi grounded on 3 July and was pulled off by the tug *Rail* on 4 July.

DIVIDENDS

Segi paid far more real and speedy dividends than either of the other diversionary assaults made by the Eastern Force on 30 June.

Beginning 10 July, it was possible to provide fighter support for all bombing missions against Munda from the Seabee-built 3,300-foot long Segi airstrip. By 15 July, when Rear Admiral Turner reluctantly took his departure from TOENAILS, our aircraft from Segi were providing daylight protection to amphibious craft during the last lap of their passage from the Russells or Guadalcanal and at the beachheads.

WICKHAM ANCHORAGE

Early in the planning stages of TOENAILS, it was hoped that an airstrip might be built on Vangunu Island to provide fighter and close air support for later phases of operations in the Middle Solomons. When actual reconnaissance indicated there were no really good airstrip sites available, Vangunu Island stayed in the plans because Wickham Anchorage off Oleana Bay on the southeast coast, two-thirds of the way from the Russells to Rendova, looked like a good place for the landing craft to bide-a-wee should they encounter very heavy weather or have engine failure beyond the capacity of their limited engineers' force to repair. At Wickham Anchorage landing craft could remain during the daytime and be given anti-aircraft protection.

The fact that the Japanese had a company and a half of troops in the vicinity of Vuru, a mile south of Wickham Anchorage, led to beefing up the Landing Force but did not change the basic intention.

Rear Admiral Fort, Second-in-Command of Task Force 31, commanded

---

⁴² APC-27 War Diary, 1–2 Jul. 1943.

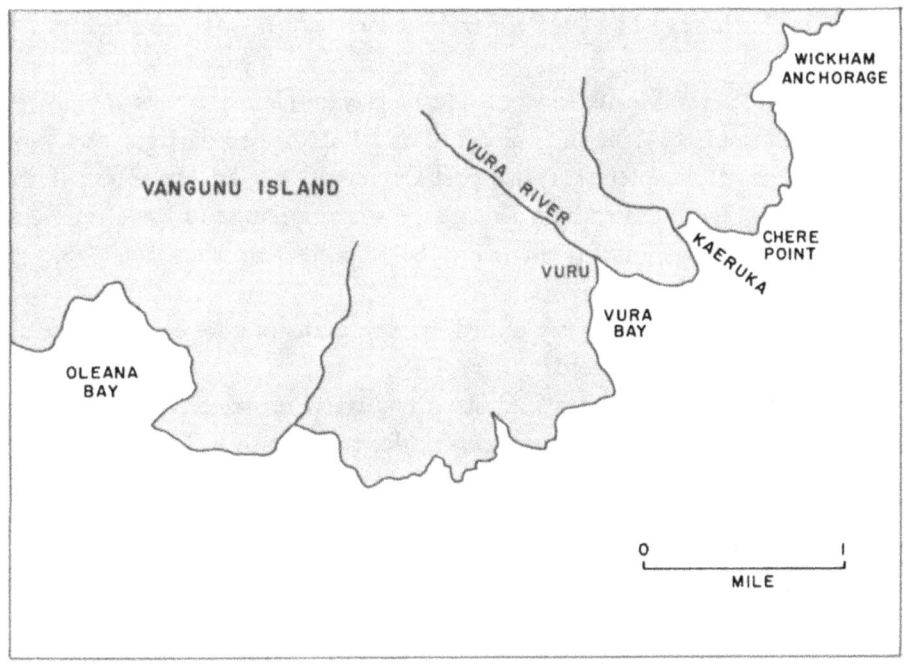

Vangunu Island and Wickham Anchorage.

the Wickham Anchorage Occupation Group, by far the largest of the three task organizations of the Eastern Task Force. His flagship was the destroyer-type minesweeper *Trever* (DMS-16), chosen because presumably she had a good surface radar, a scarce commodity in June 1943. There were two companies of Marines, a battalion of Army troops, a battery of 90-millimeter anti-aircraft guns, part of a battery of 40-millimeter and 50-caliber anti-aircraft guns, as well as the Seabees and naval base units to be landed. Two destroyer-type transports were available to land the Marines.

The Scheme of Maneuver called for the destroyer transports to put the Marines ashore during darkness at Oleana Bay three miles to the south south-westward of Wickham Anchorage, and for the Marines to march overland to make a daylight attack on the Japanese troops, reportedly numbering about 100 at Vuru. The Army troops, landing from seven LCIs, would follow close behind.

Vuru unfortunately lay between Oleana Bay where there was a good 500-yard-wide sandy beach which was not patrolled by the Japanese and Wickham Anchorage where the staging area base was to be established.

Wickham Anchorage had only a narrow beach which was patrolled by the Japanese.

There were several trails between Oleana Bay and Vuru. It was anticipated that the Marines could be in position to make a surprise daylight attack on the Japanese. A complete surprise probably could not be hoped for if the landing took place at Wickham Anchorage since the noise of lowering boats and loading troops into them could be expected to alert the Japanese patrols.[43]

While a night landing was planned for, the plans did not contemplate the miserable weather encountered.

Commander Eastern Force submitted no action report on this operation, nor did the *Trever*, *McKean* nor *Schley*. None of the ships kept a war diary and the *McKean* never even bothered to write up the Ship's Log for the morning watch on the eventful morning of June 30th, when the landings took place. The *Schley* did the best writing job of all and her Ship's Log records the following items which tell the highlights of the sad story of what happened after the *Trever*, *Schley* and *McKean* hove-to at about 0230, hopefully off of Oleana Bay.

>0256. Heavy seas running, making embarkation of Marines extremely difficult.
>
>0303. Sighted light on beach.
>
>0316. Launched all boats.
>
>* * * * *
>
>0434. Landing made at wrong beach—about 6000 yards northwest of western end of Oleana Bay.
>
>0435. Commenced steering various courses and speeds proceeding to Oleana Bay. Boat #3 and LCV following ship; unable to contact other boats.
>
>* * * * *
>
>0701. Boat #2 returned to ship with officers and crews of boats #1 and #4, and crews from two *McKean* boats. Ensign Rodner reported that boats #1 and #4 hopelessly beached on wrong beach. Marines landed.
>
>* * * * *
>
>0731. Sighted four boats high and dry on beach about 6500 yards west of Oleana Bay. Recovery of boats not deemed feasible due to rough seas, daylight and proximity of enemy forces.
>
>0745. Returned to Oleana Bay. Resumed disembarking Marines.
>
>0808. All Marines off ship.

---

[43] (a) Staff Interviews; (b) Fort.

The *McKean* Log indicates that at 0325 she began disembarking troops. There are no entries for her 0400 to 0800 watch. At 1000 it is logged that all her Marines were landed. The *Trever* logged all her Marines landed by 0925. Commander Task Group 31.3 and CTU 31.3.31 (Rear Admiral Fort) logged his arrival at 0230 and added (despite the contrary fact) "did not land troops." The troop landing was logged at 0630.

Putting together the pieces of evidence, it is apparent that those who read the radar screen on the *Trever* that night did not recognize Oleana Bay so the flagship and the two following APDs hove-to some three miles to the westward of the bay. Some of the landing boats shoved off in a downpour of rain. Darkness and choppy seas complicated the coxswain's tasks. The boats landed well to the westward of the chosen beach areas. The markers on the beach were some three miles to the eastward, so they could not be seen from shipboard.

The seven LCIs were scheduled to land their Army troops thirty minutes after the Marines went ashore. This brought the LCIs steaming through the area where the *Trever* and the two APDs were hove-to since the LCIs were proceeding far more expertly than the larger ships to the correct debarkation area. There was much confusion, but by skillful seamanship, no collisions.

Rear Admiral Fort ordered the Marines landing deferred until first light or until contact with the beach was established, but the decision was not carried out by the APDs for reasons unrecorded. The receipt of the order does not appear in the log books of his flagship, the *Trever* or the *Schley*, and as mentioned before, the *McKean* Officer of the Deck did not keep a log at this particular hour. At 0700 the LCIs landed their soldiers in good order, although a bit drenched, with all their communication equipment too wet to operate.[44]

The Marines once ashore learned that the Japanese contingent was not at Vuru but at Kaeruka, one-half mile closer to Wickham Anchorage and somewhat more numerous than the initially reported 100 troops. It was not until 3 July and after a stiff fight by the Marines and Army troops, assisted by a shelling of Chere Point just to the south of Wickham Anchorage by the *Trever*, that Commander Wickham Occupation Force could report to his impatient senior that Wickham Anchorage had been secured.[45]

---

[44] Fort.
[45] CTF 31 to COMSCOFOR, 031255 Jul. 1943.

DIVIDENDS

Even when Wickham Anchorage was secured, the beach was found to be no bonanza. APC-35 at Wickham reported that beach conditions were very bad and that there was great difficulty and delay in unloading two LCTs at one time. As a result, the 4th Echelon for Wickham was held at the Russells pending improvement of unloading conditions.[46]

THE DAY AFTER THE NIGHT BEFORE

As detailed before, while the Rendova and Onaiavisi Entrance landings were smartly accomplished and Segi Point was little more than a training exercise in difficult piloting, on 30 June the other minor occupations were having problems.

During the late morning of the 1st of July, Rear Admiral Turner reported to the Commander Third Fleet that he still had no progress report to make in regard to the Wickham Anchorage operation and no information from the Marine Advance Unit headed for Viru Harbor. At noon, he reported that the situation at Viru and Wickham "was obscure." Viru Harbor was cleared up when, about sunset on 1 July, a message came in saying that place was secured, but it was not until the morning of 3 July that the situation at Wickham Anchorage finally brightened.[47]

Wickham Anchorage faded rapidly into obscurity. Although a subordinate naval base unit and a part of a construction battalion were landed there, neither left a written record, nor did their parent organizations think their efforts at Wickham worthy of mention. So other than as a harbor of refuge, Wickham Anchorage served no useful purpose in the New Georgia campaign.[48]

JAPANESE REACTIONS TO RENDOVA

The Japanese did not attempt a Savo Island-type raid on our amphibians for nearly three days after our troops went ashore at Rendova. Then, at

---

[46] CTG 31.3 to CTF 31, 020055 Jul. 1943.

[47] (a) CTF 31 to COM 3rd Fleet, 010035 Jul.; (b) COM 4th Raiders to CG 43rd, 010600 Jul.; (c) CTF 31 to CTU 31.2.2, 012135 Jul.

[48] U.S. Bureau of Yards and Docks, *Building the Navy's Bases in World War II*, Vol. II (Washington: Government Printing Office, 1947).

0145 on 3 July, the Japanese light cruiser *Yubari* and nine destroyers swept down to the western approaches of Blanche Channel and carried out a bombardment of Rendova Harbor and the beach areas. There was negative damage to the logistic support ships still resting there. A radar-equipped night flying patrol aircraft called a "Black Cat" made contact with the Japanese task force and dropped a bomb on it without results, except probably to add to their worry factor.

Our early morning search and bombing mission by 12 B-25s with P-38s for air cover failed to locate the retiring Japanese squadron. About all the Japanese accomplished by the attack was to hammer home to us the lesson that defensive air search aircraft must be located at and controlled from the assault landing area, if fast moving light forces were to be located and turned back before reaching the assault landing areas.[49]

To bolster the Munda defenders the Japanese immediately moved about 3,000 troops from Kolombangara to Munda. Additional troops from the Northern Solomons were moved to Kolombangara and thence to Munda by almost nightly small barge movements. On 9, 11, and 12 July, another large group of 5,700 Japanese troops from the 13th Regiment were moved from Kolombangara to Bairoko and were added to those defending the Munda area.

All this troop reinforcement was accomplished despite Allied knowledge of many of the impending Japanese movements and offensive forays by our cruiser-destroyer forces into Kula Gulf on 5–6 July and 12–13 July.

TO ZANANA BEACH AND TROUBLE

Patrols moved from the islands astride Onaiavisi Entrance to Zanana Beach on 30 June and 1 July. During the night of 2 July the first large contingent, a battalion of the 43rd Division, was embarked by the amphibians at Rendova and landed at Zanana Beach. Landing craft which towed troop-loaded rubber boats behind did the chore. At Onaiavisi Entrance native guides in canoes took position at the head of columns of landing craft and piloted the lead craft around the numerous shoals and small islands to the beach. The problem of getting from Onaiavisi Entrance to Zanana Beach as it appeared prior to the actual landings is illustrated by the accompanying chart.

---

[49] AIRSOPAC War Diary, 3 Jul. 1943.

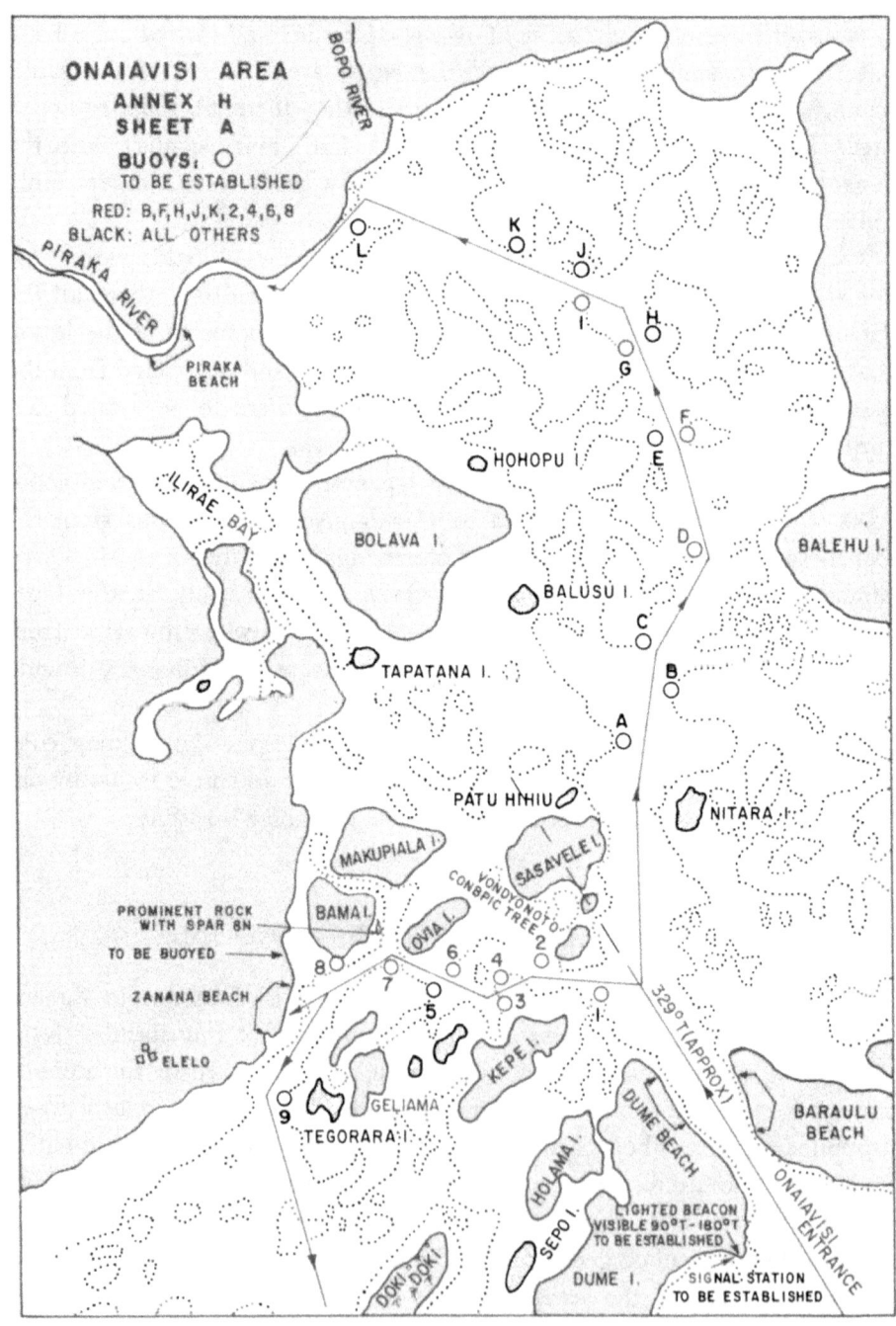

Onaiavisi Entrance and approach to Zanana Beach, New Georgia Island.

By 3 July, CTF 31 had reported to Vice Admiral Halsey that Major General Hester was well satisfied with the beach at Zanana and that the Rice Anchorage landing would be carried out the night of 5 July.[50]

By dark of 5 July, two regiments of troops were ashore on the south coast of New Georgia Island, five miles from the Munda airfield. During the night the Northern Landing Group went ashore at Rice Anchorage, on the northwest coast of New Georgia Island 15 miles north of the Munda airfield.

By 9 July, the shuttling amphibians had disembarked a fair share of another division of Army troops, the 37th Division, in the Rendova area. Early on that day our destroyers poured nearly 2,500 5-inch shells on Japanese-held positions at Munda in a total gun effort of some 5,800 rounds for that morning. Nearly a hundred planes also dropped bombs on enemy defenses around Munda airfield. All this was done without opening for the troops an easy path through the jungle, that was a combination of jungle, swamps and steep ridges, defended by well chosen strong points manned by Japanese willing to die.

By 11 July, Major General Hester had decided to use Laiana Beach, where early plans had called for landing, in lieu of Zanana Beach, three miles to the westward. By 19 July, Laiana Beach was secured and the amphibians landed Marine tanks and Army troops there.

RICE ANCHORAGE LANDINGS

Mid-June plans had called for a July Fourth amphibious landing at Rice Anchorage, 15 miles north of Munda Point, and on the New Georgia side of Kula Gulf. The actual landing was delayed until July 5th due to a necessary troop unit shift. The 4th Marine Raider Battalion lost the assignment, having been delayed by the time required to secure Viru Harbor, and was replaced by the 3rd Battalion 145th Infantry.

The tasks of the Landing Force of the Northern Landing Group were (1) to close the back door to Munda and prevent its reinforcement from Kolombangara Island by seizing Enogai Inlet and Bairoko Harbor and (2) to prevent the escape of the Munda garrison when it was placed under heavy attack from the flank and front. Rice Anchorage was chosen rather than Enogai Inlet or Bairoko Harbor because Japanese troops at these two ports were closer to Munda, and hence easier to support or reinforce.

---

[50] CTF 31 to COMSOPAC, 022225 Jul. 1943.

By and large, the purposes of the landing were not accomplished, since reinforcements from Kolombangara were continuous until the last days of the siege of Munda. When that flow ended, the Munda defenders slithered out to the west to little Baanga Island and then on to big Arundel Island, and from thence the 1,200 yards to Kolombangara.

The mission of the Northern Landing Group was to embark 2,600 Marines and Army troops at Guadalcanal and to land them at Rice Anchorage. The Escort Group Commander was Rear Admiral Ainsworth, CTG 36.1, and the Landing Force Commander was Colonel Harry B. Liversedge, USMC. The Transport Group Commander was Commander Stanley Leith. CTF 31 had directed that all transports must leave the Transport Area by 0700 on 5 July, in order to reduce the chance of daylight air raids during the return to base. The converted transports could make only 23 knots since they had but two boilers.[51]

The twelve ships making up the Transport Unit were of three different types, seven destroyer transports, two destroyer minesweepers and three

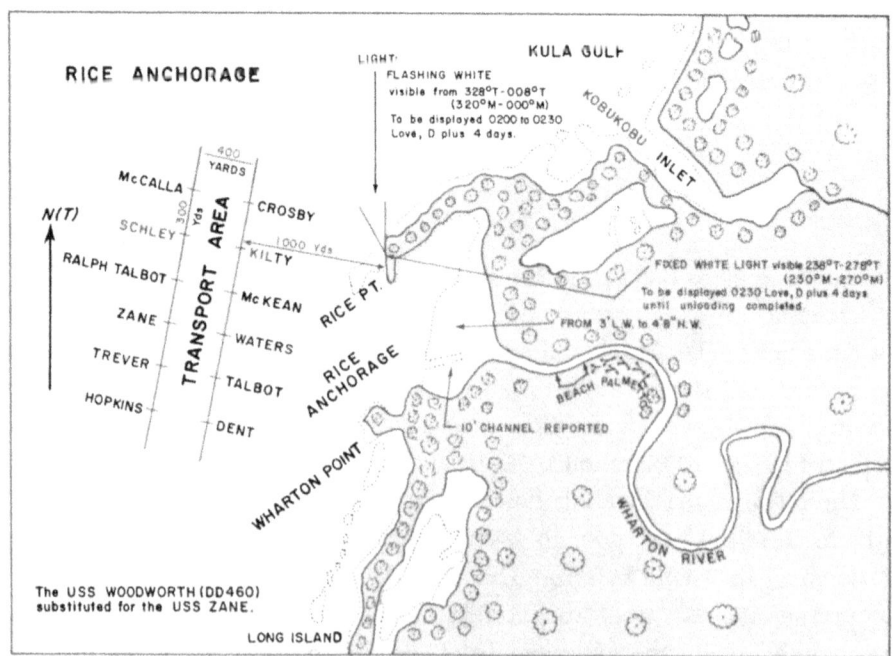

Rice Anchorage on the northwest coast of New Georgia Island.

---

[51] (a) CTG 36.1 Op Order 10–43, 1 Jul. 1943; (b) CTF 31 020242, 020422, 020556, Jul. 1943; (c) CTG 31.1 Op Order, A11–43, 10 Jul. 1943.

destroyers. The *Woodworth'* (DD-460) substituted for the damaged *Zane* (DMS-14). None of the destroyer transports or destroyer minesweepers was fitted with an SG (surface) radar, but the three destroyers in the formation would make up for the deficiency.

The radar of the *Ralph Talbot* identified Rice Point and Wharton Point and coached the formation to the Transport Area, where they hove-to about 0125.

About 0130 on 5 July, in a driving rainstorm the amphibians immediately launched all boats and began embarking the Marines and Army troops. The lights on the beach, as shown on the accompanying chart, were not due to be turned on until 0200, so the coxswains did not even have these feeble aids to assist them in the heavy rain when the first boats left for the beach at 0145.

In the hurry to unload the transports, some of the ships overloaded their landing boats with the result that the landing boats could not clear the reef blocking the entrance to Wharton River. These boats had to return to their transports to lighten their loads and make a second try. It was a case of "haste makes waste." One amphibian landed its Army company to the north of Rice Point and failed to correct the error which became known before departure. Coxswains reported a large group of native New Georgians as a welcoming party on the beach and much confusion off the beach as boats maneuvered for the best position to land next.[52]

As Commander Transports logged the matter:

> The entrance to Rice Anchorage unloading beach is over a narrow shallow bar. Many of the boats touched bottom crossing it. It was therefore found necessary to decrease the normal carrying load of the boats. The river is only seventy yards wide. It was thought that the beach was one hundred yards wide; however, only four boats at a time could land at it. There were twenty-eight ramp LCP employed in unloading twelve ships.

Soon after arrival in the Transport Area the amphibians were surprised to be illuminated by star shell and to come under fire from coastal defense guns in the Enogai Area. While Japanese guns were known to protect Bairoko Harbor, no such guns had been reported by the natives supposedly familiar with the Japanese defenses in the Enogai Area. The transports were ordered not to return this fire but to leave this chore to the two destroyer escorts, and to concentrate on disembarkation of the troops and their impedimenta.

As ships completed their unloading tasks, they cleared the anchorage area.

---

[52] Ship's Logs.

The *Radford* and the *Gwin* expended some 1,100 rounds of counter-battery fire, but since they had only the flashes of the Japanese guns as a point of aim, the Japanese batteries were still shooting at 0559—dawn—when Commander Transports, unloading having been reported completed about 0555, directed the last of the ships underway to return to base.

After their capture five days later, it was determined the Japanese guns were four 5.5-inch guns. It was discovered much sooner that one APD had failed to unload an essential radio transmitter belonging to the 3rd Battalion of the 145th Infantry of the 37th Division and that the *Trever* had two Army officers and 64 men left aboard out of seven Army officers and 209 men embarked.[53]

The Northern Landing Group's initial landing and its further logistic support brought on several gun fights between United States and Japanese cruisers and destroyers in Kula Gulf. These gun fights have gained considerable historical interest. In one, the Task Group Commander claimed the sinking of eight Japanese ships when he had actually sunk but two.[54] On the other hand, the prosaics of the amphibians and logisticians have largely been swept under the historical rug. The Landing Force Commander disappeared into the jungle and was so little heard from that when on 8 July, Rear Admiral Turner inquired of Major General Hester:

> What is Liversedge's situation?

he received back no answer until the next day, and then it read:

> No contact with Liversedge.[55]

On 12 July three fast transports of Transport Division 22 (*Kilty, Crosby* and *Schley*) with the destroyers *Woodworth* and *Taylor* as screen, returned to Rice Anchorage with further troop and logistic support. Unloading commenced about 0120 and was stopped about 0430 because of a firm desire to be under our air cover by daylight. Only a partial unloading job was done under difficult but somewhat less difficult circumstances than the first amphibious landing at Rice Anchorage.

Commander Transport Division 22 recorded his problems and disappointments as follows:

> There has been no challenge from the beach, no boats to meet us, no signs of life whatever. . . . Boats had difficulty in finding channel and some ran

---

[53] *Trever* Log.

[54] COMTHIRDFLT to CINCPAC 070626 Jul. 1943.

[55] (a) CTF 31 to Rendova, 070320 Jul. 1943; (b) Rendova to COMSOPAC to CTF 31, 080121 Jul. 1943.

aground. . . . [Boat officer] reports that our arrival was totally unexpected and the first boats were nearly fired upon. He reports great difficulties in unloading. . . . There is room for only four boats to unload at a time. . . . All unloading will have to be done by such troops as we brought with us plus boat crews and personnel sent by ships. . . . Unloading proceeding more slowly as boats become damaged and more seriously grounded. . . . Many ships' boats have not returned. . . . Have arrived at the decision to leave at 0430 regardless of the boat situation, primarily to get down into air support area by dawn. . . . All personnel have been disembarked and eighty five percent of the cargo. . . .[56]

DEPARTURE FROM THE SOLOMONS— WITH A BAD TASTE

The last newsworthy act of the TOENAILS Operation in which Rear Admiral Turner personally participated was in connection with the relief of Major General John H. Hester, U. S. Army, from his prospective command of the New Georgia Occupation Force.

In order to detail Rear Admiral Turner's advisory part in this difficult decision taken by Vice Admiral Halsey, a bit of background is essential. In the Turner personal files, there are seven despatches bearing on the matter and that is all. In the PHIBFORTHIRDFLT files, no reference to the matter could be located.

As far back as 13 June 1943, Admiral Nimitz had proposed to Admiral King that Rear Admiral Turner be relieved by Rear Admiral Wilkinson "after completion first stage New Georgia Operation," and be ordered to command the Amphibious Forces, Central Pacific and the Fifth Amphibious Force being formed up for the Central Pacific campaign.

In the planners' "future book," the first stage of the New Georgia operations was the capture of Munda, anticipated to be completed about mid-July 1943.

This future employment of Rear Admiral Turner received a favorable nod from COMINCH, and COMSOPAC was directed to issue the necessary orders to Rear Admiral Turner "at the appropriate time." [57]

On 24 June, COMINCH had directed CINCPAC that an amphibious command with its planning staff located at Pearl Harbor "must be estab-

---

[56] (a) COMTRANSDIV 22 War Diary, 12 Jul. 1943; (b) CTF 31, 110370 Jul. 1943.

[57] (a) CINCPAC to COMINCH, 130507 Jun. 1943; (b) BUPERS to CINCPAC and COMSOPAC 140833 Jun. 1943.

Construction of Bairoca Road looking north from ACORN 8 Camp entrance, leading to Munda, New Georgia.

lished at the earliest possible time," for the development and integration of amphibious plans, under Vice Admiral Spruance's command for the Central Pacific Operation.[58] Vice Admiral Halsey and Rear Admiral Turner were thus alerted that desires existed at higher levels of command for Turner's presence at Pearl Harbor at an early date.

ARMY PROBLEMS ON NEW GEORGIA

The Japanese defense of the Munda airfield approaches had been spirited. The attacks by the troops of the 43rd Division which Major General Hester commanded had not been sufficiently spirited to overcome Japanese resistance.

Very large numbers of the troops of this division had "unusual medical problems." Some 90 men had been killed by the Japanese up to 17 July,

---

[58] (a) CINCPAC to COMINCH, 130507 Jun. 1943; (b) COMINCH to CINCPAC, 241301 Jun. 1943; (c) CINCPAC Command Summary, Book Three, 24 Jun. 1943, p. 1610.

but "over 1,000 men were out of action" due to these medical problems. According to the Army's history:

> An especially large number of casualties was caused not by wounds or infectious disease but by mental disturbance. Between fifty and a hundred men were leaving the line every day with troubles which were diagnosed as 'war neuroses.' . . .[59]

Major General Oscar W. Griswold was the Commanding General of the XIV Corps and Major General Hester's immediate superior since the 43rd Division was a major part of that Corps. Lieutenant General Millard F. Harmon was the Commanding General U. S. Army Forces in SOPAC, mustering altogether about 275,000 men.[60]

When the troop offensive ashore on New Georgia gave its first evidence of slowing down, calls were made by Major General Hester for additional troops. As early as 5 July, Rear Admiral Turner was in conference on Guadalcanal with Major General Griswold and Lieutenant General Harmon in connection with moving forward part of the 37th Division, which was sailed for Rendova on the 7th and 9th of July.

Each of these four officers was directly involved in the current phase of TOENAILS as well as in planning and preparation for the assault landing on Kolombangara, and the capture of the Vila airfield which were planned to follow soon after the capture of Munda.

On this same day, 5 July, Lieutenant General Harmon recommended to Commander Third Fleet that as soon as Munda airfield was captured, the XIV Corps Commander, Major General Griswold, should take over command of the New Georgia Occupation Force, and that Major General Hester continue in command of the 43rd Division and conduct the attack on Vila.

Rear Admiral Turner immediately put in his oar backing up Major General Hester, saying that superseding Hester would be undesirable and "a severe blow to morale." He expressed his regret at having to disagree with Lieutenant General Harmon. At the same time he sent Colonel Linscott, who in the forward operational area and in the absence of Captain Anderson, was an "acting Chief of Staff," to Rendova and New Georgia to look into what the amphibians could do to ease the difficulties the Army troops were encountering in taking Munda airfield, as well as to move forward with the planning for taking Vila airfield.

---

[59] Miller, *Reduction of Rabaul* (Army), p. 120.
[60] *Ibid.*, p. 69.

There is no radio message available in which Major General Hester reported to COMSOPAC that he was ready to take over command of the New Georgia Occupation Force, and no despatch to COMSOPAC from CTF 31 suggesting that from his point of view such a moment had arrived. The ground rules for the appropriate circumstances when either commander would originate such a despatch had not been established by their common superior, Vice Admiral Halsey. This again accentuates the incompleteness of this part of the over-all Operation Plan 14–43 issued by Vice Admiral Halsey.

By 8 July the original plan for a combined assault on Munda airfield from the sea and from the flank, which earlier had been postponed, was now abandoned since the troops of the 43rd Division had not reached their jump-off positions by 8 July, and there appeared no real prospect of this happening soon.

When word of this postponement decision by Major General Hester reached Guadalcanal, Lieutenant General Harmon flew off to Noumea and a conference with Vice Admiral Halsey.

As a result of Lieutenant General Harmon's personal presentation of his views and of the continued lack of marked success of the troops on New Georgia, COMTHIRDFLT on the afternoon of 9 July sent a despatch to CTF 31 which directed that when Major General Griswold arrived in the combat area and when he was prepared to assume command,

> on orders of COMSOPAC, all ground forces, including naval units attached to the forces of occupation, will pass from the Command of CTF 31 to the Corps Commander who will assume the title of COMGEN New Georgia.[61]

Late on 13 July, Major General Griswold, who had flown up to the combat area in order to prepare himself for his operational command, added the final push to any lingering doubts Vice Admiral Halsey may have had as to the desirability of Major General Hester continuing on as a "prospective" Commander New Georgia Occupational Force, by reporting that:

> Things are going badly, and the Forty Third Division is about to fold up.[62]

Rear Admiral Turner, having received reports from Colonel Linscott, added his push by saying:

> I regret that I am compelled to agree with Griswold. From my own private advices received today from my staff officers returning from Rendova. . . .

---

[61] COMSOPAC to CTF 31, 090502 Jul. 1943.
[62] RDO Rendova to COMGENFORCES SOPAC, 130820 Jul. 1943.

Recommend immediate transfer of New Georgia Occupation Force to Griswold.[63]

At the same time, Rear Admiral Turner advised Major General Griswold:

I agree with you and have so told Halsey. Request you take command as soon as you are able to exercise it.[64]

Upon the receipt of Major General Griswold's despatch and of CTF 31's concurring despatch, COMSOPAC came immediately to the decision that "the appropriate time" had arrived and issued orders:

a. for the turn over of the command of the New Georgia Occupation Force from CTF 31 to Major General Griswold at midnight on 14 July;
b. for Rear Admiral Turner to proceed to the Central Pacific turning over to Rear Admiral Wilkinson on 15 July.[65]

This latter change occurred despite CTF 31's plea made some nine hours before the COMSOPAC detachment despatch reached the air:

In fairness to Wilkinson and me, recommend that I retain command of this operation until affairs are again going smoothly.[66]

Vice Admiral Halsey advised his subordinate who wanted to stay until affairs were going more smoothly:

Your relief by Wilkinson will be effected on 15 July as planned in view of CINCPAC's requirement for your services.[67]

TOENAILS' LESSONS AND PROFITS

(A) Logistic Support

The Navy had been much condemned for its inadequacies in logistic support during the first months of WATCHTOWER. Unlike the Guadalcanal Operation, there were 1st, 2nd, 3rd and 4th Echelon logistic support movements set up for the TOENAILS Operation and a dozen support echelons had sailed in the first 15 days of TOENAILS.

Just as Rear Admiral Turner was leaving SOPAC, Commander Landing Craft Flotillas made a report to him on the performance of landing craft in which was written the heartening logistic words:

---
[63] CTF 31 to COMSOPAC, 131400 Jul. 1943.
[64] CTF 31 to Radio Rendova, 131510 Jul. 1943.
[65] CTF 31 to COMSOPAC, 131400 Jul. 1943.
[66] COMTHIRDFLT to CINCPAC, 132320 Jul. 1943.
[67] COMTHIRDFLT to CTF 31, 132220 Jul. 1943.

588 *Amphibians Came To Conquer*

Turner Collection

A cargo of Quonset huts and prefabricated warehouses and huts unloaded (in the wrong way) at Munda.

> It appears for the first time in modern warfare that supplies have arrived with or immediately behind the Assault Troops. A good example is the airstrip at Segi. There, bulldozers were clearing a strip forty (40) minutes after the first echelon LST had beached. The flow of supplies to the front has been greater than the Advanced Bases could handle. All have requested that the flow of supplies be reduced.[68]

Enemy action, groundings and modified plans had forced many changes in the ships and landing craft originally designated for specific supporting echelon tasks. The important lesson from all this was that in order for logistic support to be delivered by amphibious ships and craft on time, a large excess of ships and craft is required over the computed space requirements for the total of personnel and tons of equipment to be moved.

For the TOENAILS Operation 36 LSTs, 36 LCIs, 72 LCTs and 28 APCs had been scheduled to be available. Fortunately plans were not based on

---

[68] Commander Landing Craft Flotillas to COMPHIBFORSOPAC FE 25–2/A3/Ser 002 of 13 Jul. 1943, subj: Performance of Landing Craft.

this number as only 12 LSTs, 26 LCIs, 43 LCTs and 16 APCs were in the area on 30 June 1943. This number was barely adequate.[69]

(B) Landing Ships and Craft

The personal worry bug to be overcome by every amphibian, coxswain, officer in charge or commanding officer was the coral shelf and the many coral heads off the few and generally narrow beaches. In due time, these coral heads would be dynamited. The beaches would be augmented with landing piers, which would be coconut log bulkheads backed up by crushed coral. But the first few days in poorly or uncharted waters were real tests.

When the first surge of TOENAILS was over, it was apparent from the reports that both landing ships and craft had turned in better than a satisfactory performance.

> The LCTs had been the most useful of all types. However, low speed (6 knots) limits their daily staging in combat areas to about 100 miles per night. . . . It is still advisable to have them underway only at night. Against a head sea, their speed is greatly reduced, sometimes to two knots. . . . The crews and officers have been standing up well in spite of operating two out of every three days.
>
> Some LSTs have transported 400 men each for short periods. . . . [LCTs] have carried as many as 250 men overnight, but in exposed positions. . . .
>
> The LCIs carry about 170 combat troops. . . . For unopposed short runs of a few hours, 350 men have been transported on a single LCI. . . . They are ideal for night landings on good beaches.
>
> The APCs, besides having proved useful as escorts, have been used to transport small groups of men. . . .
>
> The arrival of a mobile landing craft repair base unit with a floating dock has been expected for months, but they still have not arrived.[70]

(C) Night Landing Operations

Night landings on foreign shores look very well on paper and over the long history of amphibious operations have been resorted to many times. Our Navy had carried out such operations on a large scale in the North African Invasion on 8 November 1942. The Sicilian Invasion commencing 10 July 1943, eleven days after D-Day for TOENAILS was to include a large successful night landing of the assault troops.

---

[69] CTG 31.1 Loading Order 14–43 12 Jul. 1943.
[70] Commander Landing Craft Flotillas, letter, 13 Jul. 1943.

Rear Admiral Turner took a dim view of night landings prior to TOENAILS but had not closed his mind to their use. He was willing to experiment on a small scale. So the Eastern Force scheduled a night landing at Wickham Anchorage and the Western Force scheduled night landings for the Onaiavisi Entrance Unit and for the Advance Unit on Rendova.

One lesson which Admiral Turner stated he had vividly relearned during the TOENAILS Operation was the great hazard of night amphibious operations. In fact, his lack of success with them during TOENAILS soured him on night landings for any large contingent of amphibians for the rest of the war.[71]

In this connection, frequently the question has been raised as to why the major World War II amphibious assault landings in the South and Central Pacific were launched at daylight while those in the European Theater were largely launched during darkness.

It may be that the answer lies in the above observation of Admiral Turner and in the writings of Sir Roger Keyes. He was the Chief of Staff to the naval commander at the Gallipoli amphibious landing disaster in 1915. He later became an Admiral of the Fleet in the British Navy, and before and after retirement wrote extensively. His opinion was that it was "folly to storm a defended beach in daylight." A good many United States naval officers had read and been impressed by what Sir Roger Keyes wrote. In a measure, the opinion of General Vandegrift previously quoted, supports this conclusion.

In the Mediterranean, where the British influence and command lines were strong, the principle of night landings was observed during the North African, Tunisian, Sicilian and Italian campaigns.

In the South Pacific there were jungle bordered beaches (with no access roads) to contend with. In the Central Pacific there was a greater confidence in the efficiency of naval gunfire, in the dive bombing by carrier aircraft, in the quality of the close air support provided to the Marines, as well as a deeper appreciation of the essentiality of landing the troops at the appointed time and spot to facilitate the Marine and Army Scheme of Maneuver.

(D) Landing Where the Enemy Ain't

Admiral Turner later commented on Samuel Eliot Morison's statement

---
[71] Turner.

about the "folly of not taking Laiana first," and added that the decision to land at Zanana Beach instead of Laiana Beach was predicated on an acceptance, at that stage of the war, of General Vandegrift's often repeated statement that

> landings should not be attempted in the face of organized resistance, if, by any combination of march or maneuver it is possible to land unopposed and undetected.[72]

(E) Weather

Other officers pointed out that bad weather blotted out the special lights needed to guide landing craft to beaches. Special lights had been provided at Rendova, Oleana Bay and Rice Anchorage. None were visible in the manner planned.[73]

(F) Offshore Toe Holds

During the New Georgia amphibious operation an operational technique was developed which carried through the Central Pacific campaigns and on into the planning for the final attack on the Japanese homeland. This technique was pointed towards seizing toe holds on nearby islands close to but not so well defended as the main objective and making a key part of the major assault on the main objective direct from these toe holds rather than from far across the sea. They also provided a place from where artillery support could be supplied from on a round-the-clock basis.

(G) Shore Party

The Shore Party had been much condemned for its inadequacies on 7 August 1942 at Guadalcanal. Much effort had gone into making more definite its duties and increasing the number of warm bodies to carry out these duties during the next three months. On 16 October 1942, COMPHIBFORSOPAC issued a new trial operating procedure for the Shore

---

[72] (a) Turner; (b) Morison, *The Rising Sun in the Pacific* (Vol. III), p. 199; (c) COMGEN-FIRSTMARDIV, Final Report on Guadalcanal, Phase V, p. 6.

[73] (a) Staff Interviews; (b) CTF 31 Op Order A9–43, 15 Jun. 1943. Appendix (1) to Annex G.

Party. But in November 1942, the Commander Transport Division Eight still thought:

> The bottleneck of unloading is still the Shore Party. . . . At Aola Bay, the Shore Party was 800 strong (200 per ship). 400 Army, 100 Marines and 100 ACORN personnel. . . . Unloading boats on a beach is extremely strenuous physical labor and the Shore Party must be organized into reliefs if the unloading is to extend over 12 hours.[74]

Further increases in personnel as well as cleaner command lines were again tried in TOENAILS. They paid off.

(H) Force Requirements

There was one sobering lesson from TOENAILS which carried forward into future planning of assault and follow up forces for the island campaigns of the Pacific. It was expressed in a COMINCH planners memorandum of 6 August 1943:

> 2. At the termination of Japanese resistance in Munda, there were seven regimental combat teams, totaling more than 30,000 troops in our assault forces. No information differing from our initial estimate of 4 to 5,000 troops on Munda, to which reinforcements were believed to have been added for a time, has been received. However, of the Japanese on Munda only 1,671 are known to be dead and 28 captured. The overwhelming superiority of our forces in numbers and equipment had to be applied for 12 days despite air bombing and naval bombardment support before a force not more than one-seventh its size had been overcome. If we are going to require such overwhelming superiority at every point where we attack the Japanese, it is time for radical change in the estimate of the forces that will be required to defeat the Japanese now in the Southwest and Central Pacific.[75]

A STEP AWAY FROM WANTLESSNESS

How was Rear Admiral Turner holding up during the second six months of his year in the tropics? His Chief of Staff recalls:

> Most every afternoon about 5 p.m. Admiral Turner, Doyle, and Lewis went ashore for drinks before dinner. I went several times as did Hamilton Haines. They did not go to the Officers Club Bar that Marine General 'Barney' Vogel had built in the city—but went to a small restaurant run by a French woman,

---

[74] COMTRANSDIV Eight to COMPHIBFORSOPAC, letter, Nov. 1942.
[75] Captain Clarence E. Olsen, USN, to ACS (Plans), memorandum, 6 Aug. 1943.

where they had a more or less private drinking room. [The Admiral Turner Room in the Circle de Noumea, a cobwebby French Club.]

Walking there and back and walking from the dock to Admiral Halsey's morning conference is about the only exercise that Turner had, as far as I could observe while I was with him around Noumea.[76]

Regarding this period, his Flag Captain reports as follows:

The Kelly Turner Club in Noumea was where Turner and his staff drank heavily and relaxed. I was a member of this club, also its liquor supplier. Turner was lots of fun and forgot his problems here.[77]

A war correspondent who was in Noumea and in Guadalcanal at this time wrote about Rear Admiral Turner:

. . . [He] gives forth an impression of extreme weariness . . . . solemn owlish expression . . . . skinny and gaunt . . . . a chain smoker down to the last soggy half-inch . . . . face leathery and lined with character.[78]

When all was said and done, Rear Admiral Turner worked his head off in the logistical battle of the Lower Solomons and in the move to the Middle Solomons. The record of dozens of letters indicates this. It was after this initial phase of a rough and tumble contest with a first-class fighting Japanese Navy was over and won, that Rear Admiral Turner started to find in a nip at the bottle the necessary uplift to willingly wrestle another four or five hours of work each day after completing a normal 12 hours.

Like any newcomer to the tropics, he found it difficult to put in his long accustomed 18-hour working day. He had bouts with malaria, his bones ached, at times his head spun. But he kept going.[79]

Not all the members of the COMPHIBFORSOPAC Staff have the same remembrance of Rear Admiral Turner's imbibing habits in all the details. They all agree that this habit of taking a swig at a bottle, in contradistinction to a late afternoon cocktail ashore, did not take hold until after the Russells had been seized and the final planning for TOENAILS was well underway. One placed it definitely as just after his first serious bout with malaria which sent him to the hospital ship *Solace*.[80]

No member of his staff interviewed had ever seen him under the weather from drinking during this period and the majority say that the change from

---

[76] Anderson.
[77] Rodgers.
[78] Driscoll, *Pacific Victory*, pp. 58, 59.
[79] RKT Medical Record, 1942–1943.
[80] Staff Interviews.

a couple of late afternoon martinis to a swig at the bottle did not start until after Tarawa.[81]

His senior subordinate in the Solomons penned his remembrances as follows:

> He was drinking 'off hours.' On a couple of occasions it came to my attention. However, I do not believe it affected his efficiency the next day, except to make him more irritable than usual.
>
> On one of these occasions, just before TOENAILS, he was having an important presentation by an Army Brigadier who planned the Artillery setup for TOENAILS. Turner was 'bright eyed and bushy tailed' at the 0800 conference, quickly pointed out several glaring defects in the plans and had it all done over.[82]

That was par for the course.

PROBLEMS IN NEW GEORGIA PLANNING

It should be noted here that some of COMINCH planning assistants did not think Vice Admiral Halsey's final plan for TOENAILS was bold enough and made their concern a matter of record. A draft JCS despatch, calling for assault landings at Vila and Munda airfields with an attached supporting memorandum, was sent up the line in the COMINCH Plans Division to Admiral King some six weeks before the landings.

The War Plans Officer (Rear Admiral C. M. Cooke) placed his comments on this memorandum:

> We called on Halsey for some action. He has forwarded his plan. I do not feel that at this distance, we are in a position to insist on a bolder plan, to which Halsey has already given consideration and presumably rejected. There are obvious advantages to immediate seizure of Munda and Vila airfields, which from the spot, I might personally advocate.[83]

Admiral King agreed.

It also might be added that CINCPAC had preferred that the large transports not be employed for the assault landing in TOENAILS, because of the lack of strong air cover over the landing areas and a decent respect for Japanese air capabilities.

---

[81] *Ibid.*

[82] Fort.

[83] (a) COMINCH to COMSOPAC, 081329 May 1943; (b) COMSOPAC to COMINCH 090501 and 160420 May 1943; (c) Assistant Chief of Staff Plans to Admiral King, memorandum of 21 May 1943; subj: COMSOPAC TOENAILS plan.

Vice Admiral Jimmy Doyle repeats this yarn of the early days of the planning for the New Georgia Operation:

> Major General Harmon, COMGENSOPAC, came to see Rear Admiral Turner with a first draft of the Scheme of Maneuver for the New Georgia Operation Plan. General Harmon said, 'Admiral, will you look at this plan?' The Admiral took the plan and studied it hard and silently for seven or eight minutes. At the same time, I was seeing General Harmon's plan for the first time and I was galloping through a copy. When the Admiral finished going through it, he looked up and General Harmon asked, 'What do you think of the plan?' My boss replied simply but firmly, 'It stinks,' and after a pause, 'Who wrote it?' General Harmon replied, 'Admiral I did.' My boss's face lighted up and, with a twinkle in his eye, he said: 'It still stinks.' [84]

The *Washington Post,* in commenting on this story at the time of Admiral Turner's death, said he showed "more tenacity than tact." [85]

His Chief of Staff remembered that during most of the period when TOENAILS was being planned:

> Every morning at 0900, COMSOPAC (Admiral Halsey), who was based ashore, held a conference in his office, attended by his C/S and other Commands ashore (Service Commands, for instance), Senior Marine Ashore and Unit Commanders Afloat. I accompanied Admiral Turner to these conferences as did Jack Lewis and Jimmy Doyle.
>
> In general, I would say that the period from January to May 1943 was one of enforced marking time as far as the Amphibious Force was concerned. Everyone wanted to get beyond Guadalcanal but the time didn't seem propitious, mostly because of the lack of the material that was needed. . . .
>
> Both Admirals Halsey and Turner were eager to get going and make further advances to the North. Admiral Turner, however, would not set any time for such an operation as he felt that we did not have the ships or material at hand to make any such advance successfully. . . .
>
> I think it was early March that part of our Force was taken away from us. COMSOPAC received orders from COMINCH to transfer 2 APs and 2 AKAs and 1 division of troops to General MacArthur. The ships were to augment the Amphibious Force being built up by Dan Barbey in the SW Pacific. . . .
>
> Admiral Halsey wanted a target date of 1 April for the landings in New Georgia. This worried Admiral Turner a lot—for he felt that it would not be done with reasonable success with what we had, so it was postponed until later.[86]

---

[84] J. H. Doyle.
[85] *Washington Post,* 14 Feb. 1961.
[86] Anderson.

DYING ON THE VINE

In view of the successes achieved and lives saved, no more popular strategical concept came out of the Pacific War than that of by-passing Japanese-held islands or positions and letting the Japanese threat "die on the vine," while our forces directed their efforts at Japanese closer to the Japanese homeland.

The popularity has led to many claims as to who was the originator. This researcher has no idea who was the originator, but having read many thousands of despatches relating to the Pacific War, the first despatch in which he saw the expression used was in a despatch of Vice Admiral Halsey's (COMSOPAC's 110421 of July 1943) addressed to Rear Admiral Turner and asking his comments and recommendations thereon.

www.ingramcontent.com/pod-product-compliance
Lightning Source LLC
Chambersburg PA
CBHW082018300426
44117CB00015B/2266